Narrowing the U.S. Current Account Deficit
A Sectoral Assessment

ALLEN J. LENZ

assisted by

HUNTER K. MONROE
BRUCE PARSELL

Narrowing the U.S. Current Account Deficit
A Sectoral Assessment

INSTITUTE FOR INTERNATIONAL ECONOMICS
WASHINGTON, DC
JUNE 1992

Allen J. Lenz, a Visiting Fellow at the Institute for International Economics, is Director of Trade and Economics for the Chemical Manufacturers Association. He was previously Director of the Office of Trade and Investment Analysis in the International Trade Administration of the US Department of Commerce (1982–88), Staff Director of the National Security Council (1981–82), and Executive Secretary of the President's Council on International Economic Policy (1971–74). He is the author of *Beyond Blue Economic Horizons: U.S. Trade Performance and International Competitiveness in the 1990s* (1990).

INSTITUTE FOR INTERNATIONAL
ECONOMICS
11 Dupont Circle, NW
Washington, DC 20036-1207
(202) 328-9000   Telex: 261271 IIE UR
FAX: (202) 328-5432

C. Fred Bergsten, *Director*
Linda Griffin Kean, *Director of Publications*

The views expressed in this publication are those of the author. This publication is part of the overall program of the Institute, as endorsed by its Board of Directors, but does not necessarily reflect the views of individual members of the Board or the Advisory Committee.

Printed in the United States of America
94 93 92   3 2 1

Library of Congress Cataloging-
in-Publication Data

Lenz, Allen J.
    Narrowing the U.S. current account
deficit: a sectoral assessment
Allen J. Lenz.
    p.   cm.

    Includes bibliographical references
and index.

    1. Exports—United States
    2. Balance of trade—United States.
    3. United States—Manufactures.
    4. Foreign exchange—United
States.
    I. Title.
    HF3004   1992
    382'.17'0973—dc20   92-8778
                                                   CIP

ISBN 0-88132-148-6 (cloth)
ISBN 0-88132-103-6 (paper)

Contents

Preface   *C. Fred Bergsten*   **xiii**

Acknowledgments   **xvii**

1 Introduction   **1**
Objectives of the Study   3
Methodology   4
Uses of a Disaggregated Approach   6
The Critical Role of US Manufacturing   9
Organization of the Study   15
Bibliography   16

2 The US Current Account in Perspective   **17**
The Current Account Dissected   19
The Key Role of Merchandise Trade   29
Manufactures Trade and the Current Account   33
Policy Implications   35
Summary   37
Bibliography   38

3 The Role of Manufactures in Global Trade   **41**
Trade in Goods and Services   43
Manufactures Trade   43
Product Composition of Manufactures Trade   46
Manufactures Trade Shares and Flows   47
Manufactures Trade and International Capital Flows   57
Summary   58
Bibliography   60

4 An Overview of US Manufactures Trade Performance   **61**
Measuring the International Competitiveness of US
    Manufacturing   63
Trade Performance Measurements of International
    Competitiveness   69
The Effects of Foreign Direct Investment on Trade Flows   74

v

Geographical Composition of Manufactures Trade 78
Changes in the Product Composition of Manufactures Trade 84
Price and Volume Effects 88
Market Performance by Two-Digit Product Group 94
US Current Account Deficits in Perspective 98
Other Views of the Competitiveness of US-Based Manufacturing 101
The Lack of Sources of Continued Improvement 103
Summary 108
Bibliography 112

5 Individual Product Group Assessments 115

Objectives and Methodology 117
Chemicals and Related Products (SITC 5) 121
   Tables 141
Paper, Paperboard, and Articles Thereof (SITC 64) 148
   Tables 157
Textiles (SITC 65) 163
   Tables 172
Nonmetallic Mineral Manufactures (SITC 66) 179
   Tables 185
Iron and Steel (SITC 67) 192
   Tables 203
Nonferrous Metals (SITC 68) 210
   Tables 226
Manufactures of Metal (SITC 69) 233
   Tables 242
Specialized Industrial Machinery (SITC 72) 249
   Tables 262
Metalworking Machinery (SITC 73) 269
   Tables 280
General Industrial Machinery (SITC 74) 286
   Tables 295
Office Machines and Computers (SITC 75) 302
   Tables 315
Telecommunications and Sound-Reproducing Equipment
(SITC 76) 323
   Tables 335
Electrical Machinery and Parts (SITC 77) 342

Tables 355
Road Vehicles (SITC 78) and Internal Combustion
    Engines (SITC 713) 362
    Tables 384
Aircraft (SITC 792) and Aircraft Engines (SITC 714) 394
    Tables 407
Furniture (SITC 82) 416
    Tables 423
Apparel (SITC 84) 429
    Tables 440
Footwear (SITC 85) 447
    Tables 456
Professional, Scientific, and Controlling Instruments (SITC 87) 462
    Tables 470
Miscellaneous Manufactures (SITC 89) 477
    Tables 488
General Bibliography 495

6 Questionnaire Survey Results **499**
Description and Methodology 501
Export Expectations and Constraints 502
Factors Influencing Imports 512
Capital Investment and US-Based Production Capacity 517
Exchange Rate Effects 521
Conclusions 524

7 Key Findings and Policy Implications **529**
Manufactures Trade and US Current Account Performance 531
Summary of Past and Projected US Manufactures Trade
    Performance 535
US Manufactures Trade Performance: Specific Findings 540
Policy Implications 560
Bibliography 568

Appendix: Methodology and Statistics **571**
Trade Data Bases 573
Market Shares 578
The 1993 Product Group Projections 581

Tables

1.1 United States: sectoral composition of GNP, 1989   11
2.1 United States: summary of international transactions, 1981–90   20
2.2 United States: international services transactions, 1981–90   24
2.3 United States: other private services transactions, 1987 and 1990   28
2.4 United States: merchandise trade by component, 1981–90   31
3.1 Sectoral composition of world goods and services trade, 1989   44
3.2 Product composition of world trade, all commodities, 1981–89   45
3.3 Product composition of world manufactures exports, 1981–89   48
3.4 Product composition of world manufactures exports, by shares
     of total, 1981–89   49
3.5 Geographical composition of world manufactures trade, 1981–89   50
3.6 World bilateral trade flows in manufactures, 1981, 1987, and 1989   53
3.7 United States: share of world manufactures export markets,
     1981–89   54
3.8 European Community: share of world manufactures export
     markets, 1981–89   54
3.9 Japan: share of world manufactures export markets, 1981–89   55
3.10 Asian NICs: share of world manufactures export markets, 1981–
     89   55
3.11 Share of world manufactures exports taken by the United States,
     1981–89   56
4.1 United States: manufactures trade, 1981–90   70
4.2 United States: indices of competitiveness in manufactures, 1981–
     89   73
4.3 United States: geographical composition of manufactures trade,
     1981, 1987, and 1990   79
4.4 United States: geographical composition of manufactures trade,
     as shares of total, 1981, 1987, and 1990   80
4.5 United States: indices of competitiveness in industrial materials,
     1981–89   86
4.6 United States: indices of competitiveness in finished goods, 1981–89   87
4.7 United States: nominal versus real trade performance in
     manufacturing, by sector, 1982–90   90
4.8 United States: product composition of manufactures trade, 1981–87   95
4.9 United States: product composition of manufactures trade, 1987–90   96

4.10 Export growth rates necessary to achieve a $25 billion US
     manufactures trade surplus in 1993 under various import
     growth rate assumptions   99
4.11 Indices of manufacturing productivity in various industrialized
     countries, 1981 and 1989   104

     Chapter 5 tables are listed above in the Contents.

6.1 Respondents' expected changes in US exports, 1993 versus 1989 503
6.2 Respondents' US exports as a share of total US sales, 1981, 1989,
     and projected 1993   503
6.3 Portion of respondents' foreign sales met by US exports, 1981,
     1989, and projected 1993   504
6.4 Respondents' estimation of impact of 1985–90 dollar
     depreciation on 1990 export performance   505
6.5 Respondents' long-run export expectations   506
6.6 Respondents' anticipated effects of EC 1992 on US-based
     production   507
6.7 Respondents' anticipated change in exports to Eastern bloc and
     Pacific Rim ASEAN countries by mid-1990s   509
6.8 Respondents' rating of factors holding back export growth   511
6.9 Respondents' anticipated change in imports for use as inputs to
     production or for direct sale, 1993 versus 1989   512
6.10 Respondents' estimation of share of US sales accounted for by
     imports, 1981, 1989, and projected 1993   513
6.11 Trends in foreign procurement since 1985 reported by
     respondents   514
6.12 Respondents' assessment of impact of 1985–90 dollar
     depreciation on foreign procurement   515
6.13 Respondents' rating of factors holding up level of US imports 516
6.14 Respondents' assessment of effects of lack of US production
     capacity on US imports   517
6.15 Respondents' reported reasons for planned additions to
     US-based production capacity   518
6.16 Respondents' reported planned distribution of 1991 plant and
     equipment investment spending   519
6.17 Respondents' rating of factors affecting decisions to increase
     US-based production capacity   520
6.18 Respondents' estimation of effects of further significant dollar
     depreciation on exports   522

6.19 Respondents' estimation of effects of further significant dollar
depreciation on imports of production inputs and finished
goods   523
6.20 Respondents' estimates of effects of significant further dollar
depreciation on investment in US facilities   524
6.21 Respondents' estimates of effects of significant further dollar
depreciation on investment in foreign-based production   525
7.1   United States: manufactures export and import shares and share
balances, 1981 and 1989   537
7.2   World market shares of the principal exporting and importing
regions, 1989   538
7.3   United States: manufactures trade balance, actual and projected
changes, 1981–93   541
A.1   DRI import price and demand elasticities   583

To my wife Pat

They also serve who only stand and wait
and wait, and wait, and wait. . . .

Preface

The Institute for International Economics has conducted a number of studies over the years on the international trade and competitive position of the United States, including *Deficits and the Dollar: The World Economy at Risk* (1985, revised in 1987) by Stephen Marris, *United States External Adjustment and the World Economy* (1989) by William R. Cline, and my own *America in the World Economy: A Strategy for the 1990s* (1988). We held a major conference in late 1990 on the adjustment of the American (and major foreign) imbalances which produced both Paul R. Krugman's essay *Has the Adjustment Process Worked?* (1991) and a conference volume entitled *International Adjustment and Financing: The Lessons of 1985–1991* (1992).

All of these analyses have focused primarily on the macroeconomic causes and consequences of the American deficits. The microeconomic implications are obviously of great importance as well, and the present volume assesses the recent evolution and future prospects for the 21 sectors that comprise about 90 percent of US merchandise trade. In addition to the wealth of information that the book presents on these key individual indicators, which should make it an extremely useful reference, it helps provide a check on the conclusions and prescriptions that have emerged from our broader treatments of the trade issue.

Addressing as it does so many different industries, this study could not have been successfully completed without extensive assistance from a large number of experts both inside and outside the major firms in each. I join Allen Lenz in extending deep appreciation for their help at each stage of the project.

The Institute for International Economics is a private nonprofit institution for the study and discussion of international economic policy. Its purpose is to analyze important issues in that area, and to develop and communicate practical new approaches for dealing with them. The Institute is completely nonpartisan.

The Institute is funded largely by philanthropic foundations. Major institutional grants are now being received from the German Marshall Fund of the United States, which created the Institute with a generous commitment of funds in 1981, and from the Ford Foundation, the William and Flora Hewlett Foundation, the William M. Keck, Jr. Foundation, the Alfred P. Sloan Foundation, the C. V. Starr Foundation, and the United States–Japan Foundation. A number of other foundations and private corporations also contribute to the highly diversified financial resources of the Institute. About 14 percent of the Institute's resources in our latest fiscal year were provided by contributors outside the United States, including about 6 percent from Japan.

The Board of Directors bears overall responsibility for the Institute and gives general guidance and approval to its research program—including identification of topics that are likely to become important to international economic policymakers over the medium run (generally, one to three years), and which thus should be addressed by the Institute. The Director, working closely with the staff and outside Advisory Committee, is responsible for the development of particular projects and makes the final decision to publish an individual study.

The Institute hopes that its studies and other activities will contribute to building a stronger foundation for international economic policy around the world. We invite readers of these publications to let us know how they think we can best accomplish this objective.

C. FRED BERGSTEN
Director
June 1992

Acknowledgments

Of the many persons who contributed to this study, four were intimately involved in the details of its preparation for an extended period. Roger Pomeroy constructed the World Manufactures Trade Data Base and did the complex computer programming necessary to create the disaggregated time series and to extract data from a very large data base in a variety of ways.

Hunter K. Monroe and Bruce Parsell contributed greatly to all aspects of the study from design to completion. Hunter Monroe worked extensively with data base validation and table construction and authored several product group sections. Bruce Parsell managed the questionnaire survey, working closely with representatives of the trade associations that participated in the survey. He also authored several product group sections.

Michelle Ray designed and executed many of the tables, validated their content, persevered through many revisions of text and tables, and handled many other chores essential to the study's completion.

The questionnaire survey was made possible by the cooperation of 10 trade associations. I wish to express my appreciation to each association and its head for their participation. The participating associations and the individuals most directly involved were the American Iron and Steel Institute, Barry Solarz; The Association for Manufacturing Technology (formerly the National Machine Tool Builders Association), Gary Cohen; the Construction Industry Manufacturers Association, Bill Peterson; the Chemical Manufacturers Association; the Electronic Industries Association, Kevin Shannon; the Manufacturers Alliance for Productivity and Innovation, Richard McNabb; the Motor Equipment Manufacturers Association, Chris Bates; the National Association of Manufacturers, Howard Lewis; the National Forest Products Association, Alberto Goetzl; and the Rubber Manufacturers Association, Thomas Cole.

In addition, extensive discussions were held with representatives of other trade associations. These included Carl Priestland of the American Apparel Manufacturers Association, George Wino and Carlos Moore of the American Textile Manufactures Institute, Fawn Evanson of Footwear Industries of America, Bill Krist of the American Electronic Association, Irene Meister of the American Paper Institute, and John T. Eby of the Ford Motor Company.

This study draws heavily on data and expertise from the US Department of Commerce. Among the many major contributors from that agency were Sally Bath, John Henry, Martin Kohn, Bill Kolarik, Jeff Lins, Jon Menes, Tim Miles, Henry Misisco, Herta Pittman, John Rutter, Gary Teske, and Al Warner. Robert

Rogowsky and several staff members at the US International Trade Commission were also particularly helpful.

Other important information sources included Dan Bond, US Export-Import Bank; Marjorie Blumenthal, National Academy of Sciences; Doug Brackett and Joe Gerard, American Furniture Manufacturers Association; Steve Cooney, National Association of Manufacturers; Ron Duncan, World Bank; James H. Kelly; Virginia Lopez, Aerospace Industry Association; Tom Mahoney, Manufacturing Studies Board; Anthony Peters, US Bureau of Mines; Kyle Pitsor, National Electrical Manufacturers Association; Christopher Plummer, The WEFA Group; John Tilton, University of Colorado School of Mines; and Pat Williams, Telecommuncations Industry Association.

I am grateful to DRI/McGraw-Hill, Inc., and to David Blond of that organization for use of the elasticities from Mr. Blond's World Sea Trade model. John Roberts was also very helpful in resolving a number of data procurement problems.

The support of several colleagues at the Chemical Manufacturers Association was also important. Keith Christman, Jim O'Connor, Kevin Swift, Mike Walls, and several members of the association's International Trade Committee reviewed all or parts of the draft and made significant contributions.

The logistical support provided by the Chemical Manufacturers Association during the two-year tenure of the study was vital. I am deeply grateful to the Association and to its President, Robert A. Roland, for their support and cooperation.

Other organizations that provided helpful comments on the manuscript were McKinsey & Company; United Technologies Corporation; Hewlett Packard Company; IBM Corporation; The Boeing Company; and the AT&T Foundation.

Initial drafts of the study were reviewed by Walter Joelson, Kenneth Flamm, Catherine L. Mann, and J. David Richardson. Their comments and suggestions were very important factors in the evolution of the end product.

Finally, I am indebted to the Institute for International Economics and its staff for a great deal of assistance and cooperation. C. Fred Bergsten's extensive and detailed critiques of each of a series of drafts greatly improved the final product. Howard F. Rosen provided counsel and assistance during the conduct of the study. The final draft was skillfully edited by Michael Treadway and Barbara M. White.

Although many persons and organizations made this study possible and contributed to it, I am, of course, solely responsible for its shortcomings.

Allen J. Lenz

Narrowing the U.S. Current Account Deficit
A Sectoral Assessment

1

Introduction

Introduction

This study presents the results of a microeconomic, product group-by-product group assessment of problems and progress in reducing US current account deficits and the prospects for further reductions. The study's "bottom-up" analysis is intended to supplement and complement the macroeconomic, "top-down" assessments based on econometric models that are more frequently done. It identifies manufactures trade performance as the key factor in the growth of huge US current account deficits in the 1980s, in the improvement in performance that began in 1987, and in any further improvements in the 1990s. Finally, the study examines the recent trade performance of individual manufacturing industries and product groups and their prospects for the 1990s.

Objectives of the Study

The objectives of this study are to identify the contributions of individual sectors and industries to US trade performance; to assess the causes of their changing competitiveness and the resulting changes in their recent trade performance; to project future trade performance sector by sector; and to identify policy alternatives that could improve US trade performance in the future. Specific questions examined include the following:

- What basic changes have been occurring in the product composition of world trade? Which broad areas of trade—for example, services, raw materials, energy, agriculture, manufactures—and which manufactures product groups are most significant in world trade? Which are growing most rapidly? Which are declining? How do these changes affect US trade prospects?

- What basic changes have been occurring in the geographic composition of world trade in manufactures? How do these changes affect US performance and prospects? Which countries and regions are the major players in world manufactures trade?

- Which goods and services contributed most to the decline in US trade performance during the early 1980s? Which have contributed most to the reductions in US current account deficits since 1987?

- To what extent has a lack of adequate US-based production capacity constrained US exports or encouraged US imports?

- In light of the size of potential world markets and the strength of foreign competition, which manufactures product groups offer the greatest opportunities for increasing US exports or for recapture of US markets by US-based production?

- To what extent has decreased US competitiveness in particular industries affected the overall trade balance?

- How much of any improvement in US trade performance is likely to occur through export expansion and how much by recapture of US markets by US-based production?

- After adjusting for changes in exchange rates, what are the trends in the international competitiveness of US manufacturing in terms of its ability to contribute to rising US living standards?

- Within individual product groups, what are the likely main sources of improvement in US trade performance? Dollar depreciation? increased foreign direct investment in the United States? improved US productivity and price competitiveness? other factors?

- What are the policy implications for the United States and its competitors of the continued dominance of manufactures in US and world trade?

- What policy steps might facilitate further reduction of the US trade and current account deficits? What steps would improve the United States' ability to compete without a continued decline of the dollar?

Methodology

This study disaggregates the US current account into its major components, so as to examine past US trade performance at a level of detail that makes it possible to determine the relative importance and variability of each component in future performance. Merchandise trade, the key factor in current account performance, is similarly decomposed, revealing manufactures trade as the key factor in US performance in terms of both the trade account and the current account.

This study examines US performance in manufactures trade in several ways, both in the aggregate and at different levels of disaggregation. We first examine total manufactures trade and then two major groupings: basic manufactures and finished goods. We then divide manufactures into four broad areas—Standard International Trade Classifications (SITC) 5 through 8—and subsequently into the two-digit SITC product groups that fall within these four areas. We also provide more detailed information on trade performance for the three-digit subcategories within each two-digit product group.

A key part of the analysis focuses on the past and prospective performance of 21 manufactures product groups that dominated US trade performance during the 1980s and will continue to do so in the 1990s. On the basis of these assessments and other analyses, we draw general conclusions about future aggregate trade and current account performance, and about the impact of US policies on US trade performance and the manufacturing sector and on the structure and international competitiveness of the US economy.

We assess the individual product groups in three ways. Each is described briefly below.

Historical Trade Data Base   We constructed a world trade data base containing the export and import data of 26 countries (the 24 countries of the Organization for Economic Cooperation and Development [OECD] plus Taiwan and Korea) for the period 1979–89. The data base contains world manufactures trade data at the SITC one-, two-, and three-digit levels. We supplemented these data with more detailed US Department of Commerce trade statistics in SITC format for the years 1981 through 1990.[1]

Interviews   We interviewed well over 100 knowledgeable experts in a number of government agencies, trade associations, individual companies, and elsewhere to obtain their assessments of past trade performance of various industries and of their outlook for the future as well as to identify other relevant sources of information.

Mail Survey   A mail questionnaire survey conducted through 10 trade associations provided over 650 individual-company assessments of the prospects for, and key determinants of, exports, imports, and investment in plant and equipment.

---

1. See the appendix to this volume for a detailed discussion of the construction, use, and limitations of this data base.

Uses of a Disaggregated Approach

There have been few, if any, assessments of overall US trade performance utilizing a disaggregated, bottom-up approach. Most analyses of US trade are macroeconomic in approach, dealing only with large aggregates. Why decompose the current account and merchandise trade, and why analyze in detail individual manufactures trade product groups as is done in this study?

There are two basic ways in which a disaggregated analysis can aid policymaking. First, the method offers a way to learn how the trade performance of particular industries and products is affected by policies and events that shape national economic performance and trade performance in the aggregate. Second, it complements econometric, aggregated assessments of performance and outlook.

The Policymaking Uses of a Sectoral Analysis

The policies that generated a long period of US economic growth during the 1980s also contributed to the large trade and current account deficits of that period. Some elements of the US economy prospered during the 1980s, but others—particularly those facing international competition—did not do as well, and indeed some suffered. An examination of detailed, disaggregated data relating to US current account and trade performance can show which sectors and industries were most affected by foreign competition. It can identify which sectors bore the brunt of the industrial restructuring undertaken in response to lagging trade performance and which sectors are most likely to show improved trade performance in the future. It may also provide insights into the sources of some structural or macroeconomic changes, such as the long-term decline of the dollar.

Quantification of US performance in various components of the current account and of merchandise trade can put the various elements of US external transactions into proper perspective, allowing one to identify the consequences and trade-offs of US economic policies for particular sectors. Disaggregation is essential to dispel several misconceptions about US trade, for example that increased exports of services offer the prospect of large US trade gains; that high-technology exports or the targeting of a few critical technologies will solve the United States' trade problems; or that US comparative advantage in agriculture is the key to balanced US trade in the future.

Similarly, quantifying both US and world trade at various levels of disaggregation makes it possible to identify those industries and products where the United States' trade strengths and weaknesses lie, and to ascertain the size of world markets available to US exporters. The relative importance of US markets in various industries to world exporters can also be placed in proper perspective.

The findings of these microeconomic analyses may have important policy applications. For example, placing services trade and manufactures trade in proper perspective could suggest changes in domestic policies affecting each sector and international negotiating strategies regarding each. Quantifying world export markets by individual product group provides a sounder basis for assessing national trade and export strategies than simply working with aggregates. Identification of those industries and sectors most affected by fiscal, monetary, tax, regulatory, and other policies that promote net capital inflows (and therefore current account deficits) may lead to a reexamination of those policies generally. By quantifying the trade performance and potential of individual industries and products, and placing them in proper perspective with each other, one can arrive at a sounder basis both for microeconomic policies aimed at specific industries and macroeconomic policies directed to improving overall trade performance.

Using Disaggregated Analyses to Complement Macroeconomic Studies

This study projects future trade performance in each of the sectors and product groups that are most important to US trade. The projections incorporate information regarding current and projected global supply-demand conditions and other relevant factors and are based on exchange rates prevailing at the time of the analysis (September 1990–July 1991). These assessments employ a variety of quantitative and other inputs. Nevertheless, the results are ultimately subjective judgments, not the product of mathematical equations, and therefore they may exhibit the flaws of any judgmental process. Judgmental assessments can, however, incorporate information about current or projected events that will affect future supply and demand, whereas forecasting models generally must assume that no structural changes will occur during the forecast period. Disaggregated analysis may justify or challenge the models' standard assumption and may help explain why results predicted by the models may diverge from historical trends. Moreover, even when macroeconomic models identify structural changes, they do not explain them. For example, what accounts for the secular decline of the dollar, and why have the lags in trade responses following exchange rate changes lengthened? An industry-by-industry analysis may be able to predict and explain the structural changes underlying these phenomena.

The intent of this microeconomic analysis is to supplement—not replace—macroeconomic exercises. Aggregated analyses may sometimes mislead. For example, most analyses of US capital investment as a determinant of international competitiveness rely on aggregate investment series; these, however, include investments that do little to improve the competitiveness of sectors facing international competition. Examples include investments in office buildings, the financial sector, shopping malls, and other elements of retail trade.

Similarly, because US competitive strengths vary across sectors and product groups, only a disaggregated analysis can hope to identify and anticipate the effects of changes in the composition of world trade on US aggregate performance. For example, US preeminence in products with declining or small world markets cannot offset weaknesses in products that loom large and ever larger in world trade.

There are, on the other hand, several limitations to the disaggregated approach, particularly when it comes to projecting the future performance of individual product groups. The appendix in this volume reviews the specific limitations of the data bases used in the study and the statistics derived from them in some detail. Here we point to some important general limitations of the method:

- *The statistics themselves have limitations.* Trade statistics for industrialized economies are on the whole probably as good as, or better than, most other national and international statistics, such as those on consumption and output. Nevertheless, a careful perusal of disaggregated trade data will reveal errors and inconsistencies. The more disaggregated the data, the more likely it is that these problems may mislead the analyst.

- *The analyses of individual product groups do not produce testable hypotheses.* Because much of the information we collected on individual products and industries is subjective and hard to quantify, and because this study does not utilize formal models of individual product groups, our projections of trade performance are inherently subjective. Moreover, subjective judgments are necessarily imprecise when they concern the ways in which exchange rate changes can affect the trade performance of individual products. Subjective judgments cannot be used to forecast exactly how the trade balance will change in response to particular movements in exchange rates. Disaggregated analyses, however, can identify the most important sectors for international trade at an industry or product level, the key factors that determine performance, and areas of uncertainty about future performance. They can also establish the parameters of likely performance with some degree of confidence.

  Further, even if our microeconomic analyses cannot precisely quantify the effect of exchange rates on trade balances, they may at least be able to assess the sensitivity of individual product groups to the exchange rate and to indicate whether current exchange rates are likely to foster significant changes in trade performance as well as indicate the direction of those changes. In the end, readers can make their own judgments about the validity of the sectoral analyses in this volume. In some instances, that may be easier than judging the validity of econometric assessments.

■ *Aggregating the results of disaggregated analyses risks falling prey to fallacies of composition.* Not only might the conclusions drawn in some of the individual product analyses be wrong, but the whole may be different from the sum of the individual parts. This could occur if the analyses fail to capture important interactions among the individual parts. This is a significant problem with the disaggregated approach. It can be mitigated only by increasing the depth and breadth of the assessments of individual product groups and by trying to identify interrelationships among product groups. Econometric models, on the other hand, are designed precisely to pick up these interactions.

Most important, however, this study does not aim at a precise quantification of likely future overall US trade balances through aggregating the results for individual product groups. Instead, it seeks to answer the more fundamental questions set out above. For example, is the broad improvement in the US trade balance seen in recent years likely to continue at current exchange rates, and in what products and sectors is that improvement likely to occur? By answering these questions, decomposition provides analytical gains that are likely to exceed the potential losses from mistakenly embracing compositional fallacies.

The Critical Role of US Manufacturing

This study argues that manufactures trade is the primary interface between the US economy and the world economy, that manufacturing is inevitably most exposed to, and bears most of the brunt of, foreign competition, and that improved performance in manufactures trade must be the source of any major improvements in the US trade and current accounts.

What Is US Manufacturing?

The US manufacturing sector is composed of those US companies that combine labor, capital, and raw materials of various kinds to make tangible goods. The

US Department of Commerce categorizes manufacturing into 20 major groups identified by Standard Industry Codes (SICs):[2]

SIC

20 Food and kindred products

21 Tobacco products

22 Textile mill products

23 Apparel

24 Lumber and wood products

25 Furniture and fixtures

26 Paper and allied products

27 Printing and publishing

28 Chemicals and allied products

29 Petroleum refining

30 Rubber and miscellaneous plastic products

31 Leather and leather products

32 Stone, clay, glass, and cement

33 Primary metal industries

34 Fabricated metal products

35 Industrial and commercial machinery and computers

36 Electronic and other electrical equipment

38 Measuring, analyzing, and control instruments, and photographic, medical, and optical goods

39 Miscellaneous manufactures

---

2. The US Department of Commerce SIC codes combine like *activities* into industries. These codes differ from those of the SITC, a United Nations system of classification that groups the manufactured products in a way that describes the composition and flow of internationally traded goods. The SITC system is used internationally; it groups similar traded *items* into product groups and does not include the products classified under SICs 20, 21, and 29. This study uses SITC data extensively and does not use SIC data.

Table 1.1   United States: sectoral composition of GNP, 1989 (percentages of total)

Sector	In 1982 dollars	In 1989 dollars
Construction	4.4	4.8
Agriculture, forestry, and fisheries	2.4	2.2
Manufacturing	22.6	18.6
Transportation and public utilities	9.8	8.9
Wholesale trade	7.4	6.5
Retail trade	10.0	9.3
Mining	3.1	1.5
Finance, insurance, and real estate	14.7	17.2
Services	15.8	18.7
Government	10.5	11.9
Total[a]	100.0	100.0

a. Numbers do not sum to 100.0 because of small residual categories.

Source: US Department of Commerce. 1991. "Gross National Product by Industry, 1987–89." *Survey of Current Business* (April); US Department of Commerce. 1991. "Gross National Product by Industry, 1987–89," p. 25.

The Contribution of Manufacturing to US GNP

US national income identifies national income as originating in 10 sectors (table 1.1). Manufacturing remains the largest single income-originating sector when outputs are measured in constant (i.e., inflation-adjusted) 1982 dollars, with 22.6 percent of GNP; its share is almost identical to that of services (which might better be labeled "other services," since several of the other categories are services as well) when measured in terms of 1989 dollars. In current dollars, manufacturing's share of GNP has declined significantly, from 27.6 percent in 1967 to 18.6 percent in 1989. But in constant 1982 dollars manufacturing has maintained essentially the same share of GNP since 1950.

This indicates that, in real or volume terms, the proportion of manufactured goods in the US economy's total output has remained relatively constant. The divergence between the two statistics—a declining portion of total resources to produce a relatively stable portion of total output in real terms—reflects the fact that productivity growth is generally higher in manufacturing than in most other sectors of the economy. Also, manufacturing's relatively constant share of total output indicates that manufacturing is not disappearing from the United States.

Manufacturing, agricultural, forests and fisheries, and mining produce a variety of material things—tangible goods. Most of the other income-originating sectors do not make tangible goods but instead provide services of various kinds. For example, although the wholesale trade, retail trade, and government sectors deliver both goods and services to customers, they do not make goods themselves. The large "services" sector—with 18.7 percent of current-dollar GNP—

includes a wide variety of activities ranging from health spas to computer maintenance and repair.

Most kinds of services cannot be readily exported or imported and therefore do not directly face international competition (see chapter 2). US and foreign companies in such services industries as wholesale trade, retail trade, and banking often do locate in each others' markets, but when they do they usually produce and market their services there rather than export them from the home country. Hence their contribution to the export side of the US trade balance is limited at best. With few exceptions, only those industries in the manufacturing, agriculture, forestry and fisheries, and mining sectors face competition in the US market from foreign-based production. Manufacturing is by far the largest of these, and consequently it bears the brunt of international competition.

Employment and Output

Total US manufacturing employment has fluctuated with economic conditions, but at 19.6 million, employment in 1989 was about the same as in 1970. Manufacturing employment in 1990 declined to about 19.1 million, reflecting in part the slowdown in economic activity. As a percentage of total nonagricultural employment, manufacturing has declined markedly, from 33.7 percent in 1950 to only 17.3 percent in 1990. However, interpretation of these data is clouded by the fact that manufacturing firms are increasingly subcontracting to other kinds of firms many tasks that their own employees used to perform. Examples include security and cafeteria services, maintenance work, accounting, and data processing. The effect is to shift workers from firms classified as manufacturers to firms classified within services industries, with no real change in the nature of the work performed.

According to government indices, US manufacturing output in 1990 was in real terms 39.5 percent greater than in 1980 and 94.9 percent greater than in 1970. The rising output produced by a manufacturing work force that has been shrinking reflects both the more common use of service subcontractors and, more important, rising labor productivity. Rising levels of output per worker stem from a variety of factors, including improved plant and equipment and new process technologies.

The Critical Role of Manufacturing

Manufacturing plays a unique and critical role in the US economy that is often not well understood. During the 1980s, statements that the United States was becoming a services-oriented economy gained currency. This perception together with growing concerns about environmental pollution from manufacturing led some to predict—if not to welcome and advocate—a "postindustrial society" in the United States, from which manufacturing would, for the most part, have disappeared. In a 1986 cover story, *Business Week* postulated that the United States might become "a nation of hollow corporations"—one essentially devoid of manufacturing. Corporations would perform mostly design, marketing, and research in the United States and do most of their manufacturing abroad.[3] The implicit assumption was that US imports of manufactures and other goods would be paid for by exports of services.

At best, however, as will be demonstrated in chapter 2, the United States can expect only modest future surpluses in services trade. Services will not suffice to allow the United States to pay its way in the world economy while at the same time running huge deficits in oil and manufactures trade. Large manufactures deficits will inevitably translate into large current account deficits and borrowing abroad. Indeed, as chapter 2 shows, US manufactures trade surpluses will be required if the United States is to balance its international accounts in the 1990s.

Nor would continued foreign borrowing support net imports of a large portion of present US consumption of manufactured goods. Even the very large deficit in manufactures trade recorded in 1987 ($125 billion) represented only a relatively small fraction of US manufactures consumption that year. In 1987, the value added by manufacturing in current-dollar terms was $872 billion, and the value of US manufactures shipments (to domestic and foreign destinations) totaled $2,917 billion. Neither statistic accurately reflects the value of US manufactures consumption. The first captures only the value added by the manufacturing sector, whereas the second involves considerable double counting. A truly accurate measure is not available, but the value of manufactures production—including inputs from other sectors—in current-dollar terms as of 1987 was probably around 30 percent of GNP. The 1987 manufactures trade deficit of $125 billion was equivalent to 2.8 percent of GNP. This would indicate that even in 1987 the manufactures trade deficit was equivalent to less than 10 percent of US manufactured goods consumption.

Any shift of a substantial fraction of US consumption of manufactured goods to imports would therefore result in current account deficits much larger—both relatively and absolutely—than that of 1987. Political and economic forces would surely be brought to bear to keep that from happening. In effect, these forces, including the discipline of markets, will ensure that the United States will maintain a manufacturing base large enough to produce the vast majority of its consumption of manufactured goods and that manufacturing will continue to

---

3. *Business Week,* 3 March 1986, 57.

be a major part of the US economy—even if its international competitiveness must be sustained by declines in the dollar and in real wages. Those forces will not, however, ensure that US manufacturing will be world-class—a leader in manufacturing technologies and productivity capable of paying high wages— or that US manufacturing will fulfill its potential as a contributor to rising US living standards.

Clearly the US manufacturing sector must be large enough to avoid continuing large current account deficits and the adverse long-term effects on US living standards of continued borrowing abroad. But also vitally important to the long-term progress of the US economy are the catalytic effects that flow from the linkages between a world-class manufacturing sector and the other sectors of the economy. The manufacturing sector not only provides a very large market for other US industries but is the source of the vast majority of technological advances that make productivity gains possible and improve US living standards. The manufacturing sector, for example, accounts for roughly 90 percent of US patents granted and performs and bankrolls the bulk of private-sector-financed research and development (US Department of Commerce 1990). These technological advances are to be found not just in machinery, aircraft, and other heavy industries but also in textiles, papermaking, plastics, adhesives, composite materials, pharmaceuticals, and health care equipment, to name a few. Not surprisingly, therefore, manufacturing is the major source of US productivity gains.

Moreover, manufacturing plays a larger role in the US economy than GNP data indicate. As already noted, the statistic indicating that only about 18.6 percent of 1989 US GNP originated in the manufacturing sector counts only the value added by the manufacturing sector itself. It does not include the value of those inputs purchased from other sectors. In 1989, the manufacturing sector purchased some $642 billion of goods and services from other US industries to use as inputs in its production processes. It used, for example, almost one-fourth of the output of the business services, transportation and warehousing, and utilities industries, and two-thirds of the output of mining.

Manufacturing, then, is in a real sense the locomotive that pulls the other sectors of the US economy along. A strong, growing economy and rising living standards are highly unlikely without a strong, vibrant manufacturing sector. Without world-class manufacturing industries, the United States is most unlikely to be able to match the growth in living standards of its competitors. If the United States is to maintain political, economic, and military leadership, it must have a manufacturing sector that is a world leader in researching and developing new products and processes that are in turn utilized in US-based production.

In a 1990 report, however, the Office of Technology Assessment, a congressional research body, stated that "US manufacturing has never been in more trouble than it is now" (US Congress, Office of Technology Assessment 1990, 3). Weak US trade performance has been an important manifestation of this trouble. Manufacturing's trade performance during the 1990s will be an important, but not conclusive, measure of manufacturing's strength and its contributions to the US economy and living standards.

Organization of the Study

Chapter 2 of this study justifies the focus on the role of manufactures trade in the US external accounts. It begins by disaggregating US current account and merchandise trade performance. We then describe the dominant role of manufactures trade in the growth and subsequent narrowing of the US trade and current account deficits in the 1980s and project a similarly dominant role for manufactures trade in any future reductions of these deficits.

Chapter 3 provides an overview of world trade in goods and services. We present some broad statistical measures of world merchandise trade, disaggregate it into broad categories and further into specific product groups, and describe its changing composition. We identify the key role of manufactures trade in world trade, examine trends in the composition of world manufactures trade, and, using data on world export and import shares, assess in broad terms the market competitiveness of the major trading countries in manufactures trade.

Chapter 4 describes three alternative measures of competitiveness and identifies those that will be utilized in this study. The chapter gives an overview of US manufactures trade performance for 1981–90, examines the changing geographical and product composition of US exports and imports, and describes the roles of individual product groups in the 1981–87 deterioration and the 1987–90 improvement in US trade performance. We also review the effects of movements in the exchange rate and other changes on price and volume over the last decade, and we assess the outlook for productivity gains in the years just ahead.

Chapter 5 provides a detailed examination of US trade performance in the 1980s in each of 21 key manufactures product groups and discusses their prospects for the next several years.

Chapter 6 reports the findings of an extensive, detailed mail questionnaire survey that collected information from a broad range of US manufacturing firms on export, import, and investment expectations.

Chapter 7 summarizes the findings of this study and discusses their implications for US trade and economic policies.

Bibliography

US Congress. Office of Technology Assessment. 1990. *Making Things Better: Competing in Manufacturing.* 101st Cong., 2nd Sess. (April).

US Department of Commerce. US Patent and Trademark Office. 1990. "Patenting Trends In The United States, 1963–89." Washington: US Department of Commerce (August).

2

The US Current Account in Perspective

2

The US Current Account in Perspective

This chapter discusses the key role manufactures trade has played in the growth and subsequent narrowing of US trade and current account deficits since 1980. We first disaggregate the current account and analyze its principal components. We then do a similar decomposition of merchandise trade. Finally, we note the significant policy implications of manufacturing's central role.

The Current Account Dissected

The current account is the broadest measure of US international goods and services transactions.[1] The US Department of Commerce groups these trans-actions into four basic categories: merchandise trade, services, international investment income, and unilateral transfers.

From 1981 to 1987, the US current account balance moved from a $6.9 billion surplus to a $160.2 billion deficit (table 2.1). Of this $167.1 billion deterioration, 78.7 percent—$131.5 billion—was in merchandise trade. Another $23.7 billion of the decline occurred in net international investment income, reflecting the US change from the world's largest creditor country to the world's largest debtor country. Because of strong direct investment earnings, however, the international investment income account maintained a 1987 surplus of $7.6 billion.

The current account began to improve in 1988. From 1987 to 1990, the current account deficit shrank by $68.1 billion, thanks to improvements of $51.4 billion in merchandise trade, $20.0 billion in services, and $4.4 billion in international investment income; these were partly offset by a $7.7 billion increase in outward unilateral transfers.

Merchandise trade thus provided the bulk of both the 1981–87 deterioration and the 1988–90 improvement in the US current account balance. Will mer-

---

1. The current account also includes unilateral transfers (discussed below), which typically make up a very small fraction of the total.

Table 2.1 United States: summary of international transactions, 1981–90 (billions of dollars)

	1981	1982	1983	1984	1985	1986	1987	1988	1989	1990
Merchandise trade										
Exports	237.1	211.2	201.8	219.9	215.9	223.4	250.3	320.3	361.5	389.6
Imports	265.1	247.6	268.9	332.4	338.1	368.4	409.8	447.3	477.4	497.7
Balance	−28.0	−36.4	−67.1	−112.5	−122.1	−145.1	−159.5	−127.0	−115.9	−108.7
Services										
Exports	57.4	59.5	60.1	66.5	67.8	79.8	91.1	102.4	116.5	133.3
Imports	45.5	47.4	50.6	63.7	68.7	75.1	84.7	92.1	94.7	106.9
Balance	11.9	12.1	9.5	2.7	−0.9	4.7	6.4	10.3	21.8	26.4
International investment income										
Exports	85.0	85.3	82.0	92.9	82.3	81.0	90.5	110.7	128.7	130.1
Imports	53.6	57.1	54.5	69.5	66.1	70.0	82.9	105.4	126.0	118.1
Balance	31.3	28.3	27.4	23.4	16.2	11.0	7.6	5.3	2.7	12.0
of which:										
Direct investment receipts	32.6	24.7	26.8	30.0	28.3	30.9	40.6	50.4	54.0	54.4
Direct investment payments	6.9	3.2	5.6	9.2	6.1	5.4	7.2	13.6	11.5	1.8
Direct investment balance	25.7	21.6	21.2	20.8	22.2	25.5	33.4	36.8	42.5	52.6
Total goods, services, and income										
Exports	379.4	356.1	343.9	379.3	366.0	384.1	431.9	533.4	606.6	652.9
Imports	364.2	352.2	374.1	465.7	472.9	513.5	577.4	644.7	697.4	722.7
Balance	15.2	3.9	−30.2	−86.4	−106.9	−129.4	−145.5	−111.3	−90.8	−69.8
Unilateral transfers	−8.3	−9.8	−10.0	−12.6	−15.5	−16.0	−14.7	−14.9	−15.5	−22.4
Current account balance	6.9	−5.9	−40.1	−99.0	−122.3	−145.4	−160.2	−126.2	−106.3	−92.1

Source: US Department of Commerce.

chandise trade continue to be the dominant source of improvement during the 1990s? Can services or other nonmerchandise trade accounts provide major gains? A look at each of these three nonmerchandise trade components of the current account reveals their potential contributions.

Unilateral Transfers

The unilateral transfers account consists primarily of government outlays for foreign aid and other external grants as well as payments to US pensioners living abroad. Because these outlays are offset by very few receipts, the account is normally in deficit.

Movements in exchange rates do not greatly affect the unilateral transfers account. The deficit in this account rose from $8.3 billion in 1981 to $22.4 billion in 1990. Receipts from foreign governments in compensation for the costs of the Gulf War will result in a 1991 surplus in this account, but otherwise annual deficits are likely to continue in the $15 billion to $20 billion range over the next few years.

International Investment Income

The international investment income account records payments to foreign holders of several kinds of US financial assets (e.g., stocks, bonds, direct investments, bank deposits, and US Treasury securities) and payments received by US holders of similar kinds of foreign assets. In 1990, US international investment receipts were $130.1 billion and payments were $118.1 billion, resulting in a surplus of $12.0 billion.

The large surpluses seen in earlier years in US international investment income eroded during the 1980s as the United States shifted from a large creditor to a large debtor position, but not as rapidly as might have been expected. The reason is that US assets abroad typically earn higher rates of return on their book value than do foreign assets in the United States, which have typically been in place for a shorter period of time (see, e.g., Cline 1989, 97, and Bergsten and Islam, forthcoming).

In 1981 the United States earned a surplus of $31.3 billion on its international investments. By 1989, the surplus had declined to $2.7 billion (table 2.1), but weak performance of the US economy in 1990 lowered direct investment payments to foreign investors, returning the United States to a $12.0 billion surplus. The United States continued to maintain a surplus in this account through the first half of 1991.

The United States now runs deficits on the major elements of its international investments, with the exception of direct investments. The receipts in this account reflect US parent companies' share of the operating profits of their foreign affiliates. This is the principal account through which the US economy benefits from the sale of goods produced abroad by US firms' foreign affiliates; smaller amounts also enter via the services component of the current account in the form of license fees, royalties, and various service charges that these affiliates pay to their US parents. At $54.4 billion in 1990, direct investment income receipts were substantial but only a very small fraction of a much larger volume of foreign sales. Whereas one dollar of exports contributes one full dollar to the US current account balance, one dollar in foreign sales made by foreign affiliates may contribute perhaps six cents in the form of investment income, license fees and royalties, and other income (see chapter 4 for more detailed statistics).

In 1989, the $54.0 billion in investment income from US direct investments abroad greatly exceeded the $11.5 billion in payments to foreign investors for their direct investments in the United States, yielding a $42.5 billion US surplus. In 1990, the balance on direct investment income further improved by $10.1 billion. That improvement, however, stemmed from a combination of continued strong performance by US direct investments abroad (income on this investment increased by $0.4 billion) and weak performance (a $9.7 billion decline in income) by foreign direct investments in the United States. The low earnings of foreign companies from the operations of their US affiliates probably reflects the US recession that began in 1990.

US direct investments abroad in manufacturing industries earned $22.9 billion in 1990, almost half the total for all industries. The second-largest earner was the petroleum industry, with income of $10.9 billion. The large US receipts in recent years from manufacturing investments abroad are very much the heritage of large outlays in the 1960s and 1970s, a period when US manufacturing dominated its international competition. During those decades, the United States maintained substantial net outflows of direct investment capital. In recent years, however, new foreign direct investments in US manufacturing have consistently exceeded new US direct investments in manufacturing abroad by a wide margin. The gap did narrow in 1990.[2] However, if the trend that prevailed during most of the 1980s continues, the recent growth in net US earnings on direct investments may slow, and as the earnings of foreign direct investments in the United States increase, net US earnings from direct investments could begin to decline.

More immediately, a recovery of the US economy from recession is likely to increase the direct investment earnings of foreign firms from their US operations. As US indebtedness and the accompanying debt service payments continue to increase, this will probably tip the balance of the international investment income account back into deficit in the next few years. Continued strong foreign

---

2. It appears to have narrowed further through the first half of 1991. See Bergsten and Graham (1991).

economic performance may slow this deterioration by increasing foreign earnings of US direct investments abroad. In addition, any further depreciation of the dollar will increase the value of foreign earnings when translated into dollars. These factors may slow or delay further deterioration in the international investment income balance but are unlikely to halt it for very long.

Services

The third major current account category, services, is made up of a wide variety of tradeable services, mostly originating in the private sector. Exports of services in 1990 were $133.3 billion, while imports were $106.9 billion, for a balance of $26.4 billion. This account has provided sizable and growing surpluses in recent years (table 2.2).

Some analysts, citing the growth of services in the US economy and in US trade, see exports of services becoming an increasingly important source of US export earnings. However, disaggregation of the account into its seven subcategories—direct defense expenditures, US government miscellaneous services, travel, passenger fares, other transportation, royalties and license fees, and other private services—leads to the conclusion that continuing large gains are unlikely.

Defense Sales and Expenditures

Defense sales and expenditures include transfers of goods and services under military grant contracts and various overseas military expenditures. Receipts of $9.9 billion and payments (imports) of $17.1 billion in 1990 resulted in a deficit of $7.2 billion, up from $0.8 billion in 1981 (table 2.2).

Defense sales and expenditures are a function of military grants and military operations. In a more peaceful world in which elements of US military forces return to the continental United States, the deficit on this account might decline later in the 1990s. But any near-term gains are likely to be small.

US Government Miscellaneous Services

Miscellaneous government services consist of the international payments and receipts from direct defense expenditures, transfers under US marketing agency sales contracts, and various other types of government services. This subcategory will continue to have small deficits.

Table 2.2 United States: international services transactions, 1981–90 (billions of dollars)

	1981	1982	1983	1984	1985	1986	1987	1988	1989	1990
Total services										
Exports	57.4	59.5	60.1	66.5	67.8	79.8	91.1	102.4	116.5	133.3
Imports	45.5	47.4	50.6	63.7	68.7	75.1	84.7	92.1	94.1	106.9
Balance	11.9	12.1	9.5	2.7	-0.9	4.7	6.4	10.3	22.4	26.4
of which:										
Direct defense expenditures										
Exports	10.7	12.6	12.5	10.0	8.7	8.6	11.1	9.4	8.4	9.9
Imports	11.6	12.5	12.7	12.1	12.8	13.5	14.8	15.1	14.6	17.1
Balance	-0.8	0.1	-0.2	-2.1	-4.1	-4.9	-3.7	-5.8	-6.2	-7.2
US government miscellaneous services										
Exports	0.5	0.6	0.7	0.7	0.9	0.6	0.5	0.7	0.6	0.7
Imports	1.3	1.5	1.6	1.5	1.7	1.7	1.9	2.0	2.0	2.2
Balance	-0.8	-0.9	-0.9	-0.8	-0.8	-1.1	-1.4	-1.3	-1.4	-1.5
Travel										
Exports	12.9	12.4	10.9	17.1	17.7	20.3	23.4	28.9	35.2	40.6
Imports	11.5	12.4	13.1	23.3	25.2	26.7	30.0	33.1	34.5	38.7
Balance	1.4	0.0	-2.2	-6.2	-7.5	-6.4	-6.6	-4.2	0.7	1.9
Passenger fares										
Exports	3.1	3.2	3.6	4.0	4.3	5.5	6.9	8.8	10.4	12.3
Imports	4.5	4.8	6.0	5.9	6.7	6.7	7.4	7.9	8.4	9.0
Balance	-1.4	-1.6	-2.4	-1.9	-2.4	-1.2	-0.5	0.9	2.0	3.3
Other transportation										
Exports	12.6	12.3	12.6	13.8	14.7	15.5	17.0	19.0	20.7	22.4
Imports	12.5	11.7	12.2	14.8	15.6	16.7	17.8	19.5	20.7	23.4
Balance	0.1	0.6	0.4	-1.0	-0.9	-1.2	-0.8	-0.5	0.0	-1.1
Royalties and license fees										
Exports	7.3	5.2	5.3	5.6	6.0	7.3	9.1	10.8	11.9	15.3
Imports	0.7	0.6	0.7	1.0	0.9	1.1	1.4	2.1	2.2	2.6
Balance	6.6	4.6	4.6	4.6	5.1	6.2	7.7	8.7	9.8	12.7
Other private services										
Exports	10.3	13.3	14.5	15.3	15.6	22.2	23.1	24.8	29.3	32.2
Imports	3.6	4.0	4.3	5.1	5.8	8.7	11.4	12.3	11.6	13.8
Balance	6.7	9.3	10.2	10.2	9.8	13.5	11.7	12.5	17.7	18.4

Source: US Department of Commerce.

Travel, Passenger Fares, and Other Transportation

These three subcategories of the current account are interrelated. The travel account consists of expenditures by US citizens abroad and the expenditures of foreign citizens in the United States. The passenger fares account records the fares paid by US citizens to foreign carriers (mostly airlines) and by foreign passengers to US carriers. Other transportation includes port services, freight, and other charges paid by US carriers to foreign parties and similar collections by US parties from foreign carriers.

Much of total services transactions (56.5 percent of 1990 exports, 66.6 percent of imports) falls within these three subcategories. In 1990, they summed to a surplus of $4.1 billion, compared with deficits ranging up to $10.8 billion during certain years of the 1980s. The travel account alone has in fact experienced the widest variance of any services account in recent years, swinging from a modest $1.4 billion surplus in 1981 to a $7.5 billion deficit in 1985 and back to a modest $1.9 billion surplus in 1990.

The recent gains in the travel, passenger fares, and other transportation accounts are probably due partly to recent revisions in estimating techniques, which have raised the dollar amounts of both exports and imports. To the extent this is the case, the gains are a one-time adjustment, not a trend that is likely to continue. Dollar depreciation and other factors, however, have no doubt also played an important role in improving US balances.

The tourism-related accounts—travel and passenger fares—are sensitive to exchange rates, and significant further dollar depreciation would further improve their balances by deterring US travel abroad, encouraging increased foreign visits to the United States, and increasing the dollar value of the foreign-currency earnings of US air and ocean carriers. Moreover, other things being equal, rising global levels of affluence that narrow the income gaps between the United States and other countries should cause the foreign travel of residents of other countries to increase more rapidly than foreign travel by US residents. This should tilt the US travel and passenger fare accounts toward improved balances. In 1990, US travel "exports" to Japan—the expenditures of Japanese tourists and business travelers in the United States—at $7.7 billion were $5.5 billion greater than the $2.2 billion expenditures of US travelers in Japan. Even so, at $12.3 billion, Western European travelers spent more in the United States than the Japanese, as did Latin American and other Western Hemisphere (excluding Canada) visitors, at $9.2 billion. Canadian expenditures in the United States were also large, amounting to $5.7 billion. Nevertheless, the United States continues to run travel account deficits with Western Europe and the Latin American and other Western Hemisphere region.

With international air fares set by international agreements and typically denominated in dollars, dollar depreciation will not give American air carriers an advantage in the competition for passengers. It will, however, raise the dollar values of both the foreign earnings of US carriers and their foreign costs. Notwithstanding these favorable factors, travel and passenger fares, which do offer expansion potential, are relatively small accounts, with a combined 1990 two-way trade of just over $100 billion. Together they yielded a record $5.2 billion surplus in 1990, compared with a near balance in 1981. Overall, the prospects for additional gains of more than a few billion dollars in these accounts are unlikely without severe further dollar depreciation and/or a persistently weak US economy. Balances in the "other transportation" account have ranged from approximately $1 billion surpluses to approximately $1 billion deficits, and no major change is likely.

Royalties and License Fees

The sixth services subcategory, royalties and license fees, consists of the income from the sale or licensing of US technologies. Surpluses in this account have recently grown, reaching $9.8 billion in 1989 and $12.7 billion in 1990. Royalty receipts in 1990 were only 11 percent of total services receipts but provided a surplus equivalent to almost half the total services surplus.

The positive balances from royalties and license fees derive from US preeminence in the development of new technologies in earlier years and the current use of these technologies in foreign manufacturing. Recently the strong economic performance of certain foreign economies has also contributed to US surpluses in this account. The great majority of the technologies currently under license to foreign users originated in the manufacturing sector. Of total 1990 license fee and royalty receipts of $15.3 billion, $12.1 billion were receipts from the foreign affiliates of US companies. Of that $12.1 billion, foreign affiliates paid some $8.6 billion—56.2 percent of total royalty receipts—to US manufacturing firms for the use of their product and processing technologies. Another $2.6 billion, 17 percent of the total, came from licensing of industrial processes to unaffiliated foreign firms. These data highlight the key role of US direct investments abroad in generating earnings from licensing technology and the dominant role of manufacturing in income and surpluses from royalties.

The recent increases in income from royalties and licensing also partly reflect the effects of dollar depreciation; since 1985, the falling dollar has increased the dollar value of royalties and fees originally denominated in foreign currencies. Further major gains in royalties and fees not generated by the currency translation effects of additional dollar decline seem doubtful, as US technological dominance continues to recede and as both US and foreign firms in the United States utilize more and more foreign technology. Some decline in US technical dominance seems a natural result of the industrialization of other countries; as industrialization spreads, US manufacturing will inevitably become a smaller portion of total world manufacturing and will supply a smaller share of the world's advances in manufactures products and processes. The decline, however, will be accelerated if US manufacturing lags behind other key competitors in investing in new technologies.

Further dollar decline would have favorable currency translation effects on royalties and license fees but would be unlikely to have much stimulative effect on the use of US technologies abroad. Indeed, additional dollar decline could raise the dollar cost to US firms acquiring foreign technology.

Other Private Services

The seventh and final services subcategory includes a wide variety of tradeable business services such as education, financial services, insurance, income from communication services, construction contractors' fees, film rental income, management services, and consulting services. In 1990, exports of $32.2 billion and imports of $13.8 billion yielded a surplus of $18.4 billion, some $11.7 billion more than in 1981 (table 2.2).

Of the $18.4 billion surplus in other private services in 1990, $4.8 billion consisted of charges of US parent companies levied on their foreign affiliates; $13.6 billion was for services performed for nonaffiliated parties (table 2.3). Within the latter category, the 1990 education surplus of $4.4 billion was almost as large as the $5.5 billion surplus from a wide variety of business, professional, and accounting services. The surplus in education resulted from the expenditures of foreign students in the United States. Financial services netted $2.5 billion in 1990. Film rentals provided a $2.0 billion surplus.

The substantial earnings in other private services, often termed "business services," have led some to see services as a major source of export gains that would do much to improve US international transactions balances. The returns from these kinds of services are significant, but with exports making up only about 4.9 percent of total 1990 US goods and services exports, it would take huge export gains to have a major effect on overall US trade balances.

In addition, although the dollar value of many of the sales transactions is very large and very important to the firms concerned, the net return to the United States—the amount recorded as an export in the US current account—is only the US value-added portion of the transactions, which is typically only a small fraction of the total. For example, the amount credited to the US current account from an international insurance sale transaction is only the net return after claims and administrative costs outside the United States are paid. Similarly, large portions of the costs of foreign construction contracts are paid to foreign

Table 2.3 United States: other private services transactions, 1987 and 1990 (millions of dollars)

	1987			1990			Change 1987–90		
	Receipts	Payments	Balance	Receipts	Payments	Balance	Receipts	Payments	Balance
Total	23,141	11,405	11,736	32,173	13,818	18,355	9,032	2,413	6,619
Affiliated services	2,447	−530	2,977	4,333	−456	4,789	1,886	74	1,812
Unaffiliated services	20,694	11,935	8,759	27,840	14,274	13,566	7,146	2,339	4,807
Education	3,821	452	3,369	5,022	665	4,357	1,201	213	988
Financial services	3,731	2,077	1,654	4,873	2,346	2,527	1,142	269	873
Insurance	2,295	3,241	−946	1,832	1,810	22	−463	−1,431	968
Telecommunications	2,111	3,736	−1,625	2,742	5,980	−3,238	631	2,244	−1,613
Business, professiona and accounting	4,280	1,319	2,961	7,552	2,045	5,507	3,272	726	2,546
of which:									
Accounting, auditing, and bookkeeping	27	37	−10	120	37	83	93	0	93
Advertising	109	128	−19	127	246	−119	18	118	−100
Computer and data processing	649	74	575	1,085	44	1,041	436	−30	466
Data base and other information services	133	25	108	284	54	230	151	29	122
Engineering, architectural, construction	972	266	706	2,001	428	1,573	1,029	162	867
Installation, repair, and maintenance	1,087	496	591	1,942	713	1,229	855	217	638
Legal services	147	56	91	455	110	345	308	54	254
Management, consulting, and public relations	327	67	260	352	134	218	25	67	−42
Medical services	516	n.a.	516	628	n.a.	628	n.a.	n.a.	n.a.
R&D, testing, and laboratory services	177	114	63	359	211	148	182	97	85
Other business and professional	136	57	79	200	66	134	64	9	55
Other	4,456	1,110	3,346	5,819	1,428	4,391	1,363	318	1,045
of which:									
Wages of temporary workers	126	889	−763	n.a.	n.a.	n.a.	n.a.	n.a.	n.a.
Film rentals	1,095	52	1,043	2,021	70	1,951	926	18	908
Foreign governments and organizations	3,333	n.a.	3,333	n.a.	n.a.	n.a.	n.a.	n.a.	n.a.
Other	368	182	186	n.a.	n.a.	n.a.	n.a.	n.a.	n.a.

n.a. = not available

Source: US Department of Commerce, *Survey of Current Business,* September 1991.

laborers and foreign suppliers, and profits from US film rentals amount to only a small portion of the very large gross receipts.

Moreover, international competition is increasing rapidly in many of these services. For example, whereas US banks used to dominate the international banking industry, today of the world's 20 largest banks as measured by total assets, none are headquartered in the United States. Some kinds of labor-intensive services are now being imported by US firms; for example, some data entry and computer services are now handled in the Caribbean and the results transmitted electronically to the United States. Korean firms have become quite competent in handling major construction projects outside Korea. And although the United States is probably unmatched in the provision of telecommunications services, it runs large deficits in these services ($3.2 billion in 1990), partly because deregulated US telephone services offer international calls at a much lower rate than telephone services in most foreign countries provide.

A lower dollar would have positive effects on the services balance, increasing US competitiveness in some of the kinds of transactions included in the other private services account. However, the volume of exports and imports of most of these services (insurance, film rentals, consulting, management services, etc.) is likely to be only marginally affected by relatively modest exchange rate movements. The reason is that most of the costs associated with providing the services are incurred in the foreign country purchasing the service. Dollar exchange rate movements do not change these costs. A lower dollar would, however, increase the dollar value of foreign earnings originally denominated in foreign currencies.

To summarize, there is little reason to believe that the United States has a significant, enduring comparative advantage in most of these business services. Modest increases of a few billion dollars may be realized in the surpluses of some of these services in the next few years. But continuing large gains are unlikely, and the surpluses could stabilize at a level not far from that of 1990.

Looking at the broader range of services, one should expect little or no change in the royalties and license fees, defense expenditures, and other transportation accounts. Given the right conditions, however, there is potential for modest gains in travel, passenger fares, and the "other private services" account.

The Key Role of Merchandise Trade

The relatively large size of merchandise trade makes it the key to any future improvements in the US current account. Although trade in the nonmerchandise accounts is substantial, none of these accounts are likely to be a significant source of improvement in the current account in coming years. Flat or declining performance will be very likely in international investment income and unilateral transfers. Balances may improve in services, but the gains are unlikely to be large. Although some kinds of services are affected by exchange rate movements and other macroeconomic policy and performance changes, the effects are likely to be limited. For example, over the period 1981–90, the range of movement in US services balances was $27.3 billion, 17.6 percent of the sum of exports and imports of services for the midpoint year (1986), and the surplus in 1990 was only $14.5 billion higher than in 1981 (table 2.1). Over the same period, the manufactures trade balance varied within a range of $146.8 billion, 30.8 percent of the much larger sum of exports and imports of manufactures for 1986 (table 2.4).

Significant improvements in the current account balance must therefore come primarily, and perhaps exclusively, from merchandise trade. Indeed, a balanced current account later in the 1990s may require a surplus in merchandise trade to offset further deterioration in other segments of the current account, principally in international investment income.

Merchandise Trade Dissected

US merchandise trade has been in deficit since 1976, but the deficits were modest until 1983; then a rapid deterioration began and continued through 1987 (table 2.4). (Note that the merchandise trade data in table 2.4 are US Bureau of the Census data, which are configured differently from the merchandise trade data in table 2.1. See the appendix to this volume for a more detailed explanation.) A look at recent performance in the four major categories of merchandise trade as reported by the Census Bureau provides insights about the relative size and dollar value changes of different kinds of traded goods and demonstrates the dominant role of manufactures trade in merchandise trade.

- *Manufactures trade* in 1990 accounted for four-fifths of US merchandise trade: 80.1 percent of exports and 78.5 percent of imports.

- *Agricultural* products were 10.1 percent of 1990 exports and 4.5 percent of imports.

- *Mineral fuels* were 3.1 percent of exports (mostly coal) and 13.1 percent of imports (mostly crude and refined petroleum).

- *Other merchandise trade* is a group of miscellaneous items including wood, hides, skins, and paper pulp. This account made up 6.4 percent of 1990 exports and 3.9 percent of imports.

Table 2.4 further illustrates both the dominance and the fluctuations of manufactures trade performance in total US merchandise trade performance. From 1981 to 1987, probably the low point in US trade performance, the merchandise

Table 2.4 United States: merchandise trade by component, 1981–90 (billions of dollars)

	1981	1982	1983	1984	1985	1986	1987	1988	1989	1990	Change 1981–87	Change 1987–90
Total merchandise trade												
Exports	238.7	216.4	205.6	224.0	218.8	227.2	254.1	322.4	363.8	394.0	15.4	139.9
Imports	261.0	244.0	258.0	330.7	336.5	365.4	406.2	441.0	473.2	495.0	145.2	88.8
Balance	−22.3	−27.6	−52.4	−106.7	−117.7	−138.2	−152.1	−118.6	−109.4	−101.0	−129.8	51.1
Manufactures												
Exports	171.7	155.3	148.5	163.6	167.8	179.9	200.0	255.6	287.0	315.7	28.3	115.7
Imports	149.8	151.7	171.2	231.3	257.9	297.0	324.9	361.4	379.4	388.8	175.1	63.9
Balance	21.9	3.6	−22.7	−67.7	−90.1	−117.1	−124.9	−105.8	−92.4	−73.1	−146.8	51.8
Agriculture												
Exports	43.8	37.0	36.5	38.2	29.6	26.6	29.1	37.6	42.2	39.6	−14.7	10.5
Imports	17.2	15.7	16.5	19.8	20.0	21.2	20.7	21.2	22.0	22.4	3.5	1.7
Balance	26.6	21.3	20.0	18.4	9.6	5.4	8.4	16.4	20.2	17.2	−18.2	8.8
Mineral fuels												
Exports	10.3	12.8	9.6	9.5	10.1	8.2	7.8	8.6	9.9	12.3	−2.5	4.5
Imports	81.4	65.4	58.3	61.0	53.9	37.3	44.2	41.0	52.8	64.6	−37.2	20.4
Balance	−71.1	−52.6	−48.7	−51.5	−43.8	−29.1	−36.4	−32.4	−42.9	−52.3	34.7	−15.9
Other												
Exports	12.8	11.4	11.1	12.7	11.2	12.2	15.9	18.5	24.7	25.4	3.1	9.5
Imports	12.5	11.2	12.4	18.6	4.7	9.6	15.1	17.6	19.0	19.5	2.6	4.4
Balance	0.3	0.2	−1.3	−5.9	6.5	2.6	0.8	0.9	5.7	5.9	0.5	5.1

Sources: US Department of Commerce and Bureau of the Census.

trade balance declined from a deficit of $22.3 billion to one of $152.1 billion, a deterioration of $129.8 billion. The decline in the manufactures trade balance during the same period was even greater: $146.8 billion. Performance also worsened in agricultural goods, as the surplus declined to $8.4 billion, an $18.2 billion slide. Movement in the "other merchandise trade" account was marginal, only $0.5 billion, while the mineral fuels deficit actually narrowed, from $71.1 billion to $36.4 billion, an improvement of $34.7 billion. This major reduction—a result of both reduced oil import volumes and lower oil import prices—prevented the US merchandise trade deficit from being even larger and, to some extent, masked the huge deterioration in manufactures trade performance.

The merchandise trade balance improved significantly—by $51.1 billion—from 1987 to 1990 (table 2.4). The manufactures trade deficit narrowed by $51.8 billion, and the agricultural surplus increased by $8.8 billion, recouping most of the decline from its 1981 peak. The mineral fuels deficit, however, increased by $15.9 billion, as oil import volumes grew and prices rose.

With both an economic slowdown and the Gulf crisis affecting US economic performance, part of the significant 1990 improvement in manufactures trade performance may be temporary. Relatively strong growth abroad helped increase US manufactures exports by 10.0 percent over 1989, and a relatively weak US economy helped restrain growth of US manufactures imports to only 2.5 percent. On the other hand, the Gulf War pushed oil import prices during much of 1990 above earlier levels.

Further improvements in merchandise trade performance must come primarily from the manufactures trade account: the other components of merchandise trade do not offer the potential for major improvements. The 1989 agricultural surplus ($20.2 billion) was the highest since 1981 and a significant improvement over the levels of the mid–1980s. Nevertheless, it was $6.4 billion short of the $26.6 billion record of 1981. The bulk of US agricultural exports are in grains—wheat, corn, soybeans, and feed grains. US agricultural exports peaked at $43.8 billion in 1981, a time when global grain supplies were limited, driving prices upward. With exports of $42.2 billion, 1989 was the second-best year on record for US agriculture. In the meantime, however, US agricultural imports have been steadily trending upward from 1981 levels.

With exports off slightly from 1989 levels and imports rising, the agricultural surplus declined modestly in 1990 to $17.2 billion. Small further gains above the 1989 and 1990 levels may be achieved in some years, but sustained improvements will be difficult in the face of agricultural subsidies and large surplus stocks in several developed countries. These are likely to persist through the 1990s. Any improvements in the US position resulting from a successful Uruguay Round agricultural initiative are likely to occur very gradually. In the near term, grain exports to the Eastern bloc countries may rise if the necessary financing can be obtained. In the longer term, however, increased market incentives in the former Communist countries that are moving away from collectivized agriculture are likely to increase global grain production sooner or later. In all, the outlook is for supply-demand conditions that will preclude sustained US grain export bonanzas, and agricultural imports that will gradually trend upward. The likely result is continuing agricultural surpluses at around current levels, probably seldom topping $20 billion.

The US oil import bill, on the other hand, may well increase. Barring a severe US economic downturn or a major conservation effort motivated by stiff new taxes or other measures, increases in import volumes seem assured for the next several years. Import prices are difficult to predict and have declined from their Gulf War highs. But medium- and longer-term price levels above those of 1989, at least reflecting global inflation rates, seem quite likely. Oil prices have a significant impact on US imports, with each one-dollar rise in the price per barrel altering the US import bill by about $2 billion, assuming constant import volumes, which tend to be maintained in the short run. In the medium to longer term, volumes may adjust substantially to price changes.

In short, the possibility of a markedly larger oil import bill cannot be dismissed. In one view:

> Projections indicate that US oil imports will rise to perhaps 10 million barrels by 1995. At $20–25 per barrel, such an increase would add about $15–20 billion to our annual trade deficit. By 1995, at the level of $20–25 per barrel, our oil deficit *alone* would be $75–90 billion—approaching the size of the entire US trade deficit today. (Even with oil at $15 per barrel, these trade deficit effects would be massive.) (Peterson 1991).

"Other merchandise trade" will continue to be a relatively minor account that usually varies little from year to year and has only a modest effect on the overall merchandise trade balance.

Manufactures Trade and the Current Account

The above examination of the current account shows that the international investment income account and the services account will not be the critical factors in future US current account performance. Any major improvement must come primarily from the merchandise trade account. Merchandise trade performance is, in turn, dominated by manufactures trade, within which rapid changes in the size and direction of flows can occur. Absent very large oil price changes that would dramatically raise or lower the US oil import bill, US current account performance over the foreseeable future will largely reflect manufactures trade performance.

This study presumes that the elimination of large current account deficits and the accompanying foreign borrowing and effects on the manufacturing sector is a desirable goal because of the long-term contribution to US living standards. Whether or not one agrees with this goal, it is useful to determine how large an improvement in manufactures trade performance would be required to achieve balance in the US current account. The amounts involved and the difficulty of the task can be determined by projecting the changes in performance in the nonmanufacturing accounts to a future target year, subtracting those changes from the 1990 current account deficit, and treating the residual value as the improvement in manufactures trade performance required to achieve balance.

In our analysis, we chose 1993 as the target year. We did not select that particular year in a belief that current account balance will be achieved by then. It will not. Nor do we believe that a balanced account by 1993 is a necessary, or even perhaps a desirable, goal. Instead, we chose 1993 to be consistent with the projections of product groups in this study. The improvement in total manufactures trade that would be required to balance the current account then provides a benchmark for comparison with the manufactures trade performance projected in each of the product group assessments in chapter 5.

The base year from which changes to 1993 are projected is 1990. Not only are complete data for 1991 not available at this writing, but the significant improvements in the trade and current account performance of 1991 are, for the most part, the fallout of the Gulf War and the US recession rather than evidence of a new trend. Assuming an end to the US recession of 1991, the econometric models of most forecasters project that the US trade and current account deficits will expand in 1992 and 1993 from 1991 levels.[3]

Services income is the nonmerchandise trade component of the current account seen by most as having the greatest potential for improved performance. A recent econometric analysis by William R. Cline suggests increases in the services component of the current account of $11.3 billion to $21.7 billion by 1993 (Cline 1991). DRI/McGraw-Hill in its April forecast sees a 1993 improvement of $16 billion, the midpoint of the range of Cline's forecast (DRI/McGraw-Hill 1991, 73).

Cline's model projects declines in the investment income balance of $6.5 billion to $12 billion by 1993. The DRI forecast sees a worsening of less than $2 billion.

---

3. William R. Cline (1991) projects a 1991 US current account deficit of as low as $20 billion, including the effects of some $50 billion of US transfer receipts from allied payments to help finance the war. Without these payments, he estimatates the "true" 1991 current deficit at perhaps $60 billion to $70 billion. In addition, however, the US recession has affected US trade performance. Oxford Economics USA (1991) sees a 1991–93 expansion of the US current account deficit from $8 billion to $69 billion. Data Resources, Inc. sees the current account deficit expanding from $4 billion in 1991 to $84 billion in 1993 and to $104 billion in 1994 (DRI/McGraw Hill 1991a and b, 78).

Selecting the midpoints of the Cline forecasts and a value for unilateral transfers that is midway between the 1989 and 1990 levels yields the following changes from 1990 to 1993:

Services (nonfactor income)	$16.0 billion
Investment income (factor income)	− 9.0 billion
Unilateral transfers	+ 3.0 billion
Net change	$10.0 billion

The $9.0 billion investment income decline is based on a 1990 starting point that did not include the unanticipated $9.3 billion 1990 improvement in international investment income that actually occurred after the Cline and DRI analyses. This decline was due to a precipitous drop in the income of the US affiliates of foreign parents and, as noted earlier, appears to have been the temporary result of the US recession. Investment income payments to foreign parents should recover with a resumption of US economic growth. Without this atypical performance, the 1990 surplus in investment income would have been smaller and the current account deficit larger. A projection from 1990 current account component levels that included this presumably atypical investment income performance should therefore forecast a 1990–93 decline in the overall balance in US investment income that is larger than the $9.0 billion deterioration noted above.

Changes in balances in services and investment income clearly cannot be forecast with any degree of accuracy. However, given the temporary effect on investment income reflected in the 1990 current account balance and the limited opportunities for gains in the services account, it is likely that a summation of nonmerchandise trade items of the current account will show little or no change from 1990 to 1993.

Thus, assuming the scenario described above (no change in the summation of balances in the nonmerchandise trade items of the current account, no significant changes in agricultural and other balances of the merchandise trade account, and a worsening in the mineral fuels import bill of $8.0 billion), an improvement of about $100 billion in the manufactures trade balance from the 1990 level would be required to achieve balance in the current account by 1993.

Policy Implications

Large changes in the manufactures trade balance not only dominated the 1981–87 decline in US trade and current account performance and the 1987–90 improvement but will continue to dominate major changes in the future. The reason is that manufactures trade is much larger than the other components of the merchandise trade and current accounts and is more susceptible to the influences of exchange rate and other macroeconomic changes. Indeed, large swings in US external transactions balances inevitably will be manifested predominantly in the manufactures trade account.

To understand the policy significance of manufacturing's interface with the world economy, one must recognize that net international borrowing and lending are accomplished through net transfers of goods and services from the lender country to the borrower country, with the lender receiving claims on the borrower's assets. When significant changes in a country's macroeconomic policies and performance trigger consumption and investment at a level that exceeds its production, it borrows in the form of a net inflow of goods and services. For large industrialized countries, these net inflows will invariably be manifested primarily in net imports of manufactured goods.

This is what happened to the United States in the 1980s. Policy changes led to external borrowing and a large net inflow of goods and services that was manifested predominantly in changes in manufactures trade balances. The $146.8 billion 1981–87 deterioration in manufactures trade performance was equivalent to 87.9 percent of the deterioration in the current account balance overall, and to about 3.3 percent of 1987 US GNP. In 1987, net foreign borrowing—the current account deficit—was 3.5 percent of GNP.

That the effects of borrowing abroad fell primarily on US manufacturing was not a random event. Large swings in net international capital flows into and out of the United States will inevitably affect primarily the manufacturing sector, and large net borrowing abroad will entail large deficits in manufactures trade. A return to net US lending abroad will eliminate these deficits and restore surpluses in manufactures trade.

This simple conclusion has very important policy implications. In a world where most goods are readily tradeable and most services are not, the manufacturing sector is the primary interface of the US economy with the world economy. It is the sector most exposed to foreign competition. This exposure will continue to grow with the expansion of world trade and the rise in US trade as a percentage of US GNP. For example, in 1981 the sum of US exports and imports of goods and services was equivalent to 19.8 percent of GNP, and manufactures exports and imports summed to 10.5 percent of GNP. By 1990, trade in goods and services was equivalent to 20.6 percent of GNP, and manufactures trade equaled 12.9 percent of GNP. In 1981, manufactures trade was 53.2 percent of total trade in goods and services, but by 1990 it was 62.5 percent of the total.

In a world economy that is now more integrated and more competitive than ever before, manufacturing is the sector most affected by domestic and foreign economic policies. In an increasingly competitive world economy, US economic policymaking—fiscal, monetary, tax, regulatory, and other policies—must consider the vulnerability of the manufacturing sector to foreign competition. Policymakers must recognize that US policies may affect sectors insulated from foreign competition differently than they affect the manufacturing sector. The potential effects of government policies on the international competitiveness of the US manufacturing sector should be specifically considered. To date, there has not been such a focus.

Chapter 7 examines the case for an increased focus on the effects of economic policies on the international competitiveness of US manufacturing in more detail.

Summary

- From 1981 to 1987, the US current account balance, the broadest measure of US external goods and services transactions, deteriorated by $167.1 billion. Of that decline, $131.5 billion, or 78.7 percent, was manifested in merchandise trade performance. The improved performance since 1987 has also been primarily in merchandise trade.

- Only one nonmerchandise trade component of the current account—"other private services," a subcategory of the services account—offers the prospect of significantly improved performance over the next several years. Even here the improvements are uncertain and in any event are likely to be modest in relation to overall US goods and services trade, and could well be inadequate to offset the growing deficits in international investment income and other elements of the current account.

- Future improvements in US current account performance will have to come predominantly from improved performance in merchandise trade. Indeed, the nonmerchandise trade balance will worsen if US services surpluses grow less rapidly than net international investment income declines.

- A dissection of the merchandise trade account shows that the $129.8 billion 1981–87 decline (US Census Bureau basis) in merchandise trade performance was exceeded by the $146.8 billion worsening of the manufactures trade balance. A review of the prospects for other kinds of merchandise trade (principally oil imports and agricultural exports) shows little prospect of improvement in these accounts and, indeed, the potential for an enlarging oil import bill. Thus, by default, any major improvements in merchandise trade will be manifested primarily—if not solely—in improved manufactures trade performance.

- Indeed, a balanced current account by 1993—not to be expected—would be likely to require an improvement in manufactures trade of about $100 billion, from a 1990 deficit of $73 billion to a 1993 surplus of about $25 billion.

- The critical role of the manufacturing sector in US international transactions is not limited to the merchandise trade account. In 1990, US manufacturing parent companies earned $22.9 billion in investment income from the operations of their foreign affiliates. US manufacturing companies also received $8.6 billion in royalties and license fees from their foreign affiliates. US receipts for licensing of industrial processes to nonaffiliated parties added another $2.6 billion. These receipts are a heritage from earlier periods when US manufacturing was dominant in world markets. The substantial surpluses produced in both categories are unlikely to expand much further and could gradually diminish, reflecting the waning global position of US manufacturing.

- Large swings in US external balances will inevitably be manifested predominantly in the manufactures trade account. The dominant position of manufactures trade in US external balances—its key role in the current account declines of the early 1980s, the 1987–90 improvement, and future improvements—has profound implications for US economic policymaking.

- The manufacturing sector is the main interface of the US economy with the world economy. It is most exposed to, and must bear the brunt of, international competition. Large net capital inflows from foreign sources are associated with large deficits in manufactures trade and a weakened US manufacturing sector; net US capital outflows are associated with surpluses in manufactures trade and an improved environment for US manufacturing.

- Manufacturing's key role in external transactions and its vulnerability to foreign competition have been growing and will continue to grow as the world economy becomes more and more integrated and as world trade increases faster than world output. In 1981, manufactures trade was 53.2 percent of total trade in goods and services. By 1990 its share had grown to 62.5 percent. Over the same period, manufactures trade grew from 10.5 percent of US GNP to 12.9 percent.

- In an integrated world economy where one sector, manufacturing, is the key interface of the US economy with the world economy and bears the brunt of foreign competition, the vulnerability of manufacturing to changes in policy and the consequences of policy changes for the international competitiveness of US-based production should be carefully assessed.

Bibliography

Bergsten, C. Fred, and Edward M. Graham. 1991. "Strukturschwächen der US-Wirtschaft machen Auslandsanlagen erforderlich." *Handelsblatt* (Düsseldorf, 24 October). English version available from the Institute for International Economics.

Bergsten, C. Fred, and Shafiqul Islam. In press. *The United States as a Debtor Country*. Washington: Institute for International Economics.

Cline, William R. 1989. *United States External Adjustment and the World Economy*. Washington: Institute for International Economics.

Cline, William R. 1991. "The Dollar, the Budget, and US External Adjustment." Washington: Institute for International Economics (April).

DRI/McGraw-Hill. 1991a. *Review of the US Economy*. Lexington, MA: DRI/McGraw-Hill (April).

DRI/McGraw-Hill. 1991b. *Review of the US Economy*. Lexington, MA: DRI/McGraw-Hill (October).

Oxford Economics USA. 1991. *US Economic Prospects*. Wynnewood, PA: Oxford Economics USA (June).

Peterson, Peter G., with James K. Sebenius. 1991. "Rethinking America's Security: The Primacy of the Domestic Agenda." Washington: US Commission on Relations for the 21st Century (mimeographed).

US Department of Commerce, Bureau of Economic Analysis. 1990. *US Direct Investment Abroad, Operations of US Parent Companies and Their Foreign Affiliates, Preliminary 1988 Estimates*. Washington: US Department of Commerce (July).

3

The Role of Manufactures in Global Trade

3

The Role of Manufactures in Global Trade

The dominant and vulnerable role of manufactures trade in external transactions is not unique to the United States. To a substantial and increasing degree, world trade is trade in manufactured goods.

Trade in Goods and Services

According to a recent GATT report (General Agreement on Tariffs and Trade 1990, 5) world trade in goods and services was $3,775 billion in 1989 (table 3.1). At $3,095 billion, world merchandise trade was 82 percent of the total; at $680 billion, commercial services were 18 percent of total exports of goods and services (commercial services trade excludes factor income, such as international investment income). At $2,155 billion, manufactures were 57.1 percent of total exports of world goods and services and 69.6 percent of world merchandise exports.

During the 1980s, manufactures trade grew more rapidly than other elements of goods and services trade. According to GATT data, from 1980 to 1989 world manufactures exports grew at an average annual rate of 8 percent, compared with 3.5 percent for agricultural products and −4.5 percent for mining products (much of this decline was due to a fall in oil prices and trade volumes). And contrary to popular perceptions, the manufactures growth rate of 8 percent was higher than the 6.5 percent growth rate for commercial services (General Agreement on Tariffs and Trade 1990, 20).

Manufactures Trade

The disaggregated data in the World Manufactures Trade Data Base (WMTDB) constructed for this study provide additional detail on the increasing role of

43

Table 3.1 Sectoral composition of world goods and services trade, 1989

	Billions of dollars	As a percentage of:	
		Total trade	Merchandise trade
Merchandise	3,095	82.0	100.0
Agricultural	405	10.7	13.1
Mining (incl. oil)	415	10.9	13.4
Manufactures	2,155	57.1	69.6
Other	120	3.2	3.9
Commercial services	680	18.0	22.0
Transportation	225	6.0	7.3
Travel	195	5.2	6.3
Other private services and income	260	6.9	8.4
Total goods and services	3,775	100.0	122.0

Source: General Agreement on Tariffs and Trade. 1990. *International Trade 89–90,* vol. I. Geneva: General Agreement on Tariffs and Trade, table 1, p. 5

manufactures trade, defined in this study as the commodities included in Standard International Trade Classifications (SITCs) 5 through 9. According to the WMTDB, world merchandise trade exports increased from $1,664.4 billion in 1981 to $2,757.3 billion in 1989, a two-thirds increase occurring at an annual average rate of 6.5 percent (table 3.2). The WMTDB thus captures a portion of total merchandise trade equivalent to 89 percent of the amount reported by 1989 GATT data.[1]

According to the WMTDB, the nonmanufactures portion of world merchandise exports including oil decreased from $650.5 billion in 1981 to $639.6 billion in 1989, a 1.5 percent decrease (table 3.2). This occurred because mineral fuels (SITC 3, mostly oil) exports fell from $373.0 billion in 1981 to $238.6 billion in 1989, a 5.4 percent annual decline that reflected large reductions in oil prices. To avoid the effects of volatile oil prices, it is useful to separate SITC 3 from other traded products. Other items in nonmanufactures trade (SITC 0, 1, 2, and 4, mostly agricultural products) grew at a 4.7 percent annual rate, rising from $277.5 billion to $401.0 billion from 1981 to 1989. This was less than half the growth rate of manufactures trade.

Manufactures exports, besides being by far the largest category, also grew the fastest, more than doubling from $1,013.9 billion in 1981 to $2,110.3 billion in 1989, for an average annual increase of 9.6 percent. WMTDB data indicate that world manufactures exports, which accounted for 60.9 percent of world merchandise exports in 1981, increased to 75.0 percent in 1987 and 76.5 percent in 1989. Manufactures exports were 78.5 percent of non-mineral fuels merchandise trade in 1981, 83.3 percent in 1987, and 83.8 percent in 1989.

---

1. See the appendix to this volume for a discussion of product group categorizations and an explanation of the differences between the GATT and the WMTDB data.

Table 3.2 Product composition of world trade, all commodities, 1981–89 (billions of dollars except where noted)

SITC Commodity	1981	1982	1983	1984	1985	1986	1987	1988	1989	Annual growth 1981–89 (percentages)
World exports to world	1,664.4	1,556.2	1,529.9	1,630.9	1,676.9	1,855.9	2,197.8	2,571.9	2,757.3	6.5
of which:										
0 Food and live animals	152.8	139.6	137.4	142.3	138.3	162.2	180.9	207.1	215.5	4.4
1 Beverages and tobacco	16.2	16.3	15.5	15.4	16.6	19.5	23.5	26.0	28.2	7.2
2 Crude materials	101.2	89.5	90.5	98.5	94.0	99.8	119.0	145.2	153.2	5.3
3 Mineral fuels	373.0	329.8	297.7	298.1	294.0	203.3	218.4	205.1	241.5	−5.3
4 Animal and vegetable oils	7.4	6.6	7.0	9.5	8.9	6.9	7.3	8.9	8.6	1.9
5 Chemicals	123.5	117.0	122.1	131.2	136.9	162.1	195.9	238.3	246.8	9.0
6 Basic manufactures	258.5	239.1	236.0	250.0	255.0	298.3	354.5	438.3	469.0	7.7
7 Machines and transport equipment	465.7	454.7	456.6	501.2	535.1	654.3	781.9	932.9	990.0	9.9
8 Miscellaneous manufactures	144.1	142.0	144.4	158.5	170.4	217.5	269.4	310.6	334.7	11.1
9 Goods not classed by kind	22.1	21.6	22.8	26.2	27.7	31.9	46.9	59.6	69.9	15.5
Nonfuel, nonmanufactures (0–2, 4)	277.5	252.0	250.4	265.7	257.8	288.4	330.7	387.1	401.0	4.7
Manufactures (5–9)	1,013.9	974.4	981.8	1,067.1	1,125.2	1,364.1	1,648.6	1,979.6	2,110.3	9.6
US trade										
Exports	225.8	206.0	194.6	210.2	205.2	204.7	243.6	304.9	347.0	5.5
Imports	271.2	247.8	268.0	338.2	358.9	381.4	422.4	459.0	491.5	7.7
Balance	−45.4	−41.8	−73.4	−128.0	−153.7	−176.7	−178.8	−154.1	−144.6	

Source: World Manufactures Trade Data Base.

According to the WMTDB, the 1989 manufactures share of total world merchandise trade, 76.5 percent, is somewhat higher than the 69.6 percent indicated by the GATT data (table 3.1). The reason is that the WMTDB, constructed from the exports and imports of 26 industrialized and industrializing countries, captures a larger portion of total world trade in manufactures than of world trade in nonmanufactures. In fact, the $2,110.3 billion WMTDB world manufactures trade total in 1989 is 97.9 percent of the GATT valuation. The discrepancy probably reflects the fact that the WMTDB does not capture trade among countries outside the 26-country group, most of which are developing countries. A larger portion of the exports of the excluded countries is likely to consist of nonmanufactured items. By both the WMTDB and the GATT measurements, however, manufactures trade is clearly a dominant and increasing portion of total world exports of goods and services.

Product Composition of Manufactures Trade

Disaggregated data show that a growing portion of world manufactures exports consists of more highly processed items; products nearer the beginning of the processing chain account for a declining portion of the total. For example, from 1981 to 1989, exports of basic manufactures (SITC 6) increased by only 7.7 percent annually on average, and chemicals (SITC 5) by 9.0 percent (table 3.2). Both were below the 9.6 percent growth rate for manufactures as a whole (table 3.2) and significantly below the 9.9 percent rate for machinery and transport equipment (SITC 7) and the 11.1 percent rate for miscellaneous manufactures (SITC 8). These differential growth rates increased the export share of machinery and transport equipment to almost half of total manufactures exports (from 45.9 percent in 1981 to 46.9 percent in 1989), while chemicals and basic manufactures shares declined modestly (table 3.4).

There are several reasons why the more highly processed goods are likely to continue to grow as a portion of total manufactures exports. One is the globalization—some would term it the localization—of production of basic manufactures: for example, every industrializing country wants to have its own steel and chemical industries. Another reason is the smaller share of basic materials in the value of most manufactures: for example, the steel in current models of automobiles costs the manufacturer a smaller percentage of the sticker price than it did in the past. Yet a third reason is the increasing cross-trade in the parts and components that make up finished products. This cross-trade can be quite significant. For example, a manufacturer may export a component or part (a semifinished good, typically included in SITC 7 or 8) to an affiliate or supplier for inclusion in a subassembly, reimport the subassembly to be included in the finished product, and finally export the finished product. When that happens, the value of the component is included twice in the export data of the originating country and once in its import data.

These changes in the composition of manufactures trade are also reflected in more disaggregated data. At the two-digit level of detail, significant differences in growth rates among the product groups over the 1981–89 period are evident (table 3.3). Growth rates per year ranged from lows of 4.0 percent for fertilizers (SITC 56) and 5.4 percent for iron and steel (SITC 67) to a high of 18.3 percent for office machines and computers (SITC 75). Generally, trade appears to be growing more rapidly in higher than in lower-technology products. High-technology products have other advantages, including a generally higher value added. Some analysts therefore recommend that national trade strategies focus on the high-technology, high-growth items.

The relative size of product groups in international trade is also important, however. For example, professional and scientific equipment (SITC 87), a high-technology area in which the United States is strong, had a 1981–89 annual growth rate of 10.5 percent (table 3.3). Unfortunately for US export potential, however, by 1989 the product group still accounted for only 2.1 percent of world manufactures exports. Aircraft (a part of SITC 79), a high-technology industry that the United States dominates, grew at only a 7.7 percent rate from 1981 to 1989; by 1989, it was only 2.5 percent of world exports, about the same share as paper and paperboard (SITC 64). On the other hand, road vehicles (SITC 78, mostly automobiles), a product group not often regarded as high-tech and one in which US trade performance has slipped, grew at a 9.7 percent annual rate from 1981 to 1989, slightly above the 9.6 percent rate for all manufactures. In 1986, this product group made up 14.3 percent of total world manufactures exports; its share declined to 12.5 percent in 1989—still one-eighth of the world total—as the pace of US automobile imports slowed. From the standpoint of trade balances, a country may need to dominate in several high-technology, high-profile items with small world markets to offset declining performance in a larger, seemingly more mundane product group.

Manufactures Trade Shares and Flows

Developed countries dominate world manufactures trade. In 1989, the countries of the Organization for Economic Cooperation and Development (OECD) accounted for about 82 percent of world manufactures exports and took about 77 percent of world manufactures imports. In that year, 44.4 percent of total exports originated in the EC countries, but over half of these exports were to other EC countries (table 3.5). Another quarter of world manufactures exports came from Japan and the United States together. Germany was 1989's largest

Table 3.3 Product composition of world manufactures exports, 1981–89 (billions of dollars)

SITC Commodity	1981	1982	1983	1984	1985	1986	1987	1988	1989	Annual growth 1981–89 (percentages)
World exports to world of which:	1,013.9	974.4	981.8	1,067.1	1,125.2	1,364.1	1,648.6	1,979.6	2,110.3	9.6
51 Organic chemicals	31.7	29.1	32.5	35.6	37.1	41.2	49.9	62.7	66.4	9.7
52 Inorganic chemicals	15.7	15.1	14.9	15.9	16.8	18.2	20.4	23.9	24.1	5.5
53 Dyeing, tanning, and coloring	7.2	7.0	7.2	7.3	7.7	10.2	12.8	15.1	15.9	10.4
54 Medicinal and pharmaceutical products	13.3	14.5	13.9	14.1	15.4	20.0	23.7	27.1	27.2	9.4
55 Essential oils and perfume	7.0	6.7	6.8	7.2	7.6	9.6	12.0	13.8	14.6	9.7
56 Fertilizers, manufactured	7.1	5.9	6.1	7.2	7.4	7.4	8.4	10.1	9.7	4.0
57 Explosives and pyrotechnic products	0.5	0.5	0.5	0.6	0.6	0.6	0.7	1.7	1.1	10.2
58 Artificial resins and plastics	24.7	23.8	25.6	27.7	28.1	35.6	45.0	56.4	59.4	11.6
59 Chemical materials and products	16.4	14.4	14.6	15.6	16.1	19.2	23.0	27.4	28.4	7.1
61 Leather and leather manufactures	5.3	5.2	5.3	6.1	6.5	.8	9.9	9.9	10.0	8.3
62 Rubber manufactures, n.e.s.	11.2	9.9	10.1	10.7	11.2	13.7	16.7	20.3	20.4	7.7
63 Cork and wood manufactures (excl. furniture)	7.3	6.4	6.9	6.9	6.9	8.8	11.2	12.4	13.3	7.9
64 Paper, paperboard, and articles	25.2	23.8	23.6	26.1	27.5	33.9	42.2	50.3	53.2	9.8
65 Textile yarn, fabric, and madeup articles	43.6	41.1	41.0	43.5	46.1	56.2	67.8	78.3	81.8	8.2
66 Nonmetallic mineral manufactures	30.5	28.3	29.6	30.9	31.1	38.8	47.0	61.4	66.4	10.2
67 Iron and steel	64.5	59.5	52.1	57.2	60.2	63.7	70.0	91.3	98.1	5.4
68 Nonferrous metals	35.2	30.5	35.0	36.2	3.2	35.9	43.1	60.4	67.7	8.5
69 Manufactures of metal, n.e.s.	35.4	34.0	32.0	32.1	32.3	39.3	46.4	52.8	56.3	6.0
71 Power-generating machinery and equipment	35.4	35.3	34.4	36.6	38.2	44.3	52.0	62.3	66.6	8.2
72 Machinery specialized for particular industries	58.0	53.3	46.5	48.1	53.3	65.5	77.3	91.0	98.1	6.8
73 Metalworking machinery	14.2	12.1	10.4	10.9	12.6	17.6	19.8	21.7	23.1	6.2
74 General industrial machinery and equipment	57.7	53.4	49.8	49.9	52.9	65.5	77.3	93.3	101.7	7.3
75 Office and automatic data processing machines	28.8	30.6	37.9	48.8	53.7	66.5	84.9	104.4	110.3	18.3
76 Telecommunications and sound-reproducing equipment	38.9	37.9	40.2	46.0	48.4	58.8	68.6	81.9	86.1	10.4
77 Electrical machinery, apparatus, and appliances	58.5	60.6	64.5	75.5	75.1	93.6	115.4	149.8	161.3	13.5
78 Road vehicles (including air-cushion vehicles)	125.9	123.7	127.6	140.7	156.6	195.1	231.2	255.2	263.3	9.7
79 Other transport equipment	46.5	45.8	43.4	43.3	42.9	45.6	53.4	70.8	77.5	6.6
81 Sanitary, plumbing, heating, and lighting fixtures	3.1	2.9	2.9	3.0	3.2	4.2	5.4	6.6	6.3	9.4
82 Furniture and parts thereof	10.3	9.8	10.1	10.6	11.7	15.5	19.5	22.6	24.2	11.3
83 Travel goods, handbags, and similar containers	2.6	2.7	2.8	3.1	3.3	4.2	5.5	6.7	7.2	13.4
84 Articles of apparel and clothing	36.0	35.3	36.2	41.6	45.1	58.7	75.5	84.0	91.9	12.4
85 Footwear	10.1	10.5	11.0	12.3	13.3	16.7	19.9	24.3	24.5	11.7
87 Professional, scientific, and controlling instruments	20.2	20.3	20.8	22.3	25.8	31.4	36.6	42.3	44.9	10.5
88 Photographic apparatus, equipment, and supplies	19.4	17.4	17.6	18.4	18.2	23.1	27.2	31.2	33.2	7.0
89 Miscellaneous manufactures	42.3	43.0	43.0	46.9	49.7	63.7	79.8	92.9	101.8	11.6
93 Special transactions, n.e.s.	16.9	14.7	16.3	19.7	21.5	25.7	39.4	44.5	53.4	15.5
95 Armaments	3.7	5.3	4.8	5.0	4.6	4.6	6.8	6.6	6.6	7.7

Source: World Manufactures Trade Data Base.

Table 3.4 Product composition of world manufactures exports, by shares of total, 1981–89 (percentages)

SITC Commodity	1981	1982	1983	1984	1985	1986	1987	1988	1989	Change 1981–89
By one-digit SITC category:										
5 Chemicals	12.2	12.0	12.4	12.3	12.2	11.9	11.9	12.0	11.7	−0.5
6 Basic manufactures	25.5	24.5	24.0	23.4	22.7	21.9	21.5	22.2	22.2	−3.3
7 Machines and transport equipment	45.9	46.7	46.5	47.0	47.6	48.0	47.4	47.1	46.9	1.0
8 Miscellaneous manufactures	14.2	14.6	14.7	14.8	15.1	15.9	16.3	15.7	15.9	1.6
9 Goods not classed by kind	2.2	2.2	2.3	2.5	2.5	2.3	2.8	3.0	3.3	1.1
By two-digit SITC category:										
51 Organic chemicals	3.1	3.0	3.3	3.3	3.3	3.0	3.0	3.2	3.1	0.0
52 Inorganic chemicals	1.5	1.5	1.5	1.5	1.5	1.3	1.2	1.2	1.1	−0.4
53 Dyeing, tanning, and coloring	0.7	0.7	0.7	0.7	0.7	0.7	0.8	0.8	0.8	0.0
54 Medicinal and pharmaceutical products	1.3	1.5	1.4	1.3	1.4	1.5	1.4	1.4	1.3	0.0
55 Essential oils and perfume	0.7	0.7	0.7	0.7	0.7	0.7	0.7	0.7	0.7	0.0
56 Fertilizers, manufactured	0.7	0.6	0.6	0.7	0.7	0.5	0.5	0.5	0.5	−0.2
57 Explosives and pyrotechnic products	0.0	0.0	0.0	0.1	0.1	0.0	0.0	0.1	0.1	0.0
58 Artificial resins and plastics	2.4	2.4	2.6	2.6	2.5	2.6	2.7	2.8	2.8	0.4
59 Chemical materials and products	1.6	1.5	1.5	1.5	1.4	1.4	1.4	1.4	1.3	−0.3
61 Leather and leather manufactures	0.5	0.5	0.5	0.6	0.6	0.6	0.6	0.5	0.5	0.0
62 Rubber manufactures, n.e.s.	1.1	1.0	1.0	1.0	1.0	1.0	1.0	1.0	1.0	−0.1
63 Cork and wood manufactures (excl. furniture)	0.7	0.7	0.7	0.6	0.6	0.6	0.7	0.6	0.6	−0.1
64 Paper, paperboard, and articles	2.5	2.4	2.4	2.4	2.4	2.5	2.6	2.5	2.5	0.0
65 Textile yarn, fabric, and madeup articles	4.3	4.2	4.2	4.1	4.1	4.1	4.1	4.0	3.9	−0.4
66 Nonmetallic mineral manufactures	3.0	2.9	3.0	2.9	2.8	2.8	2.8	3.1	3.1	0.1
67 Iron and steel	6.4	6.1	5.3	5.4	5.3	4.7	4.2	4.6	4.6	−1.7
68 Nonferrous metals	3.5	3.1	3.6	3.4	2.9	2.6	2.6	3.1	3.2	−0.3
69 Manufactures of metal, n.e.s.	3.5	3.5	3.3	3.0	2.9	2.8	2.8	2.7	2.7	−0.8
71 Power-generating machinery and equipment	3.5	3.6	3.5	3.4	3.4	3.2	3.2	3.1	3.2	−0.3
72 Machinery specialized for particular industries	5.7	5.5	4.7	4.5	4.7	4.8	4.7	4.6	4.6	−1.1
73 Metalworking machinery	1.4	1.2	1.1	1.0	1.1	1.3	1.2	1.1	1.1	−0.3
74 General industrial machinery and equipment	5.7	5.5	5.1	4.7	4.7	4.8	5.1	4.7	4.8	−0.9
75 Office and automatic data processing machines	2.8	3.1	3.9	4.6	4.8	4.9	5.1	5.3	5.2	2.4
76 Telecommunications and sound-reproducing equipment	3.8	3.9	4.1	4.3	4.3	4.3	4.2	4.1	4.1	0.2
77 Electrical machinery, apparatus, and appliances	5.8	6.2	6.6	7.1	6.7	6.9	7.0	7.6	7.6	1.9
78 Road vehicles (including air-cushion vehicles)	12.4	12.7	13.0	13.2	13.9	14.3	14.0	12.9	12.5	0.1
79 Other transport equipment	4.6	4.7	4.4	4.1	3.8	3.3	3.2	3.6	3.7	−0.9
81 Sanitary, plumbing, heating, and lighting fixtures	0.3	0.3	0.3	0.3	0.3	0.3	0.3	0.3	0.3	0.0
82 Furniture and parts thereof	1.0	1.0	1.0	1.0	1.0	1.1	1.2	1.1	1.1	0.1
83 Travel goods, handbags, and similar containers	0.3	0.3	0.3	0.3	0.3	0.3	0.3	0.3	0.3	0.1
84 Articles of apparel and clothing	3.5	3.6	3.7	3.9	4.0	4.3	4.6	4.2	4.4	0.8
85 Footwear	1.0	1.1	1.1	1.2	1.2	1.2	1.2	1.2	1.2	0.2
87 Professional, scientific, and controlling instruments	2.0	2.1	2.1	2.1	2.3	2.3	2.2	2.1	2.1	0.1
88 Photographic apparatus, equipment, and supplies	1.9	1.8	1.8	1.7	1.6	1.7	1.7	1.6	1.6	−0.3
89 Miscellaneous manufactures	4.2	4.4	4.4	4.4	4.4	4.7	4.8	4.7	4.8	0.6
93 Special transactions, n.e.s.	1.7	1.5	1.7	1.8	1.9	1.9	2.4	2.2	2.5	0.9
95 Armaments	0.4	0.5	0.5	0.5	0.4	0.3	0.4	0.3	0.3	0.0

Source: World Manufactures Trade Data Base.

Table 3.5 Geographical composition of world manufactures trade, 1981–89 (percentages)

	1981	1982	1983	1984	1985	1986	1987	1988	1989	Change 1981–89
Share of exports to world										
United States	15.8	15.0	14.1	14.2	13.8	11.6	11.6	12.1	13.0	-2.8
Canada	3.8	3.9	4.4	4.9	4.8	4.2	3.7	3.6	3.5	-0.3
Japan	14.6	13.9	14.6	15.6	15.3	15.1	13.7	13.2	12.8	-1.8
European Community	46.9	47.6	46.3	43.6	44.2	46.8	47.3	44.3	44.4	-2.5
EC to non-EC	23.6	23.5	22.7	21.7	21.7	21.5	20.7	19.1	18.8	-4.8
Germany	15.2	16.0	15.3	14.3	14.7	16.3	16.4	15.0	14.8	-0.4
France	7.5	7.2	7.0	6.6	6.6	6.8	6.8	6.4	6.4	-1.1
Italy	6.3	6.4	6.4	6.0	6.0	6.4	6.3	5.8	6.0	-0.3
United Kingdom	6.9	7.0	6.4	6.1	6.2	6.1	6.3	6.1	6.1	-0.8
Other Western Europe	8.2	8.2	8.2	7.7	8.3	8.8	8.9	8.5	8.0	-0.2
Asian NICs[a]	4.2	4.9	5.5	6.3	6.0	6.3	7.1	8.9	8.5	4.3
Eastern Europe[b]	1.1	1.0	1.0	1.0	1.0	1.0	1.0	1.1	1.0	-0.1
Developing countries	5.1	5.0	5.6	6.2	6.2	6.0	6.4	7.3	7.6	2.5
Latin America	1.6	1.7	2.0	2.3	2.3	2.0	2.1	2.4	2.4	0.8
Rest of world	0.2	0.3	0.2	0.2	0.2	0.2	0.3	1.0	1.0	0.8
Share of imports from world										
United States	15.0	15.5	17.7	21.9	23.0	21.6	20.0	18.5	18.1	3.1
Canada	4.8	4.2	4.9	5.6	5.5	4.9	4.4	4.6	4.5	-0.3
Japan	3.0	3.0	3.2	3.5	3.2	3.2	3.7	4.3	4.7	1.7
European Community	36.6	36.8	36.6	34.3	34.6	38.3	40.7	39.7	40.3	3.7
EC from non-EC	13.9	13.6	13.8	13.2	13.1	14.1	15.0	15.3	15.5	1.7
Germany	9.0	8.9	9.2	8.5	8.4	9.5	9.9	9.3	9.4	0.4
France	6.5	6.7	6.3	5.7	5.7	6.5	6.9	6.7	6.7	0.2
Italy	3.8	3.8	3.6	3.7	3.8	4.2	4.6	4.5	4.6	0.8
United Kingdom	6.4	6.7	7.0	6.6	6.6	6.7	7.1	7.5	7.3	0.9
Other Western Europe	8.1	8.0	7.9	7.4	8.1	9.0	9.3	8.7	8.3	0.2
Asian NICs[a]	3.8	4.2	4.5	4.7	4.1	4.5	5.0	7.1	7.6	3.8
Eastern Europe[b]	2.5	2.6	2.6	2.1	2.1	2.1	1.9	1.9	1.7	-0.8
Developing countries	24.1	23.1	20.4	18.2	17.1	14.7	13.1	12.8	12.4	-11.7
Latin America	6.6	5.5	4.0	4.2	4.1	3.8	3.5	3.4	3.4	-3.2
Rest of world	0.7	1.0	0.9	0.8	0.7	0.6	0.7	1.3	1.0	0.3
Export share minus import share										
United States	0.8	-0.5	-3.6	-7.7	-9.2	-10.0	-8.4	-6.4	-5.1	-5.9
Canada	-1.0	-0.3	-0.5	-0.7	-0.7	-0.7	-0.7	-1.0	-1.0	0.0
Japan	11.6	10.9	11.4	12.1	12.1	11.9	10.0	8.9	8.1	-3.5
European Community	10.3	10.8	9.7	9.3	9.6	8.5	6.6	4.6	4.1	-6.2
Non-EC	9.8	9.9	9.0	8.5	8.6	7.4	5.7	3.8	3.3	-6.5
Germany	6.2	7.1	6.1	5.8	6.3	6.8	5.7	5.7	5.4	-0.8
France	1.0	0.5	0.7	0.9	0.9	0.3	-0.1	-0.3	-0.3	-1.3
Italy	2.5	2.6	2.8	2.3	2.2	2.2	1.7	1.3	1.4	-1.1
United Kingdom	0.5	0.3	-0.6	-0.5	-0.4	-0.6	-0.8	-1.4	-1.2	-1.7
Other Western Europe	0.1	0.2	0.3	0.4	0.2	-0.2	-0.4	-0.2	-0.3	-0.4
Asian NICs[a]	0.4	0.7	1.0	1.6	1.9	1.8	2.1	1.8	0.9	0.5
Eastern Europe[b]	-1.4	-1.6	-1.6	-1.1	-1.1	-1.0	-0.8	-0.8	-0.8	0.6
Developing countries	-19.0	-18.1	-14.8	-12.0	-10.9	-8.7	-6.7	-5.5	-4.8	14.2
Latin America	-4.9	-3.8	-2.0	-1.9	-1.8	-1.8	-1.4	-1.0	-0.9	4.0
Rest of world	-0.5	-0.7	-0.7	-0.6	-0.6	-0.4	-0.5	-0.3	-0.0	0.5

Source: World Manufactures Trade Data Base.

single-country exporter of manufactures (14.9 percent of the total), followed by the United States (13.0 percent) and Japan (12.8 percent).

Significant changes in manufactures export shares occurred during the 1980s. In 1981 the United States had a 15.8 percent share of world manufactures exports; by 1987 that share was down to 11.6 percent, but it recovered to 13.0 percent in 1989, still 2.8 percentage points below the 1981 level. The export shares of most other developed countries also declined over the period. For example, both the German and the Japanese shares declined, by 0.4 and 1.8 percentage points, respectively. These declines are an inevitable consequence of the diminishing dominance of developed countries in world manufactures markets and the increasing trade role of the Asian NICs and the developing countries.

The United States is far and away the world's largest importer of manufactured goods. Its 1989 share of 18.1 percent of world manufactures imports was almost double Germany's 9.4 percent and almost four times Japan's 4.7 percent. Japan's small share shows that it plays a much smaller role in absorbing manufactures imports than its broader importance in world trade would indicate. Even the Asian NICs (7.6 percent) now import more manufactures than Japan.

Import shares changed even more dramatically than export shares during the 1980s. In 1981 the United States took 15 percent of all world imports of manufactures. By 1985, the US share had risen to 23.0 percent, but it fell thereafter to 20.0 percent in 1987 and 18.1 percent in 1989. Although well below its peak, the US import share in 1989 was still 3.1 percentage points above the 1981 level. The import shares of the European Community, Japan, and several other developed countries also increased modestly over the 1981–87 period. The most dramatic share gain, however, was for the Asian NICs. Their import share doubled from 3.8 percent in 1981 to 7.6 percent in 1989 in only eight years.

Offsetting these increases was a marked drop in the world manufactures import share of the developing countries, which fell from 24.3 percent in 1981 to only 12.4 percent in 1989.

The international market competitiveness of individual countries and groups and the changes in their relative positions can be crudely measured by subtracting the country or group's import share from its export share. By this measure, the United States moved from a +0.8-percentage-point export-minus-import share differential in 1981, the last year in which it had a manufactures trade surplus, to −5.1 percentage points in 1989, a loss of 5.9 percentage points. By this measurement, Japan was in the strongest position of any country or region in 1989 with a positive 8.0-percentage-point export-minus-import share, even though its differential was 3.5 percentage points below the 1981 level. Germany, with a +5.4-percentage-point 1989 balance, was the second-strongest performer, although its share balance had declined by 0.8 percentage point from the 1981 level.

These statistics must be interpreted with care. For example, the calculations show the share balances of the developing countries improving from − 19.0 percentage points in 1981 to − 4.8 percentage points in 1989, a seemingly significant 14.2-percentage-point improvement. However, only 2.5 percentage points of the improvement came from increased export shares. Most of the improvement came from a declining share of world manufactures imports, from 24.1 percent in 1981 to 12.4 percent in 1989. This does not reflect increasing self-sufficiency. Instead, for most developing countries, it was the result of forgoing badly needed imports that could no longer be afforded because of the countries' need to reduce their debt burdens.

Data for the Asian NICs (Korea, Taiwan, Hong Kong, Singapore) tell a different story. These countries showed only a 0.5-percentage-point improvement in their manufactures share balances, from + 0.4 percentage points in 1981 to + 0.9 percentage points in 1989. But they accomplished this by a 4.3-percentage-point gain in export share, concurrent with a 3.8-percentage-point increase in their import share. These movements reflect a very healthy trade expansion for those economies.

World manufactures trade flows for 1981, 1987, and 1989 are summarized in table 3.6, which allows calculation of countries' trade balances and displays the breakdown of each country's export destinations and import sources. Almost 45 percent of 1989 world manufactures exports, $937.8 billion, originated in the European Community. But $541 billion of those exports, or 57.7 percent, went to destinations within the Community. This $541 billion of internal EC manufactures trade represents just over one-fourth of the world total. Thus, if one excludes intra-EC trade from the international trade figures after 1992, world manufactures trade will be reduced by over one-fourth.

Japan's dependence on the US market shows up clearly in the table. Of total 1989 Japanese manufactures exports of $270.3 billion, $93.1 billion, or 34.4 percent, went to the United States, a larger share than the 26.1 percent of 1981 but smaller than the 37.2 percent recorded in 1987. Only $47.8 billion, or 17.7 percent, of Japan's 1989 exports went to the European Community, compared with 13.8 percent in 1981. Nevertheless, in 1989, Japan's $15.8 billion in manufactures exports to Germany exceeded the $14.0 billion in US manufactures exports to Germany that year.

Tables 3.7 through 3.10 show the shares of world manufactures markets captured by the United States, the European Community, Japan, and the Asian NICs for 1981, 1987, and 1989. The US share of world manufactures exports to non-US destinations declined from 18.5 percent in 1981 to 15.8 percent in 1989 (table 3.7). Between 1981 and 1989, the United States maintained its dominant position in Canadian manufactures trade (70.6 percent) and actually increased its share in Latin America (to 52.6 percent). The US share of EC imports declined by 1.6 percentage points, from 9.4 percent in 1981 to 7.8

Table 3.6 World bilateral trade flows in manufactures, 1981, 1987, and 1989[a] (billions of dollars)

					Exporter						
Importer	World	United States	Canada	Japan	European Community	Germany	France	United Kingdom	Asian NICs	Latin America	Other
1989											
World	2,110.3	273.4	74.2	270.3	937.8	312.8	135.0	128.4	178.5	51.5	324.7
United States	382.3		62.5	93.1	74.3	24.0	10.0	15.7	67.8	32.5	52.2
Canada	97.2	68.6		6.7	8.7	2.6	1.4	1.9	5.5	1.8	5.9
Japan	97.0	25.2	1.3		19.2	7.8	2.7	3.2	23.1	3.3	24.9
European Community	865.3	67.1	4.3	47.8	541.0	169.1	79.0	60.3	31.6	9.5	164.1
Germany	194.2	14.0	0.6	15.8	101.7		21.8	14.6	8.9	2.4	50.8
France	153.0	9.5	0.5	5.2	109.4	41.5		11.8	3.6	1.4	23.4
United Kingdom	154.6	17.6	1.4	10.7	81.1	29.9	13.2		8.9	1.4	33.6
Asian NICs	137.8	27.2	1.4	50.5	21.4	7.4	3.4	4.0	21.2	2.4	13.8
Latin America	72.9	38.3	1.3	8.8	18.6	5.7	4.4	1.9	3.1		2.8
Other	457.8	47.1	3.4	63.5	254.7	96.1	34.1	41.4	26.2	2.0	60.9
1987											
World	1,648.6	191.8	60.2	225.0	817.9	270.4	112.3	103.9	116.5	34.6	202.6
United States	325.6		51.7	83.6	77.2	27.1	9.2	14.4	57.3	23.8	32.1
Canada	74.5	52.2		5.5	9.1	2.6	1.2	2.0	3.8	1.2	2.6
Japan	57.2	15.1	0.6		13.8	5.7	1.8	2.1	12.3	1.9	13.6
European Community	703.5	45.9	3.1	39.5	476.6	147.5	66.1	49.8	24.8	5.9	107.8
Germany	158.1	8.9	0.5	12.8	90.3		18.7	12.0	7.2	1.5	37.0
France	118.8	6.3	0.4	3.9	88.7	32.6		8.9	3.0	0.8	15.8
United Kingdom	111.1	11.7	1.0	8.3	66.7	24.6	9.7		6.2	0.9	16.1
Asian NICs	82.5	15.1	0.7	37.7	16.3	5.2	2.3	3.4	7.2	0.4	5.1
Latin America	59.4	27.1	1.3	8.0	19.0	6.0	4.2	2.1	1.0		3.1
Other	346.0	36.4	3.0	50.7	205.8	76.4	27.5	30.1	10.2	1.5	
1981											
World	1,013.9	159.7	38.3	148.0	498.5	154.4	75.9	70.4	42.3	16.5	110.6
United States	149.9		29.0	38.6	35.1	11.0	4.9	6.9	21.3	10.2	15.8
Canada	43.0	31.8		3.3	4.5	1.1	0.6	1.3	1.7	0.4	1.3
Japan	28.2	9.6	0.5		5.5	2.0	0.9	1.0	4.8	1.4	6.4
European Community	388.7	36.3	3.2	20.4	256.4	77.3	38.6	28.4	11.8	4.0	56.6
Germany	86.6	7.2	0.4	5.9	50.2		11.3	6.2	3.7	1.0	18.2
France	68.6	5.6	0.4	2.2	50.0	19.9		4.8	1.3	0.5	8.6
United Kingdom	60.1	8.4	1.2	4.7	33.1	10.5	5.6		3.4	0.6	8.7
Asian NICs	38.6	9.3	0.4	19.6	7.5	2.2	0.8	2.2	0.0	0.0	1.8
Latin America	67.5	32.7	2.1	10.0	20.5	5.9	3.7	2.2	0.0	0.0	2.3
Other	297.8	40.0	3.1	56.1	169.0	55.0	26.6	28.3	2.8	0.5	

a. EC exports and imports include intra-EC trade.

Source: World Manufactures Trade Data Base.

Table 3.7 United States: share of world manufactures export markets, 1981–89 (percentages)

US share of world exports to:	1981	1987	1989	Change 1981–89
World	15.8	11.6	13.0	−2.8
World other than US	18.5	14.5	15.8	−2.7
Canada	73.9	70.1	70.6	−3.3
Latin America	48.4	45.7	52.6	4.2
Mexico	67.9	74.5	74.8	6.9
Japan	34.1	26.4	26.0	−8.1
Asian NICs	24.1	18.3	19.7	−4.4
Korea	25.7	19.5	21.6	−4.1
Taiwan	27.7	18.4	21.0	−6.7
European Community	9.4	6.5	7.8	−1.6
France	8.1	5.3	6.2	−1.9
Italy	7.8	5.0	5.4	−2.4
Germany	8.3	5.6	7.2	−1.1
United Kingdom	14.0	10.6	11.4	−2.6
EC from non-EC	27.5	20.2	20.6	−6.9
Other	13.4	10.5	10.3	−3.1

Source: World Manufactures Trade Data Base.

Table 3.8 European Community: share of world manufactures export markets, 1981–89 (percentages)

EC share of world exports to:	1981	1987	1989	Change 1981–89
World	49.2	49.6	44.4	−4.8
World other than EC	38.7	36.1	31.9	−6.8
World other than US	53.6	56.0	50.0	−3.6
United States	23.4	23.7	19.4	−4.0
Canada	10.5	12.2	8.9	−1.6
Latin America	30.2	34.6	25.5	−4.7
Mexico	19.8	13.3	11.8	−8.0
Japan	19.5	24.1	19.8	0.3
Asian NICs	19.4	19.8	15.5	−3.9
Korea	13.5	17.3	12.8	−0.7
Taiwan	13.0	16.7	13.6	0.6
European Community	66.0	67.7	62.5	−3.5
France	72.9	74.7	71.5	−1.4
Italy	70.9	70.8	67.3	−3.6
Germany	58.0	57.1	52.4	−5.6
United Kingdom	55.1	60.0	52.5	−2.6
Other	56.7	59.5	55.6	−1.1

Source: World Manufactures Trade Data Base.

percent in 1989. The US share of EC imports from non-EC sources declined more dramatically, by 6.9 percentage points, from 27.5 percent in 1981 to 20.6 percent in 1989.

Consistent with the broadening of world trade participation, the EC shares of most markets also declined (table 3.8). The EC share of world exports to non-EC destinations dropped 6.8 percentage points from 1981 to 1989, more than the 2.7-percentage-point decline in the US share of world exports to non-US destinations during the same period. The European Community, however,

Table 3.9 Japan: share of world manufactures export markets, 1981–89 (percentages)

Japanese share of world exports to:	1981	1987	1989	Change 1981–89
World	14.6	13.7	12.8	−1.8
World other than US	12.7	10.7	10.3	−2.4
United States	25.7	25.7	24.4	−1.3
Canada	7.7	7.4	6.9	−0.8
Latin America	14.9	13.5	12.0	−2.9
Mexico	8.3	8.8	7.2	−1.1
Asian NICs	50.7	45.7	36.6	−14.1
Korea	56.4	56.2	39.7	−16.7
Taiwan	55.9	46.9	39.1	−16.8
European Community	5.2	5.6	5.5	0.3
France	3.2	3.3	3.4	0.2
Italy	2.3	2.9	3.0	0.7
Germany	6.8	8.1	8.2	1.4
United Kingdom	7.9	7.5	6.9	−1.0
Other	18.9	14.7	13.9	−5.0

Source: World Manufactures Trade Data Base.

Table 3.10 Asian NICs: share of world manufactures export markets, 1981–89[a] (percentages)

Asian NICs share of world exports to:	1981	1987	1989	1981–89
World	4.2	7.1	8.5	4.3
World other than US	2.4	4.5	6.4	4.0
United States	14.2	17.6	17.7	3.5
Canada	3.9	5.1	5.6	1.7
Latin America	n.a.	1.6	4.2	4.2
Mexico	n.a.	0.5	3.2	3.2
Japan	16.9	21.5	23.9	7.0
Asian NICs	n.a.	8.7	15.4	15.4
Korea	n.a.	2.5	6.4	6.4
Taiwan	n.a.	6.0	11.0	11.0
European Community	3.0	3.5	3.7	0.7
France	1.9	2.5	2.3	0.4
Italy	2.0	2.7	2.8	0.8
Germany	4.2	4.6	4.6	0.4
United Kingdom	5.6	5.6	5.7	0.1
Other	0.9	3.0	5.7	4.8

n.a. = not available

a. The Asian NICs (newly industrializing countries) are Hong Kong, Korea, Singapore, and Taiwan.

Source: World Manufactures Trade Data Base

maintained a higher 1989 share (31.9 percent) than the United States (15.8 percent), so the declines are similar in relative terms. In 1981, 51.4 percent of EC exports went to other EC countries, but by 1989 the percentage was up to 57.7 percent (table 3.6).

Japan's share of world manufactures exports declined by only 1.8 percentage points from 1981 to 1989. Its share of the US market declined even more

Table 3.11 Share of manufactures exports taken by the United States, 1981 89 (percentages)

Exporter	1981	1987	1989	Change 1981–89
World	14.8	19.8	18.1	3.3
World other than US	17.6	22.4	20.8	3.2
Canada	75.7	85.8	84.2	8.5
Latin America	61.7	68.7	63.2	1.5
Mexico	88.3	89.1	87.7	−0.6
Japan	26.1	37.2	34.4	8.3
Asian NICs	50.3	49.2	38.0	−12.3
Korea	45.9	51.7	34.8	−11.1
Taiwan	59.2	47.1	38.3	−20.9
European Community	7.1	9.4	7.9	0.8
France	6.4	8.2	7.4	1.0
Italy	7.1	9.7	9.0	1.9
Germany	7.1	10.0	7.7	0.6
United Kingdom	9.9	13.9	12.2	2.3
Other	14.3	15.8	16.1	1.8

Source: World Manufactures Trade Data Base.

modestly: Japan still provided 24.4 percent of US manufactures imports in 1989 (table 3.9). By 1989, Japan had managed to raise its share of EC imports to only 5.5 percent, but this was nevertheless about seven-tenths the size of the 7.8 percent US share. Japan's 1989 share of German imports (8.2 percent), however, surpassed the US share of that market (7.2 percent), while the US share of the UK market (11.4 percent) topped Japan's (6.9 percent).

The Asian NICs have made notable progress in raising their share of the world export market. The near doubling of their world export share from 4.2 percent in 1981 to 8.5 percent in 1989 was broadly based (table 3.10). The United States remains the key market for the NICs, which by 1989 provided 17.7 percent of US manufactures imports, almost three-fourths as much as Japan. The NICs' 23.9 percent share of Japan's much smaller manufactures imports—only modestly below the 26.0 percent US share—is also a remarkable feat. The US share of Japan's imports, however, has declined sharply since 1981, while the NICs' share has been increasing rapidly. At only 3.7 percent, NIC penetration of the EC market remains low.

The United States is a very important market for world manufactures exporters. In 1981, it took 17.6 percent of all exports by other countries (table 3.11). That figure rose to 22.4 percent in 1987, and in 1989 it was 20.8 percent. Over 84 percent of Canada's manufactures exports went to the United States in 1989. Japan sent over one-third (34.4 percent) of its manufactures exports to the United States in that year, a higher proportion than in 1981. Although only 7.9 percent of total 1989 EC exports went to the United States, 18.7 percent of EC exports to non-EC destinations were absorbed by the United States.

During the 1980s the rapid growth of US imports played a particularly important role in stimulating the growth of world manufactures trade. Of the $634.7 billion expansion of world manufactures exports from 1981 to 1987, $181.7 billion, or 28.8 percent, was absorbed by the United States. This is reflected in the expansion of US import shares from the 15.0 percent level of 1981 to 20 percent and above for the years 1984 through 1987 (table 3.5). The large increases in US imports not only resulted in significant changes in national shares of world manufactures exports and imports but did much to propel economic growth outside the United States during most of the 1980s.

Manufactures Trade and International Capital Flows

The data presented in this chapter clearly establish that manufactures trade is the dominant and most rapidly growing segment of world goods and services trade. Less obvious is the dominant role of manufactures trade in providing the counterpart to changes in net flows of financial capital. Current account balances reflect the net lender or borrower status of individual countries. Except for changes resulting from dramatic movements in oil prices, large changes in balances of non-oil-exporting countries will inevitably be manifested primarily in manufactures trade. The US transition from lender to borrower during the 1980s provides an illustration.

Movements in exchange rates, for example, will not have much impact on which countries are oil exporters and which oil importers. The geography of oil deposits largely determines which countries can export oil and which must import it, although national economic and other policies can certainly affect the development and availability of oil for export.

Agricultural trade is somewhat the same. Different economic policies may, in the long term, change the former Soviet Union from a net importer to a net exporter of grain; EC subsidies have created large grain surpluses that are exported; China has moved toward self-sufficiency in grain. But agricultural production bases are ultimately limited by geography and usually change more slowly than do production bases for manufactures.

Services trade is also inherently less responsive than manufactures trade to movements in exchange rates and is less a means of implementing changes in net capital flows than is manufactures trade. Well over half of world commercial services trade is transportation and travel (tourism). Travel is a service that does respond to exchange rate movements and other changing economic factors, but in 1989 it represented only 5.2 percent of world trade in goods and services (table 3.1). Other private services such as insurance, film rentals, education, consulting, and construction typically respond only slowly and in limited degree to exchange rate movements. The reason is partly, as we have already seen, that the major portion of the costs involved in producing many of these services (for example, insurance) is incurred in the customer country.

In the past, dramatic changes in oil prices have markedly changed net international capital flows, albeit temporarily. But except for oil price changes, net flows of international capital and the corresponding flows of manufactures trade change mainly as the result of international investors' changing perceptions of investment opportunities. These in turn are the outcome of the differing domestic and international economic policies and prospects of individual countries. Thus, because there are no other adequate means of transmitting sudden, large changes in net capital flows, changes in net international investment flows among industrialized countries will primarily affect their manufacturing sectors.

Vacillating policies or dramatic events that induce wide fluctuations in international net capital flows can cause significant and perhaps costly shifts among resources in the countries affected. Moreover, wide swings in a country's economic climate for manufacturing and uncertainty about the future climate can inhibit investment in the manufacturing sector and hurt its long-term competitiveness. Policymakers should be aware of whether a proposed policy may cause major changes in a country's net international capital flows and carefully consider how such changes may affect the sectoral composition of the economy and the employment, investment, productivity, and long-term performance of the manufacturing sector and its long-term contribution to US living standards. Foreign policymakers, whose countries' economies have long been dependent on foreign trade, seem to be more aware of this need than do their US counterparts. Although concerns about the effects of international capital flows on the manufacturing sector have not been evident in US policymaking, they have long been a major factor in resistance in Germany, Japan, and the Asian NICs to policy changes that would reduce their capital outflows.

Summary

- A continued decline in the dollar share of most nonmanufactured goods—food, beverages and tobacco, crude materials (other than mineral fuels), and animal and vegetable oils—in world merchandise trade seems assured. Exports of mineral fuels, on the other hand, have varied widely as a percentage of total world exports during the 1980s, from 22.6 percent in 1981 to 18.7 percent in 1987, mostly because of changes in oil prices. Oil prices will probably remain volatile, and oil could from time to time increase its dollar share of world trade.

- Manufactures trade dominates US merchandise trade and the US balances in trade and current accounts. It also accounts for a growing proportion of world trade in goods and services and dominates the trade performance of most industrialized countries.

- Manufactures trade is the major growth segment of world trade. It has been subject to intensifying competition as more and more countries develop their manufacturing industries and as manufactures assume a larger role in international trade.

- Gradual changes are occurring in the composition of world manufactures trade. In general, trade is growing more rapidly in the more highly processed, more finished goods. For example, world exports of chemicals and basic manufactures are increasing less rapidly than exports of transportation equipment and consumer goods.

- Individual manufactures product groups vary widely with respect to their role in world trade. The road vehicles product group is the largest product group and one of the fastest growing. A dominant international competitive position in road vehicles trade is therefore much more significant for a country's trade balance than dominance in other products.

- A few developed countries dominate world manufactures trade. In 1989, Germany produced 14.9 percent of world manufactures exports; the United States accounted for 13.0 percent and Japan 12.8 percent. Japan's large trade surpluses stem from its unusually small import share, 4.7 percent of the world total, less than the Asian NICs', about the same as Canada's, and in dramatic contrast to the 18.1 percent US share.

- Together the EC countries had a 44.4 percent share of 1989 world manufactures exports. However, almost 58 percent of those exports went to other EC countries. Excluding intra-EC exports from world trade after 1992 would reduce the dollar value of world manufactures trade by about one-fourth.

- The Asian NICs made dramatic inroads into world manufactures trade during 1981–89, strongly increasing both their import and their export shares. The relative participation in world trade by the rest of the developing world declined, however. Modest gains in export shares by developing countries were overwhelmed by declines in import shares, reflecting debt management in the form of both export expansion and the forced reduction of badly needed imports.

- Significant shifts have been occurring in the geographic composition of world manufactures trade. In addition to a marked decline in US competitiveness (a lower share of world exports, a higher share of world imports, and a -5.1-percentage-point share balance in 1989), the export shares of most developed countries have been declining modestly and their import shares rising. This reflects a decline in the dominance of developed countries in world trade in manufactures.

- Manufactures trade is the main conduit through which large changes in net international capital flows are manifested. Major changes in net international capital flows are normally caused primarily by national monetary, fiscal, tax, regulatory, and other economic policies. But whatever their cause, net changes in international capital flows affect primarily the manufacturing sectors of industrialized countries. There are two reasons for this. Not only is manufactures trade much larger than other forms of international exchange of goods and services, but also the size and direction of flows can change more rapidly than for other forms of goods and services.

- For the industrialized countries, net capital inflows generally translate into manufactures trade deficits; net outflows translate into trade surpluses. National economic policymakers should give careful consideration to the effects that large, rapid changes in the size and direction of net capital flows have on the manufacturing sector and on the structural balance of the domestic economy.

Bibliography

General Agreement on Tariffs and Trade. 1990. *International Trade 89–90.* vol. I. Geneva: General Agreement on Tariffs and Trade.

4

An Overview of US Manufactures Trade Performance

An Overview of US Manufactures Trade Performance

Manufactures trade accounted for most of the dramatic growth in the US trade and current account deficits in 1981–87 as well as for most of the narrowing of the deficits that began in 1988. It will also be the primary vehicle for further reducing US trade imbalances during the 1990s. This chapter discusses alternative methods of measuring the international competitiveness of US manufacturing, provides an overview of the recent trade performance of US manufactures, describes the geographic composition of US manufactures trade, assesses the effects of exchange rate movements and other factors on US market competitiveness in manufactures, compares recent US manufacturing productivity gains with those of its competitors, and assesses the outlook for US manufacturing. This overview of manufactures trade performance will be used as a framework for the detailed analyses of individual product groups in chapter 5.

Measuring the International Competitiveness of US Manufacturing

International competitiveness is an issue of great concern in the United States, but the term is seldom clearly defined. There are several different bases on which US competitiveness may be assessed. These include:

- US living standards

- the worldwide sales of US-owned firms, including their foreign subsidiaries

- the trade performance of US-based production.

US Living Standards

A country's living standards are the ultimate reflection of its international competitiveness. Recognizing this, the President's Commission on Industrial Competitiveness defined international competitiveness as "the degree to which a nation can, under free and fair market conditions, meet the test of international markets, while simultaneously maintaining and expanding the real incomes of its citizens" (President's Commission on Industrial Competitiveness 1985, 6).

This definition implies that a country should maintain a rough long-term cumulative balance in its international accounts, since external borrowing that enhances consumption boosts living standards in only a temporary fashion. It also excludes meeting the test by lowering the value of one's currency or restraining domestic growth, both of which strategies would help the country's balance of trade at the expense of real domestic incomes.

A rising standard of living is any country's basic economic objective. Concern about future US living standards is the underlying reason for concern about the competitiveness of US firms and US-based production.

Changes in the relative living standards of countries occur only slowly and are difficult to measure; thus, international comparisons are tenuous. Opinions differ on what is the best measure of the standard of living. One widely used measure is real income (see, e.g., Lawrence 1988). Measurements of changes in real income are, of course, influenced by the price index used to deflate the nominal income data, by the starting and ending points of the analysis, by the kind of income being measured—family income, per capita income, wage-earners' income, before- or after-tax income—and by whether one is interested in averages or the distribution of incomes. Because of the many factors involved, there is ample room for disagreement about whether real incomes are rising or falling. Probably the best that can be done is to gauge general trends, and even then there may be disagreement. Even most optimists, however, would probably agree that real incomes in the United States are rising less rapidly than in most of the post-World War II period and than in several competitor countries. The involvement of so many factors probably explains why more attention is not given to the critically important living-standards concept of competitiveness.

Sales by US-Owned Firms

In a world of instant communications and fast, low-cost transportation, large multinational companies can serve foreign markets either by exporting from the home country or by locating production in the foreign markets. Competing successfully in some important foreign markets may require locating production there rather than exporting to them. Many US companies own production facilities—foreign direct investments—in other countries, and conversely, many foreign companies have direct investments in the United States.

In a world where multinationals own a vast network of subsidiary firms and operations in each other's home countries, it is fair to ask the question, "Who is us?"[1] Does the label "American" apply only to US-owned companies located in the United States? Or does it include the foreign affiliates of US companies? And what about foreign-owned companies located and producing in the United States? The answers have important implications for US policies (Reich 1990, 53).

US trade data present a picture of sharp US decline during the 1980s and only modest partial recovery in recent years. But some argue that in today's more integrated world economy trade balances do not really matter—that a better measure of US competitiveness is the performance of *US-owned* companies, including overseas subsidiaries, in world markets. Which measure is more useful for US policymaking purposes?

The earnings of the foreign affiliates of US companies do contribute to the US current account balance and to US living standards. A comparison of the foreign earnings of US and foreign companies helps put these foreign earnings in perspective and provides a measure of the ability of US-owned companies to compete in international markets. The 1990 book value of US manufacturing direct investments abroad ($168.0 billion) was only marginally larger than the comparable book value of foreign direct investments in manufacturing in the United States ($160.2 billion).[2] However, book values often understate the real value and earning power of US investments abroad, which have generally been in place longer than foreign investments in the United States. Although modestly larger in total book value, US manufacturing direct investments abroad have consistently earned significantly more than the direct investments of foreign companies in US manufacturing. At $22.9 billion, the 1990 international investment income of US manufacturing direct investments abroad was $18.6 billion greater than the income of foreign companies from their direct investments in manufacturing in the United States. Thus, by this measure, US companies have consistently been internationally competitive.

A better and more direct measure of the competitiveness of US firms is their total sales, including the foreign sales of their affiliates. One estimate puts the

---

1. See in particular the article by that title by Robert B. Reich (1990).

2. All of the direct investment valuations in this study are on the historical cost (book value) basis traditionally used by the US Department of Commerce. Recently, the US Commerce Department has also begun to value direct investments on a current cost basis and on a market value basis, both of which typically yield higher valuations. However, historical cost is the only basis on which detailed estimates of the position of US direct investment abroad and the position of foreign direct investment in the United States are available by country, industry, and account.

total foreign sales of US companies with foreign affiliates at five times the value of their recorded US exports (Julius 1990, 81). In fact, according to *The Economist*:

> If America's "trade" balance is measured on the basis of nationality of ownership rather than residency (that is, adding the sales, net of local purchase, of overseas subsidiaries to the recorded trade balance and deducting all intra-firm flows to avoid double counting), then in 1986 America's recorded visible trade deficit of $144 billion is transformed into a $57 billion surplus. Doing the same calculations today would probably give America the world's biggest surplus. (*The Economist*, 29 March 1991, 61)

Although sales by foreign affiliates may be as profitable for individual companies as the same dollar amount of sales through US exports, they have very different effects on the home country. Corporate leadership is understandably concerned with maximizing the firm's profits, regardless of whether they come from foreign or domestic production. National leadership, however, is concerned with the welfare of the country's population—its jobs and living standards—and whether the country is borrowing or lending through its international transactions.

The foreign sales of US-owned companies make a positive contribution to the US economy and to US living standards through US receipts of international investment income and other forms of income and benefits. Moreover, as noted later in this chapter, the returns and benefits from direct investments are clearly preferable to the loss of foreign markets. Nevertheless, the strong performance of US companies abroad cannot offer much solace to policymakers concerned about the US economy, because the potential contribution to the US economy from a dollar of foreign sales by a foreign affiliate is many times smaller than that from a dollar of exports of US-based production. For example, the 1988 sales of foreign affiliates of US manufacturing firms totaled $620 billion (US Department of Commerce, Bureau of Economic Analysis 1990, table 2), but provided only $25.4 billion in US manufacturing direct investment income receipts, or about 4.1 percent. In addition, in 1988, foreign affiliates paid their US manufacturing parents royalties of $8.6 billion and service charges of $1.9 billion. Together, these amounts were equivalent to another 1.7 percent of their $620 billion of foreign sales and brought the total income in US international accounts from foreign manufacturing affiliates to $35.7 billion, about 5.8 percent of sales. Even this is small compared with $316 billion in total 1990 US manufactures exports.

Moreover, a substantial portion—typically about one-third or more—of the direct investment income portion of the earnings from direct investments is reinvested in the host country to enlarge or retain a competitive foothold there. Such reinvestments have little immediate effect on the US economy except to the extent that they finance exports of capital equipment or other goods or services from the United States.

The return to the US economy of a dollar of sales by a foreign affiliate of a US company is therefore very small compared with the return from a dollar of exports. Direct investments abroad may, however, have other, indirect positive effects on US international accounts by generating exports from US parent firms to their foreign affiliates.

Nevertheless, for US policymakers interested in US jobs and living standards, the favorable global competitive position of US-owned firms is of only limited interest since it cannot compensate for poor international competitive performance by US-based production. On the other hand, the global sales surpluses of US companies are an indicator that US management—often faulted in comparisons with Japanese and others—may not be so inept after all.

Why are US-owned businesses abroad doing so much better in international competition than US-based operations? Can it be that the United States does not provide an environment as favorable for manufacturing as do competitor countries? In a highly competitive world economy where investment capital flows to the most attractive locations, this is a key policy question.

The Trade Performance of US-Based Production

For the reasons given above, this study does not seek primarily to assess the United States' international competitiveness in terms of current or prospective living standards. Neither does it examine performance and competitiveness from the viewpoint of US firms or industries, which may be very different. For example, because of rising foreign production and sales, US firms may enjoy strong global performance even while US-based production is declining and trade deficits are rising in the same product group.

Instead, the bulk of the analysis in this study focuses on *the international trade competitiveness of US-based production of manufactures*—that is, on the present and near-term future ability of US-produced manufactures to compete in US and foreign markets. In other words, for the purposes of this study, "us" is *US-based production, whether US-owned or foreign-owned.*

International trade data describe the trade performance of the United States and competitor countries in terms of exports, imports, and trade balances. This information can be used to assess the international market competitiveness of US-based production at given points in time. For this purpose, this study considers US manufacturing "competitive" in international markets if the manufacturing sector as a whole is able to sell enough US-made manufactures in US and foreign markets to balance the US trade and current accounts, *regardless of the terms of trade,* including the dollar exchange rate. This is a convenient simplifying assumption that narrows the focus of most of this study to trade balances, rather than an analysis of how that trade performance is achieved or how it affects US living standards.

The international market competitiveness of US manufacturing as measured by trade balances is, however, a result of several factors. These include the dollar exchange rate, relative US and foreign economic growth rates, and the wages and productivity of US manufacturing relative to competitors. For policymaking purposes, what counts most is a country's international competitiveness in terms of its living standards. Analyses of the trade performance of manufacturing are most useful when put into perspective and considered along with other factors. For example, dollar depreciation aids the international market competitiveness of US goods by worsening the terms of trade, which has an adverse effect on US living standards. Similarly, contractionary policies could slow US economic growth relative to foreign growth rates, but that is an undesirable way to improve trade performance. Thus, what counts is not just good trade performance but how that performance is achieved. Strong US market performance based on productivity gains contributes to gains in living standards. Strong performance achieved by dollar depreciation can lower living standards.

Thus, despite the general focus on trade balances, the trade performance assessments in this volume are accompanied by data on exchange rates and relative prices to provide some conclusions about the effects of the performance of US-based manufacturing on US living standards. For example, continuing deficits in manufactures trade and the current account despite significant dollar depreciation and deteriorating terms of trade signal a manufacturing sector that is lagging behind its competitors in productivity gains or in its ability to adapt to changes in the product or geographic composition of markets; this will have negative effects on living standards. Assessing historical and projected performance in terms of trade balances is thus an important first step in assessing the contribution of manufacturing to US living standards.

The analyses in this study typically begin in 1981, the most recent year in which the United States experienced surpluses in both manufactures trade and the current account. Both 1980 and 1981, however, were good years for US trade and were not necessarily typical of the previous decade. Performance fluctuated during the 1970s, with relatively large deficits in some years. According to Bruce Scott (1991, 1), "US competitive decline was masked in the 1970s by a declining dollar on the one hand and inflated sales to developing countries, notably in Latin America, which were financed in large measure by unsound bank loans. . . . Without the unsound, credit based export sales the deterioration would have been more severe." In addition, US trade performance was boosted through 1981 by a high level of exports to the OPEC countries, financed by their increased revenues from higher oil prices.

Trade Performance Measurements of International Competitiveness

This study uses international trade data to measure the domestic and foreign market competitiveness of US-based production of manufactured goods. It uses both dollar trade data (exports, imports, and balances in current-dollar terms) and market share data (export and import shares of markets in percentage terms).

Trade Balance Measurements of US Performance

US trade data show a rapid growth of US trade deficits from 1981 to 1987, evidence of a growing inability of US-based manufactures production to compete against foreign-based production, both in foreign markets and in the US market. Small surpluses were typical for US manufactures trade in the 1970s and through 1982, but then performance worsened dramatically. In 1981, the manufactures trade surplus was $21.9 billion (table 4.1), but consistently deteriorating performance moved the balance to a 1987 deficit of $124.9 billion—a slide in only six years of $146.8 billion, equivalent to 3.3 percent of 1987 GNP.

The 1981–87 decline was due to both lagging US exports and very rapid import growth. From 1981 to 1987, US manufactures exports grew at an average annual rate of 2.9 percent, well below the 8.5 percent annual rate of growth of world exports to non-US destinations; meanwhile US imports grew by 14.2 percent per year (table 4.1), well above the annual world export growth rate. US performance began to improve in 1988 and continued to do so through 1990, with rapid export growth and more modest import growth narrowing the deficit by $51.8 billion (domestic and foreign exports, imports customs basis) from its 1987 low point. Export growth rates have exceeded import growth rates since 1987. Nevertheless, 1990 manufactures imports were 2.6 times those of 1981; exports that year were only 1.8 times the 1981 level. The $73 billion manufactures trade deficit in 1990 represented a decline of $95 billion from the $21.9 billion 1981 surplus and was equivalent to 1.4 percent of 1990 GNP. The large manufactures deficit persisted despite the fact that International Monetary Fund (IMF) indices of the real effective exchange rate of the dollar (deflated by relative wholesale prices, 1985 = 100) show the dollar exchange rate index in 1990 (69.6) well below its level of 1981 (83.9), when the United States had

Table 4.1 United States: manufactures trade, 1981–90 (billions of dollars except where noted)

	1981	1982	1983	1984	1985	1986	1987	1988	1989	1990	Average change 1981–87	Average change 1987–90
Exports	171.7	155.3	148.5	163.6	167.8	179.9	200.0	255.6	287.0	315.7		
Change from previous year		−16.4	−6.8	15.1	4.2	12.1	20.1	55.6	31.4	28.7	4.7	38.6
Percentage change		−9.6	−4.4	10.2	2.6	7.2	11.2	27.8	12.3	10.0	2.9	16.7
Imports	149.8	151.7	171.2	231.3	257.9	297.0	324.9	361.4	379.4	388.8		
Change from previous year		1.9	19.5	60.1	26.6	39.1	27.9	36.5	18.0	9.4	29.2	21.3
Percentage change		1.3	12.9	35.1	11.5	15.2	9.4	11.2	5.0	2.5	14.2	6.2
Balance	21.9	3.6	−22.7	−67.7	−90.1	−117.1	−124.9	−105.8	−92.4	−73.1		
Change from previous year		−18.3	−26.3	−45.0	−22.4	−27.0	−7.8	19.1	13.4	19.3	−24.5	17.3

Source: US Department of Commerce.

narrow manufactures trade and current account surpluses (International Monetary Fund 1991, 111).[3]

Trade Share Measurements of US Performance

Although the trade deficits of the 1980s are clear evidence of lagging ability of US manufacturing to compete in world (US and foreign) markets, they do not indicate how the slippage occurred, nor do they indicate the change in US international market competitiveness compared with that of other countries. World trade has grown dramatically, with many developing countries increasing their participation. In such an environment, even a country with modestly increasing trade surpluses could experience a declining relative position in international markets if its surpluses were growing more slowly than the dollar valuation of world trade.

A more complete picture of the performance of US manufactures trade relative to world markets and relative to the performance of other countries can be obtained from examining data that show changes in US and competitor-country shares of world exports. Chapter 3 provided data on US shares of total world manufactures exports, together with the shares of competitor countries (table 3.5). US export shares, however, are more precisely and usefully calculated by matching US manufactures exports against world manufactures exports to non-US destinations (i.e., world exports *excluding* those to the United States). This provides the most accurate measure of US performance in the world market that is available to US exporters. For example, dramatically higher US imports in the 1980s were the main force that greatly increased world automobile exports, but were not part of the world export market available to US automobile exporters. Thus, calculating the US share of exports to non-US destinations avoids the effects on US export shares of changes in the dollar value of US imports.

Similarly, expressing US imports as a share of world exports from non-US sources is the best measurement of import share because it avoids the effects of changes in US exports on calculations of US import shares. It is also a useful measurement of the dependence of foreign exporters on the US market.

According to data from the WMTDB created for this study, the US share of world exports to non-US destinations declined from 18.5 percent in 1981 to 14.5 percent in 1987, but then rebounded to 15.8 percent in 1989, leaving a

---

3. The Federal Reserve Board's weighted-average (nominal) exchange rate indices were 103.26 for 1981 and 89.05 for 1990. Other deflators give different real exchange rate results; for example, when deflated by the IMF's unit value of exports index, the dollar exchange rate remains above its 1981 level (see the paper by William R. Cline and following commentary in chapter 2 of Bergsten 1991).

2.7-percentage-point share loss for the entire period (table 4.2). Export shares alone, however, are an inadequate measure of changes in competitiveness because the export shares of all industrialized countries will tend to decline as developing countries industrialize and become more involved in world trade. But if a country's competitive position has not changed, declines in its export shares attributable to growth in world trade should be matched by roughly parallel declines in its import shares.

US export and import shares did not, however, move together during the 1980s. This demonstrates that fundamental changes occurred in the market competitiveness of US-based production of manufactured goods. During 1981–87, US export shares declined, but import shares rose. The US share of world imports from non-US sources rose from 18.0 percent in 1981 to 27.0 percent in 1985 before declining to 22.8 percent in 1987 and 20.9 percent in 1989, 3.0 percentage points above the 1981 level. As noted above, this measurement of the share of rest-of-the-world exports absorbed by the United States also provides an index of the dependence of foreign exporters on the US market.

Again as noted above, US performance improved after 1987. In 1988 and 1989, US exports of manufactures grew more rapidly than world exports of manufactures, raising the US export share. US imports of manufactures grew more slowly than world imports of manufactures, lowering the US import share. However, for the entire 1981–89 period for which WMTDB data are available, world exports to non-US destinations increased at an annual rate of 9.1 percent, while US exports increased at only a 7.0 percent rate (table 4.2). Similarly, the 12.3 percent annual rate of US import growth significantly exceeded the 10.2 percent annual rate of world manufactures imports from non-US sources. Together these relationships indicate a decline in relative US international market competitiveness during the period.

Because the WMTDB data in table 4.2 are denominated in dollars, they are affected by the exchange rate used in converting foreign export and import values into dollars. Other things being equal, the currency translation effects associated with a rising dollar increase the US shares of total world exports and imports because given amounts of foreign currencies translate into fewer dollars; the converse occurs with a falling dollar. The effects of the distortions introduced by exchange rate changes can, however, be minimized by subtracting the US import share from the US export share to arrive at a percentage share balance. These share balances provide a crude index of relative US competitiveness in international manufactures markets. Perhaps more usefully, changes in the share balances can indicate whether that competitiveness is improving or worsening.

The US share balance in 1981 of +0.5 percentage point reflects the manufactures trade surplus and reasonably strong market competitiveness of US manufactures in that year; the rapid 1981–86 decline to a −10.1-percentage-point share balance in 1986 evidences a dramatic decline in US competitiveness in

Table 4.2 United States: indices of competitiveness in manufactures, 1981–89 (billions of dollars except where noted)

	1981	1982	1983	1984	1985	1986	1987	1988	1989	Annual growth 1981–89 (percentages)
World exports to non-US destinations	864.4	828.0	806.9	834.8	875.8	1,074.0	1,323.0	1,612.1	1,728.0	9.1
World imports from non-US sources	858.1	834.7	844.4	922.8	987.3	1,223.6	1,471.0	1,756.5	1,866.8	10.2
US trade										
Exports	159.7	145.6	138.2	151.5	155.0	158.1	191.8	239.1	273.4	7.0
Imports	154.2	153.9	176.6	238.8	266.7	303.0	335.9	373.3	390.9	12.3
Balance	5.5	–8.3	–38.4	–87.3	–111.7	–144.9	–144.1	–134.2	–117.5	
										Change 1981–89
US share of exports to non-US destinations	18.5	17.6	17.1	18.2	17.7	14.7	14.5	14.8	15.8	–2.7
US share of imports from non-US sources	18.0	18.4	20.9	25.9	27.0	24.8	22.8	21.3	20.9	3.0
US export-minus-import share balance	0.5	–0.8	–3.8	–7.7	–9.3	–10.1	–8.3	6.4	–5.1	–5.7

Source: World Manufactures Trade Data Base.

both US and foreign markets as a result of both declining export shares and increasing import shares. The majority of the loss, however, came from the 6.8-percentage-point 1981–86 increase in the import share. In 1987, the share balance deficit narrowed modestly, mostly reflecting a decline in the import share.[4] Performance continued to improve in 1988 and 1989. Nevertheless, in 1989 the United States was still providing the market for well over one-fifth (20.9 percent) of rest-of-the-world manufactures exports but supplying only one-seventh (15.8 percent) of world exports to non-US destinations. As a result, the United States in 1989 still had a large negative share balance position (− 5.1 percentage points). This was better than in 1987, but still 5.6 percentage points worse than in 1981.

The Effects of Foreign Direct Investment on Trade Flows

In a world of instant communications and fast, low-cost transportation, large multinational corporations can produce and sell in markets around the world. Producing in foreign markets rather than exporting to them from the home country has become an increasingly important way for firms to be more competitive. Parent manufacturing multinationals establish production, sales, and service affiliates in combinations of domestic and foreign locations that they believe will put them in the strongest competitive position in important markets.

Foreign direct investment (FDI)—the ownership for purposes of control by an investor in one country of a business enterprise or property in another country—is rapidly growing as a means of transferring capital, production capabilities, and manufacturing and other technologies across national boundaries. Total world FDI grew from $518.5 billion in 1980 to $1,342.3 billion in 1989, a 159 percent increase in only nine years (Rutter 1991, appendix table 1). A substantial portion of this FDI—about one-third or more—is investment in manufacturing, indicating that international investors are establishing or acquiring significant manufacturing capabilities outside their home countries. As noted earlier, the book value of US direct investments abroad in manufacturing reached $168.0 billion in 1990; foreign direct investments in the United States in manufacturing rose in that same year to $160.2 billion.

The effects on trade flows of this trend toward the globalization of production of manufactured goods are important but difficult to quantify. When a firm locates production abroad to serve foreign markets, exports from the home

---

4. The nominal deficit peaked in 1987. The 1987 improvement in the share balance, resulting mostly from a decline in the import share, reflects in part an increase in the dollar value of rest-of-the-world imports that was more rapid than the increase in US imports that year.

country will clearly be lower than if it had retained those foreign markets and continued to serve them by exporting from the home country.

However, in an intensely competitive world, exporting to major foreign markets simply may not be enough to ensure the firm's competitiveness there; reliance on the export of domestic production may result in loss of those foreign markets. Moreover, direct investments normally lead to substantial exports from parent companies to their affiliates. In addition, parents charge their affiliates for the licensing of technology and for various other services, thereby adding to the home country's exports of services and thus to its current account balance. Thus, remaining competitive via FDI is clearly preferable to losing the foreign market altogether. Nevertheless, it is impossible to quantify the net contribution of direct investments to a country's trade performance because one cannot know what exports would have been if companies had relied solely—and perhaps unsuccessfully—on exports from the home country.[5]

US manufacturing companies were among the first to move into FDI in a big way after World War II. US companies interested in foreign markets began to move production to those markets partly in reaction to relatively higher US wage rates and operating costs, but also to respond to the encouragement of foreign governments, to hedge against exchange rate fluctuations, and to elude existing or potential foreign trade barriers.[6] The results of the questionnaire survey conducted as part of this study (see chapter 6) indicate that many companies now feel that successfully servicing and competing in major markets requires a presence in those markets.

The movement toward production in the market to be served is today a global phenomenon. Although US companies were at the forefront for much of the post-World War II period, foreign competitors have been rapidly catching up. During 1980–90, FDI in US manufacturing increased by $127 billion while US direct investment in foreign manufacturing increased by only $79 billion. Higher rates of FDI by other countries lowered the US share of world FDI from 42.5 percent in 1980 to 28.3 percent in 1989 (Rutter 1991a, appendix table 1.).

Nevertheless, the 28.3 percent US share (measured on a historical or book value basis) substantially exceeds that of any other country—the closest rivals were the United Kingdom (16.7 percent), Japan (11.5 percent), and Germany (9.1 percent). Moreover, although the book value of US manufacturers' direct investments abroad is now only slightly higher than the book value of FDI in US manufacturing, the sales, real market value, and earning power of US direct investments abroad are significantly larger than those of foreign manufacturing

---

5. For a detailed assessment of and an attempt to estimate the effects of direct investments on trade balances, see Bergsten et al. (1978, 45).

6. For further details on the motivations to foreign investments see Cantwell (1991) and Rutter (1991a).

investments in the United States; this reflects the fact that the US investments have generally been in place for a longer time. US manufacturing investments abroad consistently outearn foreign investments in the United States by large margins.

US firms remain much more likely than foreign firms to serve markets through direct investment in production facilities abroad. This has significant implications for US trade performance. In 1988, the foreign sales of the foreign affiliates of US manufacturing multinationals were $619.8 billion, or 2.4 times total US exports of manufactures (US Department of Commerce, Bureau of Economic Analysis, 1990, table 5). In contrast, the 1988 sales in the United States of the US manufacturing affiliates of foreign parents were $268 billion, equivalent to only 74 percent of total US manufactures imports (US Department of Commerce 1990, table A-7).

Although it is impossible to calculate the effects of FDI versus what might have been had firms attempted to compete by continuing to export from their home country, the effects of direct investments on US trade flows are increasing, and the multinational firms' and parent-affiliate shares of trade in US trade can be quantified in crude terms.

In 1988, the most recent year for which data are available at this writing, total US exports of US manufacturing multinationals to all foreign buyers were $174.5 billion, about 54 percent of total US manufactures exports of $322 billion (US Department of Commerce, Bureau of Economic Analysis 1990, table 57). US parent firms classified as engaged in wholesale trade exported another $27.4 billion, most of it in the form of manufactured goods, an amount equal to 8.5 percent of 1988 US manufactures exports. In addition, exports from the United States by manufacturing firms that are the US affiliates of foreign parents totaled $21 billion, equivalent to 6.5 percent of total US manufactures exports (US Department of Commerce 1990, table G-1). Thus, even allowing for some double counting, and recognizing that not all of the exports by wholesalers are manufactured goods, exports by US multinationals and the US affiliates of foreign multinationals appear to have accounted for about two-thirds of US manufactures exports in 1988.

A substantial portion of those exports consisted of trade between parent firms and their affiliates. The foreign affiliates of US parents reported shipments of $75.1 billion from their US manufacturing parents, an amount equivalent to 23.3 percent of 1988 US manufactures exports. The US manufacturing affiliates of foreign parents shipped $5.6 billion in manufactured goods to their foreign parents. In addition, US affiliates classified as engaged in wholesale trade shipped about $10 billion worth of manufactures to their foreign parents. The $15.6 billion from the last two categories is equivalent to about 4.8 percent of 1988 US manufactures exports. Thus, it appears that about 28 percent of 1988 US manufactures exports resulted from trade between parents and their affiliates.

Most of that trade (23.3 percent) consisted of the exports of US parents to their foreign affiliates. But a not-insignificant portion (4.9 percent) consisted of the exports of US affiliates to their foreign parents.

Multinationals play a similarly dominant role in US manufactures imports. The portion of total manufactures imports represented by trade between parents and affiliates (about 46 percent) is larger than the share of US export trade. This difference, however, arises in large part because imports of Japanese automobiles and some other finished manufactured goods are made by US "wholesale trade" affiliates of Japanese parent manufacturing firms. That is, a substantial portion of the imports of US affiliates from foreign firms is in the form of finished products rather than inputs to US manufacturing processes.

Much of US direct investment in manufacturing abroad is in Europe and Canada (about 70 percent), and the great majority of FDI in US manufacturing originates in Europe (78 percent) and Japan (9.5 percent). Therefore, US trade with these areas is most affected by direct investments.

The export statistics that decompose US manufacturing exports to parents and affiliates are difficult to interpret, but it appears that perhaps 30 percent of 1988 US manufactures exports to the European Community were to affiliates. The data also indicate that well over half of 1988 US manufactures exports to Canada were transactions between parents and affiliates. The great majority, $34.4 billion, consisted of exports to US-owned Canadian affiliates, with the exports of US affiliates to their Canadian parents ($5.5 billion) playing only a minor role.

Although the exact effects of FDI on trade flows cannot be calculated, we can draw some general conclusions from the above discussion:

■ The effects of FDI on trade flows and balances are already large and will continue to increase with the growth of FDI.

■ Compared with exporting to foreign markets, direct investments in foreign manufacturing facilities reduce the trade surplus (or increase the deficit) of the exporting country in the products concerned.

■ However, increased US direct investment abroad may be the best available way to gain and maintain a presence in some foreign markets and to develop enduring supplier-customer relationships that will add to US exports.

■ Increased FDI in the United States would tend to decrease US trade deficits in some product groups such as automobiles and consumer electronics and to improve the US trade balance in the longer term (see, e.g., Orr 1991, 63).

■ Because it establishes continuing parent-affiliate trade relationships, FDI *may* decrease the fluctuations in trade balances in individual product groups that occur as a result of exchange rate changes and other factors, such as changing technological leads among individual producer countries.

Perhaps most important, however, the large and growing volume of FDI in manufacturing demonstrates the ability of firms to locate and produce around the globe. As competition for world manufactures markets becomes more intense, and as communications and transportation become faster and more efficient, investment in production facilities will be less and less tied to a company's home country and will flow to those locations that offer the most efficient means of serving world markets.

Countries already compete for manufacturing investment. Increasing reliance on FDI to serve foreign markets highlights the growing importance to countries of a favorable climate for manufacturing investments. Differences in investment climate among countries strongly influence production locations, which in turn affect trade flows and balances.

Geographical Composition of Manufactures Trade

A look at US manufactures trade performance by trading partner can aid in understanding past performance and the potential effects of changes in world trade flow patterns and the dollar exchange rate.

The relative decline in imports by developing countries has significantly affected the US trade position. In 1981, one-third of US manufactures trade was with developing countries (tables 4.3 and 4.4). But trade with developing countries accounted for significantly more than one-third (41.7 percent) of the total $150.8 billion decline in the manufactures trade balance from 1981 to 1987. On the other hand, the 1987–90 improvement in the trade balance was mostly ($37.1 billion, or 88.9 percent of the total) with developed countries. Thus, whereas the 1981–87 decline was proportionately greater with developing countries, the 1987–90 improvement was proportionately less.

The 1981–87 worsening of US balances with the developing countries reflected the decline in those countries' purchasing power during the 1980s. The smaller improvement with the developing countries from 1987 to 1990 reflects both their continuing lack of purchasing power and the fact that many of them tie their currencies to the dollar, such that changes in exchange rates do not directly affect their trade with the United States.

For example, Latin America has been an important US market, and one in which the United States has been dominant. Data on Latin American trade reveal some changes that have significantly affected overall US trade performance and will continue to do so. In 1981, world exports of manufactures were $1,014 billion; exports to Latin America were $67.6 billion, or 6.7 percent of the total (chapter 3, table 3.6). More than 48 percent of 1981 world exports to Latin America ($32.7 billion) originated in the United States.

Table 4.3   United States: geographical composition of manufactures trade, 1981, 1987, and 1990 (billions of dollars)

	Rev. 2		Rev. 3		Change		
	1981	1987	1987	1990	1981–87	1987–90	1981–90
Canada							
Exports	37.74	52.34	52.19	69.19	14.60	17.00	31.45
Imports	31.13	54.29	54.21	69.59	23.16	15.38	38.46
Balance	6.60	−1.95	−2.02	−0.40	−8.56	1.62	−7.00
Japan							
Exports	9.66	15.09	15.06	28.58	5.43	13.52	18.92
Imports	37.26	83.86	83.87	89.09	46.60	5.22	51.82
Balance	−27.60	−68.77	−68.81	−60.51	−41.17	8.30	−32.91
European Community							
Exports	36.92	44.67	44.64	76.48	7.75	31.84	39.56
Imports	33.41	71.13	71.09	81.08	37.72	9.99	47.67
Balance	3.50	−26.46	−26.46	−4.60	−29.96	21.85	−8.10
Total developed countries							
Exports	98.15	125.48	125.25	196.06	27.33	70.81	97.91
Imports	110.36	224.11	223.98	257.73	113.75	33.75	147.37
Balance	−12.20	−98.62	−98.72	−61.67	−86.42	37.06	−49.47
OPEC							
Exports	16.62	7.53	7.50	10.17	−9.10	2.67	−6.45
Imports	0.61	1.76	1.76	2.71	1.15	0.95	2.10
Balance	16.01	5.76	5.74	7.46	−10.25	1.72	−8.55
Latin America							
Exports	32.75	27.14	27.10	43.20	−5.61	16.11	10.45
Imports	10.25	23.68	23.59	33.69	13.42	10.11	23.44
Balance	22.49	3.46	3.51	9.51	−19.03	6.00	−12.99
Asian NICs							
Exports	9.32	15.67	15.66	29.11	6.35	13.45	19.79
Imports	20.11	56.27	56.24	59.35	36.16	3.11	39.24
Balance	−10.79	−40.60	−40.58	−30.24	−29.81	10.35	−19.45
Other developing countries							
Exports	9.73	10.45	10.54	17.01	0.72	6.47	7.29
Imports	6.43	12.86	12.83	20.83	6.43	7.99	14.39
Balance	3.30	−2.40	−2.29	−3.81	−5.70	−1.52	−7.11
Total developing countries							
Exports	63.50	57.55	57.57	96.59	−5.95	39.02	33.09
Imports	37.20	94.16	94.01	115.84	56.96	21.83	78.64
Balance	26.30	−36.61	−36.44	−19.25	−62.91	17.19	−45.55
Centrally planned economies							
Exports	1.98	3.59	3.51	4.84	1.61	1.32	2.86
Imports	2.20	6.47	6.46	15.24	4.26	8.77	13.03
Balance	−0.23	−2.88	−2.95	−10.40	−2.65	−7.45	−10.17
World							
Exports	167.80	192.01	191.73	297.79	24.21	106.06	129.98
Imports	149.76	324.73	324.44	388.81	174.97	64.36	239.05
Balance	18.04	−132.72	−132.71	−91.02	−150.76	41.70	−109.06

Source: US Department of Commerce.

Table 4.4 United States: geographical composition of manufactures trade, as shares of total, 1981, 1987, and 1990 (percentages)

	Rev. 2		Rev. 3		Change		
	1981	1987	1987	1990	1981–87	1987–90	1981–90
Canada							
Exports	22.5	27.3	27.2	23.2	4.8	-4.0	0.7
Imports	20.8	16.7	16.7	17.9	-4.1	1.2	-2.9
Japan							
Exports	5.8	7.9	7.9	9.6	2.1	1.7	3.8
Imports	24.9	25.8	25.8	22.9	0.9	-2.9	-2.0
European Community							
Exports	22.0	23.3	23.3	25.7	1.3	2.4	3.7
Imports	22.3	21.9	21.9	20.9	-0.4	-1.1	-1.5
Total developed countries							
Exports	58.5	65.4	65.3	65.8	6.9	0.5	7.3
Imports	73.7	69.0	69.0	66.3	-4.7	-2.7	-7.4
OPEC							
Exports	9.9	3.9	3.9	3.4	-6.0	-0.5	-6.5
Imports	0.4	0.5	0.5	0.7	0.1	0.2	0.3
Latin America							
Exports	19.5	14.1	14.1	14.5	-5.4	0.4	-5.0
Imports	6.8	7.3	7.3	8.7	0.4	1.4	1.8
Asian NICs							
Exports	5.6	8.2	8.2	9.8	2.6	1.6	4.2
Imports	13.4	17.3	17.3	15.3	3.9	-2.1	1.8
Other developing countries							
Exports	5.8	5.4	5.5	5.7	-0.4	0.2	-0.1
Imports	4.3	4.0	4.0	5.4	-0.3	1.4	1.1
Total developing countries							
Exports	37.8	30.0	30.0	32.4	-7.9	2.4	-5.4
Imports	24.8	29.0	29.0	29.8	4.2	0.8	5.0
Centrally planned economies							
Exports	1.2	1.9	1.8	1.6	0.7	-0.2	0.4
Imports	1.5	2.0	2.0	3.9	0.5	1.9	2.4

Source: US Department of Commerce.

By 1989, world exports of manufactures had risen to $2,110.3 billion, a 108 percent increase over 1981 (table 3.6). World exports of manufactures to Latin America, however, were only $72.9 billion, up only 8 percent over the 1981 level. US exports to Latin America were $38.3 billion, or $5.6 billion more than in 1981; this increased the US share to 52.5 percent.

In 1981, some 20.5 percent of US manufactures exports went to Latin America, just over the 19.9 percent to Canada. But as a result of the relative decline in Latin American imports, by 1989 the share of US exports to Latin America had dropped to 14.0 percent. US imports from Latin America, however, did not similarly lag. These were $10.2 billion in 1981 but rose to $32.5 billion (table 3.6) by 1989, a 219 percent increase. The share of total US manufactures imports from Latin America also rose, from 6.8 percent in 1981 to 8.5 percent in 1989. To summarize, whereas in 1981 the US manufactures trade surplus with Latin America was $22.5 billion, in 1989 it was $5.8 billion, for a decline of $16.7 billion.

This decline was not due to a loss of US competitiveness; the US share of world manufactures exports to Latin America actually rose modestly from 1981 to 1989. It was instead due to a collapse of Latin American purchasing power—the need of Latin American debtors to contract imports and expand exports to meet debt servicing requirements. If Latin American imports had grown at the same rate as total world exports, 1989 Latin American manufactures imports from the world would have been $140 billion. Assuming a constant US share of those imports (52.5 percent), US manufactures exports to the region would have been $73.5 billion, or $35.2 billion larger than the $38.3 billion actually realized and about 38 percent of the total US manufactures trade deficit. The decline of Latin American markets, together with US absorption of large increases in Latin American manufactures exports, was thus an important factor in the overall 1981–87 decline of US trade performance, but was not caused by a loss of US competitiveness in the sense of a declining market share.[7]

Some analysts view the late 1970s through 1981 as an aberration for Latin American trade, a period when excessive lending from the United States and other developed countries unwisely inflated Latin American purchasing power above norms justified by economic conditions. This, they argue, raised US exports to Latin America above sustainable levels, temporarily helping the United States to maintain export surpluses with Latin America, even while US performance was slipping elsewhere. According to this view, the United States cannot, in the foreseeable future, expect Latin America to be as important a US export market as it was in the years before 1982, the beginning of the Latin American debt crisis.

---

7. For an examination of the effects of the Latin American debt crisis on US trade, see US Department of Commerce (1988b).

Nevertheless, given the apparent continuing strong US position in Latin American markets, an economic resurgence there could greatly improve US trade performance. However, it can be argued that such a resurgence would draw increased interest and competition from foreign producers, with uncertain results on US trade balances. Whatever assessment one makes of US trade prospects, Latin American creditworthiness has not yet, for the most part, been restored. Much of the gain in Latin American purchasing power in recent years has come from increased US imports from Latin America. US manufactures imports from Latin America were $10.3 billion in 1981, $23.6 billion in 1987, and $33.7 billion in 1990 (table 4.3). Even so, things have been improving from the US perspective. Manufactures exports to Latin America grew by $16.1 billion from 1987 to 1990, outpacing import growth by $6 billion.

Mexico, which dominates US manufactures trade with Latin America, is experiencing a strong economic recovery, with real economic growth of 2.9 percent in 1987, 3.9 percent in 1990, and a projected 4.0 percent in 1991 following several years of decline. About 54 percent of US manufactures exports to Latin America went to Mexico in 1990, and 63 percent of US manufactures imports from Latin America came from Mexico. The US manufactures trade surplus with Mexico was $9.0 billion in 1981, $0.4 billion in 1987, and $6.2 billion in 1990. Thus, $8.6 billion of the $19 billion 1981–87 decline in the US manufactures trade balance came from trade with Mexico; virtually all ($5.8 billion) of the $6.0 billion improvement in the US balance with Latin America from 1987 to 1990 was in trade with that country.

Although there are encouraging signs in some other Latin American economies, there seems to be little prospect of a return to the large US trade surpluses of 1981 and earlier. Gradual improvement seems more likely. As long as this key market remains sluggish, it will greatly handicap US efforts to expand exports and will force increased reliance on other markets.

The OPEC countries are another market in which US trade performance was strong in the 1970s but whose purchasing power has diminished. In 1990, the US manufactures balance with the OPEC countries was $8.6 billion below the 1981 level. The reason was largely that exports to those countries were $6.5 billion less than in 1981, as a result of their diminished purchasing power following the sharp decline in oil prices in 1985–86.

There have been differing rates of improvement in US trade with the developed countries as well. The US manufactures trade balance with Canada declined by $8.6 billion from 1981 to 1987 and improved by only $1.6 billion from 1987 to 1990 (table 4.3), a year in which both economies were experiencing economic slowdowns. The $7 billion 1981–90 decline in the US balance with Canada is close to the $8.5 billion expansion of the US road vehicle deficit with Canada over the same period. Given the close integration of the US and Canadian automobile industries, the United States now has, in effect, a built-in structural road vehicle deficit with Canada. Canadian automobile production is mostly by US-owned firms for the US market. There is heavy US investment in Canadian manufacturing of road vehicles and in other industries, including chemicals. Moderate exchange rate movements are likely to have little near-term effect on US-Canadian automobile trade and only modest near-term effects on trade balances in other industries where there is substantial US direct investment.

The volume of US-EC trade does not differ much from US-Canadian trade, but trade balances with the European Community changed much more during the 1981–90 period, perhaps reflecting the larger depreciation of the dollar against the EC currencies and stronger EC growth. Both the decline and the recovery in the trade balance with the European Community were much larger—a $30 billion 1981–87 decline was followed by a $21.9 billion 1987–90 recovery, more than half of the overall $41.7 billion US manufactures trade improvement.

The 1981–87 manufactures balance with Japan declined by $41.2 billion, but despite dollar depreciation against the yen of about 30 percent between 1985 and 1990, the manufactures trade deficit with Japan narrowed by only $8.3 billion from 1987 to 1990, only one-fifth of the 1981–87 decline. Half of that narrowing was in road vehicles, and much of it occurred in a very soft 1990 US automobile market. Clearly, dollar depreciation has not yet been sufficient to induce sharp cuts in the manufactures trade deficit with Japan. With 1990 Japanese manufactures exports still more than three times US exports to Japan, it will take very high growth rates of US exports to narrow the gap significantly.

The $10.4 billion 1987–90 improvement in US trade with the Asian NICs resulted from an expansion of US exports and a marked slowing of the growth of US imports as the NICs' currencies appreciated against the dollar. Offsetting these improvements, the US deficit with the centrally planned economies worsened by $7.5 billion from 1987 to 1990, largely because of a huge expansion of US imports from China; because of China's very low unit labor costs, trade with China is largely unaffected by changes in the dollar exchange rate.

The geographic composition of US manufactures trade is such that only a relatively modest portion of US trade—mostly with the European Community and the Asian NICs, which together make up just over one-third of US manufactures exports and imports—has been strongly affected by changes in the dollar exchange rate. Further marked dollar depreciation against the Japanese yen could ultimately force changes in the US-Japan balance, but the effects to date have been only modest. Dollar depreciation will not alter relationships with those developing countries that link their currencies to the dollar. Nor will it much affect trade with countries that have extremely low unit labor costs, such as China.

Changes in the Product Composition of Manufactures Trade

Changes have also been occurring in the product composition of US and world manufactures trade that may have long-term effects on US trade performance. For analytical purposes, manufactures are sometimes classified into two broad groups: chemicals (SITC 5) and basic manufactures (SITC 6) are combined and termed intermediate goods or industrial supplies (inputs that will be further processed into other products), and machinery and transport equipment (SITC 7) and miscellaneous manufactures (SITC 8) are combined and identified as finished goods (final products used by producers and consumers). These are highly imperfect descriptors. For example, the machinery and transport equipment group includes many components that will be further processed or assembled into other finished products; the chemicals group, on the other hand, includes not only chemical inputs but a vast array of final products such as cleansers and pharmaceuticals.

Nevertheless, this categorization provides a rough indication of the production technology characteristics of the two groups. The basic technologies for producing chemicals and basic manufactures typically involve the transformation of raw materials into other materials usable for further manufacturing. These transformations are usually performed by machine-controlled or machine-driven operations, requiring large-scale capital equipment such as furnaces, pumps, mixers, and presses. Compared with other types of manufacturing, a relatively limited amount of labor is needed to monitor, regulate, or service the machines and to maintain adequate flows of raw materials. In contrast, machinery and transport equipment and miscellaneous manufactures generally employ workers using specialized tools to process and assemble parts in more complex combinations. The assembly process is also likely to require a higher labor content than do processes involving only raw materials transformations (US Department of Commerce, International Trade Administration, 1988a, 17).

The finished-goods portion of total world manufactures trade has been increasing. In 1981, at $609.8 billion, SITCs 7 and 8 accounted for 60.1 percent of world manufactures exports (table 3.2). By 1989, their share had increased to $1,324.7 billion, or 62.8 percent of the world manufactures total. Changes in the broad composition of US manufactures trade have been even more significant. In a detailed examination of US manufactures trade performance, Susan Hickok (1991, 27) finds:

> Finished goods are an increasing share of U.S. imports while their share of U.S. exports has remained virtually unchanged in recent years. An examination of these divergent developments in the role of finished goods in U.S. trade suggests that U.S. comparative advantage may be moving away from finished goods and toward industrial supplies. This shift is somewhat disturbing since demand for finished goods appears to be growing rapidly while the outlook for industrial supplies is

less dynamic. A declining U.S. comparative advantage in the finished goods sector is also of concern because a strong competitive position in this sector is a sign of an economy's technological sophistication and, to some extent, its market power in the world economy.

This study presents similar findings about the composition of US exports and imports; these findings support the conclusion of a declining US comparative advantage in finished goods. From 1981 to 1989, the US deficit in industrial supplies (SITCs 5 and 6) expanded from $5 billion to $23.2 billion, an $18.2 billion deterioration (table 4.5). During the same years, however, the balance for finished goods plummeted from a $10.3 billion surplus to a $112.0 billion deficit—a decline of $122.3 billion (table 4.6).

In 1981, industrial supplies were 28.7 percent of the total US exports in SITCs 5 through 8. By 1989, the export composition had changed only marginally, with industrial supplies declining to 26.4 percent. The change on the import side, however, was much more significant. Industrial materials fell from 33.0 percent of total US SITC 5–8 imports in 1981 to 23.1 percent in 1989.

Declining US competitiveness in finished goods can also be illustrated by analyzing market shares. Over the 1981–89 period, the US share of exports of industrial supplies to non-US destinations declined by 3.1 percentage points, but the US share of imports also declined—by 1.4 percentage points—leaving a net loss in share balance of only 1.7 percentage points (table 4.5). The loss in finished goods was much more significant. Here, the export share declined by 4.4 percentage points while the import share increased by 5.1 percentage points, for a share balance decline of 9.4 percentage points (table 4.6).

Market share data also indicate that the more homogeneous industrial supplies respond more quickly than finished goods to price changes induced by changes in exchange rates. At its 1985 low point, corresponding roughly with the peak in the dollar's strength, the share balance for industrial supplies was −7.0 percentage points, but by 1989 the balance had narrowed to −1.7 percentage points, an improvement of 5.3 percentage points. However, the share balance for finished goods improved only 4.5 percentage points from its 1986 low point of −12.4 percentage points to its 1989 level of −7.9 percentage points.

Finished goods have been growing as a share of world manufactures trade because, as economies mature, demand for finished goods typically increases faster than demand for industrial supplies. Put more formally, an economy's income elasticity of demand for imported finished goods is generally greater than its income elasticity of demand for imported industrial supplies (Hickok 1991, 36). The dramatic increase in US imports of finished goods and the failure of exports to expand at a similar pace suggest a declining US comparative

Table 4.5 United States: indices of competitiveness in industrial materials, 1981–89ᵃ (billions of dollars except where noted)

	1981	1982	1983	1984	1985	1986	1987	1988	1989	Annual growth, 1981–89 (percentages)
World trade										
World exports to non-US destinations	334.8	315.4	311.0	321.6	332.4	396.9	479.8	593.4	630.3	8.2
World imports from non-US sources	342.2	323.9	326.4	351.4	366.3	435.1	518.0	632.6	667.4	8.7
US trade										
Exports	44.2	37.2	35.2	38.1	35.7	36.7	43.4	54.9	63.9	4.7
Imports	49.3	44.0	48.3	63.7	65.0	67.7	73.5	85.9	87.1	7.4
Balance	−5.0	−6.7	−13.1	−25.5	−29.4	−31.0	−30.2	−30.9	−23.2	
										Change 1981–89
US share of exports to non-US destinations (percentages)	13.2	11.8	11.3	11.9	10.7	9.2	9.0	9.3	10.1	−3.1
US share of imports from non-US sources (percentages)	14.4	13.6	14.8	18.1	17.8	15.6	14.2	13.6	13.0	−1.4
Export share minus import share (percentages)	−1.2	−1.8	−3.5	−6.3	−7.0	−6.3	−5.2	−4.3	−2.9	−1.7

a. Industrial materials are defined as SITC 5 (chemicals) and SITC 6 (basic manufactures).

Source: World Manufactures Trade Data Base.

Table 4.6 United States: indices of competitiveness in industrial materials, 1981–89ᵃ (billions of dollars except where noted)

	1981	1982	1983	1984	1985	1986	1987	1988	1989	Annual growth, 1981–89 (percentages)
World trade										
World exports to non-US destinations	509.9	493.7	476.0	490.7	519.4	649.2	800.9	966.2	1,036.0	9.3
World imports from non-US sources	496.7	491.3	497.5	549.4	597.4	760.2	919.2	1,082.4	1,154.1	11.1
US trade										
Exports	110.2	102.6	97.4	105.2	109.7	112.2	129.7	159.8	178.6	6.2
Imports	99.9	104.3	122.5	168.3	193.2	226.0	251.5	275.9	290.5	14.3
Balance	10.3	–1.6	–25.1	–63.1	–83.5	–113.8	–121.8	–116.1	–112.0	
										Change 1981–89
US share of exports to non-US destinations (percentages)	21.6	20.8	20.5	21.4	21.1	17.3	16.2	16.5	17.2	–4.4
US share of imports from non-US sources (percentages)	20.1	21.2	24.6	30.6	32.3	29.7	27.4	25.5	25.2	5.1
Export share minus import share (percentages)	1.5	–0.4	–4.2	–9.2	–11.2	–12.4	–11.2	–9.0	–7.9	–9.4

a. Finished goods are defined as SITC 7 (machines and transport equipment) and SITC 8 (miscellaneous manufactured goods).

Source: World Manufactures Trade Data Base.

advantage in finished goods. This implies that, assuming other factors remain unchanged and that the US economy grows at rates similar to those of its major trading partners, US demand for manufactures imports may grow faster than US exports of manufactured goods in the future.

Hickok (1991, 36) concludes:

> The increased sensitivity of U.S. import demand to income growth without a corresponding change on the export side implies that, in coming years, overall U.S. economic growth may have to be slower or U.S. prices lower relative to foreign prices than would otherwise be the case in order for the United States to maintain a given trade balance level. Trade adjustment through lower U.S. prices relative to foreign prices is, however, likely to be harder to achieve than in the past because of the change in U.S. import composition over the 1978–89 period. The demand for differentiated finished goods responds to significant nonprice factors and consequently tends to be less sensitive to relative price changes than does the demand for homogeneous industrial supplies.

In assessing the causes of the recent trends in US performance, Hickok (1991, 27) finds the most important factor to be:

> weak U.S. investment, as measured against the investment performance of U.S. trade partners, [which] has lowered the relative supply of capital to U.S. industry, eroding the traditionally strong competitive position of the United States in the production of finished goods.

Price and Volume Effects

An assessment of the effects of dollar exchange rate changes on the prices and volumes of exports and imports can provide additional insights. The IMF real effective exchange rate indices (based on relative wholesale prices, 1985 = 100) for 1976 to 1990 are as follows:

Year	Index
1976	80.8
1977	78.8
1978	72.8
1979	73.0
1980	73.7
1981	83.9
1982	90.3
1983	92.9
1984	98.9
1985	100.0
1986	79.8
1987	71.7
1988	69.0
1989	73.5
1990	69.6

Exchange rate indices only imperfectly reflect constantly changing exchange rate movements among trading partners. Problems inherent in constructing these indices include selecting the appropriate deflator, averaging the day-to-day movements, and adjusting the weighing of the index to reflect the constantly changing geographical composition of exports and imports. Recognizing these limits, however, the dollar exchange rate in 1990 as measured by this index (69.6) was below the average for the three years 1978–80 (73.2), a period during which US manufactures trade balances moved from deficit to surplus. The average of the indices for 1988–90 (70.7) was also below the 1978–80 average of 73.2.

The trade results for the two periods, however, were dramatically different. During 1978–80, the cumulative US manufactures trade *surplus* was $23.6 billion, an amount equivalent to 3.1 percent of combined US manufactures exports and imports for the period. On the other hand, the cumulative US manufactures trade *deficit* for 1988–90 totaled $271.3 billion, equivalent to 13.7 percent of total US manufactures exports and imports during the period. These results— achieved at roughly similar real exchange rates—are evidence not only of a substantial decline in the world market competitiveness of US manufactures in a single decade but also of a declining ability to compete at given exchange rates and the need for further dollar depreciation to restore a balanced current account.

Exchange rates are, of course, only one of many variables affecting market competitiveness as measured by trade balances. We have already noted the effects of the collapse of Latin American and OPEC markets. Differences in US and foreign economic growth rates are another important factor. However, the dramatic change in US performance is beyond what these factors are capable of explaining. To obtain further insights, the analysis can be extended to consider the effects of another important factor, namely, relative changes in export and import prices.

Export and import price indices are available from the US Bureau of Labor Statistics at the one-digit SITC level beginning in 1982 for SITCs 6 and 7, in 1983 for SITC 5, and in 1984 for SITC 8. Considering the many thousands of items in each category, these indices can measure actual price movements only crudely.[8] Accepting these limitations, table 4.7 provides these one-digit SITC price indices, adjusted to show the change from the year in which the data series became available. For example, with the base year 1983, the beginning year for SITC 5 price data, the 1990 export price index is 1.177 and the import

---

8. For a discussion of the measurement problems and inaccuracies of import price measurements see Krugman (1991).

Table 4.7 United States: nominal versus real trade performance in manufacturing, by sector, 1982–90

Sector	Base year (billions of dollars)			1990			Change from base year			
							Billions of dollars		Percentages	
	1982	1983	1984	Nominal dollars	Price index	Real dollars	Nominal	Real	Nominal	Real
Chemicals and related products (SITC 5)										
Exports		19.97		38.98	1.177	33.12	19.01	13.15	95.2	65.8
Imports		10.95		22.47	1.163	19.32	11.52	8.37	105.2	76.4
Balance		9.02		16.51		13.80	7.49	4.78	n.a	n.a.
Export-import price ratio					1.012					
Basic manufactures (SITC 6)										
Exports	17.12			31.67	1.250	25.34	14.55	8.22	85.0	48.0
Imports	33.36			59.91	1.329	45.08	26.55	11.72	79.6	35.1
Balance	-16.24			-28.24		-19.74	-12.00	-3.50	n.a	n.a.
Export-import price ratio					0.941					
Machinery and transport equipment (SITC 7)										
Exports	87.24			172.52	1.185	145.59	85.28	58.35	97.8	66.9
Imports	73.69			208.10	1.333	156.11	134.41	82.42	182.4	111.9
Balance	13.55			-35.58		-10.53	-49.13	-24.08	n.a	n.a.
Export-import price ratio					0.889					
Miscellaneous manufactured articles (SITC 8)										
Exports			19.17	39.29	1.180	33.30	20.12	14.13	105.0	73.7
Imports			42.67	81.48	1.312	62.10	38.81	19.43	91.0	45.5
Balance			-23.50	-42.19		-28.81	-18.69	-5.31	n.a	n.a.
Export-import price ratio					0.899					

n.a. = not available.

Source: Monthly Labor Review, various issues.

index is 1.163.[9] The table also shows the relationship of the 1990 adjusted export price index to the 1990 adjusted import index; for SITC 5 that ratio is 1.012. These import and export price indices, reflecting the actual nominal changes, can be compared with the changes that would have occurred if the full effects of real exchange rate movement were reflected in nominal prices. Many other effects operate on export and import prices. For example, producers' costs change, and the changing intensity of international competition affects the profit margins that sellers can extract from buyers. However, using these calculations, the amount of actual pass-throughs in each of the one-digit groups as indicated by the price indices can be compared with those indicated by exchange rate movements. The data reveal significant differences among the product groups in the effects of dollar depreciation on prices and on nominal and real trade performance following the decline of the dollar from 1982–85 levels.

Chemicals has clearly shown the best performance relative to its base year. A full pass-through of the exchange rate effects indicated by the IMF indices would have raised the cost of $1.00 of 1983 imports to $1.335 in 1990.[10] However, because exchange rates were not the only factor influencing prices, US import prices for chemicals reflected less than half of the increase that would have occurred had exchange rates been the only factor influencing prices. Moreover, export prices for US chemicals actually increased more than did import prices, raising the ratio of export prices to import prices from 1.00 in 1983 to 1.012 in 1990. Meanwhile, the chemicals trade surplus increased in nominal terms from $9.0 billion in the 1983 base year to $16.5 billion in 1990, and in volume terms to $13.8 billion. The gain reflected increases of 65.8 percent in exports and 76.4 percent in imports in volume terms. Thus, from 1983 to 1990, the data show a large increase in the nominal and real trade surpluses for chemicals and a modest improvement in the US terms of trade.

Performance in the remaining three product groups was less encouraging. Basic manufactures worsened less than the remaining two categories. From the 1982 base year to 1990, the nominal dollar deficit expanded from $16.2 billion to $28.2 billion. Import prices increased to $1.329 (1982 = $1.00), modestly more than the $1.297 effect that alone would have resulted from full implementation of exchange rate movements.[11] Export prices, however, also in-

---

9. In effect, the procedure followed here rebases each index to the first year for which data in that SITC group are available.

10. The IMF real index was 92.9 for 1983 and 69.6 for 1990. Thus, on a full pass-through of the exchange rate, it would require 1.335 of 1990 dollars to purchase the same quantity as $1.00 could purchase in 1983.

11. The 1982 IMF real exchange rate index was 90.3, and the 1990 index was 69.6, yielding a 1982-to-1990 ratio of 1.297.

creased—to $1.250—so that the real effect on relative prices was a 6.1 percent decline in the US terms of trade for basic manufactures. In this environment, exports in volume terms grew by 48.0 percent from the base year; imports grew by a more modest 35.1 percent. At $19.7 billion in real terms, the 1990 deficit was only modestly larger than the $16.2 billion deficit in the base year.

Performance was much worse in the very large machinery and transportation equipment group. Import prices rose to $1.333, slightly above the $1.297 implied by the 1982–90 dollar exchange rate movements. In part, this probably reflected the upward effects of the voluntary restraint agreement on the prices of automobiles imported from Japan as well as the effects of upscaling of these imports to larger, more luxurious, and more expensive units.[12] US export prices increased only slightly more than half as much, to $1.185, and the export-import price ratio fell by 11.1 percent, to 0.889. In nominal terms, the balance deteriorated by $49.1 billion, from a $13.6 billion surplus in 1982 to a $35.6 billion deficit in 1990. In real terms, exports grew by only 66.9 percent, while imports grew by 111.9 percent. In volume terms, the $10.5 billion 1990 deficit also represented a significant deterioration from the 1982 surplus.

The nominal balance for miscellaneous manufactures moved from a $23.5 billion deficit in 1984 to a $42.2 billion deficit in 1990. Export prices rose to only $1.18 compared with the 1984 base year, well below the $1.416 that would have resulted from full pass-through of the exchange rate movements over the period.[13] Import prices, however, rose to $1.312 relative to the base year. A decline in the export-import price ratio to 0.899 (1984 = 1.00), a 10.1 percent fall, raised export volumes by 73.7 percent, while import volumes grew by 45.5 percent. In volume terms, however, the $28.8 billion deficit exceeded the $23.5 billion level of 1984.

The implications of these volume and price index data include the following:

- In real or volume terms, the improvement in manufactures trade performance from 1987 to 1990 was much greater than in current dollars—an important plus in terms of the effects of international trade on US GNP and economic growth. The US Department of Commerce estimates that 40 percent of US economic growth in the 1987–90 period came from export expansion, and 84 percent in 1990 (US Department of Commerce, International Trade Administration 1991).

---

12. See Bergsten et al. (1987) for a discussion of how auction quotas could deprive exporters to the United States of the economic rents that accrue when quotas are simply assigned to exporters.

13. A 1984 real IMF index of 98.9 and a 1990 index of 69.6 yield a 1982-to-1990 ratio of 1.416.

- By 1990, the dollar was well below the levels of the 1982–84 base years used in this analysis. Except for chemicals, however, 1990 trade performance remained well below that in the base years, in both nominal and volume terms. Thus, except for chemicals, the significant dollar depreciation from 1982–84 levels has been inadequate to restore the market competitiveness of US-based production to the levels of those base years.

- The significant dollar depreciation since the base years has resulted in much more modest changes in US export-import price relationships. This reflects in part an ability of foreign exporters to absorb large portions of the effects of dollar depreciation and cost increases stemming from world inflation and other factors.[14] Major competitors have thus far been able to mute the effects of dollar decline by lowering or holding down the prices of their exports expressed in their national currencies. This ability implies that some foreign margins in earlier years were fat enough to absorb the effects of a dollar decline. But foreign staying power may also stem partly from the greater productivity gains of some foreign competitors—particularly Japan—and the continuing entry of new low-cost producers into manufactured products trade.

- US export price increases, reflecting cost increases and attempts to increase profit margins, also contributed significantly to narrowing the relative price effects of dollar depreciation. The changes in export-import price ratios reveal significant differences in the competitiveness of broad categories of industries and their ability to benefit from dollar depreciation. Performance has been significantly poorer in finished goods than in chemicals and basic manufactures. For example, despite the fact that 1983–90 US chemicals export price increases modestly topped import price increases, raising the chemicals export-import price ratio by 1.2 percent, the US chemicals trade surplus expanded in both nominal and volume terms. But for machinery and transportation equipment, an 11.1 percent 1982–90 decline in export-import price ratios was insufficient to stop imports from growing at almost twice the rate of exports in both nominal and volume terms.

- Machinery and transportation equipment is the sector that appears to have experienced the largest decline in its competitiveness, in the sense that a substantial decline in the relative export-import price ratio has not restored performance to anything close to earlier levels. The implication is that, absent other major changes, further dollar depreciation and relative price changes will be required to achieve further substantial improvements.

- The declines in the ratios of export prices to import prices represent a deterioration in the US terms of trade that will exert downward pressure on US

---

14. For a discussion of import prices during 1985–90, see Krugman (1991, 33).

living standards. For example, setting 1983 as a base year—the earliest year for which price index data in machinery and transportation equipment are available—if one (hypothetical) unit of exports of machinery and transportation equipment in that year was sufficient to pay for one (hypothetical) unit of imports, then by 1990 one unit of the same exports in real terms would buy less than one unit (0.889) of the same imports in real terms. That is, in 1990 a larger amount of real resources had to be given up in exports to pay for a given amount of imports than in 1983. These data and the Hickok analysis are evidence—although not conclusive in view of the short time period—of a "secular decline" in US competitiveness claimed by many analysts.[15]

■ Dollar depreciation, nevertheless, had significant effects. By 1990, dollar depreciation had resulted in major improvement in US trade performance but was inadequate to eliminate the manufactures trade deficit, let alone restore the current account or even manufactures trade to surplus. Unless nominal trade balances further improve without further changes in export-import price ratios induced by exchange rate movements—and other analyses in this study indicate this will not occur—substantial further improvements in nominal trade balances will require significant further dollar depreciation that will exert further downward pressure on US living standards.

Market Performance by Two-Digit Product Group

An overview of US trade performance on a more disaggregated product basis can also be useful before examining performance in individual product groups. The United Nations' SITC system groups like products into categories useful for analytical purposes. These differ from the SIC categories, which group similar activities into industries. The SITC system divides manufactures trade into five one-digit classes (SITC 5–9) and some 40 two-digit groups.

The dollar value of world trade activity in the somewhat arbitrarily formed individual groups varies widely. For any country, strong market competitiveness is clearly more important in the larger groups than in the smaller ones. Tables 4.8 and 4.9 show which groups have been most important to US performance and which provide the greatest opportunities for significant improvement.

Tables 4.8 and 4.9 disaggregate US manufactures exports, imports, and balances at the two-digit level of detail for 1981–87 and 1987–90. Excluding those classifications in the 9 series (which are not very useful for analytical purposes),

---

15. See, for example, the examination of the question of secular decline in Krugman (1991), which also provides an assessment of the contribution of exchange rate movements to US trade performance in the 1980s.

Table 4.8 United States: product composition of manufactures trade, 1981–87 (millions of dollars)

SITC Category	Exports 1981	Exports 1987	Exports Change 1981–87	Imports 1981	Imports 1987	Imports Change 1981–87	Balance 1981	Balance 1987	Balance Change 1981–87
5-9 Total manufactures	167,803	192,014	24,211	149,757	324,730	174,972	18,046	-132,715	-150,761
51 Organic chemicals	5,168	6,631	1,463	2,917	4,509	1,592	2,251	2,122	-129
52 Inorganic chemicals	3,203	3,131	-72	2,094	2,865	771	1,109	266	-842
53 Dyeing, tanning, and coloring	538	641	103	339	1,068	729	199	-427	-627
54 Medicinal and pharmaceutical products	2,255	3,348	1,092	833	2,360	1,528	1,423	987	-435
55 Essential oils and perfume	980	1,017	37	382	1,057	675	597	-40	-638
56 Fertilizers, manufactured	1,694	2,261	566	1,094	794	-300	600	1,467	866
57 Explosives and pyrotechnic products	90	91	1	60	107	48	31	-17	-48
58 Artificial resins and plastics	3,758	5,395	1,637	733	1,893	1,161	3,025	3,501	477
59 Chemical materials and products	3,423	3,856	433	755	1,264	510	2,668	2,592	-77
61 Leather and leather manufactures	431	636	205	571	1,055	484	-140	-419	-279
62 Rubber manufactures, n.e.s.	1,197	1,363	166	1,573	2,942	1,369	-376	-1,579	-1,203
63 Cork and wood manufactures (excl. furniture)	600	688	88	1,237	2,172	935	-637	-1,484	-847
64 Paper, paperboard, and articles	2,946	3,166	220	3,832	7,382	3,550	-886	-4,216	-3,330
65 Textile yarn, fabric, and madeup articles	3,619	2,933	-686	2,875	6,131	3,256	744	-3,198	-3,942
66 Nonmetallic mineral manufactures	2,245	2,332	88	4,887	8,972	4,085	-2,642	-6,640	-3,997
67 Iron and steel	2,878	1,290	-1,588	11,238	9,097	-2,141	-8,360	-7,807	553
68 Nonferrous metals	2,803	2,179	-624	6,950	7,957	1,007	-4,147	-5,778	-1,631
69 Manufactures of metal, n.e.s.	4,297	3,131	-1,166	4,251	8,158	3,907	45	-5,027	-5,072
71 Power-generating machinery and equipment	9,588	10,360	772	4,614	10,947	6,333	4,974	-587	-5,561
72 Machinery specialized for particular industries	14,602	9,243	-5,359	5,244	11,459	6,215	9,358	-2,215	-11,574
73 Metalworking machinery	2,190	1,639	-551	2,002	2,978	976	188	-1,339	-1,527
74 General industrial machinery and equipment	11,884	8,380	-3,504	4,855	10,568	5,712	7,029	-2,188	-9,216
75 Office and automatic data processing machines	9,743	18,641	8,897	3,563	18,413	14,850	6,181	228	-5,953
76 Telecommunications and sound-reproducing equipment	3,841	5,066	1,225	8,947	20,820	11,873	-5,106	-15,754	-10,648
77 Electrical machinery, apparatus, and appliances	11,287	16,408	5,121	9,300	24,678	15,378	1,986	-8,270	-10,256
78 Road vehicles (including air-cushion vehicles)	16,398	21,055	4,657	28,146	72,501	44,355	-11,748	-51,446	-39,698
79 Other transport equipment	16,339	17,955	1,616	3,282	5,675	2,392	13,056	12,280	-776
81 Sanitary, plumbing, heating, and lighting fixtures	329	268	-60	192	781	589	137	-513	-650
82 Furniture and parts thereof	697	624	-73	1,267	4,656	3,389	-570	-4,032	-3,463
83 Travel goods, handbags, and similar containers	83	49	-34	802	1,903	1,101	-719	-1,854	-1,135
84 Articles of apparel and clothing	1,255	1,184	-72	7,619	20,639	13,020	-6,363	-19,455	-13,092
85 Footwear	141	186	45	3,146	7,236	4,091	-3,005	-7,051	-4,045
87 Professional, scientific, and controlling instruments	6,024	7,438	1,414	1,771	4,616	2,845	4,253	2,822	-1,431
88 Photographic apparatus, equipment, and supplies	2,586	2,544	-42	3,240	5,483	2,243	-654	-2,939	-2,284
89 Miscellaneous manufactures	5,286	6,542	1,256	8,064	19,292	11,228	-2,778	-12,750	-9,972
93 Special transactions, n.e.s.	8,142	1,224	-6,918	4,820	8,082	3,262	3,322	-6,857	-10,180
95 Armaments	2,132	58	-2,074	101	107	6	2,031	-48	-2,080
96 Coins		6	3		14	14	2	-8	-10
97 Gold	3,111	1,730	-1,381	2,131	1,612	-519	980	119	-862
98/99 Low-value shipments		15,112	15,112		2,334	2,334		12,778	12,778

Source: US Department of Commerce.

Table 4.9 United States: product composition of manufactures trade, 1987–90 (millions of dollars)

SITC Category	Exports 1987	Exports 1990	Exports Change 1987–90	Imports 1987	Imports 1990	Imports Change 1987–90	Balance 1987	Balance 1990	Balance Change 1987–90
5-9 Total manufactures	191,729	297,787	106,058	324,444	388,806	64,362	-132,714	-91,019	41,696
51 Organic chemicals	7,717	10,400	2,683	5,508	7,392	1,883	2,209	3,008	799
52 Inorganic chemicals	3,789	3,816	27	2,668	3,234	565	1,121	582	-539
53 Dyeing, tanning, and coloring	952	1,588	636	1,267	1,288	22	-314	300	614
54 Medicinal and pharmaceutical products	2,718	4,103	1,385	1,509	2,500	991	1,209	1,603	394
55 Essential oils and perfume	951	1,963	1,011	982	1,323	341	-31	639	671
56 Fertilizers, manufactured	1,084	2,575	1,490	768	955	187	317	1,619	1,303
57 Explosives and pyrotechnic products	4,033	6,429	2,395	1,113	1,974	862	2,920	4,454	1,534
58 Artificial resins and plastics	1,660	2,633	973	1,327	1,773	446	333	860	527
59 Chemical materials and products	3,118	5,478	2,360	1,425	2,028	603	1,693	3,450	1,756
61 Leather and leather manufactures	529	864	335	721	867	145	-192	-3	189
62 Rubber manufactures, n.e.s.	1,078	2,079	1,000	3,145	3,544	399	-2,067	-1,466	602
63 Cork and wood manufactures (excl. furniture)	698	1,245	547	2,031	2,109	78	-1,333	-864	469
64 Paper, paperboard, and articles	3,092	4,992	1,900	7,249	8,510	1,261	-4,157	-3,519	638
65 Textile yarn, fabric, and madeup articles	3,106	4,922	1,816	5,965	6,398	432	-2,860	-1,476	1,384
66 Nonmetallic mineral manufactures	2,142	3,134	992	8,853	9,890	1,037	-6,711	-6,756	-45
67 Iron and steel	1,270	3,390	2,119	9,127	9,874	747	-7,856	-6,484	1,373
68 Nonferrous metals	2,322	5,189	2,868	7,951	9,806	1,855	-5,630	-4,617	1,013
69 Manufactures of metal, n.e.s.	3,361	5,857	2,496	7,802	8,917	1,115	-4,441	-3,060	1,381
71 Power-generating machinery and equipment	10,006	15,570	5,564	10,650	14,591	3,941	-644	978	1,622
72 Machinery specialized for particular industries	9,365	15,255	5,890	11,233	12,945	1,712	-1,868	2,310	4,179
73 Metalworking machinery	2,236	2,748	512	3,036	3,688	652	-801	-940	-140
74 General industrial machinery and equipment	8,313	15,688	7,376	11,403	14,484	3,080	-3,090	1,205	4,295
75 Office and automatic data processing machines	18,634	24,726	6,092	18,318	26,917	8,599	316	-2,192	-2,508
76 Telecommunications and sound-reproducing equipment	5,085	9,114	4,029	20,797	22,288	1,491	-15,712	-13,174	2,538
77 Electrical machinery, apparatus, and appliances	15,265	28,216	12,951	23,747	33,601	9,854	-8,482	-5,385	3,097
78 Road vehicles (including air-cushion vehicles)	20,906	29,373	8,467	72,585	72,239	-346	-51,679	-42,866	8,813
79 Other transport equipment	17,634	31,833	14,199	5,610	7,343	1,733	12,024	24,490	12,466
81 Sanitary, plumbing, heating, and lighting fixtures	311	679	368	896	1,236	339	-586	-557	28
82 Furniture and parts thereof	572	1,597	1,025	4,551	5,008	457	-3,979	-3,411	568
83 Travel goods, handbags, and similar containers	97	133	37	1,912	2,226	314	-1,815	-2,092	-277
84 Articles of apparel and clothing	1,219	2,479	1,260	20,495	25,533	5,038	-19,276	-23,054	-3,778
85 Footwear	271	479	208	7,547	9,576	2,029	-7,276	-9,097	-1,821
87 Professional, scientific, and controlling instruments	8,082	12,108	4,026	4,835	6,208	1,373	3,247	5,900	2,653
88 Photographic apparatus, equipment, and supplies	2,750	3,664	914	5,803	6,664	862	-3,052	-3,000	52
89 Miscellaneous manufactures	9,236	18,147	8,911	19,467	25,027	5,560	-10,231	-6,881	3,350
93 Special transactions, n.e.s.	1,224	2,359	1,135	8,082	12,093	4,011	-6,857	-9,733	-2,876
95 Armaments	58	87	29	107	228	121	-48	-141	-92
96 Coins	6	7	1	14	8	-6	-8	-1	7
97 Gold	1,730	2,984	1,253	1,612	1,081	-531	119	1,903	1,784
98/99 Low-value shipments	15,112	9,890	-5,222	2,334	3,442	1,107	12,778	6,448	-6,329

Source: US Department of Commerce.

there are 35 categories of manufactures trade normally utilized in describing US manufactures trade. From 1981 to 1987, US trade performance worsened in 32 of these groups and improved in 3, summing to a net worsening in the balance of $150.8 billion on a domestic exports, imports customs basis. A major portion of the decline, however, occurred in just a few product areas:[16]

	1981–87 decline (billions of dollars)
SITC	
78 road vehicles	$39.7
84 apparel and clothing	13.1
72 specialized industrial machinery	11.6
76 telecommunications and sound-reproducing equipment	10.6
77 electrical machinery	10.3
Total	$85.3

Thus, well over half (56.6 percent) of the 1981–87 manufactures trade decline occurred in these five product groups; a sixth category, general industrial machinery, contributed another $9.2 billion.

From 1987 to 1990, US manufactures trade performance improved in 28 categories and worsened in 7, for a total improvement of $41.7 billion. Improvement was modest in most product groups, however, with the gains concentrated in a few categories:

	1987–90 improvement (billions of dollars)
SITC	
79 aircraft	$12.5
78 road vehicles	8.8
5 chemicals	7.1
74 general industrial machinery	4.3
72 specialized industrial machinery	4.2
Total	$36.9

Together, these five product groups accounted for over 88 percent of the 1987–

---

16. US trade data are available in SITC format, Revision 2, through 1988. The United States implemented Revision 3 in 1989, and data for prior years through 1983 were recreated by a concordance process. This study in general assesses changes from 1981 to 1987, typically the low point of US trade performance, and then assesses changes from 1987 to 1990. Because the Revision 2 and 3 amounts may not correspond exactly at the two-digit level of detail, we have generally used Revision 2 data in assessing 1981–87 changes and Revision 3 data in assessing changes from 1987 forward.

90 improvement. Three of them (road vehicles, general industrial machinery, and specialized industrial machinery) also contributed heavily to the earlier decline. The concentration of gains and losses in a relatively few product groups facilitates the analysis of prospective performance, narrowing the range of product groups requiring the most detailed assessment. The major impact of a relatively small number of product groups on trade performance, however, does not imply an ability to fix US trade problems by dealing with only certain specific products or industries. The eight groups in the above two lists make up a very large portion of total US manufactures trade. Moreover, these product groups embrace essentially the whole spectrum of US manufacturing, from basic manufactures to automobiles to aircraft. Inputs to automobile production come from practically every manufacturing sector, and aircraft employs a broad range of manufacturing's most state-of-the-art technologies from a number of product groups.

US Current Account Deficits in Perspective

The last US current account surplus was in 1981. US performance apparently hit bottom in 1987, six years later. There was significant improvement in the three years 1987–90. Can the deterioration that occurred over the six-year period ending in 1987 be reversed by the end of the six-year period that followed 1987? It would be difficult for the United States to return to a balanced current account by 1993. Some statistical analyses can help put the difficulty of the task in perspective.

Export and Import Growth Rate Parameters of a $100 Billion Manufactures Trade Improvement

A balanced current account by 1993 would require that the US manufactures trade balance improve by about $100 billion from 1990 levels (see chapter 2), from a 1990 deficit of $73 billion to a 1993 surplus of about $25 billion. For this to occur, manufactures exports would have to grow annually at an average rate about 9.5 percentage points above the average growth of imports (table 4.10).

Can the United States achieve and sustain export growth rates of that magnitude through 1993? From 1987 to 1989, US manufactures export growth rates actually averaged 10.5 percentage points above import growth rates (table 4.1). However, 1987 export growth rates began from a very low base, surging 27.8 percent in 1988, 16.6 percentage points above the import growth rate. The 1989 export growth rate fell to 12.3 percent, and the export-import growth differential was only 7.3 percentage points. In 1990, the export growth rate continued to

Table 4.10 Export growth rates necessary to achieve a $25 billion US manufactures trade surplus in 1993 under various import growth rate assumptions

Percentages		Resulting 1993 trade[a] (billions of dollars)	
Assumed import growth rate	Matching export growth rate	Exports	Imports
−2	7.4	390.0	365.9
0	9.4	413.8	388.8
2	11.5	437.6	412.6
4	13.7	462.3	437.3
6	15.6	488.1	463.1

a. Actual 1990 manufactures exports were $315.7 billion and imports $388.8 billion.

decrease, falling to 10.0 percent, but the export-import differential rose to 7.5 percentage points as import growth fell to only 2.5 percent. With a weak US economy, the difference enlarged in the first three quarters of 1991. Over the first eight months of 1991, manufactures exports were up at an annualized rate of 7.9 percent over 1990, and imports were down 2.1 percent, resulting in a differential of 10.0 percentage points. However, at 7.9 percent, the 1991 US manufactures export growth rate is probably not much above—and possibly below—the growth rate of world manufactures exports, just as it apparently was in 1990. The implication is that in 1991 US export competitiveness was not gaining much in world markets, if at all. In short, the easier part of US export growth gains has already been achieved. Export gains, although still quite strong, have been declining, and import growth should pick up again when US economic growth resumes. Given this combination, future gains in manufactures trade are likely to be more difficult. In fact, with the value of 1990 imports 1.23 times that of exports, manufactures exports must now grow 1.23 times faster than imports simply to keep the dollar value of the deficit from enlarging.

If import growth resumes, it will be extremely difficult to eliminate the manufactures trade and current account deficits by 1993 or even in the following few years. Even a modest annual import growth rate of 4 percent would require a 13.7 percent annual export gain—well above likely world manufactures export growth rates—to achieve elimination of the deficit by 1993. The implication of table 4.10 is that a $100 billion manufactures trade improvement by 1993 is likely to require a reduction in the real volume of US imports, and possibly also a reduction in current-dollar terms (a reduction in the current-dollar value of imports from the 1990 level). At existing dollar exchange rates, a significant, sustained decline in imports is unlikely unless US economic growth rates are low or negative for a sustained period.

There is, of course, no requirement to eliminate the current account deficit by 1993. Extending the time frame for returning the external accounts to balance lowers the export-import differential required to close the gap and makes the task less formidable. The more important question is whether there is a sustainable trend of improvement in performance without continued dollar depreciation.

Market Share Parameters of a $100 Billion Manufactures Improvement

The growth rate of world exports of manufactures to non-US destinations will greatly influence the ease or difficulty with which the United States improves its manufactures trade performance. The stronger the growth of imports by other countries, the easier it will be for the United States to increase its exports.

Data available for this study allowed construction of the WMTDB only through 1989. Preliminary data compiled by the General Agreement on Tariffs and Trade indicate that world exports of manufactures grew in nominal terms by 15 percent in 1990; however, this figure reflects in part the valuation effects of dollar decline during the year rather than an increase in the volume of world trade. The WMTDB valuation of 1989 manufactures exports to non-US destinations was $1,728.0 billion (table 4.2). Increasing that by 15 percent to reflect 1990 growth and assuming 9.0 percent annual growth (the 1981–89 rate) for the years 1991 through 1993 provides a projected 1993 value of exports to non-US destinations of $2,563 billion. A $25 billion US manufactures trade surplus in that year would be about 1.0 percent of world exports and would imply a US positive share balance of about that amount.

Set against the 1989 share balance of −5.1 percentage points, this implies the need for a further improvement of about 6.1 percentage points in the US share balance to return the US current account to balance. Applying the 15 percent GATT growth percentage for world manufactures exports to 1990 US trade data, however, it appears that both the US export and import shares probably declined in 1990—the export share to about 15.2 percent, and the import share to about 18.8 percent. The net effect would be to reduce the US share balance to perhaps −3.6 percentage points. This implies the need for a further share balance improvement of some 4.6 percentage points to achieve a $25 billion surplus by 1993; this would be roughly equal to the estimated improvement achieved for the 1987–90 period. In this frame of reference, the task does not seem impossible. Again, however, increased export market shares and decreased import market shares will become consistently more difficult to achieve as foreign competitors react to market share losses and as the effects of earlier dollar depreciation dissipate and the dollar appreciation of 1989–90 takes hold.

If the United States does significantly improve its external balance, will it do so primarily by increasing its export share or by decreasing its import share?

The aggregate data do not provide many clues as to the answer. However, in a world of expanding trade with growing roles for new players, there will be a general tendency for US, Japanese, and EC shares of world exports to decline. Considering the general decline in the individual market shares of the major trading partners, the US share of some key export markets is not far from 1981 levels, and further improvement in an era of intensifying competition may be difficult. For example, the 1989 US share of the EC market was 7.8 percent, somewhat below the 1981 level of 9.4 percent (table 3.7). However, over the same period the EC share of its own market (that is, that composed of intra-EC trade) declined from 66.0 percent in 1981 to 62.5 percent in 1989 (table 3.8), reflecting the general decline in developed-country shares. Thus, further enlarging the US share of the EC market may be difficult, particularly as the European Community increases its political and economic unity.

To improve US trade performance, US exports must obviously grow more rapidly than US imports in nominal dollar terms. In market share terms, however, it will probably be increasingly difficult for the United States to achieve further gains in export share. One reason is that more and more countries are participating in the competition for world manufactures export markets, and this tends to result in declining individual-country shares; another reason is that US market share positions have already improved in some key markets while growth in imports is lagging in others. This leads to the conclusion that if the United States is to eliminate its current account deficits, US manufactures imports are likely to have to grow much more slowly than world manufactures exports and probably more slowly than US consumption of manufactures. This implies a substitution of US-based production for foreign-based production in supplying the US market.

Other Views of the Competitiveness of US-Based Manufacturing

Will manufactures trade improvements continue the gains of 1987 to 1990, achieving a $100 billion further improvement without additional dollar depreciation or US policy changes? The product group assessments in chapter 5 provide disaggregated analyses of the outlook. First, however, it is useful to look at some current perceptions about the competitiveness of US manufacturing and consider whether there is cause for longer-term optimism.

The preceding analyses may seem pessimistic about the competitiveness of US-based manufacturing. There are other, more optimistic views. For instance, according to a February 1991 *New York Times* front-page article entitled "American Revival in Manufacturing Seen in US Report":

A Government report issued yesterday suggests that the Rust Belt has staged a renaissance on the factory floor. . . . productivity—the measure of output per hours worked—climbed to a record level in 1990 . . . factories making everything from chemicals to cars now account for a robust 23.3 percent of the nation's gross national product . . . up from 20 percent in 1982, the post-World War II low . . . the new data put U.S. manufacturers on a par with those of Japan and Western Europe. . . . A related report by the Bureau of Labor Statistics showed that manufacturing productivity grew at a 3.6 percent rate during the 1980s, almost three times as fast as in the 1970s . . . some analysts suggested that manufacturing no longer needed to be sheltered with costly subsidies or import protection. . . . The report also reflects a growing consensus among many economists that the long-term problem in the nation's economy is not dilapidated, inefficient factories, but productivity growth among the white-collar service sector . . . (Nasar 1991a).

A March 1991 *Wall Street Journal* story headlined "US Manufacturers Poised for Rebound: Slimmed-Down Sector Awaits End of Recession" noted that a growing number of economists think that "US manufacturing [is] ready to lift off when the economy snaps back" (Boyle 1991).

In April 1991, another *New York Times* front-page story, with the title "Boom in Manufactured Exports Provides Hope for US Economy," related that "the lower dollar has done wonders for American industry" and that "in a quiet revolution, the United States, long derided as an industrial has-been, has become one of the world's low-cost manufacturers . . ." (Nasar 1991b).

In May, a front-page *Washington Post* story headlined "US Firms Stage Competitive Revival" stated: "American manufacturers—written off by many commentators in the 1970s and '80s as dinosaurs doomed to succumb to Japanese and other foreign rivals—have staged a remarkable comeback, reviving American competitiveness in many industries" (Richards 1991).

These and other frequently heard observations convey an image that US products are once again fully competitive in foreign markets. This view deserves analysis. The February 1991 *New York Times* article reported manufacturing as achieving "a robust 23.3 percent of gross national product . . .up from 20 percent in 1982. . . ." The article indicated "the new data put U.S. manufactures on a par with those of Japan and Western Europe." In fact, however, measurements of manufacturing's share of total US output are problematic. There are many difficulties in measuring an output stream that is made up of a flow of hundreds of thousands of products, including a great many new and constantly evolving items with rapidly changing capabilities. For example, for purposes of measuring national aggregate manufacturing production, how does one equate the production of a single desktop computer in 1990 with the production of a single mainframe computer in 1970, given that the desktop unit is probably the more powerful of the two?[17] Constant changes in quality and performance capability

---

17. For a discussion of the impact of measurement of computers on trade data, see Lawrence (1990).

pose essentially insuperable measurement problems that degrade the usefulness of productivity indices for long-term comparisons. In addition, some portion of US manufactures production during the 1980s was attributable to the US defense buildup and does not reflect output that competes in US and foreign consumer-goods markets (see, e.g., Dornbusch et al. 1988, 9).

More important, even if measured accurately, the share of total production contributed by US manufacturing is irrelevant to assessments of US competitiveness. So long as manufactures trade deficits persist, the manufacturing sector is producing fewer manufactured goods than the country is consuming and either lacks sufficient capacity or is not sufficiently competitive in US and world markets to sell enough to avoid deficits in the manufactures trade and current accounts (and to avoid continued external borrowing). A still more important question is whether the needed gains will result from US productivity gains vis-à-vis foreign competitors or must be generated by dollar depreciation.

With deficits continuing despite the dollar depreciation that has occurred since 1985, why do media reports frequently imply that US goods are fully competitive in foreign markets? The answer is that such judgments are based on anecdotal evidence. They reflect the fact that many "made-in-the-USA" manufactures are indeed very competitive in foreign markets. Many US manufacturers are enjoying a more favorable competitive position than they have for a decade. This is the result of a combination of dollar depreciation, wage restraint, and increased productivity and efficiency in response to foreign competition. Manufacturing is in a much better competitive situation than it has been for some time. But in terms of the country's broader overall needs, the manufacturing sector as a whole is not yet sufficiently competitive in US and foreign markets to eliminate the trade and current account deficits and has achieved its gains largely as a result of dollar decline to real levels at or below those of earlier periods of trade surpluses.

The Lack of Sources of Continued Improvement

What about the future? Not only have manufactures trade deficits narrowed significantly since 1987—by more than $17 billion annually between 1987 and 1990—but data for the first nine months of 1991 show significant further improvement. Will this trend continue? Are further trade gains to come? Have improvements already been made in the US manufacturing base that will pay off in continuing trade gains over the next several years? Most important, can US manufacturing continue the improvements in performance required to eliminate the trade and current account deficits *without* major policy changes and *without* further significant depreciation of the dollar? Two sources of potential improvement are examined below.

Table 4.11 Indices of manufacturing productivity in various industrialized countries, 1981 and 1989

Country	Productivity index (1985 = 100) 1981	Productivity index (1985 = 100) 1989	Change in productivity index, 1981–89 (percentages)	Country's share of US manufactures: (percentages) Exports	Country's share of US manufactures: (percentages) Imports
United States	97.9	138.0	41.0		
Canada	104.8	119.9	14.4	23.2	17.9
Japan	94.3	145.2	54.0	9.6	22.9
Belgium	94.2	132.0	40.1	2.3	1.1
Denmark	99.6	103.1	3.5	0.3	0.3
France	93.4	125.1	33.9	3.9	3.0
Germany	99.3	117.0	17.8	5.3	7.1
Italy	97.6	133.8	37.1	1.8	2.9
Netherlands	97.7	131.5	34.6	3.1	0.9
Norway	96.5	131.7	36.5	0.3	0.2
Sweden	95.8	117.6	22.8	1.0	1.2
United Kingdom	94.8	143.1	50.9	6.9	4.4
Total				57.7	61.9

Source: Monthly Labor Review (August 1991): 94.

Productivity Gains

Although measurement of changes in productivity is fraught with difficulties, such changes are an important indicator of manufacturing's international competitiveness. Consistent gains in recent years could indicate a trend of improvements in international market competitiveness that will continue. But to be a source of improved US competitiveness in world markets, US manufacturing productivity growth rates must be *higher* than those of major competitor countries. Moreover, at best the year-to-year gains that might be achieved are small, and the effects cumulate only slowly. US manufacturing productivity gains would have to exceed those of key foreign competitors for many years to improve US international market competitiveness significantly.

The numerous measurement problems that make domestic measurements of productivity changes suspect make intercountry productivity comparisons even less reliable. There is no assurance that countries measure productivity in the same way. Nevertheless, intercountry comparisons are the best tool available and are frequently used as one indicator of changes in a country's competitiveness.

According to data compiled by the US Bureau of Labor Statistics, by 1989 US manufacturing productivity had increased by 38 percent from 1982 levels (table 4.11) and 41.0 percent from its level in 1981, the beginning year for most analyses in this study. Comparing US productivity growth rates during the 1981–89 period with those of 11 competitors shows US rates above all but 2 of the group, Japan and the United Kingdom. These data have been widely cited as indicating a resurgence of the competitiveness of US manufacturing. However, the data cover only a subset of OECD countries that represent a little more than half of US manufactures trade: 57.7 percent of US manufactures exports and 61.9 percent of US imports. Not included, besides the other 13 OECD countries, are many newly industrializing and developing countries that account for large portions of US manufactures trade and that offer US manufacturers increasingly tough competition. Moreover, even the data in table 4.11 show higher US productivity gains only in comparison with a group of competitors that represent 41.5 percent of US exports; compared with the remaining countries in the group (Japan and the United Kingdom), which represent 16.5 percent of US exports, US productivity is lagging. The edge is narrower on the import side, where the data show higher US productivity gains than those of competitors providing only 34.6 percent of US imports, and lower gains than those of competitors (Japan and the United Kingdom) that provide 27.3 percent of US imports.

If one accepts these data at face value, recent US productivity gains over most other important trading partners are modest. An important exception is Canada, which has experienced only a 14.4 percent 1981–89 improvement. A more surprising exception is Germany. Notwithstanding its strong trade performance during the decade, Germany registered productivity growth of only 17.6 percent over the period according to these data.

The data highlight the importance of Canada in US manufactures trade. Canada absorbed 23.2 percent of US manufactures exports and supplied 17.9 percent of US imports. Despite the much lower Canadian productivity growth rates and a 1990 exchange rate slightly below that of 1981, the US manufactures trade balance with Canada has improved only modestly since 1987 and remains $7 billion below that of 1981 (table 4.3).

Productivity rates are only one factor influencing production locations and trade balances. Moreover, in interpreting these data, it should be recognized that the productivity figures are aggregated, representing manufactures as a whole. Over one-fourth of US manufactures exports to Canada consists of road vehicles (mostly parts and components for assembly of automobiles in Canada) and engines, and two-fifths of US manufactures imports from Canada are in these two categories. Thus, even if productivity in Canadian manufacturing as a whole is lagging behind that in the United States, Canadian automobile productivity rates might compare favorably with those in the United States. But even if the data correctly reflect US and Canadian automobile productivity changes, production locations in the integrated US-Canada automotive industry are unlikely to change in the short term. Of course, the long-term effects of slower Canadian productivity growth on road vehicle production, on other manufacturing operations, and on the US-Canada manufactures trade balance could be significant, particularly under a future North American Free Trade Agreement.

Japan is also critical in any international productivity comparison because of the large share of US manufactures imports (22.9 percent) that it supplies and because an ever-larger portion of the US manufactures trade deficit is with Japan. Japan's 54.0 percent gain in productivity from 1981 to 1989 was substantially larger than that of the United States, probably reflecting Japan's high investment levels of recent years. Again, Japan's productivity growth rates in its key export industries—including automobiles, electronics, and industrial machinery—would be particularly important but are not revealed in aggregate comparisons. Even in aggregate terms, however, the United States continues to fall behind Japan, but at a slower rate.

Important countries missing from the US Bureau of Labor Statistics productivity comparisons of OECD country data include the Asian NICs, the Latin American countries, China, and some other developing countries. As these countries intensify their efforts to industrialize and to accomplish export-led growth, many of them are likely to make rapid gains in productivity. They are also likely to enlarge their production capabilities by gaining the skills and the plant and equipment needed to make products they do not now manufacture.

In summary, the available data on productivity are both incomplete and open to varying interpretations. Taken at face value, the relatively strong US productivity growth indicated by the data for the 1981–89 period as compared with some other periods seems encouraging. However, given the mixed and incomplete results—the continuing lag behind Japanese productivity growth rates, the relatively small gains over many other competitors included in the data base, and the relatively small portion of total trade with countries where gains are registered—the data do not provide convincing evidence that US manufacturing productivity is gaining enough ground to correct the huge manufactures imbalances of the 1980s by declines in costs of production relative to those of competitors.

Investment Trends

There was great concern during the 1980s about the large US trade and current account deficits and the US transition from the world's largest creditor country to the world's largest debtor country. Some analysts dismissed these concerns, reasoning that US borrowing abroad was financing an investment boom that would make the United States more productive and more internationally competitive. These analysts saw new US investment as creating new production and export capabilities that would facilitate future exports and debt servicing.

In fact, from 1982 to 1989, inflation-adjusted spending on nonresidential plant and equipment grew by 40 percent. In the late 1980s, it averaged more than 12 percent of real GNP—a level previously seen only twice in the postwar US economy (Steindel 1991, 2). Also, real (1982 dollars) US gross fixed investment rose from $509.3 billion in 1981 to $724.5 billion in 1989.

These data indicate that there was an investment boom of sorts in the United States during the 1980s. But the highly aggregated data leave unclear what kind of investments were made. Only a small portion of total US investment goes to the manufacturing sector, which bears the brunt of international competition. A closer examination of US government statistics indicates that capital formation in the manufacturing sector during the 1980s was lackluster. Total US investment during the period was large, but most of it went into sectors other than manufacturing—sectors unlikely to contribute much to US export growth and trade deficit reduction (Kolarik 1989). Roughly 84 percent of cumulative investment during the 1980s went into nonfarm, nonmanufacturing activities. Residential housing alone absorbed about 28 percent of investment. Retail trade and the finance, insurance, and real estate sector were among those also experiencing rapid growth. Only about 16 percent of total US investment went to the manufacturing sector.

Annual real investment in US manufacturing was generally flat during the 1980s. Consequently, manufacturing's real net capital stock grew at an average annual rate of only 1.4 percent from 1980 to 1989, compared with a 3.8 percent rate from 1970 to 1979 and 4.5 percent for the decade of the 1960s. Net capital stock in wholesale trade grew at an 8.1 percent annual rate during the 1980s, retail trade at 4.9 percent, and finance, insurance, and real estate at 6.2 percent (Steindel 1991, table 1).

The data also show that large portions of capital investment spending for manufacturing during the 1980s went into information processing rather than to the factory assembly line: "toward equipping executives, managers, and professionals . . . with ever greater amounts of computational and processing power. . . . But this investment has yet to show much of a payback on the productivity front . . ." (Roach 1991, 59).

Moreover, despite inflows of new investment, the capital stock for manufacturing continued to age during the 1980s. The average age of plant and equipment rose from 10.15 years in 1980 to 11.11 years at the end of 1988, the highest figure since 1951 (Kolarik 1989).

The fact is that the bulk of capital spending during the 1980s did not go to equip US manufacturing for the task of eliminating US trade and current account deficits. Instead, the investment boom of the 1980s was largely in such areas as housing and office buildings, resale and wholesale trade, shopping malls, hotels, and financial services—sectors unlikely to do much for US manufactures trade performance or any other aspect of US trade.

These results should not be surprising. The economic policies of the early 1980s triggered massive net capital inflows and an overly strong dollar that seriously impaired the international market competitiveness of US manufacturing. These were followed in 1986 by a tax act that increased the cost of capital for US business. The 1986 tax reform act included alternative minimum tax regulations that hit capital-intensive manufacturing industries particularly hard. The combined effect of policies of the 1980s was to make investment in US manufacturing relatively less attractive than investment in some other sectors of the US economy.

The manufacturing sector's record on capital spending in the 1980s is not impressive. It does not support an expectation of sustained high productivity growth rates during the 1990s that would significantly improve US manufacturing's competitiveness against many key US competitors. It certainly does not give much hope of gaining on Japanese manufacturing, investment in which rose during the 1980s at incredibly high rates, by about 5.9 percent of GNP during 1980–87, as compared with 2.3 percent of GNP by US manufacturing. Our conclusion is that neither the productivity gains reported in recent data nor recent investment trends give reason to believe that US manufacturing productivity gains will lead to continuing improvements in trade performance. Improvements are likely to have to come from less desirable sources, such as dollar depreciation and slower US economic growth.

Summary

■ The market competitiveness of US manufactures, as assessed in this study through trade performance data, is not a measure of effects on the country's living standards. Market competitiveness is simply the ability to sell sufficient quantities in world markets to preclude large, continuing trade and current account deficits, regardless of the terms of trade.

■ Market competitiveness can be achieved through various means, including continuing dollar depreciation. Dollar depreciation, however, is unlikely to be consistent with improving US living standards because it unfavorably alters the terms of trade.

■ The market competitiveness of US manufactures has improved since its 1986–87 low point, particularly in real (volume) terms, which are what matter to immediate US economic growth and employment. However, US manufactures have not yet become sufficiently competitive to preclude large US external (i.e., current account) deficits in current-dollar terms.

■ A major portion of the 1987–90 improvement in US trade balances was in trade with the European Community. Over two-thirds of the 1981–87 decline in the deficit with the European Community was recouped from 1987 to 1990. Further gains in EC trade are likely to be increasingly difficult, however, as the effects of earlier dollar depreciation are spent.

■ From 1981 to 1987, the US share of exports to non-US destinations declined from 18.5 percent to 14.7 percent but increased to 15.8 percent by 1989. The

US share of imports from non-US sources rose from 18.0 percent in 1981 to a remarkable 27.0 percent in 1986, but decreased to 20.9 percent by 1989. Thus, in 1989 the United States was still taking more than one-fifth of world manufactures exports from non-US sources, but providing less than one-sixth of world manufactures exports to non-US destinations.

■ Changing US export-minus-import percentage share balances provide a crude measurement of changing US market competitiveness in manufactures trade. The share balance declined from 0.5 percentage points in 1981 to −10.1 percentage points in 1986. By 1989, it had recovered to −5.1 percentage points, still 5.7 percentage points below the 1981 level.

■ To achieve the $100 billion improvement in manufactures trade performance that would be needed to balance the US current account by 1993—a hypothetical target for analytical purposes—would require that US manufactures exports grow each year, 1991 through 1993, about 9.5 percent faster than US manufactures imports. Export-import growth rate differentials of this magnitude were maintained from 1987 to 1990, following the marked dollar depreciation that began in 1985. Export growth rates have been waning rapidly, however, and a recovery in the economy will lead to increased import growth rates, making a 9.5 percent differential difficult and unlikely.

■ Eliminating US current account deficits will require wresting manufactures trade export market shares from competitor countries. Rapid growth of world manufactures trade, if it occurs, will relieve the competitive pressures and facilitate enlargement of the US share of world export markets. Slower growth, however, will intensify competition for existing markets and make it more difficult to enlarge US shares.

■ Assuming world manufactures trade growth rates continue at rates typical of the 1980s, to balance its current account by 1993 the United States would need to improve its export-minus-import share balance by about 4.6 percentage points, from an estimated −3.6 percentage points in 1990 to about +1.0 percentage point in 1993. The share balance did improve by about this amount from 1987 to 1990. However, export growth rates have been declining as the effects of earlier dollar decline have been spent and as foreign competition stiffens.

■ It is likely that further significant US manufactures trade balance improvement will come about less as a result of US export growth rates that exceed world export growth rates than as a result of US import growth rates that are lower than world export growth rates. This implies that US-based production will increasingly substitute for foreign production in supplying the US market.

- Because of the large dollar values involved, or because of the large US deficits they generate, a relatively few product groups are particularly critical to US trade performance. These include road vehicles (automobiles and trucks), aircraft, chemicals, apparel, footwear, and electrical and electronic equipment.

- Rapid increases in foreign direct investment and a worldwide trend toward globalization of production are having significant but difficult-to-quantify effects on world and US trade flows.

- The United States has been a leader in direct investments in foreign-based production. The foreign sales of the foreign affiliates of US manufacturing companies in 1988 were 2.4 times total US manufactures exports. That same year, the US sales of US affiliates of foreign manufacturing companies were only 74 percent of total US manufactures imports.

- The effects of US direct investments abroad on US trade balances cannot be determined because it is impossible to determine what US exports would have been had foreign markets been served—perhaps unsuccessfully—solely by US exports. Substantial exports of US parents to their foreign affiliates and other earnings from foreign investments are clearly preferable, however, to the loss of foreign markets to foreign competitors.

- The rapidly rising foreign investment in US manufacturing reduces US trade deficits in several product groups compared with importing the same production from foreign sources.

- Coupling trade performance data with information on dollar exchange rate movements can reveal trends in the competitiveness of US-based manufactures production in the broader sense of productivity changes and other improvements relative to those of competitors. Using the combined data to analyze four broad categories of manufactures indicates that, except for chemicals, the international competitiveness of US-based production has declined significantly, as evidenced by simultaneous deterioration of both nominal and real trade balances and the terms of trade in 1990 as compared with 1982–84.

- In the early 1980s, the United States had strong competitive positions in the manufactures markets of many developing countries. Developing countries took about one-third of US manufactures exports. During the 1980s, a decline occurred in the relative purchasing power of many developing countries—particularly the Latin American and OPEC countries—that is not likely to be reversed soon. Lagging US economic performance in key markets will complicate a return to balance in the US external accounts, even though the United States has maintained its market share in these countries. Unless the Latin American market improves more rapidly than expected, eliminating US trade and current account deficits will require higher levels of performance in other geographic areas than were achieved before the decline in US trade performance of the 1980s.

■ Changes in the product composition of US and world manufactures trade appear unfavorable to the United States. The United States is losing competitiveness in finished goods, which make up a growing portion of world trade, but is doing somewhat better in industrial materials, which are slower-growing segments of manufactures trade.

■ Export and import price data indicate that exchange rate movements and other factors have only marginally lowered the relationship of US export prices to US import prices in manufactured goods compared with 1982–84. This indicates that foreign competitors are able to absorb in their export prices large portions of the effects of dollar decline, partly because of higher productivity growth rates.

■ Dollar exchange rates for 1988–90 were roughly comparable to those of 1978–80. But US manufactures trade performance was dramatically different during the two periods despite some decline in the US terms of trade. From 1978 to 1980, US manufacturing generated a cumulative trade surplus of $23.6 billion, equivalent to about 3.1 percent of US manufactures trade during the period. During the 1988–90 period, however, the cumulative deficit was $271.3 billion, equivalent to about 13.7 percent of manufactures exports and imports during the period. The situation signals a decline in the productivity of US manufacturing as compared with its foreign competition and a decline in the ability of US manufacturing to contribute to rising US living standards.

■ US manufacturing productivity gains in recent years have not been adequate to give promise of correcting the huge imbalances of the 1980s by the preferred means, namely, reducing costs of production relative to those of competitors.

■ Similarly, while there was something of an investment boom in other sectors of the US economy, manufacturing investment during the 1980s was not at particularly high levels and does not compare favorably with that of some other competitors, particularly Japan. Significant future productivity gains on key competitors should not be expected on the basis of recent levels of US investment.

■ The fall in the dollar exchange rate from 1985 to 1988 and other factors resulted in significant 1987–90 improvement in manufactures trade performance. However, the effects of that dollar decline appear to be largely spent. Overall, the implication of disaggregated trade performance and investment data for recent years is that substantial further dollar depreciation will be required to make further major reductions in manufactures trade deficits, let alone generate the surpluses that would be required to balance the US current account. This depreciation will put downward pressure on US living standards.

Bibliography

Bergsten, C. Fred, ed. 1991. *International Adjustment and Financing: The Lessons of 1985–1991.* Washington: Institute for International Economics.

Bergsten, C. Fred, Thomas Horst, and Theodore H. Moran. 1978. *American Multinationals and American Interests.* Washington: Brookings Institution.

Bergsten, C. Fred, Kimberly Ann Elliott, Jeffrey J. Schott, and Wendy E. Takacs. 1987. *Auction Quotas and United States Trade Policy.* POLICY ANALYSES IN INTERNATIONAL ECONOMICS 19. Washington: Institute for International Economics.

Boyle, Thomas F. 1991. "U.S. Manufactures Poised for Rebound." *Wall Street Journal* (22 March): A–2.

Cantwell, John. 1991. "A Survey of Theories of International Production." In Cristos N. Pitelis and Roger Sugden, eds., *The Nature of the Transnational Firm.* London and New York: Routledge.

Dornbusch, Rudiger, James Poterba, and Lawrence Summers. 1988. *The Case For Manufacturing in America's Future.* Rochester: Eastman Kodak Co.

Graham, Edward M., and Paul R. Krugman. 1991. *Foreign Direct Investment in the United States,* rev. ed. Washington: Institute for International Economics.

Hickok, Susan. 1991. "Shifting Composition of U.S. Manufactured Goods Trade." *Federal Reserve Bank of New York Quarterly Review* (Spring).

International Monetary Fund. 1991. *International Financial Statistics 1991 Yearbook.* Washington: International Monetary Fund.

Julius, DeAnne. 1990. *Global Companies and Public Policy.* London: Royal Institute of International Affairs.

Kolarik, W. F., Jr. 1989. *Investment In U.S. Manufacturing: Less Than Meets the Eye.* Washington: US Department of Commerce, Office of Trade and Investment Analysis (December).

Krugman, Paul R. 1991. *Has the Adjustment Process Worked?* POLICY ANALYSES IN INTERNATIONAL ECONOMICS 34. Washington: Institute for International Economics.

Lawrence, Robert Z. 1988. "The International Dimension." In Robert Litan, Robert Lawrence, and Charles Schultz, eds., *American Living Standards, Threats and Challenges.* Washington: Brookings Institution.

Lawrence, Robert Z. 1990. "U.S. Current Account Adjustments: An Appraisal." *Brookings Papers on Economic Activity* 2:343–82.

Nasar, Sylvia. 1991a. "American Revival in Manufacturing Seen in US Report." *New York Times* (5 February): A–1.

Nasar, Sylvia. 1991b. "Boom in Manufactured Exports Provides Hope for US Economy." *New York Times* (21 April): A-1.

Orr, James. 1991. "The Trade Balance Effects of Foreign Direct Investment in U.S. Manufacturing." *Federal Reserve Bank of New York Quarterly Review* (Summer).

President's Commission on Industrial Competitiveness. 1985. *Global Competition: The New Reality*, vol. I. Washington: Government Printing Office.

Reich, Robert B. 1990. "Who Is Us?" *Harvard Business Review* (January–February).

Richards, Evelyn. 1991. "U.S. Firms Stage Competitive Revival." *Washington Post* (20 May): A-1.

Roach, Stephen S. 1991. "Restructuring." In American Council for Capital Formation, *U.S. Investment Trends: Impact on Productivity, Competitiveness, and Growth*. Washington: American Council for Capital Formation, Center for Policy Research (April).

Rutter, John. 1991a. "Current Theories on the Motivation for Foreign Direct Investment in the United States." *TIA Staff Paper* 91–3. Washington: US Department of Commerce, International Trade Administration (May).

Rutter, John. 1991b. "Trends in International Direct Investment." *TIA Staff Paper* 91–5. Washington: US Department of Commerce, International Trade Administration (July).

Scott, Bruce R. 1991. "U.S. Competitiveness in the World Economy in the 1990s." Case Study 9-389-058. Cambridge, MA: Harvard Business School.

Steindel, Charles. 1991. "Recent Trends in Capital Formation." In American Council for Capital Formation, *U.S. Investment Trends: Impact on Productivity, Competitiveness, and Growth*. Washington: American Council for Capital Formation, Center for Policy Research (April).

US Department of Commerce. 1990. *Foreign Direct Investment in the United States: Operations of U.S. Affiliates of Foreign Companies, Preliminary 1988 Estimates*. Washington: US Department of Commerce (August).

US Department of Commerce, Bureau of Economic Analysis. 1990. *United States Direct Investment Abroad: Operations of U.S. Parent Companies and Their Foreign Affiliates, Preliminary 1988 Estimates*. Washington: US Department of Commerce (July).

US Department of Commerce, International Trade Administration, 1988a. *United States Trade: Performance in 1987*. Washington: US Department of Commerce (June).

US Department of Commerce, International Trade Administration. 1988b. *Financially Distressed LDC Debtors to the United States and Industrial West: Trends, Outlook, Implications*. Washington: US Department of Commerce (July).

US Department of Commerce, International Trade Administration. 1991. "U.S. Trade on the Rebound: Contributing to U.S. Growth and Employment." *Staff Paper* 91–4. Washington: US Department of Commerce (June).

5

Individual Product Group Assessments

5

Individual Product Group Assessments

The preceding chapters have established that manufactures trade has had a dominant role in US trade and current account performance and will continue to do so. Therefore, a thorough examination of the outlook for manufactures trade is an important way to assess future US trade and current account performance.

This chapter assesses in detail the recent trade performance of and the outlook for 21 manufactures product groups. A single analysis examines chemicals and related products (SITC 5), which is made up of nine two-digit product groups. We split one product group (SITC 71, power-generating machines) and include its parts in assessments of closely related products. Each of the remaining assessments covers a single two-digit SITC product group. Together, the analyses cover 29 of the 37 two-digit SITC product groups classified as manufactures. The analyses cover over 90 percent of 1990 US manufactures exports and imports.

We selected the product groups for analysis by considering their past and potential effects on US trade performance. We did this on the basis of the dollar values of exports, imports, and trade balances and the changes in these that each product group experienced during the 1981–90 period.

Objectives and Methodology

The objective of these analyses is to provide a detailed breakdown of world and US trade that will further an understanding of the determinants of US trade performance and of how US policies may influence that performance.

Each product analysis follows the same general pattern. We first describe the product group and review its role in world trade (size and composition, global competition patterns, and key determinants of world trade patterns). We examine next the product group's role in US trade (size, recent US performance, and US international competitiveness). We then assess the key determinants of

117

US trade performance and the trade outlook for the next few years and present our conclusions.

Analyses and tabular presentations for individual manufactures product groups focus on performance during the 1981–87, 1987–90, and 1990–93 periods. The 1981–87 period begins with the last US manufactures trade and current account surpluses and ends with the low point in US trade performance. The second period, 1987–93, is broken into two components, 1987–90 and 1990–93. The 1987–90 assessments move the analysis from the 1987 low point of US trade performance through three years of moderate recovery to 1990, the year for which the most recent US Department of Commerce data are available. Projections of 1993 performance allow us to judge the probable US position three years into the future, and six years from the 1987 low point.

The use of the 1987–93 period for the analysis and the 1993 date for projection of trade performance is not meant to imply that a return to balance by 1993 is essential or even that this would necessarily be the best policy target. It is simply a convenient analytical focal point. It is, however, useful in that it assesses the United States' ability to redress the deterioration in its performance in the same number of years that the decline occurred.

We present a standardized set of six tables for each product group. The information presented in the tables includes world trade levels and flows, export and import market shares by country or region, the geographical composition of US trade, and US international market competitiveness as measured by export shares, import shares, and share balances (export share minus import share). To provide the most complete, up-to-date information available, we used several different data series in the analyses and the tables. The analyses make extensive use of the World Manufactures Trade Data Base (WMTDB) constructed for this study, which includes data for 1981 through 1989, the latest year available. These data are in SITC Revision 2 format. US Department of Commerce data are also used extensively in other analyses for the period 1979 through 1990. These data are available from 1981 through 1988 in SITC Revision 2 format and from 1983 through 1990 in SITC Revision 3 format.

The appendix to this volume describes the various data series utilized and the reasons for discrepancies among these series. It also reviews the limitations of the WMTDB and the market share calculations drawn from it.

The reader should also be aware of the methodology and limitations of the projections of 1993 trade performance made for each product group. These projections do not utilize an econometric model. They are, instead, judgments based on analysis of all the empirical quantitative data and qualitative information collected, including the questionnaire survey data (which are summarized in chapter 6).

We made our projections in light of the following general assumptions:

- Through 1993, the dollar exchange rate remains essentially unchanged from May 1991 levels.

- The US economy returns to positive but relatively low growth rates of about 2.5 percent by mid–1992.

- Oil prices return to pre–Gulf crisis levels, subsequently increasing at rates roughly equivalent to US inflation.

- There is no major global economic downturn; the economies of other developed countries generally perform well.

In addition, the projections and the review of the 1981–90 performance give consideration to import and export elasticities graciously provided by Data Resources, Inc. (DRI) from their World Trade Service model. A tabular presentation and an explanation of these elasticities appear in the appendix.

The reader should understand that the projected results were not reached through rigorous testing of assumptions and econometric methods. Indeed, in some instances the judgments would probably override the result that might emerge through a solely formula-driven process. This is both a strength and a weakness. For example, a mathematical model that does not disaggregate to individual product groups could not take into consideration information about the effects of emerging new sources of supply that affect individual product groups. An analytical judgment of future trade balances, however, can reflect this information.

On the other hand, it is possible to lean too heavily on empirical data and qualitative assessments of industry experts. This may lead to projections that simply extrapolate past trends and miss turning points. For example, in nonmathematical projections it is difficult to anticipate the lagged effects of recent movements of exchange rates.

Changes in 1993 dollar balances are projected for each product group assessed in this chapter. Probably few of these projections will be precisely on target. But, we believe, neither are many likely to be far off the mark. One of the objectives of these projections is simply to establish orders of magnitude; that is, to establish ranges of what may be reasonably anticipated. Readers can make their own judgments as to the validity of the individual "best judgment" projections.

This chapter presents product group assessments in SITC numerical order. Tables are numbered sequentially within each product group; for example, within road vehicles (SITC 78) tables are identified as table 5.78.1, table 5.78.2, etc.

Chapter 7 presents general findings drawn from the individual product group analyses.

Individual product group analyses included in this chapter are:

SITC

5 Chemicals and related products

Basic Manufactures

64 Paper, paperboard, and articles thereof

65 Textiles

66 Nonmetallic mineral manufactures

67 Iron and steel

68 Nonferrous metals

69 Manufactures of metal, not elsewhere specified

Machinery and Transportation Equipment

72 Special industrial machinery

73 Metalworking machinery

74 General industrial machinery

75 Office machines and computers

76 Telecommunications and sound-reproducing equipment

77 Electrical machinery, not elsewhere specified, and parts (and SITC 716: electric motors and generators)

Miscellaneous Manufactures

78 Road vehicles (and SITC 713: engines)

79 Other transportation equipment (SITC 792: aircraft, and SITC 714: engines)

82 Furniture and parts

84 Clothing and accessories

85 Footwear

87 Professional, control, and scientific instruments

89 Miscellaneous manufactures

Chemicals and Related Products (SITC 5)

Chemicals has been one of US manufacturing's few strong performers, yielding continuing surpluses throughout the 1980s. These surpluses declined from 1980 through 1985, but performance improved in the latter part of the decade. The chemical trade surpluses topped $16 billion in both 1989 and 1990 and may reach $19 billion in 1991. There are signs, however, that modest trade balance declines may occur in the 1990s. Chemicals is a major factor in US trade, accounting for 13.1 percent of 1990 US manufactures exports and 5.8 percent of imports.

Description of the Product Group

Chemicals and related products (SITC 5) is a very broad grouping. The US chemical industry produces over 60,000 different products, ranging from basic organic and inorganic "commodity" chemicals used in other production processes and products to finished consumer goods such as detergents and medicines. It also includes synthetic resins, elastomers, and other specialty chemicals tailored to specific purposes.

This section examines the entire chemicals group in a more aggregated analysis than is given other product groups in this study. This is both practical and desirable because of the huge number of chemical products; the fact that many of them become inputs to other chemical products and processes, giving rise to a large volume of trade within the chemical industry itself; and the relatively stable composition of broad categories of products in chemical trade. Moreover, except for some energy-rich developing countries that still produce only basic chemical products, the trade performance of important chemical producer countries is not tied to a single chemical product but typically depends on performance across a wide spectrum of products, from basic chemicals to finished consumer goods. Further, trade in none of the major product subgroups is dominated by any one country. Finally, the major change in SITC classifications in 1989 from Revision 2 to Revision 3 substantially altered the descriptions of the two-digit product groups SITC 57 through 59, making 1981–90 comparisons in those categories difficult at the two- and three-digit levels of detail. For these reasons, this section treats the whole of chemicals and related products rather than examining some or all of the individual two-digit categories, the procedure followed in the remainder of this part of the study.

Disaggregating the chemicals group to the two-digit level of detail, the nine chemicals categories through 1988 (SITC Revision 2) are:

SITC

51 organic chemicals

52 inorganic chemicals

53 dyeing, tanning and coloring materials

54 medicinal and pharmaceutical products

55 essential oils and resinoids and perfume materials; toilet, polishing, and cleansing preparations

56 fertilizers, manufactured

57 explosives and pyrotechnic products

58 artificial resins and plastic materials, and cellulose esters and ethers

59 chemical materials and products not elsewhere specified.

In 1989, a major revision to the SITC codes (revision 3) realigned some product groups within the chemical group. The following sections were significantly changed by Revision 3 to the new definitions shown below:

57 plastics in primary forms

58 plastics in nonprimary forms

59 chemical manufactures and products.

Detailed US Department of Commerce data are available in Revision 2 format through 1988 and in Revision 3 format beginning in 1983. The changes in nomenclature should be noted in the data presentations in this section, which make use of both Revision 2 and Revision 3 data.

Role in World Trade

Size and Composition

At $246.8 billion, 1989 world exports of the nine two-digit categories of chemical products were about one-eighth of total world manufactures exports (table

5.5.1). Although a very large element in world trade, total world chemical exports were, nevertheless, about $16 billion less than the $263 billion trade in automobiles (SITC 78).

Trade in chemicals grew somewhat more slowly than world manufactures trade during the 1980s. World chemical exports grew 9.0 percent per year on average from 1981 to 1989, slightly below the 9.6 percent rate for manufactures as a whole.

Differences in the world export growth rates of individual two-digit product groups (table 5.5.1) reveal some changes during the 1980s in the composition of chemical trade. For example, exports of fertilizers grew at an annual rate of only 4.0 percent from 1981 to 1989, while the growth rate for plastic materials was 11.6 percent. Medicinals and pharmaceuticals are also increasing in importance because of high annual growth rates. Two types of basic industrial chemicals, organic chemicals and inorganic chemicals, together made up 36.7 percent of total world trade in chemicals in 1989, but this was down modestly from over 38 percent in 1981 as a result of slow growth in exports of inorganic chemicals.

Chemical production is increasingly globalized. Many industrializing countries are developing their own production capabilities for basic organic and inorganic chemicals, fertilizers, and other basic items, a factor that may slow trade growth in those items somewhat. These trends could continue to gradually reduce the relative role of basic chemicals in international trade and lower the percentage share of chemicals in world manufactures trade. Any decrease, however, is likely to be modest because continued technological advances will lead to new, higher-value specialized chemicals that will add to world trade totals, particularly as developing economies progress and increase their demand for more sophisticated chemical products.

For the foreseeable future, total trade in chemicals is likely to continue to grow at rates similar to, or slightly below, those for manufactures trade as a whole. Continued gradual changes in the composition of the trade are also likely, with basic organic chemicals probably growing somewhat more slowly than the higher-value-added products farther down the processing chain. The slow growth in basic inorganic chemicals is also likely to continue. Rising global living and health standards should, however, lead to somewhat more rapid growth in medicines and pharmaceuticals and to increased exports of various forms of plastics and "other" chemical manufactures and products.

Global Competition Patterns

The United States, with total 1989 shipments (domestic shipments and exports) of $256 billion, is by far the largest producer of chemicals in the world. Japan is second with 1989 shipments of $161 billion, and Germany is third at $85 billion. Germany, however, is the world's largest chemical exporter, with 19.5 percent of world chemical exports in 1987 and 17.8 percent in 1989 (table 5.5.2). France and the United Kingdom are other major exporters, with export shares of 9.7 percent and 8.2 percent in 1989, respectively. Japan trails behind by a substantial margin, with only 5.9 percent of world exports in 1989.

The United States share of world chemical exports declined significantly, from 18.6 percent in 1981 to 13.1 percent in 1987, but rose to 14.7 percent by 1989 (table 5.5.2). The 1985–87 decline partly reflected the weakening dollar. Other things being equal, a declining dollar increases the dollar valuation of foreign competitor exports and their calculated percentage share of world exports.

Given the effects of changing exchange rates on share calculations, as well as other shortcomings, export shares alone are an incomplete measure of changes in a country's competitiveness in international markets. Import shares are also relevant and the export-minus-import-share calculations in table 5.5.2 can provide crude year-by-year indications of the relative competitiveness of individual countries in international markets. For example, Germany, the world's largest chemical exporter, is also the world's largest importer, with 10.6 percent of world chemical imports in 1987 and 9.8 percent in 1989. But the consistently wide margins of its shares of world exports over its import shares (8.9 percentage points in 1987, 8.0 percentage points in 1989) and the fact that its positive share balance greatly exceeds that of any other competitor are evidence of Germany's strong competitiveness in international markets.

Changes in these export-minus-import margins also signal trends in a country's ability to compete in international markets. For example, the positive margin of the US export share over its import share narrowed by 6.0 percentage points from 1981 to 1987 and by 4.6 percentage points from 1981 to 1989, indicating declining competitiveness in world markets, mostly as the result of a drop in the US export share. Similar calculations show 1981–89 changes of − 1.7 percentage points for the European Community as a whole, and a − 0.1- percentage-point loss for Germany. The data also show a modest Japanese role in chemical trade (5.9 percent of 1989 world exports, 5.8 percent of imports), and a 0.4-percentage-point decline in Japan's export-minus-import share from 1981 to 1989.

Care must be exercised in interpreting these data, however. For example, the marked improvements for Latin America and the "other" country category (mostly developing countries) stem from declining import shares, not increasing export shares. The declining imports probably do not indicate increased self-sufficiency in chemicals so much as they reflect financial difficulties and a decreasing ability to afford needed imports.

Bilateral chemical trade flow patterns are summarized for 1989 in table 5.5.3. The data clearly illustrate the very large role of the European Community in world chemical exports ($144.1 billion in 1989, 58.4 percent of the world total). Also evident is the large role of intra-EC chemical trade in world chemical trade, with $83.6 billion of exports by EC countries—58 percent of the EC total—going to other EC countries. Germany, with 1989 exports of $43.9 billion and imports of $23.3 billion, had a 1989 surplus of $20.6 billion, the largest of any country, overshadowing US exports of $36.4 billion and the $15.5 billion US surplus. Generally, the table also shows the developed countries as net exporters, and the NICs and "other" countries as net importers.

Key Determinants of World Trade Patterns

Chemicals is probably more globalized than any other major manufacturing industry. That is, many basic products are produced in many countries, and chemical markets around the world are sufficiently integrated that world supply-demand relationships determine world prices for many basic products. There is a world market for chemicals that can readily be transported across oceans and over great distances. On the other hand, some basic chemicals—for example, ethylene—are so difficult to transport that they are generally produced near their point of consumption. Typically, however, difficult-to-transport chemicals are processed further to create "downstream" products that can be transported more readily. Given today's instant communications and fast, low-cost transportation, markets in one continent can now often be efficiently served by production in another.

One result is that producers are less able to pass on cost increases that stem from domestic causes. For example, neither feedstock price rises resulting from tax increases nor the costs of environmental restrictions on US producers apply to foreign competitors. Thus, companies with only domestic production facilities must bear rising costs attributable to domestic causes that foreign producers do not face. Multinational companies can switch production among their several plant locations in different parts of the world to meet changing conditions in supply, demand, or exchange rates. The result is that global supply-demand relationships and exchange rates largely determine prices, production locations, and trade and investment patterns for many chemicals. The trend to globalization is not unique to chemicals but is particularly pronounced in this product group.

Globalization of production and the resulting very strong effects of global supply-demand relationships on domestic industries stem from several factors. These include the pervasive need for chemicals in modern industrial processes, the standardized nature of many industry products, and the high R&D costs of remaining competitive in both products and production processes.

Chemicals are inputs to agricultural production and virtually all manufacturing processes and products. The construction and services industries also use chemicals. Given the essential, pervasive use of chemicals, virtually every country has at least a modest chemical industry, often beginning with production of fertilizers and related chemicals. Yet the bulk of the market economies' estimated $960 billion 1989 chemical output was accounted for by only a handful of developed nations. Combined, the United States, Japan, Canada, and the EC countries accounted for about three-fourths of that output in 1989.

About one-third of the industry's output consists of basic commodity chemicals (organic chemicals, SITC 51, and inorganic chemicals, SITC 52). The formulas and production processes for most of these products are well known. While product quality in these basic chemicals is very important, sales are largely to industrial users, and normally no characteristics differentiate one company's products from another. Therefore, competition in basic commodity chemicals is based largely on price, although service, reliability, and other factors are also important.

The industry also produces large numbers of specialized high-technology products, often covered by patents. Developing these advanced products and remaining competitive in complex production processes for the whole spectrum of chemical products requires large expenditures for R&D. These typically amount to 4 percent to 5 percent of the industry's sales, and are much higher for companies specializing in medicines, pharmaceuticals, and composite materials. The need to amortize these high costs over large sales volumes means that companies must sell in global markets to maintain their technical and competitive positions. The chemical industries of developed countries typically produce a wide variety of chemicals, ranging from basic commodity chemicals to specialty chemicals tailored to unique applications. In developing countries, domestic chemical industries generally make simpler chemicals such as fertilizers and inorganic commodity chemicals. Some countries also produce minor volumes of specialty chemicals, but they usually must import a large portion of their total requirements. As they develop industrially, however, they seek to expand their production capabilities. Just as most countries want their own "flag carrier" airlines, most want to have their own chemical industries. Those that have their own low-cost feedstocks or other raw materials want to obtain the maximum value added from their natural resources by producing not only basic organic and inorganic chemicals but also more sophisticated downstream chemical products. Those that have no particular material resource advantages nevertheless want the independence and value-added advantages of their own production facilities as well as the significant transfer of technology to be gained from developing a chemical industry.

Such factors have encouraged a global orientation among major companies and produced a worldwide market in many chemicals. To compete in major markets, however, major companies do not necessarily export but often locate production in those markets. The technology for creating both basic chemicals and most specialized chemicals can be readily transferred to, and implemented by, production facilities in many countries. This has led to widespread foreign direct investment in chemicals. Major companies often have plants producing some chemicals in several countries.

US companies led the globalization of chemical production. The book value of direct investment abroad by US chemical companies reached $38.7 billion in 1990, and foreign direct investment in the US chemical industry rose to $41.7 billion. Both values are larger than for any other manufacturing industry. Book values, however, do not accurately reflect real value and earning power, but only the amount of the original investment. In book-value terms, foreign direct investments in the US chemical industry are greater than US direct investments in foreign chemical industries. But book values typically understate the earning power of US investments abroad, which have typically been in place longer than comparable foreign investments in the United States and which in the chemical industry have generated larger earnings than foreign investments in the United States.

By the standard Department of Commerce definition (10 percent or more of the voting stock of a US company held by a single foreign entity), 29.3 percent of the US chemical industry was foreign controlled in 1988, giving chemicals one of the highest levels of foreign control among major US manufacturing industries. US chemical companies, however, also control a large number of companies in foreign countries. Sales of the foreign affiliates of US chemical companies in 1988 were $90.3 billion. The globalization of the chemical industry and its production is further illustrated by the fact that some US chemical companies now derive half or more of their income from overseas operations.

The flow of foreign direct investments in the chemical industry has not been primarily from developed to developing countries. A cross-flow of direct investment among the industrialized nations has been the main factor in the globalization of chemical production and markets. Most direct investment by the US chemical industry (50 percent of the 1990 total) is in Europe, but a substantial portion is in Canada (16.6 percent). Only about one-fifth of US chemical industry direct investment abroad is in developing countries. Similarly, most foreign direct investment in the US chemical industry is from Europe (83 percent), only 9.4 percent is from Japan, and 1.2 percent from Canada. The continuing globalization of the chemical industry manifested in worldwide direct investments seems to indicate that a relatively few large multinational companies will increasingly dominate world chemicals trade.

Direct investments in the United States by foreign companies and direct investments abroad by US chemical companies have generated a substantial trade between US chemical companies and their foreign affiliates and between US affiliates and their foreign parents. Commerce Department data for 1988 indicate that 170 US chemical industry parents had 2,867 affiliates abroad in all industries, including chemicals. In 1988 there were 1,749 US affiliates in foreign chemical industries, some with US parents outside the chemical industry. According to Commerce Department estimates, at $10.6 billion, exports in 1988 by US chemical company parents to their foreign affiliates were one-third of all US chemical exports. Exports by US affiliates to their foreign parents were another $4.0 billion, one-eighth of all 1988 US chemical exports. Similarly, $8.0 billion (39.4 percent) of 1988 US chemical imports was derived from trade between parents and affiliates. According to these estimates, trade between US parents and their foreign affiliates yielded a US surplus on chemicals of $3.1 billion in 1988, and exports of US affiliates in the United States exceeded their imports by $2.3 billion.

The international trade in chemicals between parents and affiliates in part reflects a specialization in production. For example, some specialty chemicals may be produced only in one or a few selected locations that supply the company's needs in other markets. For more common chemicals, however, multinational companies may be able to select among several production locations in different parts of the world to meet changing conditions in supply, demand, and exchange rates.

More than two-thirds of total US chemical-industry investments abroad are in Europe or Canada, and 84 percent of foreign direct investment in the United States is from Europe or Canada. Thus, the US chemicals trade between parents and affiliates is primarily with European and Canadian parents and affiliates, and a very high portion of the US chemicals trade with Europe and Canada is between parents and affiliates.

Chemical production in developed countries usually serves mainly domestic needs. There are several exceptions, however. Germany, for example, in 1989 exported 53.8 percent of its total production, mostly to other EC countries. Several developed countries with large chemical industries typically enjoy significant trade surpluses. Nevertheless, chemical industries in industrialized countries have not usually been built primarily to serve export markets. Also, until recently, developing countries created new chemicals production facilities primarily to support their domestic needs, and chemical exports were not a major factor in their export-led growth strategies. More frequently, industrializing nations following export-led growth strategies targeted other kinds of manufactures—that were less capital intensive—including apparel, textiles, and other low-technology manufactures.

Thus, until the 1980s, developing countries were not usually important competitors in chemical trade. They were export markets for the chemical industries of the developed countries and typically provided substantial surpluses for those countries. That situation still generally prevails, but during the 1980s several developing countries embarked on ambitious programs to develop globally competitive chemical industries. Those building world-class facilities included several of the industrializing countries of Asia such as Singapore, Korea, Taiwan, and Thailand. Several of the larger economies of Latin America (Argentina, Brazil, Mexico, and Venezuela) and some Middle Eastern countries have also initiated large investments in their chemical industries, primarily in petrochemicals.

The output of the large-scale petrochemical plants being constructed in the Middle and Far East will in many instances greatly exceed the domestic needs of the producer countries. Many of these facilities will depend on export markets to absorb much, if not most, of their output. Some will utilize abundant natural gas resources that would otherwise be wasted by flaring. These facilities will have very low feedstock costs—near zero marginal costs in some instances. Continued growth of these production facilities and gradual expansion to include more downstream, higher-value-added products could significantly change global competitive relationships, the locus of world chemical production, and resulting trade and investment patterns.

Role in US Trade

Recent Performance

Chemicals play an important role in US trade. Chemicals comprised 13.3 percent of US manufactures exports in 1987 and 13.1 percent in 1990. Chemical exports of $39.0 billion in 1990 were only slightly smaller than total US agricultural exports of $39.6 billion. The chemical shares of US manufactures imports have been much smaller, 5.0 percent in 1987 and 5.8 percent in 1990.

The US chemical trade surplus was $11.9 billion in 1981 (table 5.5.4). It then declined to $7.1 billion in 1985 before beginning a recovery that led it back to $10.5 billion in 1987 and new records of $15.7 billion in 1989 ($16.7 billion after an adjustment for underreporting of US exports to Canada) and $16.5 billion in 1990. Chemicals, therefore, did not contribute significantly to the major deterioration of US manufactures trade performance between 1981 and 1987. Moreover, in recent years it has been one of the few strong performers in the US manufactures trade account, second only to aircraft (SITC 792).

Although US-based chemical production was affected by the downturn in its trade balance during the 1980s, it was affected more by the decline in total US manufactures trade performance. Over the 1981–87 period, the US manufactures trade balance slid by $150.8 billion (table 4.6; domestic exports, imports customs basis), or about 3.5 percent of 1987 US GNP. Because about half of the chemical industry's US-based production is used as inputs by other US manufacturing industries, the very large 1981–87 decline in manufactures trade performance represented a very high domestic opportunity cost to the US chemical industry in lost sales. That is, the large US manufactures trade deficits were evidence of the loss of large amounts of chemical sales to other US-based manufacturing industries whose output was displaced by imports.

The United States usually achieves trade surpluses in every two-digit product group within the SITC 5 chemicals classification except dyeing, tanning, and coloring materials and essential oils, both of which are relatively small components of total chemicals trade (table 5.5.4). The major surplus categories are organic chemicals and inorganic chemicals, medicinals and pharmaceuticals, plastics, and chemical manufactures. US exports of medicinals and pharmaceuticals reached $4.1 billion in 1990, nearly double the 1981 level. Imports trebled, however, from $833 million to $2.5 billion. As a result, the surplus in this category grew only modestly, from $1.4 billion in 1981 to $1.6 billion in 1990.

Plastics, in resins and in other forms, have been important in US trade, although Revision 3 reclassifications for SITCs 57, 58, and 59 have frustrated comparisons over time, complicating the analysis. Various plastic resins and plastics in nonprimary forms have produced the largest portion of recent US chemicals trade surpluses. Together, the 1990 surpluses in plastics in primary forms and chemical materials and products totaled $7.9 billion, or 47.9 percent of the total industry surplus.

It is noteworthy, however, that a major portion of the total surpluses ($4.65 billion or 30 percent in 1989, and $3.6 billion or 21.8 percent in 1990) has typically come from basic organic and inorganic chemicals, not from high-technology or specialty chemicals. This is an important factor in evaluating prospective trade performance in the 1990s, when foreign production of these basic chemicals is expected to increase rapidly. Moreover, increasing production capabilities in basic organic chemicals in developing countries will inevitably lead, in the longer term, to foreign production of many of the downstream plastics products and other chemical manufactures and products that utilize basic organic chemical inputs.

The United States typically achieves modest surpluses in chemical trade with the other developed countries (tables 5.5.5 and 5.5.6). Balances with the European Community fluctuate narrowly between surplus and deficit, apparently depending largely on exchange rate and relative US-EC economic conditions. Japan has consistently provided substantial US surpluses: $2.3 billion in 1989 and $2.2 billion in 1990.

The developing countries, however, have been the main source of US surpluses in 1990, taking 35.3 percent of US exports and providing only 15.3 percent of US imports, leaving a $10.3 billion US surplus. Latin America has been an important factor in these surpluses, giving the United States a $4.5 billion surplus in 1990, including $1.6 billion in trade with Mexico. Also particularly noteworthy is US trade with the Asian NICs (Hong Kong, Taiwan, Korea, and

Singapore), an important source of recent US surpluses with the developing world supplying $4.0 billion in 1989 and $3.6 billion in 1990.

US International Competitiveness

The large chemical trade surpluses that were maintained through the 1980s, the 1990 surplus that topped $16 billion, and the prospect of a 1991 surplus close to $19 billion are evidence that the US chemical industry is competitive in international markets. But continuing trade surpluses—even increasing surpluses—do not necessarily provide a valid measure of whether relative US strength in international markets is waxing or waning. Table 5.5.6 provides additional indicators of the international market competitiveness of the US chemical industry. The data show that world exports of chemicals to non-US destinations grew from $114.8 billion in 1981 to $179.6 billion in 1987 and to $225.9 billion in 1989. Although US chemical exports expanded to new highs during that time, the US share of world exports to non-US destinations declined from 20.0 percent to 14.3 percent in 1987, but thereafter increased to 16.1 percent by 1989.

As noted earlier, these export share calculations are imperfect indicators of US competitiveness in world markets because they are affected by exchange rates, growth in the size of the world market, and various other factors. For example, the post-1985 share declines in part doubtless reflect the effects of the decline of the dollar during that period not just on trade volume changes but also on the mathematics of share calculations.[1] Moreover, if the world economy and world exports expand more rapidly than the US economy, a smaller US share of rapidly expanding world exports—a smaller piece of a bigger pie—becomes almost inevitable. This would not necessarily be an undesirable change or reflect a diminished position relative to other major competitors.

The shortcomings of export share measurements as indicators can be mitigated by pairing export and import shares, since both are subject to the same distortions from the effects of exchange rate movements and the growth of world trade. The US share of world imports from non-US sources—that is, the share of non-US exports taken as imports by the United States—provides both a measure of US absorption of exports from the rest of the world and a measure of the dependency of foreign exporters on the US market. The US share balance—the difference between US export and import shares—can thus provide a crude

---

1. Other things equal, dollar depreciation increases the dollar value of trade denominated in foreign currencies and hence increases the foreign shares of world exports and decreases the US share of total world exports.

indicator of US international competitiveness in world chemical trade. The US chemical industry's positive 1989 share balance of 6.2 percentage points is such an indicator (table 5.5.7).

Trends in export, import, and balance shares can also be revealing. From 1981 to 1987, while the US share of exports to non-US destinations was declining, the US share of world imports from non-US sources was increasing. The US import share grew from 9.5 percent in 1981 to 12.7 percent in 1985, before declining to 9.6 percent in 1987. It then rose to 9.9 percent in 1989. As a result of these import and export share changes, the US share balance declined from a positive 10.5 percentage points in 1981 to a positive 4.3 percentage points in 1986, before improving to 4.7 in 1987 and 6.2 in 1989. The net decline in the share balance over the 1981–87 period was 5.8 percentage points, indicating a significant deterioration in US chemical trade competitiveness during that period. The improvement from 1987 to 1989 left the US share balance still 4.3 percentage points below the 1981 level.

Key Determinants of US Trade Performance

A great many factors affect the trade performance of chemicals, a basic US industry that supplies inputs to other US industries and is more globalized than most other manufacturing industries. These key factors include:

- US and world economic growth rates

- US and global chemical supplies

- continued globalization of chemical production

- comparative costs of compliance with environmental regulations

- comparative feedstock and energy costs

- the dollar exchange rate.

Because the world consumption of and demand for chemicals closely parallel trends in US and world GNPs, both US and world economic growth rates are important to US chemical trade performance. Chemical imports are partly determined by US economic growth and, other things being equal, will continue to increase as US GNP expands. US export growth also generally parallels that of the world economy. High US economic growth rates could, however, constrain US exports if the combination of foreign and domestic demand exceeds US production capacity.

US chemical producers sometimes view export markets as residuals. This is not necessarily an irrational approach in an industry with homogeneous products and a rapid growth of global supplies. For example, in the face of limited capacity, it may be a logical business decision for a US producer to give preference to a long-standing domestic customer over a new customer halfway round the world in an area where new capacity is about to come on stream. Thus, when production reaches the limits of capacity, US customers—sometimes seen by US producers as more stable and dependable—may be given first priority on available supplies. In 1990, however, US capacity appeared generally adequate to handle both US and foreign demand in most situations.

Perhaps most important, strong world economic growth not only increases US export opportunities but puts upward pressure on export and import prices. A strong world economy also lessens pressures on the US market from the exports of other countries. Thus, a strong world economy should tend to increase US chemical trade surpluses.

World demand for chemicals fluctuates with conditions in the US and world economies. Global demand, however, is only one side of the supply-demand equation that determines prices and trade flows. If global supplies increase more rapidly than global demand, world prices will decline (perhaps substantially), competitive pressures will increase, and trade flows may change.

There are cycles in new investment in the world chemical industry. Periods of high capacity utilization and strong profits typically motivate waves of new investment that build supply beyond demand growth. Growth of global capacity may stall—or even reverse—in recession, or after periods in which supply growth exceeds demand growth. However, global capacity continues to enlarge in most years. To achieve economies of scale, additions to capacity are frequently large and require long gestation periods, often several years. In addition to capacity additions in developed countries, the continuing construction of large chemical plants in developing countries and newly industrializing countries—some of them rich in low-cost energy and feedstocks, some without their own energy sources—will have important effects. The rising construction of chemical plants in developing countries adds a new element of supply expansion. Many chemical industry analysts see ongoing supply growth outpacing demand growth to a degree that could have profound effects on world chemical production and trade patterns during the 1990s.

The large US-based chemical industry is linked to facilities in many other countries through a network of foreign direct investment in the United States and US direct investment abroad. Because production can to some extent be switched among a company's US and foreign plants to serve both its US and foreign markets, exchange rate changes have important effects on the US in- dustry's trade performance.

The globalization of the chemical industry both limits and facilitates US exports of chemicals. In surveys taken in 1989 and 1990, major US chemical companies in the United States cited "globalization of markets and production" and the perceived need to locate production facilities in important markets as the most important single factor limiting the growth of US chemical exports, and as a factor that significantly affects their decisions on investment in plant and equipment.[2] In essence, the responses indicated that, for a variety of reasons, exporting to major markets is often not as competitive as producing in those markets, and that serving export markets is not often an important reason for adding plant capacity in the United States. On the other hand, the links between US production plants and their foreign affiliates or parents facilitate US exports of products not made by the foreign plants and, perhaps, exports of products to supplement the foreign plants' production when US supplies are available at favorable prices.

In the same 1990 survey of chemical companies, increased production in Asian and other developing countries was the second most important factor inhibiting the further growth of exports. Foreign trade barriers were the third most important, but only marginally ahead of the "service and flexibility" of foreign competitors.

In ranking the factors that act to continue the inflow of US imports, the survey respondents viewed competitive foreign quality as the most important. Second was "no US source of supply" (probably referring primarily to some specialty chemicals), followed by competitive foreign service and flexibility.

In the longer term, US chemical trade performance will be very much determined by the rate of US innovations relative to those of foreign competitors, and by the costs of US-based production relative to those of competitors. A high rate of innovation, dependent on high R&D rates, provides unique new high-value-added products that can be successfully exported from US production facilities.

Many factors, including rates of investment in new production facilities and processes determine costs of production. Feedstock prices—the prices for oil and gas raw material inputs to petrochemical production—are another critically important cost factor. Taxes or other policies that drive up US feedstock costs relative to those of competitors would injure US competitiveness in chemicals.

Environmental restrictions that raise US production costs may also be an increasingly significant factor in US competitiveness. The air toxins provisions of the recently enacted Clean Air Act are projected to add almost $5 billion (in 1989 dollars) to annual chemical industry pollution abatement costs by the year 2005, raising those costs to about 2.9 percent of chemical industry shipments. Additional regulations in other areas (water, solid waste, etc.) will almost certainly raise costs still higher. Proposals for new energy taxes—some with environmental objectives—pose a major threat to the industry, both because many

---

2. The 1990 chemical industry survey is included in the manufacturing industry survey, the results of which are provided in chapter 6.

of its production processes are energy intensive and because it uses oil and gas as feedstocks in petrochemical products.

The extent to which these environmental regulations and energy taxes affect the international competitiveness of US-based chemical production will depend on the costs of US regulations and taxes compared with those of competitor countries. Comparative costs will be determined not only by the standards imposed, but by how they are imposed and by what provisions are made to offset the added costs. For example, energy and other taxes are often imposed in such a way that the initial incidence falls on the producer. This puts US-based production at a disadvantage, tending to increase imports and to discourage exports. Taxes imposed on the final product so that imports bear the same costs as domestic products do not disadvantage US-based production. Tax concessions and subsidies can also mitigate the costs of environmental compliance. Foreign governments, typically more export conscious than US administrations, may be more likely than the United States to consider the international competitiveness of their chemical industries in establishing regulations and taxes that promote a cleaner environment.

Cost disadvantages that may impair the competitiveness of the chemical industry in international markets can, over the longer term, be compensated for by dollar depreciation, albeit with undesirable effects on US living standards.

Outlook

Near-Term Outlook

In 1988 and through most of 1989, global supply-demand relationships were tight in many chemicals, prices were firm, the dollar had depreciated markedly from its earlier highs, and US chemical exports set new record highs in both years. In a 1989 survey of the chemical industry's major producers, 43 percent of the respondents indicated that "lack of capacity" was a factor in holding down the volume of US exports.

In 1990, however, the US economy slowed. That, plus the addition of new US capacity, enlarged the supply of US chemicals available for export. In the 1990 survey of the same major chemical companies, only 29 percent of the respondents indicated lack of capacity as a factor in inhibiting exports. Moreover, most of those citing capacity limitations were smaller companies with relatively small exports. In fact, only 6.4 percent of 1989 respondents with sales over $1 billion—the larger companies are the major exporters—termed lack of capacity a significant factor in restraining exports, and only 3 percent of that respondent group cited it as a significant factor in 1990.

The 1990 combination of increased availability of domestic supply, further decline in the dollar, and relatively strong global demand might have led to expectations of further growth in the 1990 US chemical trade surplus compared with the record 1989 level. In fact, however, the 1990 surplus of $16.5 billion was about $0.2 billion below the 1989 level. The surplus declined because chemical exports in 1990 rose only 4.3 percent over 1989 while imports grew by 8.5 percent.

Examination of detailed data for the first half of 1990 revealed a significant slippage (at a rate of about $1.5 billion for the year) in US exports of basic organic and inorganic chemicals to the Asian NICs as well as moderate increases in imports from them. This change appeared to reflect growing production capacity in Taiwan, Korea, and Singapore. For several years, a number of industry analysts have been projecting that new capacity being added in many developing countries—some energy rich, some not—would create global excess supplies early in the 1990s. Such excess supplies could diminish and perhaps ultimately eliminate US chemical trade surpluses.[3] Year-end 1990 data showed a decline in the basic organic chemicals surplus of about $560 million from 1989 levels. The Asian NICs were a key factor in this change. US exports to those countries were down $265 million, and imports from them up $160 million; together these changes explain about $425 million of the decline in the US organic chemicals surplus.

It is too early to project with certainty a decline in the chemical trade balance as a result of growing foreign capacity in basic industrial chemicals. In fact, US chemical exports for the first half of 1991 were up almost 14.9 percent over 1990 levels, while imports increased only by 5.5 percent. If performance continues at this rate for the full year, a surplus well above the 1990 level will result, perhaps reaching $19 billion. The export increases, however, are primarily in organic chemicals and plastics and may continue to reflect effects of the Gulf War and the US economic slowdown, which motivate increased attention to export markets by US chemical manufacturers and reduced imports. These effects are unlikely to continue much longer and, indeed, began to weaken in June 1991. Instead, growth of capacity in several developing countries clearly continues to pose a threat to traditional US exports, both to those countries that are developing new capacity and to third-country markets (Tazner, 1991, 60). Neither the actual nor the projected decline was large, and global supply and demand are difficult to project accurately. Nevertheless, the weight of the evidence is that a continuing, gradual downturn in the US basic industrial chemical

---

3. See, for example, the following: "The Far East Buildup Continues," *Chemical Week*, 20 March, 1991, 46. "Petrochemicals, Calm After the Storm," *Chemical Week*, 20 March, 1991, 34. "Petrochemical Outlook," State of the Industry Address, Second Joseph P. Leonard International Petrochemical Conference, Singapore, 20 September 1990.

trade balance, projected by many chemical industry analysts, is likely to begin soon as markets shake off the effects of the Gulf War and as new capacity continues to come on stream in the Western Pacific and elsewhere.

Rising production capabilities and living standards in developing countries should, of course, increase their demand for many specialized, higher technology chemicals that will remain beyond their production capabilities for some time. Thus, an important determinant of US trade balances with these countries may be whether their demand for imports of the more specialized chemical products rises more rapidly than their need for imports of the more basic chemicals declines.

To summarize, the Gulf War appears to have temporarily restrained the growth of basic organic chemical production by some Asian producers by interfering with their feedstock supplies, and thus to have temporarily enhanced US exports. With so many forces at work, predictions for the next few years are tenuous at best. For example, the environmental costs of US producers will rise, but the full effects of the Clean Air Act and other legislation likely in the next few years will not be reflected in industry competitiveness by 1993.

However, the chemical trade surplus will probably peak in 1991. Without further significant dollar depreciation, there seems to be little reason to expect the chemical trade surplus to grow beyond 1991. More likely, declines will begin soon and continue for several years, although the surplus will probably narrow only slowly. By 1993 the chemical trade surplus is likely to be back to or modestly below 1990 levels, although the outcome cannot be projected with confidence. More important, however, even if the surplus does not decline below 1990 levels, the gains of the 1980s will not continue. It is quite unlikely that chemicals will be a source of significant gains in manufactures trade performance for the foreseeable future, into the mid-1990s.

Longer Term Outlook

Many other factors will have important effects on US chemical trade balances during the 1990s. One is the EC 1992 process. Not only is there a large trade in chemicals between the United States and Europe, but the most important competition for US companies in third markets is often from European companies. Successful economic integration of the European Community is expected to speed European growth and raise demand there, potentially benefitting US exporters. It will, however, also tend to rationalize European production and increase its competitiveness, both in the EC market and in third-country markets. Creation of such a large trading bloc will also motivate many companies to establish production in Europe and make it more difficult for exports from the United States to compete there.

Latin America is a key market for US chemicals and one with huge unmet needs. Much of the area is, however, debt-laden and forced to restrict imports below its needs to avoid further debt increases. Growth of exports to Latin America has lagged since 1981. In 1981, US chemical exports to Latin America were $4.0 billion, 20.1 percent of total chemical exports, and the Latin American share of US chemical exports was continuing its decline, reaching 16.2 percent by 1989 (table 5.5.3). By 1990, exports to Latin America had grown by only 29 percent, to $6.2 billion, well below the 85 percent growth of total chemical exports. The US share of world chemical exports to Latin America was maintained, however, declining only modestly from 55.8 percent in 1981 to 54.6 percent in 1989. Had US chemical exports to Latin America increased at the same rate as to the rest of the world, they would have been $2.7 billion larger in 1990. A strong Latin American recovery would probably benefit US chemical exports significantly. But with some exceptions Latin American economic prospects are not bright, and rapidly growing markets in this area do not seem likely in the foreseeable future.

A North American Free Trade Agreement could benefit the US chemical industry, offering access to Mexican feedstocks, investment opportunities, and access to a growing market. Little effect on the consistent US surpluses with Mexico—$1.6 billion in 1990—seems likely, however, for several years. Chemicals is a capital-intensive industry, and lower Mexican labor costs would offer little incentive to shift to Mexico production for the US market. Nor would stricter environmental standards motivate moves to Mexico, since US companies build new facilities worldwide to meet the highest standards under which they must operate globally.

Nevertheless, direct investment in Mexico's chemical industry might be significant. Mexico has indicated a need for a $5 billion to $7 billion infusion in its petrochemical and chemical-processing industries (US Department of Commerce 1991 12–133). The long-term effects of such investment on the US-Mexican chemical trade balance would probably be positive, with Mexican growth stimulating demand for a variety of more sophisticated US chemicals.

Reduction of foreign barriers to US chemical exports would have some positive effects and should continue to be pursued. Probably more important, however, is the reduction of barriers to US direct investments abroad, a major goal of the current GATT negotiations. This is important to the chemical industry not only for the profits and license fees such investments yield but also because direct investments facilitate US exports to foreign affiliates. In the longer term, these parent-affiliate relationships are likely to be increasingly important in maintaining a strong US chemical export position.

The costs of environmental regulation in the United States and the way those costs are imposed create major uncertainties in projecting the chemical industry's long-term international competitiveness and trade performance.

Conclusions

- Chemicals make up a major portion of US manufactures trade: 13.1 percent of 1990 US manufactures exports, and 5.8 percent of imports. In 1990, exports were 39.0 billion, only slightly less than US agricultural exports, and chemicals earned a US surplus of $16.5 billion. The 1991 surplus may reach $19 billion.

- Chemicals is one of the most globalized manufacturing industries. In terms of both its world market shares and its trade surpluses, US-based chemical production is one of the most competitive of US manufacturing industries. In part this is because of the industry's extensive overseas investments and the trade flows between US producers and their foreign affiliates and parents.

- However, the relative position of the US chemical industry in world markets declined during the 1980s, and the competitive position of US based production is not strong enough to ensure continued large surpluses through the 1990s. The combination of increasing chemical production by energy-rich developing countries with very low feedstock costs and rising US production costs driven by increasing environmental restrictions and environmentally oriented energy taxes will pose continuing serious long-term threats to the competitiveness of US based chemical production in the 1990s.

- Most industry forecasters expect new sources of supply to emerge in several industrializing countries that up to now have been important markets for US exports. These new supplies will contribute to growing global overcapacity beginning in the early 1990s. This will lower global prices, intensify global competition, and tend to lower US trade surpluses.

- For a brief period late in the 1980s, US exports were modestly constrained by lack of capacity. But by the end of 1990 this was not a significant factor in holding back US chemical exports or holding up import levels.

- Enhanced ability to make direct investments in countries where such investments are now difficult, a goal of the current GATT negotiations, would aid US chemical trade performance in the longer term, increasing earnings from foreign investments and mitigating the export losses that might otherwise occur as foreign capabilities grow.

- Chemical trade is unlikely to be an important source of improved US trade performance well into the mid-1990s. At $16.5 billion, the 1990 chemical industry trade surplus was down about $0.2 billion from the 1989 record level. Based on first-half 1991 performance, a new record surplus—perhaps as much as $19 billion—seems in sight for 1991. Because US chemical trade is much affected by global supply-demand relationships, projections of future balances are tenuous. However, the industry's trade surpluses have probably peaked for the foreseeable future, and absent significant further dollar depreciation, modest declines in US surpluses seem likely for several years. A decline by 1993 to 1990 levels ($16.5 billion) or lower seems likely.

- Over the longer term, many factors will shape the industry's trade performance. These include the outcome of the GATT negotiations, negotiation of a North American Free Trade Agreement, the performance of the Latin American economies, and the costs and methods of implementing a continuing tightening of environmental regulations. With global competition continuing to increase, however, it would be optimistic to assume that chemical surpluses will continue to grow in the 1990s. Continued modest declines beyond 1993 seem more likely. In any event, chemicals is unlikely to be a source of further gains for the foreseeable future.

Bibliography

Young, Andrew, and Ian Young. 1991. "The Far East Buildup Continues." *Chemical Week* (20 March): 46–52.

Alperowicz, Natasha. 1991. "Petrochemicals: Calm After the Storm." *Chemical Week* (20 March): 34–44.

Council on Competitiveness. 1991a. "A Competitive Profile of the Drugs and Pharmaceuticals Industry." Washington: Council on Competitiveness (March).

Council on Competitiveness. 1991b. "A Competitive Profile of the Chemical and Allied Products Industry." Washington: Council on Competitiveness (March 1991).

MIT Commission on Industrial Productivity. 1989. *The Working Papers of the MIT Commission on Industrial Productivity*, vol. 1. Cambridge, MA: MIT Press.

Table 5.5.1 Chemicals: product composition of world trade, 1981–89 (billions of dollars except where noted)

SITC Product	1981	1982	1983	1984	1985	1986	1987	1988	1989	Annual growth 1981–89 (percentages)
World exports to world	123.5	117.0	122.1	131.2	136.9	162.1	195.9	238.3	246.8	9.0
of which:										
51 Organic chemicals	31.7	29.1	32.5	35.6	37.1	41.2	49.9	62.7	66.4	9.7
52 Inorganic chemicals	15.7	15.1	14.9	15.9	16.8	18.2	20.4	23.9	24.1	5.5
53 Dyes, tanning	7.2	7.0	7.2	7.3	7.7	10.2	12.8	15.1	15.9	10.4
54 Medicinal, pharmaceuticals	13.3	14.5	13.9	14.1	15.4	20.0	23.7	27.1	27.2	9.4
55 Perfume, cleaning	7.0	6.7	6.8	7.2	7.6	9.6	12.0	13.8	14.6	9.7
56 Fertilizers, manufacturing	7.1	5.9	6.1	7.2	7.4	7.4	8.4	10.1	9.7	4.0
57 Explosives, pyrotechnics	0.5	0.5	0.5	0.6	0.6	0.6	0.7	1.7	1.1	10.1
58 Plastic materials	24.7	23.8	25.6	27.7	28.1	35.6	45.0	56.4	59.4	11.6
59 Chemical materials n.e.s.	16.4	14.4	14.6	15.6	16.1	19.2	23.0	27.4	29.4	7.1
Memorandum: SITC 5 share of world manufactures exports (percentages)	12.2	12.0	12.4	12.3	12.2	11.9	11.9	12.0	11.7	Change 1981–89 −0.5

Source: World Manufactures Trade Data Base.

Table 5.5.2 Chemicals: geographic distribution of world trade, 1981–89 (percentages of total)

Country	1981	1982	1983	1984	1985	1986	1987	1988	1989	Change 1981–89
Share of exports to world										
United States	18.6	17.0	16.2	17.1	15.5	13.7	13.1	13.2	14.7	−3.9
Canada	3.2	2.9	3.0	3.2	3.0	2.5	2.4	2.6	2.6	−0.6
Japan	5.4	5.3	5.6	5.7	5.5	5.8	5.9	5.8	5.9	0.5
European Community	57.6	59.3	59.0	57.7	58.8	60.4	61.1	59.3	58.4	0.8
EC to non-EC	26.6	26.8	27.1	26.8	27.1	26.4	25.8	25.1	24.5	−2.1
Germany	17.8	18.1	18.2	17.8	17.7	19.3	19.5	18.3	17.8	0.0
France	9.8	10.0	9.7	9.6	10.0	10.3	10.4	9.9	9.7	−0.1
Italy	4.2	4.5	5.0	4.7	4.8	4.4	4.5	4.3	4.4	0.2
United Kingdom	8.8	9.1	8.6	8.4	8.9	8.8	8.8	8.5	8.2	−0.6
Other Western Europe	8.6	8.7	8.9	8.4	8.7	9.6	9.9	9.6	8.8	0.3
Asian NICs[a]	0.6	0.9	1.0	1.2	1.2	1.3	1.4	2.3	2.5	1.9
Eastern Europe[b]	1.9	1.7	1.8	1.8	2.0	1.7	1.5	1.8	1.4	−0.5
Developing countries	3.5	3.5	4.1	4.5	5.0	4.5	4.3	5.1	5.0	1.5
Latin America	1.2	1.2	1.6	1.9	1.9	1.4	1.2	1.4	1.5	0.3
Rest of world	0.3	0.3	0.2	0.2	0.2	0.3	0.2	0.4	0.4	0.2
Share of imports from world										
United States	7.7	7.9	9.0	10.5	10.6	9.2	8.2	8.2	8.4	0.7
Canada	2.8	2.7	3.3	3.4	3.1	2.8	2.6	2.7	2.8	−0.0
Japan	4.9	5.4	5.6	6.0	5.6	5.6	5.6	5.7	5.8	0.9
European Community	43.5	44.2	43.7	42.5	43.4	46.3	47.5	45.3	46.0	2.5
EC from non-EC	12.5	12.4	12.4	12.1	12.4	12.8	12.9	12.3	12.7	0.2
Germany	9.7	10.0	10.0	9.7	9.9	10.5	10.6	9.8	9.8	0.1
France	8.2	8.0	7.6	7.4	7.6	8.1	8.3	7.9	8.0	−0.2
Italy	5.6	5.8	5.9	5.8	6.0	6.5	6.7	6.5	6.6	1.0
United Kingdom	5.8	6.1	6.2	6.3	6.2	6.4	6.7	6.7	6.6	0.9
Other Western Europe	8.8	9.1	9.0	8.3	9.5	9.9	10.1	9.8	8.9	0.0
Asian NICs[a]	4.3	4.6	4.9	5.1	4.6	5.3	5.8	8.4	9.0	4.7
Eastern Europe[b]	4.0	3.7	3.3	3.1	3.3	3.1	3.1	2.9	2.7	−1.2
Developing countries	22.6	21.0	19.8	19.3	18.1	16.2	15.4	15.1	14.2	−8.4
Latin America	7.0	6.3	5.4	5.6	5.3	5.0	4.5	4.1	4.2	−2.8
Rest of world	0.2	0.3	0.3	0.4	0.4	0.4	0.3	1.4	1.1	1.0

Export share minus import share

United States	10.9	9.1	7.1	6.5	4.9	4.5	4.9	5.0	6.3	-4.6
Canada	0.4	0.2	-0.3	-0.2	-0.2	-0.3	-0.2	-0.1	-0.2	-0.6
Japan	0.5	-0.1	-0.0	-0.3	-0.1	0.2	0.3	0.1	0.1	-0.4
European Community	14.1	15.1	15.3	15.2	15.4	14.1	13.6	14.0	12.4	-1.7
Non-EC	14.1	14.4	14.7	14.7	14.7	13.6	12.9	12.9	11.8	-2.3
Germany	8.1	8.1	8.2	8.1	7.8	8.8	8.9	8.5	8.0	-0.1
France	1.6	2.0	2.0	2.2	2.4	2.2	2.1	2.0	1.7	0.1
Italy	-1.3	-1.2	-0.9	-1.0	-1.1	-2.2	-2.3	-2.2	-2.2	-0.9
United Kingdom	3.0	3.0	2.4	2.1	2.6	2.4	2.1	1.8	1.6	-1.4
Other Western Europe	-0.3	-0.4	-0.1	0.1	-0.8	-0.3	-0.2	-0.1	-0.0	0.3
Asian NICs[a]	-3.7	-3.7	-3.9	-3.9	-3.4	-4.0	-4.4	-6.1	-6.5	-2.8
Eastern Europe[b]	-2.1	-2.0	-1.5	-1.3	-1.4	-1.4	-1.6	-1.1	-1.4	0.8
Developing countries	-19.1	-17.5	-15.7	-14.8	-13.1	-11.7	-11.1	-10.0	-9.3	9.9
Latin America	-5.8	-5.1	-3.8	-3.7	-3.4	-3.6	-3.3	-2.7	-2.7	3.1
Rest of world	0.1	-0.1	-0.1	-0.3	-0.2	-0.1	-0.1	-1.0	-0.7	-0.8

a. Hong Kong, Korea, Singapore, and Taiwan.

b. Including Soviet Union.

Source: World Manufactures Trade Data Base.

Table 5.5.3 Chemicals: bilateral trade flows, 1989 (billions of dollars)

Importer	World	United States	Canada	Japan	European Community	Germany	France	United Kingdom	Asian NICs	Latin America	Other
World	246.8	36.4	6.5	14.6	144.1	43.9	24.0	20.2	6.1	3.6	35.5
United States	20.9		4.1	2.5	8.8	2.7	1.4	1.8	0.8	1.8	2.9
Canada	5.9	4.2	0.3	0.1	1.1	0.4	0.1	0.3	0.1	0.1	0.3
Japan	13.7	4.7			4.1	1.8	0.7	0.6	1.3	0.3	3.0
European Community	116.2	9.7	0.7	2.4	83.6	23.4	14.3	10.7	0.5	1.0	18.3
Germany	23.3	1.5	0.0	0.7	15.9		3.8	2.3	0.1	0.2	4.8
France	19.4	0.9	0.2	0.3	14.4	5.2		2.1	0.0	0.2	3.3
United Kingdom	15.4	1.5	0.2	0.3	10.9	3.4	2.4		0.1	0.1	2.3
Asian NICs	18.4	4.7	0.4	5.2	3.8	1.4	0.6	0.7	1.7	0.3	2.2
Latin America	10.8	5.9	0.2	0.3	3.6	1.2	0.8	0.5	0.1		0.8
Other	61.0	7.2	0.8	4.1	39.1	13.1	6.2	5.6	1.6	0.1	8.1

Source: World Manufactures Trade Data Base.

Table 5.5.4 Chemicals: product composition of US trade, 1981–90[a] (millions of dollars)

Category	SITC Rev. 2			SITC Rev. 3			
	1981	1987	Change 1981–87	1987	1990	Change 1981–90	Change 1987–90
SITC 5 Chemicals							
Exports	21,109	26,369	5,260	26,023	38,983	17,874	12,961
Imports	9,206	15,918	6,712	16,567	22,468	13,262	5,901
Balance	11,903	10,451	-1,452	9,455	16,515	4,612	7,060
of which:							
51 Organic chemicals							
Exports	5,168	6,631	1,463	7,717	10,400	5,232	2,683
Imports	2,917	4,509	1,592	5,508	7,392	4,475	1,883
Balance	2,251	2,122	-129	2,209	3,008	757	799
52 Inorganic chemicals							
Exports	3,203	3,131	-72	3,789	3,816	613	27
Imports	2,094	2,865	771	2,668	3,234	1,140	565
Balance	1,109	266	-842	1,121	582	-527	-539
53 Dyeing, tanning, and coloring							
Exports	538	641	103	952	1,588	1,050	636
Imports	339	1,068	729	1,267	1,288	950	22
Balance	199	-427	-627	-314	300	100	614
54 Medicinal and pharmaceutical products							
Exports	2,255	3,348	1,092	2,718	4,103	1,848	1,385
Imports	833	2,360	1,528	1,509	2,500	1,667	991
Balance	1,423	987	-435	1,209	1,603	180	394
55 Essential oils and perfume materials							
Exports	980	1,017	37	951	1,963	983	1,011
Imports	382	1,057	675	982	1,323	941	341
Balance	597	-40	-638	-31	639	42	671
56 Fertilizers, manufactured							
Exports	1,694	2,261	566	1,084	2,575	880	1,490
Imports	1,094	794	-300	768	955	-139	187
Balance	600	1,467	866	317	1,619	1,019	1,303
57 Explosives and pyrotechnic products				**57 Plastics in primary forms**			
Exports	90	91	0	4,033	6,429	6,338	2,395
Imports	60	107	48	1,113	1,974	1,915	862
Balance	31	-17	-48	2,920	4,454	4,424	1,534
58 Artificial resins and plastics				**58 Plastics in nonprimary forms**			
Exports	3,758	5,395	1,637	1,660	2,633	-1,125	973
Imports	733	1,893	1,161	1,327	1,773	1,041	446
Balance	3,025	3,501	477	333	860	-2,165	527
59 Chemical materials and products							
Exports	3,423	3,856	433	3,118	5,478	2,055	2,360
Imports	755	1,264	510	1,425	2,028	1,273	603
Balance	2,668	2,592	-77	1,693	3,450	781	1,756

a. Data are expressed on a domestic exports, imports customs basis. Source: US Department of Commerce.

Table 5.5.5 Chemicals: geographic composition of US trade, 1981–90[a]

	Millions of dollars				Percentages of total			
	1981	1987	1989	1990	1981	1987	1989	1990
Exports								
Canada	2,172	3,220	4,210	6,050	10.9	12.4	11.5	15.5
Japan	2,551	3,401	4,664	4,582	12.8	13.1	12.8	11.8
European Community	5,177	7,085	9,758	10,510	26.0	27.2	26.7	27.0
United Kingdom	785	1,087	1,554	1,527	3.9	4.2	4.3	3.9
Germany	927	1,177	1,515	1,775	4.7	4.5	4.2	4.6
Netherlands	1,075	1,488	2,033	2,190	5.4	5.7	5.6	5.6
Developing countries	7,392	9,306	13,450	13,762	37.1	35.8	36.9	35.3
Latin America	3,996	4,599	5,918	6,232	5.8	5.5	6.0	5.9
Mexico	1,156	1,431	2,195	2,298	5.8	5.5	6.0	5.9
Asian NICs	1,519	3,031	4,733	4,656	20.1	17.7	16.2	16.0
Total	19,925	26,022	36,485	38,983	100.0	100.0	100.0	100.0
Imports								
Canada	2,842	3,074	3,934	4,304	30.9	18.6	19.0	19.2
Japan	938	2,301	2,373	2,391	10.2	13.9	11.4	10.6
European Community	3,394	7,332	9,158	9,729	36.9	44.3	44.1	43.3
United Kingdom	738	1,503	2,030	2,072	8.0	9.1	9.8	9.2
Germany	983	2,236	2,828	3,117	10.7	13.5	13.6	13.9
France	660	1,443	1,502	1,541	7.2	8.7	7.2	6.9
Developing countries	987	2,140	3,050	3,427	10.7	12.9	14.7	15.3
Latin America	662	1,064	1,671	1,766	7.2	6.4	8.1	7.9
Mexico	233	393	582	665	2.5	2.4	2.8	3.0
Asian NICs	152	632	744	1,024	1.7	3.8	3.6	4.6
Total	9,206	16,567	20,752	22,468	100.0	100.0	100.0	100.0

a. Data are expressed on a domestic exports, imports customs basis.

Source: US Department of Commerce.

Table 5.5.6 Chemicals: US trade balances by partner country, 1981–90[a] (millions of dollars)

	Rev. 2	Rev. 3					Change
Country	1981	1983	1985	1987	1989	1990	1981–89
Canada	− 383	168	− 168	146	276	1,746	659
Japan	1,429	1,447	1,388	1,100	2,291	2,191	862
European Community	2,037	494	− 424	− 248	599	781	− 1,438
United Kingdom	− 3	− 194	− 398	− 416	− 475	− 545	− 472
Germany	− 124	− 379	− 502	− 1,059	− 1,312	− 1,342	− 1,188
Netherlands	829	469	522	907	1,321	1,423	492
France	9	− 401	− 801	− 714	− 571	649	− 580
Italy	175	31	− 149	− 79	8	7	− 167
Total developed	4,258	2,986	1,241	1,545	4,269	5,367	11
Mexico	1,361	767	957	1,037	1,613	1,633	252
Latin America	4,156	2,563	2,631	3,534	4,246	4,466	90
Asian NICs	1,266	1,514	1,321	2,398	3,988	3,632	2,722
Total developing	7,238	5,626	5,484	7,166	10,400	10,335	3,162
Total CPE	408	401	379	735	1,063	812	655
World	11,903	9,021	7,113	9,455	15,733	16,515	3,830

CPE = centrally planned economies.

a. Data are expressed on a domestic exports, imports customs basis.

Source: US Department of Commerce.

Table 5.5.7 Chemicals: indices of US competitiveness, 1981–89 (billions of dollars except where noted)

	1981	1982	1983	1984	1985	1986	1987	1988	1989	Annual growth 1981–89
World trade										
World exports to non-US destinations	114.8	108.4	111.3	118.3	123.1	147.3	179.6	218.3	225.9	8.8
World imports from non-US sources	102.3	98.2	103.6	112.0	119.3	144.0	174.6	213.5	219.8	10.0
US trade										
Exports	23.0	19.9	19.7	22.4	21.3	22.2	25.6	31.3	36.4	5.9
Imports	9.7	9.4	11.3	14.3	15.1	15.5	16.7	20.4	21.8	10.6
Balance	13.2	10.5	8.4	8.1	6.2	6.7	8.9	10.9	14.6	1.2
										Change 1981–89
US share of exports to non-US destinations (percentages)	20.0	18.4	17.7	18.9	17.3	15.1	14.3	14.4	16.1	−3.9
US share of imports from non-US sources (percentages)	9.5	9.6	10.9	12.8	12.7	10.8	9.6	9.6	9.9	0.4
Export share minus import share (percentages)	10.5	8.8	6.8	6.1	4.6	4.3	4.7	4.8	6.2	−4.3

Source: World Manufactures Trade Data Base.

Paper, Paperboard, and Articles Thereof (SITC 64)

The paper industry produces an enormous variety of products, ranging from newsprint to absorbent material for disposable diapers. The United States, historically one of the largest paper producers, is also by far the largest consumer of paper. After a significant decline in the early to mid-1980s, US trade performance in this industry began to improve in 1987. Because of large investments in upgrading and expanding US production capacity in the late 1980s and early 1990s, the US trade position should continue to improve through the mid-1990s.

Description of the Product Group

Two three-digit subcategories makeup this product group:

SITC

641 paper and paperboard

642 paper and paperboard cut to size or shape, and articles of paper or paperboard.

Unlike many classification systems, the SITC does not include pulp wood in the paper industry. Pulp wood—a basic raw material for paper production that is widely traded internationally—and waste paper are included in SITC 251 (crude materials, inedible, except fuels). In recent years the United States has had an increasing trade surplus in pulp wood and waste paper, rising from $0.2 billion in 1983 to $0.9 billion in 1988.

Role in World Trade

Size and Composition

Paper's $53.2 billion in 1989 world exports accounted for only 2.5 percent of total world manufactures exports. Paper's export dollar value placed it in the bottom third of manufacturing industries in terms of importance in world trade.

As with most basic manufactures, demand for paper products tends to closely follow changes in the growth rate of GDP. World paper exports stagnated during the early 1980s because of the sharp recession in the United States and other countries (table 5.64.1). Modest export growth in 1984 and 1985 was followed by relatively strong export growth through the rest of the 1980s. Paper exports grew by an average of 9.8 percent annually between 1981 and 1989, marginally faster than the 9.6 percent annual growth of manufactures trade.

A large majority—about four-fifths—of paper exports consists of paper and paperboard in bulk form, for example, large rolls of paper and paperboard. Cut paper products and articles of paper and paperboard account for the remaining one-fifth of world paper exports. From 1981 to 1989, exports of the more highly finished products grew by 11.2 percent annually, compared with only 9.5 percent for paper and paperboard.

Global Competition Patterns

Canada has traditionally been the largest single exporter of paper to the world, although its position has slipped somewhat in recent years (table 5.64.2). The European Community, the largest paper-exporting region, increased its share of world exports between 1981 and 1989. Germany, the largest exporter within the European Community, accounted for roughly one-third of EC exports during the period. The US share of world paper exports declined significantly during the 1980s to only 8.1 percent in 1989.

The Community's share of world paper imports during the 1980s was even larger than its share of exports, leaving it with negative export-minus-import share balances during the decade. Among Community members, Germany experienced the largest increase in share balance between 1981 and 1989 (table 5.64.2). Developing countries as a whole were the region with the most improvement. The 9.7-percentage-point improvement in their share balance, however, was largely the result of a decline in their world import share. The United States is the world's largest paper-importing country. The US export-minus-import share balance declined nearly 10 percentage points from 1981 to a low of −13.2 percentage points in 1985. The US share balance then improved by

5.5 percentage points to −7.7 percent by 1989, but remained substantially (4.3 percentage points) below the 1981 level.

Bilateral paper trade patterns are summarized in table 5.64.3. Nearly 40 percent of 1989 world exports originated in the European Community, but almost 75 percent of these went to other EC members. Germany, the second-largest exporter after Canada, exported over 70 percent of its paper products to other EC members. US exports go primarily to the European Community, Latin America, and Canada, with Japan a smaller but increasing market. The Community, Latin America, and Canada together accounted for just over 60 percent of all US exports in 1989, and Japan for an additional 12.8 percent. The United States is Canada's single largest market. US newsprint imports alone accounted for over half of Canadian paper exports.

Role in US Trade

Recent Performance

Paper products constituted only 1.7 percent of 1990 US manufactures exports and 2.2 percent of imports (table 4.9).

The United States consistently runs deficits in its paper trade, principally because of the very large newsprint imports included in the product group. US paper trade deficits grew from $0.9 billion in 1981 to $4.2 billion in 1987, before falling to $3.5 billion in 1990 (table 5.64.4).

Paper ranked in the middle third of all manufacturing industries examined in terms of value of US exports and US imports. US paper exports, despite a slump in the early to mid-1980s, grew modestly between 1981 and 1987 (table 5.64.4), and improved substantially between 1987 and 1990. Paper imports nearly doubled between 1981 and 1987, causing a $3.3 billion 1981–87 expansion in the paper trade deficit. After 1987, import growth slowed dramatically and the deficit narrowed modestly.

In addition to the items covered in this analysis, the US paper industry exports large quantities of pulp wood and waste paper. The US trade balance in wood pulp and waste paper improved by $0.8 billion between 1983 and 1988, with exports growing from $1.7 billion in 1983 to $3.7 billion in 1988. Imports of wood pulp and waste paper grew more slowly, from $1.5 billion in 1983 to $2.7 billion in 1988. Waste paper constituted just under 20 percent of SITC 251 exports but was a negligible part of imports. Data for wood pulp and waste paper (SITC 251) were not included in the WMTDB. Statistics for US trade in these items are taken from American Paper Institute (1989).

US paper exports are largely paper and packaging materials of relatively low value, which are sent primarily to Asia and Latin America (table 5.64.5). Exports to both Japan and Mexico increased relatively rapidly during the 1980s. The market-oriented, sector-specific (MOSS) negotiations produced significant tariff and nontariff concessions that aided exports to Japan. Exports to Mexico were boosted by recent tariff and nontariff concessions made by that country upon its entry into the GATT. Exports to the Asian NICs, an important US market, also grew substantially faster than average.

Canada is the dominant source of US paper imports. Canada alone provided over 85 percent of total US paper imports in 1981 (table 5.64.5). By 1990, however, Canada's share had declined to 74.0 percent. Newsprint is the single largest imported paper product, with imports from Canada accounting for roughly 55 percent of US newsprint consumption. The US Commerce Department reports that the United States imported roughly $4.4 billion of newsprint in 1989 and 1990. Newsprint imports constituted just over 50 percent of all US paper imports in 1990.

International Competitiveness

The $2.6 billion increase in the US deficit in paper trade in 1981–1990 reflects a decline in US market competitiveness. Although US producers lost some market share in the United States to foreign producers, the decline in US competitiveness manifested itself largely in poor export performance rather than an increase in the share of imports in the domestic market.

World exports to non-US destinations increased 9.5 percent annually between 1981 and 1989 (table 5.64.6). US exports grew much more slowly, only 5 percent per year. This resulted in a decline in the US share of exports to non-US destinations from 13.8 percent to 9.7 percent between 1981 and 1989. Meanwhile, the US share of imports from non-US sources—a measure of the importance of the US market to exporters outside the United States—remained stable, increasing only from 17.2 percent to 17.3 percent. US export and import performance in this period combined to cause a deterioration in the US share balance of 4.2 percentage points (table 5.64.6). However, nearly all of the change arose from the decline in the US share of world exports to non-US destinations.

Outlook

Key Determinants of US Trade Performance

Several factors will influence the competitiveness of US-based paper production in international markets and US trade performance in the 1990s. Environmental issues, including recycling and emissions (especially dioxins), are particularly important. A growing number of cities and countries require that newspapers be recycled and that newsprint used within their jurisdictions be produced from recycled materials. These regulations as well as increasing voluntary recycling efforts have produced major changes in the newsprint segment of the industry. The US Commerce Department estimates that one-third of the primary paper and paperboard mills in the United States now use waste paper as their primary fiber input. An additional 50 percent use waste materials for between 10 percent and 50 percent of their papermaking inputs.

Although there is already substantial use of recycled materials, mandatory and voluntary recycling programs have made recycled inputs available more rapidly than manufacturers have been able to incorporate them into production. In response, firms are expanding their capacity to use recycled materials. At least 37 planned expansions of mills that will use recycled paper and paperboard were announced in 1990, according to the US Commerce Department (1991). In addition, the *Journal of Commerce* reports that an estimated $1.1 billion will be spent between 1991 and 1995 to expand US deinking capacity, a major bottleneck to greater use of recycled materials (Harper 1991).

During the 1970s, the paper industry was hit relatively hard by clean air and water regulations and was one of the larger investors in environmental improvements during that period. From 1989 to 1991, spending by the paper industry on environmental improvements exceeded $1.25 billion—roughly 2.6 percent of the industry's total investment. This represented about 7 percent of total environmental outlays by US industries during the period.

Reducing dioxin levels in discharge water and trace amounts in paper products has been a primary concern in the industry. Reductions in the use of chlorine bleach in the production process and other relatively inexpensive changes have already reduced emissions of dioxin significantly. Additional reductions will be relatively more expensive as producers switch to other bleaching agents. Expenditures on reducing dioxin emissions are one example of costs that US producers sometimes face—to meet environmental, health, safety, or other regulations—that overseas producers often can avoid. The American Paper Institute estimates that the paper industry will spend more than $1 billion on R&D and in capital costs to address the dioxin issue.

A second factor influencing the competitiveness of the US paper industry into the 1990s is the plant and equipment investments made by the industry in the middle to late 1980s. Partly in response to increased penetration of the domestic market by foreign products, US paper manufacturers have recently made substantial investments to improve technology and expand production capacity. Between 1989 and 1991, investment expenditures in the paper industry have amounted to more than 10 percent of the value of industry shipments. This compares with 3.6 percent for all manufacturing in 1989 (Chemical Manufacturers Association 1990, tables 2.4 and 5.2). As a result of these investments, US plants are today fully cost competitive with production elsewhere in the world. With some excess capacity as a result of recent expansions, US producers are in a good position to take advantage of expanding opportunities in overseas markets.

A final factor that will affect the competitiveness of US manufacturers into the 1990s is the European Community's treatment of paper producers in the member countries of the European Free Trade Association (EFTA). The Scandinavian members of EFTA are major paper producers and enjoy relatively free access to EC markets. For example, the European Community imposes a 9 percent tariff on printing and writing papers, except for imports from EFTA members. Thus, although imports account for 31 percent of the EC market for paper and paperboard products, EFTA members supply about 80 percent of these imports. Elimination of the uneven tariff treatment for non-EFTA members would strengthen the US competitive position relative to EFTA producers and would increase the share of US paper in EC imports.

Outlook Through 1993

Recent trends in the US and foreign paper industries bode well for US producers in world competition. The decline of the dollar since 1985 and large capital investments in recent years have resulted in a US industry that is fully cost competitive with other major world producers. Indeed, production costs—particularly labor costs—have been rising more rapidly in Canada than in the United States. The changing relative position of US and Canadian manufacturers are reflected in the lower share of Canadian newsprint in US consumption. Much recent investment has been brought about by a change in the outlook of US producers. US manufacturers have focused mostly on the domestic market; exports have been only about 6.5 percent of shipments in recent years. However, increasing foreign competition in domestic markets, combined with the relatively sluggish growth in the domestic market, has forced US producers to look increasingly to overseas markets for growth in sales.

Even at current exchange rates, US trade performance in paper products should continue to improve. With their current excess capacity, US producers are in a good position to respond to increases in domestic and foreign demand without substantial increases in investment. Paper's US import price elasticity of demand (equal to -0.9, according to DRI estimates) places it in the middle range of industries in terms of responsiveness to changes in the dollar exchange rate (see the appendix to this volume). Additional devaluation, by increasing the US dollar price of imports, would result in roughly proportionate declines in the value of US paper imports. The DRI elasticity estimates also indicate that additional devaluation relative to the European currencies would proportionately increase the value of US exports to Europe. Devaluation against the yen, however, would result in a much less than proportionate increase in US paper exports to Japan.

It is difficult to predict the effects of several trends in the industry. Until recently, plastics have increasingly substituted for paper in containers and packaging. Growing concern about the lack of biodegradability of plastics, however, seems to have slowed this trend. McDonald's Corp.'s decision to halt the use of foam containers for its products is one example. However, the issue will continue to be a source of controversy, with the ultimate choice depending on relative prices, regulations, the success of the plastics industry in implementing effective recycling programs, and public perceptions of how packaging waste is handled.

Whereas environmental considerations are perceived as favoring paper rather than plastic in some products, its use in other products has raised environmental concerns. Lack of biodegradability and recycling difficulties have raised concerns about at least two products containing substantial inputs from the paper industry: disposable diapers and aseptic beverage containers. Some local governments have already attempted to ban the sale of these products.

The trade balance in paper products is likely to improve by $1.5 billion to $2.5 billion between 1990 and 1993, still leaving a $1 billion to $2 billion deficit. US imports will probably continue to be weak over the period, with stable or declining imports through 1992 before a return to growth in 1993. Export growth, on the other hand, fueled by relatively strong overseas growth in demand for paper, should continue to be relatively robust over the period.

Longer Term Outlook

The US paper industry is in a good position to maintain its competitive position beyond 1993. Recent and planned capital expenditures on US manufacturing facilities should allow US producers to remain fully cost competitive with major overseas competitors. In the absence of unfavorable exchange rate movements, the paper trade balance should continue to improve modestly.

Removal of unfavorable tariff treatment of non-EFTA imports by the European Community would significantly improve US export prospects to this important market and could greatly enhance the US trade position. Further expansion in the use of recycled paper products in the United States and abroad would also enhance the US paper trade position by reducing paper imports. The United States is the world leader in paper production using recycled inputs. US producers, who have invested heavily in expanding their production capacity to use recycled materials, lead foreign competitors in this area and are in a good position to exploit this growing market.

Conclusions

- World paper exports of $53.2 billion in 1989 were 2.5 percent of world manufactures exports, placing paper toward the bottom of the manufactures product groups in terms of share of world exports. Although less important than many industries in world trade, the paper industry was relatively more important in US trade, constituting 1.7 percent of 1990 manufactures exports and 2.2 percent of manufactures imports. Paper ranks near the middle in terms of value of US exports and imports.

- An increase of over $3 billion in paper's trade deficit contributed significantly to the deterioration in the US trade position between 1981 and 1987. Pulp wood and waste paper are related materials but are classed in another SITC product group. Including these items in the paper trade figures would reduce the decline in trade performance somewhat. The industry's 1987 deficit, for example, would be reduced by $0.8 billion, to $2.4 billion. Waste paper contributed $0.5 billion of the $0.8 billion surplus in wood pulp and waste paper in 1987.

- The dominant factor in US trade in paper products is imports of Canadian newsprint. In recent years, Canada has supplied over 70 percent of total US imports of paper products. By far the greater part has been newsprint. Imports from Canada supply roughly 55 percent of US newsprint consumption.

- Environmental concerns will have important effects on the paper industry in the 1990s. One of the largest changes will be in the market for newsprint. Regulations mandating the use of recycled materials in newsprint production, combined with rapid increases in the availability of recycled inputs, will continue to cause rapid shifts in the types of inputs used in paper production, particularly newsprint production. The shift to newsprint with greater recycled content will favor US producers in the domestic market. A continuing decline in the share of imported newsprint in US consumption is likely. However, growth in newsprint use will hold the absolute volume of newsprint imports about constant.

- Large investments already made to improve technology and increase capacity will benefit the US paper industry in the 1990s. These investments have allowed US producers to be fully cost competitive with major world producers. US cost competitiveness and modest excess capacity should allow US producers to rapidly exploit any additional marketing opportunities that arise overseas or domestically. The excess capacity will gradually be eliminated over the next three or four years.

■ US paper exports in 1990 were $5.0 billion, and imports $8.5 billion, yielding a trade deficit of $3.5 billion. Relatively weak import growth and stable export growth should allow the paper industry's trade balance to improve in the early to mid-1990s. An improvement of between $1.5 billion and $2.5 billion is likely between 1990 and 1993, but this will probably not be enough to generate a surplus in paper by 1993.

■ The US paper industry's large investment in upgrading and expanding production facilities will continue to give US producers an important competitive edge beyond 1993. Continuing investment, especially in capacity devoted to making products from recycled inputs, combined with a relative increase in demand for products manufactured from recycled inputs, should provide the basis for continuing modest improvement in the US paper trade balance beyond 1993.

■ Trade in wood pulp and waste paper (SITC 251) produced a surplus of $0.9 billion in 1988. Although US trade in waste paper was substantially smaller than trade in wood pulp, the huge surplus of waste paper exports over imports accounted for $0.5 billion of the surplus in wood pulp and waste paper.

■ Mandatory recycling programs in the United States are likely to add to the waste paper available for recycling and export. With the supply of waste paper growing more rapidly than the ability to use it in paper production, however, the price will remain low. Therefore, although export volumes of waste paper are likely to grow rapidly, waste paper's low value will prevent it from adding substantially to the trade surplus in wood pulp and waste paper.

Bibliography

American Paper Institute. 1989. *Statistics of Paper, Paperboard, and Wood Pulp.* New York: American Paper Institute.

Chemical Manufacturers Association. 1990. *U.S. Chemical Industry Statistical Handbook.* Washington: Chemical Manufacturers Association.

Harper, Douglas C. 1991. "Recyclers of Newspapers Are Rolling in Dough." *Journal of Commerce* (11 March): 11a.

US Department of Commerce, International Trade Administration. 1991. *U.S. Industrial Outlook.* Washington: US Department of Commerce.

Table 5.64.1 Paper, paperboard, and articles: product composition of world trade, 1981–89
(billions of dollars except where noted)

SITC Product	1981	1982	1983	1984	1985	1986	1987	1988	1989	Annual growth 1981–89 (percentages)
World exports to world of which:	25.2	23.8	23.6	26.1	27.5	33.9	42.2	50.3	53.2	9.8
641 Paper and paperboard	20.2	18.8	18.6	20.8	21.7	26.6	33.3	39.7	41.8	9.5
642 Cut paper and articles	5.0	4.8	4.8	5.0	5.4	7.0	8.6	10.6	11.6	11.2
										Change 1981–89
Memorandum: SITC 64 share of world manufactures exports (percentages)	2.5	2.4	2.4	2.4	2.4	2.5	2.6	2.5	2.5	0.0

Source: World Manufactures Trade Data Base.

Table 5.64.2 Paper, paperboard, and articles: geographic distribution of world trade, 1981–89 (percentages of total)

Country	1981	1982	1983	1984	1985	1986	1987	1988	1989	Change 1981–89
Share of exports to world										
United States	11.7	11.1	10.8	10.0	8.5	7.7	7.5	7.7	8.1	-3.6
Canada	17.6	17.3	17.6	18.3	18.3	15.8	14.7	14.4	14.9	-2.7
Japan	3.5	3.6	3.7	3.8	3.8	3.5	3.3	3.2	3.1	-0.4
European Community	33.4	34.6	34.7	34.3	35.0	37.5	38.4	37.7	38.3	4.9
EC to non-EC	9.5	9.5	9.9	10.7	11.0	10.5	10.4	10.4	10.6	1.1
Germany	10.7	11.8	12.3	12.2	12.6	13.7	14.1	13.7	13.9	3.2
France	5.8	5.8	5.8	5.9	5.9	6.3	6.4	6.1	6.3	0.5
Italy	3.2	3.1	2.9	3.3	3.2	3.4	3.4	3.4	3.8	0.6
United Kingdom	3.6	3.7	3.5	3.5	3.6	3.6	3.8	3.9	3.8	0.3
Other Western Europe	30.7	30.1	29.8	29.6	30.7	31.2	31.5	30.9	29.8	-0.9
Asian NICs[a]	0.6	0.9	1.0	1.0	1.0	1.1	1.1	2.0	1.9	1.3
Eastern Europe[b]	0.7	0.6	0.6	0.5	0.5	0.6	0.6	0.6	0.5	-0.2
Developing countries	1.2	1.3	1.6	2.4	2.2	2.5	2.5	3.0	2.8	1.6
Latin America	0.8	0.9	1.1	1.7	1.4	1.6	1.6	1.9	1.7	1.0
Rest of world	0.0	0.0	0.0	0.0	0.1	0.1	0.1	0.4	0.4	0.4
Share of imports from world										
United States	15.1	15.9	17.7	21.3	21.7	18.7	17.3	16.7	15.8	0.7
Canada	2.3	2.3	2.7	2.9	2.7	2.5	2.3	2.6	2.7	0.4
Japan	1.8	2.1	2.1	2.0	1.9	2.1	2.0	2.2	2.3	0.4
European Community	48.7	49.1	48.6	46.5	46.4	51.4	53.5	52.9	54.4	5.7
EC from non-EC	25.0	24.7	24.3	23.3	22.8	24.9	25.9	26.0	26.1	1.1
Germany	11.4	11.0	10.9	10.5	10.2	11.8	11.9	11.3	10.7	-0.7
France	7.9	8.1	8.1	7.6	7.5	8.6	8.7	8.6	8.3	0.5
Italy	2.9	3.1	3.4	3.5	3.5	3.9	4.4	4.0	4.2	1.3
United Kingdom	11.8	11.8	11.7	11.1	11.2	11.1	12.0	12.5	11.7	-0.0
Other Western Europe	6.1	6.2	6.4	6.0	6.4	7.2	7.4	7.3	6.8	0.7
Asian NICs[a]	2.2	2.4	2.6	2.7	2.6	2.8	2.9	3.9	4.4	2.2
Eastern Europe[b]	4.0	4.0	3.3	2.8	3.1	2.6	2.2	2.2	2.2	-1.8
Developing countries	17.7	16.1	14.7	13.5	13.2	11.1	10.6	10.2	9.6	-8.1
Latin America	6.0	5.2	4.5	4.1	3.6	3.2	3.1	3.1	3.2	-2.8
Rest of world	0.1	0.0	0.0	0.0	0.0	0.0	0.0	0.2	0.1	0.0

Export share minus import share

United States	−3.4	−4.8	−7.0	−11.3	−13.2	−11.0	−9.8	−9.0	−7.7	−4.3
Canada	15.3	15.1	15.0	15.4	15.5	13.3	12.4	11.8	12.1	3.1
Japan	1.7	1.5	1.6	1.8	1.9	1.4	1.4	1.0	0.8	−0.9
European Community	−15.3	−14.5	−14.0	−12.2	−11.4	−13.9	−15.0	−15.2	−16.1	−0.7
Non-EC	−15.6	−15.2	−14.4	−12.6	−11.8	−14.4	−15.6	−15.7	−15.5	0.1
Germany	−0.7	0.9	1.4	1.6	2.5	1.9	2.1	2.4	3.2	3.9
France	−2.1	−2.3	−2.3	−1.7	−1.6	−2.3	−2.3	−2.5	−2.0	0.1
Italy	0.3	−0.0	−0.5	−0.2	−0.3	−0.4	−0.9	−0.6	−0.5	−0.8
United Kingdom	−8.2	−8.1	−8.2	−7.7	−7.6	−7.5	−8.2	−8.6	−7.9	0.3
Other Western Europe	24.6	23.9	23.5	23.6	24.3	24.0	24.1	23.6	23.0	−1.6
Asian NICs[a]	−1.6	−1.5	−1.5	−1.7	−1.5	−1.7	−1.8	−1.9	−2.4	−0.9
Eastern Europe[b]	−3.3	−3.4	−2.8	−2.3	−2.5	−2.0	−1.6	−1.6	−1.7	1.6
Developing countries	−16.5	−14.8	−13.1	−11.1	−11.0	−8.6	−8.1	−7.2	−6.8	9.7
Latin America	−5.2	−4.3	−3.4	−2.4	−2.3	−1.6	−1.5	−1.3	−1.5	3.8
Rest of world	−0.1	0.0	0.0	0.0	0.0	0.0	0.0	0.2	0.3	0.4

a. Hong Kong, Korea, Singapore, and Taiwan.

b. Including Soviet Union.

Source: World Manufactures Trade Data Base.

Table 5.64.3 Paper, paperboard, and articles: bilateral trade flows, 1989 (billions of dollars)

Importer	World	United States	Canada	Japan	European Community	Germany	France	United Kingdom	Asian NICs	Latin America	Other
World	53.2	4.3	7.9	1.6	20.4	7.4	3.4	2.0	1.0	0.9	17.1
United States	9.0		6.5	0.3	0.8	0.3	0.1	0.1	0.2	0.5	0.8
Canada	1.1	0.8		0.0	0.2	0.0	0.0	0.0	0.0	0.0	0.1
Japan	1.2	0.5	0.2		0.1	0.1	0.0	0.0	0.1	0.0	0.3
European Community	28.1	0.6	0.5	0.2	14.8	5.1	2.5	1.3	0.0	0.3	11.5
Germany	6.0	0.1	0.1	0.1	2.7		0.8	0.3	0.0	0.1	2.9
France	4.6	0.0	0.0	0.0	3.1	1.3		0.3	0.0	0.0	1.3
United Kingdom	6.2	0.2	0.3	0.0	2.4	1.0	0.5		0.4	0.1	3.1
Asian NICs	2.2	0.5	0.1	0.6	0.2	0.1	0.0	0.1		0.0	0.4
Latin America	1.8	1.2	0.3	0.0	0.2	0.0	0.1	0.0	0.0		0.2
Other	9.8	0.7	0.3	0.4	4.1	1.8	0.6	0.5	0.3	0.0	3.8

Source: World Manufactures Trade Data Base.

Table 5.64.4 Paper, paperboard, and articles: product composition of US trade, 1981–90[a] (millions of dollars except where noted)

		SITC Rev. 2			SITC Rev. 3			
Category	1981	1987	Change 1981–87	1987	1990	Change 1981–90	Change 1987–90
Total							
Exports	2,946	3,166	220	3,092	4,992	2,045	1,899
Imports	3,832	7,382	3,550	7,249	8,510	4,678	1,261
Balance	− 886	− 4,216	− 3,330	− 4,157	− 3,519	− 2,632	638
of which:							
641 Paper and paperboard							
Exports	2,192	2,430	238	2,382	3,590	1,398	1,208
Imports	3,529	6,595	3,066	6,514	7,666	4,137	1,152
Balance	− 1,337	− 4,165	− 2,828	− 4,132	− 4,076	− 2,739	56
642 Cut paper and articles							
Exports	754	736	− 18	710	1,402	648	692
Imports	302	787	485	735	845	543	110
Balance	452	− 51	− 503	− 25	557	105	582

a. Data are expressed on a domestic exports, imports customs basis.

Source: US Department of Commerce.

Table 5.64.5 Paper, paperboard, and articles: geographic composition of US trade, 1981–90[a]

	Millions of dollars				Percentages of total			
	1981	1987	1989	1990	1981	1987	1989	1990
Exports								
Canada	520	591	739	1,315	17.7	19.1	17.6	26.3
Japan	259	399	536	512	8.8	12.9	12.8	10.3
European Community	555	477	634	787	18.8	15.4	15.1	15.8
United Kingdom	177	136	194	224	6.0	4.4	4.6	4.5
Germany	113	81	102	153	3.8	2.6	2.4	3.1
France	60	32	46	63	2.0	1.0	1.1	1.3
Italy	42	65	72	91	1.4	2.1	1.7	1.8
Latin America	841	796	1,148	1,218	28.5	25.7	27.4	24.4
Mexico	341	335	616	630	11.6	10.8	14.7	12.6
Asian NICs	115	250	419	450	3.9	8.1	10.0	9.0
Other	656	579	719	710	22.3	18.7	17.1	14.2
Total	2,946	3,092	4,195	4,992	100.0	100.0	100.0	100.0
Imports								
Canada	3,325	5,142	6,204	6,300	86.8	70.9	72.6	74.0
Japan	66	219	220	238	1.7	3.0	2.6	2.8
European Community	139	663	785	826	3.6	9.1	9.2	9.7
United Kingdom	45	127	141	157	1.2	1.8	1.6	1.8
Germany	30	253	320	293	0.8	3.5	3.7	3.4
France	31	79	108	121	0.8	1.1	1.3	1.4
Italy	7	67	55	70	0.2	0.9	0.6	0.8
Latin America	125	335	445	267	3.3	4.6	5.2	3.1
Mexico	88	257	376	193	2.3	3.5	4.4	2.3
Asian NICs	55	168	167	169	1.4	2.3	2.0	2.0
Other	122	722	728	710	3.2	10.0	8.5	8.3
Total	3,832	7,249	8,549	8,510	100.0	100.0	100.0	100.0

a. Data are expressed on a domestic exports, imports customs basis.

Source: US Department of Commerce.

Table 5.64.6 Paper, paperboard, and articles: indices of US competitiveness, 1981–89 (billions of dollars except where noted)

	1981	1982	1983	1984	1985	1986	1987	1988	1989	Annual growth 1981–89 (percentages)
World trade										
World exports to non-US destinations	21.4	20.0	19.4	20.5	21.6	27.6	34.9	41.7	44.2	9.5
World imports from non-US sources	23.2	22.1	22.0	24.7	26.5	32.9	40.9	48.2	52.1	10.6
US trade										
Exports	2.9	2.6	2.5	2.6	2.3	2.6	3.2	3.9	4.3	5.0
Imports	4.0	4.0	4.4	5.9	6.3	6.7	7.7	8.8	9.0	10.7
Balance	−1.1	−1.4	−1.9	−3.3	−4.0	−4.1	−4.5	−4.9	−4.7	
										Change 1981–89
US share of exports to non-US destinations (percentages)	13.8	13.2	13.1	12.7	10.8	9.4	9.1	9.3	9.7	−4.1
US share of imports from non-US sources (percentages)	17.2	17.9	19.9	23.7	23.7	20.3	18.8	18.2	17.3	0.1
Export share minus import share (percentages)	−3.4	−4.7	−6.8	−11.0	−12.9	−10.9	−9.7	−8.9	−7.6	−4.2

Source: World Manufactures Trade Data Base.

Textiles (SITC 65)

Concern about the international trade performance of the textile and apparel industries emerged earlier than in most other US manufacturing industries. The two industries are closely linked, with a majority of the output of the US textile industry going to the apparel industry. Textiles and apparel combined have a share of world manufactures trade second only to that of road vehicles. Textiles and apparel are also among the most closely watched and politically sensitive industries in international trade.

Description of the Product Group

In addition to a wide variety of fabrics, the textile industry produces a large number of products used as inputs by other industries—for example, tire cord. It also includes many final products such as carpets, tents, and rope. Textiles, as defined in SITC 65, is divided into the following three-digit subcategories.

SITC

651 textile yarn

652 cotton fabrics, woven (not including narrow or special fabrics)

653 fabrics, woven, of man-made textile materials (not including narrow or special fabrics)

654 other textile fabrics, woven (for example from silk or wool)

655 knitted or crocheted fabrics (including tubular knit fabrics, not elsewhere specified, pile fabrics, and open-work fabrics), not elsewhere specified

656 tulles, lace embroidery, ribbons, trimmings, and other small wares

657 special yarns, special textile fabrics, and related products (for example, rubberized fabrics, rope, cord, and conveyor belts)

658 made-up articles, wholly or chiefly of textile materials, not elsewhere specified (for example tarps, tents, bed linens, and curtains)

659 floor coverings, etc.

Role in World Trade

Size and Composition

World textile exports of $81.8 billion in 1989 accounted for 3.9 percent of all world manufactures exports, down from 4.3 percent in 1981 (table 5.65.1). This decline is the result of textiles' somewhat lower export growth rate relative to all manufactures.

Three of the three-digit product subcategories accounted for roughly 60 percent of world textile exports in 1989. Textile yarn, the largest of the export subcategories, accounted for one-quarter of the total. Two other subcategories— cotton fabrics and fabrics made from man-made fibers—accounted for another third. The relative importance of the three-digit subcategories remained essentially unchanged over the 1981–89 period.

Global Competition Patterns

The European Community is the largest exporting and importing region, accounting for roughly one-half of textile exports and imports between 1981 and 1989 (table 5.65.2). With its export share slightly exceeding its import share, the Community had a small positive export-minus-import share balance during the 1980s. EC intratrade is an important factor in the Community's large export and import shares. Nearly two-thirds of EC exports in 1989 went to other EC members (table 5.65.3).

Japan, which had the second-largest 1981 export share after the European Community, experienced a significant decline in exports between 1981 and 1989. This accounted for most of the decline in Japan's share balance position during the 1980s. Like Japan, the United States suffered a decline in its share balance position primarily because its export share fell. The US share of world textile exports declined steadily, falling by nearly half between 1981 and 1989 to 4.8 percent.

Both the Asian NICs and the developing countries as a group showed significant improvement in their share balances. The NICs' export share tripled between 1981 and 1989, overcoming a large increase in their import share and improving their share balance position significantly. The developing countries saw an improvement in their share balance between 1981 and 1989 that was far larger than that of any other region. Just over 20 percent of the improvement came from an increase in their export share. For most other industries analyzed in this study, the improved share balance of the developing countries has resulted almost entirely from falling shares of world imports, which typically have reflected debt problems and limited access to foreign exchange rather than improved market competitiveness.

Key Determinants of World Trade Patterns

International trade in apparel and textiles is governed by the Multi-Fiber Arrangement (MFA), which permits some deviation from GATT principles. Established in the mid-1970s, the MFA restricted trade in textiles and apparel made from cotton and man-made fibers. Implemented in the face of rising protectionist sentiment in the United States and Europe, the MFA was designed as a way to increase protection while placing limits on the extent of the restrictions. The MFA has been renewed and revised several times and broadened to cover more products. Renewal of the current MFA agreement, due in 1991, has been postponed pending the outcome of the Uruguay Round negotiations in the GATT.

The MFA is implemented through bilateral negotiations between MFA members that set maximum quantities of specific products to be imported. MFA agreements have been used almost exclusively to restrict textile exports from developing to developed countries, particularly to the United States and the European Community. The MFA gives some flexibility to exporting countries subject to quota restrictions. Because the MFA provides for quantity restrictions, usually expressed in square-meter-equivalents, rather than value restrictions, countries that export products subject to MFA agreements have often switched their exports to items of higher unit value. This has enabled them to increase the value of their exports without significantly increasing their volume of exports. In addition, US importers can switch their imports from countries that are bound by MFA quotas to those that have not filled their quotas or that have no quota restrictions. By the early 1980s, the United States had established quotas for some 80 percent of textile and apparel imports from developing countries. Many of the countries granted quotas, however, do not use them fully.

Agreements under the MFA place greater trade restrictions on apparel than on textiles. The MFA governs roughly 40 percent of world apparel trade but only about 14 percent of world textile trade. A variety of other bilateral and unilateral restrictions govern much of world textiles and apparel trade not subject to MFA regulations.

Role in US Trade

Recent Performance

US textile exports of $5.0 billion in 1990 accounted for 2.0 percent of US manufactures exports, while US imports of $6.4 billion accounted for 1.6 percent of US manufactures imports. After a sharp decline between 1981 and 1987, the US trade balance in textiles improved by $1.5 billion between 1987 and 1990. Yet the US deficit remained over $1 billion in 1990.

US textile exports are concentrated in only a few of the three-digit trade subcategories (table 5.65.4). Textile yarns, man-made textile fabrics, and specialty yarns and textile fabrics account for over 60 percent of the total. Textile yarn alone accounted for 24.9 percent of US textile exports in 1990.

US textile imports are also concentrated in a few subcategories. Cotton fabrics, man-made textile fabrics, and made-up articles of textile materials together accounted for over one-half of total US textile imports during the 1980s (table 5.65.4). Cotton fabrics is the single largest import subcategory, accounting for 17.5 percent of US textile imports in 1990.

Canada is the largest single-country market for US textiles exports (table 5.65.5), absorbing 18.4 percent of the total in 1981 and 24.3 percent in 1990. The other important export markets for US textiles are Latin America and the European Community. There was little change in the relative importance of US export markets during the 1980s.

The European Community is the largest source of US textile imports, accounting for roughly one-quarter of the total. Japan, the second-largest source of US imports in 1981, became a less significant import source during the 1980s, its share declining from 17.7 percent in 1981 to 9.0 percent in 1990. The import share of the Asian NICs, the other major source of US textile imports, remained about the same at 17.9 percent in 1990. China's share has been rising and reached 10.3 percent in 1990.

International Competitiveness

US textile exports increased by only 1 percent annually between 1981 and 1989. At the same time, world exports to non US destinations rose 8 percent annually (table 5.65.6). With US exports stagnant in the face of an expanding market, the US share of textile exports to non-US destinations fell sharply, from 8.9 percent in 1981 to 5.2 percent in 1989.

After dipping briefly in the early 1980s, the US share of world imports from non US sources rose steadily through the mid-1980s before leveling off late in the decade at 8.4 percent, only modestly above the 7.7 percent 1981 level (table 5.65.6). The increase in US textile imports in the mid-1980s provided an expanding market for exports of other countries. The US share balance position, a rough indicator of US market competitiveness, declined during the 1980s, mostly as a result of a decline in the US share of exports to non-US destinations.

Outlook

Key Determinants of US Trade Performance

The textile and apparel industries are unique among US manufacturing industries in that they have received significant protection from imports for an extended period.

As with apparel, the rapid appreciation of the dollar was a main cause of the surge in US textiles imports noted earlier. The rise in the value of the dollar, particularly against the currencies of the Asian NICs, seriously hampered the ability of US producers to compete against foreign producers. The surge of imports occurred despite the import restrictions imposed under MFA agreements. Several years of relatively weak demand during the early 1980s led to many of the import quotas not being filled. This provided room for the rapid import expansion of the mid-1980s. DRI data support the importance of import price changes in determining trade flows. An estimated import price elasticity of -1.1 indicates that a rise in the dollar's value causes a more than proportionate increase in US textile imports (see the appendix to this volume).

The rate of import growth slackened between 1987 and 1990, for several reasons. The devaluation of the dollar in the latter half of the 1980s reduced the competitive disadvantage that US producers had faced in the early 1980s. Import restrictions also became more effective. As a result of the rapid import growth of the mid-1980s, many countries had filled their import quotas, and this effectively limited further expansion. Also, 1987 was the first full year of trade under a 1986 renegotiation of the MFA that many analysts feel further tightened import restrictions.

US trade performance in textiles depends largely on international agreements governing textiles and apparel trade and on exchange rates, which set the relative prices of US- and foreign-produced goods. US textile producers also face competitive pressures because of the relative decline in their sales to US apparel producers, their primary market. During the 1980s, the US-produced share of US apparel consumption fell. This reduced the demand for both imported and domestically produced textile inputs. Thus, although higher apparel imports represented lost opportunities to domestic textile producers, there was a slight positive effect on the textile trade balance because demand for imported textile inputs was lower. Higher apparel imports, of course, increase the apparel deficit.

The movement of apparel production overseas has theoretically expanded export opportunities for US textile producers by increasing foreign demand for textile inputs imported from the United States. Thus, other things equal, a shift of apparel production overseas tends to improve the trade balance in textiles. The overall effect on US textile production, however, is strongly negative because foreign-produced apparel uses a much smaller percentage of US-produced textiles than does US-produced apparel. Therefore, the shift of apparel production overseas has both reduced the size of the market for US-produced textiles and shifted textiles marketing opportunities from the United States to foreign countries.

The shift in apparel production to foreign locations was accompanied by a decline in the prices of imported textiles relative to domestically produced textiles caused by the appreciation of the dollar during the early 1980s. This caused the share of US-produced textiles used in both domestic and overseas production of apparel to decline, increasing textile imports and reducing exports. The negative effect of the currency appreciation on the textile trade balance overwhelmed any small positive trade balance effect of the shift of apparel production to overseas locations.

Near-Term Outlook

The 1980s were a period of turmoil for US textile manufacturers. Facing intense competition from foreign producers, many US textile firms invested heavily in advanced production technologies and machinery. Indeed, investment in plant and equipment in textiles remained strong throughout the 1980s—between $1.5 billion and $1.7 billion annually from 1980 to 1986, growing to $2.0 billion by 1987, and $2.1 billion in 1989. The high cost of textile machinery forced firms to consolidate operations and increased the minimum efficient size of textile mills.

US textile manufacturers paid particular attention to improving quick-response technologies, which emphasize better communications and coordination between manufacturers and their customers—factors of particular importance in the fashion industry. The goal is to reduce the time a retailer needs to restock an item; this makes lower inventories possible and reduces retailers' losses from dead stock. Reductions in the response time of US manufacturers improve their competitive position relative to foreign producers because, coupled with the relatively shorter delivery times from US producers, this gives US-based production significant advantages.

US manufacturers also concentrated on constructing plants that could produce a variety of textiles and switch rapidly from one product to another. Textile production has traditionally been characterized by relatively long production runs of standard outputs. The ability to switch rapidly from one product to another and to use shorter production runs enables manufacturers to profitably exploit smaller market niches.

Because of the restructuring of US textile manufacturing during the 1980s, productivity in this industry increased more rapidly than in most other US manufacturing industries. US productivity growth exceeded that of most foreign producers as well. US textile manufacturers were competitive with foreign man-ufacturers as the 1990s began. Despite employment declines during the 1980s, improved productivity allowed the value of shipments to rise steadily. Between 1987 and 1990, employment in the textile industry declined by nearly 3.5 percent to 650,000, according to the US Department of Commerce, while the value of product shipments grew by 5.1 percent.

Several factors will determine US textiles trade performance during the 1990s. One is the trade stance that the European Community will adopt with the advent of EC 1992. As with many other products, there is a divergence of views among EC members on restrictions on textile imports. It is unclear whether the Com-munity will adopt textile trade regulations that are more restrictive than those currently in force or less so. Although import restrictions do not generally apply to US producers, they do affect US trade performance indirectly. That is, to the extent that the Community adopts a more restrictive textile trade policy, some of the exports of third countries that would have gone to Europe may be diverted to the US market.

The renegotiation of the MFA scheduled for 1991 has been postponed and a 20-month extension put in place until after the expected completion of the Uruguay Round of the GATT. The outcome of the round and any renegotiation of the MFA will influence US trade performance in these industries greatly. The recent improvement in US trade performance may weaken the push for more stringent import restrictions in the upcoming negotiations. But even without additional restrictions, US producers are likely to maintain their share of the domestic market unless the dollar becomes significantly stronger.

There are several reasons to be optimistic about the prospects for US trade in textiles in the 1990s. The United States is currently fully competitive in high-quality textiles and specialty fabrics, two segments that may grow significantly during the 1990s. As noted earlier, Europe is one of the principal export markets for US textiles. Many analysts are predicting significant economic growth in Europe some time after 1992. This should stimulate demand for the types of textiles of which the United States is already a significant supplier.

On a net basis, the US trade position in textiles is likely to improve slightly. The dampening effect of the 1990–91 recession on textile imports, combined with the potential for expansion in the European market, may lead to an im-provement of $0.5 billion to $0.7 billion by 1993, which would reduce the 1990 deficit of $1.4 billion to less than $1.0 billion.

Medium-Term Outlook

The improvement in the textile trade balance anticipated during the early 1990s is likely to be reversed after 1993. Much of the improvement expected during the early 1990s will come as a result of the US recession, which has reduced import growth. Strong import growth is likely to accompany economic recovery in the United States, probably beginning in 1992.

There are also some signs of a near-term slowing of economic activity in Europe. A slowdown in such an important export market would be likely to cause a decline in US export performance. In the absence of significant differences in growth rates between the United States and its major export markets, the modest improvement in the textiles trade balance foreseen during the early 1990s will probably taper off by 1992 or 1993, with little change in US balances in the years immediately thereafter.

Conclusions

- International trade in textiles and apparel together accounted for 8.3 percent of total world trade in manufactures in 1989, a share second only to road vehicles. Their large role in international trade helps make these industries among the most politically sensitive.

- Unlike most of US manufacturing, the textile industry has enjoyed some form of protection against imports for an extended time. The protection did not, however, prevent a surge of imports during the early to mid-1980s caused primarily by the sharp rise in the value of the dollar. The US textiles trade deficit bottomed at $3.2 billion in 1987, improving to a deficit of $1.4 billion in 1990.

- The overall performance of the domestic textile industry depends heavily on the performance of the domestic apparel industry, its largest customer. The shift in apparel production from the United States to overseas locations has reduced the US market for US-produced textiles substantially. The shift had little effect, however, on the trade performance of US textiles.

- In response to increasing foreign competition and a declining domestic textiles market, the US textiles industry consolidated operations and increased investment in plant and equipment during the 1980s. Investment was targeted at improving quality, flexibility, and response time.

- Industry investment during the 1980s provided for labor productivity increases greater than for US manufacturing in general and greater than for most foreign textile producers. With increased labor productivity and the decline in the dollar since 1985, US producers are now competitive with foreign manufacturers in most textile products.

- In the absence of significant changes in the exchange rate, there may be modest further improvement in the US trade position of perhaps $0.5 billion to $0.7 billion by 1993. This would come about through import reductions due to the US recession and through the expansion of the export market for man-made and specialty textiles, two areas in which US producers are most competitive.

■ Additional improvement beyond 1993 is, however, unlikely. Recovery of the US economy from the 1990–91 recession and slower economic growth in Europe, one of the major US textile markets, is likely to lead to a small but continuing US textiles trade deficit during the mid-1990s.

Bibliography

American Textile Manufacturers Institute. 1990. *Textile Hi-Lights*. Washington: American Textile Manufacturers Institute (March).

Cline, William R. 1990. *The Future of World Trade in Textiles and Apparel*, rev. ed. Washington: Institute for International Economics.

Commission of the European Communities. 1990. *Panorama of EC Industry, 1990*. Luxembourg: Commission of the European Communities.

Industry, Science and Technology Canada. 1988. *Industry Profile: Textiles*. Ottawa: Industry, Science and Technology Canada.

Truell, Peter. 1990. "House Agrees 271–149 to Curb Textile Imports." *Wall Street Journal* (19 September).

US Department of Commerce, International Trade Administration. 1988. *U.S. Industrial Outlook, 1988*. Washington: US Department of Commerce (January).

US Department of Commerce, International Trade Administration. 1989. *U.S. Industrial Outlook, 1989*. Washington: US Department of Commerce (January).

US Department of Commerce, International Trade Administration. 1990. *U.S. Industrial Outlook, 1990*. Washington: US Department of Commerce (January).

US Department of Commerce, International Trade Commission. 1990. *U.S. Trade Shifts in Selected Commodity Areas, January–June 1990*. Washington: US Department of Commerce (December).

Wolff, Alan, Thomas R. Howell, and William A. Noellert. 1985. *The Reality of World Trade in Textiles and Apparel*. Prepared for the Fiber, Fabric and Apparel Coalition for Trade (FFACT).

Table 5.65.1 Textiles: product composition of world trade, 1981–89 (billions of dollars except where noted)

SITC Product	1981	1982	1983	1984	1985	1986	1987	1988	1989	Annual growth 1981–89 (percentages)
World exports to world	43.6	41.1	41.0	43.5	46.1	56.2	67.8	78.3	81.8	8.2
of which:										
651 Textile yarn	11.3	10.6	10.8	11.9	12.8	14.7	18.0	19.3	19.7	7.3
652 Cotton fabrics, woven	5.8	5.5	5.5	6.1	6.3	7.7	9.3	9.8	10.4	7.6
653 Manmade fiber, woven	8.3	7.5	7.4	7.6	8.3	10.3	11.5	16.2	18.1	10.3
654 Other woven textiles	3.0	2.6	2.7	3.0	3.2	3.8	4.5	6.2	7.0	11.2
655 Knitted fabrics	2.0	1.9	1.9	1.8	1.9	2.5	3.1	3.3	3.8	8.4
656 Lace, ribbons, etc.	1.3	1.2	1.0	1.0	1.0	1.3	1.6	1.9	2.0	5.6
657 Special textiles	4.1	4.0	4.0	4.2	4.4	5.7	7.1	8.3	8.5	9.3
658 Textile, n.e.s.	3.4	3.0	2.9	3.1	3.5	4.2	5.1	6.1	6.4	8.2
659 Floor coverings	4.4	3.9	3.8	3.8	3.9	5.0	6.3	7.0	7.5	6.8
										Change 1981–89
Memorandum: SITC 65 share of world manufactures exports (percentages)	4.3	4.2	4.2	4.1	4.1	4.1	4.1	4.0	3.9	−0.5

Source: World Manufactures Trade Data Base.

Table 5.65.2 Textiles: geographic distribution of world trade, 1981–89 (percentages of total)

Country	1981	1982	1983	1984	1985	1986	1987	1988	1989	Change 1981–89
Share of exports to world										
United States	8.3	6.8	5.8	5.5	5.1	4.6	4.3	4.7	4.8	-3.5
Canada	0.8	0.7	0.6	0.7	0.7	0.7	0.7	0.7	0.7	-0.0
Japan	13.5	12.4	13.1	12.3	10.7	9.8	8.3	7.0	6.8	-6.6
European Community	52.2	52.3	52.2	50.9	51.1	53.3	53.1	48.6	49.5	-2.7
EC to non-EC	20.5	19.8	19.8	19.9	19.5	19.4	18.6	17.0	17.3	-3.2
Germany	12.9	13.5	13.3	13.0	13.2	14.6	14.5	13.4	13.5	0.6
France	7.2	7.1	6.8	6.7	6.8	6.9	6.7	5.9	6.1	-1.1
Italy	9.5	9.9	10.3	10.1	10.2	10.7	10.8	9.5	10.4	0.9
United Kingdom	5.4	5.1	4.7	4.6	4.8	4.5	4.6	4.4	4.4	-1.0
Other Western Europe	7.4	7.6	7.4	6.9	9.3	9.1	8.9	8.4	7.4	-0.1
Asian NICs[a]	4.9	7.7	7.9	8.9	9.0	8.9	9.7	15.5	16.0	11.2
Eastern Europe[b]	1.3	1.1	1.2	1.2	1.2	1.2	1.2	1.3	1.0	-0.3
Developing countries	11.2	10.9	11.6	13.2	12.7	12.3	13.8	13.3	12.9	1.7
Latin America	2.0	2.0	2.1	2.5	2.3	2.0	2.1	1.8	1.6	-0.3
Rest of world	0.2	0.1	0.1	0.1	0.1	0.1	0.1	0.9	1.1	0.9
Share of imports from world										
United States	7.0	6.8	8.0	10.5	10.8	10.3	9.6	8.1	7.9	0.9
Canada	3.3	2.7	3.5	3.6	3.5	3.2	3.0	2.8	2.9	-0.3
Japan	3.9	4.1	3.8	4.6	4.4	4.0	4.7	5.3	5.5	1.6
European Community	46.1	46.6	46.4	44.4	45.1	48.3	49.7	46.5	45.9	-0.2
EC from non-EC	15.2	14.9	14.9	14.2	14.3	15.2	16.2	15.3	15.0	-0.2
Germany	12.4	11.9	12.3	11.3	11.1	12.1	12.1	11.2	11.1	-1.3
France	7.9	8.4	7.8	7.4	7.6	8.3	8.2	7.6	7.6	-0.3
Italy	5.1	5.6	5.3	5.7	5.9	6.3	7.0	6.2	6.4	1.3
United Kingdom	8.1	8.2	8.6	8.2	8.5	8.2	8.5	8.4	7.6	-0.5
Other Western Europe	9.8	9.6	9.4	8.9	9.4	10.0	10.0	8.4	8.6	-1.2
Asian NICs[a]	4.4	6.1	6.7	7.2	7.0	7.1	7.4	10.6	11.5	7.2
Eastern Europe[b]	3.5	3.1	3.4	3.0	2.7	2.5	2.3	2.3	2.1	-1.4
Developing countries	19.9	18.7	17.0	15.4	15.2	13.3	12.1	13.9	14.2	-5.7
Latin America	2.9	2.5	1.9	2.0	2.0	2.0	1.8	2.1	2.2	-0.8
Rest of world	0.1	0.1	0.1	0.1	0.1	0.1	0.2	0.6	0.5	0.4

table continued next page

Table 5.65.2 Textiles: geographic distribution of world trade, 1981–89 (percentages of total) (continued)

Country	1981	1982	1983	1984	1985	1986	1987	1988	1989	Change 1981–89
Export share minus import share										
United States	1.3	-0.0	-2.2	-5.0	-5.7	-5.8	-5.3	-3.5	-3.1	-4.5
Canada	-2.5	-2.0	-2.8	-2.9	-2.8	-2.5	-2.3	-2.1	-2.2	0.3
Japan	9.6	8.3	9.3	7.7	6.4	5.8	3.6	1.7	1.4	-8.2
European Community	6.1	5.8	5.8	6.6	5.9	5.0	3.3	2.1	3.6	-2.5
Non-EC	5.4	4.8	4.8	5.7	5.2	4.2	2.4	1.7	2.4	-3.0
Germany	0.6	1.6	1.0	1.7	2.1	2.5	2.4	2.2	2.5	1.9
France	-0.7	-1.3	-1.0	-0.7	-0.8	-1.4	-1.5	-1.7	-1.5	-0.8
Italy	4.4	4.3	5.0	4.4	4.3	4.3	3.8	3.3	3.9	-0.5
United Kingdom	-2.7	-3.1	-3.8	-3.7	-3.7	-3.7	-3.9	-4.0	-3.2	-0.5
Other Western Europe	-2.4	-2.0	-2.0	-2.0	-0.2	-0.9	-1.1	-0.0	-1.2	1.2
Asian NICs[a]	0.5	1.6	1.2	1.8	2.0	1.8	2.3	4.9	4.5	4.0
Eastern Europe[b]	-2.2	-2.0	-2.2	-1.8	-1.5	-1.3	-1.1	-1.0	-1.1	1.1
Developing countries	-8.7	-7.8	-5.4	-2.2	-2.5	-1.0	1.7	-0.7	-1.4	7.3
Latin America	-1.0	-0.5	0.2	0.5	0.2	-0.0	0.3	-0.3	-0.5	0.4
Rest of world	0.1	0.0	0.0	0.0	0.0	0.0	-0.1	0.3	0.6	0.5

a. Hong Kong, Korea, Singapore, and Taiwan.

b. Including Soviet Union.

Source: World Manufactures Trade Data Base.

Table 5.65.3 Textiles: bilateral trade flows, 1989 (billions of dollars)

Importer					Exporter						
	World	United States	Canada	Japan	European Community	Germany	France	United Kingdom	Asian NICs	Latin America	Other
World	81.8	3.9	0.6	5.5	40.5	11.1	5.0	3.6	13.1	1.3	16.9
United States	6.7		0.4	0.6	1.9	0.3	0.2	0.3	1.3	0.6	1.9
Canada	2.0	0.7		0.1	0.4	0.1	0.0	0.1	0.3	0.1	0.4
Japan	4.6	0.3	0.0		1.0	0.1	0.1	0.2	1.3	0.0	2.0
European Community	38.3	0.9	0.1	0.1	26.3	6.3	3.3	2.0	1.1	0.5	8.8
Germany	9.4	0.1	0.0	0.1	5.7		0.9	0.4	0.2	0.1	3.0
France	6.4	0.1	0.0	0.1	4.9	1.2		0.3	0.1	0.0	1.2
United Kingdom	6.1	0.3	0.0	0.2	4.0	0.9	0.5		0.3	0.1	1.3
Asian NICs	8.7	0.3	0.0	2.1	0.7	0.2	0.1	0.0	4.2	0.0	1.2
Latin America	1.8	0.9	0.0	0.1	0.3	0.0	0.0	0.0	0.5	0.1	0.0
Other	19.8	0.8	0.1	2.0	10.0	4.0	1.2	0.9	4.3		2.5

Source: World Manufactures Trade Data Base.

Table 5.65.4 Textiles: product composition of US trade, 1981–90[a] (millions of dollars except where noted)

Category	SITC Rev. 2			SITC Rev. 3			
	1981	1987	Change 1981–87	1987	1990	Change 1981–90	Change 1987–90
Total							
Exports	3,619	2,933	−686	3,106	4,992	1,373	1,886
Imports	2,875	6,131	3,256	5,965	6,398	3,523	433
Balance	744	−3,198	−3,942	−2,859	−1,406	−2,150	1,453
of which							
651 Textile yarn							
Exports	902	677	−225	886	1,242	340	356
Imports	214	643	429	668	697	483	29
Balance	688	34	−654	218	545	−143	327
652 Cotton fabrics, woven							
Exports	349	292	−57	269	503	154	234
Imports	607	1,292	685	1,291	1,120	513	−171
Balance	−258	−1,000	−742	−1,022	−617	−359	405
653 Woven manmade fiber							
Exports	797	555	−242	444	673	−124	229
Imports	580	898	318	871	974	394	103
Balance	217	−343	−560	−427	−301	−518	126
654 Other woven textiles							
Exports	73	77	4	93	129	56	36
Imports	387	610	223	626	647	260	21
Balance	−314	−533	−219	−533	−517	−203	16
655 Knitted fabrics							
Exports	73	35	−38	102	218	145	116
Imports	16	73	57	99	144	128	45
Balance	57	−38	−95	3	74	17	71
656 Lace, ribbons, etc.							
Exports	93	119	26	97	185	92	88
Imports	52	132	80	115	182	130	67
Balance	41	−13	−54	−18	2	−39	20
657 Special textiles							
Exports	613	649	36	714	1,053	440	339
Imports	333	631	298	477	695	362	218
Balance	280	18	−262	237	358	78	121
658 Textile, n.e.s.							
Exports	335	282	−53	255	358	23	103
Imports	329	1,112	783	1,122	1,332	1,003	210
Balance	6	−830	−836	−867	−974	−980	−107
659 Floor coverings							
Exports	385	246	−139	246	561	176	315
Imports	357	741	384	698	606	249	−92
Balance	28	−495	−523	−452	−45	−73	407

a. Data are expressed on a domestic exports, imports customs basis. *Source:* US Department of Commerce.

Table 5.65.5 Textiles: geographic composition of US trade, 1981–90

	Millions of dollars				Percentages of total			
	1981	1987	1989	1990	1981	1987	1989	1990
Exports								
Canada	666	581	696	1,195	18.4	18.7	17.9	24.3
Japan	124	150	297	269	3.4	4.8	7.6	5.5
European Community	741	783	938	1,160	20.5	25.2	24.1	23.6
United Kingdom	271	177	273	295	7.5	5.7	7.0	6.0
Germany	92	123	139	175	2.5	4.0	3.6	3.6
Italy	70	111	75	126	1.9	3.6	1.9	2.6
Latin America	765	705	866	1,099	21.1	22.7	22.2	22.3
China	284	86	61	57	7.8	2.8	1.6	1.2
Other	1,040	802	1,039	1,142	28.7	25.8	26.7	23.2
Total	3,619	3,106	3,897	4,922	100.0	100.0	100.0	100.0
Imports								
Canada	82	271	370	402	2.9	4.5	6.1	6.3
Japan	510	705	614	577	17.7	11.8	10.1	9.0
European Community	689	1,527	1,699	1,739	24.0	25.6	27.9	27.2
United Kingdom	120	247	281	292	4.2	4.1	4.6	4.6
Germany	92	255	290	316	3.2	4.3	4.8	4.9
Italy	250	464	508	475	8.7	7.8	8.3	7.4
Latin America	261	529	555	624	9.1	8.9	9.1	9.8
Asian NICs	491	1,136	1,078	1,145	17.1	19.0	17.7	17.9
China	243	515	619	658	8.5	8.6	10.2	10.3
Other	598	1,283	1,161	1,253	20.8	21.5	19.0	19.6
Total	2,875	5,965	6,094	6,398	100.0	100.0	100.0	100.0

a. Data are expressed on a domestic exports, imports customs basis.

Source: US Department of Commerce.

Table 5.65.6 Textiles: indices of US competitiveness, 1981–89 (billions of dollars except where noted)

	1981	1982	1983	1984	1985	1986	1987	1988	1989	Annual growth 1981–89 (percentages)
World trade										
World exports to non-US destinations	40.5	38.3	37.6	39.1	41.4	50.7	61.4	71.8	75.1	8.0
World imports from non-US sources	40.0	38.3	38.6	41.4	43.4	53.6	64.4	73.1	76.9	8.5
US trade										
Exports	3.6	2.8	2.4	2.4	2.4	2.6	2.9	3.7	3.9	1.0
Imports	3.1	2.8	3.3	4.6	5.0	5.8	6.5	6.3	6.4	9.6
Balance	0.5	0.0	-0.9	-2.2	-2.6	-3.2	-3.6	-2.6	-2.6	
										Change 1981–89
US share of exports to non-US destinations (percentages)	8.9	7.3	6.3	6.1	5.7	5.1	4.8	5.1	5.2	-3.6
US share of imports from non-US sources (percentages)	7.6	7.3	8.5	11.1	11.5	10.9	10.1	8.6	8.4	0.8
Export share minus import share (percentages)	1.2	-0.1	-2.2	-5.0	-5.8	-5.8	-5.4	-3.5	-3.2	-4.4

Source: World Manufactures Trade Data Base.

Nonmetallic Mineral Manufactures (SITC 66)

Imports of diamonds, cement, china, and glassware create persistent US deficits in this group of diverse products. US economic downturns, however, temporarily reduce import demand when they occur, by reducing construction activity and lowering consumer confidence.

Description of the Product Group

Nonmetallic mineral manufactures, not elsewhere specified, includes the following subcategories:

SITC

661 cement, lime, and fabricated construction materials (excluding glass and clay materials)

662 clay construction materials and refractory construction materials (e.g., bricks and tiles)

663 mineral manufactures, not elsewhere specified

664 glass

665 glassware

666 pottery (including chinaware and porcelain)

667 pearls and precious and semiprecious stones (including diamonds).

Products in SITCs 661 through 665 are often used as construction materials. Optical fiber is included in SITC 773, electrical distribution equipment, rather than in this product group.

Role in World Trade

Size and Composition

World exports of nonmetallic mineral manufactures were $66.4 billion in 1989, or 3.1 percent of world manufactures exports (table 5.66.1). This share was relatively constant over the 1980s, with exports growing by 10.2 percent annually on average, modestly above the 9.6 percent growth rate of manufactures exports generally.

The subcategory pearls and precious and semiprecious stones consists primarily of diamonds. It accounts for almost half of world trade in this product group and has experienced rapid growth. Glass, however, was the subcategory with the most rapid growth in trade, because of strong construction demand and increased production in developing countries, particularly Southeast Asia. Cement and clay have limited importance in international trade because of their weight and bulk.

Global Competition Patterns

The European Community accounts for over half the world's exports in this product group (table 5.66.2). However, about half of the Community's trade in this group was intra-EC trade (table 5.66.3). The Community has the largest surpluses in trade in these products, and the United States the largest deficits. The United States is the largest single-country importer, with 16.2 percent of world imports in 1989, down from 23.6 percent in 1985 (table 5.66.2).

Role in US Trade

Recent Performance

This product group accounts for 0.9 percent of US manufactures exports and 1.7 percent of US manufactures imports. The US trade deficit in nonmetallic mineral manufactures deteriorated from $2.6 billion in 1981 to $6.8 billion in 1990, mostly because of import growth (table 5.66.4). Most of that deterioration occurred from 1981 to 1987. The largest contributors were pearls and precious and semiprecious stones, and cement and building products.

Canada is the largest US export market, absorbing 35.3 percent of 1990 exports. Latin America became less important as a destination for US exports during the 1980s, while exports to Japan grew (table 5.66.5). Over a third of US imports come from the European Community.

International Competitiveness

The US share of world exports to non-US destinations fell from 8.8 percent in 1981 to 6.1 percent in 1989 (table 5.66.6). The US share of imports rose to 25 percent in 1985, but by 1989 it had fallen to 17.4 percent, close to the 1981 level of 17.2 percent.

Outlook

Key Determinants of US Trade Performance

The determinants of US trade performance in this category are discussed below by subcategory.

Cement, Lime, and Building Products (SITC 661)

The trade balance in this subcategory grew from $0.2 billion to $1.0 billion over the 1980s, with most of the deterioration coming from rising imports during 1981–87 (table 5.66.4).

Cement accounts for most of US trade in this subcategory. Here, too, most of the deterioration occurred on the import side; the United States has never been a major exporter of cement. In 1990, imports accounted for 14.8 percent of US cement consumption, up from 5.4 percent in 1981. Growth in imports was particularly large from Mexico and the European Community, where producers have moved beyond being swing suppliers in times of high demand and are substituting for US domestic capacity. According to the US Commerce Department (1987, vii), imports of cement during the 1980s increased because of world overcapacity, weak world demand, strong US demand, and a surplus of water transport carriers that lowered transportation costs. Furthermore, foreign ownership of US cement production has increased from 10 percent to 70 percent over the 1980s, and given the links between foreign companies in the United States and their foreign parents, many producers can easily switch from domestic to foreign sources. More recently, a 1990 dumping levy has reduced imports from Mexico, and an investigation has been pending against Japan. The threat of protective action may be acting to restrain imports.

The cement industry is both energy- and capital-intensive. Land transport costs are high, so markets are typically regional or local. Regional markets are often more closely linked by water to foreign markets than to markets in other parts of the United States (US Department of Commerce 1987, 9). Generalizations about the US market must be interpreted in the light of these considerations.

Clay and Refractory Products (SITC 662)

Increasing imports caused the US trade balance in this subcategory to deteriorate from a small 1981 surplus of $9 million to a 1990 deficit of $254 million (table 5.66.4). This occurred despite substitution of other materials for brick in residential construction, its primary use. The import penetration of ceramic tiles increased from 47 percent to 61 percent during the 1980s, according to the US

Commerce Department (1991b, 7–11), and appears relatively insensitive to exchange rate changes.

Mineral Manufactures Not Elsewhere Specified (SITC 663)

This subcategory includes a miscellany of grinding and polishing stones as well as articles of mica, asbestos, and mineral wools. The trade balance returned to a $22 million surplus in 1990 after deteriorating by $258 million to a $49 million deficit in 1987 (table 5.66.4).

Glass and Glassware (SITCs 664 and 665)

The US trade balance in glass deteriorated by a half-billion dollars from 1981 to 1987 but thereafter recovered the loss, moving to a $299 million surplus in 1990 (table 5.66.4), largely in response to exchange rate changes. Weakness in the major consuming industries—construction and automobile manufacturing—also helped reduce the demand for glass imports. Glass containers have lost ground to plastic and metal substitutes. Flat glass is consumed primarily by the construction and automotive industries. A fall in automobile imports and a rise in US-based production of cars for the US market would increase US demand for flat glass. The US glassware industry has been shrinking under the pressure of lower-priced imports.

Pottery (SITC 666)

This subcategory consists mainly of tableware made of porcelain or china. US imports increased over the 1980s in response to the rise in the dollar, but the removal of tariff protection after the Tokyo Round also played a role. US companies produce china primarily for commercial use within the United States, although at least one company imports blank plates and decorates them for the home market. US exports are negligible, so the large deficit, $1.2 billion in 1990, is driven by demand for china used in the home (table 5.66.4).

Pearls and Precious and Semiprecious Stones (SITC 667)

Imports in this subcategory grew by $1.9 billion over the 1980s, leading to a $4.2 billion deficit in 1990. Gem diamonds account for about 85 percent of imports and a similarly large proportion of exports in this subcategory. US gem resources are not large; hence US diamond exports are produced from imported raw materials. The world diamond market is dominated by South Africa-based De Beers Consolidated Mines Ltd.; a De Beers subsidiary markets 80 percent to 85 percent of the world's gem and industrial diamonds. Its nominal rough diamond prices have not fallen on a year-to-year basis in many decades, but have in fact increased 1,800 percent in the last 40 years, according to the US Bureau of Mines (Austin 1989, 15).

US import patterns reflect the traditional roles of Belgium and Israel in diamond cutting and polishing, and that of London as a trading center for uncut diamonds. In addition, India developed a major cottage industry during the 1980s and now produces most of the world's small, inexpensive diamonds. The most important diamond mines, in terms of volumes produced, are in South Africa, the former Soviet Union, Botswana, Zaire, and Australia (Austin 1989, 12).

Elasticities calculated by Data Resources, Inc., indicate the responsiveness of US trade to changing macroeconomic conditions (see the appendix to this volume). Import demand for cement responds relatively elastically to changes in exchange rates. Import demand in the United States and abroad also responds strongly to growth in the consumption component of GNP. The response to growth in investment is minimal, contrary to what might be expected. US import demand in a category that includes clay, glass, and diamonds as well as some metal manufactures is moderately responsive to changes in import prices, but not particularly responsive otherwise. Import demand in a category that includes glassware and china as well as a number of other consumer goods is both price-elastic and responsive to growth in the consumption component of GNP.

Near-Term Outlook

Construction demand in the United States is likely to be slow for the next several years; this will help moderate the level of cement imports. A concerted program to improve US infrastructure would increase cement imports, as would a recovery of nonresidential construction. Given insignificant US production capacity, imports of china and glassware will continue to rise, unless import growth is temporarily interrupted by recession.

Rising gem prices and expanding US demand will continue to increase the US deficit in precious stones. Demand for diamonds will rise disproportionately as incomes grow worldwide. Promotional campaigns are successfully creating demand in the Far East, for instance, and diamond engagement rings are becoming customary in Japan. Increasing world demand and continued operation of the diamond cartel will lead to higher diamond prices. A recession would only temporarily slow the trend toward increasing US demand for diamonds. Assuming reasonably good economic performance, a modest increase in the US deficit of perhaps $1 billion seems likely by 1993.

Medium-Term Outlook

There is no significant prospect for reduced trade deficits in this product group, given the lack of potential for export growth or import substitution.

Conclusions

- The trade balance in most SITC 66 subcategories is a function of imports: there is little US export capability or potential for import substitution. Deficits are likely to continue to grow for the foreseeable future.

- US deficits in cement, china, glassware, and diamonds will gradually expand from current levels of around $7 billion if the US economy performs well.

- A recession lessens import demand for these items, but only temporarily. A modest increase of about $1 billion in the US deficit seems likely by 1993, with continued expansion in the deficit related to US economic growth rates.

Bibliography

Austin, Gordon T. 1989. "Gem Stones." In US Department of the Interior, Bureau of Mines, *Minerals Yearbook*. Washington: US Department of the Interior.

Commission of the European Communities. 1990. *Panorama of EC Industry, 1990*. Luxembourg: Commission of the European Communities.

Industry, Science and Technology Canada. 1988. *Industry Profiles*. Ottawa: Industry, Science and Technology Canada.

Japan Economic Journal. 1990. *Japan Economic Almanac, 1990*. Tokyo: Japan Economic Journal.

National Research Council. 1990. *Competitiveness of the U.S. Minerals and Metals Industries*. Washington: National Academy Press.

Noetstaller, Richard. 1988. "Industrial Minerals: A Technical Review." *Technical Paper* 76. Washington: World Bank.

US Department of Commerce. 1983. *A Competitive Assessment of the U.S. Ceramic and Floor Tile Industry*. Washington: US Department of Commerce.

US Department of Commerce, International Trade Administration. 1987. *A Competitive Assessment of the U.S. Cement Industry*. Washington: US Department of Commerce (July).

US Department of Commerce, International Trade Administration. 1991. *U.S. Industrial Outlook, 1991*. Washington: US Department of Commerce (January).

US Department of the Interior, Bureau of Mines. 1990. *Mineral Commodity Summaries, 1990*. Washington: US Department of the Interior (January).

US Department of the Interior, Bureau of Mines. 1991. *Minerals Yearbook, 1989*, vol. I: *International*. Washington: US Department of the Interior.

Table 5.66.1 Nonmetallic mineral manufactures: product composition of world trade, 1981–89

(billions of dollars except where noted)

SITC Product	1981	1982	1983	1984	1985	1986	1987	1988	1989	Annual growth 1981–89 (percentages)
World exports to world	30.5	28.3	29.6	30.9	31.1	38.8	47.0	61.4	66.4	10.2
of which										
661 Cement, building products	3.4	3.4	3.5	3.3	3.1	3.5	4.0	5.3	5.9	7.2
662 Clay and refractory products	3.8	3.2	3.1	3.1	3.1	3.9	4.8	5.7	6.0	5.8
663 Mineral manufactures n.e.s.	3.4	3.4	3.5	3.8	3.8	4.9	6.0	6.9	7.2	9.9
664 Glass	3.3	3.2	3.3	3.4	3.6	4.6	5.9	7.5	8.2	12.1
665 Glassware	2.9	2.8	2.8	2.9	3.0	3.8	4.5	5.0	5.3	7.7
666 Pottery	2.3	2.1	2.2	2.4	2.3	2.8	3.5	3.5	3.5	5.5
667 Diamonds, etc.	13.0	11.4	12.7	13.5	12.9	17.0	20.4	27.5	30.8	11.3
Memorandum:										Change 1981–89
SITC 66 share of world manufactures exports (percentages)	3.0	2.9	3.0	2.9	2.8	2.8	2.8	3.1	3.1	0.1

Source: World Manufactures Trade Data Base.

Table 5.66.2 Nonmetallic mineral manufactures: geographic distribution of world trade, 1981–89 (percentages of total)

Country	1981	1982	1983	1984	1985	1986	1987	1988	1989	Change 1981–89
Share of exports to world										
United States	7.4	6.6	6.1	6.2	6.0	5.0	5.0	4.8	5.1	–2.3
Canada	1.1	1.2	1.2	1.5	1.5	1.3	1.2	1.3	1.4	0.3
Japan	6.9	6.8	7.2	7.3	6.9	6.0	5.3	4.9	4.6	–2.3
European Community	58.7	59.4	58.6	55.4	54.8	56.6	56.5	51.0	50.9	–7.8
EC to non-EC	32.0	32.3	32.8	31.7	30.5	29.7	28.9	26.1	26.5	–5.5
Germany	10.0	10.5	9.9	9.2	9.8	11.0	10.8	9.2	8.7	–1.2
France	6.8	6.7	6.6	6.2	6.4	6.0	6.0	5.2	5.1	–1.7
Italy	9.4	9.3	9.5	8.9	8.9	9.0	9.2	8.2	8.1	–1.3
United Kingdom	9.8	9.9	10.2	10.0	9.0	9.6	9.3	8.7	8.1	–1.7
Other Western Europe	8.1	7.8	7.4	8.2	9.0	9.1	9.0	7.9	7.9	–0.2
Asian NICs[a]	3.1	3.7	3.8	4.4	4.4	4.2	4.8	4.9	4.7	1.6
Eastern Europe[b]	2.0	2.3	2.0	2.3	2.2	2.6	2.5	2.2	1.7	–0.3
Developing countries	12.3	11.8	13.3	14.5	15.2	15.1	15.7	16.8	18.3	6.0
Latin America	1.6	1.6	1.9	2.5	2.6	2.1	3.1	3.0	3.1	1.5
Rest of world	0.1	0.2	0.2	0.1	0.1	0.1	0.1	6.2	5.4	5.3
Share of imports from world										
United States	15.8	15.3	17.7	21.9	23.6	21.3	18.8	17.5	16.2	0.4
Canada	2.7	2.4	2.6	2.8	3.0	2.6	2.4	2.7	2.8	0.1
Japan	3.5	3.5	3.5	3.6	3.8	4.6	5.6	6.7	7.1	3.6
European Community	43.5	42.4	41.5	39.1	38.2	41.5	42.9	42.7	42.7	–0.8
EC from non-EC	17.3	16.3	17.0	16.4	15.2	16.7	16.7	18.6	18.6	1.3
Germany	8.0	7.5	7.5	6.7	6.3	7.1	7.3	6.7	6.6	–1.4
France	6.6	6.1	5.2	4.8	5.1	5.5	5.8	5.4	5.4	–1.2
Italy	2.8	2.7	2.3	2.4	2.5	2.7	3.0	3.0	3.0	0.2
United Kingdom	9.0	8.9	10.0	9.1	8.6	9.3	8.9	9.8	8.8	–0.2
Other Western Europe	9.3	9.0	8.4	9.4	9.3	10.4	10.8	10.1	9.8	0.5
Asian NICs[a]	3.9	4.6	4.3	4.2	3.9	3.7	4.0	4.7	5.2	1.3
Eastern Europe[b]	1.2	1.2	1.1	1.0	1.0	0.9	0.8	0.7	0.6	–0.6
Developing countries	18.9	20.4	19.9	16.8	16.1	14.1	13.5	13.9	14.3	–4.6
Latin America	3.2	2.5	1.6	1.6	1.7	1.5	1.5	1.3	1.4	–1.9
Rest of world	0.1	0.1	0.1	0.1	0.1	0.2	0.2	0.2	0.2	0.2

Export share minus import share

United States	−8.5	−8.7	−11.5	−15.7	−17.5	−16.3	−13.8	−12.7	−11.1	−2.6
Canada	−1.6	−1.2	−1.4	−1.3	−1.5	−1.3	−1.2	−1.4	−1.4	0.1
Japan	3.4	3.4	3.7	3.7	3.1	1.5	−0.3	−1.7	−2.5	−5.9
European Community	15.2	17.0	17.1	16.3	16.6	15.2	13.6	8.3	8.2	−7.0
Non-EC	14.6	16.0	15.8	15.3	15.3	13.0	12.2	7.5	7.9	−6.8
Germany	2.0	3.0	2.4	2.4	3.4	3.9	3.5	2.5	2.1	0.2
France	0.2	0.6	1.4	1.4	1.3	0.6	0.3	−0.2	−0.3	−0.5
Italy	6.6	6.6	7.2	6.6	6.3	6.3	6.2	5.2	5.1	−1.5
United Kingdom	0.8	1.0	0.2	0.9	0.4	0.4	0.4	−1.1	−0.7	−1.5
Other Western Europe	−1.2	−1.1	−1.0	−1.2	−0.3	−1.3	−1.8	−2.2	−1.9	−0.7
Asian NICs[a]	−0.8	−0.9	−0.5	0.2	0.5	0.5	0.8	0.2	−0.5	0.3
Eastern Europe[b]	0.7	1.1	0.8	1.4	1.3	1.7	1.6	1.4	1.1	0.3
Developing countries	−6.6	−8.6	−6.7	−2.3	−0.9	1.0	2.2	2.9	4.1	10.7
Latin America	−1.7	−0.9	0.2	0.8	0.9	0.7	1.6	1.6	1.7	3.4
Rest of world	0.1	0.1	0.1	0.0	−0.0	−0.1	−0.1	6.0	5.2	5.1

a. Hong Kong, Korea, Singapore, and Taiwan.

b. Including Soviet Union.

Source: World Manufactures Trade Data Base.

Table 5.66.3 Nonmetallic mineral manufactures: bilateral trade flows, 1989 (billions of dollars)

Importer	World	United States	Canada	Japan	European Community	Germany	France	United Kingdom	Asian NICs	Latin America	Other
										Exporter →	
World	66.4	3.4	0.9	3.0	33.8	5.8	3.4	5.4	3.1	2.0	20.2
United States	11.4		0.8	0.9	4.0	0.4	0.3	0.7	1.0	0.9	3.9
Canada	1.4	0.7		0.1	0.4	0.0	0.0	0.1	0.1	0.0	0.1
Japan	4.6	0.4	0.0		1.2	0.1	0.1	0.1	0.8	0.1	2.0
European Community	28.9	0.7	0.0	0.3	16.2	3.2	1.9	2.4	0.5	0.3	10.8
Germany	4.5	0.1	0.0	0.1	3.2		0.6	0.2	0.1	0.0	1.0
France	3.5	0.1	0.0	0.0	2.9	0.8		0.1	0.1	0.0	0.5
United Kingdom	7.8	0.2	0.0	0.1	2.8	0.4	0.3		0.1	0.0	4.7
Asian NICs	3.3	0.5	0.0	0.9	1.1	0.2	0.1	0.1	0.2	0.0	0.5
Latin America	0.9	0.4	0.0	0.0	0.4	0.1	0.1		0.0		0.1
Other	15.9	0.7	0.0	0.8	10.4	1.8	0.8	1.9	0.4	0.7	2.8

Source: World Manufactures Trade Data Base.

Table 5.66.4 Nonmetallic mineral manufactures: product composition of US trade, 1981–90[a]
(millions of dollars except where noted)

Category	SITC Rev. 2			SITC Rev. 3			
	1981	1987	Change 1981–87	1987	1990	Change 1981–90	Change 1987–90
Exports	2,245	2,332	87	2,142	3,134	889	992
Imports	4,887	8,972	4,085	8,853	9,890	5,003	1,037
Balance	−2,642	−6,640	−3,998	−6,711	−6,756	−4,114	−45
of which							
661 Cement, lime, construction materials							
Exports	132	57	−75	47	132	0	85
Imports	315	1,016	701	960	1,096	781	136
Balance	−183	−959	−776	−913	−964	−781	−51
662 Clay and refractory products							
Exports	246	185	−61	163	310	64	147
Imports	237	477	240	505	564	327	59
Balance	9	−292	−301	−342	−254	−263	88
663 Mineral manufactures, n.e.s.							
Exports	467	545	78	376	725	258	349
Imports	258	594	336	481	703	445	222
Balance	209	−49	−258	−105	22	−187	127
664 Glass							
Exports	585	597	12	590	1,059	474	469
Imports	253	771	518	757	760	507	3
Balance	332	−174	−506	−167	299	−33	466
665 Glassware							
Exports	270	180	−90	194	401	131	207
Imports	376	802	426	831	940	564	109
Balance	−106	−622	−516	−637	−539	−433	98
666 Pottery							
Exports	37	39	2	34	71	34	37
Imports	712	1,308	596	1,308	1,222	510	−86
Balance	−675	−1,269	−594	−1,274	−1,151	−476	123
667 Precious and semiprecious stones and pearls							
Exports	508	730	222	739	436	−72	−303
Imports	2,736	4,003	1,267	4,011	4,605	1,869	594
Balance	−2,228	−3,273	−1,045	−3,272	−4,169	−1,941	−897

a. Data are expressed on a domestic exports, imports customs basis.

Source: US Department of Commerce.

Table 5.66.5 Nonmetallic mineral manufactures: geographic composition of US trade, 1981–90[a]

	Millions of dollars				Percentages of total			
	1981	1987	1989	1990	1981	1987	1989	1990
Exports								
Canada	572	574	691	1,107	25.5	26.8	18.8	35.3
Japan	127	252	414	292	5.7	11.8	11.3	9.3
European Community	373	363	655	508	16.6	16.9	17.8	16.2
United Kingdom	86	61	147	136	3.8	2.8	4.0	4.3
Germany	80	61	103	104	3.6	2.8	2.8	3.3
France	58	34	64	56	2.6	1.6	1.7	1.8
Italy	28	333	47	53	1.2	15.5	1.3	1.7
Latin America	443	242	353	428	19.7	11.3	9.6	13.7
Mexico	153	87	163	225	6.8	4.1	4.4	7.2
Asian NICs	236	291	496	340	10.5	13.6	13.5	10.8
Other	494	420	1,063	459	22.0	19.6	28.9	14.6
Total	2,245	2,142	3,672	3,134	100.0	100.0	100.0	100.0
Imports								
Canada	316	710	716	701	6.5	8.0	7.0	7.1
Japan	635	821	841	739	13.0	9.3	8.2	7.5
European Community	1,684	3,097	3,460	3,535	34.5	35.0	33.7	35.7
United Kingdom	254	476	526	602	5.2	5.4	5.1	6.1
Germany	219	361	366	407	4.5	4.1	3.6	4.1
France	157	268	305	327	3.2	3.0	3.0	3.3
Italy	225	602	652	701	4.6	6.8	6.3	7.1
Latin America	226	631	775	779	4.6	7.1	7.5	7.9
Mexico	88	379	439	437	1.8	4.3	4.3	4.4
Asian NICs	315	938	782	677	6.4	10.6	7.6	6.8
Israel	564	1,075	1,336	1,209	11.5	12.1	13.0	12.2
Other	1,147	1,581	2,365	2,250	23.5	17.9	23.0	22.8
Total	4,887	8,853	10,275	9,890	100.0	100.0	100.0	100.0

a. Data are expressed on a domestic exports, imports customs basis.

Source: US Department of Commerce.

Table 5.66.6 Nonmetallic mineral manufactures: indices of US competitiveness, 1981–89
(billions of dollars except where noted)

	1981	1982	1983	1984	1985	1986	1987	1988	1989	Annual growth 1981–89 (percentages)
World trade										
World exports to non-US destinations	25.6	23.9	24.2	24.1	23.9	30.4	37.9	50.8	55.0	10.0
World imports from non-US sources	29.8	27.7	29.4	31.1	31.5	39.7	47.7	58.1	62.2	9.6
US trade										
Exports	2.2	1.9	1.8	1.9	1.9	1.9	2.3	2.9	3.4	5.4
Imports	5.1	4.6	5.6	7.3	7.9	9.0	9.5	10.7	10.8	9.9
Balance	-2.9	-2.7	-3.8	-5.4	-6.0	-7.1	-7.2	-7.9	-7.5	
										Change 1981–89
US share of exports to non-US destinations (percentages)	8.8	7.8	7.5	7.9	7.8	6.3	6.2	5.8	6.1	-2.7
US share of imports from non-US sources (percentages)	17.2	16.5	18.9	23.4	25.0	22.6	19.9	18.6	17.4	0.2
Export share minus import share (percentages)	-8.4	-8.7	-11.4	-15.5	-17.2	-16.3	-13.7	-12.8	-11.3	-2.9

Source: World Manufactures Trade Data Base.

Iron and Steel (SITC 67)

US iron and steel trade deficits were a subject of heated debate and policy actions during the 1980s. The deficits improved over the decade with the help of voluntary restraint agreements (VRAs) with major competitors, restructuring and cost-cutting in the US steel industry, strong world steel demand, and decline in US steel-consuming industries. The 1981 deficit was $8.4 billion, improving to $6.5 billion in 1990. The narrowing of the steel trade deficit came also partly in response to the fall in the dollar after 1985, but significant further improvement in the balance is not likely in the near future.

Description of the Product Group

Iron and steel (abbreviated to "steel" in the rest of this analysis) consists of the following three-digit subcategories:

SITC

671 pig iron, spiegeleisen, sponge iron, iron or steel powders and shot, and ferroalloys

672 ingots and other primary forms

673 iron and steel bars, rods, angles, shapes, and sections

674 universals, plates and sheets

675 hoop and strip

676 rails and railway track construction material

677 iron and steel wire, whether or not coated, but not insulated

678 tubes, pipes, and fittings

679 iron and steel castings, forgings, and stampings, in the rough state, not elsewhere specified.

Role in World Trade

Size and Composition

World exports of steel were \$98.1 billion in 1989, just over a third the size of world automotive exports (table 5.67.1). Steel trade growth averaged only 5.4 percent annually during 1981–89, leading to a fall in its share of world manufactures trade of 1.7 percentage points, the largest drop of any single two-digit category (table 3.4). This reflected the general tendency for trade in more finished goods to increase more rapidly than trade in basic materials. For example, trade in products containing steel, such as automobiles, exceeds direct trade in steel. Measured by volume, world steel trade growth averaged only 2 percent during 1981–88, and growth in world production averaged only 1.3 percent, according to International Iron and Steel Institute statistics (1990a and b). In comparison, from 1950 to 1970, growth in world steel production averaged 5.9 percent annually, and in the 1970s 1.9 percent.

Higher-value products, such as sheets, plates, shapes, and pipes, make up a larger share of trade in steel than do unprocessed products such as pig iron and ingots. The flat-rolled products in SITC 674 constitute the largest subcategory. The higher-value products compete more on the basis of quality, unlike nonferrous metals (SITC 68), which compete mainly on price.

Global Competition Patterns

Japan and Germany are the world's leading steel-exporting countries (table 5.67.2) and earn large surpluses in their steel trade (table 5.67.3). The US and Japanese shares of world steel exports fell during 1981–89 while the shares of the European Community and the developing countries grew (table 5.67.2). Japan uses steel much more intensively (as measured by tons consumed per unit of GNP) than other industrialized countries, largely to make automobiles, but it produces enough steel to maintain a significant trade surplus nevertheless.

From 1981 to 1989, the developing countries' share of world steel imports plummeted 11.5 percentage points, and the European Community's grew by a similar amount. The result was that the developing countries' negative share balance diminished by 17.0 percentage points. This occurred to a large extent because their domestic steel production rose, displacing imports. The positive share balances of the European Community and Japan fell, and US performance improved, with the US share of world imports declining much more than did its share of world exports. Table 5.67.2 shows the Asian NICs' share balances in deficit during 1981–89, reflecting their increasing need for steel to support both exports of other manufactures and domestic growth. The data also reflect a diversification of sources of supply for steel as well as a decline in the importance of steel as an import by developing countries, because they either became more self-sufficient in producing steel or lost the ability to pay for imports.

Key Determinants of World Trade Patterns

The world steel industry changed greatly in the 1980s. A capacity overhang developed as steel was used less intensively, as governments subsidized inefficient plants, and as new competitors emerged among the developing countries. The large integrated producers faced competition from mini-mills armed with new technology that made it more economical to produce steel from scrap. In addition, the industrialized countries have largely completed building their basic infrastructures, whereas demand in some developing countries has increased as a result of development. Korea and Brazil now rank among the top 10 countries in steel production and export tonnage, according to the International Iron and Steel Institute (1990a).

Competitive pressures led to widespread restructuring in the US and European steel industries. Japan's steel industry has only recently begun restructuring, and so far the changes there have not been as extensive as in the United States and Europe. Globally, large amounts of capacity and labor were shed in the 1980s. The US General Accounting Office (1989, 4) found that this "pattern of growth and decline in the industry around the world is broadly consistent with what would be expected from considerations of labor cost and differences in growth of demand for steel." Despite global shifts in production and consumption, the largest companies are still based in developed countries. Overcapacity, tough competition for markets, and national interest in the industry—qualities that sometimes lead to export subsidies and import restrictions—characterize the industry.

Role in US Trade

Recent Performance

US exports and imports of steel dropped sharply in the 1980s. Steel accounted for 1.2 percent of US manufactures exports and 2.6 percent of imports in 1990. The steel deficit decreased during 1981–90 from $8.4 billion to $6.5 billion as imports fell faster than exports (table 5.67.4). In 1984, the steel trade deficit reached a record high of $9.4 billion, and import penetration rose to 26 percent. Exports recovered during 1987–90, growing from $1.3 billion to $3.4 billion. Canada is the largest market for US steel exports, with 40.5 percent of the 1990 total, followed by Latin America with 24.0 percent (table 5.67.5). Japan is the largest single-country US supplier, providing 21.8 percent of 1990 US imports, but imports from Canada (15.3 percent), Latin America (12.7 percent), and the European Community (28.8 percent) are also significant.

International Competitiveness

An additional measure of the declining role of the United States in steel trade is given by the US share of world exports to non-US destinations (table 5.67.6). This share fell from 5.5 percent to 4.1 percent during 1981–89, and the US share of world imports from non-US sources fell from 19.7 percent to 12.0 percent. In other words, the United States became a less important source of export competition as well as a less important market for other countries' exports. The overall effect was a modest improvement in the steel trade deficit.

Outlook

Key Determinants of US Trade Performance

Trade data do not, however, capture crucial changes in the US steel industry. The rising dollar in the early 1980s heightened the troubles of the industry, which was already facing the challenges of new competition, new technology, and declining consumption. US firms shed a quarter of their capacity between 1982 and 1987, closing the oldest and least efficient plants. The industry lowered production costs, cutting employment and negotiating concessions in wages. Labor productivity increased dramatically during the 1980s to levels competitive with other countries. The share of US production using the state-of-the art continuous casting method grew from 20 percent in 1981 to 67 percent in 1990, according to the US Department of Commerce (1991). Wharton Econometric Forecasting Associates (Plummer 1990, 21) estimate that US costs per metric ton in the third quarter of 1990 were below those of Japan and Germany and about the same as Canada, but above those of the United Kingdom, Korea, Brazil, and Taiwan.

The 1980s also saw substantial growth in the number of US mini-mills, primarily for lower-value products. One company, Nucor, has opened a thin-slab casting plant that will make higher-value flat-rolled products. However, several mini-mills appear to have backed off from their announced plans to move upmarket, and larger integrated plants still account for 70 percent of US steel production. Foreign ownership and joint ventures have increased sharply and have provided capital and foreign technology. Several Japanese investments in the United States reflect plans to supply Japanese-owned automobile plants in the United States.

The long-term decline in the intensity of use of steel in the US and world economies reflects increased efficiency in the use of steel, reduced infrastructure investment, the availability of substitutes, and growth in less steel-intensive sectors of the economy. According to the US General Accounting Office (1989, 3), the United States now consumes half as much steel per dollar of real GNP as in 1950, and the steel industry's share of the value added by manufacturing industries has declined to one-third its 1958 level.

By 1990, conditions in the US industry had stabilized. The decline in capacity was reversed in 1989. VRAs with 27 countries including the countries of the European Community, Japan, and Korea, which took effect in 1984, helped lower imports, particularly in volume terms. The fall in the dollar and strong global demand at the end of the decade left the US steel deficit in 1990 lower than it had been in 1981, but still large at $6.5 billion. Many countries have not filled their quotas under the VRAs recently. Despite the strong response of the US steel industry to its challenges, the US share of world steel production did not return to 1981 levels. By 1991, US steel consumption had declined as important steel-consuming industries such as the automobile industry shifted production abroad.

Elasticities calculated by DRI indicate that US demand for imported steel is very responsive to changes in import prices, which might be caused by movements in exchange rates, but is not very responsive to US income growth (see the appendix to this volume). Foreign demand for US exports is less responsive to price movements but more responsive to growth in the consumption component of world GNP. A relatively open market in the United States compared with major competitors is one reason the US market is more responsive to changes in import prices.

Near-Term Outlook

Further improvement in the iron and steel trade balance will not be significant without additional dollar depreciation to levels below those of late 1991. Weak world steel demand and global overcapacity could in fact result in some enlargement of the US deficit.

The world steel industry continues to have at least 150 million tons per year overcapacity; 1989 world production was 783 million tons. A number of governments still subsidize their steel industries heavily, although some analysts see a decreasing willingness to do so. The European Community's competition commissioner, Leon Brittan, recently gave up his attempt to end protection for the European steel industry under the Treaty of Paris, according to the *Financial Times* (Leadbeater and Kellaway 1990).

Significant US export expansion is unlikely. The US steel industry is oriented toward serving domestic customers; foreign markets are viewed as vents for intermittent surplus production, not as long-term commitments. Even though transport costs are significant for steel, decisions about plant locations and closings do not indicate a concern for ease of exporting. For instance, few modern plants are located near deep-water ports. Nevertheless, the fall in the dollar exchange rate has made some companies more export oriented; USX Corp. reactivated its exports division in 1988. However, US exporters face a world steel industry that has substantial overcapacity and, in many countries, government support.

An American Iron and Steel Institute survey done for this study reported that US companies producing iron and steel expected exports to be down 20 percent in 1990 and 1993 from 1989 levels, but probably not more than that in the longer term. The survey responses identify several primary factors holding back US export growth: the ability of foreign competitors to service foreign markets, their flexibility in meeting needs, and the existence of foreign import barriers and subsidies. Capacity constraints do not restrain US exports; investment is directed primarily toward modernizing existing capacity. Additional dollar depreciation is not expected to affect exports significantly.

Most analysts expect world steel demand to grow slowly; the temporarily high demand of 1987–89 is now over, and growth is likely to return to the slow pace of the 1970s and early 1980s. The primary export destinations for US steel are Latin America, Canada, the Asian NICs, the European Community, and Japan (table 5.67.5). The American Iron and Steel Institute does not expect EC 1992 to affect exports to the European Community significantly. Intra-EC steel trade has long been open (indeed, one of the constituent organizations of the present Community is an early-1950s arrangement to liberalize coal and steel within Europe—the European Coal and Steel Community), and today it accounts for almost a third of world steel trade (table 5.67.3). The former Eastern bloc countries have not been a traditional US export destination, and there are no significant plans to export there, according to the survey. Credit problems will limit exports to the Soviet Union and China. Asian demand is expected to be stronger, although producers in these markets can be expected to defend their market shares aggressively. Japan in particular will demand more steel for public works projects. Latin American markets are depressed by the fallout from their foreign debt problems, and Latin American capacity added in brighter times is now directed more toward exports, adding to competition in world markets.

In general, demand is growing faster in developing countries than in developed countries, although the intensity of steel use for developing countries as a whole fell during 1979–87.

US steel deficits are more likely to shrink through recapture of US markets by US-based production than through export expansion; the United States is the world's largest single-country importer of steel, although Germany is a very close second (table 5.67.3). Domestic demand will most likely not grow much in 1991, because of weaknesses in major steel-consuming industries such as motor vehicles and construction. The primary sources of US imports are the European Community, Japan, Canada, and Korea (table 5.67.5); few countries are using their full quotas under the VRA program. By 1987, for the first time in many years, the price paid for steel in the United States was no longer the highest in the world, and this development is encouraging foreign exporters to shift some emphasis to other markets. According to the American Iron and Steel Institute, factors holding up the level of US imports include below-cost export prices of foreign manufacturers and US capacity constraints in some products.

US-based production, perhaps by Japanese-owned companies, may gradually replace steel imports by Japanese-owned automobile plants in the United States. However, softening world demand coupled with persisting overcapacity will probably increase foreign competition for US markets. Wharton Econometric Forecasting Associates, the Economist Intelligence Unit, the Organization for Economic Cooperation and Development, and the International Iron and Steel Institute all projected the volume of world steel production to fall in 1991. According to the International Iron and Steel Institute, it had already fallen 2.3 percent in the first nine months of 1990.

The outlook for the US trade balance in steel is contingent on several factors. First, demand for steel is sensitive to the business cycle, interest rates, and particularly the strength of steel-consuming industries. Steel consumption increases faster than GNP growth when the latter is 3 percent per year or higher, although the correlation is imperfect; recessions tend to dampen steel demand. The demand for steel depends substantially on the demand of industries that consume steel, such as construction, automobiles, and machinery. These industries are interest rate sensitive, so rising interest rates also tend to lower demand. If the United States were to undertake the major infrastructure improvement program that some argue is needed, the demand for structural steel and plate would improve.

Second, given higher profits and increased labor productivity in the industry, pressure from unions for higher wages is likely to increase. After a period of constant wages from 1982 to 1988, the United Steelworkers of America in 1989 won wage increases and limits on overtime work. USX Corp., one of the main steel exporters, renewed its labor contract without any strikes; the contract guarantees workers' pension and health benefits should the company be taken over. There are other uncertainties about labor-related costs. Some contracts provide that if inflation is higher than 3 percent, workers will receive automatic cost-of-living adjustments. Also, the industry is responsible for the health care costs of a large number of retirees from the 1980s, and these could prove high.

Third, when President George Bush renewed the steel VRAs in 1989, he committed the US government to negotiations toward an international consensus on unfair trade practices in steel. If these negotiations are successful, the resulting decrease in foreign subsidies and barriers could increase US exports and lower imports. However, many analysts consider a successful outcome to the talks unlikely. In that case, the VRAs could be renewed when they expire in 1992, even though President Bush has said he will not renew them. Although most countries are not using their existing allocations, different economic conditions or more restrictive VRAs could change this. Some industry observers believe that once the VRAs expire, developing countries will gear up to increase their sales in the US market.

Fluctuations in oil prices do not greatly affect costs in the US steel industry as petroleum products are not a major energy source for steel producers.

To summarize the likely effects of the various crosscurrents at work, a recessionary falloff in US demand and the delayed results of earlier declines in exchange rates could improve the US trade balance by up to $1 billion in 1991 and 1992, but a US recovery and increased foreign competition could easily wipe out this improvement by 1993. There is likely to be little change in the 1993 balance compared with 1990.

Medium-Term Outlook

The medium-term export outlook is difficult to predict. The industry has made great strides in modernization, although the finish line is constantly moving. Foreign steelmakers spend more than their US counterparts on R&D, but the US industry has shed its not-invented-here attitude and can often obtain foreign technology, if sometimes with a lag. To some extent, low levels of R&D reflect a recognition that steelmaking technology is mature and that resources are better directed toward incremental process innovations and market-oriented development. In this respect, the increase in the number of US steel companies run by scientists and engineers with operational experience is significant. However, one recent visitor to Japan reports continuing technological advances at a rapid rate and believes that the United States is still losing ground (Merton Flemings, Massachusetts Institute of Technology, personal communication).

In addition to government supports, foreign producers to varying degrees have advantages in labor, raw material, and capital costs. US labor productivity has increased and wage growth has been restrained, but US wages remain higher than those of most competitors.

The US steel industry is by no means doomed, but without further significant decline in the dollar, the trade deficit in steel will remain close to the $6.5 billion level. This will occur because of the persistence of a number of factors: new competitors, foreign advantages in costs and technology, declining use of steel in industrialized countries, and intense competition stemming from world overcapacity.

Conclusions

- The US iron and steel trade balance improved significantly over the 1980s as a result of substantial restructuring, the negotiation of VRAs restricting imports, and strong world demand at the end of the decade.

- The balance improved in the second half of the 1980s largely in response to the fall in the dollar and industry restructuring, but these benefits have largely been played out.

- The US industry is oriented toward domestic customers, and given declining world demand, further significant increases in exports cannot be expected.

- Global overcapacity remains large, with the help of government subsidies. Overcapacity and declining world demand will continue to generate intense competition and make the US market—the world's largest—a continued target for exporters with excess supplies.

- Without further major depreciation in the dollar, no significant improvements from the 1990 iron and steel trade deficit of $6.5 billion should be expected. A recessionary falloff in US demand and further exchange rate decline could improve the US trade balance up to $1 billion in 1991 and 1992, but a US recovery and increased foreign competition could easily wipe out this improvement by 1993.

- Looking beyond 1993, without a further significant decline in the dollar, there is little reason to expect major improvement in steel trade balances. Large deficits near 1991 levels are likely to continue.

Bibliography

Barnett, D., and R. Crandall. 1986. *Up from the Ashes: The Rise of the Steel Minimill in the United States*. Washington: Brookings Institution.
Commission of the European Communities. 1990. *Panorama of EC Industry, 1990*. Luxembourg: Commission of the European Communities.

Duncan, Ronald C., ed. 1991. *Price Prospects for Major Primary Commodities*. Washington: World Bank (in press).

Economist Intelligence Unit. 1990. *Industrial Raw Materials*. London: Business International.

Flemings, Merton, et al. 1989. "The Future of the United States Steel Industry in the International Marketplace." In *The Working Papers of the MIT Commission on Industrial Productivity*, vol. 2. Cambridge, MA: MIT Press.

Hogan, William T. 1990. *Global Steel in the 1990s: Growth or Decline*. Lexington, MA: Lexington.

Industry, Science and Technology Canada. 1988. *Industry Profiles*. Ottawa: Industry, Science and Technology Canada.

International Iron and Steel Institute. 1990a. *World Steel in Figures, 1990*. Brussels: International Iron and Steel Institute.

International Iron and Steel Institute. 1990b. *International Steel Statistical Yearbook, 1990*. Brussels: International Iron and Steel Institute.

Japan Economic Journal. 1990. *Japan Economic Almanac, 1990*. Tokyo: Japan Economic Journal.

Leadbeater, Charles. 1990a. "World Steel Output Forecast to Decline." *Financial Times* (27 September).

Leadbeater, Charles. 1990b. "Hard Times Ahead as World Steel Markets Shrink." *Financial Times* (30 October).

Leadbeater, Charles, and Lucy Kellaway. 1990. "European Steel Sector Retains Protection." *Financial Times* (19 November): 20.

Marcus, Peter, Karlis Kirsis, and Donald Barnett. 1989. *World Steel Dynamics*. New York: Paine Webber (December).

National Academy of Engineering. 1985. *The Competitive Status of the U.S. Steel Industry*. Washington: National Academy Press.

National Research Council. 1990. *Competitiveness of the U.S. Minerals and Metals Industries*. Washington: National Academy Press.

Office of Technology Assessment. 1980. *Technology and Steel Industry Competitiveness*. Washington: Office of Technology Assessment (OTA-M − 122, June).

Organization for Economic Cooperation and Development. 1990a. *Aluminum, Copper, and Steel in Developing Countries*. Paris: Organization for Economic Cooperation and Development.

Organization for Economic Cooperation and Development. 1990b. *The Iron and Steel Industry in 1988*. Paris: Organization for Economic Cooperation and Development (January).

Peters, Anthony. 1990. "Iron and Steel." In *Minerals Yearbook, 1990*, vol. 1. Washington: US Department of the Interior (September).

Plummer, Christopher. 1990. *Conquering World Steel Markets in the 1990s: Country and Product Forecasts to the Year 2000*. Bala Cynwyd, PA: Wharton Econometric Forecasting Associates (August).

Tilton, John E., ed. 1990. *World Metal Demand: Trends and Prospects*. Washington: Resources for the Future (October).

Tumazos, John C. 1990. *Steel Process Efficiency*. New York: Donaldson, Lufkin & Jenrette.

US Congress, Congressional Budget Office. 1987. *How Federal Policies Affect the Steel Industry*. Washington: Congressional Budget Office (February).

US Congress, Congressional Research Service. 1986. *The Competitiveness of American Mining and Processing*. Report prepared for the House Committee on Energy and Commerce, Subcommittee on Oversight and Investigations, Committee Print 99-FF. Washington: Government Printing Office (July).

US Department of Commerce, International Trade Administration. 1987. *Long-Term Trends and Underlying Factors Affecting Steel Consumption in the United States*. Washington: Government Printing Office (October).

US Department of Commerce, International Trade Administration. 1991. *U.S. Industrial Outlook, 1991*. Washington: Government Printing Office (January).

US Department of the Interior, Bureau of Mines. 1990. *Mineral Commodity Summaries, 1990*. Washington: US Department of the Interior (January).

US General Accounting Office. 1989. *The Health of the U.S. Steel Industry*. Washington: General Accounting Office (GAO/NSIAD-89−193, July).

US International Trade Commission. 1989. *Effects of Voluntary Restraint Agreements in Steel*. Washington: US International Trade Commission.

Wharton Econometric Forecasting Associates. 1990. "Executive Summary: U.S. and World Steel." Bala Cynwyd, PA: Wharton Econometric Forecasting Associates (31 August).

Yano, Ichiro, ed. 1989. *Nippon: A Charted Survey of Japan 1989/90*. Tokyo: Tsuneta Yano Memorial Society.

See also the following periodicals: *American Metal Market, Iron Age Manufacturing Management, Iron and Steel Engineer, Metal Bulletin, Steel Times International, World Steel Intelligence,* and the US International Trade Commission's annual surveys and monthly reports on the US steel industry.

Table 5.67.1 Iron and steel: product composition of world trade, 1981–89 (billions of dollars except where noted)

SITC Product	1981	1982	1983	1984	1985	1986	1987	1988	1989	Annual growth 1981–89 (percentages)
World exports to world	64.5	59.5	52.1	57.2	60.2	63.7	70.0	91.3	98.1	5.4
of which:										
671 Pig iron, etc.	3.9	3.1	3.1	3.9	4.0	4.2	4.4	6.8	8.7	10.6
672 Ingots, etc.	6.4	5.4	5.4	6.2	7.1	7.9	9.6	12.5	16.0	12.2
673 Iron, steel shapes	11.6	10.3	9.6	10.3	11.4	11.7	11.6	16.3	15.9	4.0
674 Plates, sheets	18.0	16.8	16.8	18.1	18.2	20.0	23.3	28.7	32.1	7.5
675 Hoop, strip	2.4	2.2	2.2	2.4	2.4	2.9	3.4	2.5	2.4	0.0
676 Railway track, etc.	0.7	0.6	0.5	0.1	0.6	0.6	0.7	1.4	0.7	−0.1
677 Wire not insulated	1.6	1.3	1.3	1.5	1.5	1.8	2.0	2.4	2.7	7.0
678 Tubes, pipes, etc.	19.1	18.0	11.6	12.1	13.0	12.6	12.5	16.5	17.7	−0.9
679 Castings, etc.	0.9	0.8	0.7	0.8	0.8	0.9	1.0	2.5	2.0	10.2
Memorandum:										
SITC 67 share of world manufactures exports (percentages)	6.5	6.1	5.3	5.4	5.3	4.7	4.2	4.6	4.6	−1.8

Source: World Manufactures Trade Data Base.

Table 5.67.2 Iron and steel: geographic distribution of world trade, 1981–89 (percentages of total)

Country	1981	1982	1983	1984	1985	1986	1987	1988	1989	Change 1981–89
Share of exports to world										
United States	4.5	3.6	2.8	2.4	2.0	1.7	1.9	2.3	3.6	−0.8
Canada	3.1	2.8	2.6	3.0	2.9	2.7	2.9	2.2	1.8	−1.2
Japan	25.9	26.3	24.6	24.2	22.6	19.9	18.0	16.9	15.1	−10.7
European Community	50.7	50.1	50.1	48.9	50.3	52.7	53.3	49.2	50.9	0.2
EC to non-EC	27.9	25.7	25.6	25.4	26.3	23.5	23.0	19.9	19.6	−8.3
Germany	16.0	16.5	15.3	14.8	15.7	16.7	16.9	15.1	15.4	−0.6
France	10.0	9.4	9.3	9.2	9.2	9.6	9.5	8.8	8.9	−1.1
Italy	6.4	6.5	6.3	5.9	5.9	6.0	5.9	5.0	6.0	−0.5
United Kingdom	3.8	3.8	3.9	3.6	4.0	4.3	5.1	4.8	5.0	1.2
Other Western Europe	7.6	7.9	8.9	9.0	10.7	11.0	11.7	11.6	10.3	2.7
Asian NICs[a]	1.8	2.8	3.3	3.6	3.2	3.0	3.2	5.9	5.9	4.1
Eastern Europe[b]	1.8	1.7	1.9	2.1	1.9	2.2	2.3	2.7	2.5	0.8
Developing countries	3.8	4.1	5.0	6.3	6.0	6.3	6.7	9.3	9.2	5.5
Latin America	1.4	1.8	2.7	3.6	2.9	3.1	3.2	4.5	4.7	3.3
Rest of world	0.0	0.1	0.0	0.1	0.1	0.1	0.1	0.4	0.7	0.6
Share of imports from world										
United States	18.7	16.5	14.2	20.6	18.2	14.7	13.9	13.2	11.6	−7.1
Canada	3.1	1.8	1.9	2.3	2.5	2.1	2.3	2.8	2.3	−0.8
Japan	1.7	1.9	2.6	3.3	2.4	2.7	3.5	5.0	5.1	3.5
European Community	30.2	32.5	34.0	31.8	32.1	39.4	40.4	39.0	41.6	11.4
EC from non-EC	7.0	8.3	8.7	8.1	8.4	10.3	10.2	10.1	11.1	4.0
Germany	8.2	8.4	9.9	8.7	8.9	10.9	10.7	10.2	10.9	2.7
France	6.2	6.6	6.6	6.1	5.9	6.9	7.2	6.7	6.9	0.8
Italy	3.6	3.9	4.0	4.3	4.2	5.4	5.9	5.8	6.7	3.1
United Kingdom	3.4	3.9	3.7	3.5	3.6	4.1	4.4	4.7	4.7	1.3
Other Western Europe	6.6	6.8	6.9	6.6	8.0	9.0	9.6	8.6	8.1	1.5
Asian NICs[a]	4.8	4.3	5.1	5.1	4.2	5.0	6.4	8.4	9.9	5.1
Eastern Europe[b]	6.7	7.9	8.5	7.1	7.0	6.6	6.4	5.4	4.3	−2.5
Developing countries	27.7	27.6	26.0	22.3	24.9	20.1	17.0	17.2	16.2	−11.5
Latin America	6.8	5.2	2.7	2.7	2.5	2.3	2.5	2.2	2.3	−4.5
Rest of world	0.1	0.0	0.3	0.2	0.3	0.1	0.1	0.2	0.3	0.2

Export share minus import share

United States	-14.3	-12.9	-11.4	-18.2	-16.2	-13.0	-12.0	-10.9	-8.0	6.2
Canada	0.0	1.0	0.7	0.8	0.4	0.6	0.6	-0.7	-0.5	-0.5
Japan	24.2	24.4	22.1	20.9	20.2	17.2	14.5	11.9	10.0	-14.2
European Community	20.5	17.6	16.1	17.1	18.2	13.3	12.9	10.2	9.3	-11.2
Non-EC	20.9	17.4	16.8	17.3	17.9	13.2	12.8	9.9	8.5	-12.4
Germany	7.8	8.1	5.4	6.0	6.8	5.8	6.2	4.9	4.5	-3.3
France	3.8	2.8	2.7	3.1	3.3	2.7	2.3	2.1	2.0	-1.8
Italy	2.8	2.6	2.3	1.6	1.7	0.5	-0.1	-0.7	-0.8	-3.6
United Kingdom	0.4	-0.1	0.2	0.1	0.4	0.2	0.7	0.2	0.3	-0.1
Other Western Europe	1.0	1.1	2.0	2.4	2.7	2.0	2.1	3.0	2.2	1.2
Asian NICs[a]	-3.0	-1.5	-1.9	-1.5	-1.0	-2.0	-3.2	-2.5	-4.0	-1.1
Eastern Europe[b]	-5.0	-6.2	-6.7	-5.0	-5.1	-4.4	-4.1	-2.7	-1.8	3.2
Developing countries	-24.0	-23.5	-21.0	-16.0	-18.9	-13.7	-10.2	-7.9	-7.0	17.0
Latin America	-5.4	-3.4	-0.0	0.9	0.4	0.8	0.7	2.3	2.4	7.8
Rest of world	-0.0	0.1	-0.3	-0.1	-0.2	0.1	0.0	0.3	0.4	0.4

a. Hong Kong, Korea, Singapore, and Taiwan.

b. Including Soviet Union.

Source: World Manufactures Trade Data Base.

Table 5.67.3 Iron and steel: bilateral trade flows, 1989 (billions of dollars)

Importer	World	United States	Canada	Japan	European Community	Germany	France	United Kingdom	Asian NICs	Latin America	Other
						Exporter					
World	98.1	3.5	1.8	14.9	50.0	15.1	8.8	4.9	5.7	4.6	17.7
United States	11.1		1.6	2.4	3.2	0.9	0.7	0.4	0.9	1.3	1.7
Canada	2.0	0.8		0.2	0.5	0.1	0.1	0.1	0.1	0.3	0.2
Japan	5.4	0.3			0.2	0.0	0.0	0.0	2.3	0.8	1.8
European Community	41.8	0.4	0.1	0.4	30.7	8.0	5.6	2.8	0.2	1.0	9.0
Germany	11.0	0.0	0.0	0.1	7.2		1.7	0.8	0.1	0.3	3.4
France	7.1	0.0	0.0	0.0	6.0	1.7		0.4	0.0	0.1	1.1
United Kingdom	4.6	0.1	0.0	0.2	3.3	1.2	0.5		0.0	0.1	1.0
Asian NICs	8.5	0.5	0.0	4.1	0.8	0.2	0.1	0.2	0.6	0.9	1.5
Latin America	2.3	0.8	0.0	0.4	0.9	0.3	0.2	0.1	0.1		0.1
Other	27.1	0.9	0.1	7.4	13.7	5.5	2.0	1.2	1.6	0.3	3.3

Source: World Manufactures Trade Data Base.

Table 5.67.4 Iron and steel: product composition of US trade, 1981–90[a] (millions of dollars)

Category	SITC Rev. 2 1981	SITC Rev. 2 1987	SITC Rev. 2 Change 1981–87	SITC Rev. 3 1987	SITC Rev. 3 1990	Change 1981–90	Change 1987–90
Total							
Exports	2,878	1,290	-1,588	1,270	3,390	512	2,120
Imports	11,238	9,097	-2,141	9,127	9,874	-1,364	747
Balance	-8,360	-7,807	553	-7,857	-6,484	1,876	1,373
of which							
671 Pig iron, etc.							
Exports	77	67	10	71	147	70	76
Imports	861	628	233	627	1,063	202	436
Balance	-784	-561	-223	-556	-916	-132	-360
672 Ingots and other primary forms							
Exports	155	34	121	69	214	59	145
Imports	371	613	-242	527	606	235	79
Balance	-216	-579	363	-458	-393	-177	65
673 Iron, steel shapes							
Exports	345	156	189	103	647	302	544
Imports	1,739	1,711	28	2,137	2,157	418	20
Balance	-1,394	-1,555	161	-2,034	-1,510	-116	524
674 Universals, plates and sheets							
Exports	663	362	301	164	401	-262	237
Imports	2,853	3,955	-1,102	1,645	1,448	-1,405	-197
Balance	-2,190	-3,593	1,403	-1,481	-1,046	1,144	435
675 Hoop, strip							
Exports	98	67	31	162	302	204	140
Imports	104	188	-84	470	727	623	257
Balance	-6	-121	115	-308	-425	-419	-117
676 Rails and railway track construction material							
Exports	70	27	43	194	541	471	347
Imports	109	66	43	1,717	1,408	1,299	-309
Balance	-39	-39	0	-1,523	-867	-828	656
677 Iron and steel wire, not insulated							
Exports	74	57	17	27	56	-18	29
Imports	317	408	-91	66	105	-212	39
Balance	-243	-351	108	-39	-49	194	-10
678 Tubes, pipes, and fittings							
Exports	1,252	436	816	44	95	-1,157	51
Imports	4,846	1,502	3,344	408	388	-4,458	-20
Balance	-3,594	-1,066	-2,528	-364	-293	3,301	71
679 Castings, forgings, and stampings							
Exports	144	84	60	436	987	843	551
Imports	38	26	12	1,530	1,971	1,933	441
Balance	106	58	48	-1,094	-984	-1,090	110

a. Data are expressed on a domestic exports, imports customs basis. *Source:* US Department of Commerce.

Table 5.67.5 Iron and steel: geographic composition of US trade, 1981–90

	Millions of dollars				Percentages of total			
	1981	1987	1989	1990	1981	1987	1989	1990
Exports								
Canada	778	466	634	1,374	27.0	36.7	19.3	40.5
Japan	43	48	270	212	1.5	3.8	8.2	6.3
European Community	278	164	350	362	9.7	12.9	10.6	10.7
United Kingdom	105	46	99	108	3.6	3.6	3.0	3.2
Germany	31	37	42	60	1.1	2.9	1.3	1.8
France	41	17	33	54	1.4	1.3	1.0	1.6
Italy	34	27	115	57	1.2	2.1	3.5	1.7
Latin America	1,086	312	730	815	37.7	24.6	22.2	24.0
Asian NICs	122	77	456	228	4.2	6.1	13.9	6.7
Korea	30	20	317	150	1.1	1.6	9.7	4.4
Other	570	203	847	399	19.8	16.0	25.8	11.8
Total	2,877	1,270	3,287	3,390	100.0	100.0	100.0	100.0
Imports								
Canada	1,388	1,579	1,657	1,506	12.4	17.3	15.6	15.3
Japan	3,864	2,228	2,476	2,155	34.4	24.4	23.4	21.8
European Community	3,779	2,495	3,055	2,846	33.6	27.3	28.8	28.8
United Kingdom	342	275	413	392	3.0	3.0	3.9	4.0
Germany	1,224	762	887	865	10.9	8.3	8.4	8.8
France	689	527	730	664	6.1	5.8	6.9	6.7
Italy	483	226	241	252	4.3	2.5	2.3	2.6
Latin America	539	919	1,225	1,254	4.8	10.1	11.6	12.7
Asian NICs	567	652	647	754	5.0	7.1	6.1	7.6
Korea	489	491	479	574	4.4	5.4	4.5	5.8
Other	1,101	1,254	1,538	1,359	9.8	13.7	14.5	13.8
Total	11,238	9,127	10,598	9,874	100.0	100.0	100.0	100.0

a. Data are expressed on a domestic exports, imports customs basis.

Source: US Department of Commerce.

Table 5.67.6 Iron and steel: indices of US competitiveness, 1981–89 (billions of dollars except where noted)

	1981	1982	1983	1984	1985	1986	1987	1988	1989	Annual growth 1981–89 (percentages)
World trade										
World exports to non-US destinations	52.4	51.0	44.4	45.6	49.7	54.6	60.0	79.2	87.1	6.6
World imports from non-US sources	61.8	59.1	50.4	56.1	60.1	63.6	68.8	90.3	96.1	5.7
US trade										
Exports	2.9	2.2	1.5	1.3	1.2	1.1	1.3	2.1	3.5	2.6
Imports	12.1	10.1	7.4	11.9	11.2	9.6	9.8	12.3	11.5	-0.6
Balance	-9.2	-7.9	-5.9	-10.6	-10.0	-8.5	-8.5	-10.2	-8.0	
										Change 1981–89
US share of exports to non-US destinations (percentages)	5.5	4.2	3.3	2.9	2.5	2.0	2.2	2.7	4.1	-1.4
US share of imports from non-US sources (percentages)	19.7	17.2	14.7	21.1	18.7	15.0	14.2	13.6	12.0	-7.7
Export share minus import share (percentages)	-14.2	-13.0	-11.4	-18.2	-16.2	-13.0	-12.0	-10.9	-7.9	6.3

Source: World Manufactures Trade Data Base.

Nonferrous Metals (SITC 68)

The United States runs substantial, persistent deficits in most nonferrous metals and imports more than half its consumption of silver, platinum, zinc, nickel, and tin. The 1980s were a difficult decade for the nonferrous metals industry, but the US copper industry managed dramatic cost reductions, and the US share of world silver production grew quickly. Aluminum trade has returned to near balance, although the industry must import almost all of its raw materials. Metals prices are hard to predict. A fall in metals prices and a slowdown in the US economy would probably lead to some reduction in the deficit. A recovery in US metals-consuming industries would enlarge the deficit. However, the US metals and related mining industries have been declining for a long time, and significant improvement is highly unlikely.

Description of the Product Group

Nonferrous metals consists of:

SITC

681 silver, platinum, and other metals of the platinum group

682 copper

683 nickel

684 aluminum

685 lead

686 zinc

687 tin

688 uranium depleted of U-235, thorium, and their alloys

689 tungsten, molybdenum, tantalum, magnesium, and other base metals and cermets (bonded ceramic-metallic mixtures).

This product group includes semifabricated articles such as bars, rods, pipes, foils, plates, and wire; metal manufactures are recorded under SITC 69 and elsewhere. Nonmonetary gold is recorded under SITC 97 (Revision 2). Coins that are not legal tender are recorded under SITC 96. Ores and scrap are recorded under SITC 2. Trade in uranium and thorium is small in dollar terms and is not included in this analysis; the subcategory was deleted in SITC Revision 3.

Role in World Trade

Size and Composition

World exports of nonferrous metals were $67.7 billion in 1989 (table 5.68.1). These exports grew relatively slowly during 1981–89, and their share of world manufactures exports fell, from 3.5 percent to 3.2 percent. The developed economies have gradually been reducing the intensity of their use of metals, as measured by tons consumed per unit of GNP. Metal-consuming industries have economized on the use of metals by substituting plastics and other materials. Because refining and smelting are energy intensive, rising costs for energy and pollution abatement have tended to increase the prices of metals compared with substitutes.

Aluminum, copper, and silver are the most important nonferrous metals in world trade. World exports of aluminum grew during the 1980s at a rapid 12.7 percent annual rate, in part because of aluminum's use as a lightweight and recyclable substitute for other metals in, for example, beverage containers. The intensity with which the world economy uses aluminum remained fairly constant during the 1980s, while the intensity of use of other metals such as steel and copper fell. Also, higher aluminum prices increased the dollar value of the quantities traded.

Global Competition Patterns

The largest exporters of nonferrous metals in 1989 were Germany, Canada, and Latin America; the largest importers were the United States, Japan, Germany, and France. The developing countries and Canada are large net exporters of nonferrous metals, while the European Community, the United States, and Japan are large net importers (table 5.68.2). The roles of most countries in metals trade did not change greatly on balance over the 1980s; the largest change was the increase in the Asian NICs' negative share balance by 5 percentage points, reflecting rapid growth in metal-consuming industries in those countries.

Most minerals trade flows from the developing countries and Canada to the industrialized countries, particularly if intra-EC trade is excluded (table 5.68.3). The United States, Japan, and Germany all run significant minerals trade deficits.

Key Determinants of World Trade Patterns

The intensity with which nonferrous metals are used in the industrialized economies has fallen since 1973 (Tilton 1990, 305). However, the developing countries have increased their intensity of use over that period. The United States and the United Kingdom also use most metals less intensively than Germany and Japan, possibly because the United States and the United Kingdom import metal-intensive products, have a larger share of services in their GNP, and currently invest less in metal-intensive capital goods.

World trade patterns are further discussed below by subcategory.

Role in US Trade

Recent Performance

Nonferrous metals accounted in 1990 for 1.7 percent of exports and 2.5 percent of imports in US manufactures trade. The US trade deficit in nonferrous metals increased from $4.1 billion in 1981 to $5.9 billion in 1989, but narrowed to $4.6 billion in 1990 (table 5.68.4). Canada, with its abundant mineral and energy resources, accounted for two-fifths of US imports in 1990 (table 5.68.5). The primary US export destinations were Japan, Canada, and the European Community. Deteriorating trade balances in several metal-consuming industries, such as automobiles, reduced US demand for metals imports and the scrap and ores used to make them. As already noted, the US aluminum industry imports almost all of its raw materials, and most US zinc ore is exported before processing.

Almost all the metals in this product group are traded on commodity exchanges in New York and London, and their prices are volatile. Changes in the US trade balance measured in dollars are often a result of these price changes. Speculation and investment demand frequently receive the blame for price volatility, but inelastic short-run responses of metal supply and demand to external shocks also play an important role. Consuming industries do not alter their production plans with every change in metals prices, nor do the mining industries alter production plans with every change in refining prices. Moreover, smelting industries have long lead times to discover and develop new deposits, and they incur high costs when shutting down. Also, governments now own a significant proportion of production capacity, and to meet their social objectives they often do not cut production in surplus periods. As a result, small shifts in the nearly vertical short-run demand and supply curves require large changes in prices to clear markets. Shifts are most common in demand, because of the cyclical nature of metals-consuming industries: construction, capital equipment, consumer durables, and transportation. Political unrest, strikes, and bad weather can create shortages in supply, particularly now that more of the industry is located in developing countries.

Supply and demand are more elastic in the long run, so short-term price fluctuations do not necessarily reflect long-run trends. Theoretically, inventories and futures markets can smooth out short-run deviations, but high interest costs and short time horizons in futures markets limit their effectiveness. The United States has lost its former dominant position in world metal production, except for molybdenum and magnesium. In 1989, the United States imported more than half of its silver, platinum, zinc, nickel, and tin consumption. The causes of decline in US smelting and refining are discussed below in tandem with the causes of the poor health of US mining. The high transport costs for ores link the prospects of the two industries, and both face similar energy and labor costs and regulations.

A Congressional Research Service study found that the US mining and processing industry has declined significantly, but that it is too soon to announce its death (US Congress, Congressional Research Service 1986, 141). At one time, the United States had the largest, shallowest, highest-grade, and easiest-to-refine ore deposits in the world excluding the Soviet Union as well as lower labor costs per unit of output, better technologies, and cheaper energy than the rest of the world. A long list of factors, however, have greatly reduced or eliminated the US comparative advantage in mining and smelting. According to the National Research Council (1990, 52), these include depletion of resources, new discoveries abroad, high labor costs, the application of more efficient "greenfield" mine designs and equipment, the diffusion of technology and sophisticated management techniques, the movement of consuming industries to other countries, greater substitution away from metals and greater economy in the use of metals in the United States, increasing US electricity costs and development of less expensive sources abroad, stricter US regulations to protect the environment and workers' health, safety, and other rights, the desire of developing countries to process their own ores, the consequent emergence of government-owned companies, and the availability of concessionary capital to firms in developing countries (National Research Council 1990, 52).

In many metals, the United States became the swing supplier, the one that had to cut production when prices fell. This occurred because US costs increased relative to competitors' costs and because foreign government-controlled companies stay in the market even when prices fall to maintain employment or obtain foreign exchange. As comparative advantage shifted and as the dollar rose to its 1985 peak, overcapacity became apparent and the US nonferrous metals industry went through a tough period. In response, technology was improved, and nontechnological ways to cut costs—plant closings, wage cuts, labor force reductions, and reduced R&D budgets—were implemented to such an extent that little further cost reduction is now considered possible in those areas. According to many analysts, however, the United States is now no longer the swing supplier and is less vulnerable to price fluctuations than before.

The United States does retain a number of advantages vis-à-vis some competitors: higher productivity, lower internal transport costs, a lower tax burden, fewer government restrictions, a stronger resource base than Europe or Japan, greater availability of scrap, and market-determined input prices. Real US electricity prices have been falling, but some foreign aluminum producers still have access to cheaper (often hydroelectric) energy sources. Despite the ability of the US metals industry to weather the very difficult 1980s, it is highly unlikely that the United States will ever return to its previously dominant position.

International Competitiveness

The US share of world metals trade declined in the 1980s (table 5.68.6). US imports accounted for about one-sixth of the market for world exports from non-US sources in 1989, although that share had fallen by 5.3 percentage points since 1981. The US share of world exports to non-US destinations also fell, but by a smaller amount, to 8.2 percent in 1989.

Outlook

Key Determinants of US Trade Performance

The following sections analyze each metal separately. Because many metals are jointly mined or are substitutes for one another, the separation is not always clean.

Silver and Platinum (SITC 681)

The United States is the second-largest producer of silver in the world; the other big producers are Mexico, Peru, the former Soviet Union, and Canada. However, US production of silver is not sufficient to meet domestic consumption needs. The 1990 nominal dollar price of silver was at a 15-year low and was half its 1981 price; nonetheless, US silver production increased because silver is often a by-product of gold, copper, zinc, and lead mining. This effect has been even greater for other countries whose ores have richer by-products. Silver is used primarily for photographic purposes; much of US silver "consumption" leaves the country as exports of photographic film (this may change if new, electronics-based photographic technologies enter the market as expected). Silver is also used in electrical and electronic goods, jewelry, and silverware. In addition to utilitarian considerations, market conditions for this precious metal reflect the attitudes of investors and speculators.

South Africa and the former Soviet Union produce most of the world's platinum, palladium, and rhodium. The United States produces only small amounts of metals in the platinum group and relies heavily on imports. Platinum is used as a catalyst by the automotive and chemical industries, for electrical and electronic goods, and for jewelry. World demand exceeded supply in the late 1980s but was projected by Johnson Matthey (1990), an investment firm, to fall short of supply in 1990.

Copper (SITC 682)

The US trade balance in copper improved in dollar terms from 1981 to 1990, although the US share of world production fell. The United States still manages to meet 65 percent to 70 percent of its copper needs domestically; it remains the largest refiner of copper but has dropped to second place in production of copper ore. The main copper producers are Chile, the United States, Canada, the former Soviet Union, Zaire, Zambia, Poland, Peru, and the Philippines.

Several forces precipitated restructuring in the US copper industry in the 1980s. The decade began with substantial world overcapacity, and world inventories continued to grow through 1982. Demand fell short of expectations, particularly during the 1981–82 world recession. Also, miniaturization and the use of substitutes such as aluminum and fiber optics cut into copper consumption over the longer term. On the supply side, inertia in the discovery and development process meant a lag in the effect that the slowdown in demand had on capacity additions. In spite of falling prices and growing inventories, production in developing countries increased, led particularly by government-owned companies, which often had institutional financing. Also, developing countries sought to capture more of the value added by copper production and became less willing to supply unprocessed ore.

Factors internal to the United States also played an important role. Many of the US smelters and refineries that shut down were outdated, and others did not comply with environmental regulations, according to the Office of Technology Assessment (US Congress, Office of Technology Assessment 1990). Labor costs were high, technology was lagging, and the quality of US copper ore was lower than that of foreign competitors and was declining.

In any case, the US industry bore the brunt of adjustment to the slowdown in world demand. In 1978 and 1984, the US International Trade Commission found that imports had substantially injured the US copper industry, although no protective action was taken. The US copper industry recovered toward the end of the 1980s as a result of higher prices and extensive cost-cutting. High-cost facilities were closed, labor costs were cut, and a cost-efficient technology—solvent extraction-electrowinning—was widely adopted. Producers in other countries have also lowered their costs, but not to the same extent.

The world overcapacity problem has largely been resolved. Copper inventories in the market economies fell from 1982 through 1987 but have been fairly constant since then. The 1990 nominal dollar price of copper was 50 percent above the 1981 price. Because of supply problems, world demand exceeded supply in 1989, and it should continue to do so for the next few years. A significant share of world copper production now comes from politically unstable areas, and supply disruptions have become common.

Nickel (SITC 683)

The US nickel trade deficit enlarged over the 1980s by $0.7 billion, to a 1989 deficit of $1.3 billion, but recovered strongly in 1990 to a $0.9 billion deficit (table 5.68.4). The United States has had no nickel ore production since 1986 and has shed a substantial amount of smelting and refining capacity. US consumption of nickel has declined recently as a result of decreased demand for stainless steel, its primary use. The primary nickel producers are Canada, the former Soviet Union, New Caledonia (a French overseas territory in the Pacific), the United States, Indonesia, Cuba, and South Africa. About 40 percent of world production is directly or indirectly state controlled and does not readily respond to market forces, according to Industry, Science and Technology Canada (1988, 2). Market-economy nickel inventories increased from 1980 to 1982 and have been falling since then.

Aluminum (SITC 684)

US aluminum trade returned to near balance in 1990 after deteriorating to a deficit of $1.6 billion during the 1980s (table 5.68.4). However, the industry must import nearly all its raw materials (which are recorded in SITC 28). Even though the United States has few remaining bauxite resources and high energy costs, it is the second-largest aluminum refiner and the largest smelter among the market economies. The largest aluminum-consuming industries are those that make containers and packaging and transportation equipment, and the construction and electrical industries. Over time, some aluminum users have shifted to plastics and composites. However, as noted above, there has also been substitution from other metals to aluminum because of its low weight and recyclability.

The world aluminum smelting and refining industry underwent substantial restructuring in the 1980s as a result of overcapacity and shifting competitiveness. The main aluminum producers are now the United States, the former Soviet Union, Canada, Australia, Brazil, China, and Norway; the industry remains concentrated. Japan was the world's second-largest producer of primary aluminum at the outset of the 1980s but is now largely out of that business. Comparative advantage in aluminum production has shifted from the United States, Japan, and some European countries to Australia and Brazil, according to the Congressional Research Service (US Congress, Congressional Research Service 1986, 115). However, the process of restructuring is not yet complete. A study by Bird Associates found that 7 percent of primary aluminum production capacity in the market economies is uneconomic, mostly in Europe (Gooding 1990c).

Even though the US share of the world's aluminum smelting fell in the 1980s, the US industry maintained its role in fabrication and marketing. US producers also retain a large role in aluminum smelting, but their dependence on foreign sources of ores and concentrates, unlike other metals industries, makes them vulnerable to the effects of increasing shipping costs and strikes. Electricity, which accounts for a quarter of operating costs, has become available in some countries at lower prices than in the United States. Also, governments directly or indirectly control around a third of the world's aluminum capacity and tend not to cut production during surplus periods. Foreign subsidies and trade barriers also limit US export opportunities, according to the US Commerce Department. Because of this policy and a narrowing of the comparative disadvantage of the United States, US companies became the swing suppliers for a period. In spite of these disadvantages, five years of restructuring have left the US industry much more competitive. The aluminum smelting industry managed to reduce energy and labor costs substantially in the late 1980s, but unlike with copper, capacity did not recover to original levels.

Lead (SITC 685)

Despite a 50 percent increase in the price of lead, the small US trade deficit in lead narrowed slightly during 1981–90 (table 5.68.4). US trade in this metal is small compared with other nonferrous metals. The production of lead as a by-product of zinc, particularly in other countries, has recently led to a large world oversupply of lead. Because lead and zinc deposits are found together less often in the United States than in competitor countries, US lead producers are often at a disadvantage.

Transportation equipment accounts for three-quarters of US lead consumption; its primary use there is in electrical batteries. In addition, lead is used in oxides, ammunition, cathode tubes, paints, crystal, and gasoline. The use of lead has dropped for health and environmental reasons and because substitutes have become more widely available.

The primary lead producers are the former centrally planned economies, Australia, the United States, Canada, Mexico, and Peru. Large US deposits of lead ore can be profitably mined using mechanical means, which has helped the US industry compete against countries with lower labor costs. However, US deposits produce few valuable by-products. Recycled lead, most of it from used batteries, accounts for 65 percent of US lead production. Environmental regulations have been less burdensome for the lead and zinc industry than for other certain metals. In particular, standards limiting sulfur emissions into the atmosphere have not been burdensome because the sulfur can be captured and sold in the form of sulfuric acid; important markets for the acid fortunately happen to be nearby. Also, US lead and zinc ores are relatively clean.

Zinc (SITC 686)

The US trade deficit in zinc grew over the 1980s, mostly after 1987, reaching $1.0 billion in 1990 (table 5.68.4). Some of the deterioration can be attributed to the 75 percent increase in the nominal dollar price of zinc from 1981 to 1990.

US production of zinc ore is growing quickly, but, unable to match subsidized foreign competitors, the US industry has largely lost the ability to process zinc ore. The Red Dog Mine in Alaska will soon be the largest zinc-producing mine in the world, according to the US Commerce Department, and most of its output will be exported in unprocessed form. Deposits in the United States are of lower grade and have fewer valuable by-products than deposits abroad, but US labor is more productive. As US deposits have become depleted, US smelting and refining plants, which have mostly been located in the interior of the country, have had trouble obtaining other sources of supply. Excess smelting capacity worldwide has increased competition to obtain zinc ore, driving its price up. As mentioned above, environmental regulations have so far not been as burdensome for the US lead and zinc industries as for other metals. Although the United States is a small producer compared with other countries, it is the largest producer of zinc from scrap. The United States uses zinc less intensely than other countries, although indirect imports of products containing zinc probably account for most of the difference.

World zinc demand and prices are at record levels. However, US zinc consumption has grown slowly over the 1980s. The main zinc consumers are the transportation and construction industries, increasingly for use in galvanized steel, although zinc is also used for die casting and brass. The US market for zinc alloy has shrunk as imports of products containing zinc have increased. Over time, particularly in the 1970s, zinc users have also substituted lighter-weight materials and have learned to use the metal more efficiently.

Tin (SITC 687)

The United States has never had significant tin resources, and essentially all requirements must be imported. The largest tin producers are Brazil, Malaysia, Indonesia, and China. The most common uses of tin are as a coating on steel sheets, solder, white metal and pewter, chemicals, bronze, and tinning. With the help of falling prices, the US trade balance in tin improved over the 1980s from a deficit of $0.6 billion in 1981 to a deficit of $0.2 billion in 1990 (table 5.68.4). The drop in prices was initially the result of the 1981 recession, but price supports under the International Tin Agreement collapsed later in the 1980s.

Other Nonferrous Metals (SITC 689)

The deficit in this miscellaneous category fell from $197 million in 1981 to $59 million in 1990 (table 5.68.4). The United States is a net exporter and the world's largest producer of molybdenum. The United States produces a much smaller volume of molybdenum than of most other metals, but because of its high prices, the United States usually produces a higher dollar value of molybdenum than of lead or zinc. The United States is also a large producer and net exporter of magnesium. The United States has no economic sources of chrome and man-ganese domestically and also imports tungsten and tantalum.

According to import price and demand elasticities calculated by DRI, US demand for imports of nonferrous metals is not very sensitive to changes in import prices, such as might be caused by changes in the exchange rate (see the appendix to this volume). Movements in import prices have a counterin-tuitive effect on demand for US exports of nonferrous metals; the foreign price elasticities are positive or only slightly negative. These might result from the insignificance of US export potential in this area, or it might be that a strong dollar damages US metals-consuming industries so much that US nonferrous metals exports increase. On the other hand, the trade balance in this product group is very responsive to growth in the consumption component of GNP, implying that faster growth abroad than in the United States will have strongly positive effects on this trade balance.

Near- and Medium-Term Outlook

The United States does not have a big export presence in most of these metals, nor does it have much potential to increase exports, except perhaps in semi-fabricated products. Most progress will therefore have to come in the form of reduced imports. Price volatility makes predictions difficult, but if World Bank projections of falling metals prices are borne out (Duncan 1991), the dollar value of the US trade deficit should also fall, even if the physical volume of exports and imports remains relatively stable. Several important metals-consuming industries are already weak, particularly the automotive and construction industries, and a further downturn in the US economy would reduce industrial demand for metals even more. On the other hand, a large program to rebuild and expand US infrastructure would increase demand for most metals. Substitution in and out of these metals will continue to occur on an incremental, or part-by-part basis, and will alter demand conditions only slowly; the net effect on the trade deficit over the next few years is likely to be small in any event.

In the longer run, the combination of higher wages, higher energy costs, lower-quality ores, and a return to strong demands for metals implies that the United States will remain a net importer of metals for the foreseeable future. The United States is unlikely to gain a significant technological edge unless innovations are peculiarly suited to US resources. Technology transfer in the metals industry is almost immediate, because most innovations are developed by equipment vendors; the United States is a net exporter of mining machinery and equipment.

The near- and medium-term outlook is further discussed by individual metal below.

Silver and Platinum (SITC 681)

The US trade deficit in this category, $1.9 billion in 1990, can be expected to improve in 1991. The silver trade balance will improve as mining of silver as a by-product increases, with some offset from falling prices. However, the US silver deficit will remain near its 1991 level for the foreseeable future.

A surplus of platinum may cause prices to continue the fall begun in 1990 and thereby lead to a reduction in the dollar value of the platinum trade deficit. In the short term, slowed US automobile production will be demanding fewer catalytic converters, which contain platinum, but the amount of platinum in each converter is increasing. Weak consumer confidence will also hurt demand for jewelry. In the longer term, the platinum deficit will continue near 1991 levels.

Copper (SITC 682)

Stimulated by strong foreign demand compared with that in the United States and increased US production capacity, the US trade deficit in copper, $0.5 billion in 1990, should improve, particularly in semifabricated products. Copper demand in Japan and Germany is already outstripping those countries' domestic capacities. In the longer term, Japan's Ministry of International Trade and Industry expects US copper demand to grow slowly through the year 2000 compared with the rest of the world, but Asian demand to grow faster than world demand, at over 6 percent annually (Gooding 1990a). Stronger copper demand abroad will tend to improve the US copper trade deficit.

Except for a new large smelter in Texas, US production will be relatively stable; the trade balance will be largely determined by domestic demand. US producers have probably lowered costs sufficiently to become competitive and will no longer be the swing suppliers, the ones that have to cut production first when prices go down. The trade deficit is more likely to decrease through falling prices than through changes in actual quantities exported and imported. Analysts project that capacity in the market economies will exceed consumption in the early 1990s, making falling prices probable. In fact, the surplus probably exists already but has been masked by various supply problems.

Nickel (SITC 683)

Reduced demand or lower nickel prices offer the only hope for improvement in the nickel deficit. Lower prices are indeed probable, given that several forecasters expect world nickel supply to exceed demand for the next few years (Gooding 1990b). Some nickel producers will cut capacity at present prices, but falling prices should still reduce the dollar size of the US deficit.

Aluminum (SITC 684)

The US balance in aluminum should improve, particularly in semifabricated products. Foreign demand for aluminum has been strong and should continue to grow more quickly than US demand, according to forecasts (see, e.g., Bourke 1990). Projections are that in the market economies (and particularly in Asia) aluminum demand, which is now slightly above capacity, will continue to grow more quickly than capacity. One reason that foreign demand will grow more quickly is that the United States has largely completed the shift to aluminum beverage cans, while other countries have not.

If prices fall, the high production costs of European producers should make them the swing suppliers, assuming that governments are willing to let them shut down production. However, rising prices are more probable. The United States is highly unlikely to add new capacity, given its higher electricity costs. Capacity expansions are, however, planned in a number of countries with low energy costs. Industry officials expect continued growth in world production of around 2 percent to 3 percent over the next several years. The 1990–91 Gulf crisis caused some analysts to lower their projections.

Lead (SITC 685)

US demand for lead for automotive batteries will be weak. The US Bureau of Mines has forecast zero growth in US lead demand through the year 2000. Therefore, the US trade balance in lead should continue to improve. Future environmental regulations that would reduce US lead production and increase imports are, however, a strong possibility.

Zinc (SITC 686)

The US trade balance in zinc is expected to improve. The Japanese Ministry of International Trade and Industry projects that zinc demand will grow more slowly in the United States through the year 2000 than in the rest of the world, particularly Asia.

The outlook for tin and other nonferrous metals is similar to that for zinc.

Conclusions

■ The United States runs persistent deficits in almost all nonferrous metals. The only large category near balance is aluminum, but almost all raw materials for aluminum refining (bauxite and alumina) are imported.

■ The US metals and related mining industries have been declining for a long time, and significant improvement is highly unlikely, given relatively high US electricity and labor costs, the lack of significant new deposits, and the mobility of technology.

■ Falling prices and a slowdown in the US economy would help reduce the metals deficit. A recovery in metals-consuming industries or a concerted program to rebuild US infrastructure would, however, enlarge the deficit.

■ The US trade deficit will remain near the 1990 level of $4.6 billion for the foreseeable future, with fluctuations in the balance largely a function of changes in prices and international economic growth rates.

Bibliography

Atwell, Wayne. 1990a. *Copper Perspectives: Back to the Future*. New York: Gold-man Sachs (11 September).

Atwell, Wayne. 1990b. *Steel and Nonferrous Focus with Monthly Statistics*. New York: Goldman Sachs (October).

Bourke, William. 1990. "Aluminum Industry Year-End Review and 1991 Out-look." Richmond, VA: Reynolds Metal Company (12 December).

Brook Hunt & Associates. 1984. *Western World Copper Costs and Production Strategy 1975–85*. 5 vols. London: Brook Hunt & Associates (December).

Campbell, Gary. 1989. "The Response of U.S. Copper Companies to Changing Market Conditions." *Resources Policy* 15, no. 4 (December): 320–36.

Campbell, Gary, Anil Jambekar, and Brian Frame. 1986. "Zinc Processing in the USA: An Analysis of a Declining Industry." *Resources Policy* 12, no. 4 (December): 317–34.

Commission of the European Communities. 1990. *Panorama of EC Industry, 1990*. Luxembourg: Commission of the European Communities.

Dammert, Alfredo, and Jasbir G.S. Chhabra. 1990. "The Lead and Zinc Indus-tries: Long Term Prospects." *World Bank Staff Commodity Working Paper* 22. Washington: World Bank.

Duncan, Ronald C., ed. 1991. *Price Prospects for Major Primary Commodities*. Wash-ington: World Bank (in press).

General Agreement on Tariffs and Trade. 1990. *Background Studies: Trade in Natural-Resource Products: Nickel*. Washington: UNIPUB.

Gooding, Kenneth. 1990a. "Japan Worried About Metals Supply." *Financial Times* (12 October).

Gooding, Kenneth. 1990b. "Nickel and Tin Cuts Forecast." *Financial Times* (5 December): 28.

Gooding, Kenneth. 1990c. "Uneconomic Aluminum Production Capacity Put at 7 Per Cent." *Financial Times* (5 December): 28.

Gooding, Kenneth. 1990d. "Record Aluminum Demand Forecast in 1991." *Financial Times* (13 December).

Gooding, Kenneth. 1991a. "Silver Price to Fall Further.'" *Financial Times* (8 January): 26.

Gooding, Kenneth. 1991b. "Metal Output Surges Forecast." *Financial Times* (9 January): 26.

Gooding, Kenneth. 1991c. "Nickel Supply Forecast to Move into Surplus This Year." *Financial Times* (1 February): 24.

Industry, Science and Technology Canada. 1988. *Industry Profiles*. Ottawa: In-dustry, Science and Technology Canada.

International Lead and Zinc Study Group. 1990. "World Lead and Zinc Supplies and Demand 1989–1991." Geneva: International Lead and Zinc Study Group (October).

Japan Economic Journal. 1990. *Japan Economic Almanac, 1990*. Tokyo: Japan Economic Journal.

Johnson Matthey. 1990. "Platinum: 1990 Interim Review." London: Johnson Matthey.

Mardones, Jose Luis, Enrique Silva, and Christian Martinez. 1985. "The Copper and Aluminum Industries." *Resources Policy* 11, no. 1 (March):3–16.

National Research Council. 1990. *Competitiveness of the U.S. Minerals and Metals Industries*. Washington: National Academy Press.

Organization for Economic Cooperation and Development. 1990a. *Mining and Metallurgy Investment in the Third World: The End of Large Projects?* Paris: Organization for Economic Cooperation and Development.

Organization for Economic Cooperation and Development. 1990b. *Aluminum, Copper, and Steel in Developing Countries*. Paris: Organization for Economic Cooperation and Development.

Peck, Merton, ed. 1988. *The World Aluminum Industry in a Changing Energy Era*. Washington: Resources for the Future.

Porter, K. E., and Paul R. Thomas. 1988. "The International Competitiveness of United States Copper Production." *Minerals Issues, 1988*. Washington: US Department of the Interior.

Radetzki, Marian. 1985. *State Mineral Enterprises: An Investigation into Their Impact on International Mineral Markets*. Washington: Resources for the Future.

Radetzki, Marian, and Kenji Takeuchi. 1989. "Growth Patterns in Copper Consumption in Industrializing Countries." *World Bank Staff Commodity Working Paper* 21. Washington: World Bank.

Shearson Lehman Brothers. 1990. *Annual Review of the World Aluminum Industries*. New York: Shearson Lehman Brothers.

"Slight Growth is Forecast for Aluminum." 1990. *Journal of Commerce* (13 December): 12A.

"Survey: Aluminum." 1990. *Financial Times* (24 October).

Takeuchi, Kenji, John E. Strongman, and Shunichi Maeda. 1986. "World Copper Industry: Its Changing Structure and Future Prospects." *World Bank Staff Commodity Working Paper* 15. Washington: World Bank.

Tan, C. Suan. 1987. "An Econometric Analysis of the World Copper Market." *World Bank Staff Commodity Working Paper* 20. Washington: World Bank.

Tilton, John E., ed. 1990. *World Metal Demand: Trends and Prospects*. Washington: Resources for the Future (October).

US Congress, Congressional Research Service. 1986. *The Competitiveness of American Metal Mining and Processing*. Report prepared for the House Committee on Energy and Commerce, Subcommittee on Oversight and Investigations, Committee Print 99-FF. Washington: Government Printing Office (July).

US Congress, Office of Technology Assessment. 1988. *Copper: Technology and Competitiveness*. Washington: Government Printing Office (OTA-E – 367, September).

US Congress, Office of Technology Assessment. 1990. *Nonferrous Metals: Industry Structure*. Washington: Government Printing Office (OTA-BP-E – 62, September).

US Department of Commerce, International Trade Administration. 1986. *The Effect of Electricity Rates on the Competitiveness of the United States Primary Aluminum Industry*. Washington: Government Printing Office.

US Department of Commerce, International Trade Administration. 1989. *Zinc Alloy and Die Castings: A Measure of Indirect Imports and Their Impact*. Washington: Government Printing Office (December).

US Department of Commerce, International Trade Administration. 1991. *U.S. Industrial Outlook, 1991*. Washington: Government Printing Office (January).

US Department of the Interior, Bureau of Mines. 1991a. *Mineral Commodity Summaries, 1991*. Washington: US Department of the Interior (January).

US Department of the Interior, Bureau of Mines. 1991b. *Minerals Yearbook, 1989*, vol. I: *International*. Washington: US Department of the Interior (in press).

See also the following periodicals: *American Metal Market, Metal Bulletin, Metals Week, American Mining Congress Journal, Engineering & Mining Journal, World Metal Statistics*.

Table 5.68.1 Nonferrous metals: product composition of world trade, 1981–89 (billions of dollars except where noted)

SITC Product	1981	1982	1983	1984	1985	1986	1987	1988	1989	Annual growth 1981–89 (percentages)
World exports to world	35.2	30.5	35.0	36.2	33.2	35.9	43.1	60.4	67.7	8.5
of which										
681 Silver, platinum	5.9	4.1	6.0	4.8	3.9	4.8	5.8	6.8	6.7	1.7
682 Copper	10.1	8.9	9.5	9.5	9.2	9.9	11.5	17.6	22.5	10.6
683 Nickel	2.3	1.9	1.6	1.8	1.8	1.7	2.0	2.9	3.9	6.9
684 Aluminum	10.9	10.4	12.3	13.7	12.7	14.8	18.4	26.4	28.4	12.7
685 Lead	1.0	0.9	0.8	0.8	0.7	0.6	0.9	1.1	1.1	1.1
686 Zinc	1.6	1.5	1.6	2.1	1.8	1.5	1.7	2.8	3.8	11.5
687 Tin	2.0	1.4	1.5	1.7	1.5	1.0	0.9	1.2	1.3	−4.9
689 Other nonferrous metals	1.3	0.8	0.8	1.1	1.2	1.0	1.1	1.6	1.8	4.1
Memorandum:										Change 1981–89
SITC 68 share of world manufactures exports (percentages)	3.5	3.1	3.6	3.4	2.9	2.6	2.6	3.1	3.2	−0.3

Source: World Manufactures Trade Data Base.

Table 5.68.2 Nonferrous metals: geographic distribution of world trade, 1981–89 (percentages of total)

Country	1981	1982	1983	1984	1985	1986	1987	1988	1989	Change 1981–89
Share of exports to world										
United States	8.0	7.3	6.0	5.9	5.8	4.5	5.1	6.0	6.9	−1.0
Canada	9.0	8.9	9.2	9.2	9.2	8.8	8.5	8.1	8.3	−0.7
Japan	3.8	3.8	4.3	3.9	4.2	4.1	3.9	3.4	3.1	−0.6
European Community	37.0	37.4	36.8	35.6	36.4	38.6	37.2	33.9	35.1	−2.0
EC to non-EC	14.6	14.1	15.6	14.6	13.7	13.8	13.0	11.2	10.9	−3.7
Germany	9.9	10.6	10.6	10.6	11.2	12.2	12.1	10.7	10.7	0.7
France	5.8	5.3	5.2	5.3	5.3	5.5	5.5	5.1	5.4	−0.4
Italy	2.0	2.0	2.1	2.0	2.4	2.5	2.4	2.4	2.6	0.6
United Kingdom	6.9	7.1	7.0	6.1	5.4	6.3	5.7	4.9	4.8	−2.1
Other Western Europe	10.4	10.2	10.7	11.5	12.0	12.2	13.1	13.6	12.0	1.5
Asian NICs[a]	0.4	0.5	0.8	0.8	0.7	0.8	1.0	1.9	2.1	1.7
Eastern Europe[b]	3.0	3.5	3.4	3.9	3.2	3.8	4.4	4.9	5.1	2.1
Developing countries	25.1	24.6	25.1	24.9	24.2	23.5	22.6	23.8	23.1	−2.0
Latin America	9.5	9.7	10.4	10.5	9.3	9.1	8.5	10.0	10.5	1.0
Rest of world	0.1	0.0	0.0	0.1	0.1	0.1	0.1	0.5	0.4	0.3
Share of imports from world										
United States	20.2	17.2	21.6	22.5	20.7	20.9	18.2	16.5	15.5	−4.7
Canada	2.2	1.9	2.0	2.2	2.3	2.0	2.0	2.5	2.6	0.4
Japan	11.7	11.7	11.6	12.4	11.5	9.4	12.4	14.5	13.7	2.1
European Community	45.2	46.8	43.5	41.9	43.4	45.3	44.4	43.5	45.7	0.4
EC from non-EC	23.6	24.0	22.6	20.8	21.3	21.0	20.2	21.0	22.3	−1.3
Germany	11.7	12.5	11.7	12.3	12.7	12.9	12.2	11.9	12.9	1.2
France	8.3	8.3	7.3	7.0	7.4	7.9	7.7	7.8	8.2	−0.1
Italy	5.5	5.7	5.2	5.5	5.6	5.9	6.3	6.2	6.6	1.1
United Kingdom	8.2	8.6	8.6	7.2	7.1	7.1	7.2	7.0	7.0	−1.2
Other Western Europe	7.0	7.0	6.8	6.7	7.8	8.5	9.0	7.8	7.1	0.2
Asian NICs[a]	2.3	2.9	3.4	3.6	3.6	4.3	5.2	8.0	8.8	6.6
Eastern Europe[b]	1.5	1.4	1.0	1.4	1.1	0.8	0.8	1.0	0.6	−0.9
Developing countries	8.3	9.0	8.3	7.8	8.3	7.3	6.5	5.5	5.3	−3.0
Latin America	2.3	1.7	1.0	1.2	1.5	1.3	1.3	1.1	1.1	−1.1
Rest of world	1.4	1.6	1.6	1.1	1.1	1.4	1.2	0.4	0.2	−1.2

table continued next page

Table 5.68.2 Nonferrous metals: geographic distribution of world trade, 1981–89 (percentages of total) (continued)

Country	1981	1982	1983	1984	1985	1986	1987	1988	1989	Change 1981–89
Export share minus import share										
United States	-12.2	-9.9	-15.6	-16.6	-14.9	-16.5	-13.1	-10.5	-8.6	3.7
Canada	6.8	7.0	7.3	7.0	6.9	6.8	6.4	5.6	5.7	-1.1
Japan	-7.9	-7.9	-7.3	-8.5	-7.3	-5.3	-8.5	-11.2	-10.6	-2.7
European Community	-8.2	-9.4	-6.7	-6.3	-7.0	-6.7	-7.2	-9.6	-10.6	-2.4
Non-EC	-9.0	-10.0	-7.0	-6.2	-7.7	-7.2	-7.2	-9.8	-11.4	-2.4
Germany	-1.8	-1.9	-1.0	-1.7	-1.5	-0.8	-0.1	-1.2	-2.3	-0.5
France	-2.5	-3.0	-2.1	-1.7	-2.0	-2.4	-2.2	-2.7	-2.8	-0.4
Italy	-3.6	-3.7	-3.2	-3.4	-3.2	-3.4	-3.8	-3.9	-4.1	-0.5
United Kingdom	-1.3	-1.5	-1.6	-1.1	-1.7	-0.8	-1.4	-2.2	-2.2	-0.9
Other Western Europe	3.5	3.2	3.9	4.8	4.1	3.6	4.1	5.8	4.8	1.4
Eastern Europe[b]	-1.8	-2.4	-2.7	-2.8	-2.9	-3.5	-4.2	-6.1	-6.8	-4.9
Asian NICs[a]	1.5	2.1	2.4	2.5	2.2	3.0	3.5	3.8	4.5	3.0
Developing countries	16.8	15.6	16.8	17.1	15.9	16.2	16.1	18.3	17.8	1.0
Latin America	7.2	8.0	9.4	9.3	7.8	7.7	7.2	8.9	9.4	2.1
Rest of world	-1.3	-1.6	-1.5	-1.1	-1.0	-1.3	-1.1	0.1	0.2	1.5

a. Hong Kong, Korea, Singapore, and Taiwan.

b. Including Soviet Union.

Source: World Manufactures Trade Data Base.

Table 5.68.3 Nonferrous metals: bilateral trade flows, 1989 (billions of dollars)

Importer	World	United States	Canada	Japan	European Community	Germany	France	United Kingdom	Asian NICs	Latin America	Other
World	67.7	4.7	5.6	2.1	23.7	7.2	3.6	3.2	1.4	7.1	23.1
United States	10.2		4.1	0.5	1.3	0.3	0.2	0.4	0.1	1.9	2.3
Canada	1.5	1.1		0.0	0.1	0.0	0.0	0.0	0.4	0.0	0.2
Japan	9.4	1.4	0.4		0.5	0.1	0.1	0.3	0.1	1.6	5.0
European Community	31.7	0.7	0.6	0.1	16.3	4.3	2.7	1.8	0.0	2.6	11.3
Germany	8.9	0.1	0.0	0.0	3.8		0.9	0.7	0.0	0.8	4.0
France	5.7	0.1	0.0	0.0	3.5	1.1		0.3		0.5	1.5
United Kingdom	4.6	0.2	0.2	0.0	2.1	0.8	0.3		0.6	0.4	1.7
Asian NICs	5.3	0.6	0.2	1.1	0.4	0.2	0.0	0.1		0.7	1.7
Latin America	0.8	0.5	0.0	0.0	0.2	0.1	0.0	0.0	0.0		0.0
Other	8.8	0.4	0.3	0.4	4.8	2.2	0.6	0.7	0.2	0.1	2.6

Source: World Manufactures Trade Data Base.

Table 5.68.4 Nonferrous metals: product composition of US trade, 1981–90ª (millions of dollars except where noted)

Category	SITC Rev. 2			SITC Rev. 3			
	1981	1987	Change 1981–87	1987	1990	Change 1981–90	Change 1987–90
Total							
Exports	2,803	2,179	-624	2,322	5,189	2,386	2,867
Imports	6,950	7,957	1,007	7,951	9,806	2,856	1,855
Balance	-4,147	-5,778	-1,631	-5,629	-4,617	-470	1,012
of which							
681 Silver, platinum							
Exports	470	253	-217	247	376	-94	129
Imports	1,656	1,666	10	1,666	2,322	666	656
Balance	-1,186	-1,413	-227	-1,419	-1,946	-760	-527
682 Copper							
Exports	396	352	-44	384	1,213	817	829
Imports	1,302	1,568	266	1,552	1,757	455	205
Balance	-906	-1,216	-310	-1,168	-544	362	624
683 Nickel							
Exports	286	107	-179	111	228	-58	117
Imports	867	573	-294	575	1,114	247	539
Balance	-581	-466	115	-464	-886	-305	-422
684 Aluminum							
Exports	1,272	1,186	-86	1,269	2,860	1,588	1,591
Imports	1,354	2,860	1,506	2,859	2,845	1,491	-14
Balance	-82	-1,674	-1,592	-1,590	16	98	1,606
685 Lead							
Exports	26	12	-14	11	71	45	60
Imports	90	138	48	138	93	3	-45
Balance	-64	-126	62	-127	-22	42	105
686 Zinc							
Exports	15	12	-3	13	47	32	34
Imports	553	592	39	586	1,019	466	433
Balance	-538	-580	-42	-573	-972	-434	-399
687 Tin							
Exports	50	21	-29	13	53	3	40
Imports	644	270	-374	271	256	-388	-15
Balance	-594	-249	345	-258	-203	391	55
689 Other nonferrous metals							
Exports	287	234	-53	272	341	54	69
Imports	484	289	-195	304	400	-84	96
Balance	-197	-55	142	-32	-59	138	-27

a. Data are expressed on a domestic exports, imports customs basis. *Source:* US Department of Commerce.

Table 5.68.5 Nonferrous metals: geographic composition of US trade, 1981–90

	Millions of dollars				Percentages of total			
	1981	1987	1989	1990	1981	1987	1989	1990
Exports								
Canada	575	699	1,068	1,353	20.5	30.1	21.3	26.1
Japan	657	581	1,440	1,571	23.4	25.0	28.8	30.3
European Community	714	442	709	768	25.5	19.0	14.2	14.8
United Kingdom	188	147	204	222	6.7	6.3	4.1	4.3
Germany	110	82	126	135	3.9	3.5	2.5	2.6
France	107	69	114	122	3.8	3.0	2.3	2.4
Italy	48	33	73	72	1.7	1.4	1.5	1.4
Latin America	457	283	540	536	16.3	12.2	10.8	10.3
Mexico	300	172	368	367	3.2	6.8	11.0	12.1
Asian NICs	91	158	551	628	3.2	6.8	11.0	12.1
Other	309	159	696	333	11.0	6.8	13.9	6.4
Total	2,803	2,322	5,004	5,189	100.0	100.0	100.0	100.0
Imports								
Canada	2,197	2,830	4,758	3,927	31.6	35.6	43.7	40.0
Japan	300	437	389	462	4.3	5.5	3.6	4.7
European Community	839	1,221	1,332	1,332	12.1	15.4	12.2	13.6
United Kingdom	209	262	350	391	3.0	3.3	3.2	4.0
Germany	245	358	368	431	3.5	4.5	3.4	4.4
France	138	128	183	172	2.0	1.6	1.7	1.8
Italy	32	74	44	38	0.5	0.9	0.4	0.4
Latin America	1,296	1,323	1,888	1,462	18.6	16.6	17.3	14.9
Mexico	291	470	707	503	4.2	5.9	6.5	5.1
Asian NICs	60	55	66	54	0.9	0.7	0.6	0.6
Other	2,258	2,085	2,456	2,569	32.5	26.2	22.6	26.2
Total	6,950	7,951	10,889	9,806	100.0	100.0	100.0	100.0

a. Data are expressed on a domestic exports, imports customs basis.

Source: US Department of Commerce.

Table 5.68.6 Nonferrous metals: indices of US competitiveness, 1981–89 (billions of dollars except where noted)

	1981	1982	1983	1984	1985	1986	1987	1988	1989	Annual growth 1981–89 (percentages)
World trade										
World exports to non-US destinations	28.3	25.3	27.7	28.3	26.6	28.7	35.5	50.8	57.5	9.3
World imports from non-US sources	32.0	28.2	32.8	34.8	32.2	35.7	42.0	59.1	65.9	9.4
US trade										
Exports	2.8	2.2	2.1	2.1	1.9	1.6	2.2	3.6	4.7	6.7
Imports	7.1	5.2	7.6	8.4	7.1	7.9	8.1	10.5	11.0	5.7
Balance	−4.3	−3.0	−5.5	−6.3	−5.2	−6.3	−5.9	−6.8	−6.4	
										Change 1981–89
US share of exports to non-US destinations (percentages)	9.9	8.8	7.6	7.5	7.2	5.6	6.1	7.2	8.2	−1.7
US share of imports from non-US sources (percentages)	22.1	18.5	23.1	24.0	22.2	22.1	19.3	17.8	16.8	−5.3
Export share minus import share (percentages)	−12.2	−9.7	−15.5	−16.5	−15.0	−16.5	−13.2	−10.6	−8.6	3.6

Source: World Manufactures Trade Data Base.

Manufactures of Metal (SITC 69)

This SITC category includes a variety of products, made primarily from iron, steel, or aluminum, that are used extensively in construction and in the production of other goods. Restructuring of the world steel industry (discussed under SITC 67) significantly affected trade in metal manufactures. Production shifted significantly from Japan, the European Community, and the United States to newly emergent steel producers, which enjoyed cost advantages thanks to relatively low labor costs and more efficient production.

Description of the Product Group

Eight three-digit groups make up this miscellaneous group of metal manufactures.

SITC

691 structures and parts of structures, not elsewhere specified, of iron, steel or aluminum (e.g., door and window frames, shutters, balustrades, plates, strips, rods, angles, shapes, sections, tubes, and the like, prepared for use in structures)

692 metal containers for storage and transport (cans, casks, drums, boxes, vats, etc.)

693 wire products (excluding insulated electrical wiring) and fencing grills

694 nails, screws, nuts, bolts, rivets, and the like, of iron, steel, or copper

695 tools for use in the hand or in machines (shovels, picks, hoes, scythes, saws, wrenches and spanners, files, hammers, vices, pliers, etc.)

696 cutlery (razors, scissors, spoons, forks, knives, and knife blades)

697 household equipment of base metal, not elsewhere specified (nonelectric kitchen stoves, water heaters, etc., pots, pans, etc.)

699 manufactures of base metal, not elsewhere specified (safes, pins, needles, buckles, springs, anchors, chain, etc.).

Role in World Trade

Size and Composition

Metal manufactures, with 1989 world exports of $56.3 billion, is in the midrange of the industries examined in terms of value of world exports (table 5.69.1). Along with the iron and steel industry, metal manufactures experienced one of the lowest export growth rates of all the two-digit industries. World exports of metal manufactures expanded by only 6.0 percent annually on average over the 1981–89 period, compared with the 9.6 percent average annual growth of world manufactures exports overall. The rather slow growth of metal manufactures exports resulted in a decline in its share of world manufactures exports, from 3.5 percent in 1981 to 2.7 percent in 1989.

Roughly one-half of world metal manufactures trade in 1989 was in two of the three-digit SITC groups. The miscellaneous subcategory (SITC 699) accounted for one-third of total exports (table 5.69.1), and hand tools accounted for an additional 18 percent. These two subcategories increased their combined share from 45 percent in 1981 to 53 percent in 1989. The third-largest subcategory of metal manufactures, structures and parts, experienced a decline in exports between 1981 and 1989. The remainder of the three-digit subcategories for metal manufactures had stable and relatively small export shares.

Global Competition Patterns

The European Community dominates world exports of metal manufactures. It accounted for roughly one-half of all world exports of these products during the 1980s (table 5.69.2). Germany was by far the largest exporter within the European Community, accounting for roughly one-third of EC metal manufactures exports during the 1980s; unlike the European Community as a whole, Germany increased its share of world exports between 1981 and 1989. Significant exporters outside the European Community include the Asian NICs, Japan, and the United States. There was a major shift in the shares of exports among these countries. Both Japan and the United States showed significant declines in export shares, while the Asian NICs increased their share substantially over the 1981–89 period.

The European Community was also the largest importing region during the 1980s. Its share of world imports of metal manufactures grew from 33.0 percent in 1981 to 42.8 percent in 1989. Germany was the largest importer within the Community, accounting for about 10 percent of world metal manufactures imports in 1989 and nearly one-quarter of all EC imports. The United States was, however, by far the largest single-country importer of metal manufactures during the 1980s. Other significant importing areas in 1989 included Canada, the Asian NICs, and the developing countries.

Mostly as a result of the rapid increase in its share of world imports, the European Community's export-minus-import share balance declined substantially between 1981 and 1989. The United States and Japan also experienced significant declines in share balances.

The developing countries, in contrast, experienced a large improvement in their export-minus-import share balance. This increase reflects the severe cutback in imports many of these countries suffered during the 1980s. The developing countries' share of world imports of metal manufactures dropped from 32.7 percent in 1981 to only 13.4 percent in 1989. This 19.3-percentage-point drop accounted for nearly all the increase in the developing countries' export-minus-import share balance. Increased domestic production of metal manufactures and, more important, import constraints resulting from debt problems were responsible for this dramatic drop.

Table 5.69.3 shows world trade flows for metal manufactures in 1989 and illustrates the dominance of the European Community in metal manufactures trade. Nearly 60 percent of 1989 EC exports went to other EC members. In fact, intra-EC trade accounted for nearly one-third of all world exports. Table 5.69.3 also indicates the importance of the United States as a world metal manufactures importer. The United States was the destination for nearly 45 percent of all exports from the Asian NICs, one-third of Japanese exports, and over 80 percent of Canadian exports.

Key Determinants of World Trade Patterns

Demand for metal manufactures is derived largely from demand for goods that use these products as inputs. Only about one-third of the output in this industry consists of goods for final consumption. The major uses for these products are in transportation equipment (primarily aircraft and automobiles), industrial equipment, and construction. Factors affecting trade in transportation equipment (SITCs 78 and 79) and industrial equipment (SITCs 72, 73, and 74) are discussed elsewhere in this study.

A substantial portion of metal manufactures consists of bulky items for which shipping costs are a relatively large portion of the total purchase price. This is true especially for metal structures and metal containers. For these items, markets tend to be local or regional rather than national or international.

Standardized commodities make up a fairly large part of the international trade that does occur in this product group. These are relatively low-technology items that are manufactured to specifications common to many markets. Such items are concentrated in the subcategories wire products and nails and other fasteners and to a lesser extent in hand tools and cutlery. For these products, price is a prime purchase consideration. Because firms compete primarily on the basis of price, manufacturing costs are of critical importance in determining world trade patterns.

Steel and other metals account for more than 50 percent of production costs in this product group. Hence, areas with access to relatively cheap steel have an advantage in the production of these goods. Recent restructuring in the world steel industry (described elsewhere in this volume) has had major effects on trade patterns for metal manufactures. Many of the newly emergent steel producers (China, the Asian NICs, Brazil) also promote the production of higher-value-added metal manufactures. Exports of these products, rather than of steel or semifinished steel products, are seen as a way to increase foreign-currency earnings.

Labor is usually the second-largest production cost, accounting for 15 percent to 20 percent of total production costs for many products. The relatively low wage rates in many of the new steel-producing countries is a second reason why they have become important exporters of metal manufactures.

Fluctuations in exchange rates are also important in determining trade patterns for the commodity-type products in this group. Exchange rate changes affect the relative prices of imported and domestically produced goods. As price is the dominant factor in the purchase decision for these types of products, fluctuations in exchange rates can cause relatively rapid changes in sources of supply.

A final, relatively small segment of the metal manufactures industry consists of specialty items that are manufactured to customer specifications. These products have relatively small production runs and are often produced by small manufacturing concerns employing fewer than 20 people. Factors such as quality, delivery schedules, and the ability to meet product specifications, rather than price, tend to be determining factors in purchase decisions for these goods. The importance of delivery schedules and close relationships between suppliers and customers often favor local producers over distant producers and limit the amount of international trade in these goods.

Role in US Trade

Recent Performance

Although the product group ranks in the top half of all US manufactures groups by amount of exports, metal manufactures play a less important role in US manufactures exports than in world manufactures exports generally. US exports of metal manufactures of $5.9 billion in 1990 accounted for 2.0 percent of all US manufactures exports. This contrasts with the category's 2.8 percent share of world manufactures trade in the same year. Imports of metal manufactures were $8.9 billion in 1990, or 2.3 percent of all US manufactures imports.

The 1981–87 period saw a dramatic deterioration in the US trade balance in metal manufactures (table 5.69.4). Exports declined more than 25 percent, while imports, which had nearly equaled exports in 1981, nearly doubled. As a result, from near balance, the US trade position deteriorated to a deficit of $5.0 billion by 1987.

From 1987 to 1990, US metal manufactures exports increased twice as much as did imports, reducing the US trade deficit by $1.4 billion. Nevertheless, the 1990 US trade balance was still $3.1 billion in deficit, compared with the nearly balanced position of 1981.

US exports of metal manufactures were concentrated in tools, structures and parts, and miscellaneous metal manufactures. These three subcategories together accounted for nearly 75 percent of all US metal manufactures in 1981 (table 5.69.4). There was some redistribution of exports among the three during the 1980s, with structures and parts declining substantially relative to the other two and the miscellaneous category becoming more important.

Canada is the major market for US exports of manufactures of metal, taking 37.3 percent of the 1990 total (table 5.69.5). The Asian NICs provide over one-fourth of US imports.

International Competitiveness

Table 5.69.6 presents additional evidence of the declining role of the United States in world trade in metal manufactures. World exports of metal manufactures contracted sharply in the early 1980s. Not until 1986 did world exports to non-US destinations surpass their 1981 level. US exports recovered even more sluggishly and in 1989 were still slightly below their 1981 level. The slow US export recovery resulted in a significant decline in the US share of exports to non-US destinations, from 14.5 percent in 1981 to 9.4 percent in 1989.

The United States accounted for a rising share of imports originating outside the United States during the 1980s. Increasing from 14.6 percent of the total from non-US sources in 1981, the US share peaked at 23.6 percent in 1985, before declining to 18.2 percent in 1989, still 3.6 percentage points above 1981. The declining US share of exports and its increasing share of imports together contributed to the 8.7-percentage-point decline in its export-minus-import share balance between 1981 and 1989.

Outlook

Key Determinants of US Trade Performance

Two key factors affecting US metal manufactures trade performance during the 1980s were raw materials costs and exchange rates. As discussed in the section on iron and steel, during much of the 1980s US steel prices were substantially above world prices—the result of "voluntary" restrictions on exports to the US market. Because steel is an important component in metal manufactures, the high cost of steel in the United States put US metal manufacturers at a competitive disadvantage. This was one cause of the substantial shift in the production of metal manufactures from the United States to newly emergent steel producers.

US trade performance is also sensitive to changes in the value of the US dollar. DRI import price elasticity estimates place metal manufactures in the midrange of industries in terms of sensitivity to changes in import prices (see the appendix to this volume). The estimated import price elasticity of -1.1 indicates that US imports of metal manufactures would increase roughly proportionately to declines in import prices. The sharp runup in the value of the US dollar during the early to mid-1980s caused a substantial decline in the price of imported metal manufactures relative to domestically produced items and contributed to the decline in US market competitiveness.

Near-Term Outlook

US imports of metal manufactures will grow only slowly through 1993, because domestic US demand in two of the key markets for metal manufactures (transportation equipment and construction) is likely to remain weak through at least 1991 and recover only slowly thereafter. The aircraft industry, a large consumer of metal manufactures, will probably continue to experience strong demand. The US industry, however, has been operating at capacity and is unlikely to expand, thus limiting growth in demand from this sector.

The restructuring of the US steel industry should help improve US exports. The US domestic price of steel has recently fallen relative to world prices and in early 1991 was equivalent to or below world prices. This will increase the market competitiveness of US producers of metal manufactures.

The Canada-US Free Trade Agreement is likely to be somewhat beneficial to US producers. Canadian tariffs on metal manufactures have generally been higher than US tariffs. The combination of reduced tariffs and the proximity of US producers to major Canadian markets should increase net exports to Canada.

It is most likely that the US trade balance for metal manufactures will show minor improvement in 1991. However, the deficit should begin to increase again by 1993 as the effects of the US economic recovery assert themselves. Thus, the 1993 US deficit is likely to be roughly the same as in 1990.

Medium-Term Outlook

The technology for metal manufactures is widely available and is not changing rapidly. Most items are easily manufactured with only modest capital investments. These characteristics, in addition to the commodity nature of much of the output in this industry, mean that raw material and labor costs are the most important determinants of the location of production. The expansion of production capacity for metal manufactures in many of the newly emergent steel producers—which often have substantially lower labor costs—will continue to place strong competitive pressures on US producers.

Recovery of the US economy from the recession of the early 1990s will lead to a recovery in the growth of US imports. US economic recovery and strong competitive pressures from overseas are likely to cause the US trade deficit in metal manufactures to grow modestly after 1993.

Significant changes in exchange rates could cause significant changes in the US trade balance in this product group because of the sensitivity of metal manufactures trade to changes in import prices.

Conclusions

■ Three industry groups—construction, industrial machinery, and transportation equipment—account for most of demand for metal manufactures. Export growth for the majority of the industries within these three groups was below the average for all manufactures during the 1980s. The relatively slow growth of its major markets caused metal manufactures' share of world manufactures exports to decline from 3.5 percent in 1981 to 2.7 percent in 1989.

■ Only a small part of metal manufactures output is traded internationally. High shipping costs relative to value, particularly for metal containers and structural metal, dictate local or regional markets for many of these products.

■ A substantial shift in production occurred during the 1980s. Japan, the European Community, and the United States all lost export share to the Asian NICs and the developing countries. Many of the countries that have increased their share of world exports are newly emergent steel producers that have promoted the production of metal manufactures as a way to increase the value added of their exports. Labor costs, although not as important as steel costs, are still an important competitive factor in metal manufactures production. The relatively low wage rates in many of the newly emergent steel-producing countries have helped them compete effectively in international markets.

■ Metal manufactures make up a smaller part of US exports than of world exports. US metal manufactures exports of $4.4 billion in 1989 were only 1.8 percent of all 1989 US manufactures exports. Metal manufactures constituted 2.7 percent of all world manufactures exports in the same year.

■ Poor export performance and rapid import growth ensured a substantial deterioration of the US metal manufactures trade balance during the 1980s. From near balance in 1981, the US position deteriorated to a deficit of $3 billion in 1990. US domestic steel prices that exceeded world prices and adverse exchange rate movements during the early to mid-1980s caused the sharp deterioration in US trade performance.

■ Slack US demand in key markets (particularly construction and transportation equipment) will ensure slow import growth of metal manufactures during the early 1990s. Meanwhile, relatively strong economic performance in the major US export markets of Japan and the European Community should allow for continued export growth. The recent narrowing of the US trade deficit in this product group is likely to end in 1991 or 1992, returning the 1993 deficit to about the $3 billion 1990 level. After that, economic recovery in the United States will probably allow import growth sufficient to cause a modest growth in the US metal manufactures trade deficit into the mid-1990s.

Bibliography

Commission of the European Communities. 1990. *Panorama of EC Industry, 1990.* Luxembourg: Commission of the European Communities.

Industry, Science and Technology Canada. 1988a. *Industry Profile: Metal Stampings, Closures and Containers.* Ottawa: Industry, Science and Technology Canada.

Industry, Science and Technology Canada. 1988b. *Industry Profile: Wire and Wire Products.* Ottawa: Industry, Science and Technology Canada.

US Department of Commerce, International Trade Administration. 1988. *U.S. Industrial Outlook, 1988.* Washington: Government Printing Office (January).

US Department of Commerce, International Trade Administration. 1989. *U.S. Industrial Outlook, 1989*. Washington: Government Printing Office (January).

US Department of Commerce, International Trade Administration. 1990. *U.S. Industrial Outlook, 1990*. Washington: Government Printing Office (January).

Table 5.69.1 Manufactures of metal: product composition of world trade, 1981–89 (billions of dollars except where noted)

SITC Product	1981	1982	1983	1984	1985	1986	1987	1988	1989	Annual growth 1981–89 (percentages)
World exports to world	35.4	34.0	32.0	32.1	32.3	39.3	46.4	52.8	56.3	6.0
of which										
691 Structures and parts	7.8	7.7	6.3	5.3	5.0	5.8	6.5	6.6	7.2	–1.1
692 Metal storage, containers	2.2	2.1	2.3	2.2	1.9	2.4	2.8	3.3	3.6	6.2
693 Wire (nonelectrical), fencing	1.9	1.7	1.7	1.6	1.8	2.0	2.3	2.8	3.0	6.0
694 Nails, screws, nuts, etc.	2.7	2.5	2.5	3.0	3.0	3.7	4.5	5.3	5.8	10.0
695 Tools (hand and machine)	5.9	5.7	5.5	5.7	6.1	7.3	8.9	9.6	10.2	7.1
696 Cutlery	1.4	1.2	1.2	1.2	1.3	1.5	1.8	2.1	2.2	5.8
697 Household equipment	3.5	3.5	3.2	3.3	3.3	4.0	4.6	5.1	5.1	4.9
699 Other	10.0	9.4	9.3	9.8	10.2	12.8	15.6	17.9	19.6	8.8
Memorandum:										Change 1981–89
SITC 69 share of world manufactures exports (percentages)	3.5	3.5	3.3	3.0	2.9	2.9	2.8	2.7	2.7	–0.8

Source: World Manufactures Trade Data Base.

Table 5.69.2 Manufactures of metal: geographic distribution of world trade, 1981–89 (percentages of total)

Country	1981	1982	1983	1984	1985	1986	1987	1988	1989	Change 1981–89
Share of exports to world										
United States	12.8	11.2	10.5	10.7	8.9	6.8	6.8	7.3	7.9	−4.9
Canada	2.8	2.5	2.6	3.4	3.3	3.0	2.9	3.0	3.1	0.3
Japan	12.6	13.0	12.6	12.2	11.0	10.3	8.1	8.3	8.3	−4.3
European Community	53.8	54.6	53.8	51.2	52.7	55.3	55.5	52.0	52.7	−1.0
EC to non-EC	29.8	30.1	29.5	27.5	26.9	25.2	24.1	21.5	21.5	−8.2
Germany	16.2	17.0	17.3	16.3	17.4	19.8	19.9	19.0	18.9	2.7
France	9.0	8.6	8.4	8.0	7.6	7.5	7.2	6.5	6.7	−2.4
Italy	9.9	9.5	9.9	9.1	9.0	9.8	9.8	9.1	9.6	−0.4
United Kingdom	7.0	7.2	6.3	6.1	6.5	5.5	5.5	5.1	5.0	−2.0
Other Western Europe	10.0	10.1	10.4	10.1	11.4	11.9	12.3	11.7	10.8	0.8
Asian NICs[a]	4.6	5.3	6.6	8.3	8.4	8.4	9.7	12.3	11.3	6.6
Eastern Europe[b]	0.6	0.5	0.6	0.6	0.7	0.8	0.8	0.8	0.7	0.1
Developing countries	2.1	2.2	2.4	3.0	3.1	3.1	3.6	4.6	4.8	2.7
Latin America	0.5	0.6	0.7	1.0	1.0	1.0	1.1	1.3	1.4	0.9
Rest of world	0.1	0.1	0.1	0.2	0.2	0.2	0.2	0.3	0.3	0.2
Share of imports from world										
United States	12.5	13.4	14.9	19.5	21.0	18.9	18.0	17.6	16.3	3.9
Canada	4.4	3.8	4.4	5.3	5.4	4.7	4.5	5.2	5.4	1.0
Japan	1.5	1.6	1.8	1.9	1.8	1.9	2.1	2.4	2.8	1.3
European Community	33.0	32.7	33.0	32.8	34.1	39.4	42.2	41.7	42.8	9.8
EC from non-EC	10.3	9.8	10.0	10.3	10.3	11.5	12.4	12.7	13.2	2.9
Germany	7.6	7.4	7.9	7.7	7.9	9.4	9.8	9.3	9.8	2.2
France	6.3	6.4	6.1	5.8	6.3	7.3	8.0	7.8	7.9	1.6
Italy	2.9	2.7	2.6	2.6	2.8	3.3	3.5	3.6	3.8	0.9
United Kingdom	4.6	4.8	5.1	5.6	5.7	5.9	6.5	6.9	6.9	2.3
Other Western Europe	9.5	9.5	9.5	9.3	10.2	11.8	12.7	11.8	11.1	1.7
Asian NICs[a]	3.0	3.3	3.8	4.1	3.6	3.3	3.3	4.4	4.9	1.9
Eastern Europe[b]	2.2	2.5	3.0	1.9	1.9	2.0	2.1	1.9	1.8	−0.4
Developing countries	32.7	31.4	28.5	23.5	20.4	16.6	13.8	13.7	13.4	−19.3
Latin America	6.7	5.3	3.9	3.8	3.4	3.3	3.0	3.0	3.4	−3.3
Rest of world	0.1	0.0	0.0	0.0	0.0	0.0	0.0	0.1	0.1	0.1

table continued next page

Table 5.69.2 Manufactures of metal: geographic distribution of world trade, 1981–89 (percentages of total) (continued)

Country	1981	1982	1983	1984	1985	1986	1987	1988	1989	Change 1981–89
Export share minus import share										
United States	0.4	-2.1	-4.4	-8.8	-12.1	-12.1	-11.3	-10.3	-8.4	-8.8
Canada	-1.6	-1.3	-1.8	-1.9	-2.1	-1.7	-1.5	-2.2	-2.2	-0.6
Japan	11.2	11.4	10.9	10.3	9.2	8.4	6.0	5.8	5.6	-5.6
European Community	20.8	21.9	20.9	18.4	18.6	15.9	13.4	10.4	9.9	-10.8
Non-EC	19.4	20.4	19.5	17.2	16.6	13.7	11.7	8.9	8.3	-11.1
Germany	8.6	9.6	9.4	8.7	9.5	10.4	10.1	9.7	9.1	0.5
France	2.7	2.2	2.4	2.2	1.3	0.2	-0.8	-1.4	-1.2	-4.0
Italy	7.1	6.8	7.3	6.5	6.2	6.6	6.3	5.5	5.8	-1.3
United Kingdom	2.5	2.4	1.1	0.5	0.8	-0.5	-1.0	-1.8	-1.9	-4.3
Other Western Europe	0.6	0.6	0.9	0.8	1.2	0.1	-0.3	-0.1	-0.3	-0.9
Asian NICs[a]	1.7	2.0	2.8	4.2	4.8	5.1	6.4	7.9	6.4	4.7
Eastern Europe[b]	-1.5	-2.0	-2.4	-1.3	-1.2	-1.2	-1.3	-1.0	-1.0	0.5
Developing countries	-30.6	-29.3	-26.1	-20.5	-17.3	-13.5	-10.2	-9.1	-8.7	22.0
Latin America	-6.2	-4.8	-3.3	-2.8	-2.3	-2.2	-1.9	-1.7	-2.0	4.2
Rest of world	0.0	0.0	0.1	0.1	0.1	0.2	0.1	0.2	0.2	0.1

a. Hong Kong, Korea, Singapore, and Taiwan.

b. Including Soviet Union.

Source: World Manufactures Trade Data Base.

Table 5.69.3 Manufactures of metal: bilateral trade flows, 1989 (billions of dollars)

Importer					Exporter						
	World	United States	Canada	Japan	European Community	Germany	France	United Kingdom	Asian NICs	Latin America	Other
World	56.3	4.4	1.8	4.7	29.7	10.6	3.8	2.8	6.3	0.8	8.7
United States	9.5		1.5	1.6	1.7	0.6	0.3	0.3	2.8	0.7	1.2
Canada	2.1	1.2		0.1	0.3	0.1	0.0	0.1	0.3	0.0	0.2
Japan	1.5	0.3			0.3	0.1	0.0	0.0	0.6	0.0	0.3
European Community	24.9	1.0	0.0	0.6	17.6	5.9	2.1	1.4	1.1	0.1	4.5
Germany	5.8	0.2	0.1	0.2	3.3		0.6	0.3	0.3	0.0	1.8
France	4.6	0.1	0.0	0.1	3.7	1.4		0.2	0.1	0.0	0.7
United Kingdom	3.9	0.3	0.0	0.2	2.4	0.9	0.3		0.3	0.0	0.6
Asian NICs	2.3	0.3	0.1	0.9	0.5	0.2	0.1	0.1	0.4	0.0	0.2
Latin America	2.0	1.0	0.1	0.1	0.6	0.1	0.2	0.1	0.1		0.1
Other	14.1	0.6	0.1	1.3	8.7	3.6	1.1	0.9	1.2	0.0	2.3

Source: World Manufactures Trade Data Base.

Table 5.69.4 Manufactures of metal: product composition of US trade, 1981–90[a] (millions of dollars except where noted)

Category	SITC Rev. 2			SITC Rev. 3		Change 1981–90	Change 1987–90
	1981	1987	Change 1981–87	1987	1990		
Total							
Exports	4,297	3,131	-1,166	3,361	5,857	1,560	2,496
Imports	4,251	8,158	3,907	7,802	8,917	4,666	1,115
Balance	46	-5,027	-5,073	-4,441	-3,060	-3,106	1,381
of which							
691 Structures and parts							
Exports	972	265	-707	181	381	-591	200
Imports	182	319	137	295	215	33	-80
Balance	790	-54	-844	-114	166	-624	280
692 Metal storage and transport containers							
Exports	284	222	-62	183	401	117	218
Imports	80	206	126	215	256	176	41
Balance	204	16	-188	-32	145	-59	177
693 Wire (excluding insulated electrical wiring), fencing grills							
Exports	191	70	-121	69	198	7	129
Imports	410	561	151	553	626	216	73
Balance	-219	-491	-272	-484	-429	-210	55
694 Nails, screws, nuts, etc.							
Exports	263	246	-17	376	650	387	274
Imports	758	1,301	543	1,297	1,461	703	164
Balance	-495	-1,055	-560	-921	-810	-315	111
695 Tools (hand and machine)							
Exports	932	657	-275	625	1,125	193	500
Imports	639	1,175	536	1,228	1,496	857	268
Balance	293	-518	-811	-603	-371	-664	232
696 Cutlery							
Exports	81	61	-20	61	183	102	122
Imports	321	468	147	397	446	125	49
Balance	-240	-407	-167	-336	-263	-23	73
697 Household equipment of base metal, n.e.s.							
Exports	317	269	-48	264	353	36	89
Imports	570	1,012	442	989	1,143	573	154
Balance	-253	-743	-490	-725	-790	-537	-65
699 Manufactures of base metal, n.e.s.							
Exports	1,256	1,341	85	1,603	2,566	1,310	963
Imports	1,284	3,101	1,817	2,827	3,274	1,990	447
Balance	-28	-1,760	-1,732	-1,224	-708	-680	516

a. Data are expressed on a domestic exports, imports customs basis.

Source: US Department of Commerce.

Table 5.69.5 Manufactures of metal: geographic composition of US trade, 1981–90

	Millions of dollars				Percentages of total			
	1981	1987	1989	1990	1981	1987	1989	1990
Exports								
Canada	951	1,019	1,300	2,182	22.1	30.3	23.8	37.3
Japan	130	218	334	355	3.0	6.5	6.1	6.1
European Community	677	742	978	1,072	15.8	22.1	17.9	18.3
United Kingdom	204	233	328	351	4.7	6.9	6.0	6.0
Germany	129	145	243	271	3.0	4.3	4.4	4.6
France	87	76	123	137	2.0	2.3	2.2	2.3
Italy	63	55	61	71	1.5	1.6	1.1	1.2
Latin America	1,187	649	1,064	1,216	27.6	19.3	19.5	20.8
Mexico	554	320	708	862	12.9	9.5	12.9	14.7
Asian NICs	197	231	339	393	4.6	6.9	6.2	6.7
Other	1,155	502	1,453	639	26.9	14.9	26.6	10.9
Total	4,297	3,361	5,468	5,857	100.0	100.0	100.0	100.0
Imports								
Canada	732	1,332	1,449	1,363	17.2	17.1	16.1	15.3
Japan	1,166	1,359	1,677	1,584	27.4	17.4	18.7	17.8
European Community	862	1,507	1,688	1,762	20.3	19.3	18.8	19.8
United Kingdom	173	228	273	289	4.1	2.9	3.0	3.2
Germany	271	555	578	626	6.4	7.1	6.4	7.0
France	134	191	215	238	3.2	2.4	2.4	2.7
Italy	92	204	227	235	2.2	2.6	2.5	2.6
Latin America	143	418	662	708	3.4	5.4	7.4	7.9
Mexico	92	282	452	499	2.2	3.6	5.0	5.6
Asian NICs	939	2,416	2,431	2,320	22.1	31.0	27.1	26.0
Taiwan	503	1,612	1,615	1,561	11.8	20.7	18.0	17.5
Other	409	770	1,066	1,180	9.6	9.9	11.9	13.2
Total	4,251	7,802	8,973	8,917	100.0	100.0	100.0	100.0

a. Data are expressed on a domestic exports, imports customs basis.

Source: US Department of Commerce.

Table 5.69.6 Manufactures of metal: indices of US competitiveness, 1981–89 (billions of dollars except where noted)

	1981	1982	1983	1984	1985	1986	1987	1988	1989	Annual growth 1981–89 (percentages)
World trade										
World exports to non-US destinations	31.3	29.8	27.5	26.4	26.2	32.4	38.6	43.8	46.8	5.2
World imports from non-US sources	31.0	30.1	28.8	29.1	30.2	36.9	43.7	49.6	51.8	6.6
US trade										
Exports	4.5	3.8	3.3	3.4	2.9	2.7	3.1	3.9	4.4	−0.2
Imports	4.5	4.6	4.9	6.4	7.1	7.7	8.6	9.7	9.4	9.7
Balance	0.0	−0.8	−1.6	−3.0	−4.2	−5.0	−5.5	−5.8	−5.0	
										Change 1981–89
US share of exports to non-US destinations (percentages)	14.5	12.9	12.2	13.0	10.9	8.2	8.1	8.8	9.4	−5.1
US share of imports from non-US sources (percentages)	14.6	15.3	16.9	22.1	23.6	20.8	19.8	19.5	18.2	3.6
Export share minus import share (percentages)	−0.1	−2.4	−4.8	−9.1	−12.7	−12.6	−11.7	−10.7	−8.8	−8.7

Source: World Manufactures Trade Data Base.

Specialized Industrial Machinery (SITC 72)

The products included in SITC 72 (formally referred to as "machinery specialized for particular industries") are used in a wide variety of construction and production processes. As with general industrial machinery (SITC 74), demand depends largely on the overall level of economic activity. Specialized industrial machinery played an important role in US manufactures trade performance during the 1980s. Its $11.6 billion trade balance decline between 1981 and 1987 was the third largest of the two-digit manufacturing categories.

Description of the Product Group

SITC 72 contains a diverse group of products. The industry is divided into several three-digit subcategories:

SITC

721 agricultural machinery (excluding tractors) and parts thereof

722 tractors (other than those in 744.11 and 783.2; tractors used in agriculture are the largest part of this group)

723 civil engineering and contractors' plant and equipment and parts thereof, not elsewhere specified (includes bulldozers, excavators, pile drivers, and road rollers)

724 textile and leather machinery and parts thereof, not elsewhere specified

725 paper-mill and pulp-mill machinery, paper-cutting machines and other machinery for the manufacture of paper articles and parts thereof, not elsewhere specified

726 printing and bookbinding machinery and parts thereof, not elsewhere specified

727 food-processing machines (excluding domestic) and parts thereof, not elsewhere specified

728 other machinery and equipment specialized for particular industries and parts thereof, not elsewhere specified (includes machine tools specialized

for particular industries; equipment for sorting, crushing, or mixing stones or earth; machinery for the rubber and artificial plastic materials industries; and machinery for the tobacco industry).

Role in World Trade

Size and Composition

Specialized industrial machinery has one of the largest shares of world manufactures exports. With total world exports of $98.1 billion in 1989, the product group accounted for 4.7 percent of all world manufactures exports (table 5.72.1), tying with general industrial machinery (SITC 74) for the fifth-largest share of world manufactures exports. World exports of specialized industrial machinery grew at an average annual rate of 6.2 percent from 1981 to 1989, substantially below the 9.6 percent rate for all manufactures. As a result, the group's 1989 share of world exports is below that of 1981, when it accounted for 5.7 percent of all world manufactures exports.

Civil engineering equipment, "other" specialized industrial machinery, and agricultural equipment together accounted for nearly three-fourths of world trade in specialized industrial machinery in 1981. Their share dropped, however, to roughly 60 percent by 1989 (table 5.72.1). World exports of both tractors and civil engineering equipment fell between 1981 and 1987, reducing their share in specialized industrial machinery exports substantially. Exports of tractors and civil engineering equipment recovered between 1987 and 1989, although 1989 exports of tractors were still below their 1981 level.

Global Competition Patterns

The European Community has the largest shares of both exports and imports of specialized industrial machinery of any country or region. The Community's share of world exports rose between 1981 and 1989 to just over 50 percent (table 5.72.2). An even larger increase in the share of world imports, however, caused a decline in the Community's export-minus-import share balance between 1981 and 1989. Nonetheless, the Community continued to enjoy the largest positive share balance of any country or region in 1989. The developing countries experienced the largest gain in share balance, 20.5 percentage points, from 1981 to 1989. Virtually the entire change resulted from a contraction in the import share from 39.4 percent to 19.4 percent. This reflected severe restrictions on imports as a result of a lack of foreign exchange.

The United States experienced the most dramatic decline—16.2 percentage points—in share balance in specialized industrial machinery between 1981 and

1989. Nearly three-fourths of the decline resulted from a reduction in the US share of world exports, although a modest increase in the US import share also contributed.

Bilateral trade flows are summarized in table 5.72.3. As with most of the industries examined in this study, a large share of EC exports (45.7 percent in 1989) go to other members of the Community. The Community was the most important export market for the United States, closely followed by Canada and Latin America. The Community was also the largest source of imports into the United States.

Key Determinants of World Trade Patterns

The technology used to produce specialized industrial machinery tends to be well known and generally available. Hence, few producers or regions enjoy an advantage in the marketplace because of lower production costs due to superior technology.

Exchange rates play an important role in determining trade in specialized industrial machinery. Buyers can often purchase a particular kind of machine—usually with similar features and capabilities—from a variety of sources in different countries. Thus, purchase decisions tend to focus on cost, quality, and after-sale service considerations. Competition among suppliers is stiff.

Other factors also strongly influence purchase decisions. The high unit cost of many of the goods in this category forces most buyers to finance their purchases. Thus, financing provisions—including availability of financing, interest rates, and loan guarantees—are also important.

For many applications the overall quality or reliability of the machinery is critical. With nearly all machinery in this category used in construction, mining, or other production processes, unscheduled downtime can be costly to the user. Thus, a reputation for quality can be an important marketing feature. The parts and service network available for machinery used in production processes is also of great importance. Sellers with well-established service networks have an advantage over those with poor parts or service availability.

Role in US Trade

Recent Performance

With exports of $15.3 billion in 1990 (table 5.72.4), or 5.1 percent of total manufacturing exports, specialized industrial machinery was the seventh-largest

US manufactures export category. Imports of $13.4 billion in 1990 made this product group the ninth-largest manufactures import category, accounting for 3.5 percent of US manufactures imports.

US exports of specialized industrial machinery swung widely during the 1980s. Exports dropped from $14.6 billion in 1981 to only $9.3 billion in 1983, remained essentially unchanged through 1987, and then grew dramatically through 1990. Relatively rapid import growth during this period led to a massive decline in the trade balance for this industry. From a surplus of over $9 billion in 1981, specialized industrial machinery slid to a deficit of more than $2 billion by 1987. The recovery in export performance between 1987 and 1990 helped move the account back to a modest $1.8 billion surplus by 1990 but made up for only about 30 percent of the $11.6 billion decline between 1981 and 1987.

Sharp export reductions to Latin America and OPEC, the two most important US export markets, caused a substantial portion of the US trade deterioration and accounted for over 80 percent of the 1981–87 decline in US exports. Severe debt problems forced many Latin American countries to sharply reduce imports in the early to mid-1980s. The reduction in oil demand accompanying the worldwide recession in the early 1980s caused many OPEC countries to scale back their construction programs and thus their demand for specialized industrial machinery. Although these two regions accounted for the vast majority of the 1981–87 US export decline, they accounted for less than 40 percent of the 1987–90 improvement. Since 1987, US exports to Latin America and the OPEC countries have stabilized, and these markets appear unlikely to regain soon their previously large role in US exports.

Civil engineering equipment experienced the largest trade swings of any three-digit subcategory in this group. In 1981, this subcategory accounted for over 40 percent of US specialized industrial machinery exports and more than one-half of the trade surplus. By 1987, exports of civil engineering equipment had fallen to less than 45 percent of the 1981 level; imports, meanwhile, more than doubled. The resulting $4.7 billion decline in the trade balance for engineering equipment accounted for 40 percent of the decline in the overall trade balance for specialized industrial machinery. A strong export surge between 1987 and 1990 made up only about 45 percent of the ground lost in the first part of the decade.

Agricultural equipment, the second-largest trade subcategory in this product group, also experienced a severe decline in trade performance from 1981 to 1987. Fairly strong import growth together with poor export performance increased the trade deficit in this subcategory by $2.6 billion. The $0.4 billion improvement for agricultural equipment and tractors combined between 1987 and 1990 recouped only 13.7 percent of the decline in the balance between 1981 and 1987.

International Competitiveness

The $11.6 billion decline in the trade balance for specialized industrial machinery between 1981 and 1987 was exceeded among manufactures product groups only by road vehicles and apparel . Improvement of $3.7 billion between 1987 and 1990 still left the US balance $7.5 billion below the 1981 level. The massive fall in the trade balance indicates a substantial decline in US competitiveness in specialized industrial machinery.

A decline in the US export-minus-import share balance is another indicator of a decline in US market competitiveness. World exports to non-US destinations increased on average by 8.5 percent annually between 1981 and 1989, but US exports declined by an average of 1.6 percent annually over the same period (table 5.72.6). Consequently, the US share of world exports to non-US destinations fell dramatically from 1981 to 1989.

US imports of specialized industrial machinery increased by an average of 16.9 percent per year between 1981 and 1989, substantially faster than the 13.1 percent annual increase in world imports from non-US sources (table 5.72.6). The result was a modest increase in the US share of world imports from non-US sources between 1981 and 1987. Relatively slow US import growth since 1987 has allowed the US import share to decline to 15.7 percent, which is still above the 12.9 percent 1981 level.

The export and import performance of specialized industrial machinery caused one of the largest declines in percentage share balance of any US manufacturing industry between 1981 and 1987. Poor export performance accounted for three-fourths of the decline. A leveling off of the decline in the US export share and a continuing decline in the US import share beginning in 1984 allowed a modest improvement in the US percentage share balance between 1987 and 1989, although at 0.8 percent in 1989 it remained far below its 16.3 percent position of 1981.

Outlook

Key Determinants of US Trade Performance

Despite the diversity of machinery included in this product group, several factors that help determine trade performance are common to the different subcategories. As noted earlier, few producers enjoy an advantage in the marketplace because of superior technology. Production costs are, however, an important factor in determining US trade performance. Steel is a major input in many of the products in this group, and the cost of steel therefore makes up a large share of total production costs. For some products, it is the largest single cost, exceeding the cost of labor. Until recently, steel prices in the United States have been significantly higher than world prices, partly as a result of "voluntary" restraint agreements in the steel industry. Higher prices for steel put US manufacturers of products for which steel is a major cost component at a disadvantage. By 1987, however, steel prices in the United States had dropped relative to world prices, improving the cost competitiveness of US producers of goods that use large amounts of steel.

Fluctuations in exchange rates can alter the relative prices of US- and foreign-built machines in both the US and overseas markets. Because price is an important consideration in the purchase decision, exchange rate fluctuations can cause major changes in trade flows among the principal supplier countries, which include Germany, Japan, Italy, and the United States.

The availability of financing and the terms at which it is offered are an important part of the overall cost to the user of specialized industrial machinery. Firms based overseas are often able to offer more attractive financing packages, because of either lower interest rates or government guarantees and assistance, than US-based producers can.

Perceptions of quality and reliability are also crucial for much of the machinery in this product group. Virtually all specialized industrial machinery is used in construction or in production processes. Downtime due to equipment failure or excessive maintenance requirements, as noted above, is costly. Firms are thus often willing to pay a premium for equipment that is perceived to be more reliable or of higher quality. The United States generally has a good reputation for quality in overseas markets for specialized industrial machinery.

A related factor is the availability of spare parts and service. In some uses, the ability to make repairs quickly is vital. In agriculture, for example, having equipment unavailable for even a week or two during critical seasons can mean the difference between a profit and a loss for the year. Considerations of parts and service availability may therefore overshadow small differences in purchase price. Although US manufacturers have often lagged behind foreign competitors in developing overseas sales and service networks, they have recently focused on improving their networks. This should strengthen their competitive position in coming years.

A final factor affecting US trade performance for many types of specialized industrial machinery is product liability. Much of the machinery in this product group is used in relatively hazardous occupations such as agriculture and mining. As a result, manufacturers of specialized industrial machinery often face legal action resulting from injuries or deaths suffered while using their machinery. The US legal system typically results in damage awards much larger than those in other countries. US-based firms are more exposed to legal liability costs than foreign-based producers, which sell a smaller proportion of their output in the US market.

Near-Term Outlook

One major factor determining US trade performance in recent years has been the poor export performance in two of the largest US export markets. Over 80 percent of the 1981–87 US export decline occurred in Latin America and the "other" country category, which is dominated by the OPEC countries (table 5.72.5). Neither region had regained its 1981 export levels by 1990. The share of US exports going to these markets fell from 57.2 percent in 1981 to 41.8 percent in 1990.

These export markets are unlikely soon to regain the importance they had at the beginning of the 1980s. Continuing debt problems in many Latin American countries will constrain their ability to import. Although large reconstruction programs in Kuwait will provide some stimulus for exports to the OPEC group, relatively low oil prices anticipated in the near term are likely to limit export growth to other OPEC countries.

Agricultural equipment used in the United States—and in a few other markets such as Canada and Australia—differs from that used in other countries because of differences in farm size. The size of the average farm in the United States is 175 hectares (432 acres). In Europe it is only 8 to 25 hectares, and Japanese farms are even smaller. This has led the United States to produce and use equipment that is well adapted to large-scale, capital-intensive agricultural production but ill suited for the smaller operations typical of many foreign countries.

US producers have tended to specialize in the highly sophisticated and specialized equipment used in large-scale farming. Production of simpler, less sophisticated equipment, suitable for use in smaller-scale operations, has largely shifted overseas. The United States, for example, dominates in the production of tractors of over 100 horsepower, sales of which are limited to a few markets with farms large enough to use them effectively. Production of the smallest tractors (below 40 horsepower) has shifted to Asia, and particularly Japan. Relatively high production costs in the United States—particularly steel and unit labor costs—combined with the relatively strong dollar in the early 1980s caused US manufacturers to abandon the production of small tractors. Production of medium-sized tractors (40 to 100 horsepower) has substantially shifted to Europe, although the producers are often subsidiaries of US firms.

With the production of smaller tractors largely located outside the United States, there is unlikely to be much change in US trade performance in this subcategory through 1993. Limited export markets for US production and continued imports of small tractors virtually assure a continued deficit. The trade balance is most likely to continue to deteriorate slowly, perhaps by $0.1 billion to $0.2 billion per year through 1993.

The United States is stronger in exporting agricultural machinery other than tractors. Relatively stable import growth combined with some improvement in export growth is likely to allow a $0.2 billion to $0.3 billion annual improvement in the trade balance through 1993, for an overall improvement of up to $1.0 billion. The combined effect of changes in trade performance of these two three-digit subcategories is therefore likely to be modest—no more than $0.1 billion to $0.2 billion annually through 1993.

Civil engineering equipment includes a broad variety of equipment used in the construction and mining industries. A recent US Commerce Department competitiveness study of one part of this subcategory, mining machinery, lists the strength of the dollar as the most important factor accounting for the loss of US market share to European and Japanese producers during the early 1980s (US Department of Commerce 1986).

Many of the products in this subcategory are sold in markets that are very price competitive, and relatively small changes in the exchange rate can have substantial effects on purchase decisions. DRI elasticity data support the notion that US demand for civil engineering equipment is quite sensitive to import prices. With an import price elasticity of demand equal to -1.5, a change in exchange rates that alters import prices can be expected to produce a more than proportionate change in US sales of imported civil engineering equipment. The DRI elasticities also suggest that at least some export markets—Japan in particular—are sensitive to changes in exchange rates. Japan's imports of civil engineering machinery change roughly in tandem with changes in the domestic Japanese price of imported goods. Thus, an appreciation of the yen against the dollar that changes yen prices can be expected to significantly increase US sales in the Japanese market. Trade performance during 1987–90 supports the accuracy of these elasticity estimates. Japan, however, is not a major importer of specialized industrial machinery, taking only 6.4 percent of 1990 US exports.

Prospects for US exports of civil engineering machinery are relatively good. The effects of the 1989–90 dollar decline have probably not yet been fully realized. Exploration for and production of minerals have been growing more rapidly overseas than in the United States. Developing countries in particular have been active in minerals exploration and production in recent years. Thus, growing export markets relative to the domestic market should provide good opportunities for US-based producers to increase exports. A critical factor in increasing overseas sales will be the provision of after-sales service and support.

A sluggish domestic economy will limit the sales of residential and commercial construction equipment in the United States and will constrain imports. Rebuilding Kuwaiti infrastructure destroyed or damaged during the Gulf War, on the other hand, should boost US exports of construction equipment substantially, especially since Kuwait has announced a policy of directing contracts toward countries that were active in the effort to remove Iraqi forces from Kuwait.

There will be continued improvement in the trade balance for civil engineering equipment through 1993. Relatively strong export growth combined with weak imports should allow the trade balance to improve in this subcategory by at least $0.5 billion annually. This would increase the subcategory's trade surplus from $2.8 billion in 1990 to perhaps $4.5 billion to $5.0 billion by 1993.

European producers took the technological lead in textile machinery with the introduction of new spinning and weaving equipment in the mid-1970s. US producers still lag behind European producers in this important segment of the textile machinery industry. European technological leadership, combined with an aggressive sales effort, the establishment of a substantial service network in the United States, and the relatively high value of the US dollar in the early 1980s, rapidly eroded the position of US textile machinery manufacturers relative to European producers. The prospects for significant improvement are dim. There is likely to be little change—either improvement or deterioration—in the US trade balance in textile machinery.

Of the remaining three-digit subcategories, only the miscellaneous category is likely to experience any substantial change in its trade balance. Many developing countries are moving toward additional ore processing at mine sites. This should improve the export prospects for ore-processing equipment, an important part of this subcategory. Continued improvement of $0.3 billion to $0.5 billion per year in the trade balance for this subcategory should result in a $1.0 billion to $1.5 billion increase in the surplus.

The rest of the three-digit categories combined are likely to experience little change in trade balances through 1993. Imports of paper machinery are likely to remain stable or decline because of the end of the current investment cycle in the industry. Continued export growth may improve the trade balance for paper machinery by $0.1 billion to $0.2 billion per year. There may be a small deterioration in the trade balance for printing machinery. Sales of printing machinery depend heavily on activity in the advertising business. With the end of the recession anticipated and with the 1992 elections in the United States, there is likely to be a surge in demand for printing equipment. Thus, imports, which have been flat since 1987, are likely to begin to increase again. The increase in imports is likely to exceed export growth, leading to a small deterioration in the trade balance for printing machinery. The remaining category, food-processing machinery, is unlikely to experience a significant change.

Combined, the results for the three-digit subcategories indicate a moderate trade improvement for specialized industrial machinery. The projected $1.0

billion to $1.3 billion annual improvement would result in a roughly $3 billion increase over 1990's $1.8 billion trade surplus, raising the 1993 surplus to about $5 billion.

Medium-Term Outlook

The international value of the dollar will continue to be one of the most important factors in US trade performance. Changes in exchange rates can cause significant changes in trade flows in specialized industrial machinery. Further improvements are likely to come from export expansion and import stabilization. Significant parts of the industry shifted overseas during the 1980s, however, and production of some of these products is unlikely to return to the United States, even with substantial additional dollar devaluation.

In a number of product lines—particularly agricultural and civil engineering equipment—efforts by US producers to improve sales and service networks may begin to pay dividends overseas.

Neither full implementation of EC 1992 nor a North American Free Trade Area (NAFTA) is likely to substantially affect US trade performance in this product group. Many major US producers of specialized industrial machinery have already established a presence in the European Community, so full implementation of EC 1992 is unlikely to cause a major additional shift of production there. Agreement on NAFTA is also unlikely to substantially affect US trade performance. Mexico is already a significant US export market, and there are few barriers to US exports of specialized industrial machinery to Mexico. The United States does not import significant amounts of specialized industrial machinery from Mexico, and Mexico does not possess any significant production advantages over the United States. Therefore, it is unlikely that there would be a significant shift of production from the United States to Mexico as a result of a NAFTA.

Medium-term US trade prospects for specialized industrial machinery will be determined largely by the exchange value of the dollar, economic growth in the United States relative to its major competitors, and market conditions for products produced using specialized industrial machinery. If the dollar remains at about its late-1991 level, the rapid improvement in US trade performance between 1987 and 1990 will taper off through 1993, with the trade balance stabilizing and a surplus of $5 billion to $6 billion likely to emerge by 1995.

Changes in world minerals prices, in agricultural prices, or in European agricultural policies could significantly alter US trade performance in this product group. Depressed world prices for minerals or agricultural commodities would substantially reduce world demand for products in which US exports are concentrated.

Conclusions

■ US trade performance in specialized industrial machinery was among the poorest of all two-digit categories between 1981 and 1987. The $11.6 billion decline in the trade balance for specialized industrial machinery was the third-largest decline and accounted for 7.7 percent of the $150.8 billion decline in US manufactures trade performance.

■ Sharp reductions in exports to Latin America and the OPEC countries accounted for a large part of the 1981–87 decline in US trade performance. Their combined shares of US exports dropped from 57.2 percent in 1981 to 43.7 percent in 1987 and have remained about constant through 1990. Ongoing debt problems in Latin America are likely to continue to restrict US export opportunities in this important market. There are somewhat better prospects for increasing US exports to the OPEC countries, especially with increased Kuwaiti demand for specialized industrial machinery. However, the relatively low oil prices projected for the near to medium term are likely to prevent a return of OPEC's freer spending patterns of the late 1970s.

■ The decline in the dollar's value since 1985 has been largely responsible for improved US trade performance since 1987. The $3.7 billion improvement since 1987—a result of both export expansion and import stabilization—is, however, less than one-third of the 1981–87 decline.

■ The production of some product and component lines—for example, agricultural tractors—shifted overseas during the early to mid-1980s in response to the overvalued dollar. Dollar devaluation to date has been insufficient to return the manufacture of many of these products to the United States. For many of these products, there is little prospect that production will return to the United States.

■ Prospects for additional improvement in the specialized industrial machinery trade balance are good through 1993. Small improvements across most of the three-digit categories should result in a roughly $1 billion annual improvement in the specialized industrial machinery trade balance between 1991 and 1993, leaving the United States with a trade surplus of roughly $5 billion in that year.

■ Prospects for US trade in specialized industrial machinery after 1993 are more uncertain. In the absence of significant changes in exchange rates, the US trade position is likely to stabilize at roughly its 1993 level. Substantial additional devaluation would provide further improvement, much of it through increased exports. But a substantial portion of the production of components and finished goods that shifted overseas in the early to mid-1980s is unlikely to return to the United States, given the exchange rates that are likely to prevail during the period. Thus, imports are unlikely to decline significantly.

■ Changes in market conditions facing products produced using specialized industrial machinery could be important for US trade performance beyond 1993. Agricultural and mineral prices, for example, fluctuate substantially and affect demand for agricultural and mining equipment, both in the United States and overseas. Generally, increases in agricultural and mineral prices would tend to increase exports of agricultural and mining equipment and improve the US trade position in this category, whereas declines in agricultural and mineral prices would worsen the US trade position.

Bibliography

Carroll, Irwin, Peggy Haggerty, and Brian A. Morsch. 1990. "Preserving the Vital Base: America's Semiconductor, Materials and Equipment Industry" (Working Paper of the National Advisory Committee on Semiconductors). Washington: Government Printing Office.

Commission of the European Communities. 1990. *Panorama of EC Industry, 1990.* Luxembourg: Commission of the European Communities.

Industry, Science and Technology Canada. 1988. *Industry Profile: Commercial Printing.* Ottawa: Industry, Science and Technology Canada.

US Department of Commerce, International Trade Administration. 1985a. *A Competitive Assessment of the U.S. Construction Equipment Industry.* Washington: US Department of Commerce (February).

US Department of Commerce, International Trade Administration. 1985b. *A Competitive Assessment of the U.S. Oil Field Equipment Industry.* Washington: US Department of Commerce (February).

US Department of Commerce, International Trade Administration. 1985c. *A Competitive Assessment of the U.S. Farm Machinery Industry.* Washington: US Department of Commerce (March).

US Department of Commerce, International Trade Administration. 1986. *A Competitive Assessment of the U.S. Mining Machinery Industry.* Washington: US Department of Commerce (October).

US Department of Commerce, International Trade Administration. 1987. *A Competitive Assessment of the U.S. Textile Machinery Industry.* Washington: US Department of Commerce (January).

US Department of Commerce, International Trade Administration. 1988. *U.S. Industrial Outlook, 1988.* Washington: Government Printing Office (January).

US Department of Commerce, International Trade Administration. 1989a. *U.S. Industrial Outlook, 1989*. Washington: Government Printing Office (January).

US Department of Commerce, International Trade Administration. 1989b. *A Competitive Assessment of the U.S. Paper Machinery Industry*. Washington: US Department of Commerce (March).

US Department of Commerce, International Trade Administration. 1990a. *U.S. Industrial Outlook, 1990*. Washington: Government Printing Office (January).

US Department of Commerce, International Trade Administration. 1990b. *U.S. Trade Shifts in Selected Commodity Areas, January–June 1990*. Washington: US Department of Commerce (December).

Table 5.72.1 Specialized industrial machinery: product composition of world trade, 1981–89

(billions of dollars except where noted)

SITC Product	1981	1982	1983	1984	1985	1986	1987	1988	1989	Annual growth 1981–89 (percentages)
World exports to world	58.0	53.3	46.5	48.1	53.3	65.5	77.3	91.0	98.1	6.8
of which										
721 Agricultural, except tractors	5.1	4.6	4.2	4.4	4.4	5.0	5.6	6.5	7.0	4.0
722 Tractors, nonroad	6.3	5.1	4.5	4.3	4.2	4.4	4.8	5.7	5.7	–1.3
723 Civil engineering equipment	16.3	15.5	11.5	11.0	12.1	13.0	13.2	16.4	18.1	1.3
724 Textile, leather machinery	8.4	7.5	7.1	7.7	8.7	11.9	15.6	16.9	17.6	9.7
725 Paper and pulp mill machinery	2.3	2.1	1.9	2.0	2.5	3.2	4.0	4.8	5.5	11.5
726 Printing and bookbinding	3.5	3.2	3.1	3.3	3.9	5.4	6.9	8.3	9.3	13.0
727 Food machinery, nondomestic	2.1	1.9	1.8	1.8	2.1	2.6	3.2	3.5	3.6	7.1
728 Other	14.0	13.3	12.4	13.7	15.6	20.2	24.1	28.9	31.4	10.6
Memorandum:										Change 1981–89
SITC 72 share of world manufactures exports (percentages)	5.7	5.5	4.7	4.5	4.7	4.8	4.7	4.6	4.7	–1.0

Source: World Manufactures Trade Data Base.

Table 5.72.2 Specialized industrial machinery: geographic distribution of world trade, 1981–89 (percentages of total)

Country	1981	1982	1983	1984	1985	1986	1987	1988	1989	Change 1981–89
Share of exports to world										
United States	26.5	25.1	19.9	20.0	18.6	14.0	12.0	13.1	14.2	−12.3
Canada	3.5	3.1	3.2	3.4	3.0	2.5	2.3	2.1	2.0	−1.4
Japan	10.2	10.2	12.7	13.6	14.0	13.8	13.6	13.9	14.6	4.4
European Community	48.2	49.6	51.1	49.7	50.2	54.6	55.7	53.5	52.4	4.2
EC to non-EC	31.7	31.5	31.8	31.3	31.5	33.1	31.8	29.1	28.5	−3.2
Germany	19.0	20.0	21.4	20.9	21.4	24.5	24.8	23.3	23.2	4.2
France	6.2	6.1	6.4	5.5	5.2	5.6	5.5	5.5	5.4	−0.8
Italy	7.7	8.0	8.7	8.6	9.0	10.0	10.3	10.2	9.6	1.9
United Kingdom	8.6	8.5	7.6	7.5	7.5	6.9	7.0	6.6	6.4	−2.2
Other Western Europe	9.7	9.9	10.6	10.6	11.2	12.1	13.1	12.8	12.0	2.3
Asian NICs[a]	0.4	0.9	1.1	1.3	1.3	1.4	1.8	2.7	2.8	2.4
Eastern Europe[b]	0.6	0.5	0.5	0.5	0.6	0.7	0.5	0.7	0.5	−0.1
Developing countries	0.6	0.5	0.7	0.8	0.8	0.7	0.8	1.4	1.1	0.5
Latin America	0.3	0.3	0.4	0.5	0.4	0.4	0.4	0.6	0.6	0.3
Rest of world	0.1	0.1	0.1	0.1	0.1	0.1	0.2	0.2	0.2	0.1
Share of imports from world										
United States	9.5	9.3	11.4	16.2	15.9	15.5	15.1	14.4	13.4	3.9
Canada	7.4	5.9	6.3	6.9	6.9	6.0	5.8	5.4	5.1	−2.3
Japan	1.4	1.5	1.7	1.8	1.6	1.6	1.9	2.3	2.4	1.0
European Community	24.4	25.8	28.1	27.0	26.9	30.0	34.1	34.8	34.2	9.8
EC from non-EC	7.9	8.1	8.9	8.7	8.6	9.2	10.6	11.4	11.1	3.2
Germany	4.1	4.0	5.1	4.7	4.8	5.4	5.5	5.4	5.6	1.5
France	5.4	5.8	5.9	5.2	5.1	5.8	6.5	6.7	6.8	1.4
Italy	3.0	2.8	2.7	2.8	2.9	3.4	4.2	4.1	3.8	0.9
United Kingdom	4.2	5.0	5.8	5.8	5.6	5.2	6.0	6.7	6.3	2.1
Other Western Europe	7.6	7.7	8.1	7.7	9.3	10.3	10.5	9.2	8.8	1.3
Asian NICs[a]	4.4	5.4	5.6	6.2	5.5	5.9	7.3	8.9	10.7	6.3
Eastern Europe[b]	3.9	4.6	4.3	3.8	4.0	4.8	4.1	4.3	4.3	0.4
Developing countries	39.4	37.5	32.9	28.2	27.8	24.6	20.2	19.4	19.4	−20.0
Latin America	11.9	9.6	5.7	5.8	6.3	6.0	5.1	5.0	4.8	−7.1
Rest of world	0.0	0.1	0.0	0.0	0.0	0.0	0.0	0.1	0.1	0.0

table continued next page

Table 5.72.2 Specialized industrial machinery: geographic distribution of world trade, 1981–89 (percentages of total) (continued)

Country	1981	1982	1983	1984	1985	1986	1987	1988	1989	Change 1981–89
Export share minus import share										
United States	17.0	15.8	8.5	3.8	2.7	-1.5	-3.2	-1.3	0.8	-16.2
Canada	-4.0	-2.8	-3.1	-3.6	-3.8	-3.5	-3.4	-3.3	-3.1	0.9
Japan	8.8	8.7	11.0	11.8	12.4	12.2	11.8	11.7	12.2	3.4
European Community	23.9	23.7	23.0	22.7	23.3	24.5	21.6	18.7	18.2	-5.7
Non-EC	23.8	23.5	22.9	22.6	22.9	23.9	21.2	17.8	17.4	-6.4
Germany	14.9	16.0	16.3	16.2	16.6	19.1	19.2	17.9	17.5	2.7
France	0.8	0.3	0.6	0.4	0.1	-0.2	-1.1	-1.3	-1.4	-2.2
Italy	4.7	5.2	6.0	5.8	6.1	6.6	6.1	6.1	5.8	1.1
United Kingdom	4.4	3.6	1.9	1.7	1.9	1.8	1.1	-0.2	0.1	-4.4
Other Western Europe	2.1	2.2	2.5	2.9	1.9	1.8	2.6	3.6	3.1	1.0
Asian NICs[a]	-4.0	-4.6	-4.5	-4.9	-4.2	-4.5	-5.5	-6.2	-7.9	-3.9
Eastern Europe[b]	-3.3	-4.1	-3.9	-3.2	-3.5	-4.1	-3.6	-3.7	-3.8	-0.5
Developing countries	-38.8	-37.0	-32.3	-27.4	-26.9	-23.9	-19.4	-18.1	-18.3	20.5
Latin America	-11.6	-9.3	-5.3	-5.3	-5.8	-5.6	-4.7	-4.4	-4.2	7.3
Rest of world	0.1	0.0	0.1	0.1	0.1	0.1	0.1	0.1	0.1	0.1

a. Hong Kong, Korea, Singapore, and Taiwan.

b. Including Soviet Union.

Source: World Manufactures Trade Data Base.

Table 5.72.3 Specialized industrial machinery: bilateral trade flows, 1989 (billions of dollars)

Importer	Exporter										
	World	United States	Canada	Japan	European Community	Germany	France	United Kingdom	Asian NICs	Latin America	Other
World	98.1	14.0	2.0	14.3	51.4	22.7	5.3	6.3	2.7	0.6	13.1
United States	13.2		1.6	3.6	5.6	2.6	0.6	1.0	0.5	0.4	1.5
Canada	4.0	2.5		0.3	0.8	0.3	0.1	0.1	0.1	0.0	0.3
Japan	2.7	0.9	0.0		1.1	0.7	0.1	0.1	0.3	0.0	0.4
European Community	35.0	3.1	0.1	2.0	23.5	9.7	2.6	2.5	0.3	0.1	5.9
Germany	6.0	0.6	0.0	0.5	2.9		0.6	0.4	0.1	0.0	2.0
France	6.9	0.5	0.0	0.3	5.1	2.4		0.6	0.1	0.0	1.0
United Kingdom	6.1	0.8	0.0	0.5	3.9	2.0	0.5		0.1	0.0	0.8
Asian NICs	7.9	1.5	0.0	3.6	1.7	0.8	0.2	0.2	0.6		0.5
Latin America	5.0	2.4	0.1	0.3	1.8	0.6	0.2	0.1	0.1		0.4
Other	30.3	3.5	0.2	4.5	17.0	7.9	1.7	2.1	1.0	0.0	4.2

Source: World Manufactures Trade Data Base.

Table 5.72.4 Specialized industrial machinery: product composition of US trade, 1981–90[a] (millions of dollars except where noted)

Category	SITC Rev. 2			SITC Rev. 3			
	1981	1987	Change 1981–87	1987	1990	Change 1981–90	Change 1987–90
Total							
Exports	14,602	9,243	−5,359	9,365	15,255	653	5,890
Imports	5,244	11,459	6,215	11,233	13,440	8,196	2,207
Balance	9,358	−2,216	−11,574	−1,868	1,815	−7,543	3,683
of which							
721 Agricultural machinery excluding tractors							
Exports	1,420	868	−552	883	1,553	133	670
Imports	637	759	122	719	904	267	185
Balance	783	109	−674	164	649	−134	485
722 Tractors, nonroad							
Exports	2,102	625	−1,477	625	921	−1,181	296
Imports	643	1,076	433	1,076	1,504	861	428
Balance	1,459	−451	−1,910	−451	−583	−2,042	−132
723 Civil engineering equipment							
Exports	6,310	2,793	−3,517	3,257	5,238	−1,072	1,981
Imports	1,086	2,239	1,153	2,543	2,410	1,324	−133
Balance	5,224	554	−4,670	714	2,827	−2,397	2,113
724 Textile, leather machinery							
Exports	697	667	−30	838	1,046	349	208
Imports	977	1,842	865	1,794	2,118	1,141	324
Balance	−280	−1,175	−895	−956	−1,072	−792	−116
725 Paper mill and pulp mill machinery							
Exports	341	303	−38	303	574	233	271
Imports	254	463	209	463	764	510	301
Balance	87	−160	−247	−160	−190	−277	−30
726 Printing and bookbinding machinery							
Exports	776	663	−113	641	1,169	393	528
Imports	408	1,139	731	1,163	1,200	792	37
Balance	368	−476	−844	−522	−31	−399	491
727 Food processing machinery, nondomestic							
Exports	390	331	−59	343	451	61	108
Imports	111	295	184	342	374	263	32
Balance	279	36	−243	1	77	−202	76
728 Other							
Exports	2,566	2,994	428	2,474	4,303	1,737	1,829
Imports	1,129	3,644	2,515	3,133	3,670	2,541	537
Balance	1,437	−650	−2,087	−659	633	−804	1,292

a. Data are expressed on a domestic exports, imports customs basis.

Source: US Department of Commerce.

Table 5.72.5 Specialized industrial machinery: geographic composition of US trade, 1981–90[a]

	Millions of dollars				Percentages of total			
	1981	1987	1989	1990	1981	1987	1989	1990
Exports								
Canada	2,712	2,173	2,446	3,125	18.6	23.2	17.9	20.5
Japan	552	394	877	973	3.8	4.2	6.4	6.4
European Community	2,178	2,010	3,067	3,411	14.9	21.5	22.5	22.4
United Kingdom	584	526	786	885	4.0	5.6	5.8	5.8
Germany	371	360	551	633	2.5	3.8	4.0	4.1
France	399	342	528	541	2.7	3.7	3.9	3.5
Italy	181	169	220	268	1.2	1.8	1.6	1.8
Latin America	3,709	1,814	2,312	2,627	25.4	19.4	16.9	17.2
Asian NICs	810	695	1,498	1,360	5.5	7.4	11.0	8.9
Other	4,641	2,279	3,444	3,759	31.8	24.3	25.2	24.6
Total	14,602	9,365	13,644	15,255	100.0	100.0	100.0	100.0
Imports								
Canada	1,337	1,218	1,556	1,387	25.5	10.8	12.0	10.7
Japan	804	2,917	3,605	3,336	15.3	26.0	27.8	25.8
European Community	2,239	5,352	5,738	6,275	42.7	47.6	44.3	48.5
United Kingdom	431	949	1,038	1,073	8.2	8.4	8.0	8.3
Germany	1,078	2,630	2,720	3,059	20.6	23.4	21.0	23.6
France	185	560	576	594	3.5	5.0	4.4	4.6
Italy	306	620	764	790	5.8	5.5	5.9	6.1
Latin America	139	258	376	343	2.7	2.3	2.9	2.6
Asian NICs	115	420	432	412	2.2	3.7	3.3	3.2
Other	610	1,068	1,252	1,192	11.6	9.5	9.7	9.2
Total	5,244	11,233	12,959	12,945	100.0	100.0	100.0	100.0

a. Data are expressed on a domestic exports, imports customs basis.

Source: US Department of Commerce.

Table 5.72.6 Specialized industrial machinery: indices of US competitiveness, 1981–89 (billions of dollars except where noted)

	1981	1982	1983	1984	1985	1986	1987	1988	1989	Annual growth 1981–89 (percentages)
World trade										
World exports to non-US destinations	52.6	48.7	41.3	41.1	45.4	55.9	66.0	78.8	86.0	8.5
World imports from non-US sources	42.0	39.5	36.5	39.0	43.9	57.1	68.5	81.8	87.7	13.1
US trade										
Exports	15.4	13.4	9.3	9.6	9.9	9.2	9.2	11.9	14.0	−1.6
Imports	5.4	4.8	5.2	7.8	8.6	10.4	11.9	13.6	13.8	16.9
Balance	10.0	8.6	4.1	1.8	1.3	−1.2	−2.7	−1.7	0.2	
										Change 1981–89
US share of exports to non-US destinations (percentages)	29.2	27.5	22.4	23.4	21.9	16.4	14.0	15.1	16.5	−12.7
US share of imports from non-US sources (percentages)	12.9	12.3	14.3	20.1	19.6	18.2	17.4	16.6	15.7	2.8
Export share minus import share (percentages)	−0.1	−2.4	−4.8	−9.1	−12.7	−12.6	−11.7	−10.7	−8.8	−8.7

Source: World Manufactures Trade Data Base.

Metalworking Machinery (SITC 73)

Metalworking machinery includes a wide variety of machinery used to manufacture metal items. The largest part of the industry, accounting for over 75 percent of world trade in metalworking machinery, is machine tools and parts. Machine tools are used to shape metal and other materials. Although not a large part of total world trade, machine tools are used directly or indirectly in the manufacture of virtually all products.

Description of the Product Group

Metalworking machinery can be divided into two broad subcategories: machine tools and other metalworking machinery. Metalworking machinery other than machine tools includes primarily machinery used for casting, rolling, welding, or brazing metal. Machine tools are power-driven machines that are not hand held and are used to cut, form, or shape metal. They vary enormously in complexity, from simple manually controlled lathes to multistation, computer-controlled machining centers. The machine tool subcategory can be further divided into numerically controlled (NC) and non-NC machine tools. Numerical controls—a US-developed technology—are control systems that operate a machine by means of numerically coded programs inserted or fed into the system manually or electronically.

Four three-digit commodity groups make up the metalworking machinery product group:

SITC

731 machine tools working by removing metal or other material

733 machine tools for working metal, sintered metal carbides, or cermets, without removing material

735 parts, not elsewhere specified, and accessories suitable for use solely or principally with the machines falling within headings 731 and 733

737 metalworking machinery (other than machine tools) and parts thereof, not elsewhere specified; this subcategory includes machinery used for casting, rolling, or welding metal.

Revision 3 of the SITC expanded the former single category of machine tools, SITC 736, into the present categories 731, 733, and 735.

Role in World Trade

Size and Composition

World exports of metalworking machinery were $14.2 billion in 1981 and accounted for 1.4 percent of world manufactures exports (table 5.73.1). World trade in these products contracted sharply after 1981 in response to the world-wide economic slowdown. By 1983, metalworking machinery exports had fallen to $10.4 billion, 26 percent below their 1981 level. From that trough, exports expanded steadily. It was not until 1986, however, that world exports exceeded their 1981 level. By 1989, world metalworking machinery exports had reached $23.1 billion. Growth in metalworking machinery exports, at 6.2 percent per year on average, lagged behind the 9.6 percent average annual growth in manufactures exports overall.

Global Competition Patterns

The European Community is by far the largest exporter of metalworking machinery, accounting for about half of world exports during the 1980s (table 5.73.2). Germany was the largest single exporter, with about 25 percent of world exports. Japan increased its share of the world export market from 16.1 percent in 1981 to 21.5 percent in 1989. Over the same period the US share of the world market declined from 15.4 percent to 9.9 percent. The East Asian NICs also showed substantial improvement, increasing their share of world exports from 1.8 percent in 1981 to 4.0 percent in 1989.

The European Community was also the largest metalworking-machinery importing region. The Community accepted 33.9 percent of 1989 world imports, a substantial increase from its 28.4 percent share in 1981 (table 5.73.2). Although the United States is not the largest consumer of machine tools (both Japan and the Soviet Union exceed the United States in this regard), it is the largest single-country importer. Its import share increased dramatically from 14.7 percent in 1981 to 22.0 percent in 1985, before shrinking to 15.1 percent in 1989. Only two other countries imported more than $1 billion worth of machine tools in 1987: the Soviet Union and Germany. Germany accounted for 8.4 percent of world metalworking machinery imports in 1989, up from 6.8 percent in 1981. Other significant importers include the East Asian NICs (11.8 percent of 1989 world imports), France (6.5 percent), and the developing countries (15.8 percent).

Since 1985, when it passed the European Community, Japan has had the largest positive export-minus-import share balance in metalworking machinery (table 5.73.2). From 14.0 percentage points in 1981, Japan increased its share balance to 19.1 percentage points in 1989. Virtually all of Japan's improvement resulted from the 5.3-percentage-point increase in its export share during the 1980s.

The European Community, particularly Germany, was the only other area with large positive export-minus-import share balances. Although the Community's share balance declined substantially between 1983 and 1987, Germany's declined by much less.

By 1989, the United States, the former Soviet Union, the Asian NICs, and the developing countries had the largest negative export-minus-import share balances. The 5.9-percentage-point drop in the US share balance position, from 0.7 percentage points in 1981 to −5.2 percentage points in 1989, was the largest for any country. The steep decline in the US export share caused over 90 percent of the decline in the US share balance position.

Like the United States, the Asian NICs experienced a substantial deterioration in their share balance position. Their deterioration, however, resulted from a rapid increase in their share of world imports rather than a decline in their export share. The developing countries improved their share balance position more than any other country or region. With negligible exports, however, their share balance reflects declining imports almost exclusively.

Intra-EC trade dominates world trade flows in metalworking machinery (table 5.73.3). Over 20 percent of world exports were from one EC member to another in 1989. The United States was the Community's most important single-country non-EC market. The United States was also the largest single-country export market for Japan, the Asian NICs, and Canada. The most important export markets for the United States were Latin America, Canada, the European Community, and the Asian NICs.

Key Determinants of World Trade Patterns

The 1980s were a decade of transition for the machine tool industry, and that transition strongly influenced world trade patterns. Much of the production of lower-priced, standardized machines shifted from the United States and Europe to Japan and, more recently, to the Asian NICs. Traditionally, the vast majority of machine tools were built in response to customers' orders and manufactured to customers' specifications. Backlogs of orders developed in periods of high demand and were reduced when demand became slack. Fluctuations in the order backlogs helped to even out production and employment despite the large fluctuations in demand.

After establishing a significant presence in domestic and foreign markets, Japanese machine tool producers began standardizing machines that had previously been custom built. They were able to achieve economies of scale and reduce production costs. With favorable exchange rates, good-quality machines, lower prices, and, equally important, reductions in delivery times, Japanese producers became important competitors in the US market in the late 1970s.

The Japanese are now facing competition from other producers. Japanese domination of the market for relatively inexpensive, standardized machine tools is being challenged by Korea, Taiwan, China, and Brazil. The Japanese are also increasingly moving into markets in which US and German producers are most competitive: those in custom-made, high-precision tools. Because these machines are more specialized, they require a local engineering presence, which several Japanese firms have established.

Role in US Trade

Recent Performance

Metalworking machinery's share of US manufactures exports declined from 1.3 percent in 1981—about the same as metalworking machinery's share in world trade—to 0.8 percent in 1987. Between 1981 and 1989, US manufactures exports overall grew on average by 7.0 percent annually while metalworking machinery exports grew by an average of only 0.5 percent annually.

There was a shift in importance among markets for US exports of these goods during the 1980s, with the East Asian NICs becoming much more important customers (table 5.73.5). Their share of US metalworking machinery exports nearly doubled, from 7.1 percent in 1981 to 13.1 percent in 1990. A substantial part of the increase in these exports went to Korea, whose share of the US export market grew from just over 1 percent to nearly 8 percent between 1981 and 1987, and increased another full percentage point between 1987 and 1989. Japan was another country whose share of the US export market grew significantly, from 4.4 percent in 1981 to 7.6 percent in 1990. Meanwhile Germany's share rose from 3.5 percent to 6.8 percent.

While the importance of export markets in Europe and Asia increased during the 1980s, the two largest export markets for the United States declined in importance. In 1981 Canada and Latin America accounted for over half of all US metalworking machinery exports. By 1990 their combined share had fallen to 35 percent.

US import growth averaged a moderate 7.1 percent per year between 1981 and 1989 (table 5.73.6), although there were wide fluctuations from year to year. Between 1981 and 1983, for example, imports actually declined by one-fourth, to $1.5 billion. In the next year imports increased by 36.7 percent. Further increases of 36.3 percent in 1985 and 17.7 percent in 1986 resulted in 1986 imports of $3.4 billion, over twice the level of the low point in 1983. The large fluctuations in US imports reflect the cyclical nature of the market for metalworking machinery. The 1981–83 decline in imports resulted from the severe recession in the United States in the early 1980s. The subsequent increase in US imports coincided with economic recovery in the United States. The increase in imports and a decline in domestic production resulted in imports capturing a larger percentage of domestic machine tool consumption. Imports' share of consumption rose from 24.9 percent in 1981 to 47.6 percent in 1987 (National Machine Tool Builders Association 1989b, 126).

Japan is the largest source of metalworking machinery imported into the United States. From 36.1 percent in 1981, Japan's share of US imports in this category increased to over one-half by 1989 before declining to 41.3 percent in 1990. The growth in Japan's market share came largely at the expense of the miscellaneous category of countries. The EC share of US imports declined from 30.6 percent to 26.8 percent between 1981 and 1989 but then rebounded to 32.8 percent in 1990. Roughly half of US imports from the European Community are from Germany. Canada, the United Kingdom, and Italy have the next largest shares. Other important US suppliers include the East Asian NICs, primarily Taiwan.

Declines in US metalworking machinery exports through the mid-1980s reinforced the effect of substantial import growth on the US trade balance. From a small surplus of $0.2 billion in 1981, a peak year for US metalworking machinery exports, the US balance declined to a deficit of $1.3 billion by 1987 (table 5.73.4). A $0.6 billion decline in metalworking machinery exports accounted for about one-third of the $1.5 billion decline in the trade balance. The other two-thirds came from a $1.0 billion increase in imports.

US exports in this product group increased from 1983 to 1990, reversing the steep 1981–83 decline. By 1990 US exports were $2.7 billion, roughly 25 percent above their 1981 level. In 1990 US imports declined for the first time in a decade. Despite that decline and some increase in exports, the 1990 US trade deficit in metalworking machinery was still nearly $1.0 billion.

International Competitiveness

The substantial decline in the US metalworking machinery trade balance is one indication of a decline in US international competitiveness. A decline in the US share of world exports is another. While world exports to non-US destinations increased by an average of 6.1 percent annually from 1981 through 1989, US exports increased by an annual average of 0.5 percent (table 5.73.6). The US share of world exports to non-US destinations dropped dramatically, from 18.0 percent in 1981 to 9.8 percent by 1987, but recovered to 11.6 percent in 1989.

The US share of imports from non-US sources varied over the 1981–89 period but ended the period below the 1981 level. From 17.6 percent in 1981, the US import share increased to a high of 24.9 percent in 1985 before declining to 16.7 percent in 1989.

The decline in exports and strong import growth through 1985 caused a sharp deterioration in the US export-minus-import share balance (table 5.73.6). Beginning with nearly identical export and import shares in 1981, the US share balance deteriorated sharply to −12.1 percentage points by 1985. A falling US share of imports from non-US sources allowed the US share balance to improve to −5.1 percentage points in 1989.

Outlook

Key Determinants of Trade Performance

The domestic machine tool industry is composed of a large number of small firms. The 1987 US Department of Commerce Census of Manufacturers listed 652 establishments in the machine tool industry, with total employment of 46,400 persons. However, 43 percent of these firms employed fewer than 20 people. The 1987 figures indicate a significant contraction from the previous Census of Manufacturers in 1982, when employment, at 77,800, was approximately two-thirds higher.

The US industry has been strongly affected by the restructuring of the industry around the world. Much of the production of relatively simple, less expensive metalworking machinery has shifted to Japan and the East Asian NICs. Although several US machine tool producers offer broad product lines, many concentrate in niche markets or on custom-built, computer-controlled machine tools, and on the integration of two or more machine tools into machine centers with automatic transfer of materials between stations. The United States is particularly strong in peripherals and software applications.

A survey of US machine tool builders done in conjunction with this study indicates several factors that hinder US trade performance. A number of industry analysts interviewed cited the US product liability system as a major competitive disadvantage to US producers. Data from the National Machine Tool Builders Association bear this out, showing that in 1988 the median machine tool builder spent seven times more on product liability than on research. Over half of all respondents to the machine tool industry survey conducted for this study indicated that product liability costs were either extremely important or very important to their decisions whether to increase US-based production capacity. Of the 11 potential factors listed in the survey question, only the projected level of domestic demand was ranked as more important.

US machine tool builders were also asked to rank factors that limited the growth of US exports of machine tools. Nearly 45 percent of respondents indicated that a lack of knowledge of foreign markets was either extremely important or very important in limiting export growth. This response probably reflects the small size of most US firms (the median US firm in this industry has annual sales of about $6 million) and the limited financial resources available to them, which make it difficult to establish foreign sales networks.

A similar proportion of respondents also ranked foreign import barriers as an important limitation on export growth. A third factor, listed by 37 percent of the respondents as either extremely or very important, was a lack of competitive export financing. These two factors indicate the differences in treatment US machine tool builders and their foreign competitors receive from their national governments. Many foreign governments have targeted their domestic machine tool industry to receive government assistance, including support for investment and R&D, various protective import barriers, and the provision of low-interest, government-guaranteed loans for export sales.

Firms were also asked to rank the importance of factors that encouraged imports of machine tools into the United States. The most important factor, with 52 percent of respondents ranking it as extremely or very important, was that foreign goods were very competitive in terms of quality. Roughly 35 percent of respondents ranked the following factors as extremely or very important: foreign competitors selling below cost to retain US markets in the hope of regaining price competitiveness, no US source of supply for some products, and the competitiveness of foreign service and flexibility in meeting customers' needs.

A recurring theme in the survey results and in interviews with industry analysts is the lack of financial resources available to US producers, which limits their ability to compete internationally. Although US machine tool builders spend significantly on investment and R&D, restricted and volatile cash flows make long-term planning difficult. During the 1980s, for example, US machine tool consumption fluctuated erratically between about $2.5 billion and $5.5 billion annually. Firms also face difficulties in trying to finance long-term projects through borrowing rather than through retained earnings. Few banks are willing to lend to firms in a mature industry that is facing intense competition from

Japan and is subject to sharp sales fluctuations. The same factors also limit these firms' ability to raise funds through equity financing.

Two factors combined in the mid-1980s to allow Japanese exports to the United States to expand rapidly. First, the economic recovery after 1982 created a large increase in domestic demand for machine tools. US producers were unable to meet this surge in demand, and order backlogs grew rapidly. Japan, concentrating on mass production of standard machines, offered much shorter delivery times on some types of machines. The rise in the value of the dollar at the same time reduced the price of imported machines relative to US-produced machines. The combination of these two factors caused many US purchasers to shift to non-US sources.

Near-Term Outlook

Several factors will affect US trade performance in machine tools in the early 1990s. One of these is the effect of full implementation of EC 1992. In recent years the European Community has been the largest export market for US producers. Many US producers believe that exporting to Europe is likely to become more difficult after EC 1992 is implemented. One problem is that many of the decisions concerning standards for machine tools within the European Community are yet to be made. There is some fear that certification will be required at the port of entry rather than in the United States. This uncertainty makes planning for exports to the European market difficult, as the production of machine tools often requires a substantial lead time.

The effects of economic liberalization in Eastern Europe and its integration into the world economy are uncertain. There will be a large market for machine tools in Eastern Europe and the Soviet Union as the former Eastern bloc nations attempt to modernize their production facilities. However, financing problems may substantially dampen expression of this demand. There may be some resort to barter arrangements, which have been used previously with the Soviet Union and in some developing countries. Germany will be in the best position to exploit these new markets because of its previous experience in exporting to the Soviet Union and its relatively close ties to Eastern Europe. Some US producers, particularly those willing and able to put together nontraditional financing packages, may also do well in Eastern Europe. Our survey results indicate some optimism about the Eastern European market. Over 40 percent of machine tool industry respondents reported that, although they have not previously exported to Eastern Europe, they plan to do so in the future.

A relaxation of export restrictions on sensitive technologies may also benefit US manufacturers. The United States is most internationally competitive in the types of machines whose exports have been restricted under COCOM (Coordinating Committee for Multilateral Export Control) rules. In addition, industry members feel the US government has tended to interpret COCOM restrictions more stringently than its COCOM partners, to the detriment of US exports. Thus, the expected easing of restrictions would be particularly beneficial to US producers and should increase US exports. However, until the new regulations have been formulated, the extent of the benefit to US producers remains uncertain.

US trade performance in the early 1990s depends on the level of economic growth in the United States relative to its competitors. The relatively slow growth expected in the United States in the early 1990s will limit import growth, while relatively strong growth overseas, if it occurs, should provide stable or expanding export markets. Thus, in the absence of significant changes in exchange rates, the United States is likely to continue the modest improvement in the metalworking machinery trade balance begun in 1990, with an improvement of perhaps $100 million to $200 million per year through 1993. This would result in a 1993 trade deficit of $0.3 billion to $0.6 billion.

Medium-Term Outlook

The United States will continue to face stiff competition into the mid-1990s. Japanese producers, for example, are working very hard at standardizing the production of specialized machine tools. One goal is to design a set of standard castings that can be adapted to any tool made, instead of having to create a new casting for each tool from scratch. US producers are limited in their ability to invest in the development of this technology by their lack of access to financial capital.

Recovery from the 1990–91 recession is likely to lead to a surge in imports as US manufacturers increase their purchases of metalworking machinery. Thus, even with continued export expansion, it is unlikely that a modest trade balance improvement in the early 1990s will continue after 1993.

Conclusions

■ Despite its relatively small role in world trade, metalworking machinery is critical to determining the international competitiveness of manufacturing industries.

■ The US international trade position in metalworking machinery declined substantially during the 1980s. The US share of world exports to non-US destinations fell sharply, from 18.1 percent in 1981 to 11.7 percent in 1989.

- During the 1980s US producers faced intense competition from Japanese and other East Asian producers in the market for standardized machine tools. The rise in the dollar, combined with the successful move to mass production of these machines in Asia, caused a shift in production from the United States to Asia. This was one of the primary causes of the rapid increases in imports to the United States during the 1980s.

- The emergence of new producers in the lower end of the market, including the Asian NICs, ensures that competitive pressures in this industry will be intense. As a result, US producers are unlikely to regain a substantial share of this market.

- The United States remains a strong competitor in the market for high-quality, computer-controlled machine tools. Several developments, including the opening up of markets in Eastern Europe and the potential relaxation of export restrictions, suggest continued growth of US exports.

- US trade performance in the early 1990s depends on the level of economic growth in the United States relative to its competitors. In the absence of large changes in economic growth rates or exchange rates, the United States is likely to continue the modest improvement in its trade balance in metal-working machinery, with an improvement of perhaps $100 million to $200 million per year.

- A slowdown in the United States accompanied by continued growth in Europe and Asia would add to the improvement in the US trade balance in this industry. Such an outcome would, however, be damaging to the large number of US firms with few or no exports. If many of these firms should fail, the ultimate result when the US economy recovers could be a surge of imports replacing the output that the failed US companies would have produced.

Bibliography

Auerbach, Stuart. 1990a. "Dresser's High Road to Success." *Washington Post* (15 May): D1.

Auerbach, Stuart. 1990b. "High-Tech Sales Plan Unveiled, Bush Liberalizes E. Europe Policy." *Washington Post* (7 June): E1.

Auerbach, Stuart. 1990c. "High-Tech Trade Curbs Eased for Eastern Europe." *Washington Post* (8 June): F1.

Commins, Kevin. 1990. "Export Boom Fails to Heal Machine Tool Industry's Ills." *Journal of Commerce* (7 September).

Commission of the European Communities. 1990. *Panorama of EC Industry, 1990.* Luxembourg: Commission of the European Communities.

Guenther, Gary L. 1986. *Machine Tools: Imports and the U.S. Industry, Economy, and Defense Industrial Base.* Washington: Congressional Research Service, Library of Congress (July).

Industry, Science and Technology Canada. 1988. *Industry Profile: Machine Tools and Tooling.* Ottawa: Industry, Science and Technology Canada.

March, Artemis. 1989. "The U.S. Machine Tool Industry and its Foreign Competitors." *MIT Commission on Industrial Productivity Working Paper.* Cambridge, MA: MIT Press.

Milbank, Dana. 1991. "U.S. Machine Tool Makers Posted Gains Overseas in 1990, Slipped Domestically." *Wall Street Journal* (4 March): A2.

National Machine Tool Builders Association. 1989a. *Economic Briefing Book.* McLean, VA: National Machine Tool Builders Association (15 May).

National Machine Tool Builders Association. 1989b. *The Economic Handbook of the Machine Tool Industry, 1989–1990.* McLean, VA: National Machine Tool Builders Association.

National Machine Tool Builders Association. 1989c. *Survey of Major Export Markets: Europe 1992.* McLean, VA: National Machine Tool Builders Association (September).

US Congress, Office of Technology Assessment. 1989. *Holding the Edge: Maintaining the Defense Technology Base.* Washington: US Congress (April).

US Department of Commerce, International Trade Administration. 1988. *U.S. Industrial Outlook, 1988.* Washington: Government Printing Office (January).

US Department of Commerce, International Trade Administration. 1989. *U.S. Industrial Outlook, 1989.* Washington: Government Printing Office (January).

US Department of Commerce, International Trade Administration. 1990. *U.S. Industrial Outlook, 1990.* Washington: Government Printing Office (January).

US International Trade Commission. 1990. *U.S. Trade Shifts in Selected Commodity Areas, January–June 1990.* Washington: US International Trade Commission (December).

Table 5.73.1 Metalworking machinery: product composition of world trade, 1981–89 (billions of dollars except where noted)

SITC	Product	1981	1982	1983	1984	1985	1986	1987	1988	1989	Annual growth 1981–89 (percentages)
	World exports to world	14.2	12.1	10.4	10.9	12.6	17.6	19.8	12.7	23.1	6.2
	of which										
736	Machine tools	11.1	9.4	8.1	8.6	10.0	14.1	15.7	17.4	18.8	6.8
737	Other machinery	3.1	2.8	2.4	2.4	2.8	3.7	4.4	4.2	4.3	4.3
											Change 1981–89
	Memorandum: SITC 73 share of world manufactures exports (percentages)	1.4	1.2	1.1	1.0	1.1	1.3	1.2	1.1	1.1	−0.3

Source: World Manufactures Trade Data Base.

Table 5.73.2 Metalworking machinery: geographic distribution of world trade, 1981–89 (percentages of total)

Country	1981	1982	1983	1984	1985	1986	1987	1988	1989	Change 1981–89
Share of exports to world										
United States	15.4	13.6	11.0	11.0	10.2	8.5	8.3	9.1	9.9	−5.5
Canada	1.5	2.2	1.4	2.0	1.7	1.4	1.0	0.8	0.7	−0.8
Japan	16.1	13.7	16.5	21.3	23.6	23.5	20.8	20.1	21.5	5.4
European Community	50.6	53.0	51.8	47.0	45.7	47.6	50.2	49.0	48.6	−1.9
EC to non-EC	32.6	34.9	34.2	31.3	29.8	30.1	30.5	29.4	28.2	−4.5
Germany	24.4	26.4	26.3	23.1	22.1	24.6	25.6	24.1	24.1	−0.3
France	5.1	4.7	5.1	4.2	3.9	3.6	3.4	3.9	3.5	−1.6
Italy	8.6	8.6	8.9	8.1	8.6	8.6	9.4	8.9	9.6	0.9
United Kingdom	7.0	7.5	6.0	6.2	5.4	4.8	5.7	5.9	4.8	−2.2
Other Western Europe	12.0	13.3	14.9	14.0	14.1	14.7	15.1	14.9	12.9	0.9
Asian NICs[a]	1.8	2.0	2.3	2.7	2.6	2.3	2.8	3.8	4.0	2.2
Eastern Europe[b]	1.9	1.5	1.2	1.0	1.2	1.2	1.2	1.5	1.3	−0.6
Developing countries	0.7	0.7	0.8	0.8	0.9	0.8	0.8	2.1	0.9	0.3
Latin America	0.2	0.2	0.4	0.3	0.4	0.3	0.2	0.2	0.2	0.0
Rest of world	0.1	0.1	0.1	0.1	0.1	0.1	0.1	0.2	0.2	0.2
Share of imports from world										
United States	14.7	15.7	14.7	19.3	22.0	18.9	15.4	15.1	15.1	0.5
Canada	7.1	4.8	4.8	5.7	5.6	5.8	5.0	4.2	3.8	−3.3
Japan	2.1	2.4	2.3	2.3	2.3	2.1	1.8	2.0	2.4	0.3
European Community	28.4	29.4	27.9	27.3	27.0	31.0	33.8	31.8	33.9	5.5
EC from non-EC	11.2	11.8	11.7	12.1	12.1	14.0	14.6	13.4	14.5	3.3
Germany	6.7	6.6	7.0	6.6	7.3	8.9	9.2	7.9	8.3	1.6
France	5.9	5.9	5.5	4.8	4.7	5.4	6.0	6.0	6.4	0.5
Italy	3.4	2.9	2.9	2.8	2.7	3.1	4.4	4.0	4.3	0.9
United Kingdom	4.9	5.4	5.0	5.3	5.2	5.3	4.6	5.6	5.8	0.9
Other Western Europe	10.3	9.3	8.8	8.2	8.8	10.1	10.7	9.5	9.2	−1.1
Asian NICs[a]	4.7	3.8	5.3	5.5	5.4	5.9	7.3	9.9	11.7	7.0
Eastern Europe[b]	7.8	8.7	12.0	8.3	7.1	7.0	7.4	9.9	7.5	−0.3
Developing countries	24.9	25.5	24.4	23.1	20.2	18.2	18.0	17.3	15.8	−9.0
Latin America	9.6	8.8	5.7	6.0	4.5	4.2	5.6	5.0	4.1	−5.5
Rest of world	0.0	0.0	0.0	0.0	0.0	0.0	0.0	0.0	0.0	0.0

table continued next page

Table 5.73.2 Metalworking machinery: geographic distribution of world trade, 1981–89 (percentages of total) (continued)

Country	1981	1982	1983	1984	1985	1986	1987	1988	1989	Change 1981–89
Export share minus import share										
United States	0.7	-2.2	-3.7	-8.3	-11.9	-10.4	-7.1	-6.0	-5.2	-6.0
Canada	-5.7	-2.6	-3.4	-3.7	-4.0	-4.4	-4.0	-3.5	-3.1	2.5
Japan	14.0	11.3	14.3	19.1	21.4	21.4	19.0	18.1	19.1	5.0
European Community	22.2	23.6	23.9	19.8	18.7	16.6	16.4	17.2	14.8	-7.5
Non-EC	21.4	23.0	22.5	19.2	17.6	16.1	16.0	15.9	13.6	-7.8
Germany	17.7	19.8	19.3	16.6	14.8	15.6	16.4	16.3	15.8	-1.9
France	-0.8	-1.1	-0.3	-0.6	-0.8	-1.8	-2.6	-2.1	-3.0	-2.1
Italy	5.2	5.7	6.0	5.3	6.0	5.6	5.1	4.9	5.2	0.0
United Kingdom	2.1	2.2	1.1	0.9	0.2	-0.4	1.1	0.3	-1.0	-3.0
Other Western Europe	1.6	4.0	6.1	5.9	5.3	4.6	4.4	5.4	3.7	2.0
Asian NICs[a]	-2.9	-1.8	-3.0	-2.8	-2.8	-3.6	-4.5	-6.1	-7.7	-4.8
Eastern Europe[b]	-5.9	-7.2	-10.8	-7.2	-6.0	-5.8	-6.2	-8.5	-6.2	-0.4
Developing countries	-24.2	-24.8	-23.6	-22.3	-19.3	-17.4	-17.2	-15.2	-14.9	9.3
Latin America	-9.4	-8.6	-5.3	-5.7	-4.2	-3.9	-5.5	-4.8	-3.9	5.5
Rest of world	0.1	0.1	0.1	0.1	0.1	0.1	0.1	0.1	0.2	0.1

a. Hong Kong, Korea, Singapore, and Taiwan.

b. Including Soviet Union.

Source: World Manufactures Trade Data Base.

Table 5.73.3 Metalworking machinery: bilateral trade flows, 1989 (billions of dollars)

Importer	World	United States	Canada	Japan	European Community	Germany	France	United Kingdom	Asian NICs	Latin America	Other
						Exporter					
World	23.1	2.3	0.2	5.0	11.2	5.5	0.8	1.1	0.9	0.1	3.5
United States	3.5		0.1	1.7	1.0	0.5	0.1	0.2	0.2	0.0	0.3
Canada	0.7	0.3		0.1	0.2	0.1	0.0	0.0	0.0	0.0	0.1
Japan	0.6	0.2	0.0		0.2	0.1	0.0	0.0	0.1	0.0	0.1
European Community	8.2	0.5	0.0	0.9	4.7	2.0	0.4	0.5	0.2	0.0	1.7
Germany	2.1	0.1	0.0	0.3	0.9		0.1	0.1	0.0	0.0	0.8
France	1.5	0.0	0.0	0.1	1.1	0.5		0.1	0.0	0.0	0.3
United Kingdom	1.3	0.2	0.0	0.2	0.7	0.4	0.1		0.0	0.0	0.2
Asian NICs	2.2	0.4	0.0	1.2	0.3	0.2	0.0	0.0	0.1		0.1
Latin America	1.0	0.4	0.0	0.1	0.4	0.1	0.0	0.0	0.0	0.0	0.1
Other	7.0	0.4	0.0	1.0	4.4	2.5	0.3	0.4	0.2		1.0

Source: World Manufactures Trade Data Base.

Table 5.73.4 Metalworking machinery: product composition of US trade, 1981–90[a] (millions of dollars except where noted)

	SITC Rev. 2			SITC Rev. 3			
Category	1981	1987	Change 1981–87	1987	1990	Change 1981–90	Change 1987–90
Total							
Exports	2,190	1,639	−551	2,236	2,748	558	512
Imports	2,002	2,978	976	3,036	3,688	1,686	652
Balance	188	−1,339	−1,527	−800	−940	−1,128	−140
of which							
731 Machine tools removing metal (Rev. 3)							
Exports				461	665		204
Imports				1,460	1,861		401
Balance				−999	−1,196		−197
733 Machines tools working but not removing metal (Rev. 3)							
Exports				272	442		170
Imports				493	511		18
Balance				−221	−69		152
735 Parts, n.e.s., and accessories (Rev. 3)							
Exports				600	751		151
Imports				545	587		42
Balance				55	164		109
736 Machine tools (Rev. 2)							
Exports	1,583	1,170	−413				
Imports	1,804	2,440	636				
Balance	−221	−1,270	−1,049				
737 Other metalworking machinery and parts							
Exports	606	469	−137	903	889	283	−14
Imports	198	538	340	539	729	531	190
Balance	408	−69	−477	364	160	−248	−204

a. Data are expressed on a domestic exports, imports customs basis.

Source: US Department of Commerce.

Table 5.73.5 Metalworking machinery: geographic composition of US trade, 1981–90[a]

	Millions of dollars				Percentages of total			
	1981	1987	1989	1990	1981	1987	1989	1990
Exports								
Canada	537	419	401	515	24.5	18.7	15.4	18.7
Japan	96	159	204	208	4.4	7.1	7.8	7.6
European Community	415	483	615	678	18.9	21.6	23.6	24.7
United Kingdom	145	145	232	199	6.6	6.5	8.9	7.2
Germany	77	133	150	188	3.5	5.9	5.8	6.8
France	57	51	53	71	2.6	2.3	2.0	2.6
Italy	37	58	57	64	1.7	2.6	2.2	2.3
Latin America	595	452	453	465	27.2	20.2	17.4	16.9
Asian NICs	156	295	424	361	7.1	13.2	16.3	13.1
Other	391	428	506	521	17.9	19.1	19.4	19.0
Total	2,190	2,236	2,603	2,748	100.0	100.0	100.0	100.0
Imports								
Canada	126	167	260	248	5.8	5.5	6.7	6.7
Japan	791	1,385	1,959	1,522	36.1	45.6	50.5	41.3
European Community	670	959	1,038	1,209	30.6	31.6	26.8	32.8
United Kingdom	182	154	176	222	8.3	5.1	4.5	6.0
Germany	275	537	572	670	12.6	17.7	14.7	18.2
France	47	36	55	63	2.1	1.2	1.4	1.7
Italy	100	165	143	161	4.6	5.4	3.7	4.4
Latin America	19	17	28	33	0.9	0.6	0.7	0.9
Asian NICs	140	198	243	227	6.4	6.5	6.3	6.2
Other	444	310	352	449	20.3	10.2	9.1	12.2
Total	2,190	3,036	3,880	3,688	100.0	100.0	100.0	100.0

a. Data are expressed on a domestic exports, imports customs basis.

Source: US Department of Commerce.

Table 5.73.6 Metalworking machinery: indices of US competitiveness, 1981–89 (billions of dollars except where noted)

	1981	1982	1983	1984	1985	1986	1987	1988	1989	Annual growth 1981–89 (percentages)
World trade										
World exports to non-US destinations	12.2	10.3	9.0	8.8	10.0	14.3	16.7	18.8	19.6	6.1
World imports from non-US sources	11.9	10.6	9.2	9.6	11.6	16.2	18.2	20.8	21.7	7.8
US trade										
Exports	2.2	1.6	1.1	1.2	1.3	1.5	1.6	2.0	2.3	0.5
Imports	2.1	1.9	1.5	2.1	2.9	3.4	3.1	3.4	3.6	7.1
Balance	0.1	−0.3	−0.4	−0.9	−1.6	−1.9	−1.5	−1.5	−1.3	
										Change 1981–89
US share of exports to non-US destinations (percentages)	18.0	15.8	12.7	13.6	12.8	10.5	9.8	10.5	11.6	−6.4
US share of imports from non-US sources (percentages)	17.6	18.3	16.7	22.0	24.9	20.9	17.0	16.6	16.7	−0.9
Export share minus import share (percentages)	0.4	−2.5	−4.0	−8.4	−12.1	−10.4	−7.2	−6.1	−5.1	−5.5

Source: World Manufactures Trade Data Base.

General Industrial Machinery (SITC 74)

General industrial machinery and equipment includes a broad variety of products that are used extensively in construction and for the transportation of materials. Demand for these products depends largely on the overall level of economic activity and more specifically on building construction, mining, and public works activity such as road and airport construction and water and sewage improvements.

Description of the Product Group

General industrial machinery and equipment is divided into the following three-digit groups:

SITC

741 heating and cooling equipment

742 pumps for liquids and liquid elevators

743 pumps (other than for liquids), compressors, and fans

744 mechanical handling equipment (work trucks, cranes, hoists, and conveyors)

745 other nonelectrical machinery, tools, and mechanical apparatus (powered hand tools, vending machines, etc.)

746 ball and roller bearings

747 taps, cocks, valves, and similar appliances for pipes, boiler shells, tanks, vats, and the like

748 transmission shafts and cranks; bearing housings and plain shaft bearings; gears and gearing; ball screws; gear boxes and other speed changers

749 nonelectric parts and accessories of machinery.

The present (Revision 3) subcategories 746, 747, and 748 were included under SITC 749 in Revision 2.

Role in World Trade

Size and Composition

With world exports of $101.7 billion, general industrial machinery accounted for 4.8 percent of world manufactures exports in 1989 (table 5.74.1). World exports of general industrial machinery grew substantially more slowly from 1981 to 1989 (by an average of 7.3 percent annually) than world exports of all manufactures (9.6 percent annually on average).

Despite large dollar-value changes in exports for the two-digit category overall, the relative positions of the three-digit subcategories changed little during the 1980s (table 5.74.1). Nonelectric machinery parts and accessories, a miscellaneous category, was consistently the largest of the three-digit subcategories, followed by heating and cooling equipment; mechanical handling equipment; pumps, compressors, and fans; and other nonelectrical machinery.

Global Competition Patterns

The European Community had a large and growing share of general industrial machinery exports during the 1980s (table 5.74.2). Its import share also rose. Nevertheless, the European Community still retained a strong 19.2-percentage-point share balance in 1987 and a 16.4-percentage-point balance in 1989. Germany is the largest single-country exporter, with 22 percent of 1989 exports, followed by Japan (15.5 percent) and the United States (12.8 percent). The United States is by far the largest importer, with 13.2 percent of 1989 world imports.

The developing countries as a group experienced the largest improvements in share balance position during the past decade, with a rise of nearly 20 percentage points between 1981 and 1989. Despite this marked improvement, at −15.0 percentage points the 1989 share balance of the developing countries remained substantially negative. Moreover, their improved share balance did not indicate a greater ability to compete in world markets but resulted almost entirely from a sharp drop (18.1 percentage points) in their import share. This drop reflected severe limits on the amount of foreign exchange available to purchase imports.

The United States experienced by far the largest decline in its share balance: a drop of 11.0 percentage points between 1981 and 1989. A fall in the US share of world exports accounted for nearly 60 percent of the worsening of the US share balance position.

Table 5.74.3 shows 1989 world trade flows for general industrial machinery and reveals a $14.2 billion German surplus in 1989, compared with a $13.4

billion surplus for Japan and a $0.7 billion US deficit. More than half of all exports from the European Community go to other EC members. The United States is the largest single-country export market for the European Community. The United States, the Asian NICs, and the European Community are the major markets for Japanese exports.

Key Determinants of World Trade Patterns

Overall demand for general industrial machinery is governed largely by the level of economic and investment activity in industrialized countries. Choice among potential sources of supply of general industrial machinery is determined largely by price and perceptions of quality and reliability. The technology for producing the majority of the products included in general industrial machinery is well known and relatively stable. Reliability is often a crucial factor, particularly in the chemical and petroleum industries, where companies rely on various pumps and other types of materials-handling equipment to maintain constant control over the flow of materials through production processes. Any disruption due to the failure of pumps or other materials-handling equipment tends to be lengthy and costly to resolve.

Role in US Trade

Recent Performance

US exports of general industrial machinery were $15.7 billion in 1990 and accounted for 5.3 percent of US manufactures exports. US imports of $14.5 billion in 1990 accounted for 3.7 percent of all US manufactures imports. From 1981 to 1987, world exports of general industrial machinery increased while U.S exports fell; US imports, however, more than doubled (table 5.74.4). These trends moved the United States from a $7.0 billion 1981 surplus to a $2.2 billion 1987 deficit, the seventh-largest decline among two-digit categories during that period. By 1990, however, exports had rebounded, yielding a $1.2 billion surplus.

Whereas world exports of general industrial machinery are fairly evenly divided among the various three-digit subcategories, US exports have been strongest in heating and cooling equipment and pumps (other than for liquids), compressors, and fans. The largest decline in US exports occurred in mechanical handling equipment. This subcategory accounted for 45.4 percent of the decline in exports for the entire product group between 1981 and 1987.

Canada is the most important single export market for the United States for general industrial machinery (table 5.74.5). After Canada, the European Community (particularly Germany and the United Kingdom), Mexico, and Japan are most important. OPEC (mainly Saudi Arabia) is an important market for US exports of pumps for liquids because of the importance of the oil industry and the long experience of US manufacturers in that industry.

US general industrial machinery imports expanded rapidly between 1981 and 1987, providing a significant outlet for the increase that occurred in world exports during the period. Import expansion was particularly important in pumps (other than for liquids), compressors, and fans and in mechanical handling equipment (table 5.74.4). US import growth slowed after 1987.

US imports of general industrial machinery from Japan, Germany, and the East Asian NICs grew rapidly during the 1980s (table 5.74.5). US imports of mechanical handling machinery from the East Asian NICs, especially Korea, grew particularly strongly. Much of the increase in imports from the NICs reflects a shift in production from the United States to areas with lower costs. In many cases the rapid growth in exports to the United States represents a buildup of production in the NICs from very low levels.

International Competitiveness

The US share of world exports to non-US destinations fell from 20.8 percent in 1981 to 12.4 percent in 1987 before improving to 14.8 percent in 1989 (table 5.74.6). Total world imports from non-US sources increased by $24.2 billion from 1981 to 1987 (table 5.74.6) while US imports increased by $5.9 billion. Thus, the United States absorbed 24.4 percent of the increase in world imports of general industrial machinery from non-US sources between 1981 and 1987. The surge in US imports can also be seen in the increase in the US share of world imports from non-US sources. In 1981, the United States absorbed 10.8 percent of total world imports of general industrial machinery from non-US sources, 15.5 percent by 1987, and 15.7 percent by 1989. These changes in export and import performance are reflected in the large decline in the US share balance during the 1980s (table 5.74.6).

Outlook

Key Determinants of US Trade Performance

Given the importance of price in purchase decisions and the widespread global production capabilities of many of the items in this trade category, changes in exchange rates play an important role in determining US trade performance in general industrial machinery. Indeed, the decline in US trade performance during the early 1980s closely tracks the strengthening of the dollar against the other major currencies during that period, just as the more recent improvements in US trade performance parallel the decline of the dollar from 1985 on.

With an import price elasticity of demand equal to -1.5, general industrial machinery ranks in the top one-third of the industries examined in terms of responsiveness to changes in import prices. This indicates that additional depreciation of the US dollar would be relatively effective in limiting the growth of imports in this industry.

DRI elasticity data (see the appendix to this volume) also indicate that the general industrial machinery industry is relatively sensitive to increased domestic and foreign investment. General industrial machinery has the fifth-highest elasticity of demand with respect to changes in investment spending in other countries and the third highest elasticity of demand with respect to changes in domestic investment spending—that is, increased investment in foreign economies should raise US exports more than proportionately, while increased investment in the United States should increase US imports more than proportionately.

Although further dollar devaluation would improve the trade balance of this product group further, some of the domestic markets lost to foreign competitors during the early 1980s are likely to remain out of the reach of US producers. A large share of the manufacturing of mechanical handling equipment, for example, moved overseas during the early 1980s and is unlikely to be reestablished without significant further sustained dollar devaluation. In addition, much of the manufacturing capability remaining in the United States relies on foreign sources for a number of components, because US manufacturers, squeezed by the rising dollar during the early 1980s, sought to reduce costs by shifting to overseas sources for these components and products.

In addition to the effects of the strengthening dollar, the "voluntary" restraint agreements in the steel industry increased the domestic price of steel. Because steel is an important component of the costs of production in this industry, the rise in steel prices put US producers at a disadvantage. Because the capacity to manufacture certain components and final products in this category no longer exists in the United States, the effects of additional marginal dollar decline on US trade balances will be smaller than if a self-contained US industry remained.

Near-Term Outlook

Some markets that were important to US exports in earlier years are performing poorly. In 1981, Latin America imported $5.4 billion of general industrial machinery from the world, half of it from the United States. By 1987, however, Latin American imports from the world had declined to $3.6 billion, with $1.6

billion, or 44 percent of the total, from the United States. By 1990, US exports to Latin America were still only $2.5 billion, a half-billion below the 1981 level and only 15.8 percent of the US total, compared with one-fourth of the total in 1981. The weakening of the important Latin American market has had significant effects on US exports.

Similarly, US exports to OPEC countries were $2.3 billion in 1981, but only $1.0 billion in 1990. The rebuilding of the Kuwaiti oil fields and other infrastructure should spur US exports of general industrial machinery over the next several years. However, lowered purchasing power in other OPEC countries and in Latin America will limit US exports, as will any slackening in investment in other major markets.

Recent developments may help US general industrial machinery producers more than their foreign competitors. The phasing out of chlorofluorocarbons (CFCs) as the refrigerant in cooling equipment has motivated substantial research and the development of alternative refrigerants. Cooling systems must be redesigned to work with alternative refrigerants, and US manufacturers have an opportunity to exploit the growing market for both new cooling systems and conversions of existing systems. The market for cooling equipment, particularly for replacement and modifications, will be growing and changing rapidly during the 1990s and should put US producers in a strong competitive position because of their early experience with cooling equipment using alternative refrigerants.

A second area with substantial room for further improvement is pumps for liquids. The chemical and oil industries are two major industries that use large quantities of industrial pumps. Many developing countries are now developing their own chemical production capabilities, and as new facilities are built, the demand for pumps will increase. Also, revisions in environmental regulations are likely in the 1990s, both in the United States and elsewhere. This will lead to the modification of existing plants and to a corresponding increase in the demand for industrial pumps. The destruction of the Kuwaiti oil facilities during the 1991 Gulf War will also increase demand for a variety of oil field equipment, including industrial pumps. Kuwait has announced a policy favoring members of the alliance when awarding contracts for reconstruction, thus giving US producers an edge.

The third area that may well see an increase in demand in coming years is pumps (other than liquid), compressors, and fans. Products in this subcategory (such as electrostatic precipitators, i.e., scrubbers) are used extensively by electric utilities for pollution abatement. Demand for pumps, compressors, and fans increased substantially during the 1970s as various pollution abatement requirements came into effect. Demand is likely to surge again during the 1990s as US pollution standards are tightened. More important, restrictions on emissions are likely to become more stringent in other parts of the world, particularly in Europe, during the 1990s. Because US firms have experience in building equipment for pollution abatement, they are in a good position to capture a substantial share of the market for such equipment in other countries.

Developments in general industrial machinery markets should allow an improvement in the trade balance of at least $0.5 billion annually and possibly as much as $1.0 billion annually through 1993. This would result in a 1993 trade surplus in this product group of roughly $3 billion to $4 billion.

Medium-Term Outlook

Many of the issues driving US trade performance in general industrial machinery in the near term will continue to be important beyond 1993. One of the most important is the exchange value of the US dollar. Exchange rate fluctuations strongly influence world trade flows for general industrial machinery.

In the absence of unfavorable changes in the value of the dollar, the United States should remain in a strong competitive position in general industrial machinery. World demand should remain strong for many of the products of which the United States is a major world supplier. These include new and remanufactured cooling equipment using alternative refrigerants, industrial pollution-control equipment, and industrial pumps used in the chemical and petroleum industries. Relatively strong demand in these markets should result in a continuing improvement in the US general industrial machinery trade balance.

Conclusions

■ Trade performance in general industrial machinery contributed significantly to the deterioration in US trade performance between 1981 and 1987. The $9.2 billion decline in the trade balance for general industrial machinery accounted for about 6 percent of the decline in the manufactures trade balance between 1981 and 1987.

■ The deterioration in US trade performance was caused largely by the rise of the dollar against the currencies of key competitors in the early 1980s. The dollar appreciated just as US demand was recovering from the effects of the economic slowdown in the early 1980s. Thus, much of the increase in US purchases went to foreign producers as the dollar price of goods manufactured overseas fell relative to the price of domestically made goods.

■ With the dollar declining during the late 1980s, the United States regained some of the market it had lost. Trade performance improved by $4.3 billion between 1987 and 1990, recouping about 47 percent of the 1981–87 loss in the trade balance. The majority of the improvement has come from improved export performance, although relatively slow import growth has also helped.

- The production of some product and component lines shifted overseas during the early to mid-1980s in response to the overvalued dollar. Dollar devaluation to date has been insufficient to return the manufacture of many of these products to the United States, and substantial additional devaluation would be required to do so.

- Prospects for additional improvement in the general industrial machinery trade balance are good. Between 1990 and 1993, world demand is expected to remain strong in several of the three-digit subcategories in which the United States is a strong competitor. More stringent environmental regulations, both in the United States and overseas, are expected to spur demand for pumps of all types, compressors, and fans. US producers are in a strong competitive position in these markets because of their previous experience in providing equipment to meet environmental regulations.

- Growth in chemical production outside the United States and reconstruction of oil facilities in the Middle East will also spur export sales of pumps for liquids.

- Demand in Latin America, a key US market, will continue to be sluggish because of continuing austerity programs brought on by large debt burdens.

- Trade performance is likely to improve by $0.5 billion to $1.0 billion per year between 1990 and 1993, resulting in a trade surplus by 1993 of roughly $3 billion to $4 billion.

- Because of the sensitivity of trade in general industrial machinery to exchange rates, the exchange value of the dollar will largely determine US trade performance beyond 1993. If the dollar maintains roughly its late-1991 relationship to the currencies of its major competitors, favorable trends in individual markets should provide continuing modest improvements in the US trade position in general industrial machinery beyond 1993.

Bibliography

Commission of the European Communities. 1990. *Panorama of EC Industry, 1990.* Luxembourg: Commission of the European Communities.

Industry, Science and Technology Canada. 1988a. *Industry Profile: Construction Machinery.* Ottawa: Industry, Science and Technology Canada.

Industry, Science and Technology Canada. 1988b. *Industry Profile: Materials Handling Equipment.* Ottawa: Industry, Science and Technology Canada.

US Department of Commerce, International Trade Administration. 1985a. *A Competitive Assessment of the U.S. Ball and Roller Bearings Industry.* Washington: US Department of Commerce (February).

US Department of Commerce, International Trade Administration. 1985b. *A Competitive Assessment of the U.S. Oil Field Equipment Industry.* Washington: US Department of Commerce (February).

US Department of Commerce, International Trade Administration. 1986. *A Competitive Assessment of the U.S. Mining Machinery Industry.* Washington: US Department of Commerce (October).

US Department of Commerce, International Trade Administration. 1988. *U.S. Industrial Outlook, 1988.* Washington: Government Printing Office (January).

US Department of Commerce, International Trade Administration. 1989. *U.S. Industrial Outlook, 1989.* Washington: Government Printing Office (January).

US Department of Commerce, International Trade Administration. 1990. *U.S. Industrial Outlook, 1990.* Washington: Government Printing Office (January).

US International Trade Commission. 1990. *U.S. Trade Shifts in Selected Commodity Areas, January–June 1990.* Washington: US International Trade Commission (December).

Table 5.74.1 General industrial machinery: product composition of world trade, 1981–89 (billions of dollars except where noted)

SITC Product	1981	1982	1983	1984	1985	1986	1987	1988	1989	Annual growth 1981–89 (percentages)
World exports to world	57.7	53.4	49.8	49.9	52.9	65.5	77.3	93.3	101.7	7.3
of which										
741 Heating, cooling equipment	11.2	10.6	10.1	9.5	9.3	11.2	13.2	16.8	18.5	6.5
742 Pumps for liquid	5.5	5.2	4.6	4.5	4.8	5.7	6.7	8.5	9.3	6.7
743 Other pumps, centrifugal	8.8	7.9	7.7	7.7	8.1	9.7	11.7	15.2	16.4	8.1
744 Handling equipment	10.3	9.6	8.2	8.3	8.8	11.0	12.5	14.0	15.4	5.2
745 Nonelectrical machinery, tools	6.6	6.2	6.2	6.6	6.8	8.8	10.4	12.1	13.0	8.9
749 Nonelectrical machine parts	15.1	13.8	12.8	13.3	14.5	18.4	21.9	26.5	29.4	8.7
										Change 1981–89
Memorandum: SITC 74 share of world manufactures exports (percentages)	5.7	5.5	5.1	4.7	4.7	4.8	4.7	4.7	4.8	– 0.9

Source: World Manufactures Trade Data Base.

Table 5.74.2 General industrial machinery: geographic distribution of world trade, 1981–89 (percentages of total)

Country	1981	1982	1983	1984	1985	1986	1987	1988	1989	Annual growth 1981–89
Share of exports to world										
United States	19.1	18.3	16.0	16.3	14.5	11.1	10.8	11.6	12.8	-6.3
Canada	1.7	1.6	2.0	2.3	2.0	1.8	1.7	1.9	1.9	0.2
Japan	15.2	13.9	15.2	15.9	14.9	14.3	13.4	15.4	15.5	0.3
European Community	51.2	53.3	53.4	51.7	53.6	57.2	57.6	54.1	53.5	2.3
To non-EC	30.4	32.0	31.9	30.5	31.2	31.3	29.5	26.7	26.2	-4.2
Germany	19.5	20.7	20.4	20.1	21.3	24.0	24.1	22.4	22.0	2.4
France	7.9	8.0	8.0	7.5	7.6	7.5	7.3	6.7	6.8	-1.1
Italy	8.3	8.6	9.6	9.1	9.3	9.8	10.5	9.5	9.7	1.4
United Kingdom	7.8	7.9	7.1	6.9	7.2	6.8	6.6	6.8	6.4	-1.4
Other Western Europe	9.9	10.4	10.3	10.1	10.9	11.5	11.7	10.9	10.0	0.1
Asian NICs[a]	1.2	0.9	1.5	1.9	2.0	1.9	2.4	3.2	3.2	2.0
Eastern Europe[b]	0.4	0.4	0.4	0.4	0.4	0.5	0.4	0.5	0.4	-0.1
Developing countries	0.8	0.9	0.9	1.1	1.4	1.5	1.8	2.5	2.4	1.6
Latin America	0.3	0.4	0.4	0.6	0.7	0.8	0.9	1.0	1.2	0.9
Rest of world	0.1	0.1	0.1	0.1	0.2	0.2	0.2	0.2	0.2	0.1
Share of imports from world										
United States	8.6	8.4	9.6	13.3	14.5	14.0	13.6	13.0	13.2	4.6
Canada	4.5	4.0	4.1	4.9	4.8	4.2	4.0	5.7	5.8	1.4
Japan	1.7	2.0	2.0	2.2	2.1	1.9	2.0	2.3	2.5	0.8
European Community	30.5	31.3	31.6	31.1	31.9	35.8	38.4	37.1	37.1	6.7
To non-EC	10.3	10.6	10.6	10.7	10.8	11.3	11.6	11.3	11.5	1.2
Germany	6.2	6.3	6.7	6.5	6.7	7.8	8.2	7.5	7.6	1.4
France	6.4	6.5	6.3	5.9	6.1	6.8	7.4	7.1	7.0	0.6
Italy	3.2	3.1	3.0	3.1	3.2	3.8	4.2	4.1	4.2	0.9
United Kingdom	4.8	5.2	5.5	5.8	6.0	5.9	6.1	6.4	6.3	1.5
Other Western Europe	9.5	9.3	9.3	9.4	10.5	11.8	12.5	10.8	10.0	0.5
Asian NICs[a]	4.7	4.8	4.7	5.5	5.0	4.9	5.7	8.1	9.2	4.6
Eastern Europe[b]	3.9	4.7	4.9	3.8	3.7	3.9	3.4	3.5	3.1	-0.8
Developing countries	35.4	33.6	31.9	27.8	25.8	22.2	19.1	18.2	17.3	-18.1
Latin America	9.2	7.3	4.7	4.9	5.1	4.8	4.4	4.3	4.2	-5.0
Rest of world	0.0	0.0	0.0	0.0	0.0	0.0	0.0	0.1	0.1	0.1

Export share minus import share

United States	10.5	9.9	6.4	2.9	0.0	-2.8	-2.7	-1.4	-0.5	-11.0
Canada	-2.8	-2.4	-2.1	-2.7	-2.8	-2.5	-2.4	-3.8	-3.9	-1.1
Japan	13.5	11.9	13.2	13.7	12.8	12.4	11.4	13.1	13.0	-0.6
European Community	20.8	22.0	21.8	20.6	21.7	21.3	19.2	17.0	16.4	-4.4
To non-EC	20.2	21.4	21.2	19.8	20.4	20.1	17.9	15.4	14.7	-5.4
Germany	13.3	14.3	13.7	13.5	14.5	16.2	16.0	14.9	14.4	1.0
France	1.5	1.4	1.7	1.6	1.5	0.7	-0.1	-0.4	-0.2	-1.7
Italy	5.0	5.5	6.6	6.0	6.1	6.0	6.2	5.4	5.5	0.5
United Kingdom	3.0	2.7	1.6	1.1	1.2	0.9	0.5	0.4	0.1	-2.9
Other Western Europe	0.4	1.1	1.0	0.7	0.3	-0.4	-0.8	0.2	0.0	-0.4
Asian NICs[a]	-3.4	-3.9	-3.2	-3.6	-3.0	-3.0	-3.3	-4.9	-6.0	-2.6
Eastern Europe[b]	-3.4	-4.3	-4.6	-3.4	-3.3	-3.4	-2.9	-3.0	-2.7	0.7
Developing countries	-34.6	-32.7	-31.0	-26.7	-24.4	-20.7	-17.3	-15.7	-15.0	19.6
Latin America	-8.9	-7.0	-4.3	-4.3	-4.4	-4.0	-3.5	-3.3	-3.0	6.0
Rest of world	0.1	0.1	0.1	0.1	0.2	0.2	0.1	0.2	0.1	0.1

a. Hong Kong, Korea, Singapore, and Taiwan.

b. Including Soviet Union.

Source: World Manufactures Trade Data Base.

Table 5.74.3 General industrial machinery: bilateral trade flows, 1989 (billions of dollars)

Importer	World	United States	Canada	Japan	European Community	Germany	France	United Kingdom	Asian NICs	Latin America	Other
World	101.7	13.0	2.0	15.7	54.4	22.3	6.9	6.5	3.3	1.2	12.1
United States	13.7		1.7	4.3	4.2	1.8	0.4	0.9	1.4	1.0	1.2
Canada	4.0	2.7		0.3	0.6	0.2	0.1	0.1	0.1	0.1	0.2
Japan	2.3	0.8	0.0		0.7	0.4	0.1	0.1	0.3	0.0	0.4
European Community	39.5	2.8	0.1	2.1	27.7	10.8	3.6	2.8	0.3	0.1	6.2
Germany	8.1	0.6	0.0	0.5	4.5		1.1	0.7	0.1	0.1	2.3
France	7.5	0.4	0.0	0.2	5.8	2.7		0.6	0.0	0.0	0.9
United Kingdom	6.5	0.8	0.0	0.4	4.2	1.8	0.6		0.1	0.0	0.9
Asian NICs	8.0	1.5	0.0	4.0	1.6	0.7	0.6	0.3	0.4	0.0	0.4
Latin America	4.5	2.3	0.0	0.5	1.5	0.5	0.2	0.1	0.0	0.0	0.2
Other	29.6	2.8	0.1	4.6	18.0	8.0	2.3	2.1	0.6	0.0	3.5

Source: World Manufactures Trade Data Base.

Table 3.74.4 General industrial machinery: product composition of US trade, 1981–90 (millions of US dollars)

Category	SITC Rev. 2			SITC Rev. 3			
	1981	1987	Change 1981–87	1987	1990	Change 1981–90	Change 1987–90
Total							
Exports	11,884	8,380	-3,504	8,313	15,688	3,804	7,375
Imports	4,855	10,567	5,712	11,403	14,484	9,629	3,081
Balance	7,029	-2,187	-9,216	-3,090	1,205	-5,824	4,295
of which							
741 Heating, cooling equipment							
Exports	2,538	1,999	-539	1,976	3,610	1,071	1,634
Imports	403	1,273	870	1,511	1,814	1,411	303
Balance	2,135	726	-1,409	465	1,795	-340	1,330
742 Pumps for liquid							
Exports	1,182	928	-254	928	1,542	360	614
Imports	675	895	220	895	1,219	544	324
Balance	507	33	-474	33	323	-184	290
743 Other pumps, centrifuges							
Exports	1,989	1,426	-563	1,644	3,101	1,112	1,457
Imports	938	2,152	1,214	2,341	3,142	2,204	801
Balance	1,051	-726	-1,777	-697	-41	-1,092	656
744 Mechanical handling equipment							
Exports	2,790	1,198	-1,592	786	2,179	-611	1,393
Imports	739	1,846	1,107	1,783	2,061	1,322	278
Balance	2,051	-648	-2,699	-997	118	-1,933	1,115
745 Nonelectrical machinery and tools							
Exports	1,394	1,155	-239	1,124	2,008	614	884
Imports	555	1,528	973	1,522	1,643	1,088	121
Balance	839	-373	-1,212	-398	365	-474	763
746 Ball or roller bearings (Rev. 3)							
Exports				312	652		340
Imports				718	895		177
Balance				-406	-243		163
747 Taps, cocks, valves, and similar appliances (Rev. 3)							
Exports				711	1,231		520
Imports				1,215	1,656		441
Balance				-504	-425		79
748 Transmission shafts and cranks, etc. (Rev. 3)							
Exports				366	811		445
Imports				935	1,446		511
Balance				-569	-635		-66
749 Nonelectrical machine parts (Rev. 3)							
Exports	1,989	1,674	-315	466	555	-1,434	89
Imports	1,543	2,873	1,330	483	607	-936	124
Balance	446	-1,199	-1,645	-17	-52	-498	-35

a. Data are expressed on a domestic exports, imports customs basis.

Source: US Department of Commerce.

	Millions of dollars				Percentages of total			
	1981	1987	1989	1990	1981	1987	1989	1990
Exports								
Canada	2,398	2,200	2,745	4,669	20.2	26.5	21.0	29.8
Japan	384	400	833	840	3.2	4.8	6.4	5.4
European Community	1,876	1,732	2,847	3,152	15.8	20.8	21.7	20.1
United Kingdom	446	497	844	880	3.8	6.0	6.4	5.6
Germany	379	341	581	665	3.2	4.1	4.4	4.2
France	305	244	449	528	2.6	2.9	3.4	3.4
Italy	143	142	227	250	1.2	1.7	1.7	1.6
Latin America	2,937	1,626	2,330	2,476	24.7	19.6	17.8	15.8
Mexico	1,268	811	1,228	1,365	10.7	9.8	9.4	8.7
Asian NICs	667	626	1,513	1,684	5.6	7.5	11.6	10.7
OPEC	2,312	748	1,010	1,095	19.5	9.0	7.7	7.0
Other	1,310	981	1,817	1,772	11.0	11.8	13.9	11.3
Total	11,884	8,313	13,095	15,688	100.0	100.0	100.0	100.0
Imports								
Canada	775	1,258	1,731	1,722	16.0	11.0	12.0	11.9
Japan	1,164	3,324	4,118	3,861	24.0	29.2	28.5	26.7
European Community	1,827	3,764	4,462	4,730	37.6	33.0	30.8	32.7
United Kingdom	443	699	950	927	9.1	6.1	6.6	6.4
Germany	722	1,727	1,948	2,148	14.9	15.1	13.5	14.8
France	185	270	372	378	3.8	2.4	2.6	2.6
Italy	244	632	694	734	5.0	5.5	4.8	5.1
Latin America	131	653	991	1,034	2.7	5.7	6.8	7.1
Mexico	88	442	725	738	1.8	3.9	5.0	5.1
Asian NICs	202	890	922	846	4.2	7.8	6.4	5.8
OPEC	490	1,564	1,765	1,604	10.1	13.7	12.2	11.1
Other	468	840	1,403	1,532	9.6	7.4	9.7	10.6
Total	4,855	11,403	14,470	14,483	100.0	100.0	100.0	100.0

a. Data are expressed on a domestic exports, imports customs basis.

Source: US Department of Commerce.

Table 5.74.6 General industrial machinery: indices of US competitiveness, 1981–89 (billions of dollars except where noted)

	1981	1982	1983	1984	1985	1986	1987	1988	1989	Annual growth 1981–89 (percentages)
World trade										
World exports to non-US destinations	52.9	49.2	45.3	43.8	46.1	57.1	67.6	80.9	88.8	6.6
World imports from non-US sources	46.7	43.9	42.1	42.7	46.6	59.6	70.9	83.7	90.6	8.6
US trade										
Exports	11.0	9.8	8.0	8.1	7.7	7.3	8.4	10.8	13.0	2.1
Imports	5.1	4.6	4.9	6.9	8.1	9.6	11.0	12.7	14.3	13.7
Balance	5.9	5.2	3.1	1.2	-0.4	-2.3	-2.6	-1.9	-1.3	
										Change 1981–89
US share of exports to non-US destinations (percentages)	20.8	19.9	17.6	18.5	16.7	12.8	12.4	13.4	14.8	-6.0
US share of imports from non-US sources (percentages)	10.8	10.5	11.7	16.2	17.4	16.1	15.5	15.2	15.7	4.9
Export share minus import share (percentages)	10.0	9.4	5.8	2.3	-0.7	-3.3	-3.1	-1.8	-0.9	-10.9

Source: World Manufactures Trade Data Base.

Office Machines and Computers (SITC 75)

World exports of computers and office machines increased nearly fourfold from 1981 to 1989, making this the fastest-growing product group during the 1980s. The United States began the 1980s with a $6 billion trade surplus in this category, but by 1990 this had slid to a $2 billion deficit. Also, the US export-minus-import share balance fell more in this category than in any other. The industry is typical of high-technology industries in that the United States originated the basic technology but now faces competition from foreign firms able to generate a steady stream of enhancements in the product itself and in its production.

Description of the Product Group

SITC 75 consists of:

SITC

751 office machines

752 automated data processing machines (computers)

759 parts and accessories.

The office machines subcategory includes typewriters, calculators, and photocopiers. Facsimile (fax) machines are included not in the office machines subcategory but in telecommunications equipment. The computers subcategory includes most general-purpose computers. Special-purpose computers are included in many other products recorded in other categories, such as telecommunications equipment (SITC 76), electromedical equipment (SITC 77), and scientific and professional instruments (SITC 87). Semiconductors are recorded under SITC 776, and software under SITC 898.

Role in World Trade

Size and Composition

World exports of office machines, computers, and parts and accessories increased from $28.8 billion in 1981 to $110.3 billion in 1989, for an annual growth rate of 18.3 percent compared with 9.6 percent for manufactures as a whole. Most of the growth was in computers and in parts and accessories (table 5.75.1). The product group's share of world manufactures exports increased from 2.8 percent in 1981 to 5.2 percent in 1989. US imports accounted for some 25 percent of the growth in world computer trade, but even if US imports are excluded, world computer exports grew more strongly than manufactures exports as a whole.

Global Competition Patterns

Despite its precipitous decline from 34 percent of world exports in 1981, the United States remained only narrowly behind Japan as the world export leader in 1989, followed by the Asian NICs, the United Kingdom, and Germany. The largest shares of imports in 1989 went to the United States (23.0 percent), the United Kingdom (10.8 percent), and Germany (10.6 percent), with Japan taking only a trivial 3.9 percent of the total (table 5.75.2). Major changes took place in world export and import shares during the 1980s. In 1981, the export share of the United States exceeded its import share by 21.6 percentage points. By 1989, however, the import share exceeded the export share by 2.0 percentage points, and the US export-minus-import share balance had declined by 23.6 percentage points. The share balances of Japan and the NICs improved by 5.9 percent and 9.4 percent, respectively. Their improvement occurred mostly on the export side as the shares of all other major countries fell. The share balances of the developing countries also rose as their share of imports dropped 6.3 percentage points. The European Community had the largest negative share balance in 1989 (− 11.4 percentage points). True to its usual form in electronics items, Japan ran a substantial surplus of $19.1 billion in this product group in 1989 (table 5.75.3).

Key Determinants of World Trade Patterns

As these statistics show, the world computer industry was one of the most rapidly evolving in the 1980s, which were a period of enormous technological advance and structural change in the industry. During the 1980s, computing moved from the back office to people's desktops and homes. The manufacturing of computers, still rather customized in 1981, became much more commodity-like by 1987.

Two major segments of the computer industry, personal computers and work-stations, were of minimal importance in 1981. Today, computers retailing for less than $15,000 account for more than half of US computer shipments. The price-to-performance ratio has fallen quickly for most products, and the range and quality of off-the-shelf software has improved enormously, enlarging consumer markets dramatically.

The computer industry has often been targeted by governments eager to promote fast-growing high-technology industries in their countries (see, e.g., Flamm 1987 and 1988). The US military financed early computer R&D, and military demand was crucial in getting the industry off the ground in the United States after World War II. Governments in Europe and Japan have encouraged the development of indigenous computer industries, with Japan the more successful. Government procurement preferences for domestic computers played a large role in Japan, a lesser role in Europe (Flamm 1987, 178). However, the government funds less of that country's industrial computer R&D than is the case in the United States or Europe (Flamm 1987, 177). Evaluating the wisdom of industry targeting is beyond the scope of this book, but it is indisputable that the actions of governments have an important impact on computers.

Another important trend in the international computer industry is increasing international collaboration in R&D, manufacturing, and sales. This has several goals: to obtain increasingly competitive foreign technology, to circumvent protection and government restrictions on procurement, to share the increasing costs and risks of R&D, and to make product lines complementary. A US Commerce Department study (1990, 5), citing studies by the Massachusetts Institute of Technology, the Institute for Defense Analysis, and the National Academy of Sciences, argues that increased collaboration has accelerated the international diffusion of US technology. Foreign governments have also obtained US electronics technology by making their purchases contingent on "offsets," for instance, by demanding that military jets purchased from the United States be made in part in the purchasing country. However, Japan has without question become an important developer of commercial computer technology, on a par with the United States (Flamm 1987, 176).

In addition, there is a strong movement toward common standards, which allow computer equipment made by different suppliers to be connected together into networks and to use the same software and components. Sometimes standardization occurs as companies seek allies against competing standards; IBM made its PC (personal computer) standard available to other computer makers when it entered the personal computer market in 1981. Buyers now aggressively demand standardization. The IBM PC standard has had compelling and visible effects on the price and availability of not only computers themselves but also software, peripherals, and service. The European Community also encouraged standardization by putting legal pressure on IBM to disclose the technical details of its products, particularly its mainframe interface specifications (Flamm 1987, 168).

The move toward common standards, particularly at the low end of the market, has favored Asian producers, which excel in producing large volumes of commodity-like products. For instance, many IBM PC-compatible products and parts have become commodity-like, with many producers, particularly at the lower end of the market, competing mainly on price instead of unique product characteristics. The competition is so great that IBM has abandoned its PC standard and developed a new, proprietary "PS" standard. The large markets created by common standards have also sped up innovation of software and other products that work on existing standards, and the development of technologies that can most easily serve as the standard for the next generation. Standards have reduced the degree to which buyers become locked in to a single supplier through investments in equipment, software, and skills. Although support among users and suppliers for common standards has grown quickly, proprietary systems such as the IBM PS computers and the Apple Macintosh continue to be very successful. The same is true of the more powerful systems.

Role in US Trade

Recent Performance

Office machines and computers in 1990 accounted for 8.3 percent of US manufactures exports and 6.9 percent of imports. The US trade balance in this product group fell from a $6.2 billion surplus in 1981 to a $2.2 billion deficit in 1990, despite a 145 percent nominal increase in exports (table 5.75.4). Most of the deterioration occurred in computers and, to a lesser extent, in computer parts and accessories. Imports of office machines also grew, primarily photocopiers and parts.[1]

The principal export destinations for US computers in 1990 were Canada, Japan, the United Kingdom, the NICs, and Germany (table 5.75.5). Japan and the NICs increased in importance as destinations during the 1980s. The principal sources for US imports were Japan, the NICs (particularly Singapore and Taiwan), the European Community, and Canada. A number of US and foreign-

---

1. Unfortunately the shift from Revision 2 to Revision 3 appears to have introduced some spurious volatility into the three-digit disaggregation (see the appendix to this volume).

owned companies have border plants in Mexico and are highly export oriented, not always toward the US market. For instance, 95 percent of IBM's Mexican production in 1987 was exported, although not all to the United States, according to an IBM annual report cited in Nunez (1990, 97).

International Competitiveness

The sharp fall in the US computer trade surplus reflects the significantly changed role of the United States in world trade in these products. The US share of exports to non-US destinations fell from 39.5 percent in 1981 to 28.0 percent in 1989 (table 5.75.6). Meanwhile, the US share of imports from non-US sources increased from 20.1 percent to 30.8 percent. The result of these changes was a 22.2-percentage-point 1981–89 decline in the US share balance, to − 2.8 percentage points. A return of the US trade balance to the large surplus of 1981 would require significant displacement of foreign-based production in US and world markets, an unlikely event.

Outlook

Key Determinants of US Trade Performance

The market share of US-owned companies, including their production in foreign plants, declined in almost all categories, as table 5.75.7 indicates.

In assessing US trade prospects, data on the world market shares of US-based production of these items would be more useful than data on the world market shares of US-owned companies. The US trade balance measures the difference between US based production and US consumption. US-owned computer companies supply foreign markets more through foreign production than through exports from the United States. In the five major foreign computer markets, US companies had a 45 percent share of 1986 sales of assembled computers, but exports of assembled computers from the United States account for only two-fifths of these foreign sales, according to the US Commerce Department. The book value of assets of foreign affiliates of US companies in the office machine and computer category grew from $15.7 billion in 1982 to $49.0 billion in 1988. These foreign subsidiaries do import some components from the United States; however, because US-owned companies were moving production offshore in most of the categories in table 5.75.7 during the 1980s, the share of US-based production unambiguously declined in most categories, reflecting partly the lagged effects of the rising dollar.

The reasons for the decline in the market share of US-based production are complex and hard to disentangle but include the following. First, US-owned companies lost market share to foreign-based competitors that combined aggressive pricing strategies with a steady stream of enhancements in their products and production processes. Asian companies built upon their success in component technologies, such as semiconductor and display technologies. Second, US-owned companies moved their production abroad for business reasons: to be near markets, to take advantage of lower labor costs, or to manufacture to unique local standards. Third, US-owned companies responded to pressure from foreign governments to manufacture locally. Governments have a number of ways to apply such pressure, including government procurement preferences, regulations, the threat of protection, and membership in research consortia. Observers disagree about the relative importance of these factors, but the lost market share of US-based production will not be easily regained.

Evaluations of each of the three-digit subcategories follow.

Office Machines

This subcategory accounted for only 3 percent of the product group's total exports but 10 percent of imports in 1990 (table 5.75.4). Photocopiers and parts make up the majority of US trade in this category. A number of new Asian competitors entered the US market or consolidated their positions in the 1980s. Several large Japanese factories now make photocopiers in the United States, but the main component, the image-transferring device or "engine," is imported.

Computers

Computers accounted for 56 percent of exports and 57 percent of imports in the product group in 1990. US government data classify computers by retail price only. This is unfortunate because different types of computers overlap in price. However, even with the best of data, the distinctions among personal computers, workstations, minicomputers, mainframes, and supercomputers have blurred. Improvements in performance can make one type of computer competitive with computers in the next higher category, and falling prices can narrow the range between higher- and lower-priced computers. Despite these problems, much can be learned by examining US computer trade by product.

These figures, from the Bureau of Economic Analysis, are subject to currency translation effects. Worldwide sales of personal computers grew very quickly during the 1980s. The IBM PC standard introduced in 1981 achieved wide acceptance, and many parts, accessories, and even lower-value computers became commoditized. A number of producers compete on the basis of price; PC profit margins are thin, and IBM, as noted, has shifted to its own proprietary standard. Apple succeeded with a proprietary technology by making its Macintosh computers easier to use; its innovations have been widely copied. Most US PC manufacturers are highly export oriented, but foreign companies make many of their components (table 5.75.7). The popularity of the IBM PC standard appears to have favored high-volume Asian suppliers.

Workstation machines, which are faster and have better-quality graphics than personal computers, are the next higher type of computer in performance and price. Workstations were originally intended for scientists and engineers but are moving into business applications. Four US producers—Sun Microsystems, Apollo, Digital, and Hewlett-Packard—dominate this quickly growing market, and there has been little competition from foreign producers, according to a US Commerce Department analyst. Japanese companies are more competitive only in memory and display design and manufacturing.

The minicomputer and mainframe markets remain large, but they have not grown as quickly as markets for lower-value products. Minicomputers have been under technological attack from below and above, as workstations and networked PCs have improved their capabilities and mainframe costs have fallen. At the same time, the improved performance of minicomputers has put them in competition with mainframes. The primary manufacturers of minicomputers, IBM and Digital, still rely on US-based production, and little production moved abroad in the 1980s. Using production locations both inside and outside the United States, US-owned companies still make 60 percent to 70 percent of world mainframes.

Supercomputers receive a great deal of public attention because of their unusually high performance. They have played a large role in trade negotiations, but at present they make up less than 1 percent of world computer sales (table 5.75.7). The United States holds the dominant position in this market, although its share is falling. Government buyers, particularly in Japan, have shown a strong preference for locally produced supercomputers; the US government and government-funded organizations have also shown an evident, albeit less-pronounced, preference for US-made computers. Nongovernment purchasers in United States also tend to favor well-established local companies because postpurchase service, including software updates, is important. Here, too, local preference is less pronounced in the United States than in Japan.

Parts and Accessories

These accounted for 41 percent of 1990 exports and 33 percent of imports in the product group. US exports of parts and accessories more than doubled in nominal terms from 1981 to 1990, but have not grown as fast as world exports because US companies abroad have increased their local sourcing of parts. In addition, almost all manufacturing of peripherals by US-owned companies has moved abroad. Imports of parts have increased as high-volume Asian parts makers have captured market share, and a multitude of assemblers and "systems integrators" have sprung up in the United States. The drop in the US duty rate from 3.9 percent to zero in 1987 may also have played a small role.

Foreign Direct Investment

Foreign direct investment in the United States in office and computing machines grew from $0.4 billion to $2.7 billion from 1980 to 1988, according to the US Department of Commerce. The factories of foreign companies in the United States produce peripherals, PCs, and laptops. Some observers warn that Japanese acquisitions of existing companies focus on cash-hungry companies possessing technology in which Japan is behind. However, the shift of Asian production to the United States helps improve the trade balance to the extent that it adds value in the United States instead of abroad. But according to the US Commerce Department, subsidiaries, particularly Japanese subsidiaries, of foreign electronics companies in the United States increased their imports of parts faster than their sales during 1980–86. Some observers predict that, as time goes on, Asian-owned computer parts makers will increase the US content of their production, following the pattern of the automobile industry. Another (anonymous) observer suggests that dumping rulings are easier to obtain on final assembly than on parts, so that the motivation to make parts in the United States is reduced. The Commerce Department expects continued growth of foreign direct investment in computers in the United States.

According to the Commerce Department, a lack of export financing has hurt US computer exports, particularly for large-scale projects in developing countries (US Department of Commerce 1986, 53.). One financing problem is that many large systems no longer meet the Export-Import Bank's requirement of 85 percent US content, and some US firms have instead obtained financing from foreign governments and therefore shipped from their foreign subsidiaries.

According to data from DRI, US and foreign demand for imports of computers has one of the most elastic responses of any industry to changes in import prices and growth in domestic consumption (see the appendix to this volume). In other words, changes in exchange rates and differentials between US and foreign growth are likely to have particularly large effects on the computer trade balance.

Near-Term Outlook

The computer and office machine trade balance is likely to continue to deteriorate through the mid-1990s as growing imports of parts, peripherals, and high-value photocopiers offset exports of workstations. Faster growth abroad and the decline in the dollar during 1990 will be positive influences, particularly given the price elasticity of computer trade. Nevertheless, a deterioration of around $3 billion in the industry's trade balance by 1993 seems likely. Capacity constraints do not appear to be a problem limiting US exports.

Foreign manufacturers appear to be shifting production of low-value photocopiers to US plants. However, producers in Japan are focusing more on the high end of the market, and the dollar value of imports is more than likely to increase.

Because the PC market is more saturated in the United States than abroad, US sales are growing more slowly than sales abroad. On the other hand, fast growth in the laptop, portable, and notebook segments will play to Asian strength in this area, increasing US imports of parts.

US domination of the workstation segment of the market should result in increasing exports, particularly with IBM's entry into the market; several Japanese entrants, however, are also probable. Fast growth is also likely as workstations make inroads into professional markets traditionally served by PCs and minicomputers. The workstation market has moved quickly from proprietary to nonproprietary systems. Hewlett-Packard and Sun Microsystems have licensed their proprietary technology to Asian producers in an effort to set the *de facto* market standard, as IBM did in the PC market. However, Asian producers have a history of succeeding through high-volume strategies in markets in which standards have been set and price competition is more important. Already several clones of US-made machines are on the market, and a flood of Asian imports could be in store if the history of the PC market is a guide.

No significant changes are expected in the US mainframe and minicomputer trade positions. Lower-line mainframes will face competition from multiprocessor/microprocessor computers, which are now being made by US companies using some foreign parts.

Falling defense budgets will hurt demand for supercomputers, but increased scientific demand should offset this fall. Less expensive alternatives such as parallel processing will also erode profit margins. Europe should continue to be a strong market for the United States. Trade negotiations with Japan may result in a few more sales there. However, Japanese companies have introduced several very fast computers that will compete in Japan and in global markets.

Medium-Term Outlook

Several analysts project that demand for computers will grow more quickly outside the United States. However, a study by McKinsey and Company also concludes that the fast growth the world computer industry experienced in the 1980s is ending. It states that "while the outlook for fundamental demand remains strong, the ability of the world economy to continue absorbing rapidly increasing expenditures on computer technology is reaching a practical limit" (McKinsey & Co. 1990, 1). However, not all analysts agree with predictions of a slowdown, and certainly some segments of the market, such as workstations and laptops, should continue to grow rapidly. The McKinsey study also predicts that, based on historical patterns, half of the current leaders in the world computer industry will not exist in their present form in five to ten years (McKinsey & Co. 1990, 1).

The worldwide move to common standards in computers of all kinds may continue to reduce the US role as the advantage shifts to high-volume, low-cost producers that compete well on price. There is little reason to expect significant improvement in the trade balance in the foreseeable future. A significant technological edge will become increasingly necessary to earn high returns.

Conclusions

- The 1980s was a period of enormous technological advance and structural change in the computer industry. During that period, computing moved from the back office to individual desks and homes, and manufacturing of computers, fairly customized in 1981, became much more commodity-like at the low end of the product scale.

- The US share balance of world trade in computers and office machines experienced the greatest fall of any product category in the 1980s, from +21.6 percentage points in 1981 to −2.0 percentage points in 1989.

- The strong market position of US-owned production—often located abroad—should not be confused with the declining position of US-based production.

- The success of high-volume Asian producers in making standardized personal computers and parts, one of the fastest-growing industry segments, contributed a great deal to the decline in the US computer trade balance and the move from surplus to deficit.

- Competition will continue to intensify in this highly dynamic industry, particularly if common standards cause computers and parts to compete on the basis of price.

- The computer and office machine trade balance is likely to continue to deteriorate by around $3 billion through 1993, to a deficit of about $5 billion, as growing imports of parts, peripherals, and photocopiers offset export improvements in other areas, such as workstations.

- The longer-term outlook for US trade in computers and office equipment is negative; market growth will slow and competition will intensify. Deficits could continue to enlarge beyond 1993.

- Computers offer a classic illustration of the fact that technological leadership in a product does not ensure a trade surplus in that product. US-invented and even US-owned technologies can be utilized in foreign production, with US trade deficits the result. Thus, a strong trade position requires not just competitive US-owned and US-developed technology, but also competitive US-based manufacturing.

Bibliography

Cane, Alan. 1990. "Coming to Terms with 'Old' Age." *Financial Times* (13 November): 22.

Clausing, Don P. 1989. "The U.S. Semiconductor, Computer and Copier Industries." In *Working Papers of the MIT Commission on Industrial Productivity*, vol. 2. Cambridge, MA: MIT Press.

Computer Business Equipment Manufacturers Association. 1990. *1990 Annual Report*. Washington: Computer Business Equipment Manufacturers Association.

Council on Competitiveness. 1990. *Sectoral Profile: Computer Systems*. Washington: Council on Competitiveness (July).

Electronics Industries Association of Japan. *Facts and Figures on the Japanese Electronics Industry*. Tokyo: Electronics Industries Association of Japan.

Commission of the European Communities. 1990. *Panorama of EC Industry, 1990*. Luxembourg: Commission of the European Communities.

Flamm, Kenneth. 1987. *Targeting the Computer: Government Support and International Competition*. Washington: Brookings Institution.

Flamm, Kenneth. 1988. *Creating the Computer: Government, Industry, and High Technology*. Washington: Brookings Institution.

Flamm, Kenneth. 1989. "The Computer Industry in Industrialized Economies: Lessons for the Newly Industrializing." *Industry Series* 8. Washington: World Bank (February).

Goldfarb, Debra. 1990. "Protectionism or Realpolitik: The Japanese Supercomputer Market." Framingham, MA: IDC (November).

Industry, Science and Technology Canada. 1988. *Industry Profiles*. Ottawa: Industry, Science and Technology Canada.

Institute for Defense Analysis. 1988. *Microelectronics Manufacturing Technology: A Defense Perspective: Final Report of the Defense Microelectronics Technology Base Project*. Washington: Institute for Defense Analysis (April).

Japan Economic Institute of America. 1990. *Japan's Expanding U.S. Manufacturing Presence*. Washington: Japan Economic Institute of America (December).

Japan Economic Journal. 1990a. *Japan Economic Almanac, 1990*. Tokyo: Japan Economic Journal.

Japan Electronics Almanac. 1990. Tokyo: DEMPA Publications.

Japan Electronics Industry Development Association. 1990. *Long-Term Prospects for the Electronics Industry*. Translation by the American Electronics Association Japan Office. Tokyo: Japan Electronics Industry Development Association (March).

McKinsey and Co. 1990. *The 1990 Report on the Computer Industry*. New York: McKinsey & Co.

National Academy of Engineering. 1984. *The Competitive Status of the U.S. Electronics Industry*. Washington: National Academy Press.

National Academy of Sciences. 1986. *The Positive Sum Strategy: Harnessing Technology for Economic Growth*. Washington: National Academy Press.

National Research Council. 1990. *Keeping the U.S. Computer Industry Competitive*. Washington: National Academy Press.

Nunez, Wilson Peres. 1990. "The Electronic Industry." In *Foreign Direct Investment and Industrial Development in Mexico*. Paris: Organization for Economic Cooperation and Development.

Office Information Technology Association of America. 1986. *The Impact of the Computer Software and Services and Computer Hardware Industries in the U.S. Economy*. Prepared by DRI, Inc. Arlington, VA: Office Information Technology Association of America.

Organization for Economic Cooperation and Development. 1990. *Technology and Global Competition: The Challenge for Newly Industrializing Economies*. Paris: Organization for Economic Cooperation and Development (January).

Quick, Finan & Associates. 1989. *Evaluation of U.S. and Japanese Market and Trade Data: Report to the American Electronics Association*. Washington: Quick, Finan & Associates (10 October).

"Survey on Personal Computers and Software." 1990. *Financial Times* (25 September).

US Department of Commerce, International Trade Administration. 1986. *A Competitive Assessment of the U.S Microcomputer Systems Industry*. Washington: US Department of Commerce (August).

US Department of Commerce, International Trade Administration. 1990. *The Competitive Status of the U.S Electronics Sector.* Washington: US Department of Commerce (January).

US Department of Commerce, International Trade Administration. 1991. *U.S. Industrial Outlook, 1991.* Washington: US Department of Commerce (January).

See also the following periodicals: *Office Products Analyst, Today's Office, Modern Office Technology, Electronics, Electronic Business, Electronic News, Information Week, PC Week, Info Systems, Datamation, Info World.*

Table 5.75.1 Office machines and computers: product composition of world trade, 1981–89
(billions of dollars except where noted)

SITC Product	1981	1982	1983	1984	1985	1986	1987	1988	1989	Annual growth 1981–89 (percentages)
World exports to world	28.8	30.6	37.9	48.8	53.7	66.5	84.9	104.4	110.3	18.3
of which										
751 Office machines	6.0	5.4	5.8	6.5	6.6	7.5	8.4	9.7	10.5	7.2
752 Computers (ADP)	13.0	14.4	17.9	23.6	25.9	33.3	43.1	53.3	61.0	21.3
759 Parts and accessories	9.9	10.2	12.8	16.6	19.3	23.4	30.6	41.4	39.5	18.9
										Change 1981–89
Memorandum: SITC 75 share of world manufactures exports (percentages)	2.8	3.1	3.9	4.6	4.8	4.9	5.1	5.3	5.2	2.4

Source: World Manufactures Trade Data Base.

Table 5.75.2 Office machines and computers: geographic distribution of world trade, 1981–89 (percentages of total)

Country	1981	1982	1983	1984	1985	1986	1987	1988	1989	Change 1981–89
Share of exports to world										
United States	34.0	33.2	30.7	29.8	27.7	23.1	22.0	22.1	21.0	–13.0
Canada	3.2	3.1	3.0	2.9	2.6	2.0	2.2	2.1	2.0	–1.2
Japan	15.0	15.4	18.6	20.2	19.6	22.0	21.3	21.6	21.2	6.2
European Community	39.3	39.2	36.2	34.1	37.2	38.2	38.1	34.3	35.0	–4.2
EC to non-EC	12.9	12.9	11.8	11.4	12.8	12.4	11.4	10.1	9.9	–3.0
Germany	11.0	10.6	9.5	8.0	9.1	10.1	9.3	7.6	7.7	–3.4
France	6.4	5.5	5.3	4.7	4.8	5.5	5.7	4.7	4.7	–1.7
Italy	4.1	4.2	3.5	3.0	3.9	3.8	3.4	3.3	2.9	–1.2
United Kingdom	8.8	9.1	8.2	8.4	9.0	7.9	8.7	9.0	9.1	0.3
Other Western Europe	3.6	3.5	3.6	2.8	3.1	3.2	2.9	2.7	2.6	–1.1
Asian NICs[a]	2.7	3.4	6.0	8.0	7.5	9.4	11.6	14.8	15.0	12.3
Eastern Europe[b]	0.1	0.1	0.1	0.1	0.0	0.1	0.1	0.0	0.0	–0.1
Developing countries	1.9	2.0	1.7	1.8	1.8	1.4	1.5	2.1	2.6	0.7
Latin America	1.5	1.5	1.2	1.2	1.2	0.9	0.9	1.1	1.2	–0.3
Rest of world	0.1	0.1	0.1	0.2	0.4	0.5	0.4	0.3	0.3	0.3
Share of imports from world										
United States	12.3	13.8	18.2	22.7	21.9	22.5	22.3	22.1	23.0	10.7
Canada	8.1	8.0	7.1	7.6	6.1	5.2	5.1	4.7	4.6	–3.5
Japan	3.6	3.2	2.8	2.8	2.9	2.6	2.6	3.2	3.9	0.4
European Community	49.9	49.8	48.5	45.2	46.5	47.2	48.2	46.8	46.4	–3.5
EC from non-EC	25.9	26.0	25.7	24.9	24.4	24.4	24.8	25.3	24.7	–1.2
Germany	11.7	10.8	10.8	9.6	10.3	10.9	10.8	10.0	10.6	–1.1
France	9.4	9.9	8.8	7.3	7.5	8.1	8.2	7.9	7.5	–1.9
Italy	5.5	5.0	4.3	4.3	4.9	4.8	5.2	5.0	4.4	–1.2
United Kingdom	11.2	11.7	12.0	11.2	10.7	9.9	10.5	10.7	10.8	–0.3
Other Western Europe	8.5	8.1	7.8	6.8	7.7	8.3	8.3	8.0	7.5	–1.0
Asian NICs[a]	3.1	3.5	4.3	4.6	4.4	4.3	4.6	6.4	6.0	2.9
Eastern Europe[b]	0.9	0.7	0.6	0.4	0.4	0.5	0.5	0.6	0.7	–0.1
Developing countries	10.8	10.3	8.6	7.8	8.1	7.0	6.1	5.9	5.2	–5.6
Latin America	4.7	4.0	2.6	2.7	3.0	2.6	2.3	2.3	2.0	–2.8
Rest of world	0.0	0.0	0.0	0.0	0.0	0.0	0.0	0.0	0.0	0.0

Export share minus import share

United States	21.6	19.3	12.5	7.2	5.9	0.6	-0.3	-0.0	-2.0	-23.6
Canada	-4.8	-4.8	-4.2	-4.8	-3.5	-3.1	-2.9	-2.7	-2.6	2.3
Japan	11.5	12.2	15.8	17.4	16.7	19.4	18.6	18.4	17.3	5.9
European Community	-10.7	-10.6	-12.2	-11.1	-9.3	-9.0	-10.1	-12.5	-11.4	-0.7
Non-EC	-13.0	-13.0	-13.9	-13.5	-11.7	-12.0	-13.4	-15.2	-14.7	-1.7
Germany	-0.7	-0.2	-1.2	-1.6	-1.2	-0.9	-1.5	-2.4	-2.9	-2.2
France	-3.0	-4.4	-3.5	-2.6	-2.7	-2.6	-2.5	-3.2	-2.8	0.1
Italy	-1.4	-0.8	-0.8	-1.3	-1.0	-1.0	-1.8	-1.7	-1.4	0.0
United Kingdom	-2.4	-2.6	-3.8	-2.8	-1.7	-2.1	-1.8	-1.7	-1.7	0.7
Other Western Europe	-4.9	-4.6	-4.2	-4.0	-4.6	-5.1	-5.4	-5.4	-5.0	-0.1
Asian NICs[a]	-0.4	-0.1	1.7	3.4	3.2	5.1	7.0	8.4	9.0	9.4
Eastern Europe[b]	-0.7	-0.5	-0.5	-0.4	-0.4	-0.4	-0.4	-0.5	-0.7	0.0
Developing countries	-8.9	-8.3	-6.9	-6.0	-6.2	-5.6	-4.6	-3.8	-2.6	6.3
Latin America	-3.3	-2.5	-1.5	-1.6	-1.8	-1.6	-1.3	-1.2	-0.8	2.5
Rest of world	0.1	0.1	0.1	0.2	0.4	0.5	0.3	0.3	0.3	0.2

a. Hong Kong, Korea, Singapore, and Taiwan.

b. Including Soviet Union.

Source: World Manufactures Trade Data Base.

Table 5.75.3 Office machines and computers: bilateral trade flows, 1989 (billions of dollars)

Importer	World	United States	Canada	Japan	European Community	Germany	France	United Kingdom	Asian NICs	Latin America	Other
World	110.3	23.2	2.2	23.4	38.6	8.5	5.2	10.0	16.6	1.3	5.0
United States	27.5		1.6	12.1	3.1	0.6	0.3	1.1	8.8	0.8	1.0
Canada	3.9	2.6		0.5	0.2	0.0	0.0	0.0	0.4	0.2	0.1
Japan	4.3	3.0	0.0		0.3	0.1	0.1	0.1	0.6	0.1	0.2
European Community	52.4	10.3	0.5	6.8	27.7	5.8	3.6	6.8	4.4	0.1	2.6
Germany	12.2	2.3	0.0	2.5	5.4		1.1	1.8	1.3	0.0	0.7
France	8.2	1.3	0.0	0.7	4.9	1.3		1.4	0.5	0.0	0.7
United Kingdom	10.9	3.0	0.1	1.5	4.9	1.2	0.8		1.1	0.0	0.4
Asian NICs	6.1	2.4	0.0	2.0	0.4	0.1	0.0	0.1	1.0	0.0	0.2
Latin America	2.2	1.7	0.0	0.2	0.3	0.1	0.1	0.0	0.1	0.0	0.0
Other	14.0	3.2	0.1	1.9	6.7	1.8	1.0	1.8	1.3	0.0	0.8

Source: World Manufactures Trade Data Base.

Table 5.75.4 Office machines and computers: product composition of US trade, 1981–90[a]
(millions of dollars except where noted)

Category	SITC Rev. 2			SITC Rev. 3			
	1981	1987	Change 1981–87	1987	1990	Change 1981–90	Change 1987–90
Total							
Exports	9,743	18,640	8,897	18,634	24,726	14,983	6,092
Imports	3,562	18,410	14,848	18,318	26,917	23,355	8,599
Balance	6,181	230	−5,951	316	−2,192	−8,373	−2,508
of which							
751 Office machines							
Exports	556	457	−99	534	791	235	257
Imports	1,475	2,410	935	2,541	2,693	1,218	152
Balance	−919	−1,953	−1,034	−2,007	−1,902	−983	105
752 Computers							
Exports	4,967	8,643	3,676	8,577	13,804	8,837	5,227
Imports	703	7,074	6,371	12,587	15,424	14,721	2,837
Balance	4,264	1,569	−2,695	−4,010	−1,620	−5,884	2,390
759 Parts and accessories							
Exports	4,220	9,540	5,320	9,523	10,130	5,910	607
Imports	1,384	8,926	7,542	3,190	8,800	7,416	5,610
Balance	2,836	614	−2,222	6,333	1,330	−1,506	−5,003

a. Data are expressed on a domestic exports, imports customs basis.

Source: US Department of Commerce.

Table 5.75.5   Office machines and computers: geographic composition of US trade, 1981–90[a]

	Millions of dollars				Percentages of total			
	1981	1987	1989	1990	1981	1987	1989	1990
Exports								
Canada	1,274	2,835	2,572	3,436	13.1	15.2	11.1	13.9
Japan	753	1,702	3,001	3,352	7.7	9.1	12.9	13.6
European Community	4,655	8,338	10,314	10,605	47.8	44.7	44.5	42.9
United Kingdom	1,209	2,276	3,017	2,947	12.4	12.2	13.0	11.9
Germany	1,088	1,850	2,339	2,525	11.2	9.9	10.1	10.2
France	840	1,076	1,274	1,378	8.6	5.8	5.5	5.6
Italy	338	690	683	665	3.5	3.7	2.9	2.7
Latin America	953	1,362	1,688	1,823	9.8	7.3	7.3	7.4
Asian NICs	547	1,784	2,393	2,288	5.6	9.6	10.3	9.3
Other	1,561	2,613	3,216	3,222	16.0	14.0	13.9	13.0
Total	9,743	18,634	23,184	24,726	100.0	100.0	100.0	100.0
Imports								
Canada	521	1,167	1,696	1,893	14.6	6.4	6.6	7.0
Japan	1,649	8,755	11,150	11,006	46.3	47.8	43.4	40.9
European Community	604	2,081	2,303	2,366	17.0	11.4	9.0	8.8
United Kingdom	126	668	827	804	3.5	3.6	3.2	3.0
Germany	185	555	444	522	5.2	3.0	1.7	1.9
France	76	159	228	247	2.1	0.9	0.9	0.9
Italy	67	245	304	233	1.9	1.3	1.2	0.9
Latin America	145	508	842	776	4.1	2.8	3.3	2.9
Asian NICs	520	5,444	8,660	9,610	14.6	29.7	33.7	35.7
Hong Kong	263	583	925	812	7.4	3.2	3.6	3.0
Korea	58	768	1,410	1,351	1.6	4.2	5.5	5.0
Singapore	67	2,177	3,708	4,355	1.9	11.9	14.4	16.2
Taiwan	131	1,916	2,618	3,092	3.7	10.5	10.2	11.5
Other	124	363	1,028	1,266	3.5	2.0	4.0	4.7
Total	3,563	18,318	25,679	26,917	100.0	100.0	100.0	100.0

a. Data are expressed on a domestic exports, imports customs basis.

Source: US Department of Commerce.

Table 5.75.6 Office machines and computers: indices of US competitiveness, 1981–89 (billions of dollars except where noted)

	1981	1982	1983	1984	1985	1986	1987	1988	1989	Annual growth 1981–89 (percentages)
World trade										
World exports to non-US destinations	24.7	25.8	30.2	37.4	41.8	51.0	64.9	79.1	82.8	16.3
World imports from non-US sources	18.1	19.7	24.9	32.8	37.6	49.1	63.3	77.6	85.2	21.4
US trade										
Exports	9.7	10.2	11.6	14.6	14.9	15.3	18.6	23.1	23.2	11.5
Imports	3.7	4.4	7.0	11.2	11.9	15.1	19.0	23.1	26.3	27.8
Balance	6.0	5.8	4.6	3.4	3.0	0.2	−0.4	−0.0	−3.1	
										Change 1981–89
US share of exports to non-US destinations (percentages)	39.5	39.4	38.5	38.9	35.7	30.1	28.7	29.1	28.0	−11.5
US share of imports from non-US sources (percentages)	20.1	22.4	28.0	34.0	31.6	30.7	30.0	29.7	30.8	10.7
Export share minus import share (percentages)	19.4	17.0	10.5	4.9	4.1	−0.6	−1.3	−0.6	−2.8	−22.2

Source: World Manufactures Trade Data Base.

Table 5.75.7　US-owned companies' share of worldwide electronics markets, 1984 and 1987

Product	Percent of total 1984	Percent of total 1987	World market, 1987 (billions of dollars)
Photocopiers	40	36	$13.4
Computers	78	69	121.0
Personal computers	75	64	47.2
Laptop computers	85	57	1.6
Supercomputers	96	77	1.1
Displays	11	8	8.2
Flat panel displays	25	15	2.4
Floppy drives	35	2	2.5
Hard drives (<300 MB)	73	65	8.2
Hard drives (<40 MB)	70	60	2.3
Dot matrix printers	10	8	4.8
Software	70	70	44.5
Operating systems	90	90	16.4
Database management	100	95	2.8
Spreadsheets	100	100	0.9

MB = megabytes.

Source: US Department of Commerce, International Trade Administration. 1990. *The Competitive Status of the US Electronics Sector.* Washington: US Department of Commerce (April): 17.

Telecommunications and Sound-Reproducing Equipment (SITC 76)

The US trade deficit in telecommunications and sound-reproducing equipment (consumer electronics) increased from $5.1 billion in 1981 to $13.3 billion in 1990. This occurred because of the success of Asian electronics producers in US markets, partly facilitated by the breakup of American Telephone and Telegraph Co. (AT&T). A number of products that are now major imports did not exist or were unimportant in 1981: facsimile (fax) machines, cordless telephones, telephone answering machines, videocassette recorders (VCRs), camcorders, and compact disc (CD) players; few of these are made in the United States. Significant improvement in this category will require greater openness in foreign telecommunications equipment markets and increased production of consumer electronics items in the United States, probably by Asian companies.

Description of the Product Group

Telecommunications and sound-reproducing equipment consists of:

SITC

761 television receivers

762 radio broadcast receivers, including receivers incorporating sound recorders or reproducers

763 gramophones, other sound recorders and reproducers, and VCRs

764 telecommunications equipment, not elsewhere specified, and parts and accessories of items in SITC 76.

For analytical purposes it is useful to divide this category into consumer electronics (SITC 761, 762, and 763) and telecommunications equipment (SITC 764). Telecommunications equipment includes a mix of consumer electronic items and industrial equipment with different trade characteristics. For example, this subcategory includes not only telephone handsets, camcorders, fax machines, and telephone answering machines—clearly items with widespread consumer applications—but also switching equipment used by offices and telephone companies. It also includes a significant number of items that are not telecommunications equipment, but are consumer electronics parts and accessories, such as loudspeakers.

Several items that might be considered consumer electronics products are recorded elsewhere. Personal computers are recorded under SITC 75, electronic games and musical instruments under SITC 89, electronic watches under SITC 88, and most electronic parts and components, as well as fiber optics, under SITC 77. Trade in telecommunications services, such as international telephone calls, is not classified within the SITC system.

Role in World Trade

Size and Composition

World exports of goods in this product group were $86.1 billion in 1989, constituting 4.1 percent of world manufactures exports (table 5.76.1). During 1981–89, world export growth in this category averaged 10.4 percent per year, modestly higher than the 9.6 percent average growth of world manufactures exports. However, because much of the growth was in exports to the United States, world exports of these products to non-US destinations grew at an annual rate of only 9.8 percent (table 5.76.6).

The subcategory with the largest share (over half) and the fastest growth in exports was telecommunications equipment, parts, and accessories. However, a large part of this trade involves goods not commonly thought of as telecommunications equipment. For example, roughly half of the $11.6 billion in US imports in this subcategory in 1989 consisted of consumer electronics parts and accessories.

Global Competition Patterns

The flow of world trade in this product group changed dramatically during 1981–89 (table 5.76.2). The US share of exports fell 1.0 percentage point below 1981 levels, while the European Community's share fell by 3.6 percentage points. Japan's share fell 9.5 percentage points but still accounted for roughly a third of world exports. Because world exports doubled, no large country's exports actually fell in dollar terms. The big export-share winners were the NICs, whose share increased by 11.7 percentage points to 20.1 percent. On the import side, the major shifts were the 3.0-percentage-point increase in the US import share and the very large drop in the import share of the developing countries. The import shares of the European Community and the NICs both increased slightly.

The already negative share balance of the United States deteriorated by 4.0 percentage points to -18.3 percent, with three-fourths of this decline occurring on the import side. By contrast, the fall in Japan's positive share balance took place almost exclusively through a fall in its export share. The negative share balance of the developing countries fell 16.9 percentage points because of lower imports, probably more as a result of lost purchasing power than because of import substitution. The European Community is the second-largest exporter of these products after Japan, but more than half of EC exports remain within the Community (table 5.76.3). Japan has generated huge surpluses in this category, with 1989 exports of $27.4 billion and imports of only $2.8 billion yielding a $24.6 billion surplus.

Key Determinants of World Trade Patterns

Although Japan's share of world exports has fallen, Japanese-owned firms, with operations in many countries, dominate every major consumer electronics market and have achieved substantial economies of scale. It is probably no coincidence that NIC exports rose as Japanese exports fell. Other Asian countries, especially the NICs, are becoming significant production bases, particularly for older technologies. Some but certainly not all of these production facilities are Japanese owned.

Asian companies have not achieved the same dominance in telecommunications equipment for industrial use; US manufacturers of these products have been increasingly successful at selling in foreign markets. However, they often choose to serve these markets from foreign production facilities because differing foreign technical standards reduce the economies of scale of producing at home and because government-owned telephone companies abroad mandate local production. US subsidiaries abroad typically still obtain some components and parts from the United States. Companies from Japan and the Asian NICs have been more successful at serving foreign markets from their home country: their more consumer-oriented products are usually bought for home or office use by individuals who have less of a bias toward locally made goods.

Role in US Trade

Recent Performance

This product category accounted for 3.1 percent of US manufactures exports in 1990 and 6.0 percent of US manufactures imports. The US trade deficit in telecommunications and sound-reproducing equipment deteriorated from $5.1 billion in 1981 to $15.8 billion in 1987, but improved modestly to $13.3 billion by 1990 (table 5.76.4). The deterioration was spread fairly evenly among the four subcategories. Exports and imports grew by similar percentages from 1981 to 1990. Most of the imports came from Japan, the NICs, and Mexico, although Japan's share fell significantly from 1981 to 1990 (table 5.76.5). Imports from Mexico, a growing portion of the total, come mostly from *maquiladora* plants near the US border. Bilateral deficits in 1990 were with Japan ($8.5 billion), the NICs ($3.7 billion), and Mexico ($1.4 billion).

International Competitiveness

US imports grew 12.4 percent annually on average during 1981–89, increasing the US share of world imports from non-US sources to 29.7 percent from 27.1 percent (table 5.76.6). US exports grew by an average of 9.1 percent annually, but because world exports to non-US destinations grew more quickly—at a 9.8 percent annual rate—the US share of world exports fell from 13.1 percent to 12.4 percent.

Outlook

Key Determinants of US Trade Performance

Consumer electronics accounted for most of the 1981–87 deterioration in US trade in this product group. Growing imports of stereo systems, VCRs, tape decks, loudspeakers, and particularly newer products such as CD players and camcorders were major factors. The domestic market share of US-owned consumer electronics companies is now minimal, and the substantial majority of US-based production is foreign owned and draws heavily on imported parts and components. One study estimates the value added of US-owned consumer electronics companies to be 5 percent of US sales (Staelin et al. 1989, 1). One of the few areas in which US-based production by US-owned companies is important is loudspeakers.

In some consumer electronics products, US demand is supplied primarily by imports. For instance, a study for the American Electronic Industries Association indicates that, in 1988, imports from Japan supplied 77 percent of US VCR consumption, with another 4 percent provided by US-based production of Japanese firms (Quick, Finan & Associates 1989). Korea is also an important source of US imports of VCRs. The United States imported 11.7 million VCRs from all countries in 1988 (Electronic Industries Association 1990a).

In some other products, US-based production by foreign-owned firms is more significant: foreign direct investment in the United States in the radio, TV, and communications equipment industries grew from $1.1 billion in 1980 to $4.6 billion in 1988 (US Department of Commerce, International Trade Administration and National Communications Information Administration 1990, 47). For instance, US-based production accounted for 67 percent of US apparent consumption of color and black-and-white TVs in 1989 (US Department of Commerce 1990). The rest are imported, with Mexico the largest source. US-based production of color TVs by Japanese firms accounted for 34 percent of apparent US consumption in 1988, while imports from Japan fell to only 1 percent of apparent US consumption (Quick, Finan & Associates, 1989). These statistics accord with a statement by the chairman of Sony (Morita 1991) that nearly 100 percent of its color TVs sold in the United States are made in California. The only remaining US-based TV manufacturer, Zenith, produces most of its sets in Mexico (Graham and Krugman 1991, 53). Mexico was a bigger source of US TV imports in 1988 than the NICs as a group. Many TV parts are also made in the United States; the United States had a trade surplus in TV picture tubes in 1989. The inflow of foreign investment in consumer electronics that made this possible is slowing, according to the Commerce Department (1991, 38-12).

The deterioration over the 1980s in US trade in telecommunications equipment resulted in part from the US deregulation of telecommunications. A recent US Commerce Department study found that "much of the telecommunications trade problem results from asymmetrical access to telecommunications markets in the United States and overseas" resulting from unilateral deregulation of the US markets (US Department of Commerce, International Trade Administration and National Communications Information Administration 1990, 74). Once consumers were permitted to buy their own telephones, they began buying imports that cost less or had new features, such as cordless telephones. In addition, the "Baby Bells" created by divestiture were prohibited from discriminating in favor of AT&T when buying network equipment, and the market share of a Canadian company, Northern Telecom, climbed quickly as a result. However, the role of deregulation should not be overemphasized. Northern Telecom makes much of its equipment in the United States, although newer entrants may not do so. Fast growth in markets that were open to imports before deregulation, such as those for answering machines and faxes, also played an important role.

A greater proportion of higher-value telecommunications equipment for business and industry use is manufactured or assembled in the United States. US-based production of fax machines and answering machines has never been great, and success in opening foreign markets will neither increase exports nor reduce US imports of these products. Two North American producers, AT&T and Northern Telecom, continue to dominate the network equipment market primarily through US-based production, with a small presence by other foreign producers. The United States also remains strong in producing communications satellites and some mobile radio systems.

Table 5.76.7 gives a rough, but far from ideal, indication of the position of US companies in world electronics markets. Most available statistics give market shares by company, not by country of production. A product bought in the United States is an import if it was made abroad, even by a US-owned company, and is not an import if it was made in the United States, even if the producer is a foreign-owned company. In addition, available statistics are often insufficient to assess the relative importance of "screwdriver" assembly plants that import their parts as opposed to those that obtain sources locally. For instance, AT&T's foreign equipment sales increased from $200 million in 1986 to $1.2 billion, but it supplies many foreign markets from foreign production facilities, often in order to satisfy foreign government procurement preferences for their local products (Marx 1991, 7). Nonetheless, AT&T's facilities obtain around a third of their parts and components from the United States, and sales by US-owned facilities abroad have led to US exports.

Proposed legislation would allow the Baby Bells to engage in manufacturing, adding to US production capabilities. However, the contribution this would make to the US trade balance depends on whether these new producers draw parts and components from foreign or domestic sources.

Elasticities supplied by DRI (see the appendix to this volume) indicate that US demand for consumer electronics imports (SITC 761-63) is extremely responsive to changes in import prices, such as might be caused by movements in exchange rates. However, notwithstanding the sharp fall in the yen-dollar exchange rate since early 1985, the dollar prices of most consumer electronics items imported from Japan and other sources have continued to decline; this is evidence of continued advances in technology and productivity gains in production abroad. Import demand is also very responsive to growth in the consumption component of GNP, as would be expected for a group of consumer durable goods. Statistically significant elasticities could not be computed for US consumer electronics exports, underlining the improbability of much progress in this area.

Telecommunications Equipment

Near-Term Outlook

The Telecommunications Industry Association and several other telecommunications trade associations believe that US trade in telecommunications equipment is turning around and that balanced trade in that component of the product group is possible in 1991. According to US Commerce Department statistics, US exports of telecommunications equipment increased at a 27 percent annual rate from 1987 to 1990, while import growth slowed from 19 percent to less than 2 percent. As a result, the deficit was $2.5 billion in 1987, $1.8 billion in 1989, and $0.8 billion in 1990. This projection, however, does not imply a balance in this subcategory, which includes other products. The deficit for the subcategory as a whole was $3.7 billion in 1990 compared with $4.3 billion in 1987. The US Commerce Department is not quite as optimistic as the telecommunications associations about the outlook for US trade in telecommunications equipment.

Medium-Term Outlook

US-based production of higher-value telecommunications equipment for business and industrial use should remain highly competitive. US-based production capacity for lower-value telecommunications equipment, such as telephone handsets, fax machines, answering machines, and cordless telephones, is not great, but transplanted Japanese production has been increasing for fax machines, telephone sets, and small switching systems. The move to US production of switching systems came in response to a finding of dumping. According to the US Commerce Department study, the United States is at a disadvantage in these products in terms of technology and efficiency, not in labor costs (US Department of Commerce, International Trade Administration and National Communications Information Administration 1990, 12). This implies that more production could be shifted to the United States with well-managed application of better technology (perhaps through increased US-based production by foreign companies). Industry sources, however, disagree with this assessment. AT&T sees itself as the market leader in cordless telephones and answering machines. Many of its products in these lines are manufactured offshore, primarily because of lower labor costs, but incorporate US design, technology, and manufacturing processes.

In addition, the Baby Bells created by the breakup of AT&T have moved aggressively into foreign markets and have bought a number of foreign telephone companies; these acquisitions could lead to exports of US parts and equipment. Also, foreign telecommunications equipment markets are growing more quickly than those in the United States. The remaining barriers to US exports are, however, significant, and the United States is most competitive in network equipment, the market least likely to be opened. Moreover, several foreign producers are making a concerted effort to break into the US market for network equipment, and the private nature of US telephone companies makes them more willing than their government-owned foreign counterparts to buy from foreign suppliers. In third-country markets, particularly in developing countries, foreign producers benefit significantly from subsidized government export financing and from tied aid packages, according to the Commerce Department (US Department of Commerce, International Trade Administration and National Communications Information Administration 1990, 16). The liberalization of public procurement as a result of EC 1992 and the worldwide growth of private networks could increase opportunities for US sales to foreign buyers not influenced by national procurement biases. However, new European standards could potentially limit US exports of products if they do not interconnect with networks and other products.

Consumer Electronics

Near-Term Outlook

The outlook for consumer electronics (SITC 761, 762, and 763) is less optimistic. At current exchange rates, increased US-based manufacturing is realistic only for some products, and much of the production that is leaving Japan is staying within Asia or going into screwdriver plants in Mexico near the US border. Roughly 60 percent of US color TV consumption is already manufactured or assembled in the United States, primarily by foreign-owned firms. The MIT study states that economies of scale are greater in Japan, which produced nearly three times as many TVs as the United States in 1983 (Staelin et al. 1989, 17). US production of CD players is minimal, and the initial burst of demand for this new product does not appear to have played out yet. About 10 percent of US consumption of VCRs already is met by domestically assembled or manufactured products, but US production can be significantly increased only if more essential components are made in the United States. In the longer term, however, other new digital products, such as high-definition television (HDTV) and digital radio could follow the same pattern of large volumes of imports and minimal US production. Two products that are already selling well in Japan are digital audio tape (DAT) players and Sony's Data Discman, a handheld device that displays books on CD.

Falling prices for consumer electronics products have helped slow growth in the value of imports, particularly for VCRs, but the decline in VCR prices is not expected to continue in this maturing market, and the introduction of new products and the replacement of old machines may stimulate continued demand for VCRs. Declining US automobile demand may temporarily reduce imports of automotive audio electronics.

To determine the potential improvement in the trade balance in this product group by 1993, one could reasonably—albeit optimistically—assume elimination of the telecommunications equipment trade deficit of $0.8 billion by 1993 and achievement of a surplus of $1 billion. It is also conceivable that consumer electronics imports will continue to drop as a result of falling VCR and auto electronics demand and prices and increased US-based production of other products such as TVs, resulting in, perhaps, a $2 billion improvement in those components of the deficit. Thus, under optimistic assumptions, a $4 billion improvement over 1990 levels is conceivable at present exchange rates, perhaps lowering the 1993 deficit to $9.3 billion.

Medium-Term Outlook

The underlying long-term trend in the US electronics industry, however, is one of declining competitiveness. As popular new products become available, increased US trade deficits are likely. Some analysts take Japanese dominance in consumer electronics for granted through the 1990s. One or more hot-selling new electronic "fad" items—HDTV is a possibility—could boost US deficits in this product group to new highs (see, e.g., "Consumer Electronics: Purveyors of Dreams," *The Economist*, 13 April 1991, Survey section). According to a Japanese study, Japan will surpass the United States in electronics production by 1995 (Japan Electronics Industry Development Association 1990). Large deficits of around $10 billion or more are likely to persist until further dollar depreciation or other factors—for example, antidumping cases or political pressures—force the return to the United States of a still larger portion of production for the US market, including new products that otherwise will be likely to increase US deficits.

Conclusions

- The rise of the dollar through 1985 played an important role in the deterioration of the US trade balance in telecommunications and sound-reproducing equipment.

- Much of former US consumer electronics production capability disappeared during the 1980s as a result of foreign competition. Now some of that capability is being restored, often by inward foreign direct investment. This investment frequently, but not always, takes the form of screwdriver assembly plants utilizing imported components.

- In both consumer electronics and telecommunications equipment there is some hope for further increases in US-based production by Japanese producers responding to the lower dollar and findings of dumping.

- Large deficits of around $10 billion or more are likely to persist until further dollar depreciation or other factors, such as antidumping cases or political pressures, force the return to the United States of a still larger portion of production for the US market. Japan is likely to retain global economies of scale in R&D and production that will ensure continuing large imports from Japan and periodic surges in imports as Japanese companies develop new consumer products. Also, US telecommunications equipment markets are most likely to remain more open than those abroad.

- The United States continues to be very strong in telecommunications network equipment, mobile communications, and satellites for industrial users, but foreign producers selling to US private-sector network operators will have a much easier time of it than US-based suppliers selling to government-owned network operators abroad.

- Under optimistic assumptions, the US deficit in this product group could narrow by as much as $4 billion by 1993, to a deficit of about $9.3 billion.

- However, the underlying long-term trend in US-based electronics production is one of declining competitiveness. Given a reasonably strong US economy, the trade balance could easily stagnate at the 1990 level of $13.3 billion, or deteriorate with the introduction of new products such as DAT and eventually HDTV and digital radio, and with continued imports of fax machines, answering devices, TVs, VCRs, automotive electronics, and home music systems and products. Failure to shift production of these goods to the United States, successful entry by foreign producers into the US market for network equipment, and failure to pry open foreign telecommunications equipment markets would also help to ensure continued large deficits.

Bibliography

"Consumer Electronics: Purveyors of Dreams." 1991. *The Economist* (13 April) Survey section.

Council on Competitiveness. 1990a. *Sectoral Profile: Electronic Components and Equipment.* Washington: Council on Competitiveness (March).

Council on Competitiveness. 1990b. *Sectoral Profile: Telecommunications.* Washington: Council on Competitiveness (May).

Cowhey, Peter. "Telecommunications." 1990. In Gary C. Hufbauer, ed., *Europe 1992: An American Perspective.* Washington: Brookings Institution.

Electronic Industries Association. 1990a. *Consumer Electronics Annual Review 1990 Edition: Industry Facts and Figures.* Washington: Electronic Industries Association.

Electronic Industries Association. 1990b. *EIA 1990 Electronic Market Data Book.* Washington: Electronic Industries Association.

Japan Economic Journal. 1990. *Japan Economic Almanac, 1990.* Tokyo: Japan Economic Journal.

Electronics Industries Association of Japan. *Facts and Figures on the Japanese Electronics Industry.* Tokyo: Electronics Industries Association of Japan.

Commission of the European Communities. 1990. *Panorama of EC Industry, 1990.* Luxembourg: Commission of the European Communities.

Graham, Edward M., and Paul R. Krugman. 1991. *Foreign Direct Investment in the United States,* 2nd ed. Washington: Institute for International Economics.

Industry, Science and Technology Canada. 1988. *Industry Profiles.* Ottawa: Industry, Science and Technology Canada.

Japan Electronics Almanac. 1990. Tokyo: DEMPA Publications.

Japan Electronics Industry Development Association. 1990. *Long-Term Prospects for the Electronics Industry.* Translation by the American Electronics Association Japan Office. Tokyo: Japan Electronics Industry Development Association (March).

Marx, William B., Jr. 1991. "Case Study: AT&T Network Systems." *International Economic Insights* 2, no. 1 (January–February).

Morita, Akio. 1991. "Proposal to Reevaluate U.S.-Japan Trade" (mimeographed, 14 February).

National Academy of Engineering. 1984. *The Competitive Status of the U.S. Electronics Industry.* Washington: National Academy Press.

Quick, Finan & Associates. 1989. *Evaluation of U.S. and Japanese Market and Trade Data: Report to the American Electronics Association.* Washington: Quick, Finan & Associates (10 October).

Staelin, David H. 1989. "The Decline of U.S. Consumer Electronics Manufacturing: History, Hypotheses, and Remedies." In *The Working Papers of the MIT Commission on Industrial Productivity,* vol. 1. Cambridge, MA: MIT Press.

"Survey: Telecommunications." *The Economist.* 10 March 1990.

US Department of Commerce. 1990. *Current Industrial Reports: Radio & TV Receivers, Phonographs & Related Equipment.* Washington: US Department of Commerce (MA36M, October).

US Department of Commerce, International Trade Administration and National Communications Information Administration. 1990. *U.S. Telecommunications in a Global Economy: Competitiveness at a Crossroads.* Washington: US Department of Commerce (August).

US Department of Commerce, International Trade Administration. 1986. *A Competitive Assessment of the U.S. Central Office Digital Switch Industry.* Washington: US Department of Commerce (September).

US Department of Commerce, International Trade Administration. 1990. *The Competitive Status of the U.S. Electronics Sector: From Materials to Systems.* Washington: US Department of Commerce (April).

US Department of Commerce, International Trade Administration. 1991. *U.S. Industrial Outlook, 1991.* Washington: US Department of Commerce (January).

Table 5.76.1 Telecommunications and sound-reproducing equipment: product composition of world trade, 1981–89
(billions of dollars except where noted)

SITC Product	1981	1982	1983	1984	1985	1986	1987	1988	1989	Annual growth 1981–89 (percentages)
World exports to world	38.9	37.9	40.2	46.0	48.4	58.8	68.6	81.9	86.1	10.4
of which										
761 Televisions	5.3	4.3	4.4	5.3	5.9	6.2	7.1	11.4	12.7	11.4
762 Radios and stereos	6.2	4.5	4.6	5.5	5.3	6.2	7.1	10.4	10.4	6.7
763 Phonographs, recorders	7.7	8.3	8.4	10.4	10.7	13.0	12.4	15.0	14.9	8.6
764 Telecommmunications and other	19.7	19.1	20.5	22.1	23.8	29.6	36.7	45.1	48.5	11.9
										Change 1981–89
Memorandum: SITC 76 share of world manufactures exports (percentages)	3.8	3.9	4.1	4.3	4.3	4.3	4.2	4.1	4.1	0.2

Source: World Manufactures Trade Data Base.

Table 5.76.2 Telecommunications and sound-reproducing equipment: geographic distribution of world trade, 1981–89
(percentages of total)

Country	1981	1982	1983	1984	1985	1986	1987	1988	1989	Change 1981–89
Share of exports to world										
United States	9.9	10.1	9.4	8.5	8.6	7.5	7.4	8.0	8.9	−1.0
Canada	2.4	2.7	2.9	3.4	3.1	2.3	2.0	1.5	1.6	−0.8
Japan	41.3	37.4	40.6	44.2	44.3	42.3	36.7	34.4	31.8	−9.5
European Community	25.5	25.2	22.9	20.0	20.8	23.5	24.8	21.6	21.9	−3.6
EC to non-EC	13.4	13.6	12.0	10.6	11.1	11.2	11.5	9.9	9.7	−3.6
Germany	8.8	8.9	7.8	6.8	7.2	8.5	9.0	7.4	7.2	−1.6
France	3.0	3.2	3.4	3.0	3.3	3.2	3.6	3.1	3.4	0.3
Italy	1.9	2.2	2.1	2.0	2.0	2.2	2.0	1.7	1.7	−0.2
United Kingdom	4.1	4.1	3.7	3.3	3.5	3.5	3.8	3.8	4.2	0.1
Other Western Europe	5.8	6.2	5.5	4.8	5.3	5.6	5.8	5.8	5.8	0.0
Asian NICs[a]	11.7	12.0	14.0	14.3	12.6	13.7	17.3	21.1	20.1	8.4
Eastern Europe[b]	0.2	0.2	0.2	0.1	0.2	0.2	0.2	0.2	0.2	−0.0
Developing countries	3.2	3.6	4.5	4.6	4.9	4.9	5.7	6.9	8.7	5.5
Latin America	2.4	2.6	3.3	3.4	3.5	3.4	3.4	3.7	3.5	1.1
Rest of world	0.1	2.7	0.1	0.1	0.2	0.1	0.1	0.8	1.0	0.9
Share of imports from world										
United States	24.1	25.0	29.7	36.9	38.5	35.6	30.7	27.5	27.1	3.0
Canada	3.9	3.5	4.2	4.8	4.1	3.8	3.3	3.3	3.6	−0.2
Japan	1.2	1.2	1.2	1.2	1.1	1.3	1.7	2.3	3.0	1.8
European Community	31.1	31.2	28.6	23.7	23.0	28.2	32.5	32.7	32.7	1.7
EC from non-EC	19.7	20.1	18.0	14.6	14.2	16.8	20.1	20.8	20.4	0.8
Germany	7.4	7.3	7.3	6.3	5.8	7.0	8.2	7.9	7.9	0.5
France	4.7	4.8	3.7	3.1	2.9	3.9	4.5	4.7	4.6	−0.1
Italy	3.4	3.4	2.7	2.6	2.7	3.2	3.9	4.0	3.9	0.5
United Kingdom	6.8	7.5	7.4	5.6	5.5	5.9	6.6	6.9	6.9	0.1
Other Western Europe	6.3	6.2	5.5	5.1	5.8	6.8	7.3	7.0	6.8	0.5
Asian NICs[a]	6.1	6.5	6.6	6.5	5.3	5.7	6.6	8.9	8.7	2.6
Eastern Europe[b]	0.5	0.5	0.5	0.5	0.5	0.6	0.8	0.9	1.0	0.5
Developing countries	25.4	24.4	22.1	19.5	20.0	16.3	15.6	14.5	13.9	−11.4
Latin America	7.7	6.2	4.4	4.4	4.6	5.0	5.0	5.1	5.1	−2.6
Rest of world	0.0	0.0	0.0	0.0	0.0	0.0	0.0	1.6	1.7	1.7

Export share minus import share

United States	-14.2	-14.9	-20.3	-28.3	-29.9	-28.1	-23.3	-19.6	-18.3	-4.0
Canada	-1.5	-0.9	-1.4	-1.4	-1.0	-1.6	-1.3	-1.8	-2.0	-0.6
Japan	40.1	36.2	39.4	43.0	43.3	41.0	34.9	32.1	28.8	-11.3
European Community	-5.6	-6.0	-5.7	-3.7	-2.1	-4.7	-7.7	-11.1	-10.8	-5.2
Non-EC	-6.3	-6.6	-5.9	-4.0	-3.1	-5.7	-8.6	-10.9	-10.7	-4.4
Germany	1.4	1.6	0.5	0.5	1.4	1.5	0.8	-0.5	-0.7	-2.1
France	-1.6	-1.5	-0.3	-0.1	0.4	-0.6	-0.9	-1.5	-1.2	0.4
Italy	-1.5	-1.1	-0.7	-0.6	-0.7	-1.1	-1.9	-2.3	-2.2	-0.7
United Kingdom	-2.7	-3.4	-3.7	-2.3	-2.1	-2.4	-2.9	-3.1	-2.7	0.0
Other Western Europe	-0.6	0.0	0.1	-0.3	-0.5	-1.2	-1.5	-1.3	-1.0	-0.4
Asian NICs[a]	5.7	5.5	7.4	7.8	7.3	8.0	10.7	12.2	11.4	5.7
Eastern Europe[b]	-0.4	-0.3	-0.4	-0.3	-0.4	-0.5	-0.6	-0.7	-0.8	-0.5
Developing countries	-22.1	-20.8	-17.6	-14.9	-15.1	-11.5	-9.9	-7.6	-5.2	16.9
Latin America	-5.3	-3.6	-1.1	-1.0	-1.2	-1.7	-1.7	-1.4	-1.7	3.7
Rest of world	0.0	2.6	0.1	0.1	0.1	0.1	0.1	-0.8	-0.7	-0.7

a. Hong Kong, Korea, Singapore, and Taiwan.

b. Including Soviet Union.

Source: World Manufactures Trade Data Base.

Table 5.76.3 Telecommunications and sound-reproducing equipment: bilateral trade flows, 1989 (billions of dollars)

					Exporter						
Importer	World	United States	Canada	Japan	European Community	Germany	France	United Kingdom	Asian NICs	Latin America	Other
World	86.1	7.6	1.4	27.4	18.8	6.2	2.9	3.6	17.3	3.0	10.6
United States	24.2		0.9	9.9	0.9	0.2	0.2	0.3	7.0	2.7	2.8
Canada	2.5	0.8		0.8	0.1	0.0	0.0	0.0	0.6	0.1	0.2
Japan	2.8	0.8	0.0		0.1	0.0	0.0	0.0	1.6	0.0	0.3
European Community	28.3	1.7	0.1	7.2	10.5	3.8	1.5	1.7	3.9	0.2	4.8
Germany	6.6	0.3	0.0	2.3	1.9		0.6	0.5	1.0	0.0	1.1
France	3.8	0.1	0.0	0.8	1.8	0.9		0.3	0.5	0.0	0.6
United Kingdom	6.1	0.7	0.1	1.6	1.1	0.5	0.2		1.0	0.1	1.5
Asian NICs	6.6	0.9	0.0	3.9	0.4	0.1	0.0	0.1	1.1	0.0	0.2
Latin America	4.5	1.9	0.1	0.8	0.6	0.2	0.2	0.1	0.8		0.2
Other	17.1	1.5	0.2	4.7	6.3	2.0	1.0	1.3	2.2	0.0	2.1

Source: World Manufactures Trade Data Base.

Table 5.76.4 Telecommunications and sound-reproducing equipment: product composition of US trade, 1981–90[a] (millions of dollars except where noted)

Category	SITC Rev. 2 1981	SITC Rev. 2 1987	Change 1981–87	SITC Rev. 3 1987	SITC Rev. 3 1990	Change 1981–90	Change 1987–90
Exports	3,841	5,067	1,226	5,085	9,188	5,347	4,103
Imports	8,948	20,821	11,873	20,798	22,520	13,572	1,722
Balance	−5,107	−15,754	−10,647	−15,713	−13,333	−8,226	2,380
of which							
761 TVs							
Exports	394	253	−141	259	487	93	228
Imports	851	1,715	864	5,047	2,257	1,406	−2,790
Balance	−457	−1,462	−1,005	−4,788	−1,770	−1,313	3,018
76381 Video recorders (VCRs)							
Exports	91	95	4	100	329	238	229
Imports	1,072	3,228	2,156	448	3,754	2,682	3,306
Balance	−981	−3,133	−2,152	−348	−3,425	−2,444	−3,077
762 Radios and radio-cassette recorders							
Exports	117	157	40	157	411	294	254
Imports	1,683	4,310	2,627	5,034	4,684	3,001	−350
Balance	−1,566	−4,153	−2,587	−4,877	−4,273	−2,707	604
763 Recorders, phonographs, etc.							
Exports	300	248	−52	225	402	102	177
Imports	2,090	5,459	3,369	1,944	3,986	1,896	2,042
Balance	−1,790	−5,211	−3,421	−1,719	−3,584	−1,794	−1,865
764 Telecommunications equipment							
Exports	3,030	4,409	1,379	4,444	7,887	4,857	3,443
Imports	4,324	9,337	5,013	8,773	11,594	7,270	2,821
Balance	−1,294	−4,928	−3,634	−4,329	−3,706	−2,412	623

a. Data are expressed on a domestic exports, imports customs basis.

Source: US Department of Commerce.

Table 5.76.5 Telecommunications and sound-reproducing equipment: geographic composition of US trade, 1981–90

	Millions of dollars 1981	Millions of dollars 1987	Millions of dollars 1989	Millions of dollars 1990	Percentages of total 1981	Percentages of total 1987	Percentages of total 1989	Percentages of total 1990
Exports								
Canada	444	629	803	1,361	11.6	12.4	10.5	14.9
Japan	182	409	848	907	4.7	8.0	11.1	10.0
European Community	930	979	1,725	2,094	24.2	19.3	22.5	23.0
United Kingdom	272	384	745	709	7.1	7.6	9.7	7.8
Mexico	461	642	1,161	1,380	12.0	12.6	15.1	15.1
Asian NICs	407	621	892	1,186	10.6	12.2	11.6	13.0
Other	1,417	1,805	2,240	2,186	36.9	35.5	29.2	24.0
Total	3,841	5,085	7,669	9,114	100.0	100.0	100.0	100.0
Imports								
Canada	382	687	950	973	4.3	3.3	4.1	4.4
Japan	4,785	10,588	10,056	9,390	53.5	50.9	43.4	42.1
European Community	260	584	707	687	2.9	2.8	3.0	3.1
Germany	61	149	165	141	0.7	0.7	0.7	0.6
Mexico	800	1,737	2,669	2,776	8.9	8.4	11.5	12.5
Asian NICs	2,478	5,935	6,069	4,925	27.7	28.5	26.2	22.1
Hong Kong	292	693	653	496	3.3	3.3	2.8	2.2
South Korea	548	2,026	2,220	1,708	6.1	9.7	9.6	7.7
Singapore	459	852	1,258	1,271	5.1	4.1	5.4	5.7
Taiwan	1,178	2,363	1,938	1,451	13.2	11.4	8.4	6.5
Malaysia	73	372	893	1,230	0.8	1.8	3.9	5.5
Other	169	894	1,838	2,307	1.9	4.3	7.9	10.4
Total	8,947	20,797	23,182	22,288	100.0	100.0	100.0	100.0

a. Data are expressed on a domestic exports, imports customs basis.

Source: US Department of Commerce.

Table 5.76.6 Telecommunications and sound-reproducing equipment: indices of US competitiveness, 1981–89
(billions of dollars except where noted)

	1981	1982	1983	1984	1985	1986	1987	1988	1989	Annual growth 1981–89 (percentages)
World trade										
World exports to non-US destinations	29.4	28.9	28.0	28.6	30.7	38.3	47.7	58.8	61.9	9.8
World imports from non-US sources	33.9	33.1	35.2	40.4	45.3	54.6	63.7	75.7	79.0	11.2
US trade										
Exports	3.8	3.8	3.8	3.9	4.1	4.4	5.1	6.5	7.6	9.1
Imports	9.2	9.3	11.6	16.4	19.1	21.2	21.3	22.7	23.5	12.4
Balance	-5.4	-5.5	-7.8	-12.5	-15.0	-16.8	-16.2	-16.2	-15.8	
										Change 1981–89
US share of exports to non-US destinations (percentages)	13.1	13.3	13.5	13.7	13.5	11.5	10.6	11.1	12.4	-0.7
US share of imports from non-US sources (percentages)	27.1	28.1	33.0	40.7	42.2	38.7	33.4	30.0	29.7	2.6
Export share minus import share (percentages)	-14.0	-14.8	-19.5	-27.0	-28.7	-27.2	-22.8	-18.9	-17.3	-3.3

Source: World Manufactures Trade Data Base.

Table 5.76.7 US-owned companies' share of world consumer electronics and telecommunications equipment markets, 1985 and 1988

Product	Percent of total 1985	Percent of total 1988	World market, 1987 (billions of dollars)
Consumer electronics	19	12	37.2
Telecommunications equipment			88.0
Central office switching	25	20	4.8
Fiber optics	75	50	3.0
PBXs	38	35	7.8
Data PBXs	71	62	0.2
Facsimile	0	0	3.1
Key telephone systems	35	30	5.7
Voice mail systems	98	96	0.6
Local area networks	99	100	2.4
Data modems	66	52	3.2
Statistical multiplexors	73	69	0.5

PBXs = private branch exchanges.

Source: US Department of Commerce, International Trade Administration and National Communications Information Administration 1990, as corrected.

Electrical Machinery and Parts (SITC 77)

This category contains a potpourri of heavy electrical equipment, electromedical equipment, home appliances, electronic parts, and electrical goods not elsewhere specified. It is one of the larger categories, accounting for about 9 percent of US manufactures trade.

The US balance of trade in this category fell from a $2.0 billion surplus in 1981 to a $5.4 billion deficit in 1990. Exports improved significantly in 1990 and should continue to do so in 1991. Export growth will nonetheless be slowed by the nationally oriented procurement practices of foreign utility companies, differing national technical standards, and increasing foreign competition in electromedical equipment, appliances, and electronic parts.

Description of the Product Group

Electrical machinery and parts consists of:

SITC

771 electric power machinery (other than the rotating electric plant of heading 716) and parts thereof, not elsewhere specified

772 electrical apparatus for making and breaking electrical circuits, for the protection of electrical circuits, or for making connections to or in electrical circuits, resistors, printed circuits, switchboards other than telephone switchboards, and control panels, not elsewhere specified

773 equipment for distributing electricity

774 electrical apparatus for medical purposes and radiological apparatus

775 household types of electrical and nonelectrical equipment, not elsewhere specified

776 thermionic, cold cathode and photocathode valves and tubes, including TV picture tubes, diodes, transistors, and similar semiconductor devices, and electronic microcircuits

778 electrical machinery and apparatus, not elsewhere specified, including batteries, lamps, hand tools with electric motors, and capacitors.

This category includes a wide range of electrical products with disparate characteristics, uses, and industry structures. Therefore, we discuss the three-digit subcategories separately under "Outlook" rather than as a group under "Key Determinants of World Trade Patterns," as in other sections of this chapter.

Many electrical products are not classified within this product group. Electric power-generating equipment and electric motors are recorded under SITC 716 but are discussed in this section because they are often made by the same companies, sold to the same customers, and subject to the same economic influences. Office machines and computers are classified in SITC 75, and telecommunications and sound-reproducing equipment in SITC 76. SITC 776 does not record all electronic parts; for instance, some computer parts are classified under SITC 759.

Role in World Trade

Size and Composition

World exports of electrical machinery and parts were $161.3 billion in 1989 (table 5.77.1). This was equivalent to 7.6 percent of world manufactures exports in 1989, up from 5.8 percent in 1981. Growth of world exports in this product group averaged 13.5 percent per year during this period, significantly higher than the 9.6 percent average for manufactures exports as a whole.

Global Competition Patterns

The largest subcategories within electrical equipment in 1989 were electronic parts and electrical switchgear. World exports of electronic parts grew most rapidly, at a rate of 20.4 percent per year, enlarging this subcategory to one-third of the total product group by 1989. This growth occurred as electronics production was globalized and Asian producers increased assembly operations in other countries.

Exports are dominated by Japan, the United States, Germany, and the Asian NICs, in that order (table 5.77.2). The European Community is listed as a large exporter, but three-fifths of EC exports remain within the Community (table 5.77.3). Japan's surplus in these products in 1989 was $26.1 billion; Germany's was $9.0 billion. The US and EC export-minus-import share balances in electrical equipment fell by 5.6 and 6.8 percentage points, respectively, from 1981 to 1989, as the share balances of developing countries (excluding the NICs) increased by 13.2 percentage points (table 5.77.2). This improvement in the share balances of the developing countries occurred almost entirely through reduced imports, as slow growth and indebtedness caused their purchasing power to collapse. The export share of the NICs rose by 7.0 percentage points, but their imports rose by even more.

Role in US Trade

Recent Performance

This product group accounts for 9.5 percent of 1990 US manufactures exports and 8.6 percent of imports. The overall deterioration from 1981 to 1990 was spread relatively evenly across the three-digit product subcategories. The US trade balance in these goods deteriorated from a $2.0 billion surplus in 1981 to a $8.5 billion deficit in 1987 (table 5.77.4). The deficit then narrowed to $5.4 billion in 1990. Generators and motors (SITC 716), like SITC 77, also did not completely recover from the large deterioration of 1981–87.

Major US export destinations in 1990 included Canada, the European Community, the NICs, and Mexico (table 5.77.5). The shares of US exports going to Canada and the NICs grew over the decade, while the share going to developing countries outside of Latin America fell sharply. The major sources for US imports were Japan, the European Community, the Asian NICs, and Mexico.

International Competitiveness

The US share of world exports to non US destinations fell slightly over the 1981–89 period from 19.2 percent to 18.6 percent (table 5.77.6). The US share of world imports from non-US sources grew quickly during the 1980s from 19.2 percent in 1981, reaching a peak of 30.2 percent in 1984 before declining to 24.0 percent in 1989. The US export-minus-import share balance deteriorated from 0.0 percent to −5.4 percent over the same period, mostly because of the increase in the import share.

Outlook

Key Determinants of US Trade Performance

The trade determinants for various three-digit categories are discussed below.

Heavy Electrical Equipment (SITC 771, 772, and 773 and parts of 71)

The trade balance in each of these subcategories fell by over a billion dollars during 1981–87, and improvement through 1990 did not offset this deterioration (table 5.77.4). Movements in the dollar appear to have caused much of these fluctuations, but clearly other factors were at work.

Because of its high levels of energy consumption, the United States is the world's largest consumer of equipment for generating, transmitting, and distributing electricity; historically it has also been one of the largest producers of this equipment. Heavy electrical equipment is purchased primarily by electric utilities, and to a lesser degree by heavy industries and other independent power sources. Demand for generators is in turn determined by the demand for electricity and the reserve capacity of utilities; demand for transmission and distribution equipment depends on the amount of new construction and replacement needs. Demand for both is relatively price inelastic.

US shipments of generators (SITC 716) have been growing slowly over the last six or seven years as utilities have worked off the large reserve capacity margins that resulted from overly optimistic projections of energy demand. Purchases of transmission and distribution equipment have grown more quickly to allow the utilities to buy electricity from each other and from independent power sources. In both areas, however, substantial excess capacity in particular product lines resulted from earlier energy demand projections that proved too high.

Utilities in Europe and Japan rarely buy from US or other foreign sources because of national procurement preferences, differing national technical standards, and other nontariff barriers. Other things being equal, US buyers—even though privately owned—also prefer domestic producers because postpurchase service is important. However, this preference is less pronounced in the United States than in most competitor countries. To the extent that foreign barriers to electrical equipment trade are greater than US barriers, foreign manufacturers may be able to cover the high fixed costs of producing heavy electrical equipment by charging high prices at home while tapping export markets and charging lower prices abroad, thereby increasing their total volume of production.

Long-term relationships are common between developed-country suppliers and developing-country buyers, in response to buyer needs for long-term finance, engineering assistance, and compatibility with existing systems. As a result, competition among developed-country suppliers for new customers is fierce, and lost market share is hard to regain. Export finance plays an important role; the US industry would like to see more competitive loans from the US Export-Import Bank and faster responses to counteroffers from foreign export banks (US Department of Commerce 1986, 60). Many developing countries use European standards because of their earlier colonial ties to European countries.

Even under the most open trade policies, the inertia of old standards and established buyer-seller relationships would restrict the potential for increased US exports of particular products.

There are allegations that the International Electrical Association (IEA) acts as a cartel to hold up prices for electrical equipment, particularly in sales to developing countries (US Congress, House Committee on Interstate and Foreign Commerce 1980). US companies cannot join the IEA because of a 1947 antitrust consent decree; thus, foreign companies can allegedly earn excess profits when a US company does not bid but charge low prices when one does. The US industry contends that this practice allows foreign suppliers to charge high prices at home to subsidize lower prices in other markets—a significant advantage in an industry where the fixed costs of production are very large. Although these allegations have not been verified, bid-rigging has a long history in the electrical industry. One US industry official expressed the hope that increased competition as a result of EC 1992 would undermine the IEA's ability to act as a cartel.

Because of substantial world excess capacity in many product lines, further restructuring of the industry in the United States and abroad is probable. In some products, either the United States or Europe alone could satisfy total world demand. General Electric Co. sold its transformer business to Westinghouse in 1987, and Westinghouse in turn sold its US operations to a Swiss company, ASEA Brown Boveri Ltd., which is now the dominant producer in the United States. Although foreign ownership is common in the industry, production is not globalized: all steps of production usually take place in one plant.

Fiber optics have a small but growing share of total trade in wiring and cabling systems (SITC 773). The United States is competitive in fiber optics, but now that Japan has completed its backbone network, Japanese producers will look more to foreign markets. Increasing competition is also coming from Europe, and world capacity exceeds demand. The United States has nearly completed its longer-distance networks, but growing demand will come from local telecommunications and computer networks. If implemented, a proposal to build a national high-speed data network in the United States would greatly increase US demand for fiber optics.

According to the US Department of Commerce, US manufacturers of electric motors (SITC 716) have substantial excess capacity, in part because of the decline of the US machine tool, farm, and construction machinery industries, and increased imports of products that contain motors (US Department of Commerce 1988a, xi). As a result, some rationalization of excess capacity is most likely. Different technical standards abroad limit the ability of US producers to achieve the economies of scale necessary to produce profitably for export over the long term. EC 1992 could reduce some of these problems if it implements new common standards.

Electromedical and Radiological Apparatus (SITC 774)

The US trade balance in this subcategory deteriorated from $0.6 billion in 1981 to $0.1 billion in 1987 and improved by a similar amount through 1990 (table 5.77.4).[1] The US electromedical equipment industry is highly export oriented and has originated most important recent innovations in this area, such as magnetic resonance imaging (see, e.g., Health Industry Manufacturers Association, in press). However, foreign competition has intensified, particularly from Japan, Germany, the Netherlands, and the United Kingdom. Japanese manufacturers have more experience in making lower-cost, lower-performance equipment; the Japanese government has historically reimbursed the medical expense of using this equipment at a lower rate, providing an incentive to use less-sophisticated equipment. However, the US industry is already developing more lower-priced equipment in response to US cost containment. Foreign technical standards and government procurement policies as well as US export controls can impede US exports.

The industry is highly regulated and is affected by government policies ranging from nuclear safety to health expense reimbursement. US demand for electromedical and radiological apparatus has been constrained by efforts of the government and insurance companies to contain health care costs. For instance, according to the US Commerce Department, less expensive low- and midfield magnetic resonance imaging equipment is being used more widely, and many health insurers do not reimburse for the more expensive positron emission tomography (US Department of Commerce 1990b, 51–57). The effects of cost containment are partly offset by the increasing demand for medical care of an aging US population, and by the desire of hospitals to avoid malpractice suits and to sell themselves as providing the best possible health care.

Appliances (SITC 775)

The US appliances trade deficit enlarged from $0.1 billion in 1981 to $0.9 billion in 1990 (table 5.77.4). Demand for these consumer durables, which include refrigerators and washers, is closely tied to consumer confidence, since their purchase can usually be delayed. Over time, the increasing number of women in the US work force has greatly expanded demand for labor-saving devices with easy maintenance. Exports of large appliances to European markets face significant nontariff barriers in the form of safety testing and other red tape, and

---

1. The shift from Revision 2 to Revision 3 makes comparisons over time difficult; the United States had a surplus in 1987 according to Revision 2 and a deficit in Revision 3.

exports to Japan confront complex electrical standards and other kinds of protection. Although not all of these policies explicitly discriminate against foreign products, they can greatly reduce economies of scale for foreign suppliers by shortening production runs.

Electronic Parts (SITC 776)

The US balance in electronic parts deteriorated over the 1980s as Asian parts suppliers became more competitive, and the deficit widened to $1.6 billion in 1990 (table 5.77.4). In addition, Asian suppliers have been accused of selling semiconductor chips below cost; these accusations led to the US-Japan Semiconductor Trade Agreement in 1986. Asian electronics companies with US-based assembly operations have also shown a tendency to import parts and components into the United States.

A study for the American Electronics Association indicated that, in 1988, 24 percent of US consumption of memory chips (by all companies) were imported from Japan and another 5 percent were made by Japanese companies in the United States (Quick, Finan & Associates 1989). This pattern does not hold for all parts: Japanese companies primarily use their US factories to make electron (TV) tubes for the US market. Also US producers remain strong in making certain kinds of semiconductors, despite lost ground in some products like DRAM memory chips.

The market share of US semiconductor companies improved in 1990 after many years of decline, according to Dataquest, a market research company (Skapinker 1991). The National Advisory Committee on Semiconductors attributes the decline to the high cost of US capital, weakness in the education of the work force, difficulties in enforcing US intellectual property rights abroad, the ability of foreign competitors to benefit from their home countries' closed markets and liberal antitrust laws, and the movement of consumer electronics production to other countries (National Advisory Committee on Semiconductors 1989, 17).

The EC 1992 project will not directly affect trade in electronic parts, but some US exporters are concerned that antidumping levies, local-content requirements, and stricter rules of origin will raise the effective level of protection and force companies to invest in the European Community instead of exporting from the United States. According to the *Panorama of EC Industry 1990,* "the new EC regulation requiring that semiconductors be 'diffused' in Europe in order to satisfy local origin requirements has also led to the establishment of new production facilities in Europe by foreign producers as they seek to take advantage of the growing European market for electronics" (Commission of the European Communities 1990, 12–13).

Electrical Machinery and Apparatus, Not Elsewhere Specified (SITC 778)

This category includes batteries, lamps, hand tools with motors, and capacitors. US trade performance deteriorated considerably over the 1980s but improved thereafter to a 1990 deficit of $1.1 billion (table 5.77.4). The international markets for most of these products are very competitive. Because the products are commodity-like, the trade balance has responded quite readily to changes in the value of the dollar. Competition from producers of low-priced hand tools in developing countries has increased. Foreign-owned companies have, however, been increasing their US-based production of hand tools, particularly of low-end products, according to the US Commerce Department (1990a, 21–27).

Near-Term Outlook

The variety of products in this category makes any group forecast tenuous. Taken together, however, an overall improvement in the trade balance of up to $3 billion by 1993 is possible. That would improve the performance of the product group significantly but not by enough to eliminate the $5.4 billion 1990 deficit.

Industry representatives are optimistic about the industry's prospects, and strong export growth is likely in some sectors. However, of the $3.1 billion 1987–90 improvement, over half ($1.7 billion) was in electrical machinery not elsewhere specified (table 5.77.4). The gain resulted from strong export growth and a stagnation of imports. However, imports of hand tools, which are included in this subcategory, are likely to begin to grow again with a recovery of the economy. Also, performance in the largest component in the electrical machinery group—tubes, transistors, and semiconductor devices—actually worsened marginally from 1987 to 1990.

For the product group as a whole, first-half 1991 exports were up 8.2 percent over the first half of 1990, whereas imports were up only 3.5 percent. At these rates, a 1991 improvement of about $1 billion seems in prospect. However, the low import growth rate is probably very much related to the US recession, and export growth rates in this product group have been fading.

Given current trends and conditions and the strong competition from Japan and the Asian NICs, it will be difficult to sustain the $1 billion improvement that is likely for 1991 into the following years. A $3 billion improvement by 1993 is certainly possible, but the gain is likely to be less if US economic growth picks up.

Heavy Electrical Equipment (SITCs 771 to 773)

The electrical industry is optimistic about exports in this subcategory in the near future, particularly given the strong 1990 performance. The privatization of the British electrical system should open up markets for US exports. Already, a non-British company, Siemens, has for the first time won a contract in the United Kingdom to supply power generation equipment. A strong government procurement code resulting from the Uruguay Round could also open up markets for US exports.

On the import side, high oil prices, energy conservation, and slow residential and nonresidential construction will all tend to reduce US demand for heavy electrical equipment. The North American Electric Reliability Council (1990, 6) projects growth in electricity demand at 2 percent annually over the next decade. However, the demand for transmission systems will increase more quickly as electric utilities increase their reliance on "remote generation sources, capacity purchases and sales, and economy energy transfers," according to the US Commerce Department (1990a, 24-2).

There is substantial world overcapacity in some products, such as large transformers, because of overoptimistic projections of energy demand in the past and high costs of exiting from the industry. The US industry may be at a disadvantage relative to European producers when the shakeout comes: exit costs are higher there; European governments are more likely to prevent plant closures; and demand from Eastern Europe, if it can be financed, could sustain European producers through the shakeout.

Even though national standards differ, the technologies employed throughout the world are similar. The United States has an advantage in producing amorphous metals for transformers, which significantly lower operating costs; difficulty selling into the Japanese market led the US government to extract promises that the Japanese government would no longer target this technology. However, since Japanese utilities rarely buy US transformers, only the amorphous metal would be exported from the United States, so the dollar effects on exports would be small. The development of high-temperature superconductors could dramatically improve the energy efficiency of electrical equipment. The strong US position in superconductor research may pay off if researchers can solve the difficult problems of commercializing the technology.

Trade in electrical machinery is particularly unresponsive to changes in import prices, according to elasticities supplied by DRI (see the appendix to this volume). The trade balance in these products is much more responsive to consumption and investment growth, so faster growth abroad should help reduce US trade deficits in this area.

Electromedical Equipment (SITC 774)

According to a US Commerce Department study (1988b, xvi), US manufacturers no longer have a technological advantage over their foreign competitors, but they do have a small advantage in other areas such as financing, service, and maintenance. Japanese companies are most likely to have an increasing presence in international markets, on the basis of their increasing numbers of Food and Drug Administration approvals and patents in the United States, their experience in making lower-cost, lower-performance equipment, and their success in other electronics products.

German and Japanese companies are, however, expanding their US-based production capability in response to the lower dollar. Also, the National Electrical Manufacturers Association (1990b, 13) does not project much growth in US demand, and European and Japanese demand is growing more quickly.

Appliances (SITC 775)

US demand for appliances in 1991 is at its lowest level in years. The industry is at a low point in its replacement cycle, and weak consumer confidence continues to restrain demand. The appliance trade balance is particularly responsive to changes in import prices and growth in consumption. As a result, weak demand for imports and the dollar depreciation that occurred during 1989–90 should improve the appliances trade balance in the short term.

Electronic Parts (SITC 776)

A study for the American Electronics Association projected that the US-Japan trade balance in metal oxide semiconductor memories would deteriorate over the next five years (Quick, Finan & Associates 1989). The study also estimated that the share of Japanese imports in US consumption of electron tubes would increase from 9 percent to 24 percent from 1988 to 1993. Continued improvement in the US semiconductor market share would improve the balance, particularly since the Semiconductor Industry Association projects that world semiconductor sales will grow quickly in 1991 and 1992. The outlook for semiconductors also depends on what happens when the US-Japan trade agreement dealing with semiconductors expires in 1991. Renewal of the pact is likely to have the support of chip users, who are pleased with the likely elimination of the "fair market value" pricing system. However, the high investment levels of the Japanese semiconductor industry in the 1980s will make large improvements in the US trade balance difficult.

US import demand for parts and other electrical machinery is not very responsive to changes in import prices but is moderately responsive to growth in US consumption, according to elasticities supplied by DRI (see the appendix to this volume). Foreign import demand is also moderately responsive to growth in foreign consumption but is more responsive to changes in import prices.

Electrical Machinery and Apparatus, Not Elsewhere Specified (SITC 778)

Sluggish residential construction and resale markets will reduce demand by construction professionals and new homeowners for imports of power-driven hand tools. US producers have a small technological edge in batteries and hand tools, particularly as US-made rechargeable batteries and cordless tools become more popular.

Medium-Term Outlook

Competition will be keen in this product group, which represents a substantial part of world manufactures trade. US trade prospects are uncertain at best in the largest single subcategory—electronic parts, including tubes, transistors, and semiconductor devices—which accounts for about one-third of US trade in this category. There is little reason for optimism that whatever gains may be achieved by 1993 will expand in later years or even be sustained. The product group, however, is diverse, and any forecast is highly uncertain.

Conclusions

- The US trade balance in this product group deteriorated by $10.3 billion from 1981 to 1987, making it one of the largest losers among US manufacturing industries. However, the deficit narrowed by $3.1 billion from 1987 to 1990.

- US-based production remains competitive in heavy electrical equipment, electromedical equipment, and appliances.

- Prospects for improvement in electrical equipment exports are good, building on a strong 1990 performance.

- Improvement in exports will nonetheless be tempered by the nationally oriented procurement practices of foreign utilities, different technical standards in other countries, and increasing foreign competition in electromedical equipment, appliances, and electronic parts.

- Imports should increase in the subcategories of electrical transmission and distribution equipment, electronic parts, and electromedical equipment.

- An overall improvement of about $1 billion is likely in 1991 and, on optimistic assumptions, up to $3 billion by 1993. This would result in a 1993 deficit of about $2.5 billion, still about $4.5 billion short of the $2 billion surplus of 1981.

- In the longer term, intensifying competition is the only certainty. There is, however, little reason to anticipate continuing significant US gains in this product group.

Bibliography

"Chip Sales are Forecast." 1990. *New York Times* (27 September).

Commission of the European Communities. 1990. *Panorama of EC Industry, 1990.* Luxembourg: Commission of the European Communities.

Council on Competitiveness. 1990. *Sectoral Profile: Electronic Components and Equipment.* Washington: Council on Competitiveness (March).

Health Industry Manufacturers Association. 1991. *Competitiveness of the US Health Care Technology Industry.* Washington: Health Industry Manufacturers Association.

Industry, Science and Technology Canada. 1988. *Industry Profiles.* Ottawa: Industry, Science and Technology Canada.

Japan Electronics Almanac. 1990. Tokyo: DEMPA Publications.

Japan Electronic Journal. 1990. *Japan Economic Almanac, 1990.* Tokyo: Japan Economic Journal.

National Advisory Committee on Semiconductors. 1989. "A Strategic Industry at Risk." Arlington, VA: National Advisory Committee on Semiconductors (November).

National Electrical Manufacturers Association. 1990a. *Annual Report.* Washington: National Electrical Manufacturers Association. (November).

National Electrical Manufacturers Association. 1990b. *Facts and Figures 1990.* Washington: National Electrical Manufacturers Association.

North American Electric Reliability Council. 1990. *Electricity Supply and Demand for 1990–1999.* Princeton, NJ: North American Electric Reliability Council.

Office of Technology Assessment. 1984. *Federal Policies and the Medical Device Industry.* Washington: Office of Technology Assessment (October).

Quick, Finan & Associates. 1989. *Evaluation of U.S. and Japanese Market and Trade Data: Report to the American Electronics Association.* Washington: Quick, Finan & Associates (10 October).

"The Shrinking U.S. Electric Equipment Market." 1986. *IEEE Spectrum* (September): 63–65.

Skapinker, Michael. 1991. "Western Chipmakers Raise Market Share." *Financial Times* (3 January): 12.

US Congress, House, Committee on Interstate and Foreign Commerce. 1980. *The International Electrical Association: A Continuing Cartel.* Report prepared by Barbara Epstein and Richard Newfarmer. 96th Cong., 2nd sess.

US Department of Commerce, International Trade Administration. 1985. *A Competitive Assessment of the U.S. Electric Power Generating Equipment Industry.* Washington: Government Printing Office (October).

US Department of Commerce, International Trade Administration. 1986. *A Competitive Assessment of the U.S. Transformer Industry.* Washington: Government Printing Office (February).

US Department of Commerce, International Trade Administration. 1988a. *A Competitive Assessment of the U.S. Electric Motor Industry.* Washington: US Department of Commerce (August).

US Department of Commerce, International Trade Administration. 1988b. *A Competitive Assessment of the Medical Diagnostic Imaging Industry.* Washington: US Department of Commerce (November).

US Department of Commerce, International Trade Administration. 1990a. *U.S. Industrial Outlook, 1990.* Washington: Government Printing Office (January).

US Department of Commerce, International Trade Administration. 1990b. *A Competitive Assessment of the U.S. Electronics Sector.* Washington: US Department of Commerce (April).

US Department of Commerce, International Trade Administration. 1991. *U.S. Industrial Outlook, 1991.* Washington: Government Printing Office (January).

US Department of Energy, Energy Information Administration. 1990. *Annual Outlook for U.S. Electric Power 1990: Projections Through 2010.* Washington: US Department of Energy.

See also the following periodicals: for information on heavy electrical equipment, *Electrical World* and *IEEE Spectrum;* for information on electromedical equipment, *Medical Device and Diagnostic Industry, Health Industry Week,* and *Biomedical Business International;* for information on appliances, *Dealerscope Merchandising Magazine* and *HFD: The Weekly Home Furnishings Newspaper.*

Table 5.77.1 Electrical machinery and parts: product composition of world trade, 1981–89
(billions of dollars except where noted)

SITC Product	1981	1982	1983	1984	1985	1986	1987	1988	1989	Annual growth 1981–89 (percentages)
World exports to world	58.5	60.6	64.5	75.5	75.1	93.6	115.4	149.8	161.3	13.5
of which										
771 Transformers	3.5	3.4	3.4	3.6	3.8	4.7	5.7	7.8	8.5	11.7
772 Switchgear and parts	12.3	11.9	12.2	13.3	13.5	17.4	21.2	27.0	28.7	11.2
773 Electrical distribution machinery	5.4	5.1	5.1	5.0	5.6	6.5	7.7	10.6	12.2	10.7
774 Electromedical equipment	2.9	3.0	3.2	3.3	3.8	5.0	5.7	6.5	6.3	10.2
775 Household equipment	8.2	7.4	7.7	8.3	8.7	11.0	13.4	18.1	18.8	11.0
776 Electronic parts	12.5	13.9	16.6	22.8	20.6	24.1	31.4	49.7	55.1	20.4
778 Other	13.7	13.0	13.3	14.9	15.6	20.2	24.7	30.3	32.9	11.6
Memorandum:										Change 1981–89
SITC 77 share of world manufactures exports (percentages)	5.8	6.2	6.6	7.1	6.7	6.9	7.0	7.6	7.6	1.9

Source: World Manufactures Trade Data Base.

Table 5.77.2 Electrical machinery and parts: geographic distribution of world trade, 1981–89 (percentages of total)

Country	1981	1982	1983	1984	1985	1986	1987	1988	1989	Change 1981–89
Share of exports to world										
United States	16.2	18.3	18.3	18.1	16.4	14.5	14.2	14.2	14.8	–1.4
Canada	1.3	1.1	1.1	1.5	1.6	1.3	1.2	1.4	1.5	0.2
Japan	18.1	16.1	18.4	20.7	19.6	19.8	19.1	19.3	19.5	1.4
European Community	43.9	42.7	39.4	35.0	38.5	40.9	40.6	36.6	36.3	–7.6
EC to non-EC	22.1	21.3	19.3	16.8	18.1	18.2	17.3	15.8	15.5	–6.6
Germany	15.8	15.5	14.2	12.6	14.0	15.8	15.6	14.0	14.0	–1.8
France	7.7	7.2	6.8	6.0	6.4	6.6	6.5	5.7	5.4	–2.3
Italy	5.8	5.6	5.4	4.5	4.7	4.9	5.1	4.6	4.8	–1.1
United Kingdom	5.9	6.1	5.4	5.0	5.8	5.3	5.4	5.2	5.0	–0.9
Other Western Europe	7.3	7.2	6.8	5.7	6.4	7.2	7.3	6.6	5.7	–1.6
Asian NICs[a]	6.1	7.2	7.8	9.5	9.0	8.6	9.7	13.2	13.1	7.0
Eastern Europe[b]	0.5	0.5	0.4	0.4	0.4	0.5	0.5	0.5	0.4	–0.1
Developing countries	6.6	7.0	7.8	9.0	8.1	7.2	7.3	7.7	8.0	1.4
Latin America	2.4	2.3	2.8	3.2	3.3	3.0	3.0	2.9	3.1	0.8
Rest of world	0.1	0.1	0.2	0.3	0.3	0.3	0.4	1.1	1.0	0.9
Share of imports from world										
United States	15.6	16.6	19.3	23.9	23.1	21.3	20.9	20.2	19.7	4.1
Canada	3.8	3.4	4.0	4.3	4.1	3.6	3.4	4.3	4.6	0.8
Japan	3.0	2.9	3.1	3.4	3.1	2.9	3.1	3.3	3.8	0.7
European Community	34.6	33.2	31.9	30.4	32.5	35.2	36.3	33.7	33.7	–0.9
EC from non-EC	13.6	13.0	12.9	13.4	14.0	14.2	14.8	14.6	14.7	1.1
Germany	8.8	8.2	8.1	7.7	8.3	9.0	9.1	8.2	8.3	–0.6
France	6.4	6.2	5.6	5.1	5.5	6.1	6.5	5.9	5.7	–0.7
Italy	3.5	3.4	3.2	3.2	3.5	3.9	4.3	4.2	4.3	0.7
United Kingdom	5.8	6.1	6.4	6.5	6.9	6.6	6.9	6.6	6.4	0.6
Other Western Europe	8.3	7.8	7.4	6.7	7.9	8.5	8.5	7.5	7.1	–1.2
Asian NICs[a]	6.6	7.7	9.2	10.0	8.8	9.9	11.1	14.4	15.0	8.4
Eastern Europe[b]	1.8	1.5	1.5	1.1	1.2	1.2	1.1	1.1	1.0	–0.8
Developing countries	25.1	25.3	22.5	19.0	17.8	16.2	14.6	13.6	13.3	–11.8
Latin America	6.6	5.8	4.6	4.6	4.4	4.3	4.0	4.0	4.1	–2.5
Rest of world	0.0	0.0	0.0	0.0	0.1	0.1	0.1	1.1	1.1	1.0

Export share minus import share										
United States	0.6	1.7	−1.0	−5.7	−6.7	−6.8	−6.7	−5.9	−4.9	−5.6
Canada	−2.5	−2.3	−2.9	−2.9	−2.5	−2.3	−2.2	−2.9	−3.1	−0.6
Japan	15.1	13.1	15.3	17.3	16.5	16.9	16.0	16.0	15.8	0.7
European Community	9.4	9.5	7.5	4.7	6.0	5.7	4.2	2.9	2.6	−6.8
Non-EC	8.5	8.3	6.4	3.4	4.1	4.0	2.5	1.2	0.8	−7.7
Germany	7.0	7.3	6.2	4.9	5.7	6.7	6.5	5.9	5.7	−1.3
France	1.3	0.9	1.1	0.9	1.0	0.5	0.0	−0.3	−0.3	−1.6
Italy	2.3	2.1	−2.2	1.2	1.2	1.0	0.8	0.4	0.5	−1.8
United Kingdom	0.1	0.0	−1.0	−1.5	−1.1	−1.3	−1.5	−1.4	−1.4	−1.5
Other Western Europe	−1.0	−0.6	−0.5	−1.0	−1.6	−1.3	−1.2	−0.9	−1.3	−0.4
Asian NICs[a]	−0.5	−0.5	−1.4	−0.5	0.2	−1.3	−1.4	−1.2	−1.9	−1.4
Eastern Europe[b]	−1.3	−1.1	−1.1	−0.7	−0.8	−0.8	−0.6	−0.6	−0.6	0.7
Developing countries	−18.6	−18.4	−14.7	−10.0	−9.7	−9.0	−7.3	−5.9	−5.3	13.2
Latin America	−4.2	−3.5	−1.8	−1.4	−1.1	−1.3	−1.1	−1.1	−1.0	3.3
Rest of world	0.1	0.1	0.1	0.2	0.2	0.2	0.3	0.0	−0.1	−0.2

a. Hong Kong, Korea, Singapore, and Taiwan.

b. Including Soviet Union.

Source: World Manufactures Trade Data Base.

Table 5.77.3 Electrical machinery and parts: bilateral trade flows, 1989 (billions of dollars)

Importer	World	United States	Canada	Japan	European Community	Germany	France	United Kingdom	Asian NICs	Latin America	Other
					Exporter						
World	161.3	23.9	2.4	31.5	58.6	22.5	8.6	8.1	21.1	5.1	18.7
United States	32.4		2.0	9.1	4.0	1.8	0.5	1.0	7.8	4.7	4.7
Canada	5.6	3.8		0.3	0.4	0.2	0.1	0.1	0.5	0.2	0.5
Japan	5.4	1.9	0.0		0.8	0.4	0.1	0.2	2.2	0.0	0.5
European Community	56.6	4.9	0.1	5.3	33.6	12.0	5.2	4.2	3.7	0.2	8.9
Germany	13.5	1.1	0.0	1.9	6.2		1.3	1.3	1.1	0.0	3.0
France	9.8	0.7	0.0	0.5	6.6	2.7		0.8	0.5	0.0	1.4
United Kingdom	10.3	1.4	0.1	1.4	4.9	2.0	0.8		0.9	0.0	1.6
Asian NICs	22.0	4.3	0.1	10.2	2.2	0.8	0.3	0.5	4.5	0.0	0.8
Latin America	7.1	4.6	0.1	0.9	1.2	0.4	0.3	0.1	0.2		0.1
Other	32.2	4.5	0.1	5.7	16.4	7.0	2.1	2.1	2.2	0.0	3.1

Source: World Manufactures Trade Data Base.

Table 5.77.4 Electrical machinery and parts: product composition of US trade, 1981–90ᵃ (millions of dollars except where noted)

Category	SITC Rev. 2			SITC Rev. 3			
	1981	1987	Change 1981–87	1987	1990	Change 1981–90	Change 1987–90
SITC 77 Electrical machinery and parts							
Exports	11,287	16,408	5,121	15,265	28,216	16,929	12,951
Imports	9,300	24,678	15,378	23,747	33,601	24,301	9,854
Balance	1,987	-8,270	-10,257	-8,482	-5,385	-7,372	3,097
of which							
771 Transformers							
Exports	342	332	-10	451	1,058	716	607
Imports	480	1,662	1,182	1,640	1,654	1,174	14
Balance	-138	-1,330	-1,192	-1,189	-596	-458	593
772 Switchgear and parts							
Exports	2,025	2,735	710	2,765	5,515	3,490	2,750
Imports	1,294	3,456	2,162	3,456	5,949	4,655	2,493
Balance	731	-721	-1,452	-691	-435	-1,166	256
773 Electrical distribution machinery							
Exports	678	1,266	588	1,347	2,065	1,387	718
Imports	566	2,174	1,608	2,024	2,953	2,387	929
Balance	112	-908	-1,020	-677	-888	-1,000	-211
774 Electromedical and radiological apparatus							
Exports	984	1,519	535	807	1,818	834	1,011
Imports	385	1,414	1,029	1,120	1,728	1,343	608
Balance	599	105	-494	-313	89	-510	402
775 Household electrical and nonelectrical equipment							
Exports	835	741	-94	723	1,540	705	817
Imports	951	2,615	1,664	2,090	2,480	1,529	390
Balance	-116	-1,874	-1,758	-1,367	-940	-824	427
776 Tubes, transistors, semiconductor devices, etc.							
Exports	3,940	6,686	2,746	6,620	11,401	7,461	4,781
Imports	3,964	8,182	4,218	8,139	12,967	9,003	4,828
Balance	-24	-1,496	-1,472	-1,519	-1,566	-1,542	-47
778 Electrical machinery, n.e.s.							
Exports	2,483	3,130	647	2,552	4,820	2,337	2,268
Imports	1,660	5,175	3,515	5,277	5,869	4,209	592
Balance	823	-2,045	-2,868	-2,725	-1,050	-1,873	1,675
SITC 716 Rotating electrical plant of motors and generators							
Exports	1,443	904	-539	825	1,615	172	790
Imports	532	1,238	706	1,267	1,924	1,392	657
Balance	911	-334	-1,245	-442	-309	-1,220	133

a. Data are expressed on a domestic exports, imports customs basis.

Source: US Department of Commerce.

Table 5.77.5   Electrical machinery and parts: geographic composition of US trade, 1981–90

	Millions of dollars				Percentages of total			
	1981	1987	1989	1990	1981	1987	1989	1990
Exports								
Canada	1,616	2,435	3,752	6,428	14.3	16.0	14.8	22.8
Japan	590	1,031	1,925	2,058	5.2	6.8	7.6	7.3
European Community	2,417	2,941	4,865	5,357	21.4	19.3	19.1	19.0
United Kingdom	605	948	1,437	1,562	5.4	6.2	5.7	5.5
Germany	634	691	1,134	1,168	5.6	4.5	4.5	4.1
France	379	464	725	908	3.4	3.0	2.9	3.2
Italy	212	232	436	505	1.9	1.5	1.7	1.8
Latin America	2,081	2,797	4,560	4,688	18.4	18.3	17.9	16.6
Mexico	1,126	2,086	3,477	3,606	10.0	13.7	13.7	12.8
Asian NICs	1,411	2,694	4,297	4,863	12.5	17.6	16.9	17.2
Malaysia	757	1,210	1,414	1,544	6.7	7.9	5.6	5.5
Other	2,415	2,157	4,618	3,278	21.4	14.1	18.2	11.6
Total	11,287	15,265	25,431	28,216	100.0	100.0	100.0	100.0
Imports								
Canada	754	1,814	2,443	3,323	8.1	7.6	7.6	9.9
Japan	1,997	6,424	9,217	8,903	21.5	27.1	28.5	26.5
European Community	1,245	3,424	4,297	4,598	13.4	14.4	13.3	13.7
United Kingdom	239	690	844	937	2.6	2.9	2.6	2.8
Germany	475	1,429	1,882	2,024	5.1	6.0	5.8	6.0
France	174	501	573	603	1.9	2.1	1.8	1.8
Italy	98	202	266	298	1.1	0.9	0.8	0.9
Latin America	1,266	3,184	4,648	4,997	13.6	13.4	14.4	14.9
Mexico	1,006	2,810	4,202	4,574	10.8	11.8	13.0	13.6
Asian NICs	2,079	5,632	7,237	7,009	22.4	23.7	22.4	20.9
Malaysia	953	1,372	1,795	1,767	10.2	5.8	5.6	5.3
Other	1,006	1,897	2,701	3,004	10.8	8.0	8.4	8.9
Total	9,300	23,747	32,338	33,601	100.0	100.0	100.0	100.0

a. Data are expressed on a domestic exports, imports customs basis.

Source: US Department of Commerce.

Table 5.77.6 Electrical machinery and parts: indices of US competitiveness, 1981–89 (billions of dollars except where noted)

	1981	1982	1983	1984	1985	1986	1987	1988	1989	Annual growth 1981–89 (percentages)
World trade										
World exports to non-US destinations	49.3	50.7	52.2	57.6	58.5	74.7	92.6	120.6	128.9	12.8
World imports from non-US sources	49.5	49.9	53.2	62.8	64.3	82.0	101.6	132.3	140.3	13.9
US trade										
Exports	9.5	11.1	11.8	13.7	12.3	13.5	16.4	21.3	23.9	12.2
Imports	9.5	10.4	12.9	19.0	18.4	21.0	25.4	32.0	33.7	17.1
Balance	0.0	0.7	-1.1	-5.3	-6.1	-7.5	-9.0	-10.7	-9.8	
										Change 1981–89
US share of exports to non-US destinations (percentages)	19.2	21.9	22.6	23.8	21.0	18.1	17.7	17.7	18.6	-0.6
US share of imports from non-US sources (percentages)	19.2	20.9	24.3	30.2	28.6	25.6	25.0	24.2	24.0	4.8
Export share minus import share (percentages)	0.0	1.0	-1.7	-6.4	-7.6	-7.5	-7.3	-6.6	-5.4	-5.4

Source: World Manufactures Trade Data Base.

Road Vehicles (SITC 78) and Internal Combustion Engines (SITC 713)

Road vehicles make up by far the largest single manufactures product group in world trade, and this group has been by far the most important in the deterioration of US trade performance. The 1987 road vehicles deficit was $51.4 billion, over 1.1 percent of US GNP that year. The deficit narrowed to $42.9 billion by 1990 and was a major factor in the 1987–90 improvement in manufactures trade performance. Road vehicles will also play a critical role in US trade performance during the 1990s. Indeed, substantial further reduction of the road vehicles deficit will be essential if there is to be significant further improvement in the US current account and trade deficits.

Description of the Product Group

Road vehicles as identified in SITC 78 include:

SITC

781 passenger cars

782 motor vehicles for the transport of goods (trucks) and other special-purpose vehicles

783 road motor vehicles not elsewhere specified

784 parts and accessories of motor vehicles

785 motorcycles

786 trailers and semitrailers.

Passenger cars and trucks are often lumped together in one statistic, but it is useful to separate them for analytical purposes. Parts and accessories make up a subcategory of growing importance. Trade in internal combustion engines and engine parts (SITC 713) has become increasingly important as car and truck production and assembly have become more globalized. For these reasons, we include it in this section of the analysis rather than with the rest of SITC 71, power-generating machinery.

Role in World Trade

Size and Composition

At $263.3 billion (table 5.78.1), world exports of road vehicles to all destinations made this by far the largest single two-digit manufactures category in 1989. Road vehicles constituted 9.5 percent of total world 1989 goods exports, up from 7.6 percent in 1979. As a result of a 9.7 percent average annual growth from 1981 to 1987, slightly above the 9.6 percent rate for manufacturing as a whole, road vehicles were 12.5 percent of world 1989 manufactures exports, up from 12.4 percent in 1979. In 1986, however, when US imports were at their peak, road vehicles constituted 14.3 percent of world manufactures exports. World exports of road vehicles have grown primarily in passenger cars, which increased at a 12.2 percent annual rate from 1981 to 1989. In 1989, exports of passenger cars were 55 percent of total exports in this product group, and parts and accessories were 25 percent of the total.

The increasing importance and rapid growth of world trade in parts and accessories reflect the growth in shipments of parts and components from major automobile producers to foreign markets for assembly of finished vehicles. To a lesser extent, it is also due to the growing aftermarket for parts for finished vehicles previously exported.

World exports of trucks are relatively small ($33.4 billion in 1989, 12.7 percent of the SITC 78 total), and world truck exports have grown modestly, averaging only 5.0 percent per year over 1981–89. The remaining subcategories, motorcycles and trailers, have made only minor contributions to world trade and have had negligible growth since 1981.

World exports of internal combustion engines have also grown more rapidly than world exports generally. As with parts and accessories, this growth reflects the export of major components from the producer country to other countries in which automobiles are assembled for sale in those markets. Exports of engines to all world destinations grew from $14.9 billion in 1981 to $33.4 billion in 1989, for an average rate of 9.7 percent per year (table 5.78.1).

Given its large size relative to other categories, this product group is clearly important in determining overall US trade performance. For example, a 20 percent share of 1989 world exports of road vehicles would have generated $53 billion of exports; office machines and computers would have required a 48 percent share of world exports to generate the same dollar value in exports.

Thus, the United States might need very large market shares and surpluses in several other product groups to offset poor performance in road vehicles.

Global Competition Patterns

The United States long led the world in production and exports of motor vehicles. However, the rapid decline of its leadership is evident in its declining shares of world exports during the 1980s. In 1981, the United States had a 12.8 percent share of world road vehicle exports. By 1989, that share had declined to 9.7 percent (table 5.78.2). Japan's share rose from 19.3 percent in 1979 to 26.8 percent in 1981 and 27.8 percent in 1986 before declining to 25.4 percent in 1987 and 23.4 percent in 1989. Over the 1981–89 period, the EC share of world exports also fluctuated, declining from 46.2 percent in 1981 to a low of 38.8 percent in 1985 before recovering to 47.9 percent in 1989.

The shift in world trade patterns is shown even more dramatically in the geographic composition of world imports. In 1981, the United States absorbed 23.3 percent of world road vehicle exports. Its share rose to 37.6 percent in 1985, but then fell to 32.6 percent in 1987 and 28.2 percent in 1989.

Together, declining US export shares and increasing import shares reflect a marked change in world trade patterns. The US share balance (export share minus import share) indicates that US producers of road vehicles have lost much of their ability to compete in US and foreign markets. From 1981 to 1987, the US share balance declined from − 10.5 percentage points to − 23.3 percentage points, a 12.8-percentage-point loss. By 1989, the share balance deficit had improved to − 18.5 percentage points, still 8.0 percentage points below the 1981 level.

Share balance calculations show Japan and Germany as clear winners during the 1981–89 period. Japan, with positive share balances of 24.3 percentage points in 1987 and 21.5 percentage points in 1989, was the biggest winner, even though its 1981 balance, at 26.4 percentage points, was larger. Japan's performance is the result not only of its large export share but also of its trivial share of world road vehicle imports (1.9 percent in 1989).

At 15.4 percentage points in 1987, Germany's share balance was also strong, but it weakened to 14.6 percentage points in 1989. The import share of the developing countries declined markedly, from 25.9 percent in 1981 to 9.5 percent in 1987 and 9.6 percent in 1989. This reflected primarily a decreased ability to afford imports rather than greater domestic production capabilities.

Table 5.78.3 summarizes world trade flows of road vehicles and internal combustion engines in 1989. It highlights the major role of the United States as an importer and Japan's dependence on exports to the United States. Of Japan's $61.6 billion in road vehicle exports in 1989, $29.3 billion (47.6 percent) went to the United States. With $5.1 billion in imports, Japan had a $56.5 billion road vehicle surplus in that year. In contrast, Germany's $6.3 billion in exports to the United States was only 10.9 percent of its road vehicle exports in 1989, with $33.7 billion (58.4 percent) going to other EC countries. With imports of $18.6 billion, Germany had a $39.1 billion road vehicle surplus.

Japan is also the largest exporter of engines and engine parts (table 5.78.3). Its exports have been rising rapidly and reached $6.4 billion in 1989. This rise reflects not only growing sales of repair parts but also increasing overseas assembly operations, particularly in the United States.

Globalization of World Automobile Production

Many events led to the changes in trade patterns in this product group during the 1980s. World exports of automobiles and auto parts and assemblies rose rapidly because world automobile sales and production increased rapidly, the locations of both assembly and production of components became more diversified, and exports played a larger role in building a motor vehicle industry in some countries. Open US markets and huge US automobile trade deficits (table 5.78.4) provided much of the stimulus for these changes.

The United States led the world in road vehicle production for many years. Total Japan-based production first surpassed that of the United States in 1980 as US production declined markedly, mirroring the US recession that year. But although US production had recovered by 1984, it did not reach earlier levels and remained below that of Japan. In 1988, the United States produced 11.2 million cars and trucks; Japan produced 12.7 million units, just over one-fourth of total world production of 48.1 million and about 1.5 million more units than the United States. At 4.6 million units, Germany was third in world production, and France, at 3.7 million units, was fourth.

There are great differences, however, between US and Japanese uses of domestic production. Apparent consumption in the United States in 1988 was 15.6 million cars and trucks. US production was only 11.2 million; exports were 1 million (mostly to Canada), and imports were 5.4 million. In Japan, in contrast, production was 12.7 million units, but consumption was only 6.8 million. Exports were 6.1 million and imports only 200,000. Thus, US consumption was 139 percent of production; Japanese consumption was only 54 percent of total production.

The US market was important to Japan throughout the 1980s. In unit terms, however, Japan's exports to the United States peaked in 1986 at 3.4 million cars and trucks. The portion of total Japanese car and truck production exported to the United States peaked the same year at 28 percent, and by 1988 had declined to 20.9 percent. The countries producing motor vehicles exported more than 19 million units in 1988, with Japanese manufacturers accounting for slightly less than one-third of the total.

Deficits with Japan have dominated US trade performance in road vehicles for a long time. In 1981, the bilateral deficit with Japan was 138 percent of the total US deficit in road vehicles and engines; in 1989, the $31.1 billion deficit with Japan was 63 percent of the total in these categories, and 51 percent of US passenger car imports were from Japan. In 1990, the road vehicle deficit with Japan was $25.9 billion, still 60 percent of the total.

Germany is the world's second-largest car and truck exporter, with 2.7 million vehicles, 13.9 percent of the world total, in 1988. The US market has also played an important role in Germany's automobile sales. US imports of passenger cars from Germany reached 366,543 units and $9 billion in 1987, and imports of parts and accessories rose to $900 million. By 1989, however, US imports from Germany were down to 221,000 units, and the bilateral deficit was dramatically lower at $5.3 billion, although it increased modestly in 1990 to $5.7 billion (table 5.78.5). (World production data are from Motor Vehicle Manufacturers Association of the United States 1990, 1991.)

The United States during the 1980s was also the primary market for the growth of Korea's automobile industry. From only $6 million in 1985, US imports from Korea grew to $2.6 billion in 1988 before declining significantly to $1.6 billion in 1989 and $1.1 billion in 1990. In 1988, Korea exported 53 percent of its production, the vast majority of that to the United States.

The US and Canadian automobile industries have long been integrated. Canada is by far the largest market for US exports in this product group. However, the United States persistently runs road vehicle deficits with Canada: $9.8 billion in 1989 and $8.6 billion in 1990. Each of the "Big Three" US automakers (GM, Ford, and Chrysler) maintains significant production facilities in Canada. There is specialization in production, and a large cross-trade in vehicles and parts exists between the two countries. Canada is, however, a relatively small market. The great bulk of Canadian production is exported to the United States, which incurs consistently large deficits in its trade with Canada. In its 1989 trade with Canada, for example, the United States exported 730,000 cars and trucks, but imported 1.65 million. The Big Three produced 1.83 million cars and trucks in Canada in 1989, but most of this was exported to the United States, with only 96,500 units remaining in Canada. The 1990 passenger-car deficit with Canada was $7.7 billion, and the truck deficit was $4.2 billion.

US exports of parts and accessories to Canada are also large: $8.9 billion in 1990, for a US surplus of $3.2 billion. But this does not necessarily signal an improvement in the overall road vehicle balance with Canada, since increases in this subcategory usually reflect greater Canadian production of motor vehicles for export back to the United States. US-Canada trade in internal combustion engines also yields US surpluses, $1.0 billion in 1990. Most of the engines, however, return to the United States in the form of car and truck imports from Canada.

Growing Mexican production is also serving the US market. Each of the US Big Three has production facilities in Mexico, and some of their Mexican production goes to the United States. In 1989, US car and truck exports to Mexico were 4,500 units, but imports were 143,000, resulting in a US deficit of $1.1 billion in cars and $87 million in trucks. As with Canada, rising US surpluses in parts and accessories ($1.6 billion in 1990) do not necessarily presage a net improvement in the overall balance in road vehicles with Mexico. The United States is also a net importer of internal combustion engines from Mexico, with a 1990 deficit of $182 million.

Key Determinants of World Trade Patterns

Production of road vehicles and internal combustion engines is capital intensive. Such production must pull together an enormous variety of manufacturing and other technologies utilizing many different design, manufacturing, marketing, and other skills. A country with a strong, internationally competitive automobile industry—an industry, not just assembly plants or a single company with export capabilities—is therefore likely to possess a strong, internationally competitive manufacturing sector.

The ability to design and manufacture high-quality vehicles for mass markets at competitive prices remains the key to international competitiveness in automobiles and trucks. Outside of housing, an automobile is the most expensive purchase most consumers make. Very few car buyers are insensitive to price. Differences in automobile quality and styling are quite small and probably decreasing, at least over most of the price range. In the long run, except perhaps at the top of the price scale, price competitiveness—the outgrowth of costs of production—is the most critical factor in international competition and is determined primarily by a producer's productivity relative to its wage rates and by exchange rates.

Nevertheless, national policies can greatly influence production locations and trade patterns. During much of the 1980s, a voluntary restraint agreement restricted the quantity of Japanese automobile exports to the United States. Quotas also held Japanese imports at artificially low levels in some European countries. Although Japan has not applied import quotas, Japanese automobile markets have been extremely difficult to penetrate for a variety of reasons.

Political pressures can also influence production locations and trade patterns. For example, much of the movement to the United States of Japanese production for the US market probably did not occur because production in the United States became more economically efficient than production in Japan. Japanese-based production for the US market is still competitive, as the continuing flow of imports from Japan shows. Of more immediate significance has been Japanese concern that tighter quotas might be imposed, as well as anticipation that the dollar will ultimately decline to a level that would make Japanese-based production noncompetitive in the US market. Long ago, when the United States was strong in road vehicle production, US car and truck manufacturers had similar concerns and took similar measures, setting up plants in Canada and Europe. Recently the Japanese—now the strongest automobile producers—have been moving more quickly to establish production in US and European markets, a trend that will continue.

Role in US Trade

The 1981–87 Slide in Performance

It is difficult to overrate the importance of road vehicle and engine trade in US trade performance. In 1987, road vehicles accounted for 8.3 percent of total US exports and 11.0 percent of manufactures exports, up significantly from 6.8 percent and 9.8 percent, respectively, in 1981. Imports, however, have had an even more dramatic effect on US trade. In 1987, road vehicle imports were 17.8 percent of total imports and 22.3 percent of manufactures imports, up from 10.8 percent and 18.8 percent, respectively, in 1981.

These changes reflected a deterioration in US trade performance over the 1981–87 period that, in dollar terms, was far larger than in any other single category of US trade. From 1981 to 1987, the US deficit in road vehicles moved from an already sizable $11.7 billion to $51.4 billion, a $39.7 billion decline (table 5.78.4). Most of the change came from a $27.7 billion enlargement of the deficit in passenger cars, but the truck deficit increased by $4.2 billion, and parts and accessories moved from a $4.9 billion surplus to a $2.8 billion deficit, a decline of $7.7 billion. Engine exports increased only marginally from 1981 to 1987, but imports grew rapidly, with the balance declining by $4 billion, to a $2.1 billion deficit. Road vehicle balances slid with every major trading partner (table 5.78.5)

The 1987–90 Improvement

US performance in road vehicles improved markedly from 1987 to 1990, by $8.8 billion, with the dollar value of exports up 40.5 percent and imports declining by 0.5 percent (table 5.78.4). The deficit shrank by $5.9 billion for passenger cars and by $0.4 billion for trucks. The parts and accessories account improved by $4 billion, and internal combustion engines by $793 million.

In bilateral terms, the 1987–90 improvement in road vehicles was dominated by a $4.4 billion narrowing of the deficit with Japan and a $3.8 billion improvement in trade with Germany. In 1990, the US road vehicle deficit with Japan was $25.9 billion; that with Germany was $5.7 billion. The deficit in internal combustion engines also narrowed, from $2.2 billion in 1987 to $1.4 billion in 1990. The engine deficit with Japan, however, increased modestly, from $1.8 billion in 1987 to $2.5 billion in 1990.

International Competitiveness

Table 5.78.6 shows key indicators of US competitiveness in road vehicles and engines. World exports of road vehicles to non-US destinations grew from $96.2 billion in 1981 to $153.6 billion in 1987 and $189.6 billion in 1989. The US share of these exports declined from 16.8 percent in 1981 to 14.0 percent in 1987 and 13.5 percent in 1989. US imports, on the other hand, played a key role in the growth of trade in road vehicles, rising from $29.5 billion in 1981 to $74.6 billion in 1987, but declining to $73.9 billion in 1989. The US share of imports from non-US sources moved from 27.0 percent in 1981 to 43.9 percent in 1985 before declining to 36.5 percent in 1987 and 31.6 percent in 1989.

Subtracting the US import shares from its export shares, the US margin moved from − 10.2 percentage points in 1981 to − 22.4 percentage points in 1987 and − 18.1 percentage points in 1989. These data show a marked worsening of the US competitiveness position from 1981 to 1987 and significant improvement from 1987 to 1989. US-based production of road vehicles has not been in a strong competitive position in international markets. Because international trade in this product group is so large, further improvement is essential if major gains are to occur in the US trade and current accounts.

Over the 1981–89 period, the US share of world exports of engines declined from 31.8 percent to 20.5 percent, while its share of world imports from non-US sources rose from 20.8 percent to 31.1 percent.

Outlook

Key Determinants of US Trade Performance

The large road vehicle deficits of the 1980s were generated by a massive penetration of US markets by imported automobiles. The United States runs deficits

with every major motor-vehicle-producing country. The 1990 deficit in road
vehicles was distributed among major US suppliers as follows:

	Billions of dollars
Canada	8.63
Japan	25.94
United Kingdom	0.97
Germany	5.74
Korea	1.05
Mexico	0.42
Other	0.12
Total	42.87

Improvement in US balances in road vehicles and internal combustion engines
during the 1990s will depend primarily on US-based production recapturing a
larger share of the US market. US exports of road vehicles are likely to play
only a modest role in improving US trade performance.

Increases in US exports of finished cars and trucks in the next several years
are possible, but are likely to be relatively minor. The United States is unlikely
to become a major exporter of road vehicles, other than to Canada. Significant
favorable changes in the deficit with Canada are unlikely since the Canadian
market is one-tenth that of the United States. Therefore, Canadian production
will continue to be largely for export to the United States. Moreover, a large
portion of US exports of parts and accessories to Canada returns to the United
States in the form of finished automobiles and trucks. The size of the US deficit
with Canada is, therefore, influenced primarily by the quantity of US domestic
car and truck sales, not by Canadian sales levels or by modest changes in the
US-Canada exchange rate.

Indeed, the integration of US and Canadian automobile production results in
a structural US deficit, with the number of assembled units imported from
Canada consistently exceeding those exported to Canada. In 1978, the net US
deficit in car and truck trade with Canada was 508,000 units. The deficit declined
to 205,000 units in 1979, but in the 1982–89 period it has ranged from a low
of 525,000 units in 1987 to a high of 922,000 units in 1989. There is little
prospect of a fundamental change in this pattern in the near term.

Nor does Europe, with its highly competitive market, excess production capacity, on-the-scene production by US companies, and growing Japanese production seem a ready market for US exports. Some specialty vehicles—minivans
and convertibles—will continue to be exported, but not in large quantities.
Significant US penetration of the Japanese market, even via Japanese nameplates
made in the United States, will be even more difficult.

There may be some increases in US exports to the developing countries, although the depressed economies of many of these countries is likely to preclude major expansions. Cutbacks in imports by developing countries, particularly Latin America and the OPEC countries, have significantly hurt US exports in several categories of manufactures, including road vehicles. The United States exported $3.3 billion in road vehicles to Latin America in 1981 but only $3.0 billion in 1989. In 1981, before the debt crisis in the developing world began to affect world trade, Latin America imported $7.4 billion worth of road vehicles from the world; 44.6 percent of the total came from the United States, 22.5 percent from Japan, and 24.8 percent from the European Community. In 1989, Latin American imports from the world were down to $6.3 billion. Moreover, the US share of those imports was down to $3.0 billion, or 36.5 percent, while Japan's rose to 29.3 percent and the EC share to 29.1 percent.

In 1981, US road vehicle exports to developing countries were $5.5 billion, one-third of the $16.4 billion total to all world destinations (table 5.78.4). The OPEC countries (including those in Latin America) took $3.4 billion. By 1990, total US road vehicle exports to the world were 1.8 times the 1981 level, but exports to developing countries, at $6.4 billion, were only 16 percent higher than in 1981. OPEC countries were hurt by the collapse of oil prices, and exports to them, at only $51 million, had almost disappeared. Moreover, the $4.1 billion in exports to Latin America was only modestly above the $3.4 billion of 1981; that gain came from a $1.9 billion increase in exports to Mexico, much of which returned to the United States in the form of an increased imports of cars and trucks from Mexico.

Thus, during the 1980s, US road vehicle exports suffered a setback in trade with the developing countries, particularly with Latin America. The prospects for a major restoration of Latin American or OPEC purchasing power in the foreseeable future are modest.

Thus, better US trade performance in this product group will have to occur primarily by *US-based production* supplying a larger portion of the US market. Nonetheless, the US-owned portion of that production may decline. A rapid decline in US imports is, however, unlikely. The road vehicle deficit with Germany has improved from $9.5 billion in 1987 to $5.7 billion in 1990. The 10 percent luxury tax imposed on 1 January 1991 on automobiles over $30,000 could hurt some German exports. However, without further significant dollar depreciation from mid-1991 levels, only modest further reductions in US imports from Germany and other countries of the European Community are likely.

Modest increases in imports from Mexico and the bilateral deficit with Mexico also seem likely as production there expands. In the long term, a North American Free Trade Agreement could trigger substantial investment in Mexican car and truck production intended to serve the US market, some of that investment from Japan and other foreign producers. Tariffs play a modest role in US automobile imports, mitigating the incentive that a free trade agreement with Mexico would provide automakers to produce in Mexico to serve the US market. The automobile duty rate is 2.5 percent. The much higher rate on trucks (25 percent) can be a major factor in truck trade.

Imports from Korea have declined since their 1987 peak, but greater Korean penetration of the US market is possible if new Korean models prove successful.

For US companies—the Big Three—the critical question is whether they can halt and then reverse the increased penetration of the US market by Japanese imports and increasing US-based Japanese production. Probably the majority of analysts expect the Japanese share of the US market to continue to increase and the share of the Big Three US producers to continue to decline through the 1990s. Some think it will be extremely difficult, and probably impossible, for the US companies with their aging unionized labor force and older plants to get their labor costs down to those of Japanese transplants that operate with younger, nonunion, more flexible labor forces in newer, more modern plants. Moreover, competitive bidding by individual state and local governments to lure new investments puts older, established production locations at a further disadvantage. Because most new investments are Japanese, this competition for new investment—in the form of various kinds of tax breaks, loans, land grants, and other kinds of subsidies—makes Big-Three production even less cost competitive.

Comments by industry leaders give credence to the views of those who see a continuing decline in the share of the Big Three. In the spring of 1991, Chrysler chairman Lee Iacocca petitioned President Bush to cap the Japanese market share, including both imports and cars made in the United States, projecting that "unless the Japanese cut back their export shipments...their market share will rocket up to 40 percent or more" and that "at a Japanese share of 40 percent in a depressed industry, Chrysler is gone and Ford could be mortally wounded from a competitive standpoint. Even GM is at risk. . . ." (Brown 1991).

According to a *Wall Street Journal* article, Ford chairman Harold A. Poling "says that Japan should roll back exports of cars, trucks and other goods to cut its trade surplus with the US by 25% a year for the next four years." The same article notes that GM stops short of endorsing a market-share cap, citing a GM statement that "Market shares are determined by competition" (White and Mitchell 1991).

Should the US road vehicle deficit grow further, quotas on imports from Japan might be tightened, possibly restricting not only imports from Japan but also Japanese production in the United States. However, except for GM's Saturn venture, there is little evidence that the Big Three are making large investments in a drive to regain market share, and indeed the Big Three are rounding out their product lines by adding their own nameplates to vehicles imported from other countries. Therefore, the application of quotas to US-based production by foreign companies or other major restrictions that would seriously hamper continued Japanese penetration of the US market seems most unlikely.

Whatever the progress of the Big Three in the struggle for the US market, the focus of this examination is on the role of road vehicles in the US external accounts. Japan remains the key to narrowing US deficits in road vehicles and engines.

The appendix to this volume presents elasticities for passenger cars and parts provided by Data Resources Incorporated (DRI). The DRI-calculated price elasticity of imports for parts is negligible (-0.1), but that for passenger cars is high (-1.8). That is, a 1 percent rise in US import prices would reduce US passenger car imports by 1.8 percent. Movements in the exchange rate do not affect imports by themselves; what is important is how much of the effect of exchange rate movements is passed on to the consumer. To date, Japanese companies have successfully maintained competitive prices in the US market, notwithstanding a major appreciation of the yen from its mid-1980s levels.

German producers are thought to be in a tight squeeze between their production costs and the prices they can charge in the US market. German automakers might well have to pass on most of the effects of any future dollar depreciation. But the deficit with Germany has become much smaller, and if exchange rates remain at or near their late 1991 levels, the prestige market served by much of the imports from Germany may not lose many more buyers. In a strong US automobile market, even some moderate dollar depreciation— say 5 to 10 percent—from the levels of December 1991 would probably have only moderate effects in reducing the $5.7 billion 1990 bilateral road-vehicle deficit with Germany. Japan's increasing role in the luxury car market, however, poses a threat to German market share in the United States.

Japan's situation seems quite different. Moderate dollar depreciation against the yen is likely to have little if any effect. It is widely believed that most Japanese producers could continue to profit in the US market even should the dollar weaken as much as 10 percent to 15 percent from the December 1991 rate (around 130 yen to the dollar). Moreover, most Japanese producers have the financial resources to pursue long-term market-share goals even at the expense of current profits. If this analysis is correct, a major further dollar depreciation against the yen, by perhaps 20 percent or more, would be required to make Japanese-based production for the US market sufficiently costly to diminish imports from Japan sharply. Without such depreciation, the US deficit with Japan over the next several years will be shaped not by modest variations in exchange rates but by long-term Japanese market objectives, the methods Japanese automakers choose to pursue these objectives, and US policy responses.

US-Japan Trade

At $28.4 billion, the 1990 deficit with Japan remains the largest component of the deficit in road vehicles and internal combustion engines—about 64 percent of the total—and the key variable in US trade in these product groups (table 5.78.5). Because the United States has been unable to make significant inroads into Japan's markets, the deficit with Japan will have to be narrowed principally through displacing imports from Japan with US-based production. The question is whether this will occur through production by the US Big Three or through Japanese production in the United States. A detailed examination of recent data and historical trends can provide some insights about likely future trends.

Key factors that will determine US-Japan road vehicle and engine trade balances during the 1990s include the following:

- the strength of the US car and truck markets (i.e., the total number of units sold)

- Japan's level of penetration of the US market, both by exports from Japan and by units produced in the United States, and the competitiveness of units produced by the US Big Three

- the division of the Japanese share of the US market between US-based car and truck production and imports from Japan

- the US content (engines, parts, components) of Japanese car and truck production in the United States

- the unit values of car and truck imports from Japan

- the level of US exports.

A great many events that cannot be foreseen will determine how the above factors interact and what trade balances will result. Some trends favor continuation of the recent improvements in the US-Japan bilateral balance. US quality and competitiveness, for example, are generally improving, and major projects such as the introduction of GM's new Saturn automobile could significantly improve the market share of the Big Three. Moreover, Japanese production in the United States is growing quite rapidly and, to the extent it substitutes for imports, should improve US trade performance. There are, however, a number of reasons to believe that, without further significant appreciation of the yen, there will be little if any improvement in the next several years in the US Japan bilateral balance in road vehicles and engines.

Table 5.78.7 reviews recent Japanese performance in the US market and projects 1990 and 1995 performance in terms of numbers of cars and trucks. The 1995 projection for automobile imports from Japan is an official US Department of Commerce estimate (US Department of Commerce 1991). Estimates of 1995 truck imports and car and truck transplant production are from unofficial sources. The projection assumes no further major depreciation of the dollar against the yen from the mid-1991 level of around 135 yen per dollar. Key elements in the projection for 1995 are the following:

- The total 1995 US car and truck market in which Japan will share is forecast at 16.3 million units, somewhat larger than the recession-depressed 1990 level of about 14.1 million units.

- Car and truck imports from Japan do not decline, but remain constant at the 1989 levels of 1.9 million and 0.5 million units, respectively.

- Japanese production in the United States rises by 1995 to 2.1 million automobiles and 0.4 million trucks.

- The total Japanese share (transplant production plus imports) of the US market continues to increase.

- In effect, Japanese production in the United States *supplements but does not replace* exports from Japan, which essentially remain at 1989 levels.

The result of the 1995 outcome projected by table 5.78.7 would be a continuing decline in the share of the US car and truck markets supplied by imports from Japan, from 16.9 percent in 1988 to 14.7 percent in 1995. On the other hand, a significant increase in penetration of the US market by Japanese vehicles from US- and Japanese-based production would occur. Japan's market share from the two production bases would rise to 37.4 percent of automobiles and 16.1 percent of trucks, for a combined 30.1 percent share of cars and trucks. The projected rise in share is based on several facts and judgments, including the following:

- Japanese production in the United States is very competitive with production of the Big Three in terms of quality and costs. Japanese plants in the United States are generally newer, and their productivity is higher. Labor costs per hour are lower, partly because workers are younger and have less seniority and incur lower health benefit costs.

- Japanese nameplates can continue to increase market share, based on US impressions of Japanese quality, style, and service. US quality has been rising, but public perception lags behind reality. Japanese penetration of US markets has been heaviest in younger age groups. According to a J.D. Powers study, "Generally older drivers prefer domestic makes, while younger ones, especially in their 20's, prefer foreign makes." The same study found that 80 percent of the cars bought by people 65 years of age and older are domestic brands, while only 14 percent of the people in that age group buy foreign makes. The shift is even more dramatic in the 25-to-34 age group. There 56 percent drive domestic models, while about 46 percent drive cars made by foreign manufacturers. (Levin 1991). The negatives for the Big Three are obvious. As generations more loyal to domestic manufacturers pass on, Detroit will have to improve its batting average with succeeding generations, or its market share will continue to fall.

■ To date, growth in Japanese market share has been achieved without widespread use of price-cutting or other competitive practices employed by US automakers. Japanese producers still have this strategy to fall back on if necessary. Also, Japanese marketing has not yet fully exploited several market categories (for example, the US Midwest and fleet sales).

■ US automobile companies will continue to import small cars produced in Japan.

■ Except for GM's Saturn project, there is little evidence of price and capital investment policies by US companies directed at regaining market share.

■ A primary objective of Japanese companies is likely to continue to be increased market share from the combination of US- and Japan-based production. Sensitive to criticisms of their US-based operations and anxious to avoid further restrictions, Japanese companies will strive to avoid production cutbacks in their US transplants when US markets are weak and, whenever practical, will control inventories by holding down imports. But within economic and political constraints, Japanese companies will continue to prefer Japanese-based production and will strive to avoid the large cutbacks in Japanese-based production that a major reduction in exports from Japan to the United States would entail.

■ There have been very large capital expenditures in new plant and equipment in Japan to improve productivity. Thus, without further major depreciation of the dollar, exporting from Japan to the United States will remain profitable.

Japan has informally continued the restraints on exports to the United States previously imposed by a voluntary restraint agreement. In recent years, automobile imports from Japan have declined below the self-imposed limit of 2.3 million units. Thus, the quotas are no longer a major factor in US-Japan automobile trade, although in some cases (for example, Toyota) individual-company quotas may continue to constrain exports to the United States somewhat. In general, however, the combination of rising US production of Japanese transplants and exports within the self-imposed quotas has released Japanese companies from the prior constraints on market share imposed by the US quotas. The combination of US-based production and exports from Japan can now provide a basis for further expansion of the Japanese share of the US market. Assuming no further major dollar decline, there seems little reason to expect that the increased market share projected in table 5.78.7 will not be reached by 1995. In fact, it could easily be exceeded. Indeed, some observers believe that Japanese companies, concerned about a US backlash if the market share of the big three diminishes too rapidly, have already been moderating their penetration of the US market and will continue to do so. According to a *Washington Post* article:

> Recent remarks by a top Honda executive, Shoichiro Irimajiri, tend to support the theory that politics is influencing Japanese industry's plans. "At the end of the 1980s, we realized that our production system had advanced too far compared to the Big Three or European manufacturers," Irimajiri said at a Honda press gathering in early January.
>
> A few days earlier, he told the Japan Economic Journal: "If we do our best, the Japanese share [of the US car market] could grow indefinitely. But we should not push so hard as to drive U.S. rivals out of the market." (Blustein 1991)

Japan's automakers, however, may be in a difficult position. Market demand is declining at home, and the domestic industry is still so dependent on export markets that substantial declines in exports from Japan could damage it. According to the *Wall Street Journal*:

> For the first time since they emerged as major exporters in the 1960s, Japan's automobile manufacturers confront trouble in each of their major markets. In the U.S., they face sagging car demand related to the recession. In Europe, they are holding down exports to avoid antagonizing policy makers drafting trade laws for the emerging single market. And in Japan booming demand over the past three years has given way to a cyclical decline that experts say may not slacken until 1993.
>
> These problems come at a time when labor costs are rising and many of Japan's large manufacturers, in defiance of warnings from Japan's Ministry of International Trade and Industry, have embarked on ambitious capital-spending programs that could add 800,000 vehicles to Japan's 13.4 million vehicle annual domestic production capacity in the next two years.
>
> This widening gap between supply and demand has put the squeeze on Japanese manufacturers who only a year ago seemed invulnerable. Industry experts say adverse market conditions may lead to layoffs and plant closings—drastic measures in Japan—and speed the restructuring of the nation's auto industry. (Chandler 1991)

To obtain an estimate of the US-Japan bilateral deficit, the unit import volumes projected in table 5.78.7 can be translated into dollars. Projecting to 1995 to utilize the US Department of Commerce estimates, the US-Japan dollar trade balance will be determined primarily by the number of units imported but also by unit prices. From 1983 to 1988, the average value of automobiles imported from Japan increased from $6,987 to $10,222, a 46 percent rise, for an average annual increase of about 7.5 percent. Trucks rose from $3,531 to $5,380 per unit over the same period, a 52.4 percent increase, for an average annual growth rate of about 9 percent. Unit price increases are likely to continue, reflecting both inflation and continued upscaling of the production exported from Japan.

For example, 1.9 million automobiles imported from Japan in 1995 at a unit price of $13,500 (a 4.0 percent annual increase from 1988 to 1995) would carry a price tag of $25.65 billion. Similarly, 500,000 trucks at an average unit price of $7,500 (4.5 percent annual price growth from 1988 levels) would raise the value of imports to $3.75 billion.

US imports of engines and parts and accessories will also be important in the bilateral trade balance in the 1990s. The 1990 engine deficit with Japan was $2.5 billion. Imports of parts and accessories were $5.3 billion in 1990, yielding a US deficit with Japan of $4.8 billion. US auto parts producers are, according to several sources, beginning to make some headway in supplying Japanese producers in the United States. Some observers believe that the tide is about to turn, as Japanese production in the United States begins to rely increasingly on parts and accessories made in the United States. Also, Japanese engine production in the United States is increasing, as manifested in the $600 million narrowing of the 1990 deficit from 1989.

Nevertheless, as annual Japanese car and truck production in the United States doubles to about 2.5 million units by 1995, and as the number of Japanese vehicles in use in the United States continues to cumulate, the demand for engines and parts and accessories for Japanese automobiles will grow rapidly. Japanese plans for switching to US sources are unclear, and we lack a solid basis for forecasting trends over the next few years. However, Japanese automobile manufacturers maintain intensely close, demanding relationships with their suppliers. Switching to US-based suppliers will probably be a slow process, involving Japanese efforts to have their new suppliers meet their standards. Without marked dollar depreciation to provide a further incentive to move Japanese production more rapidly to the United States, it seems likely that US-based production of parts and engines for Japanese transplants will lag behind demand and that the deficit in these two categories will not improve significantly from the $7.3 billion level of 1990.

A very detailed analysis of US-Japan automobile and parts trade sees the most likely US auto parts deficit more than doubling the 1990 level by 1994 (University of Michigan Transportation Research Institute 1991, iii). This study, however, assumes a more moderate expansion in the parts deficit by 1993—only about $1.7 billion from 1990. Political pressures, on the other hand, could alter Japanese plans and result in a more rapid switch to US-based production.

Exports, imports, and balances obviously cannot be confidently forecast beyond 1993. However, using US Department of Commerce projections of 1995 US car and truck sales and import volumes, some useful approximations can be developed. Without major further dollar depreciation, and without either quotas that would restrict the penetration of the US market by imports and Japanese transplants or a self-imposed slowing by Japanese producers of their penetration of the US market, 1995 US deficits in trade with Japan in road vehicles and engines seem likely to be close to what is projected in table 5.78.8.

The projected $37 billion deficit compares with an actual 1990 deficit with Japan of $28.4 billion in these items—an $8.6 billion expansion in nominal dollar terms, but probably little, if any, change relative to nominal US GNP. In 1993, the target year for forecasts for other product groups in this study, the deficit will probably be only moderately lower. In 1993, modestly lower dollar values for car and truck imports will probably be offset by higher imports of engines and parts and accessories. These imports are likely to be lower in 1995, when US-based production for Japanese transplants will probably be larger.

Projections by several other sources do not vary widely from those presented above. Table 5.78.9 summarizes seven projections done over the last few years. Some of the forecasts were made as long ago as 1989, and others as recently as May 1991, and the years for which the forecasts were made also vary. Price growth and other assumptions used in the forecasts also differed, and for most of the estimates, no detail is available on the breakdown into automobiles, trucks, and parts. There is, however, significant agreement on projected levels of US-based Japanese production and on the level of US imports from Japan. Except for the Fuji Research Institute projection, which does not include trucks, all forecasters see Japan's exports to the United States—a critical factor in the bilateral trade balance—at above 2.0 million vehicles a year, not far from the 1989 level. In effect, this reflects a judgment that US transplants will supplement, not replace, exports of finished vehicles from Japan and that Japan's share of the US market will continue to grow. Thus, much of the differences in the forecasts stems from assumptions about future unit prices of imported vehicles and expectations about the level of parts imports.

So long as US motor vehicle imports from Japan remain at 2 million or more units annually, a significant reduction in the US bilateral deficit in this product group is not in the cards. Inflation and upscaling in the imported units alone would raise import prices and therefore lead to some nominal growth. If the ranges indicated by these volume projections are correct, auto parts will be a key variable in setting the level of the deficit, which will remain large over the next several years.

Near- and Medium-Term Outlook

Examination of empirical data and other information leads to the conclusion that, over the next several years, US deficits in road vehicles and engines will grow somewhat, reversing the 1987–90 improvements. The bilateral deficit with

Japan in 1993 is likely to be about $35 billion, significantly higher in current-dollar terms than the $28.4 billion 1990 deficit. Japan's market share will rise above current levels. However, to reduce political tensions, Japanese companies may keep the lid on the road vehicle deficit and may moderate their drive to expand market share. The March 1992 announcement that Japan will limit its exports of automobiles to the United States to 1.65 million in fiscal year 1992 may signal such an intent.

Robert Z. Lawrence (1990) concludes that Japanese transplants will reduce the 1992 US trade deficit between $9.3 billion and $15.4 billion from what it would have been if these same units had been imported from Japan. Continued US pressures may speed the movement to the United States of Japanese assembly operations and the production of the engines, parts, and accessories to support those operations. But such a shift takes time, and Japan's plans for dividing its production locations between Japan and the United States for 1993 probably cannot now be greatly changed.

There is little room for improvement in balances with other trading partners. A $5 billion to $8 billion expansion of the deficit for road vehicles and engines from the 1990 level seems likely; this would mean a 1993 deficit of $49 billion to $52 billion.

Longer-Term Outlook

Little if any reduction in the deficit for road vehicles with Japan is likely over the next several years because of Japanese reticence to give up the benefits of Japanese-based production and the long lead times needed to shift production from Japan. It is widely believed that Japanese-based vehicle production could compete in US markets at exchange rates of 120 yen to the dollar or even lower. Nevertheless, there is no inherent economic or technical advantage to Japanese-based production of road vehicles that will indefinitely sustain the export of 2 million vehicles per year to the United States and the accompanying large US deficits. Economic and political factors will significantly narrow the US deficit sooner or later, perhaps by the end of the 1990s. However, this will occur primarily through increased Japanese production in the United States for the US market. The end of the decade is likely to see the total Japanese market share (imports plus US-made Japanese nameplates) substantially above current levels.

Road vehicle trade is not just a US-Japan issue, but also a Japan-EC issue. Some observers feel that, with no restraints, the Japanese would capture an even higher share of the market in Europe than they have in the United States. Some form of continued EC restrictions seems likely, however. A possible Japanese countermove would be to export Japanese transplant production from the United States to Europe. Such a strategy would help the US trade balance.

In any case, trade imbalances in road vehicles are a world issue, and one that is likely to continue for several years.

Conclusions

- The US trade deficit in road vehicles and engines has narrowed significantly, from $53.9 billion in 1987 to $44.3 billion in 1990, because of a combination of economic and political factors. It is unlikely to narrow further, however, without additional economic or political incentives. Indeed, it is likely to expand again, perhaps to between $49 billion and $52 billion in 1993.

- Most of the improvement since 1987 does not appear to be due to the relatively low sales of road vehicles in 1989 and 1990. Rather, the share of imports in total US vehicle unit sales has declined modestly since 1987. At the same time, the market share held by foreign producers has increased as a result of the combination of foreign imports and production in the United States by Japanese-controlled companies. Over the next several years, increased demand in the US automobile market will probably cause modest increases in the number of units imported from depressed 1990 levels. The unit prices of these imports will increase, as will the value of parts, components, and engines imported to support Japanese production in the United States. These factors will enlarge the deficit above 1990 levels, to around the record 1987 level.

- The large deficits in road vehicles and engines were not caused by lack of US plant capacity. On the contrary, several US plants of US companies have closed while new Japanese plants have been opening. This indicates the problem is a lack of *competitive* US plants.

- Yen appreciation has not yet been adequate to force Japanese companies to shift most of their production for the US market to the United States. The early-December 1991 yen-dollar rate was virtually unchanged from the December 1987 rate. Japanese production has moved to the United States mostly to escape quotas that at one time significantly restrained imports, to hedge against future dollar declines, and to temper political ill will that could lead to the reimposition of quotas.

- The strong appreciation of the deutsche mark has resulted in major price increases and significantly lower sales of German automobiles in the United States. Appreciation of the Korean won after its earlier undervaluation has also affected Korean competitiveness in the United States, but quality problems, rising domestic wages, and domestic production difficulties have probably also been important in Korea's diminished role.

- Changes in exchange rates are unlikely to have major effects on US balances with Canada and Mexico in the foreseeable future because of the integration of production in those countries with US-based production.

- Latin America's debt problems and OPEC's diminished purchasing power have reduced exports to two markets that used to be important to US car and truck producers. This loss is unlikely to be reversed in the next several years.

- Export expansion is unlikely to be a major factor in improved US performance. Further significant improvements will have to occur mostly at Japan's expense and will come about primarily by the substitution of US-based production of Japanese nameplates for Japan-based production.

- In 1985, the United States took 43.9 percent of the rest of the world's exports of road vehicles. In 1989, it took 28.2 percent. This share will decline further as more production for the US market moves to the United States.

- For the next several years, Japan's currently planned rising production in the United States will largely supplement rather than replace Japanese-based production for the United States. However, Japanese production in the United States has lowered US deficits from what they would have been had the US market been supplied only by Japanese-based production. Japanese production in the United States in 1990 was about 1.6 million units, probably reducing the US deficit by around $10 billion compared with what it would have been had the United States imported those units from Japan.

- Political considerations may motivate Japanese actions to slow the increase in the Japanese share of the US market and to maintain the quantity of car, truck, and parts imports from Japan at roughly current levels. This would moderate the size of the bilateral deficit in dollar terms, holding it at or not far above current levels. Indeed, Japan's March 1992 decision to lower the limitation on its exports of automobiles to the United States may signal a less aggressive approach to US markets and an intent to restrain the growth of the bilateral road vehicle deficit. Over the longer term, however, either a further major appreciation of the yen or some form of restrictions—explicit or implicit—would probably be required to force a significant reduction in US imports from Japan.

- A critical factor in the size of the US road vehicle deficits with Japan over the next few years is the degree to which the assembly of vehicles in the United States will be supported by parts and components made in the United States. This is difficult to predict. The speed with which Japan switches production of engines and parts and components to the United States will do much to determine the US deficit on parts and accessories and internal combustion engine trade. Again, further major dollar depreciation against the yen would motivate speeding the transition to US-based production. Continued US political pressures, however, may also speed the move.

■ The dollar will probably have to depreciate to levels well below those of the early 1980s in order to reduce the deficits in road vehicles and engines to significantly lower levels. This is a sign of long-term decline in the international market competitiveness of the US road vehicle industry.

■ Japanese surpluses in road vehicle trade will be a key world issue during the 1990s. US-Japan and Japan-EC automobile trade will remain controversial. However, there is no inherent, permanent economic or technical advantage in Japan-based production. Economic and political factors will probably combine to substantially reduce the US road vehicles deficit with Japan some time by the end of the decade. This will occur primarily through the movement to the United States of production of Japanese cars and trucks for the US market and will be accompanied by an increase in the combined market share of Japan's US-based production and imports from Japan.

Bibliography

Blustein, Paul. 1991. "Is Japan Easing Up on US Auto Makers? Export Cuts Seen as a Sign of 'Consideration'." *Washington Post* (22 February): C1.

Brown, Warren. 1991. "Bush Is Cool to Iacocca Bid for Cap on Japan Auto Sales." *Washington Post* (26 March): C1.

Chandler, Clay. 1991. "Japanese Auto Makers Face Lean Times: Market Demand Is Declining at Home and Abroad." *Wall Street Journal* (11 March): A11.

Lawrence, Robert Z. 1990. "Foreign Affiliated Automakers in the United States: An Appraisal." Arlington, VA: Automobile Importers of America (March).

Levin, Doron P. 1991. "Detroit Strives to Regain Lost Generation of Buyers." *New York Times* (9 April).

Motor Vehicle Manufacturers Association of the United States. 1990. *World Motor Vehicle Data, 1990 Edition*. Detroit: Motor Vehicle Manufacturers Association of the United States.

US Department of Commerce. 1991. "Automobile Sales and Market Shares in the United States, 1989–95." Washington: US Department of Commerce (11 January).

University of Michigan Transportation Research Institute, Office for the Study of Automotive Transportation. 1991. "The US-Japan Automotive Bilateral 1994 Trade Deficit." Ann Arbor: University of Michigan (UMTRI 91-20, May).

White, Joseph B., and Jacqueline Mitchell. 1991. "Detroit Rolls Out Old Ploy: Quotas." *Wall Street Journal* (14 January): B1.

Table 5.78.1 Road vehicles and engines: product composition of world trade, 1981–89 (billions of dollars except where noted)

SITC	Product	1981	1982	1983	1984	1985	1986	1987	1988	1989	Annual growth 1981–89 (percentages)
SITC 78:	Road vehicles										
	World exports to world	125.9	123.7	127.6	140.7	156.6	195.1	231.2	255.2	263.3	9.7
	of which										
781	Passenger cars	57.8	59.7	65.6	71.6	81.8	106.3	123.2	139.4	144.8	12.2
782	Trucks	22.5	21.1	18.7	20.2	22.3	25.4	28.2	32.0	33.4	5.0
783	Other road vehicles	4.0	3.4	2.4	2.5	2.5	2.7	3.6	5.6	5.7	4.6
784	Parts and accessories	32.5	31.4	33.5	38.7	41.5	50.2	62.6	66.6	66.9	9.4
785	Motorcycles	6.1	5.2	5.0	5.1	5.1	5.9	6.8	6.6	7.4	2.5
786	Trailers	3.1	2.7	2.2	2.2	2.3	2.6	3.2	5.1	6.1	9.0
SITC 713:	Engines										
	World exports to world	14.9	14.5	15.3	17.5	17.8	20.5	24.2	30.5	31.2	9.7
Memorandum:											Change 1981–89
	SITC 78 share of world manufactures exports (percentages)	12.4	12.7	13.0	13.2	13.9	14.3	14.0	12.9	12.5	0.0

Source: World Manufactures Trade Data Base.

Table 5.78.2 Road vehicles: geographic distribution of world trade, 1981–89 (percentages of total)

Country	1981	1982	1983	1984	1985	1986	1987	1988	1989	Change 1981–89
Share of exports to world										
United States	12.8	11.1	11.3	12.4	12.4	9.6	9.3	9.9	9.7	-3.1
Canada	8.7	10.6	12.9	15.3	14.9	12.3	10.1	10.4	9.9	1.2
Japan	26.8	24.9	25.7	26.7	27.4	27.8	25.4	24.0	23.4	-3.3
European Community	46.2	47.4	44.2	39.2	38.8	43.1	46.4	45.9	47.9	1.7
EC to non-EC	21.5	21.0	18.7	17.5	17.2	17.3	17.4	15.7	15.6	-6.0
Germany	20.7	23.0	20.9	18.7	18.9	21.1	22.4	21.4	21.9	1.2
France	8.7	8.0	7.6	6.7	6.3	6.9	7.3	7.1	7.4	-1.3
Italy	4.2	3.7	3.7	3.3	3.0	3.5	3.8	3.9	4.3	0.1
United Kingdom	4.9	4.4	3.7	3.2	3.2	3.0	3.5	3.5	3.8	-1.1
Other Western Europe	4.1	4.2	3.9	4.0	3.9	4.3	4.5	4.3	4.0	-0.1
Asian NICs[a]	0.2	0.5	0.7	0.9	1.0	1.4	1.9	3.3	2.6	2.4
Eastern Europe[b]	0.4	0.4	0.4	0.3	0.3	0.3	0.4	0.4	0.4	-0.0
Developing countries	0.8	0.9	0.9	1.1	1.3	1.4	1.9	1.9	2.0	1.2
Latin America	0.5	0.6	0.6	0.9	1.0	1.0	1.5	1.5	1.5	1.1
Rest of world	0.1	0.1	0.1	0.1	0.1	0.1	0.2	0.1	0.2	0.1
Share of imports from world										
United States	23.3	25.9	29.7	34.9	37.6	36.2	32.6	30.1	28.2	4.9
Canada	9.5	8.7	11.2	13.2	13.5	11.3	10.0	9.6	8.9	-0.6
Japan	0.4	0.4	0.5	0.5	0.5	0.7	1.1	1.5	1.9	1.5
European Community	31.0	31.9	31.5	27.3	26.3	32.0	36.3	37.3	39.2	8.3
EC from non-EC	6.7	6.5	6.6	6.1	5.6	7.1	7.7	8.1	8.4	1.7
Germany	5.6	5.3	6.0	5.2	4.7	6.3	7.0	7.2	7.4	1.8
France	5.3	5.9	5.5	4.5	4.4	5.2	6.1	6.3	6.8	1.5
Italy	4.9	4.6	3.4	3.5	3.4	3.9	4.8	5.0	5.5	0.7
United Kingdom	5.4	6.4	6.9	5.8	5.6	6.0	6.3	8.0	8.1	2.7
Other Western Europe	6.4	6.6	6.5	5.5	6.0	7.2	7.8	7.8	7.7	1.4
Asian NICs[a]	1.3	1.1	1.2	1.2	0.8	1.0	1.6	2.2	2.4	1.1
Eastern Europe[b]	0.6	0.7	0.4	0.4	0.4	0.4	0.3	0.4	0.5	-0.1
Developing countries	25.9	22.8	17.7	15.2	13.2	10.1	9.5	10.0	9.6	-16.3
Latin America	5.9	4.0	2.6	3.0	3.0	2.7	2.8	2.5	2.4	-3.5
Rest of world	0.1	0.3	0.2	0.1	0.1	0.1	0.1	0.1	0.1	-0.1

table continued next page

Table 5.78.2 Road vehicles: geographic distribution of world trade, 1981–89 percentages of total) (continued)

Country	1981	1982	1983	1984	1985	1986	1987	1988	1989	Change 1981–89
Export share minus import share										
United States	-10.5	-14.8	-18.5	-22.5	-25.2	-26.6	-23.3	-20.1	-18.5	-8.0
Canada	-0.9	1.9	1.7	2.1	1.4	1.0	0.1	0.8	1.0	1.8
Japan	26.4	24.4	25.2	26.2	26.9	27.0	24.3	22.4	21.5	-4.9
European Community	15.2	15.5	12.7	11.9	12.5	11.1	10.1	8.6	8.7	-6.6
Non-EC	14.8	14.6	12.1	11.5	11.7	10.2	9.7	7.7	7.2	-7.7
Germany	15.1	17.7	14.9	13.4	14.1	14.8	15.4	14.3	14.6	-0.5
France	3.3	2.1	2.0	2.2	1.9	1.7	1.2	0.8	0.6	-2.8
Italy	-0.7	-0.9	0.3	-0.2	-0.4	-0.4	-1.0	-1.2	-1.2	-0.5
United Kingdom	-0.5	-2.0	-3.2	-2.6	-2.3	-3.0	-2.9	-4.5	-4.3	-3.8
Other Western Europe	-2.3	-2.4	-2.6	-1.6	-2.1	-2.9	-3.3	-3.6	-3.7	-1.4
Asian NICs[a]	-1.1	-0.6	-0.5	-0.3	0.2	0.4	0.3	1.1	0.3	1.3
Eastern Europe[b]	-0.2	-0.3	-0.0	-0.1	-0.1	-0.1	0.1	0.0	-0.1	0.1
Developing countries	-25.2	-21.9	-16.8	-14.1	-11.9	-8.7	-7.6	-8.1	-7.6	17.5
Latin America	-5.4	-3.4	-2.0	-2.2	-2.0	-1.7	-1.3	-1.0	-0.9	4.5
Rest of world	-0.0	-0.1	-0.1	0.0	0.0	0.1	0.2	0.1	0.2	0.2

a. Hong Kong, Korea, Singapore, and Taiwan.

b. Including Soviet Union.

Source: World Manufactures Trade Data Base.

Table 5.78.3 Road vehicles and engines: bilateral trade flows, 1989 (billions of dollars)

Importer	World	United States	Canada	Japan	European Community	Germany	France	United Kingdom	Asian NICs	Latin America	Other
SITC 78: Road vehicles											
World	263.3	25.5	26.1	61.6	126.0	57.7	19.4	9.9	7.0	4.0	13.0
United States	73.7		25.6	29.3	9.8	6.3	0.7	1.4	3.8	3.1	2.0
Canada	20.7	15.9		2.9	0.9	0.6	0.1	0.1	0.4	0.2	0.4
Japan	6.3	3.0	0.1		3.5	2.8	0.2	0.3	0.5	0.0	0.2
European Community	5.1	0.9	0.0	10.7	85.1	33.7	14.0	6.1	0.9	0.6	7.1
Germany	6.1	1.0	0.1	3.8	12.2		3.0	1.5	0.1	0.1	1.7
France	106.6	2.1	0.1	0.9	16.0	6.1		1.5	0.1	0.0	1.2
United Kingdom	18.6	0.4	0.0	2.5	15.8	8.0	3.0		0.5	0.0	1.4
Asian NICs	18.6	0.7	0.0	2.4	1.9	0.9	0.3	0.2		0.0	0.2
Latin America	20.6	0.4	0.0	1.4	1.6	0.5	0.5	0.2	0.2		0.1
Other	44.8	2.7	0.2	14.9	23.2	12.8	3.7	1.7	0.8	0.0	3.0
SITC 713: Internal combustion engines											
World	31.2	4.8	2.0	6.4	12.3	4.8	2.7	2.2	0.2	2.4	3.1
United States	7.7		2.0	2.9	1.2	0.7	0.1	0.3	0.0	1.4	0.2
Canada	2.8	1.9		0.3	0.2	0.0	0.1	0.0	0.0	0.4	0.1
Japan	0.3	0.1	0.0		0.1	0.0	0.0	0.0	0.0	0.0	0.1
European Community	12.0	1.1	0.0	0.8	7.1	2.2	1.9	1.3	0.1	0.5	2.3
Germany	2.9	0.1	0.0	0.1	1.3		0.4	0.5	0.0	0.2	1.1
France	1.6	0.1	0.0	0.1	1.1	0.4		0.2	0.0	0.1	0.1
United Kingdom	1.8	0.3	0.0	0.3	1.0	0.5	0.2		0.0	0.0	0.2
Asian NICs	1.2	0.2	0.0	0.6	0.3	0.1	0.0	0.1		0.0	0.0
Latin America	1.6	0.9	0.0	0.2	0.5	0.1	0.2	0.1	0.0		0.0
Other	5.5	0.6	0.0	1.6	2.8	1.6	0.4	0.4	0.0	0.0	0.4

Source: World Manufactures Trade Data Base.

Table 5.78.4 Road vehicles and engines: product composition of US trade, 1981–90ᵃ (millions of dollars except where noted)

| | SITC Rev. 2 | | | SITC Rev. 3 | | | |
Category	1981	1987	Change 1981–87	1987	1990	Change 1981–90	Change 1987–90
SITC 78 Road vehicles							
Exports	16,397	21,054	4,657	20,906	29,373	12,976	8,467
Imports	28,145	72,500	44,355	72,584	72,239	44,094	−345
Balance	−11,748	−51,446	−39,698	−51,678	−42,866	−31,118	8,812
of which							
781 Passenger motor cars							
Exports	4,025	6,947	2,922	6,965	10,170	6,145	3,205
Imports	17,963	48,619	30,656	48,613	45,943	27,980	−2,670
Balance	−13,938	−41,672	−27,734	−41,648	−35,773	−21,835	5,875
782 Trucks							
Exports	2,417	2,483	66	2,461	2,959	542	498
Imports	3,792	8,018	4,226	8,291	8,383	4,591	92
Balance	−1,375	−5,535	−4,160	−5,830	−5,424	−4,049	406
783 Other road vehicles							
Exports	424	402	−22	402	557	133	155
Imports	401	697	296	700	647	246	−53
Balance	23	−295	−318	−298	−90	−113	208
784 Parts and accessories							
Exports	9,177	10,925	1,748	8,295	14,755	5,578	6,460
Imports	4,258	13,771	9,513	13,375	15,825	11,567	2,450
Balance	4,919	−2,846	−7,765	−5,080	−1,071	−5,990	4,009
785 Motorcycles							
Exports	98	147	49	1,224	460	362	−764
Imports	1,696	1,301	−395	1,377	1,239	−457	−138
Balance	−1,598	−1,154	444	−153	−779	819	−626
786 Trailers							
Exports	256	149	−107	1,557	471	215	−1,086
Imports	35	94	59	228	201	166	−27
Balance	221	55	−166	1,329	271	50	−1,058
SITC 713 Internal combustion engines							
Exports	4,113	4,241	128	4,082	5,689	1,576	1,607
Imports	2,268	6,389	4,121	6,321	7,135	4,867	814
Balance	1,845	−2,148	−3,993	−2,239	−1,446	−3,291	793

a. Data are expressed on a domestic exports, imports customs basis.

Source: US Department of Commerce.

Table 5.78.5 Road vehicles and engines: geographic composition of US trade, 1981–90

	Millions of dollars				Percent of total			
	1981	1987	1989	1990	1981	1987	1989	1990
Exports								
78 Road vehicles								
Canada	8,567	15,029	15,891	17,465	52.2	71.8	62.3	59.5
Japan	166	325	852	1,399	1.0	1.5	3.3	4.8
European Community	1,131	1,292	2,087	2,551	6.8	6.1	8.1	8.7
Germany	238	379	724	982	1.4	1.8	2.8	2.7
Other	6,534	4,260	6,649	7,958	39.8	20.3	26.0	27.9
Total	16,398	20,906	25,479	29,373	100.0	100.0	100.0	100.0
781 Passenger cars								
Canada	3,168	5,776	6,252	6,032	78.7	82.9	64.7	59.3
Japan	49	92	431	759	1.2	1.3	4.4	7.4
European Community	95	321	821	1,065	2.3	4.6	8.5	10.4
Germany	38	114	331	493	0.9	1.6	3.4	4.8
Other	713	776	2,147	2,314	17.7	11.1	22.2	22.7
Total	4,025	6,965	9,651	10,170	100.0	100.0	100.0	100.0
782 Trucks								
Canada	520	1,831	2,157	1,806	21.5	74.4	69.6	61.0
Japan	17	12	25	50	0.7	0.4	0.8	1.6
European Community	101	50	78	161	4.1	2.0	2.5	5.4
Germany	15	15	28	61	0.6	0.6	0.9	2.0
Other	1,779	568	836	942	73.6	23.0	27.0	31.8
Total	2,417	2,461	3,096	2,959	100.0	100.0	100.0	100.0
784 Parts and accessories								
Canada	4,657	5,588	7,013	8,888	50.7	67.3	59.8	60.2
Japan	90	145	317	500	0.9	1.7	2.7	3.3
European Community	894	677	999	1,078	9.7	8.1	8.5	7.3
Germany	175	155	298	331	1.9	1.8	2.5	2.2
Mexico	1,469	832	1,953	2,856	16.0	10.0	16.6	19.3
Other	2,067	1,053	1,426	1,433	22.5	12.6	12.1	9.7
Total	9,177	8,295	11,708	14,755	100.0	100.0	100.0	100.0
713 Engines								
Canada	1,658	1,922	1,859	2,790	40.3	47.0	38.6	49.0
Japan	88	81	114	114	2.1	1.9	2.3	2.0
European Community	702	689	1,077	995	17.0	16.8	22.4	17.5
Germany	77	98	142	152	1.8	2.4	2.9	2.6
Mexico	345	367	472	509	8.3	8.9	9.8	8.9
Other	1,319	1,023	1,284	1,281	32.0	25.0	26.7	22.5
Total	4,112	4,082	4,806	5,689	100.0	100.0	100.0	100.0

table continued next page

Table 5.78.5 Road vehicles and engines: geographic composition of US trade, 1981–90 (continued)

	Millions of dollars				Percent of total			
	1981	1987	1989	1990	1981	1987	1989	1990
Imports								
78 Road vehicles								
Canada	8,928	20,520	25,725	26,091	31.7	28.2	35.7	36.1
Japan	13,476	30,647	28,918	27,336	47.8	42.2	40.2	37.8
European Community	4,585	13,500	9,487	10,347	16.2	18.5	13.2	14.3
Germany	3,119	9,923	6,026	6,721	11.0	13.6	8.3	9.3
Other	1,157	7,918	7,733	8,465	4.1	10.9	10.7	11.7
Total	28,146	72,585	71,863	72,239	100.0	100.0	100.0	100.0
781 Passenger cars								
Canada	4,297	10,256	12,960	13,758	23.9	21.0	28.9	29.9
Japan	9,677	21,867	20,259	19,548	53.8	44.9	45.3	42.5
European Community	3,415	10,896	6,741	7,536	19.0	22.4	15.0	16.4
Germany	2,659	8,965	5,051	5,871	14.8	18.4	11.2	12.7
Other	573	5,594	4,742	5,101	3.1	11.5	10.6	11.1
Total	17,962	48,613	44,702	45,943	100.0	100.0	100.0	100.0
782 Trucks								
Canada	1,974	3,725	5,492	6,024	52.0	44.9	63.9	71.8
Japan	1,809	4,243	2,762	1,915	47.7	51.1	32.1	22.8
European Community	6	178	115	146	0.1	2.1	1.3	1.7
Germany	4	23	23	33	0.1	0.2	0.2	0.3
Other	3	145	221	298	0.0	1.7	2.5	3.5
Total	3,792	8,291	8,590	8,383	100.0	100.0	100.0	100.0
784 Parts and accessories								
Canada	2,259	5,810	6,622	5,706	53.0	43.4	40.4	36.0
Japan	518	3,801	5,212	5,342	12.1	28.4	31.8	33.7
European Community	1,062	2,275	2,471	2,480	24.9	17.0	15.0	15.6
Germany	414	890	924	777	9.7	6.6	5.6	4.9
Mexico	202	645	1,073	1,227	4.7	4.8	6.5	7.7
Other	217	844	988	1,070	5.0	6.3	6.0	6.7
Total	4,258	13,375	16,366	15,825	100.0	100.0	100.0	100.0
713 Engines								
Canada	706	1,618	2,025	1,753	31.1	25.5	25.5	24.5
Japan	476	1,832	3,196	2,575	20.9	28.9	40.3	36.0
European Community	812	1,355	1,127	1,443	35.8	21.4	14.2	20.2
Germany	348	735	606	954	15.3	11.6	7.6	13.3
Mexico	101	966	824	691	4.4	15.2	10.4	9.6
Other	173	550	750	673	7.6	8.7	9.4	9.4
Total	2,268	6,321	7,922	7,135	100.0	100.0	100.0	100.0

a. Data are expressed on a domestic exports, imports customs basis.

Source: US Department of Commerce.

Table 5.78.6 Road vehicles, and engines: indices of US competitiveness, 1981–89 (billions of dollars except where noted)

	1981	1982	1983	1984	1985	1986	1987	1988	1989	Annual growth 1981–89 (percentages)
SITC 78: Road vehicles										
World trade										
World exports to non-US destinations	96.2	91.5	88.1	89.3	96.9	121.5	153.6	177.2	189.6	8.8
World imports from non-US sources	109.3	108.7	110.2	118.8	135.3	171.8	204.6	222.5	234.2	10.0
US trade										
Exports	16.1	13.8	14.4	17.5	19.4	18.7	21.6	25.3	25.5	5.9
Imports	29.5	32.1	37.6	48.5	59.4	70.3	74.6	75.0	73.9	12.1
Balance	−13.4	−18.3	−23.2	−31.0	−40.0	−51.6	−53.0	−49.7	−48.4	Change 1981–89
US share of exports to non-US destinations (percentages)	16.8	15.1	16.3	19.6	20.0	15.4	14.0	14.3	13.5	−3.3
US share of imports from non-US sources (percentages)	27.0	29.5	34.1	40.8	43.9	40.9	36.5	33.7	31.6	4.6
Export share minus import share (percentages)	−10.2	−14.4	−17.8	−21.2	−23.9	−25.6	−22.4	−19.4	−18.1	−7.9
SITC 713: Engines										
World trade										
World exports to non-US destinations	12.9	12.4	11.9	12.7	12.7	14.8	17.5	22.8	23.5	7.8
World imports from non-US sources	11.2	10.8	11.4	13.3	14.0	16.8	20.6	24.9	26	11.1
US trade										
Exports	4.1	3.9	3.6	4.2	4.3	4.0	4.2	5.2	4.8	2.0
Imports	2.3	2.4	3.4	4.7	5.2	5.6	6.5	7.9	8.1	17.0
Balance	1.8	1.5	0.2	−0.5	−0.9	−1.6	−2.3	−2.7	−3.3	Change 1981–89
US share of exports to non-US destinations (percentages)	31.8	31.2	30.0	33.0	33.5	26.7	24.2	22.8	20.5	−11.3
US share of imports from non-US sources (percentages)	20.8	22.5	30.0	35.7	37.3	33.1	31.7	31.9	31.1	10.3
Export share minus import share (percentages)	11.0	8.7	0.0	−2.7	−3.8	−6.4	−7.5	−9.1	−10.6	−21.6

Source: World Manufactures Trade Data Base.

Table 5.78.7 Road vehicles: US sales and Japanese market shares, 1988–90 and projected 1995

	1988		1989		1990		1995[a]	
	Millions of units	Percentages of total	Millions of units	Percentages of total	Millions of units	Percentages of total	Millions of units	Percentages of total
US sales								
Cars	10.5		9.8		9.3		10.7	
Trucks	5.1		4.9		4.8		5.6	
Total	15.7		14.7		14.1		16.3	
of which:								
Exports from Japan								
Cars	2.0	19.2	1.9	19.4	1.7	18.5	1.9	17.8
Trucks	0.6	12.1	0.5	10.4	0.6	12.6	0.5	8.9
Total	2.6	16.9	2.4	16.4	2.3	16.5	2.4	14.7
Japanese production in US								
Cars	0.8	7.6	1.0	10.2	1.4	15.1	2.1	19.6
Trucks	0.1	1.9	0.1	2.0	0.2	3.7	0.4	7.1
Total	0.9	5.7	1.1	7.5	1.6	11.2	2.5	15.3
Total Japanese sales in US								
Cars	2.8	26.8	2.9	29.6	3.1	33.5	4.0	37.4
Trucks	0.7	14.1	0.6	12.4	0.8	16.3	0.9	16.1
Total	3.5	22.6	3.5	23.9	3.9	27.6	4.9	30.1

a. Forecast by US Department of Commerce, Office of Automotive Affairs, January 1991.

Source: Base data derived from *Ward's Automotive Reports*, various issues.

Table 5.78.8   Road vehicles: projected trade balance with Japan, 1995

Product	Billions of dollars
Automobiles	
1.9 million units imported @ $13,500[a]	25.65
Less 0.1 million units exported @ $13,500	1.35
	25.65
Trucks	
0.5 million units imported @ $7,500[b]	3.75
Parts, accessories, and engines	
US imports	9.00
Total 1995 deficit	37.05

a. Assumes annual price increases of 4 percent per year.

b. Assumes annual price increases of 4.5 percent per year.

Source: US Department of Commerce.

Table 5.78.9   Alternative projections of US-Japan bilateral road vehicle trade

Researcher and date of forecast	Forecast year	Millions of units			Nominal deficit (billions of dollars)
		US-based Japanese production	US imports from Japan	Japanese imports from US	
Nomura Research, September 1989	1995	2.2	2.75	0.2	40.5
Fuji Research Institute, February 1989	1994	2.08	1.27	0.13	24.2
Robert Z. Lawrence, March 1990	1992	2.23	2.14	n.a	30.2
Industrial Bank of Japan, June 1990	1995	2.29	2.06	0.34	27.6
Ariyoshi Okumura, Industrial Bank of Japan June 1990	1995	2.35	2.2	0.1	n.a.
Michigan Report, September 1989	1993	2.32	2.8	0.13	35.7
Allen J. Lenz, May 1991	1995	2.5	2.4	0.1	37.1[a]

n.a. = not available.

a. Of which $24.3 billion in passenger cars and $3.8 billion in trucks.

Source: The data are drawn principally from Japan-US Business Council, "Views and Proposals Concerning the Michigan Report," 29 June 1990.

Aircraft (SITC 792) and Aircraft Engines (SITC 714)

Other transportation equipment (SITC 79) includes aircraft (SITC 792). In 1990, this category provided the largest volume of US exports and the largest US trade surplus of any two-digit category, $23.7 billion. It will continue to play a very important role in US trade performance.

The United States is probably more dominant in this trade category than any other. But the US market share fell in the 1980s and is not expected to grow in the near future. The aerospace trade surplus will increase only in parallel with growth in the world market. World aircraft and engine exports are only one-fourth the size of world automotive exports. The potential contribution of aircraft surpluses to improved overall US trade performance is, therefore, limited. Alone it cannot counterbalance automotive and other large trade deficits.

Description of the Product Group

Aircraft is part of a larger category, other transport equipment (SITC 79), which consists of:

SITC

791 railway vehicles and associated equipment

792 aircraft, associated equipment, and parts

793 ships, boats, and floating structures.

This section examines only aircraft (SITC 792), which makes up about 62 percent of world exports and almost all of US trade in this category. The aircraft subcategory includes large commercial transports (jetliners), military aircraft, commuter planes, helicopters, and small planes. This analysis also includes jet engines, which make up most but not all of trade in SITC 714 (engines not based on internal combustion). US trade figures for aircraft omit the country of destination for some military exports, for national security reasons.

Role in World Trade

Size and Composition

World exports of aircraft were $53.0 billion in 1989; world exports of aircraft engines were $18.5 billion (table 5.79.1). During 1981–89, world aircraft exports grew slowly, and their share of world manufactures exports fell by nearly half a percentage point. Trade in aircraft parts and engines grew more quickly than trade in assembled aircraft.

In interpreting these and other statistics on aircraft transactions, one must remember that these products are inherently "lumpy": large commercial transports cost millions of dollars each and are made by only three firms worldwide: two US firms and one European. This lumpiness may cause statistics to fluctuate widely and can make year-to-year comparisons misleading.

Global Competition Patterns

World aircraft exports are dominated by the United States and the European Community, which collectively account for almost 90 percent of the total (table 5.79.2). US exports generally exceed EC exports. Unlike the United States, which enjoys a large aircraft trade surplus, the Community's aircraft exports are balanced by large imports. Half of the Community's aircraft exports stay within the Community, in part because the Airbus Industrie consortium produces and assembles aircraft in several countries (table 5.79.3). Since US exports are not matched by large imports, the United States has consistently run very large surpluses.

Key Determinants of World Trade Patterns

World aircraft trade patterns are determined largely by the sales of the US firms Boeing Co. and McDonnell Douglas Corp. and the Airbus Industrie consortium of the European Community. Similarly, exports by General Electric Co. and Pratt & Whitney in the United States and by Rolls Royce Ltd. in the United Kingdom account for half of world aircraft engine exports (table 5.79.3).[1] Production of military aircraft for export is also concentrated in the United States and the European Community.

---

1. SITC 714 includes some products other than jet engines.

Trade share data through 1989 do not fully reflect the success of Airbus in world markets. According to the US Commerce Department, the share of Airbus in orders for large transports increased from 7 percent to 27 percent over the 1980s. Statistics detailing aircraft orders can accurately predict future deliveries of large commercial aircraft, and these suggest that Airbus will have around a 30 percent market share for the next several years.

Any discussion of aircraft trade that focused only on trade in assembled aircraft would be incomplete. The increasing trade in parts and engines reflects the globalization of aircraft production: most aircraft contain parts from many countries (see, e.g., Aerospace Industries Association of America 1988). Also, airlines usually buy engines separately for their new and used aircraft. US exports and imports of both parts and engines doubled during 1981–89, and the United States now exports more parts and engines by dollar value than complete aircraft. A substantial portion of each large transport manufactured in the United States is of foreign origin and design, and development costs are increasingly being shared internationally. Indeed, according to one study, "It is safe to say that no large transport will ever be designed or built solely within national boundaries again. Boeing has stated flatly that it will no longer consider such huge undertakings without foreign partners" (March 1989).

The use of foreign partners and subcontractors has been encouraged by the high risk inherent in aircraft production, the national procurement practices of foreign-flagship airlines, improved foreign technical capabilities, and, in the case of military aircraft, demands of government buyers. Because of the large up-front capital requirements, long breakeven times, and uncertain demand, development of a new commercial transport entails "betting the company."

A side effect of globalization has been to reduce entry barriers by allowing companies from several countries to each make only a part of an aircraft. Globalization of the aircraft industry has occurred not through direct investment and the creation of multinationals, but through subcontracting, joint ventures, and licensing. The increased number of shifting and overlapping strategic alliances between companies has aided the international transfer of technology. World markets for aircraft are highly integrated; trade is large relative to production, and transport costs for the finished product are, of course, low.

The US content of an American-made large commercial transport is around 60 percent. Foreign-made aircraft also include US parts and engines, but as a result of a conscious policy of de-Americanization, the US content of Airbus aircraft fell from 30 percent for the A300 to 22 percent for the A320. The US content in the A330 and A340 should be higher, although actual results will depend on the buyer's choice of engines.

Increasing exports of aircraft parts and engines have helped the US trade balance, as the trade figures indicate. However, the globalization of production implies that the historical dominance of US manufacturers is slipping. For instance, the United States no longer dominates engine production as it does airframes, and US companies now make engines in cooperation with foreign partners on relatively equal terms. These factors, plus the penetration of world markets by Airbus, limit the future growth of US aircraft and engine surpluses.

Role in US Trade

Recent Performance

Aircraft is consistently the largest US export and largest surplus category. Aircraft accounted for 10 percent of US manufactures exports in 1990, but less than 2 percent of manufactures imports.

The trade balances in both aircraft and engines improved very slightly from 1981 to 1987 (table 5.79.4). The balance for parts showed the strongest performance, increasing by $1.2 billion. Imports doubled in almost all subcategories, but export growth—although smaller in percentage terms—kept the balance from deteriorating. Within the aircraft subcategory, the United States trades large amounts of commercial transports, military aircraft, parts, commuter planes, and business jets. By comparison, trade in helicopters, small planes, and satellites is small. Much of world aircraft and engine trade is between the United States and the European Community (table 5.79.5). More than one-third of US aircraft exports go to the European Community, and only about one-tenth to Japan. Half of US imports come from the European Community.

The aircraft trade balance improved remarkably from 1987 to 1990, with the surplus increasing from $12.3 billion to $23.7 billion. The improvement occurred on the strength of a 78 percent increase in exports and a 39 percent growth in imports, which started from a much smaller base.

International Competitiveness

The US share of world exports of aircraft and parts to non-US destinations rose from 55.4 percent in 1981 to 60.4 percent in 1987 (table 5.79.6), but fell to 49.1 percent in 1989. However, the US share of imports from non-US sources increased by even more in percentage terms, implying that the United States has become a much more important market for foreign exporters. The United States absorbed 28.1 percent of aircraft exports from the rest of the world in

1987. The US aircraft import share fell to 19.1 percent in 1989, however. Similar trends were evident for aircraft engines, with the United States taking over one-third of engine exports from the rest of the world in 1989.

Outlook

Key Determinants of US Trade Performance

Growing sales by the Airbus consortium have increased US imports of large commercial transports and heightened competition in export markets. Imports did not become significant until 1979 and have continued to increase since then, accounting for 20 percent of US purchases of large transport aircraft in 1989. Despite these inroads, the two largest US manufacturers continue to dominate world sales of Western-made commercial transport aircraft, with a world market share of 71 percent according to the US Commerce Department. The large transports of the two major US producers make up a third of US aerospace exports. The industry is highly export oriented, delivering more than half of its production to foreign customers.

Although the fall in the dollar after 1985 affected aerospace trade, Airbus prices its large commercial transports in dollars, and the consortium attempts to maintain its dollar prices in spite of exchange rate movements. The German government has promised to protect the German partner in Airbus from exchange rate movements with an exchange rate guarantee. Thus, a decline in the dollar exchange rate increases the German subsidy costs. The dollar has a more immediate effect on subcontracting, which is not necessarily priced in dollars. In addition, trade flows respond to most stimuli only with a relatively long lag, because of multiyear order backlogs and the time it takes to produce and deliver an aircraft.

Trade in military aircraft primarily reflects government policies and the state of international relations. The US trade surplus in military aircraft has been declining over a long period as several foreign countries have developed the ability to make their own aircraft. As world defense spending falls, declining demand and fierce competition in third markets will exacerbate this longstanding trend. The production of military aircraft is increasingly globalized, and access to technology has become much broader, but not to the same extent as for commercial aircraft. Government purchasers of military aircraft commonly place conditions on sales, such as requirements for the transfer of technology and domestic production. The trend toward joint production of military aircraft has decreased US exports of complete aircraft but has increased exports of parts. France and the United Kingdom have the capability to produce their own military aircraft, and Brazil, Taiwan, Israel, and Japan are progressing rapidly.

The increased use of hub-and-spoke systems by US airlines since airline deregulation has increased US demand for large commuter aircraft, which are not made domestically but are often imported from the European Community and Brazil. Imports of business jets have also increased, although the United States has some strong entries in this category. Third World debt and weak African economies have cut into these natural markets for small aircraft. US production of small airplanes is a fraction of historical levels, in part because of excessively high product liability insurance costs. The United States imports a small number of planes in kit form; the buyer then carries the liability for the assembly.

Most of the improvement in US trade in aircraft from 1987 to 1990 occurred in large transport aircraft, as deliveries were made on foreign orders placed earlier. The trade balance on planes weighing more than 15,000 kg improved by $9.9 billion, despite the introduction of the Airbus A320 and the Fokker F-100 into the US market in 1989 and the fall in military exports from $3.6 billion to $1.8 billion (US Department of Commerce, International Trade Administration 1991, 22-2). Orders for large transport aircraft began to climb after the early 1980s, reaching record highs in 1988 and again in 1989. Airlines had been holding back in the early 1980s, in part because of high oil prices, and when the logjam broke, most came through with big orders. Aircraft became easier to finance when banks began lending on the basis of the resale value of used airplanes, which had been rising. Also, "finance leases" became common. These arrangements, in which investors take a 20 percent equity stake in aircraft and then lease them to airlines, create substantial tax benefits in Japan. Over half of the aircraft bought in the last five years were financed in this way. The rise in the trade surplus from 1989 to 1990 was, however, exaggerated by the effects of a strike at British Aerospace, which lowered US Airbus imports in 1990, and a strike at Boeing, which lowered US exports in 1989.

Other subcategories also played a role in improved performance. The balance on parts rose $1.9 billion from 1987 to 1990, while the balance on engines improved by $0.6 billion. Continuing domestic demand for commuter aircraft to serve hub airports and the turnaround in the business jet market caused the US trade surplus in airplanes weighing from 2,000 to 15,000 kg to fall by $1.2 billion.

Near-Term Outlook

Multiyear order backlogs for the three makers of commercial transports—Boeing, McDonnell Douglas, and Airbus—mean that production rates will primarily determine aircraft exports and imports for the next several years. Boeing increased monthly production rates in 1990 from 31 to 34 planes and to 38 planes in 1991; Airbus has also increased production, partly to recover from the British

Aerospace strike. To the extent that market shares remain roughly the same, the US trade balance will increase in parallel with world deliveries. Airbus has achieved its target of a 30 percent market share, and its chairman has said that his new target is 40 percent. Boeing projects that world deliveries of large transport aircraft by all firms will increase from the 1988–89 levels of roughly $20 billion a year to over $41 billion a year (in 1990 dollars) during the period 1990–2005 (Boeing Commercial Airplane Group 1991). Deliveries averaged $16 billion in 1990 dollars from 1970 to 1990.

Airbus also projects significant growth in deliveries but is less optimistic than Boeing (Airbus Industrie 1991). Both projections are based on assumptions of booming demand for air travel, particularly in Asia, and high rates of aircraft replacement because of age, new noise regulations, and lower costs for fuel and crew salaries in new aircraft. The better financial performance of non-US airlines compared with US airlines, measured in revenue passenger miles, will have a positive effect on the trade balance, because foreign airlines will be buying more aircraft. An offsetting factor will be the need to replace the larger proportion of older planes in the US fleet.

Continued globalization is likely to continue to push up the foreign content of US aircraft and the associated US imports of engines and parts. The aftereffects of the 1990–91 Gulf crisis could temporarily lead to significantly higher military aircraft exports to the Middle East. The United States will continue to import large commuter aircraft; a US-based production capacity for these aircraft is not expected. Imports of business jets may fall as a result of corporate belt-tightening.

The governments of the United States and the European Community are discussing reductions in European subsidies to the member companies of the Airbus consortium. The United States is filing a complaint with the General Agreement on Tariffs and Trade (GATT) about the exchange rate guarantee for the German partner of the consortium. It is highly unlikely, however, that these companies would be required to pay back past subsidies at market rates of interest; a study for the US Commerce Department found that they would lack the financial capacity to do so (US Department of Commerce, International Trade Administration 1990). In practice, Airbus is here to stay, and reductions in future subsidies will affect neither the market share of planes already in production nor US aircraft trade balances in the near future.

A rough estimate of the potential dollar increase in the aircraft trade surplus for the next few years can be made in the following manner. Boeing has forecast roughly a $6 billion increase by 1993 in yearly deliveries of large transports over 1990 levels. Following present patterns, US producers can be expected to deliver 70 percent of those planes and export half of them, raising aircraft exports by $2 billion each year. However, imports of Airbus aircraft would increase by about $0.5 billion, reducing the increase in the US surplus to $1.5 billion. Assuming, optimistically, that increased imports of parts and engines to make

US planes are matched by increased exports of parts and engines and that balances on military, business, and commuter aircraft improve by $1.5 billion, a $3 billion improvement in the aircraft trade surplus is in prospect by 1993. A one-time jump in military aircraft exports to the Middle East might also help improve the balance, but only for a year or two. With the aircraft and engine balance at $26 billion in 1990, a $1 billion improvement is likely in 1991, depending on whether the companies happen to make more foreign or domestic deliveries that year. An improvement to a $29 billion surplus by 1993 is within reach.

Medium-Term Outlook

The US aircraft market is expected to remain the world's largest single-country market for some time, but growth rates are expected to be greater in the Asia-Pacific region. The European market, although growing, is constrained by air traffic congestion, overregulation, and poorly coordinated air traffic control. EC 1992 will not greatly affect aerospace trade, but partial airline deregulation coincident with EC 1992 could increase demand. In the longer run, Europe-wide aerospace standards could displace US aerospace standards in other regions, to the detriment of US exports.

High oil prices during the Gulf crisis slowed aircraft orders only after several months. The decision to order a transport is a long-term one, and new aircraft are more fuel efficient. The Gulf crisis had more of an impact on airline finances than on orders. Furthermore, air travel falls disproportionately in recessions. Because US airlines seem to be in greater trouble than foreign airlines, the net impact on the aircraft trade balance could be positive. There are also indications that flat growth in the resale value of jets has tightened airline financing. However, Airbus expects that new worldwide orders for commercial jet airliners will drop from the 1,000 + levels of the past three years to between 100 and 200 for the next few years (Betts and Leadbeater 1991).

The Middle Eastern market was strong before the Gulf crisis. Eastern Europe and the Soviet Union may become new markets; in October 1990, the US government proposed that some types of aircraft and engines, including the Boeing 747, be dropped from export control lists. The industry feels that export controls in some cases unnecessarily limit US export opportunities, as does insufficient export financing.

Aerospace trade is relatively free of formal barriers as a result of the 1979 Agreement on Trade in Civil Aircraft under the GATT; a successful Uruguay Round would have little impact on aircraft trade. In particular, trade barriers are not significant for large transport aircraft, but development and production subsidies have kept the Airbus consortium afloat despite its long history of losses. Airbus, on the other hand, charges that US aircraft manufacturers benefit indirectly from defense spending and other sources. Some argue that Airbus has provided competition for the concentrated US industry, resulting in lower prices and cost cutting. There has been some tendency for government-owned airlines to "buy national"; this creates a significant trade barrier, because many airlines are government owned (although there has been a move toward privatization in recent years). In addition, governments have been known to use landing rights at their airports to encourage private airlines to buy domestically. Preference for domestic products has encouraged the trend toward joint ventures and licensing. Offsets and countertrade are problems, but are less serious.

Airbus may have an edge in the introduction of new aircraft. It began delivery on the A340 in late 1991 and on the A330 about a year after that. McDonnell Douglas delivered its first MD-11, a wide-bodied airliner, late in 1990. Boeing announced the beginning of its 777 program in December 1990; the 777, however, will not be available for delivery until after 1994. Boeing's planned production partners include three Japanese companies—Mitsubishi, Fuji, and Kawasaki—which will make around 20 percent of the aircraft. Japanese producers are expected to play gradually increasing roles in making components and subassemblies and may develop strengths in avionics, but it is highly unlikely that they will become competitors in airframes in the 1990s.

The aerospace industry has the highest level of private R&D spending of all US industries, and government R&D funding no longer plays a key role. Current planes use technology that is, for the most part, 10 to 25 years old. The R&D budget of the National Aeronautics and Space Administration (NASA) devotes less money to aeronautics than it used to. US Department of Defense requirements have increasingly diverged from civilian needs, and the military no longer plays the role in testing new technologies to the extent that it once did. The aerospace industry has often been at the cutting edge of many manufacturing technologies, and other industries often use its innovations.

Japan has been trying to break into the aerospace industry for some time, and its Ministry of International Trade and Industry (MITI) has allocated several hundred million dollars to research on materials and engines for a hypersonic transport. A consortium of all the current market leaders—including General Electric, Pratt & Whitney, SNECMA, and Rolls Royce—will do research on the hypersonic engines. In Europe, Airbus aircraft are in some ways more technologically sophisticated than US planes, and the European Community is discussing a program for Strategic Measures in Aeronautical Research and Technology (EUROMART). The MIT Commission on Industrial Productivity (1989, 1) sums up the longer-term outlook: "The US position, though preeminent, has been declining and is likely to slip further."

Conclusions

- At $26 billion, the overall US aircraft and engines surplus in 1990 was the largest of any product category, equivalent to the bilateral US deficit with Japan in road vehicles.

- The aerospace trade surplus has increased rapidly and should continue to rise over the next few years as a result of booming demand for aircraft. Future increases, however, will be modest, resulting from a growing world market rather than from increased market share.

- World aerospace exports in 1989 were only one-fourth the size of world automotive exports, but the world aircraft market is expected to grow rapidly.

- Negative factors affecting the longer-term US aircraft trade balance, such as the globalization of production, new competition, and the effects of airline deregulation, have been masked by the recent rapid growth in world demand for large transports.

- The short-term US outlook is positive for large transports, parts, engines, and perhaps military aircraft, while deterioration is likely for business and commuter planes.

- The United States will continue to import commuter aircraft to service the hub-and-spoke systems that developed after airline deregulation; the development of US-based commuter aircraft production is not expected.

- The long-term trend of falling surpluses in military aircraft will continue, although the aftermath of the Gulf crisis could boost exports to the Middle East.

- There are long lags in the effects of exchange rate changes on aircraft deliveries, because of long order and production times and Airbus's attempts to maintain dollar prices. Trade flows of engines and parts are more responsive to exchange rates.

- Airbus is here to stay, and competition in components and parts, particularly from Japan, will continue to intensify.

- The US position, although preeminent, has been declining and is likely to slip further. Nevertheless, aircraft and engines have been a major US surplus item, totaling $26 billion in 1990. If world market conditions remain favorable, the surplus could rise to $29 billion by 1993.

- Although large surpluses should continue through the 1990s, aircraft does not appear to provide a continuing source of further major gains. It will not provide a substitute for improved performance in other product groups.

Bibliography

Aerospace Industries Association of America. 1983. *National Benefits of Aerospace Exports*. Washington: Aerospace Research Center (June).

Aerospace Industries Association of America. 1988. *The U.S. Aerospace Industry and the Trend Toward Internationalization*. Washington: Aerospace Research Center (March).

Aerospace Industries Association of America. 1989a. *U.S. Aerospace Technology Development: Stepping Up the Pace*. Washington: Aerospace Industries Association (July).

Aerospace Industries Association of America. 1989b. *Technology Readiness*. Washington: Aerospace Research Center (September).

Aerospace Industries Association of America. 1991. *Aerospace Facts and Figures, 1990–1991*. Washington: Aerospace Research Center (in press).

Airbus Industrie. 1990. *Market Perspectives for Civil Jet Aircraft*. Airbus Industrie (March).

Betts, Paul. 1990. "Aircraft Industry Faces Hard Landing." *Financial Times* (10 October).

Betts, Paul, and Charles Leadbeater. 1991. "Airbus Sees Sharp Fall in Orders for Jet Airlines." *Financial Times* (18 February): 1.

Boeing Commercial Airplane Group. 1991. *Current Market Outlook: World Travel Market Demand and Airplane Supply Requirements*. Seattle: Boeing Commercial Airplane Group (February).

Commission of the European Communities. 1988. *Toward a Programme of Strategic Measures in Aeronautical Research and Technology for Europe*. Brussels: Commission of the European Communities (June).

Commission of the European Communities. 1990. *Panorama of EC Industry, 1990*. Luxembourg: Commission of the European Communities.

Council on Competitiveness. 1990. *Aerospace: Sectoral Profile*. Washington: Council on Competitiveness (July).

General Aviation Manufacturers Association. 1991. *General Aviation Statistical Databook—1990 Edition*. Washington: General Aviation Manufacturers Association (in press).

Hayward, Keith. 1986. *International Collaboration in Civil Aerospace*. London: Frances Pinter.

Industry, Science and Technology Canada. 1988. *Industry Profiles*. Ottawa: Industry, Science and Technology Canada.

Japan Economic Journal. 1990. *Japan Economic Almanac, 1990*. Tokyo: Japan Economic Journal.

"Japanese Firms to Co-Produce New Jetliner With Boeing Co." 1990. *Washington Post* (8 December): C8.

March, Artemis. 1989. "The U.S. Commercial Aircraft Industry and Its Foreign Competitors." In *The Working Papers of the MIT Commission on Industrial Productivity*, vol. 1. Cambridge, MA: MIT Press.

Mowery, David C. 1987. *Alliance Politics and Economics: Multinational Joint Ventures in Commercial Aircraft*. Cambridge, MA: Ballinger.

National Academy of Engineering. 1985. *The Competitive Status of the U.S. Civil Aviation Manufacturing Industry*. Washington: National Academy Press.

Office of Science and Technology Policy. 1985. "National Aeronautical R&D Goals: Technology for America's Future." Washington: Office of Science and Technology Policy (March).

Society of Japanese Aerospace Companies. 1990. *Aerospace Industry in Japan: 1989–1990*. Tokyo: Society of Japanese Aerospace Companies.

"Survey on Aerospace." 1990. *Financial Times* (29 August).

US Department of Commerce, Bureau of the Census. 1987. *1987 Census of Manufactures, Aerospace Equipment, Including Parts*. Washington: US Department of Commerce.

US Department of Commerce, Bureau of the Census. 1990a. *New Complete Aircraft and Aircraft Engines (Except Military)*. Current Industrial Report, M37G series. Washington: US Department of Commerce.

US Department of Commerce, Bureau of the Census. 1990b. *Aerospace Industry (Orders, Sales, and Backlog)*. Current Industrial Report. Washington: US Department of Commerce (MA37D series).

US Department of Commerce, International Trade Administration. 1984a. *Brazilian Government Support for the Aerospace Industry*. Washington: Government Printing Office (November).

US Department of Commerce, International Trade Administration. 1984b. *Canadian Government Support for the Aerospace Industry*. Washington: Government Printing Office (November).

US Department of Commerce, International Trade Administration. 1984c. *A Competitive Assessment of the U.S. Civil Aircraft Industry*. Washington: Government Printing Office (March).

US Department of Commerce, International Trade Administration. 1986. *A Competitive Assessment of the U.S. General Aviation Industry*. Washington: Government Printing Office (June).

US Department of Commerce, International Trade Administration. 1988. *A Competitive Assessment of the U.S. Civil Helicopter Industry*. Washington: Government Printing Office (April).

US Department of Commerce, International Trade Administration. 1990. *An Economic and Financial Review of Airbus Industrie*. Prepared by Gellman Research Associates. Washington: Government Printing Office (September).

US Department of Commerce, International Trade Administration. 1991. *U.S. Industrial Outlook, 1991*. Washington: Government Printing Office (January).

US Department of Transportation. 1985. *Emerging Sources of Foreign Competition in the Commercial Aircraft Manufacturing Industry*. Washington: US Department of Transportation.

Wilbur Smith Associates. 1990. *Economic Impact of Civil Aviation on the U.S. Economy*. Washington: Wilbur Smith Associates (October).

See also the following periodicals: *Aviation Week, Air and Cosmos, Air Transport World, Flight International, Interavia*.

Table 5.79.1 Aircraft, parts, and engines: product composition of world trade, 1981–89 (billions of dollars except where noted)

SITC Product	1981	1982	1983	1984	1985	1986	1987	1988	1989	Annual growth 1981–89 (percentages)
SITC 792: Aircraft and parts World exports to world	29.2	27.9	26.4	26.1	29.5	29.8	33.2	44.3	53.0	7.7
SITC 714: Engines World exports to world	8.5	9.1	8.8	8.9	9.7	11.5	13.8	16.2	18.5	10.2
Memorandum:										
SITC 792 share of world manufactures exports (percentages)	2.9	2.9	2.7	2.4	2.6	2.2	2.0	2.2	2.5	−0.4
SITC 714 share of world manufactures exports (percentages)	0.8	0.9	0.9	0.8	0.9	0.8	0.8	0.8	0.8	0.0

Source: World Manufactures Trade Data Base.

Table 5.79.2 Aircraft, parts and engines; geographic distribution of world trade, 1981–89 (percentages of total)

Country	1981	1982	1983	1984	1985	1986	1987	1988	1989	Change 1981–89
Share of exports to world										
United States	50.5	42.2	46.2	41.8	48.2	50.8	53.7	45.2	44.6	−5.9
Canada	3.5	4.4	3.8	3.8	4.3	5.5	4.7	3.3	2.0	−1.6
Japan	0.4	0.6	0.6	0.5	0.4	0.5	0.7	0.7	0.7	0.3
European Community	34.8	43.4	39.3	42.8	35.7	36.7	33.7	38.6	43.0	8.2
EC to non-EC	20.5	24.7	23.6	24.9	21.4	21.1	18.3	22.2	23.5	2.9
Germany	11.5	16.4	12.8	14.6	11.3	9.5	10.9	11.5	13.7	2.2
France	6.9	9.3	8.4	10.7	8.2	7.7	9.4	10.3	11.9	5.0
Italy	3.7	3.8	3.6	4.1	3.6	3.5	3.5	3.5	4.2	0.5
United Kingdom	8.9	10.3	10.9	10.9	10.6	13.7	7.0	7.6	6.6	−2.3
Other Western Europe	0.9	0.7	0.9	1.2	1.4	1.8	2.2	1.9	1.5	0.6
Asian NICs[a]	0.3	0.0	0.1	0.2	0.3	0.2	0.2	0.4	0.7	0.4
Eastern Europe[b]	0.0	0.1	0.0	0.0	0.1	0.1	0.1	0.0	0.0	−0.0
Developing countries	1.7	1.6	1.5	1.5	1.4	2.5	1.5	1.9	1.5	−0.2
Latin America	0.6	0.4	0.3	0.2	0.2	0.5	0.6	0.8	0.8	0.2
Rest of world	7.5	7.0	7.7	8.2	8.4	2.0	3.2	7.9	5.9	−1.6
Share of imports from world										
United States	9.9	10.3	8.4	12.8	14.0	16.0	14.7	12.6	11.5	1.6
Canada	5.3	3.4	4.3	5.0	5.8	5.7	4.7	6.9	4.2	−1.1
Japan	4.7	3.0	6.0	3.9	5.8	6.4	5.7	4.6	3.4	−1.3
European Community	33.4	34.3	35.3	33.1	32.4	31.0	31.2	34.8	38.3	4.9
EC from non-EC	19.8	15.8	16.6	17.0	20.0	15.7	14.8	17.8	19.8	−0.1
Germany	15.0	18.1	17.6	15.4	14.1	13.6	15.2	13.4	16.2	1.2
France	4.1	3.2	3.6	2.5	2.2	3.5	3.9	6.1	5.2	1.1
Italy	3.3	2.6	2.5	3.7	3.8	3.6	3.6	2.7	3.4	0.1
United Kingdom	5.1	5.3	5.8	7.1	8.2	5.9	3.2	5.9	3.2	−1.9
Other Western Europe	4.8	3.5	5.9	4.4	5.0	6.0	5.1	4.8	5.2	0.4
Asian NICs[a]	3.8	3.1	1.8	1.0	1.7	0.8	0.7	6.2	6.9	3.1
Eastern Europe[b]	0.1	0.1	0.2	0.1	0.1	0.1	0.0	0.0	0.7	0.6
Developing countries	22.6	23.5	20.2	23.6	19.5	20.7	17.6	13.2	17.3	−5.3
Latin America	7.3	3.9	3.0	2.9	3.3	3.9	4.6	4.1	5.1	−2.1
Rest of world	13.0	16.9	16.3	15.1	15.4	10.7	18.7	14.5	9.1	−3.9

Export share minus import share									
United States	40.6	31.9	37.8	29.0	34.2	34.8	39.0	32.6	33.1	-7.6
Canada	-1.8	1.0	-0.5	-1.2	-1.5	-0.2	0.0	-3.6	-2.3	-0.5
Japan	-4.3	-2.4	-5.4	-3.4	-5.4	-5.9	-5.0	-4.0	-2.6	1.7
European Community	1.4	9.1	4.0	9.7	3.3	5.7	2.5	3.7	4.6	3.2
Non-EC	0.7	8.9	7.0	7.9	1.4	5.4	3.6	4.5	3.7	3.0
Germany	-3.5	-1.7	-4.8	-0.8	-2.8	-4.1	-4.3	-1.9	-2.5	0.9
France	2.8	6.1	4.8	8.2	6.0	4.2	5.5	4.2	6.7	3.9
Italy	0.4	1.2	1.1	0.4	-0.2	-0.1	-0.1	0.7	0.8	0.4
United Kingdom	3.8	5.0	5.1	3.8	2.4	7.8	3.8	1.8	3.4	-0.4
Other Western Europe	-3.9	-2.9	-5.0	-3.2	-3.6	-4.2	-2.9	-2.9	-3.7	0.2
Asian NICs[a]	-3.5	-3.1	-1.7	-0.8	-1.4	-0.6	-0.5	-5.7	-6.3	-2.8
Eastern Europe[b]	-0.1	-0.1	-0.2	-0.1	-0.0	0.0	0.1	0.0	-0.7	-0.6
Developing countries	-20.9	-21.9	-18.7	-22.1	-18.1	-18.2	-16.1	-11.4	-15.8	5.1
Latin America	-6.7	-3.5	-2.7	-2.7	-3.1	-3.4	-4.0	-3.3	-4.3	2.4
Rest of world	-5.5	-9.9	-8.6	-6.8	-7.0	-8.7	-15.5	-6.6	-3.2	2.3

a. Hong Kong, Korea, Singapore, and Taiwan.

b. Including Soviet Union.

Source: World Manufactures Trade Data Base.

Table 5.79.3 Aircraft, parts, and engines: bilateral trade flows, 1989 (billions of dollars)

Importer	World	United States	Canada	Japan	European Community	Germany	France	United Kingdom	Asian NICs	Latin America	Other
SITC 792: Aircraft and parts											
World	53.0	23.6	1.0	0.4	22.8	7.2	6.3	3.5	0.4	0.4	4.4
United States	4.9		0.8	0.3	2.9	0.2	1.9	0.0	0.2	0.2	0.5
Canada	1.5	1.4		0.0	0.1	0.0	0.1	0.0	0.0	0.0	0.1
Japan	2.3	2.0	0.0		0.1	0.0	0.1	0.0	0.1	0.0	0.0
European Community	23.6	9.2	0.2	0.0	10.4	6.6	1.3	0.0	0.0	0.2	3.6
Germany	3.8	2.2	0.0	0.0	1.4		0.7	0.1	0.0	0.0	0.1
France	7.6	0.9	0.0	0.0	6.4	5.6			0.0	0.0	0.3
United Kingdom	5.6	2.6	0.0	0.0	1.4	0.5	0.2		0.0	0.0	1.6
Asian NICs	3.2	2.6	0.0	0.0	0.6	0.0	0.6	0.0			0.0
Latin America	2.5	1.7	0.0	0.0	0.8	0.3	0.2	0.0	0.0		0.0
Other	15.1	6.8	0.1	0.0	7.9	0.2	0.2	3.4	0.0	0.0	0.3
SITC 714: Engines											
World	18.5	7.0	1.0	0.3	8.4	1.3	0.9	4.4	0.5	0.1	1.2
United States	4.4		0.6	0.1	3.0	0.4	0.3	1.8	0.3	0.1	0.4
Canada	1.0	0.6		0.0	0.3	0.0	0.0	0.2	0.0	0.0	0.1
Japan	0.7	0.6	0.0		0.1	0.0	0.0	0.1	0.0		0.0
European Community	7.9	3.7	0.2	0.1	3.0	0.5	0.3	1.3	0.2	0.1	0.7
Germany	1.2	0.5	0.0	0.0	0.6		0.1	0.3	0.0	0.0	0.1
France	2.8	1.8	0.1	0.0	0.9	0.2		0.4	0.0	0.0	0.0
United Kingdom	2.0	0.8	0.0	0.1	0.6	0.2	0.1		0.0		0.0
Asian NICs	0.8	0.6	0.0	0.0	0.2	0.0	0.0	0.1		0.0	0.4
Latin America	0.6	0.3	0.1	0.0	0.2	0.0	0.1	0.1	0.0		0.0
Other	3.0	1.2	0.1	0.1	1.6	0.3	0.2	0.9	0.0	0.0	0.1

Source: World Manufactures Trade Data Base.

Table 5.79.4 Aircraft, parts, and engines: product composition of US trade, 1981–90[a] (millions of dollars except where noted)

Category	SITC Rev. 2			SITC Rev. 3			
	1981	1987	Change 1981–87	1987	1990	Change 1981–90	Change 1987–90
792 Aircraft							
Exports	14,738	16,904	2,166	16,903	30,064	15,326	13,161
Imports	2,805	4,483	1,678	4,582	6,378	3,573	1,796
Balance	11,933	12,421	488	12,321	23,686	11,753	11,365
of which							
7920 Aircraft							
Exports	10,213	9,944	−269				
Imports	1,598	2,066	468				
Balance	8,615	7,878	−737				
7921 Helicopters							
Exports				529	676		148
Imports				109	186		77
Balance				420	490		70
7922 Airplanes, 2,000 kilograms or less							
Exports				152	154		2
Imports				27	36		9
Balance				125	117		−8
7923 Airplanes, 2,000 to 15,000 kilograms							
Exports				1,981	1,246		−735
Imports				1,370	1,798		428
Balance				611	−553		−1,164
7924 Airplanes, greater than 15,000 kilograms							
Exports				7,415	17,540		10,125
Imports				551	815		264
Balance				6,864	16,725		9,861

table continued next page

Table 5.79.4 Aircraft, parts, and engines: product composition of US trade, 1981–90ᵃ (millions of dollars except where noted) (continued)

Category	SITC Rev. 2			SITC Rev. 3			
	1981	1987	Change 1981–87	1987	1990	Change 1981–90	Change 1987–90
7925 Spacecraft, including satellites							
Exports				39	598		559
Imports				10	0		−10
Balance				29	598		569
7928 Aircraft, n.e.s., and associated equipment							
Exports	239	314	75	135	296	56	161
Imports	2	52	50	147	204	202	57
Balance	237	262	25	−12	91	−146	103
7929 Parts							
Exports	4,286	6,645	2,359	6,652	9,554	5,268	2,902
Imports	1,205	2,365	1,160	2,368	3,338	2,133	970
Balance	3,081	4,280	1,199	4,284	6,216	3,135	1,932
714 Engines							
Exports	2,960	4,570	1,610	4,456	7,449	4,489	2,993
Imports	1,542	2,922	1,380	2,591	4,986	3,444	2,395
Balance	1,418	1,648	230	1,865	2,463	1,045	598

a. Data are expressed on a domestic exports, imports customs basis.

Source: US Department of Commerce.

Table 5.79.5 Aircraft, parts, and engines: geographic composition of US trade, 1981–90

	Millions of dollars				Percentages of total			
	1981	1987	1989	1990	1981	1987	1989	1990
Exports								
792 Aircraft								
Canada	976	665	1,380	1,447	6.6	3.9	5.8	4.8
Japan	1,310	1,893	2,012	3,482	8.9	11.2	8.5	11.6
European Community	3,915	4,873	9,213	11,347	26.6	28.8	39.0	37.7
United Kingdom	786	1,675	2,552	3,895	5.3	9.9	10.8	13.0
Germany	1,055	958	2,244	2,062	7.2	5.7	9.5	6.9
France	680	360	852	1,320	4.6	2.1	3.6	4.4
Latin America	1,782	1,371	1,692	2,090	12.1	8.1	7.2	7.0
Asian NICs	948	1,088	2,586	2,498	6.4	6.4	10.9	8.3
Other	5,807	7,014	6,755	9,200	39.4	41.5	28.6	30.6
Total	14,738	16,904	23,638	30,064	100.0	100.0	100.0	100.0
714 Engines								
Canada	262	409	636	687	8.8	9.2	9.1	9.2
Japan	183	396	571	634	6.2	8.9	8.1	8.5
European Community	1,383	2,079	3,720	4,300	46.7	46.7	53.1	57.7
United Kingdom	308	521	825	954	10.4	11.7	11.8	12.8
France	548	936	1,772	1,909	18.5	21.0	25.3	29.6
Other	1,133	1,572	2,080	1,828	38.3	35.3	29.7	24.6
Total	2,961	4,456	7,007	7,449	100.0	100.0	100.0	100.0
Imports								
792 Aircraft								
Canada	742	1,209	1,239	1,766	26.5	26.4	21.3	27.7
Japan	179	239	384	441	6.4	5.2	6.6	6.9
European Community	1,525	2,583	3,452	3,222	54.4	56.4	59.3	50.5
United Kingdom	417	1,097	991	1,201	14.9	23.9	17.0	18.8
Germany	62	137	151	164	2.2	3.0	2.6	2.6
France	685	949	1,712	1,027	24.4	20.7	29.4	16.1
Other	359	551	749	948	12.8	12.0	12.9	14.9
Total	2,805	4,582	5,824	6,377	100.0	100.0	100.0	100.0
714 Engines								
Canada	470	442	566	706	30.5	18.0	14.3	14.2
Japan	9	39	40	n.a.	0.6	1.6	1.0	n.a.
European Community	1,028	1,816	2,931	3,653	66.7	73.9	74.1	73.3
United Kingdom	868	750	1,032	1,394	56.3	30.5	26.1	28.1
France	118	831	1,547	1,724	7.7	33.8	39.1	34.5
Other	35	161	416	627	2.3	6.6	10.5	12.5
Total	1,542	2,458	3,953	4,986	100.0	100.0	100.0	100.0

n.a. = not available.

a. Data are expressed on a domestic exports, imports customs basis.

Source: US Department of Commerce.

Table 5.79.6 Aircraft, parts, and engines: indices of US competitiveness, 1981–89 (billions of dollars except where noted)

	1981	1982	1983	1984	1985	1986	1987	1988	1989	Annual growth 1981–89 (percentages)
SITC 792 and 714: Aircraft, parts, and engines										
World trade										
World exports to non-US destinations	33.3	32.8	31.4	30.8	33.6	35.1	40.1	49.5	62.2	8.1
World imports from non-US sources	19.5	21.3	19.5	20.2	20.4	22.7	24.3	35.8	41.6	9.9
US trade										
Exports	17.7	15.0	15.5	14.3	17.8	19.0	22.5	25.8	30.6	7.1
Imports	4.3	4.2	3.3	4.7	6.1	7.5	7.5	8.6	9.9	10.9
Balance	13.3	10.8	12.2	9.6	11.7	11.5	15.0	17.2	20.7	
										Change 1981–89
US share of exports to non-US destinations (percentages)	53.0	45.6	49.4	46.4	52.9	54.1	56.0	52.1	49.2	–3.8
US share of imports from non-US sources (percentages)	22.3	19.7	16.8	23.1	29.9	33.0	30.9	24.0	23.8	1.5
Export share minus import share (percentages)	30.8	25.9	32.6	23.3	23.0	21.1	25.1	28.1	25.4	–5.4
SITC 792: Aircraft and parts										
World trade										
World exports to non-US destinations	26.6	25.5	24.3	23.8	26.3	26.4	29.6	36.9	48.1	7.7
World imports from non-US sources	14.3	16.0	14.6	15.0	14.3	15.3	16.1	26.2	30.7	10.0
US trade										
Exports	14.7	11.8	12.2	10.9	14.2	15.1	17.9	20.0	23.6	6.1
Imports	2.8	2.8	2.1	3.0	3.6	4.5	4.5	5.5	5.9	9.8
Balance	11.9	9.0	10.1	7.9	10.6	10.6	13.4	14.5	17.7	
										Change 1981–89
US share of exports to non-US destinations (percentages)	55.4	46.2	50.1	45.9	54.1	57.3	60.4	50.5	49.1	–6.3
US share of imports from non-US sources (percentages)	19.6	17.3	14.4	20.3	25.2	29.6	28.1	21.1	19.1	–0.5
Export share minus import share (percentages)	35.8	28.9	35.7	25.6	28.9	27.7	32.3	29.4	30.0	–5.8

SITC 714: Engines

									Change 1981–89
World trade									
World exports to non-US destinations	6.7	7.3	7.1	7.0	7.3	8.7	10.5	12.6	14.1	9.7
World imports from non-US sources	5.2	5.3	4.9	5.2	6.1	7.4	8.2	9.6	10.9	9.7
US trade										
Exports	3.0	3.2	3.3	3.4	3.6	3.9	4.6	5.8	7.0	11.4
Imports	1.5	1.4	1.2	1.7	2.5	3.0	3.0	3.1	4.0	12.7
Balance	1.4	1.8	2.1	1.7	1.1	0.9	1.6	2.7	3.0	
US share of exports to non-US destinations (percentages)	44.3	43.4	46.5	48.3	48.9	44.9	43.5	46.3	49.8	5.5
US share of imports from non-US sources (percentages)	29.6	26.2	23.9	32.4	40.5	40.0	36.1	32.4	36.6	7.0
Export share minus import share (percentages)	14.7	17.2	22.6	15.9	8.4	4.9	7.4	13.9	13.2	−7.3

Source: World Manufactures Trade Data Base.

Furniture (SITC 82)

US furniture imports soared during the 1980s as the techniques for transporting furniture improved and costs fell, as developing countries entered this labor-intensive industry, and as the quality of foreign products increased. Imports quadrupled during 1981–90 to $5.0 billion. With exports growing but still modest, the result was a substantial $3.4 billion 1990 deficit.

Description of the Product Group

This product group is not subdivided into three-digit subcategories. The group includes home furniture, office furniture, and special-purpose furniture such as hospital beds, dental chairs, and automobile seats.

Role in World Trade

Size and Composition

Furniture accounted for 1.1 percent of world manufactures exports, with 1989 world exports of $24.2 billion (table 5.82.1). Annual growth in world furniture exports averaged 11.3 percent during 1981–89, well above the 9.6 percent annual rate for manufactures as a whole.

Global Competition Patterns

Italy, France, and Germany are the largest exporters of furniture; the United States, Germany, and France are the largest importers (table 5.82.2). Japan's exports are negligible, but its import share has been growing rapidly, from 2.3 percent in 1981 to 5.0 percent in 1989. Trade patterns changed considerably from 1981 to 1989. On the export side, the share of the Asian NICs rose 3.0 percentage points, and that of the European Community dropped 3.3 percentage points. However, the big changes were on the import side. The US share of world imports jumped from 13.4 percent to 21.4 percent, while that of the developing countries dropped by a similar amount. One interpretation of these figures is that exports were redirected to the US market as the markets in developing countries dried up. The United States, Japan, and the United Kingdom are major net importers. The Asian NICs and developing countries are the large net exporters.

An examination of trade flows confirms the large roles of US and EC imports (table 5.82.3). EC exports in 1989 were 59.3 percent of the world total, and imports 46.1 percent. Most of the Community's imports—three-fourths of the total—come from other EC countries, and most of its exports—60 percent of the total—stay in the EC market, reflecting both longstanding trade patterns and the still relatively high transportation and inventory costs of furniture.

Key Determinants of World Trade Patterns

In the past, high transportation and inventory costs, due to furniture's bulk and fragility, insulated the production of developed countries from low-wage competition. However, this protection has slowly diminished as transportation costs have fallen, as packing methods have been perfected for shipping knocked-down (unassembled) furniture in containers, as inventory management techniques have improved, and as developing countries have become more competitive. As a result, production has been shifting to lower-wage countries, such as Taiwan and Mexico, and furniture trade has been expanding rapidly. Also, several Far Eastern countries discovered they had an inexpensive source of lumber when methods for killing the fungus in rubberwood, previously a scrap item, were developed in the 1970s. Taiwan must import rubberwood from rubber-producing countries, such as Indonesia and Malaysia, and furniture production has recently been moving to those countries, with some assistance from unfavorable Taiwanese government policies.

Developed countries, however, remain strong producers in markets where styling and quality is important. For instance, Italy has been very successful in upholstered home furniture. The Danish style is particularly well suited to automated production and knocked-down shipments in containers. Manufacturers in developed countries often obtain their parts from developing countries, according to industry officials. Improved techniques for packing and shipping the parts of knocked-down furniture have increased trade in parts (US International Trade Commission 1984, xii). However, some types of furniture such as chests of drawers cannot be easily knocked down.

Trade in upholstered furniture is hampered because the risk of damage in transport is greater and because many customers want to special-order particular styles and fabrics. It is often necessary to have a unique product to overcome transport costs and foreign tariff barriers. National differences in tastes can also impede trade in furniture, although the size of the US market and its receptiveness to foreign styles permit foreign producers to manufacture for the US market on an efficient scale (US Department of Commerce 1985). On the other hand, US retailers have become much less willing to hold inventories, to the disadvantage of foreign manufacturers, which cannot deliver as quickly as domestic suppliers can.

International trade in office furniture is impeded by the need to meet customer specifications and to develop personal client relationships. For instance, systems furniture, which is made up of modular acoustical screens and panels, must meet the specifications of architects and interior designers. Canada has nevertheless been able to sell systems furniture in the US market because of its proximity. Similarities between US and Canadian usage and manufacturing techniques have also encouraged US-Canada trade. Italy and Denmark have succeeded in the US market through sound design, and Germany through functionality. The largest US manufacturers tend to service foreign markets through production by foreign affiliates, which helps them meet local tastes with local brand names. International trade is more common in standardized office furniture sold on a retail basis through catalogues or showrooms. Indeed, it can be difficult to distinguish imported furniture and parts from domestic goods sold from the same catalogue. Taiwan has been able to utilize its cost advantage more successfully in standardized office furniture than in custom-made products. However, US products remain competitive in this area.

Home furniture is most often sold in showrooms, and price is usually an important factor. A number of factors, including disposable income, demographics (particularly of new householders), house sizes, changing consumer tastes, interest rates, and consumer confidence, affect demand for household furniture (US International Trade Commission 1984, 25).

The use of newer technologies, particularly computerized and numerically controlled equipment, has made furniture production less labor intensive. However, many kinds of furniture do not lend themselves to mass production and automation, so manufacturing remains intensive in labor, which is often unskilled (US International Trade Commission 1984, xii). These technologies have also increased the efficient scale of operation of furniture plants. Nonetheless, furniture firms remain relatively small and specialized compared with other industries (European Commission 1990). Technologies are relatively similar around the world (US Department of Commerce 1985, 6).

Role in US Trade

Furniture exports accounted for 0.5 percent of US manufactures exports in 1990 and 1.3 percent of manufactures imports. However, the sector played a significant role in the deterioration of the US trade balance, as the furniture trade deficit grew from $0.6 billion in 1981 to $4.0 billion in 1987 (table 5.82.4). More important, the balance recovered only slightly during 1987–90, despite strong export growth. The deficit was $3.4 billion in 1990 as compared with only $0.6 billion in 1981.

As imports grew over the decade, their sources did not change greatly (table 5.82.5). The European Community remains the source of about one-fifth of US imports. Mexico and Italy managed to double their share of the US import market, each from around 5 percent to around 11 percent. Imports from Taiwan also shot up during 1981–87 but fell off slightly after 1987.

The US share of world exports to non-US destinations declined from 7.7 percent in 1981 to 5.7 percent in 1989. More significantly, the US share of world imports from non-US sources grew from 14.3 percent to 22.7 percent from 1981 to 1989, reflecting the increased importance of the US market to foreign furniture exporters (table 5.82.6).

Outlook

Key Determinants of US Trade Performance

As noted earlier, falling transportation and inventory costs have made the North American market less insulated from foreign competition. The market structure of the home furniture industry, with largely independent retailers buying from a large number of specialized suppliers, also facilitated imports (US International Trade Commission 1984, 25). The high level of competition and ease of entry into the US furniture industry, evidenced by a long history of profits below the average for manufacturing, also helped sales into the US market by foreign firms. Most US companies now complement their US-made product lines with foreign pieces. In the 1980s, foreign companies began manufacturing furniture that appeared American rather than identifiably French or English. Foreign manufacture of American-style furniture is now a common practice.

Mexican *maquiladora* plants have been successful in producing lower-value home furniture for the US market; many of these operations shifted from US production to take advantage of lower wages and to avoid environmental regulations in California, according to an industry representative. Furniture trade with Europe has been more dollar sensitive. Imports of upmarket upholstered leather furniture from Italy grew quickly in the 1980s. The growing popularity of ready-to-assemble furniture from Scandinavia has played a part in increasing imports, but these items remain low-end, entry-level products, and sales of assembled furniture are still more important. Growth in US white-collar employment and in the health industries has raised demand for imports of office and hospital furniture, respectively. US imports of high-value furniture for the home have also increased.

US exports improved after 1987, but not by enough to offset the growth in imports earlier in the decade. Exports to Canada jumped $0.4 billion in 1990 after tariffs were removed under the Canada-US Free Trade Agreement. Household imports declined after 1988; according to unpublished US Commerce Department figures. US exports are constrained by differences in tastes in other countries, such as preferences for heavier furniture and wardrobes in Europe or for smaller furniture to fit smaller homes in Japan.

The US furniture industry has responded aggressively to the surge in imports. US manufacturers have rationalized their operations, adopted newer technologies, and shed their provincial attitude. Relationships that US furniture firms formed with foreign suppliers are now being turned around to increase foreign sales. US Commerce Department analysts feel that recent consolidation in the US industry will result in a more efficient scale of production and a stronger export position (US Department of Commerce 1991, 38-5). One sign of the US industry's improved position is that it is increasingly obtaining parts in the United States.

Elasticities supplied by DRI indicate that import demand in a category of consumer goods including furniture is moderately sensitive to changes in import prices (see the appendix to this volume). Such changes in import prices might be caused by movements in exchange rates. Import demand is fairly responsive to growth in the consumption component of GNP. Demand for US exports abroad is less sensitive to prices and consumption growth, although Canadian demand is more sensitive to the import prices of US goods.

Near-Term Outlook

One industry official noted that the soft domestic market is shifting more attention to export markets. The European and Japanese furniture markets have been growing at around 15 percent per year, more quickly than the US market, and this may help improve the US trade balance. The EC 1992 project will not homogenize European tastes in furniture in the near term, so the "single European market" will not attract imports in the same way that the large, homogeneous US market has. However, only 15 percent of European offices use systems furniture, as compared with 44 percent in the United States; US strength in making these products should therefore lead to increased exports to Europe as old buildings are refurbished. Reduction of Canadian tariffs under the free trade agreement should stimulate further growth in exports to that market. Improvement of up to $1 billion in the balance by 1993 can be expected.

Medium-Term Outlook

US furniture manufacturers still have room to improve their competitiveness. Many companies have not completed their shift to more globally oriented strategies. For instance, wider use of the just-in-time inventory system would speed production and improve quality, while catering to customers' special requirements. The United States will, however, continue to run deficits in furniture for the foreseeable future, because of the labor intensity of furniture production, the lack of a US technological advantage, and the quality and styling of some developed-country competitors.

Conclusions

- Several factors caused US furniture imports to soar in the early 1980s: the techniques for transporting furniture improved and costs fell; developing countries entered this labor-intensive industry; and the quality of foreign products improved.

- The partial US trade performance recovery after 1987 reflected the fall in the dollar after 1985 and an aggressive response by the US industry to foreign competition that increased US exports.

- The US deficit is likely to narrow by around $1 billion by 1993 from the 1990 level of $3.4 billion, as a result of faster growth in foreign markets, improved efficiency in the US industry, increased reliance on US sources for parts, and elimination of Canadian tariff barriers under the Canada-US Free Trade Agreement.

- The United States will, however, continue to run deficits of around $2 billion to $3 billion in furniture for the foreseeable future because of the labor intensity of furniture production, the lack of a US technological advantage, and the quality and styling of some developed-country competitors.

Bibliography

Commission of the European Communities. 1990. *Panorama of EC Industry, 1990.* Luxembourg: Commission of the European Communities.
Industry, Science and Technology Canada. 1988. *Industry Profiles.* Ottawa: Industry, Science and Technology Canada.
US Department of Commerce, International Trade Administration. 1985. *A Competitive Assessment of the U.S. Wood and Upholstered Furniture Industry.* Washington: Government Printing Office (March).

US Department of Commerce, International Trade Administration. 1991. *U.S. Industrial Outlook, 1991.* Washington: Government Printing Office (January).

US International Trade Commission. 1984. *Competitive Assessment of the U.S. Wood and Upholstered Household Furniture Industry.* Report to Subcommittee on Trade of the House Committee on Ways and Means. Investigation No. 332-170. US International Trade Commission Publication 1543 (June).

See also the periodical *Furniture Today.*

Table 5.82.1 Furniture and parts: world trade, 1981–89 (billions of dollars except where noted)

Product	1981	1982	1983	1984	1985	1986	1987	1988	1989	Annual growth 1981–89 (percentages)
World exports to world	10.3	9.8	10.1	10.6	11.7	15.5	19.5	22.6	24.2	11.3
Memorandum: SITC 82 share of world manufactures exports (percentages)	1.0	1.0	1.0	1.0	1.0	1.1	1.2	1.1	1.1	0.1

Source: World Manufactures Trade Data Base.

Table 5.82.2 Furniture and parts: geographic distribution of world trade, 1981–89 (percentages of total)

Country	1981	1982	1983	1984	1985	1986	1987	1988	1989	Change 1981–89
Share of exports to world										
United States	6.8	6.5	5.9	5.9	6.1	4.4	4.3	4.9	4.5	−2.2
Canada	2.3	2.6	3.1	3.9	4.2	3.8	3.4	3.5	4.1	1.8
Japan	1.8	1.8	1.9	1.8	1.8	1.3	0.9	1.7	1.5	−0.3
European Community	62.6	63.7	61.4	58.9	58.5	60.4	59.8	58.1	59.3	−3.3
EC to non-EC	26.1	27.3	26.7	27.5	28.2	26.3	24.1	22.2	22.4	−3.7
Germany	17.2	17.6	16.5	15.6	15.8	17.6	17.2	16.0	15.5	−1.6
France	5.7	5.9	5.8	5.3	5.3	5.3	5.3	5.4	5.5	−0.2
Italy	20.2	20.2	19.6	18.6	18.3	18.8	18.6	18.6	20.4	0.2
United Kingdom	4.2	4.3	3.9	3.6	4.0	3.4	3.3	3.1	3.3	−0.9
Other Western Europe	11.5	10.1	11.1	11.5	11.8	11.4	11.3	10.7	9.5	−2.0
Asian NICs[a]	6.0	6.2	7.5	8.5	8.2	9.4	10.2	9.6	9.0	3.0
Eastern Europe[b]	4.8	4.6	4.5	4.5	4.3	4.4	4.5	4.3	4.0	−0.7
Developing countries	5.8	5.2	6.4	7.1	7.2	6.7	7.3	8.9	9.6	3.8
Latin America	0.9	0.8	1.2	1.7	1.9	2.0	2.0	2.5	2.8	2.0
Rest of world	0.0	0.0	0.1	0.0	0.0	0.1	0.1	0.1	0.1	0.1
Share of imports from world										
United States	13.4	14.3	19.9	26.0	30.1	27.8	25.1	22.3	21.4	8.1
Canada	2.7	1.9	2.3	2.5	2.4	2.3	2.2	3.3	3.8	1.2
Japan	2.3	3.1	2.6	2.8	2.6	2.7	3.3	4.4	5.0	2.7
European Community	47.7	46.0	43.7	39.7	37.5	41.9	45.1	45.7	46.1	−1.6
EC from non-EC	12.2	11.3	11.1	10.6	9.7	10.2	11.1	11.3	11.3	−0.9
Germany	13.5	12.2	12.3	11.2	10.0	10.9	12.0	12.1	12.6	−0.8
France	11.5	12.6	11.3	9.8	9.3	10.8	11.2	11.1	10.8	−0.6
Italy	1.2	1.1	1.0	1.1	1.0	1.2	1.4	1.5	1.6	0.5
United Kingdom	6.8	7.0	7.2	7.2	6.9	7.1	7.2	7.6	7.3	0.6
Other Western Europe	12.9	13.1	12.6	12.1	12.0	13.7	14.8	14.2	13.6	0.7
Asian NICs[a]	0.9	1.2	1.3	1.3	1.6	1.3	1.1	1.4	1.7	0.8
Eastern Europe[b]	0.8	0.7	0.4	0.3	0.4	0.4	0.3	0.6	0.4	−0.4
Developing countries	18.3	18.7	16.3	14.1	12.2	9.1	7.3	7.2	6.9	−11.4
Latin America	2.5	2.3	1.8	2.1	2.1	2.0	1.8	2.1	2.0	−0.5
Rest of world	0.0	0.0	0.0	0.0	0.0	0.0	0.0	0.0	0.0	0.0

Export share minus import share

United States	−6.6	−7.7	−14.0	−20.1	−24.0	−23.3	−20.9	−17.4	−16.9	−10.3
Canada	−0.4	0.7	0.8	1.4	1.8	1.5	1.2	0.2	0.3	0.6
Japan	−0.5	−1.2	−0.7	−1.0	−0.8	−1.4	−2.4	−2.7	−3.5	−3.0
European Community	14.9	17.8	17.7	19.1	21.0	18.5	14.7	12.4	13.2	−1.7
Non-EC	13.9	16.0	15.7	17.0	18.5	16.1	13.1	10.8	11.1	−2.8
Germany	3.7	5.4	4.2	4.4	5.8	6.6	5.2	3.9	2.9	−0.8
France	−5.8	−6.7	−5.5	−4.5	−4.0	−5.5	−6.0	−5.7	−5.3	0.4
Italy	19.0	19.1	18.6	17.5	17.4	17.6	17.3	17.1	18.8	−0.3
United Kingdom	−2.6	−2.7	−3.4	−3.6	−2.9	−3.7	−3.8	−4.5	−4.1	−1.5
Other Western Europe	−1.4	−3.0	−1.5	−0.6	−0.3	−2.3	−3.6	−3.6		−2.6
Asian NICs[a]	5.1	5.0	6.2	7.2	6.6	8.1	9.1	8.2	7.3	2.2
Eastern Europe[b]	3.9	3.9	4.1	4.2	3.9	4.0	4.2	3.8	3.6	−0.3
Developing countries	−12.5	−13.5	−9.9	−6.9	−5.0	−2.4	0.0	1.7	2.7	15.2
Latin America	−1.6	−1.5	−0.6	−0.4	−0.2	0.0	0.2	0.4	0.8	2.4
Rest of world	0.0	0.0	0.0	0.0	0.0	0.0	0.0	0.1	0.1	0.1

a. Hong Kong, Korea, Singapore, and Taiwan.

b. Including Soviet Union.

Source: World Manufactures Trade Data Base.

Table 5.82.3 Furniture and parts: bilateral trade flows, 1989 (billions of dollars)

Importer	World	United States	Canada	Japan	European Community	Germany	France	United Kingdom	Asian NICs	Latin America	Other
World	24.2	1.1	1.0	0.4	14.4	3.8	1.3	0.8	2.2	0.7	4.6
United States	4.9		0.9	0.2	1.2	0.2	0.1	0.1	1.4	0.6	0.7
Canada	0.7	0.3		0.0	0.2	0.0	0.0	0.0	0.1	0.0	0.1
Japan	1.1	0.1	0.0		0.2	0.1	0.0	0.0	0.5	0.0	0.3
European Community	11.7	0.2	0.0	0.0	8.9	2.2	0.8	0.4	0.2	0.0	2.4
Germany	3.2	0.0	0.0	0.0	2.0		0.2	0.1	0.0	0.0	1.1
France	2.9	0.0	0.0	0.0	2.4	0.5		0.1	0.0	0.0	0.4
United Kingdom	1.8	0.1	0.0	0.0	1.3	0.3	0.2		0.1	0.0	0.3
Asian NICs	0.4	0.1	0.0	0.1	0.1	0.0	0.0	0.1		0.0	0.0
Latin America	0.5	0.3	0.0	0.0	0.1	0.0	0.1	0.0	0.0		0.0
Other	5.0	0.1	0.0	0.1	3.6	1.3	0.3	0.2	0.1	0.0	1.0

Source: World Manufactures Trade Data Base.

Table 5.82.4 Furniture and parts: US trade, 1981–90[a] (millions of dollars except where noted)

Category	SITC Rev. 2 1981	1987	Change 1981–87	SITC Rev. 3 1987	1990	Change 1981–90	Change 1987–90
Exports	697	624	−73	572	1,597	900	1,025
Imports	1,267	4,656	3,389	4,551	5,008	3,741	457
Balance	(570)	(4,032)	−3,462	−3,979	−3,411	−2,841	568

a. Data are expressed on a domestic exports, imports customs basis.

Source: US Department of Commerce.

Table 5.82.5 Furniture and parts: geographic composition of US trade, 1981–90

	Millions of dollars 1981	1987	1989	1990	Percentages of total 1981	1987	1989	1990
Exports								
Canada	174	166	277	718	25.0	29.0	21.4	45.0
Japan	13	30	70	79	1.9	5.2	5.4	4.9
European Community	98	96	149	180	14.1	16.8	11.5	11.3
United Kingdom	35	39	65	80	5.0	6.8	5.0	5.0
Germany	19	21	35	41	2.7	3.7	2.7	2.6
France	12	13	21	23	1.7	2.3	1.6	1.4
Italy	3	4	5	7	0.4	0.7	0.4	0.4
Latin America	167	164	331	432	24.0	28.7	25.5	27.1
Mexico	67	90	236	325	9.6	15.7	18.2	20.4
Asian NICs	16	31	63	58	2.3	5.4	4.9	3.6
Other	229	85	406	130	32.9	14.9	31.3	8.1
Total	697	572	1,296	1,597	100.0	100.0	100.0	100.0
Imports								
Canada	361	1,025	1,179	1,209	28.5	22.5	24.0	24.1
Japan	31	206	137	166	2.4	4.5	2.8	3.3
European Community	257	1,041	1,043	1,106	20.3	22.9	21.2	22.1
United Kingdom	45	92	79	93	3.6	2.0	1.6	1.9
Germany	46	217	185	199	3.6	4.8	3.8	4.0
France	15	63	63	69	1.2	1.4	1.3	1.4
Italy	63	426	516	534	5.0	9.4	10.5	10.7
Latin America	80	363	617	662	6.3	8.0	12.5	13.2
Mexico	65	304	530	578	5.1	6.7	10.8	11.5
Asian NICs	299	1,364	1,292	1,152	23.6	30.0	26.3	23.0
Other	239	552	653	713	18.9	12.1	13.3	14.2
Total	1,267	4,551	4,921	5,008	100.0	100.0	100.0	100.0

a. Data are expressed on a domestic exports, imports customs basis.

Source: US Department of Commerce.

Table 5.82.6 Furniture and parts: indices of US competitiveness, 1981–89 (billions of dollars except where noted)

	1981	1982	1983	1984	1985	1986	1987	1988	1989	Annual growth 1981–89 (percentages)
World trade										
World exports to non-US destinations	9.1	8.7	8.4	8.3	8.9	11.9	15.2	18.0	19.3	9.9
World imports from non-US sources	9.7	9.4	9.7	10.5	11.8	15.6	19.4	22.1	23.4	11.7
US trade										
Exports	0.7	0.6	0.6	0.6	0.7	0.7	0.8	1.1	1.1	5.8
Imports	1.4	1.4	2.0	2.9	3.7	4.5	5.1	5.2	5.3	18.2
Balance	−0.7	−0.8	−1.4	−2.3	−3.0	−3.8	−4.3	−4.1	−4.2	
										Change 1981–89
US share of exports to non-US destinations (percentages)	7.7	7.4	7.1	7.5	8.0	5.8	5.4	6.2	5.7	−2.0
US share of imports from non-US sources (percentages)	14.3	15.2	21.1	27.4	31.5	28.8	26.0	23.6	22.7	8.4
Export share minus import share (percentages)	−6.6	−7.8	−14.0	−19.9	−23.5	−23.0	−20.6	−17.4	−17.0	−10.4

Source: World Manufactures Trade Data Base.

Apparel (SITC 84)

Concern about the international trade performance of the US apparel and textile industries predates that about other US manufacturing industries. Agreements governing the conduct of international trade in apparel and textiles (SITC 65, reviewed separately in this study) have been in effect since the late 1950s. Apparel and textiles are second only to road vehicles in their combined share of world manufactures trade. Apparel trade has generated large US deficits, rising to $23.1 billion in 1990. Apparel and textiles are also among the most closely watched and politically sensitive trade items.

Description of the Product Group

The apparel product group is composed of seven three-digit subcategories. Those listed below are the Revision 2 subclassifications.

SITC

842 outer garments, men's and boys', of textile fabrics (other than knitted or crocheted)

843 outer garments, women's, girls', and infants', of textile fabrics (other than knitted or crocheted)

844 undergarments of textile fabrics (other than knitted or crocheted goods)

845 outer garments and other articles, knitted or crocheted, not elastic or rubberized

846 undergarments, knitted or crocheted

847 clothing accessories of textile fabrics (other than knitted or crocheted)

848 articles of apparel and clothing accessories of fabrics other than textiles; headgear of all materials.

These classifications changed substantially in 1987 with the introduction of Revision 3 of the SITC. For comparison, the three-digit subcategories under

Revision 3, used in analyses in this study employing US Department of Commerce data for 1987–90, are listed below:

841 men's or boys' coats, jackets, suits, blazers, trousers, shorts, shirts, underwear, knitwear, and similar articles of textile fabrics, not knitted or crocheted

842 women's and girls' coats, capes, jackets, suits, blazers, trousers, shorts, shirts, underwear, and similar articles of textile fabrics, not knitted or crocheted

843 men's or boys' coats, capes, jackets, suits, blazers, trousers, shorts, shirts, underwear, nightwear, and similar articles of textile fabrics, knitted or crocheted

844 women's or girls' coats, capes, jackets, suits, blazers, trousers, shorts, shirts, underwear, nightwear, and similar articles of textile fabrics, knitted or crocheted

845 articles of apparel of textile fabrics, whether or not knitted or crocheted, not elsewhere specified

846 clothing accessories, of textile fabrics, whether or not knitted or crocheted (other than those for babies)

848 articles of apparel and clothing accessories of other than textile fabrics; headgear of all types

Role in World Trade

Size and Composition

World exports of apparel were $91.9 billion in 1989 (table 5.84.1). Apparel's 4.4 percent share of world manufactures made it one of the 10 largest manufactures trade items, exceeding trade in telecommunications and in aircraft but lagging behind trade in road vehicles and special industrial machinery. Apparel exports grew by an average of 12.4 percent annually during 1981–89, substantially faster than manufactures trade as a whole. This resulted in an increase in apparel's share of world manufactures trade from 3.5 percent in 1981 to 4.4 percent in 1989.

The largest category of apparel in world trade is women's garments, which accounted for just over one-quarter of all world apparel exports in 1989. Lagging just behind women's garments in importance is knit garments. Men's outer garments was the only other three-digit group accounting for more than 15 percent of world apparel trade.

Global Competition Patterns

In 1989, the largest world apparel exporters were the European Community, the Asian NICs, and the "other" category, consisting mostly of developing countries. These three areas accounted for nearly 90 percent of world apparel exports in 1989. The major importers were the European Community, the United States, and Japan, which together accounted for over 80 percent of world apparel imports in 1989 (table 5.84.2).

The United States and Japan, both with only small shares in world apparel exports, experienced large and growing negative export-minus-import share balances during the 1980s. The European Community, despite having the largest share of world apparel exports, also experienced large negative share balances during the 1980s (table 5.84.2).

The developing countries, which improved their share balances in all of the two-digit SITC product groups examined in this study, were the only group that experienced a large improvement in their share balance position in apparel during the 1980s. This improvement resulted largely from a substantial expansion in their share of world exports rather than a contraction in their share of imports, as in most other cases.

Table 5.84.3 indicates that a majority of apparel trade by the European Community is among EC member countries. Over 70 percent of EC exports, for example, were to other EC countries in 1989. Similarly, almost one-half of total EC imports were from other EC countries. This table also highlights the importance of the United States as an export market for many countries. Roughly one-half or more of all exports from Latin America, the Asian NICs, and Canada went to the United States in 1989.

Role in US Trade

Recent Performance

US apparel exports in 1990 were $2.5 billion, less than 1 percent of US manufactures exports. US apparel imports equaled $25.5 billion in 1990, or 6.6 percent of all US manufactures imports (table 5.84.4).

US exports did not benefit from the rapid growth in world apparel trade during the 1980s. Between 1981 and 1987, apparel exports from the United

States fell by 5.4 percent while world exports more than doubled. US apparel imports, meanwhile, grew much faster than world apparel trade between 1981 and 1987, nearly tripling in value.

The rapid deterioration in US trade performance in the early to mid-1980s slowed after 1987. Between 1987 and 1990, exports doubled while annual import growth slowed dramatically, from over 15 percent on average between 1981 and 1987 to about 7 percent on average between 1987 and 1990. The deficit, however, continued to grow, reaching $23.1 billion in 1990.

Three of the three-digit subcategories—men's and boys' nonknitted outer garments, knitted undergarments, and apparel and accessories of nontextile materials and headgear of all materials—accounted for roughly 60 percent of all US apparel exports. Knitted undergarments constitute the largest single export subcategory, accounting for about 20 percent of the total in recent years (table 5.84.4).

US apparel imports have been concentrated in women's, girls', and infants' nonknitted outer garments, knitted or crocheted outer garments: and knitted or crocheted undergarments. These three subcategories account for roughly two-thirds of US imports (table 5.84.4). Women's outer garments were the largest single import subcategory, alone accounting for nearly one-third of US apparel imports.

Mexico, the largest single-country market for US exports, absorbed nearly 20 percent of US exports during the 1980s (table 5.84.5). Latin America's share of the US export market increased substantially meanwhile, from 47.7 percent in 1981 to 54.6 percent in 1990. Much of the increase to Latin America was, however, in cut pieces, which are assembled there and then reexported to the United States. US exports to Japan also increased substantially during the 1980s. By the end of the decade, Japan was the second-largest single-country market for US exports, absorbing 12.0 percent of the total in 1990. The only other significant market for US apparel was the European Community, which in 1990 absorbed 15.7 percent of US exports.

As a group, the Asian NICs are by far the most important source of apparel imports into the United States, although their share declined from 62.3 percent in 1981 to 40.6 percent in 1990 (table 5.84.5). Hong Kong is the largest single-country source of apparel imports, followed by China, Korea, and Taiwan. China and Latin America are the two areas that have significantly increased their share of the US import market recently. China has rapidly developed its textile, apparel, and footwear industries in an attempt to increase hard-currency earnings through exports. US imports of Chinese apparel rose eightfold between 1981 and 1990. China increased its import share from 5.6 percent of US apparel imports in 1981 to 13.6 percent by 1990. A large part of the increase in imports from Latin America is due to the increasing use of overseas plants to assemble cut parts shipped from the United States. Shipments of cut parts to foreign assemblers increase US exports, but when the finished products are returned to the United States, reflecting the value added by foreign assemblers, they increase imports by even more.

International Competitiveness

The US trade balance in apparel suffered one of the largest declines during the 1980s of any of the manufacturing industries examined. This deterioration is one indication of the decline in US international competitiveness in apparel trade. Another is the decline in the US export-minus-import share balance. From − 18.6 percentage points in 1981, the US share balance declined to − 34.0 percentage points in 1985 before improving to − 26.7 percentage points in 1989 (table 5.84.6). The majority of the decline in the US share balance resulted from the substantial rise in the US share of world imports from non-US sources.

 Employment in the domestic industry fell 16.7 percent between 1981 and 1986 and has since remained about constant, at just over 1 million. Labor productivity growth was below the average for US manufacturing but sufficient to allow for a modest increase in domestic output over the period. (For a discussion of labor productivity in the apparel and textile industries, see Cline 1990, 88.) Domestic shipments of apparel increased by just over 1 percent per year from 1981 to 1987, nowhere near enough to prevent an increase in imports' share of the US market from roughly 15 percent in 1981 to over 30 percent in 1987.

Outlook

Key Determinants of US Trade Performance

Apparel and textiles are unique among US manufacturing industries in that they have received significant protection from imports over an extended period of time. Other manufacturing industries have on occasion received protection, but generally not for as long.

US trade in apparel and textiles is governed by the Multi-Fiber Arrangement (MFA); by the early 1980s, the United States had bilateral restraint agreements under the MFA with 34 countries covering 80 percent of textile and apparel imports from developing countries.[1] Originally implemented in the mid-1970s, the MFA extended protection already provided to cotton products to include

---

1. This discussion of the MFA draws heavily on Cline (1990).

apparel and textiles made from man-made fibers. With protectionist sentiments rising in the United States and Europe, the MFA was designed to provide a mechanism for increased protection while limiting the severity of the restrictions.

The MFA basically depends on bilateral agreements between importing countries and their suppliers to limit the quantities of specific products—expressed in square-meter equivalents—that may be imported. The quantitative restrictions under the MFA provide some flexibility for exporting countries subject to quota restrictions to switch their exports from lower- to higher-unit-value items. This has enabled exporters to increase the value of their exports while staying within the volume restrictions. In addition, US importers can switch from countries bound by restrictive agreements to countries not yet bound by agreements. The MFA agreements place greater trade restrictions on apparel than on textiles trade. The MFA governs roughly 40 percent of world apparel trade but only about 14 percent of world textile trade. A variety of other bilateral and unilateral restrictions govern much of world trade not coming under MFA regulations. The MFA has been renewed several times; its re-renewal in 1991 was postponed pending the outcome of the Uruguay Round negotiations in the GATT.

An important influence on US trade in apparel in recent years has been trade under the provisions of section 807 of the US tariff schedule.[2] Under these provisions, US manufacturers are permitted to ship cut fabric pieces overseas to be assembled and reexported to the United States. Duty is assessed only on the value added during assembly. To qualify for consideration under section 807, only assembly operations during which the product is not "substantially transformed" may be performed outside the United States. Data identifying apparel imports permitted under section 807 have been collected since 1987. Between 1987 and 1989, these imports increased much more rapidly than apparel imports generally, and grew by 51.5 percent (from $1.34 billion to $2.1 billion) over the period while overall apparel imports increased by 19.9 percent. Trade under section 807 can be expected to continue to expand as US manufacturing firms seek to lower their costs by exporting their most labor-intensive manufacturing operations to low-wage areas. To the extent that this provision makes US-based production more competitive, it may somewhat restrain US import growth. The effects on the overall balance, however, are likely to be modest.

Several factors account for the rapid surge in imports noted earlier. As with textiles, the rapid appreciation of the dollar was the main cause of the import surge. Labor costs account for a larger share of costs in the apparel industry than for any other major manufacturing industry. Thus, the US apparel industry is at a greater disadvantage vis-à-vis low-wage producers than other industries. Already facing intense competition from lower-wage foreign producers, US pro-

---

2. Section 807 was recently replaced by section 9802.00.80 of the Harmonized Tariff Schedule, but the provisions continue to be popularly referred to as "section 807."

ducers found their ability to compete seriously hampered by the rise in the value of the dollar, particularly against the currencies of the East Asian NICs.

DRI elasticities data support the importance of import price changes in determining trade flows, reporting a calculated import elasticity of − 1.4 (see the appendix to this volume). An estimated import price elasticity greater than − 1.0 indicates that a rise in the dollar's value would cause a more than proportionate increase in US apparel imports.

The surge of imports occurred despite the import restrictions imposed under MFA agreements. Several years of relatively weak demand during the early 1980s led to many of the import quotas going unfilled. This provided room for the rapid import expansion in the mid-1980s.

The rate of import growth slackened between 1987 and 1990 for several reasons. First, the devaluation of the dollar in the latter half of the 1980s reduced the competitive disadvantage that US producers faced. Second, wages in some of the main competitor countries rose. Third, import restrictions became more effective. As noted earlier, one reason imports were able to grow so rapidly in the mid-1980s was that many countries subject to import quotas under MFA agreements had unfilled quotas. As a result of the rapid import growth in the mid-1980s, many countries filled their import quotas, putting a limit on further expansion. Also, 1987 was the first full year of trade under a new MFA agreement negotiated in 1986. Most analysts feel that the new agreement provided some additional tightening of import restrictions.

Outlook Through 1993

The overwhelming priority of US apparel manufacturers in the 1990s will be to increase labor productivity by applying new technology. There has been some success to date in adapting computer-aided design (CAD) and computer-aided manufacturing (CAM) to apparel manufacture. This technology has been useful in design, pattern making, and cutting, but its application to sewing operations, the most labor-intensive aspect of production, has been much less successful. Despite ongoing research, it has been particularly difficult to design machines that can reliably manipulate single pieces of cut fabric.

With sewing proving particularly difficult to automate, section 807 apparel trade is likely to grow rapidly during the 1990s. Although MFA agreements restrict 807 trade, there are arrangements for quota increases for 807 trade with participants in the Caribbean Basin Initiative. Not only will the search for cost reductions force US manufacturers to rely increasingly on foreign assembly of apparel, but changing labor-market conditions in the United States will increase the push to have the labor-intensive portions of apparel manufacturing done overseas. Many manufacturers already report significant shortages of labor for sewing operations in the United States.

As with textiles, investment in "quick-response" technologies will be important in the 1990s. These technologies emphasize the improvement of communications and coordination between manufacturers, distributors, and retailers. Quick-response technologies lower investment in inventory and allow manufacturers to respond rapidly to style and fashion trends, creating potentially significant advantages over distant overseas producers. Although reductions in delivery times can be critically important for some segments of the industry, especially in the fashion industry where limited production runs are common, they will be much less important for the industry overall.

Despite the more modest ($0.6 billion) 1990 increase in the apparel trade deficit, there is little prospect for sustained improvement during the early 1990s. Although the increased application of technology to apparel production shows some promise, such changes are unlikely to come rapidly enough to significantly affect US trade performance in the early to mid-1990s.

Although growth of the apparel trade deficit slowed in 1990, without a significant decline in the value of the dollar the apparel deficit will probably continue to rise from its $23.1 billion 1990 level. Assuming US economic recovery, the increases are likely to be in the range of $0.5 billion to $1 billion annually between 1990 and 1993.

Longer-Term Outlook

Several factors argue in favor of a continuing deterioration in US trade performance. US economic growth, rising prices, and greater spending power will raise US apparel consumption and imports.

Limited additional dollar devaluation is unlikely to help the competitive position of US manufacturers substantially. Unlike in textiles, the capital requirements for apparel manufacturing are modest. Should additional devaluation occur, lack of access to financial resources or machinery would probably not greatly limit expansion. Manufacturers, already facing labor shortages at the prevailing wages in some areas, would be likely to find that the problems of acquiring additional low-wage labor prevent them from substantially increasing output. If US manufacturers were to raise wages to attract additional workers, any competitive gains from the reduction in the value of the dollar would be likely to be lost through higher domestic costs. As manufacturers search for other alternatives, trade under the provisions of section 807 is likely to grow rapidly into the mid-1990s. Although imports under this provision add less to US deficits than do imports with no US content, 807 trade is likely to be a source of continuing deterioration in US trade performance.

Now that much of US apparel production has gone offshore, it would take a major technological breakthrough or marked further dollar depreciation against the currencies of key developing countries for apparel manufacturers to increase the portion of total US consumption supplied by US-based production. Absent either of these developments, the apparel trade deficit should be expected to continue to grow modestly beyond 1993, with deficit growth paralleling US economic growth rates.

Conclusions

- International trade in apparel and textiles together accounted for 8.3 percent of total world trade in manufactures in 1987, a share second only to that of road vehicles. The prominence of textiles and apparel in international trade has made them among the most politically sensitive trade items. The United States is a major apparel importer, taking 29.9 percent of world imports from non-US sources in 1989.

- Unlike much of US manufacturing, the apparel industry has enjoyed some form of protection against imports for an extended period. This did not, however, prevent a surge of imports during the mid-1980s. The sharp rise in the value of the dollar was the primary cause of the import surge. Imports accounted for 15 percent of the value of the domestic market in 1981 but more than 30 percent by 1987.

- In response to the import surge, US manufacturers have attempted to become more competitive by increasingly relying on overseas contractors to perform the most labor-intensive portions of apparel manufacturing. Cut pieces are shipped overseas, where they are sewn together and then returned to the United States. Increased use of this kind of arrangement—given special treatment under the MFA regime by section 807 of the US tariff schedule—as an alternative to US processing will continue to add modestly to trade deficits in apparel.

- Despite efforts to automate the most labor-intensive parts of apparel manufacturing, the prospects for substantial improvements in labor productivity are modest. Because of their small size, many US producers are not able to invest in some of the more costly technologies currently available.

- Although growth of the apparel trade deficit slowed in 1990, without a significant decline in the value of the dollar there are likely to be continued increases in the apparel deficit from its $23.1 billion level of 1990. The increase is likely to be in the range of $1.5 billion to $3 billion between 1990 and 1993.

- Although entry into the apparel industry is easy, additional modest dollar devaluation is unlikely to be large enough to significantly improve the prospects for US trade in apparel. Even though such a devaluation would improve the competitive position of US firms, the need for additional labor would tend to increase wage costs, which would largely negate any benefits from devaluation.

- Given the labor-intensive nature of apparel production and the existing and potential production capabilities in low-wage developing countries, apparel production is one of the manufacturing industries least likely to enjoy a resurgence in the United States—absent an unlikely technological breakthrough. Continued modest growth in the apparel deficits should be expected for the foreseeable future.

Bibliography

American Apparel Manufacturers Association. 1990. *U.S. 807 Apparel Imports*. Arlington, VA: American Apparel Manufacturers Association (April).

Cline, William R. 1990. *The Future of World Trade in Textiles and Apparel*, rev. ed. Washington: Institute for International Economics.

General Agreement on Tariffs and Trade. 1989. *Demand, Production and Trade in Textiles and Clothing*. Geneva: General Agreement on Tariffs and Trade (25 September).

Fee, Jonathan M. 1989. *807 Apparel Assembly. Special Report 1*. Arlington, VA: American Apparel Manufactures Association (December).

Hochswender, Woody. 1990. "Hong Kong Worries an Industry." *New York Times* (7 May): D5.

Industry, Science and Technology Canada. 1988. *Industry Profile: Clothing*. Ottawa: Industry, Science and Technology Canada.

Commission of the European Communities. 1990. *Panorama of EC Industry, 1990*. Luxembourg: Commission of the European Communities.

Pei-Tse Wu. 1991. "US Apparel Makers Split Over Mexican Trade Pact." *Journal of Commerce* (4 April): 1.

Resnick, Rosalind. 1990. "A Stitch in Time...." *North American International Business* (July): 36–40.

Shapiro, Eben. 1991. "This is Not a Rags to Riches Story." *New York Times* (5 January): 29.

US Department of Commerce, International Trade Administration. 1988. *U.S. Industrial Outlook, 1988*. Washington: Government Printing Office (January).

US Department of Commerce, International Trade Administration. 1989. *U.S. Industrial Outlook, 1989*. Washington: Government Printing Office (January) 1989.

US Department of Commerce, International Trade Administration. 1990. *U.S. Industrial Outlook, 1990*. Washington: Government Printing Office (January).

US International Trade Commission. 1990. *U.S. Trade Shifts in Selected Commodity Areas, January–June 1990*. Washington: US International Trade Commission (December).

Wexner, Leslie H. 1990. "How Congress Raises the Price of Your Clothes." *Washington Post* (11 September): A19.

Wolff, Alan, Thomas R. Howell, and William A. Noellert. 1985. *The Reality of World Trade in Textiles and Apparel*. Prepared for the Fiber, Fabric and Apparel Coalition for Trade (FFACT).

World Bank. 1989. "Garments: Global Subsector Study." *Industry Series Paper* 19. Washington: World Bank (December).

Table 5.84.1 Clothing and accessories: product composition of world trade, 1981–89 (billions of dollars except where noted)

SITC Product	1981	1982	1983	1984	1985	1986	1987	1988	1989	Annual growth 1981–89 (percentages)
World exports to world	36.0	35.3	36.2	41.6	45.1	58.7	75.5	84.0	91.9	12.4%
of which										
842 Men's outerwear	6.7	5.6	5.6	6.3	6.6	8.8	11.2	13.8	15.4	11.0%
843 Women's outerwear	9.2	7.4	7.8	8.9	10.1	13.3	16.4	20.1	24.3	12.9%
844 Undergarments	2.3	1.6	1.5	1.9	2.3	2.7	3.3	5.1	6.4	13.6%
845 Outerwear, knit	8.0	7.0	7.2	8.1	8.8	12.5	16.2	20.0	22.3	13.7%
846 Undergarments, knit	4.3	3.5	3.7	3.9	4.1	5.5	7.4	9.7	10.5	11.8%
847 Textile accessories	1.6	1.5	1.5	1.6	1.8	2.4	2.9	2.9	3.8	11.6%
848 Nontextile accessories	3.8	2.7	2.7	3.2	3.6	4.4	6.0	8.9	10.0	12.8%

	1981	1982	1983	1984	1985	1986	1987	1988	1989	Change 1981–89
Memorandum: SITC 84 share of world manufactures exports (percentages)	3.5	3.6	3.7	3.9	4.0	4.3	4.6	4.2	4.4	0.8

Source: World Manufactures Trade Data Base.

Table 5.84.2 Clothing and accessories: geographic distribution of world trade, 1981–89 (percentages of total)

Country	1981	1982	1983	1984	1985	1986	1987	1988	1989	Annual growth 1981–89
Share of exports to world										
United States	3.5	2.8	2.4	2.0	1.6	1.5	1.5	1.9	2.3	–1.2
Canada	0.6	0.6	0.5	0.6	0.6	0.5	0.5	0.4	0.5	–0.1
Japan	1.6	1.5	1.8	1.8	1.6	1.2	0.9	0.7	0.6	–0.9
European Community	38.0	38.2	37.4	34.2	35.0	37.5	36.1	33.6	32.3	–5.7
To non-EC	13.4	13.3	13.3	13.0	13.8	13.8	12.6	12.0	11.7	–1.7
Germany	7.0	7.1	7.0	6.3	6.4	7.1	6.6	6.4	6.1	–0.8
France	5.3	5.1	4.8	4.2	4.3	4.3	4.0	3.9	4.0	–1.3
Italy	11.9	12.4	12.4	11.5	11.8	12.8	11.9	10.8	10.4	–1.5
United Kingdom	4.6	4.2	3.6	3.2	3.4	3.1	3.1	3.0	2.6	–2.0
Other Western Europe	7.4	7.0	6.5	5.8	8.4	8.1	8.4	6.7	7.6	0.1
Asian NICs[a]	30.7	32.1	32.2	35.0	31.7	29.2	28.7	31.3	28.4	–2.3
Eastern Europe[b]	2.8	2.7	2.6	2.4	2.3	2.3	2.2	2.0	1.8	–1.0
Developing countries	17.0	16.8	18.4	19.8	20.6	21.6	23.5	24.1	28.4	11.4
Latin America	2.4	2.0	2.4	2.7	2.9	2.7	2.9	3.3	3.6	1.3
Rest of world	0.2	0.2	0.2	0.2	0.2	0.1	0.1	0.1	0.1	0.0
Share of imports from world										
United States	22.2	23.7	28.3	34.4	35.8	31.7	29.2	27.8	29.1	7.0
Canada	2.3	2.3	2.8	3.1	2.8	2.6	2.3	2.3	2.5	0.2
Japan	5.0	5.1	4.1	4.6	4.5	4.9	6.2	8.2	10.0	5.1
European Community	49.5	47.4	44.8	39.9	39.1	43.5	45.5	44.7	42.7	–6.7
To non-EC	24.7	22.8	21.5	19.6	18.5	20.6	22.9	23.6	22.8	–1.8
Germany	19.5	18.4	18.2	16.5	15.5	17.6	18.6	17.5	16.3	–3.2
France	6.7	7.1	6.6	5.7	6.0	7.0	7.4	7.3	7.1	0.5
Italy	2.0	1.9	1.7	1.5	1.7	2.0	2.2	2.3	2.3	0.2
United Kingdom	7.9	7.3	6.6	6.4	6.0	5.9	6.0	6.7	6.5	–1.5
Other Western Europe	11.8	11.9	11.3	10.2	10.5	11.3	11.5	10.5	9.5	–2.3
Asian NICs[a]	0.5	0.7	0.7	0.6	0.7	0.6	0.6	0.8	1.1	0.6
Eastern Europe[b]	1.4	1.2	1.0	1.0	1.1	0.9	0.6	0.9	0.6	–0.8
Developing countries	6.6	7.0	6.4	5.5	5.0	4.2	3.7	4.1	3.9	–2.7
Latin America	2.1	2.2	1.7	1.6	1.6	1.5	1.3	1.6	1.8	–0.3
Rest of world	0.1	0.1	0.2	0.1	0.0	0.0	0.0	0.2	0.1	0.1

table continued next page

Table 5.84.2 Clothing and accessories: geographic distribution of world trade, 1981–89 (percentages of total)   (continued)

Country	1981	1982	1983	1984	1985	1986	1987	1988	1989	Annual growth 1981–89
Export share minus import share										
United States	−18.7	−20.9	−25.9	−32.4	−34.2	−30.2	−27.7	−26.0	−26.8	−8.2
Canada	−1.7	−1.7	−2.3	−2.5	−2.3	−2.1	−1.9	−1.9	−2.0	−0.3
Japan	−3.4	−3.6	−2.3	−2.8	−2.9	−3.7	−5.3	−7.4	−9.4	−6.0
European Community	−11.5	−9.1	−7.4	−5.7	−4.1	−6.0	−9.4	−11.1	−10.4	1.1
To non-EC	−11.3	−9.6	−8.3	−6.6	−4.6	−6.9	−10.3	−11.6	−11.2	0.2
Germany	−12.6	−11.4	−11.2	−10.2	−9.2	−10.5	−12.0	−11.1	−10.2	2.3
France	−1.3	−2.0	−1.8	−1.6	−1.7	−2.7	−3.4	−3.4	−3.1	−1.8
Italy	9.9	10.5	10.7	10.0	10.1	10.8	9.7	8.5	8.1	−1.8
United Kingdom	−3.3	−3.1	−3.0	−3.2	−2.6	−2.9	−2.9	−3.7	−3.8	−0.5
Other Western Europe	−4.4	−4.9	−4.8	−4.5	−2.1	−3.2	−3.1	−3.8	−1.9	2.4
Asian NICs[a]	30.2	31.3	31.5	34.4	31.0	28.6	28.1	30.4	27.4	−2.9
Eastern Europe[b]	1.4	1.6	1.6	1.5	1.2	1.4	1.6	1.2	1.3	−0.2
Developing countries	10.4	9.8	12.0	14.3	15.6	17.4	19.9	20.0	24.5	14.1
Latin America	0.3	−0.2	0.7	1.1	1.3	1.2	1.5	1.8	1.9	1.6
Rest of world	0.1	0.0	0.0	0.0	0.1	0.1	0.1	0.0	0.0	−0.1

a. Hong Kong, Korea, Singapore, and Taiwan.

b. Including Soviet Union.

Source: World Manufactures Trade Data Base.

Table 5.84.3 Clothing and accessories: bilateral trade flows, 1989 (billions of dollars)

Importer	World	United States	Canada	Japan	European Community	Germany	France	United Kingdom	Asian NICs	Latin America	Other
World	91.9	2.1	0.5	0.6	26.7	5.6	3.6	2.4	26.1	3.3	29.6
United States	26.9		0.4	0.2	1.9	0.1	0.2	0.2	12.3	3.1	9.1
Canada	2.2	0.1		0.0	0.3	0.1	0.1	0.0	1.1	0.0	0.6
Japan	9.1	0.2	0.0		1.0	0.1	0.3	0.1	5.1	0.2	2.8
European Community	39.6	0.3	0.0	0.1	19.0	3.1	2.0	1.4	5.4	0.2	14.6
Germany	15.2	0.0	0.0	0.1	5.7		0.5	0.3	2.3	0.1	7.0
France	6.8	0.0	0.0	0.0	3.4	0.5		0.2	0.4	0.0	2.9
United Kingdom	5.8	0.0	0.0	0.0	2.2	0.5	0.2		1.8	0.0	1.7
Asian NICs	0.9	0.0	0.0	0.1	0.4	0.0	0.1	0.1	0.3	0.0	0.0
Latin America	1.6	1.3	0.0	0.0	0.2	0.0	0.1	0.0	0.1		0.0
Other	11.6	0.1	0.0	0.1	7.0	2.2	0.9	0.5	1.9	0.0	2.5

Source: World Manufactures Trade Data Base.

Table 5.84.4 Clothing and accessories: product composition of US trade, 1981–90[a] (millions of dollars except where noted)

Category	SITC Rev. 2			SITC Rev. 3			
	1981	1987	Change 1981–87	1987	1990	Change 1981–90	Change 1987–90
Exports	1,208	1,143	−65	1,219	2,479	1,270	1,260
Imports	7,619	20,639	13,020	20,495	25,533	17,914	5,038
Balance	−6,411	−19,496	−13,085	−19,276	−23,054	−16,643	−3,778
of which							
841 Menswear, nonknit							
Exports				258	625		367
Imports				4,018	5,262		1,244
Balance				−3,760	−4,637		−877
842 Men's outerwear, nonknit / 842 Women's wear, nonknit							
Exports	198	216	19	190	348		158
Imports	1,073	2,733	1,659	5,746	7,250		1,504
Balance	−876	−2,516	−1,641	−5,556	−6,901		−1,345
843 Women's outerwear, nonknit / 843 Men's wear, knit							
Exports	195	193	−3	85	200		115
Imports	2,466	6,181	3,716	761	748		−13
Balance	−2,271	−5,989	−3,718	−676	−548		128
844 Undergarments, nonknit / 844 Women's wear, knit							
Exports	64	92	29	67	146		79
Imports	737	1,631	894	2,053	2,091		38
Balance	−673	−1,538	−865	−1,986	−1,945		41
845 Outerwear, knit / 845 Apparel, n.e.s., knit or nonknit							
Exports	169	145	−24	259	588		329
Imports	1,143	4,284	3,142	5,427	6,795		1,368
Balance	−974	−4,139	−3,166	−5,168	−6,207		−1,039
846 Undergarments, knit / 846 Clothing accessories, textile							
Exports	326	225	−101	92	247		155
Imports	1,239	3,259	2,020	614	835		221
Balance	−913	−3,034	−2,121	−522	−588		−66
847 Textile accessories							
Exports	65	60	−5				
Imports	149	417	268				
Balance	−84	−357	−273				
848 Nontextile accessories / 848 Nontextile apparel and accessories							
Exports	191	211	20	267	325		57
Imports	812	2,134	1,322	1,875	2,552		677
Balance	−621	−1,923	−1,302	−1,608	−2,227		−619

a. Data are expressed on a domestic exports, imports customs basis.

Source: US Department of Commerce.

Table 5.84.5 Clothing and accessories: geographic composition of US trade, 1981–90

	Millions of dollars				Percentages of total			
	1981	1987	1989	1990	1981	1987	1989	1990
Exports								
Canada	73	55	109	218	6.0	4.5	5.2	8.8
Japan	85	102	212	297	7.0	8.4	10.2	12.0
European Community	270	155	270	390	22.4	12.7	12.9	15.7
United Kingdom	93	23	43	87	7.7	1.9	2.1	3.5
OPEC	103	40	63	64	8.5	3.3	3.0	2.6
Saudi Arabia	18	17	29	32	1.5	1.4	1.4	1.3
Mexico	209	228	375	392	17.3	18.7	17.9	15.8
Latin America	577	779	1,311	1,354	47.7	63.9	62.8	54.6
Asian NICs	20	31	39	46	1.7	2.6	1.9	1.9
Other developing countries	24	21	36	45	2.0	1.7	1.7	1.8
Other	57	37	47	65	4.7	3.0	2.3	2.6
Total	1,208	1,219	2,087	2,479	100.0	100.0	100.0	100.0
Imports								
Canada	76	273	260	247	1.0	1.3	1.1	1.0
Japan	276	374	228	159	3.6	1.8	0.9	0.6
European Community	415	1,721	1,732	1,777	5.4	8.4	7.1	7.0
Italy	192	882	899	896	2.5	4.3	3.7	3.5
Latin America	660	1,884	2,963	3,261	8.7	9.2	12.1	12.8
Asian NICs	4,743	10,263	10,992	10,359	62.3	50.1	44.8	40.6
Hong Kong	1,874	3,836	3,953	3,991	24.6	18.7	16.1	15.6
South Korea	1,325	3,032	3,598	3,257	17.4	14.8	14.7	12.8
Singapore	150	472	625	623	2.0	2.3	2.5	2.4
Taiwan	1,394	2,923	2,816	2,489	18.3	14.3	11.5	9.7
China	834	3,048	4,201	4,897	11.0	14.9	17.1	19.2
Other developing countries	427	1,986	2,895	3,469	5.6	9.7	11.8	13.6
Other	188	946	1,287	1,364	2.5	4.6	5.2	5.3
Total	7,619	20,495	24,559	25,533	100.0	100.0	100.0	100.0

a. Data are expressed on a domestic exports, imports customs basis.

Source: US Department of Commerce.

Table 5.84.6 Clothing and accessories: indices of US competitiveness, 1981–89 (billions of dollars except where noted)

	1981	1982	1983	1984	1985	1986	1987	1988	1989	Annual growth 1981–89
World trade										
World exports to non-US destinations	27.9	26.9	26.0	27.3	29.5	40.5	53.8	60.4	65.0	11.2
World imports from non-US sources	35.2	34.9	35.8	41.5	44.4	58.0	74.4	81.2	87.7	12.1
US trade										
Exports	1.3	1.0	0.9	0.8	0.7	0.9	1.1	1.6	2.1	6.6
Imports	8.1	8.5	10.4	14.6	16.2	18.7	22.1	23.1	26.2	15.8
Balance	−6.9	−7.5	−9.5	−13.8	−15.5	−17.8	−21.0	−21.5	−24.1	
										Change 1981–89
US share of exports to non-US destinations (percentages)	4.5	3.7	3.4	3.1	2.5	2.2	2.1	2.58	3.2	−1.3
US share of imports from non-US sources (percentages)	23.1	24.5	29.1	35.2	36.5	32.2	29.7	28.4	29.9	6.8
Export share minus import share (percentages)	−18.6	−20.8	−25.7	−32.1	−34	−30	−27.6	−25.82	−26.7	−8.1

Source: World Manufactures Trade Data Base.

Footwear (SITC 85)

The US footwear industry has faced intense competition for at least 20 years, and its share of the US market has steadily shrunk. Although it is not a large part of international trade, footwear has contributed substantially to US manufactures deficits and is likely to continue to do so in the 1990s.

Description of the Product Group

Footwear is given only one three-digit SITC subcategory: SITC 851, all footwear. In other statistical classifications the industry is frequently divided into two major subcategories: nonrubber footwear and rubber or rubber-soled fabric footwear. The nonrubber segment of the footwear industry is by far the larger of the two, accounting for 78.6 percent of total footwear consumption in the United States on a volume basis in 1989 (US International Trade Commission 1990c, tables 1 and 6). Because most nonrubber footwear items are priced higher than rubber footwear, they account for an even larger percentage of the value of consumption, roughly 90 percent in 1989.

Role in World Trade

Size and Composition

Footwear is not a large part of world manufactures trade. World industry exports of $24.5 billion in 1989 gave footwear only a 1.2 percent share of total world manufactures exports. Nonetheless, footwear trade has grown substantially more rapidly than manufactures trade generally. From 1981 to 1989, overall trade in manufactures increased by an average of 9.6 percent annually, while trade in footwear grew by 11.7 percent annually on average (table 5.85.1). Much of the growth in footwear trade was fueled by US imports.

Global Competition Patterns

The European Community is the largest footwear-exporting region, although the Asian NICs are increasingly challenging its dominance. From 52.8 percent of world footwear exports in 1981, the European Community's market share declined to 41.6 percent in 1989 (table 5.85.2). Italy has the largest share of exports within the European Community. The market share of the East Asian NICs grew rapidly, from 24.7 percent in 1981 to 32.8 percent in 1989. The other significant exporting group was the developing countries, which substantially increased their export share from 10.9 percent in 1981 to 19.0 percent in 1989. The important exporting countries within this group are China, Thailand, Indonesia, and Malaysia.

The European Community's share of world imports declined slightly during the 1980s (table 5.85.2). Because of the much larger decline in its export share, however, the Community's share balance declined substantially.

The Asian NICs, with a positive 1989 export-minus-import share balance of 30.6 percentage points, enjoyed the largest improvement in this measure of any country or group. This success resulted primarily from their rising share of world exports; their import share actually increased slightly.

The US export-minus-import share position declined significantly from 1981 to 1989, although less than the European Community's. A rise in the US share of world imports during the 1980s was responsible for virtually the entire deterioration.

World footwear trade patterns are summarized in table 5.85.3. Two features stand out. First, in 1989 one-quarter of total world trade in footwear consisted of intratrade within the European Community. Second, the US market is very important to the Asian NICs, absorbing 60 percent of their exports. An even higher share, roughly 75 percent, of Latin America's exports go to the United States.

Role in US Trade

Recent Performance

US footwear exports were $488 million in 1990, an insignificant fraction (less than 0.5 percent) of total US manufactures exports (table 5.85.4). Despite the large percentage increases in footwear exports in recent years, their relatively small absolute size has not been enough to prevent increases in the industry's trade deficit. Footwear imports reached $9.1 billion in 1990, roughly 2.4 percent of all US manufactures imports that year.

Despite a significant increase in per capita footwear consumption during the 1980s, domestic footwear production fell. In nonrubber footwear, for example, per capita consumption rose from roughly 3.2 pair per person in 1981 to about 4.7 pair per person in 1987 (unpublished US Department of Commerce data).

The volume of domestic production declined over the same period by 39.5 percent, from roughly 380 million pair in 1981 to 230 million pair in 1987. The value of domestic nonrubber footwear production fell from $4.8 billion in 1981 to $3.5 billion in 1987, for a decline of 27.1 percent (volume data are from US International Trade Commission 1985 and 1990a).

The combination of a decline in domestic production and a steep rise in imports resulted in an increase (in volume terms) in the share of domestic consumption supplied by imports from 50.6 percent in 1981 to 81.6 percent in 1987 for the nonrubber segment of the footwear market. Imports also accounted for the majority of consumption in the rubber footwear subcategory, where over 60 percent (in volume terms) of consumption was imported in 1987.

Because imports tend to be relatively low-unit-value items, the import share in domestic consumption by value is substantially lower. Nonetheless, this measure also shows substantial growth. In nonrubber footwear, for example, imports accounted for 34.6 percent of the value of consumption in 1981 and grew to 67.4 percent of consumption by 1987.

A change in the sources of imports accompanied the surge in imported footwear during the 1980s. As the 1980s opened, Taiwan and Korea, both relatively low-unit-value producers, had supplanted Western Europe and Brazil as the largest suppliers to the US market. Both have been moving into the production of higher-quality footwear more recently. The production of the cheapest footwear has been shifting to China, whose exports of footwear to the United States have increased dramatically. From being the fifth-largest exporter (in volume terms) to the United States in 1987, China became the third-largest in 1989, just behind Korea and Taiwan. With more and more low-unit-value footwear production shifting to China, many analysts feel that China will soon be the largest footwear exporter to the United States in volume terms. Although China lags further behind Korea and Taiwan when imports are measured on a value basis, the expansion in its exports to the United States has been as dramatic in value as in volume.

Exports from the United States (table 5.85.5) go primarily to Latin America, the European Community, Canada, and Japan. Cut footwear parts constitute a large part of US exports. These parts exports go largely to Latin America and the Caribbean, where they are assembled and exported back to the United States as finished or partly finished goods. This arrangement is advantageous to US producers because under (what used to be) section 807 of the US tariff schedules import duties are assessed only on the value added during assembly. US firms are thus able to contract out the most labor-intensive portions of footwear manufacturing.

The rapid deterioration of the trade balance in footwear that occurred between 1981 and 1987 eased between 1987 and 1990. After a decline of $4.0 billion from 1981 to 1987, the footwear trade balance deficit grew an additional $1.4

billion from 1987 to 1990, bringing the total deficit to $8.7 billion (table 5.85.4). After declining steadily for 20 years, domestic production appears to have stabilized in the past few years. A small decline in apparent consumption in quantity terms has come at the expense of imports, which fell by 8.2 percent (in volume terms) from 1987 to 1989. Imports rebounded, however, in 1990, rising by $0.8 billion. While quantities declined, the value of imports continued to rise (21.2 percent fromt 1987 to 1990) as the Asian NICs shifted to the export of higher-unit-value footwear (tables 5.85.4 and 5.85.5).

International Competitiveness

The large and growing footwear trade deficits of the 1980s provide evidence that the US footwear industry has not been competitive in the US or international markets. World exports to non-US destinations grew over 10 percent per year on average between 1981 and 1989 (table 5.85.6). US exports during the same period grew 17.7 percent annually but from a very small base, increasing the US share of exports to non-US destinations to a modest 2.4 percent of the total.

Examination of US import data confirms the US footwear industry's lack of competitiveness. The United States is the largest single importer of footwear. Its share of world footwear imports from non-US sources increased from 31.6 percent in 1981 to a peak of 44.7 percent in 1985 (table 5.85.6) but then fell to 36.5 percent by 1989. The growth in US imports provided a major stimulus to the growth in world footwear trade. World imports from non-US sources grew $13.9 billion between 1981 and 1989 (table 5.85.6). The US market alone absorbed $5.6 billion, or 40 percent, of the increase.

Outlook

Key Determinants of US Trade Performance

An important influence on US footwear trade in recent years has been section 807 trade. To qualify for 807 consideration, only assembly operations, during which the product may not be "substantially transformed," may be performed outside the United States. Trade under section 807 can be expected to continue to expand as US manufacturing firms seek to lower their costs by exporting the most labor-intensive part of footwear manufacturing to low-wage areas.

Several other factors were important to US trade performance during the 1980s. Some analysts cite the expiration of orderly marketing agreements (OMAs) with Taiwan and Korea in June 1981 as one important factor. During the four years the agreements were in effect, imports increased by less than 2.0 percent on a volume basis. Nevertheless, domestic production declined 9.2 percent during that period, resulting in a modest increase in imports' share of nonrubber footwear consumption from 46.4 percent to 50.6 percent (on a volume basis).

The expirations of the OMAs were only one of several factors that encouraged imports. For a significant portion of the time the OMAs were in effect, the US economy was in a deep recession, and this helped cause footwear consumption to drop. Consumption of nonrubber footwear, for example, fell from 3.8 pair per person in 1977 to 3.2 pair per person in 1981. Total nonrubber footwear consumption declined from 793.6 million pair in 1977 to 740.6 million pair in 1981. In such a contracting market, it is hardly surprising that footwear imports showed little growth.

The expiration of the OMAs coincided with the economy's recovery from the recession. Footwear consumption rebounded rapidly with the economic recovery, partly reflecting purchases delayed during the recession. Nonrubber footwear consumption, which suffered an absolute decline between 1977 and 1981, increased by 10.3 percent from 1981 to 1982 (in volume terms). Despite the recovery in demand, domestic production continued to fall while imports grew rapidly. The share of consumption of nonrubber footwear supplied by imports rose from 50.6 percent in 1981 to 58.7 percent in 1982.

It is unclear how effective the OMAs would have been in limiting import growth had they been retained. The OMAs applied only to Korea and Taiwan. Although these countries are the largest source of footwear imports into the United States, imports from other areas in Asia have been growing rapidly in recent years, as already noted. Had the OMAs remained in force at levels that effectively limited imports from Korea and Taiwan, it is likely that production would have shifted more rapidly to other Asian countries.

The rise in the strength of the dollar during the early 1980s reinforced the effects that the economic recovery and the expiration of the OMAs had on import growth. The dollar's rise, especially against the Taiwanese dollar and the Korean won, reduced the dollar cost of imports, leading US consumers to substitute the relatively cheaper footwear produced abroad for domestic products. As a result, domestic production declined through 1986. The subsequent decline in the dollar beginning in 1985 helped to stabilize domestic production and imports' share of the market.

DRI elasticity data support the importance of exchange rates in determining footwear trade patterns. With an import price elasticity of -1.5, footwear is among the most import price sensitive of the product groups examined. The DRI figure suggests that a change in the dollar exchange rate causes a more than proportionate change in US footwear imports (see the appendix to this volume).

Finally, a shift in tastes added to import demand in the early 1980s. There was a rapid increase in the relative demand for athletic and more casual styles of footwear. Imports account for a relatively large share of consumption of these types of footwear.

Near-Term Outlook

The US footwear market has stabilized since 1989. The shakeout of domestic producers appears to be largely over, and the rapid growth in imports and consumption of the mid-1980s has leveled off. The remaining US producers are relatively strong and are competitive under current market conditions.

The outlook for the industry in the 1990s is mixed, however. Without substantial dollar appreciation, domestic manufacturers should maintain their share of the market or perhaps increase it slightly. The trade deficit in footwear, however, is likely to continue to increase. Because imports are so much greater than exports, even a small percentage increase in imports will swamp much larger percentage increases in exports. If exports, for example, grow 36 percent between 1990 and 1993 and imports grow only 11 percent, the trade deficit in footwear would still grow by 10.3 percent ($748 million) over the period. Other things being equal, price increases alone are likely to keep the trade deficit growing. The US deficit in footwear is likely to increase by $0.2 billion to $0.4 billion per year between 1990 and 1993, resulting in a 1993 footwear trade deficit of $9.0 billion to $9.5 billion.

A prolonged recession in the United States, on the other hand, would tend to narrow the trade deficit. The footwear industry is strongly cyclical, with per capita consumption declining in response to declines in economic activity. If disposable income should fall, consumers may begin to substitute toward relatively less expensive shoes within a given category. As imported footwear tends to be more competitive than domestically produced footwear at the less expensive end of a given category, the effect would be a substitution toward imports. Nevertheless, a recession in the United States would also cause a decline in overall demand for footwear, and this effect could more than cancel out the effects of a shift toward lower-cost imports. Because changes in the footwear deficits are driven largely by changes in imports, this would result in a small decline in the deficit.

A recession in major US export markets could, however, slightly increase the US deficit in footwear. The United States exports high-priced footwear. A recession in US export markets would cause consumers there to shift to lower-cost items. Thus US exporters would be likely to lose market share to lower-cost imports from other countries. The increase in the deficit would be relatively small because US export performance is a relatively minor factor in US trade performance. A 50 percent reduction in exports from 1990 levels, for example, would add only $244 million to the trade deficit in footwear, less than 3 percent of the overall deficit in 1990.

Discussions with industry experts indicate that EC 1992 is likely to have either a neutral or a slightly negative effect on domestic US manufacturers. The final rules to be implemented have not yet been established. There is some concern that the Community will impose limits by country on footwear imports. As the United States holds only a small share of the EC market, it is unlikely that limits on US-made shoes would be imposed. Import restrictions may, however, divert to the United States footwear exports that would have gone to the Community. This could cause a small, one-time increase in import penetration.

China is likely to continue to push aggressively to increase its footwear exports during the early to mid-1990s. This is unlikely to have any large negative effects on domestic US producers or on trade balances, because the United States does not produce the low-cost footwear exported by China. Increases in imported Chinese footwear will come at the expense of imports from other countries, particularly from Korea and Taiwan.

Medium-Term Outlook

Overall, without a significant strengthening of the dollar, the prospects for further significant increases in import penetration of the US footwear market in the early to mid-1990s appear small. The footwear market has stabilized after rapid changes during the 1980s. The remaining manufacturing capacity in the United States appears relatively robust and should be able to compete effectively with imports, given the changes that are likely in the market over the next few years. It is unlikely, however, that US manufacturers will be able to recapture any substantial part of the domestic market lost to imports during the 1980s. At current exchange rates, the investment in new capacity that would be required to recapture US markets is not to be expected. However, without a sharp recession or large changes in the value of the dollar, the trade balance for footwear is likely to continue to deteriorate modestly into the mid-1990s.

Conclusions

■ Although only a small part of US trade, footwear added substantially to the US deficit in manufactures. Footwear constituted 2.4 percent of manufactures imports to the United States in 1989 and less than 0.5 percent of US exports. At $8.7 billion, the 1990 footwear deficit was at a new high and was the third-largest among two-digit manufactures product groups.

- The United States accounts for over 35 percent of world footwear imports, making it the largest single importer. Rapid growth in the US market has provided substantial stimulus to the world market. The United States accounted for about 40 percent of the growth in the world market for footwear between 1981 and 1989.

- The 1980s witnessed a substantial reshuffling of import sources for footwear. During the 1980s, the European Community's importance as a source for footwear imports declined, and the Asian NICs and China became the major sources for US footwear imports.

- The rapid increase in demand for footwear resulting from the recovery from the recession in the early 1980s, combined with the sharp rise in the dollar against other currencies, caused US footwear imports to rise sharply. A change in tastes favoring imported types of footwear and the expiration of OMAs with Taiwan and Korea also contributed to the increase.

- Declining domestic production and the increase in imports caused a rapid increase in imports' share of domestic US consumption and a substantial deterioration in the US trade balance in footwear.

- Domestic producers, after substantial downsizing during the 1980s, are competitive with foreign producers in the lines of shoes they make. Some types of footwear, however, are no longer produced in the United States. It is unlikely that production of lower-priced footwear, now concentrated in the Asian NICs and China, would return to the United States even with substantial further devaluation of the dollar.

- The US deficit in footwear is likely to increase by $0.2 billion to $0.4 billion per year between 1990 and 1993. Imports are so much greater than exports that even modest percentage increases in volume or unit prices will overwhelm any likely increase in exports. A 5 percent annual increase in imports, for example, would require exports to triple between 1990 and 1993 to hold the trade deficit constant.

- Although US producers should continue to be competitive in the lines of shoes they make, continued increases in imports of types of footwear no longer produced in the United States virtually ensure a continued modest increase in the footwear trade deficit beyond 1993.

Bibliography

Commission of the European Communities. 1990. *Panorama of EC Industry, 1990.* Luxembourg: Commission of the European Communities.

Footwear Industries of America. 1990. *Current Highlights.* Washington: Footwear Industries of America (27 February).

Industry, Science and Technology Canada. 1988. *Industry Profile: Footwear.* Ottawa: Industry, Science and Technology.

US Department of Commerce, International Trade Administration. 1988. *U.S. Industrial Outlook, 1988.* Washington: Government Printing Office (January).

US Department of Commerce, International Trade Administration. 1989. *U.S. Industrial Outlook, 1989.* Washington: Government Printing Office (January).

US Department of Commerce, International Trade Administration. 1990. *U.S. Industrial Outlook, 1990.* Washington: Government Printing Office.

US International Trade Commission. 1984. *Nonrubber Footwear: Report to the President on Investigation No. TA − 201 − 50.* Washington: US International Trade Commission (July).

US International Trade Commission. 1985. *Nonrubber Footwear: Report to the President on Investigation No. TA − 201 − 55.* Washington: US International Trade Commission (July).

US International Trade Commission. 1990a. *Nonrubber Footwear Quarterly Statistical Report.* Washington: US International Trade Commission (March).

US International Trade Commission. 1990b. *Nonrubber Footwear Quarterly Statistical Report.* Washington: US International Trade Commission (June).

US International Trade Commission. 1990c. *Nonrubber Footwear Quarterly Statistical Report.* Washington: US International Trade Commission (September).

US International Trade Commission. 1990d. *U.S. Trade Shifts in Selected Commodity Areas, January–June 1990.* Washington: US International Trade Commission (December).

World Bank. 1990. "Footwear: Global Subsector Study." *Industry Series Paper* 34. Washington: World Bank (June).

Table 5.85.1 Footwear: product composition of world trade, 1981–89 (billions of dollars except where noted)

SITC Product	1981	1982	1983	1984	1985	1986	1987	1988	1989	Annual growth 1981–89 (percentages)
World exports to world	10.1	10.5	11.0	12.3	13.3	16.7	19.9	24.3	24.5	11.7
Memorandum: SITC 85 share of world manufactures exports (percentages)	1.0	1.1	1.1	1.2	1.2	1.2	1.2	1.2	1.2	Change 1981–89 0.2

Source: World Manufactures Trade Data Base.

Table 5.85.2 Footwear: geographic distribution of world trade, 1981–89 (percentages of total)

Country	1981	1982	1983	1984	1985	1986	1987	1988	1989	Change 1981–89
Share of exports to world										
United States	1.4	1.1	0.9	0.9	0.8	1.0	1.1	1.2	1.5	0.1
Canada	0.3	0.4	0.4	0.3	0.3	0.2	0.2	0.2	0.3	−0.1
Japan	0.7	0.7	0.6	0.5	0.4	0.3	0.2	0.2	0.2	−0.5
European Community	52.8	53.3	50.6	47.7	48.5	49.3	47.0	40.8	41.6	−11.3
EC to non-EC	22.1	22.2	22.0	21.9	22.8	20.7	17.9	15.5	16.4	−5.8
Germany	3.5	3.6	3.6	3.1	3.6	3.6	3.6	3.6	4.2	0.7
France	5.2	4.8	4.4	4.2	4.4	4.2	3.7	3.2	3.1	−2.1
Italy	31.3	33.4	31.3	28.4	28.2	28.8	26.6	21.9	21.9	−9.3
United Kingdom	2.3	1.9	1.7	1.6	1.6	1.5	1.5	1.5	1.5	−0.8
Other Western Europe	7.5	7.1	6.6	6.0	6.1	6.2	5.6	5.4	4.7	−2.8
Asian NICs[a]	24.7	26.3	29.3	30.4	30.2	31.5	33.2	37.4	32.8	8.1
Eastern Europe[b]	2.6	2.2	2.0	1.9	1.9	1.7	1.6	1.6	1.5	−1.1
Developing countries	10.9	10.0	11.1	13.5	13.0	11.2	12.5	15.2	19.0	8.1
Latin America	6.2	5.6	6.7	9.3	8.5	6.7	6.8	6.6	7.9	1.7
Rest of world	0.1	0.1	0.1	0.1	0.1	0.1	0.1	0.1	0.1	0.0
Share of imports from world										
United States	31.1	33.9	37.8	42.7	44.2	40.1	37.5	35.5	35.8	4.7
Canada	3.1	2.9	3.0	2.9	2.7	2.8	2.7	2.6	2.8	−0.3
Japan	3.0	2.8	2.6	3.0	2.8	2.9	3.9	4.9	4.8	1.8
European Community	43.1	40.8	38.6	34.6	33.8	38.1	40.6	39.7	39.0	−4.1
EC from non-EC	12.0	10.2	10.4	9.5	9.2	10.1	12.3	14.3	14.0	2.0
Germany	15.6	14.5	13.8	12.4	11.8	13.5	14.5	13.6	14.0	−1.5
France	7.7	7.6	7.0	6.1	6.4	7.6	8.2	7.8	7.5	−0.1
Italy	1.4	1.3	1.6	1.3	1.6	1.7	2.0	2.2	2.2	0.8
United Kingdom	8.1	7.6	7.3	6.8	6.3	6.3	6.4	6.8	6.5	−1.6
Other Western Europe	9.7	9.2	8.5	7.8	7.7	8.5	8.7	8.2	8.1	−1.6
Asian NICs[a]	0.8	1.2	1.2	1.1	1.1	0.9	0.9	1.5	2.2	1.4
Eastern Europe[b]	2.1	2.1	1.8	1.9	2.8	2.1	1.4	2.6	1.7	−0.4
Developing countries	5.7	5.8	5.5	4.9	4.0	3.6	3.3	4.0	4.6	−1.1
Latin America	1.0	1.4	0.9	0.8	0.7	0.7	0.6	0.9	1.4	0.4
Rest of world	0.0	0.0	0.0	0.0	0.0	0.2	0.2	0.3	0.1	0.1

table continued next page

Table 5.85.2 Footwear: geographic distribution of world trade, 1981–89 (percentages of total) (continued)

Country	1981	1982	1983	1984	1985	1986	1987	1988	1989	Change 1981–89
Export share minus import share										
United States	-29.8	-32.8	-36.9	-41.8	-43.4	-39.1	-36.5	-34.3	-34.3	-4.6
Canada	-2.8	-2.5	-2.6	-2.6	-2.3	-2.6	-2.4	-2.4	-2.6	0.2
Japan	-2.3	-2.1	-2.0	-2.5	-2.4	-2.6	-3.7	-4.7	-4.6	-2.3
European Community	9.7	12.5	12.0	13.1	14.7	11.3	6.4	1.1	2.5	-7.2
Non-EC	10.1	12.0	11.6	12.4	13.5	10.7	5.6	1.2	2.4	-7.8
Germany	-12.0	-11.0	-10.2	-9.3	-8.3	-9.9	-10.9	-10.0	-9.8	2.3
France	-2.5	-2.8	-2.5	-2.0	-2.0	-3.4	-4.5	-4.7	-4.4	-1.9
Italy	29.9	32.1	29.7	27.1	26.6	27.1	24.6	19.7	19.8	-10.2
United Kingdom	-5.8	-5.7	-5.6	-5.2	-4.7	-4.8	-4.9	-5.3	-5.0	0.8
Other Western Europe	-2.2	-2.1	-1.9	-1.8	-1.6	-2.3	-3.2	-2.8	-3.4	-1.2
Asian NICs[a]	24.0	25.1	28.0	29.3	29.2	30.5	32.3	36.0	30.6	6.6
Eastern Europe[b]	0.5	0.1	0.1	-0.1	-0.9	-0.5	0.2	-1.0	-0.1	-0.6
Developing countries	5.2	4.1	5.6	8.7	9.0	7.6	9.2	11.1	14.4	9.2
Latin America	5.2	4.2	5.8	8.4	7.8	6.0	6.2	5.7	6.5	1.3
Rest of world	0.1	0.1	0.1	0.1	0.1	-0.1	-0.1	-0.2	0.0	-0.1

a. Hong Kong, Korea, Singapore, and Taiwan.

b. Including Soviet Union.

Source: World Manufactures Trade Data Base.

Table 5.85.3 Footwear: bilateral trade flows, 1989 (billions of dollars)

					Exporter						
Importer	World	United States	Canada	Japan	European Community	Germany	France	United Kingdom	Asian NICs	Latin America	Other
World	24.5	0.4	0.1	0.1	10.2	1.0	0.8	0.4	8.0	1.9	3.9
United States	9.1		0.1	0.0	1.3	0.0	0.1	0.0	4.8	1.5	1.4
Canada	0.6	0.0		0.0	0.2	0.0	0.0	0.0	0.3	0.1	0.1
Japan	1.1	0.0			0.2	0.0	0.1	0.0	0.8	0.0	0.2
European Community	9.5	0.1	0.0	0.0	6.2	0.5	0.4	0.2	1.2	0.3	1.7
Germany	3.4	0.0	0.0	0.0	2.2		0.1	0.0	0.3	0.1	0.8
France	1.9	0.0	0.0	0.0	1.3	0.1		0.0	0.2	0.1	0.3
United Kingdom	1.4	0.0	0.0	0.0	0.9	0.0	0.0		0.2	0.1	0.2
Asian NICs	0.5	0.0	0.0	0.0	0.1	0.0	0.0	0.0	0.3	0.0	0.0
Latin America	0.3	0.2	0.0	0.0	0.1	0.0	0.0	0.0	0.1	0.0	0.0
Other	3.4	0.0	0.0	0.0	2.2	0.5	0.2	0.1	0.6	0.1	0.5

Source: World Manufactures Trade Data Base.

Table 5.85.4 Footwear: product composition of US trade, 1981–90[a]
(millions of dollars except where noted)

Category	SITC Rev. 2			SITC Rev. 3			
	1981	1987	Change 1981–87	1987	1990	Change 1981–90	Change 1987–90
Exports	141	186	45	271	479	338	208
Imports	3,146	7,236	4,090	7,547	9,576	6,430	2,029
Balance	−3,005	−7,050	−4,045	−7,276	−9,097	−6,092	−1,821

a. Data are expressed on a domestic exports, imports customs basis.

Source: US Department of Commerce.

Table 5.85.5 Footwear: geographic composition of US trade, 1981–90

	Millions of dollars				Percentages of total			
	1981	1987	1989	1990	1981	1987	1989	1990
Exports								
Canada	21	23	33	57	14.9	8.5	8.9	11.9
Japan	20	53	44	48	14.2	19.6	11.9	10.0
European Community	26	70	83	129	18.4	25.8	22.5	26.9
United Kingdom	5	7	16	19	3.5	2.6	4.3	4.0
Germany	4	8	9	21	2.8	3.0	2.4	4.4
France	6	10	16	23	4.3	3.7	4.3	4.8
Italy	4	32	24	24	2.8	11.8	6.5	5.0
Latin America	43	85	151	140	30.5	31.4	40.9	29.2
Asian NICs	3	15	28	47	2.1	5.5	7.6	9.8
Other	28	25	30	58	19.9	9.2	8.1	12.1
Total	141	271	369	479	100.0	100.0	100.0	100.0
Imports								
Canada	22	44	55	53	0.7	0.6	0.7	0.6
Japan	25	10	7	5	0.8	0.1	0.1	0.1
European Community	834	1,453	1,332	1,533	26.5	19.3	15.9	16.0
United Kingdom	13	28	34	43	0.4	0.4	0.4	0.4
Germany	11	23	31	28	0.3	0.3	0.4	0.3
France	64	102	56	47	2.0	1.4	0.7	0.5
Italy	506	861	816	984	16.1	11.4	9.7	10.3
Latin America	440	1,225	1,401	1,453	14.0	16.2	16.7	15.2
Asian NICs	1,568	4,382	4,312	4,211	49.8	58.1	51.4	44.0
Taiwan	862	2,478	2,005	1,528	27.4	32.8	23.9	16.0
South Korea	632	1,775	2,183	2,573	20.1	23.5	26.0	26.9
China	42	143	721	1,477	1.3	1.9	8.6	15.4
Other	215	290	565	844	6.8	3.8	6.7	8.8
Total	3,146	7,547	8,393	9,576	100.0	100.0	100.0	100.0

a. Data are expressed on a domestic exports, imports customs basis.

Source: US Department of Commerce.

Table 5.85.6 Footwear: indices of US competitiveness, 1981–89 (billions of dollars except where noted)

	1981	1982	1983	1984	1985	1986	1987	1988	1989	Annual growth 1981–89 (percentages)
World trade										
World exports to non-US destinations	7.0	7.0	6.9	7.2	7.6	10.1	12.5	15.4	15.5	10.5
World imports from non-US sources	10.2	10.7	11.2	12.6	13.7	16.9	20.1	23.5	24.1	11.4
US trade										
Exports	0.1	0.1	0.1	0.1	0.1	0.2	0.2	0.3	0.4	17.7
Imports	3.2	3.7	4.3	5.4	6.1	6.9	7.7	8.4	8.8	13.5
Balance	−3.1	−3.6	−4.2	−5.3	−6.0	−6.7	−7.5	−8.2	−8.4	
										Change 1981–89
US share of exports to non-US destinations (percentages)	2.0	1.7	1.5	1.6	1.5	1.7	1.7	1.8	2.4	0.4
US share of imports from non-US sources (percentages)	31.6	34.4	38.3	43.2	44.7	40.6	38.0	36.0	36.5	4.9
Export share minus import share (percentages)	−29.6	−32.7	−36.8	−41.6	−43.2	−38.9	−36.3	−34.2	−34.1	−4.5

Source: World Manufactures Trade Data Base.

Professional, Scientific, and Controlling Instruments (SITC 87)

Professional, scientific, and controlling instruments include a variety of equipment falling into two broad groups. The first consists of equipment used primarily to measure, analyze, and test other materials and equipment. Equipment in this product group is increasingly used in production processes to provide feedback, to allow better control, and to improve product quality. The second group includes medical equipment and devices, except for electromedical and radiological apparatus included in SITC 774. Also of growing importance to this segment of SITC 87 is the increased monitoring of health, safety, and environmental hazards.

Description of the Product Group

Professional, scientific, and controlling instruments contains four three-digit categories:

SITC

871 optical instruments and apparatus (telescopes and microscopes)

872 medical instruments and appliances, not elsewhere specified (medical equipment, excluding equipment included in SITC 774—electric apparatus for medical purposes and radiological apparatus)

873 meters and counters, not elsewhere specified (gas, electric, and liquid meters, etc.)

874 measuring, checking, analyzing, and controlling instruments and apparatus, not elsewhere specified, as well as parts and accessories, not elsewhere specified, of the instruments and apparatus of subcategories 873 and 874 (this includes survey and navigational equipment, chromatographs, spectrometers, etc.).

Role in World Trade

Size and Composition

Professional, scientific, and controlling instruments held a relatively small but stable share of world manufactures exports during the 1980s. At $44.9 billion in 1989, these products accounted for 2.1 percent of total world manufactures exports (table 5.87.1). World exports of these items grew slightly faster than exports of manufactures generally during the 1981–89 period, by an average of 10.5 percent annually compared with the 9.6 percent annual growth rate for all manufactures.

Exports of professional, scientific, and controlling instruments are dominated by one subcategory, measuring and controlling instruments. This subcategory includes a wide variety of equipment used to test materials and equipment and to control production processes. It accounted for over 70 percent of all professional, scientific, and controlling instruments exports during the 1980s. Medical instruments account for nearly all the remaining exports in this product group, or nearly 20 percent of the total in 1989. The remaining two subcategories, optical instruments and meters and counters, together accounted for less than 10 percent of world trade in this group of products during the period examined.

Global Competition Patterns

The European Community held the largest shares of world exports and imports of professional, scientific, and controlling instruments during the 1980s and enjoyed a small positive export-minus-import share balance (table 5.87.2). This product group is one of the few in which the United States has a larger export share than any other country, 24.1 percent in 1989; the next-largest was that of Germany at 18.0 percent. The United States, however, had a lower share of world exports than in 1981 while Japan, Germany, and the Asian NICs had higher shares.

The developing countries experienced the largest improvement in export-minus-import share balances of any region. As in so many other cases, this improvement reflects a sharp decline in the developing countries' share of world imports. Their decline in import share accounted for 90 percent of the improvement in the developing countries' share balance between 1981 and 1989.

The United States experienced the largest decline in its export-minus-import share balance of any country or region examined. An increase in the US share of world imports accompanied the decline in its export share. Despite the substantial deterioration in its share balance between 1981 and 1989, the United States enjoyed the largest positive share balance position of any country in 1989.

World trade flows in professional, scientific, and controlling instruments for 1989 are shown in table 5.87.3. Roughly half of EC exports go to other EC countries. The United States, the most important external market for EC exports, accounts for about 22.4 percent of EC exports to external markets. Similarly, the United States is the single most important market for Canada, Latin America, Japan, and the Asian NICs. The European Community is the second-largest importer from these regions. The Community is the most important market for US exports. Japan and Canada were the next most important, accounting for over 10 percent of US exports each.

Key Determinants of World Trade Performance

Demand for many products in this group is largely dependent on investment in plant and equipment and spending on R&D. New and replacement equipment usually incorporates some products that fall within this group. Environmental controls (heating and cooling) in buildings, for example, are part of SITC 874. Thus, new building construction as well as renovations require inputs from this subcategory. Similarly, R&D spending often involves upgrades or new purchases of products in the three subcategories that make up the first part of this product group.

Countries or regions that are experiencing rapid growth (e.g., Asia) or are rebuilding their industrial plants (e.g., Eastern Europe) are likely to be areas of strong growth for sales of scientific and controlling instruments. On the other hand, countries with sluggish economies, such as the United States in the early 1990s, offer only modest opportunities for increased sales.

Price competition is relatively less important for many of the products in these subcategories than for other manufactures. Nonprice factors such as reliability, accuracy, and in some applications the ability to operate in harsh environments are of primary importance. Also, for many applications instruments must be customized. In particular, the increasing integration of monitoring and testing functions within the production process often requires custom software to provide feedback from the test equipment to the production process.

The emphasis on technical sophistication of much of the output in this group— plus the need to modify standard components or custom-design instruments for particular applications—has resulted in the concentration of production in countries with the technological resources, both physical and human, to produce these instruments: the United States, the European Community, and Japan. There has been relatively little movement of production of these products to low-wage areas because labor costs are a relatively small component of production costs.

Demand for products in the second subgroup within this product group, medical instruments and appliances excluding equipment included in SITC 774, is determined by the level of health care expenditures. One important trend in the United States, Europe, and Japan is the aging of their populations, which increases demand for health services. Compared with many manufactures, world demand for medical instruments is relatively stable over business cycles. World demand should also grow steadily because of the aging populations in major markets and because of increasing incomes and access to medical care in some areas of the world.

Nonetheless, there is increasing price competition among producers of these goods as the United States and other countries attempt to control the cost of health care. This has prompted research on new products that reduce the cost of providing health services (for example, new noninvasive diagnostic techniques).

Role in US Trade

Recent Performance

Professional, scientific, and controlling instruments are significantly more important in US trade than in world trade. Accounting for roughly 4 percent of US manufactures exports in 1990, the product group was the ninth-largest export category for US manufactures. Between 1981 and 1987, a period of stagnant or negative export growth for many US manufactures, US exports of professional, scientific, and controlling instruments increased by nearly 25 percent (table 5.87.4). Exports have grown more rapidly since 1987, increasing roughly 50 percent, to $12.1 billion, in 1990.

Despite a steady increase in exports during the early to mid-1980s, an even more rapid increase in imports resulted in a substantial decline in the US trade balance for this product group. Imports more than doubled from 1981 to 1987. Combined with modest export growth, this reduced the trade surplus for this category from $4.3 billion in 1981 to $2.8 billion in 1987. In the late 1980s, a sharp decline in import growth and a spurt in exports allowed a significant improvement in the US trade balance in these goods. Import growth declined from over 20 percent per year between 1981 and 1987 to less than 10 percent annually between 1987 and 1990. The trade balance improved by $2.7 billion over the same period to a 1990 surplus of $5.9 billion, one of the largest US trade surpluses for any manufacturing industry.

The vast majority of US trade in this product group is in measuring instruments and apparatus and in medical instruments, which together accounted for 95 percent of US exports of professional, scientific, and controlling instruments in 1990 (measuring instruments alone accounted for 71 percent). The same two subcategories also accounted for 89 percent of 1990 US imports of products in this group, with measuring instruments alone accounting for 65 percent of the total.

The European Community is the most important trading partner for the United States, accounting for roughly 35 percent of US exports and imports (table 5.87.5). Within the Community, Germany is the most important source of (15.4 percent of total imports) and destination for (7.9 percent of total exports) US professional, scientific, and controlling instruments.

Japan was the United States' second-largest trading partner in goods in this category. Japan has accepted an increasing share of US professional, scientific, and controlling instruments exports in recent years. Its share of US imports, on the other hand, remained roughly constant during 1981–90. US exports to Canada, the most important single-country market after Japan, fluctuated substantially over the period, while the share of US imports from Canada declined.

International Competitiveness

The declining US export share in world markets is one indication of the US decline in market competitiveness in this category. World exports to non-US destinations increased 9.8 percent annually between 1981 and 1989 while US exports grew by only 7.7 percent per year (table 5.87.6). This resulted in a decline in the US share of exports to non-US destinations, from 33.4 percent in 1981 to 28.4 percent in 1989.

The rising importance of the United States as an importer also indicates a decline in US competitiveness. From 13.0 percent of imports from non-US sources in 1981, the US import share rose rapidly to 19.3 percent in 1985 and then gradually declined to 17.3 percent in 1989. The US export and import performance combined to reduce the US share balance from 20.4 percentage points in 1981 to 11.1 percentage points in 1989.

Outlook

Key Determinants of US Trade Performance

A key factor determining US trade performance in the near term is the differential in growth rates between the United States and its major trading partners. Demand for scientific and controlling instruments is largely determined by investment in plant and equipment and expenditures on R&D. The slack US economy during the early 1990s will limit investment and R&D expenditures, thus limiting demand for scientific and controlling instruments. Import growth, therefore, can be expected to be modest through the early 1990s. Relatively robust growth in the primary US export markets, the European Community and Japan, should help maintain US export performance.

The large changes in exchange rates during the 1980s affected US trade performance in professional, scientific, and controlling instruments less than in other manufacturing industries. An import price elasticity of zero, as estimated by DRI (see the appendix to this volume), indicates that the value of US imports in this product group as a whole is unaffected by changes in import prices. US Department of Commerce sources, however, indicate that the exchange rate changes were important to the trade performance of some parts of the industry. The United States lost much of its production of optical instruments at least in part because of a decline in its price competitiveness due to the rise of the dollar during the early and mid-1980s. The rise in the dollar, however, did force US producers to streamline production, improve product quality, and modify products in response to customer demands.

Several developments in the industry helped the United States maintain its strong export position in the world during the 1980s and should help it maintain that position in the 1990s. There has been an increasing emphasis on systems that both monitor and control production processes. These systems incorporate a number of sensors that continuously test products, monitor the production process, and adjust production through feedback mechanisms to meet given parameters. Manufacturers are increasingly installing such systems in an effort to improve product quality and increase their ability to compete in international markets. US firms are particularly strong in the development of the hardware and software required for these systems.

Also helping to raise demand for products in this group is increased monitoring of the workplace for health, safety, and environmental hazards. Many firms, particularly in the United States, have increased this monitoring in an effort to avoid liability suits over worker injury or environmental damage. Greater emphasis on health, safety, and environmental issues in markets outside the United States provides an expanding market for this area of US expertise.

Manufacturers of electrical test equipment are under pressure to keep pace with the rapid changes in the electronics industry. Innovations in electronic equipment require new test equipment, providing another source of increased demand.

Near-Term Outlook

The substantial $5.9 billion 1990 US trade surplus in professional, scientific, and controlling instruments is likely to increase through 1993. Sluggish US economic performance in the early 1990s will limit US import growth through 1991 and into 1992. An investment surge in Europe anticipated with the movement toward full implementation of EC 1992, the rebuilding of Eastern Europe, and continued strong growth in Asian markets should allow US firms to maintain the strong export performance of recent years. A shift in demand within the product group toward the types of products in which the United States is particularly competitive will also help to increase US exports.

Probable annual export increases of roughly $1.0 billion will be partly offset by import growth of roughly $0.5 billion annually, resulting in an annual improvement in the trade balance of about $0.5 billion. This improvement will increase the 1990 trade surplus of $5.9 billion to a 1993 total of $7.5 billion.

Medium-Term Outlook

Professional and scientific instruments are likely to maintain or perhaps increase their share of world manufactures trade. The growing emphasis on various aspects of quality (reliability, uniformity, durability, etc.) for many manufactures has caused manufacturers to increase product testing and to integrate testing into the production process.

The prospects for US trade performance in professional and scientific instruments are good beyond 1993. Continuing US technological strength and continuing evolution of products should provide a solid basis for continued strong US export performance. However, US economic recovery is likely to boost import growth above the levels of the early 1990s. Thus, the annual increase in the US trade surplus expected in the early 1990s is likely to taper off after 1993. The United States should, however, be able to maintain its share of world exports, allowing its trade surplus to remain constant or perhaps increase slightly.

Conclusions

- Professional, scientific, and controlling instruments is composed of two types of products: equipment used for testing, measuring, or analyzing other products or equipment, and nonelectrical medical equipment and instruments. The United States has historically been a strong international competitor in both areas, with a 1990 surplus of $5.9 billion in the product group overall.

- Although it accounts for a relatively small portion of world manufactures exports, this product group increased its share of world exports during the 1980s. This trend will probably continue in the 1990s. As firms continue to strive for better product quality and performance as well as to reduce hazards to workers' health and the environment, they will increase their use of testing and monitoring equipment.

- Despite some decline during the 1980s, the United States remained the world's largest exporter of professional, scientific, and controlling instruments. Because nonprice factors (quality, custom design, etc.) are relatively important determinants of sales in this product group, the rapid appreciation of the dollar in the early to mid-1980s hurt US producers of precision instruments less than it hurt US producers of many other manufactures.

- The technical sophistication of many of the products in this category and the demand for custom-designed instruments and monitoring systems serve to concentrate production in countries with the technological resources to produce them. With its technological resources, both physical and human, the United States should maintain its position as a leading producer and exporter of professional, scientific, and controlling instruments in the foreseeable future.

- Relatively slow US economic growth during the early 1990s should limit US imports, while relatively robust economic growth in the major US trading partners should help maintain strong export performance. An expected increase in the US trade surplus of $1.5 billion by 1993 should lift the surplus in this category to roughly $7.5 billion by 1993.

- Economic recovery in the United States is likely to cause import growth to increase relative to that foreseen for the early 1990s. US technological expertise combined with a relative increase in demand for some of the products in which the United States is particularly competitive should provide for continued strong US export performance. Overall, the United States should be able to maintain or even increase its 1993 trade surplus through the 1990s.

Bibliography

Commission of the European Communities. 1990. *Panorama of EC Industry, 1990.* Luxembourg: Commission of the European Communities.

Industry, Science and Technology Canada. 1988. *Industry Profile: Instrumentation.* Ottawa: Industry, Science and Technology Canada.

US Department of Commerce, International Trade Administration. 1988. *U.S. Industrial Outlook, 1988.* Washington: Government Printing Office (January).

US Department of Commerce, International Trade Administration. 1989. *U.S. Industrial Outlook, 1989.* Washington: Government Printing Office (January).

US Department of Commerce, International Trade Administration. 1990. *U.S. Industrial Outlook, 1990.* Washington: Government Printing Office (January).

Table 5.87.1 Professional, scientific, and controlling instruments: product composition of world trade, 1981–89 (billions of dollars except where noted)

SITC Product	1981	1982	1983	1984	1985	1986	1987	1988	1989	Annual growth 1981–89 (percentages)
World exports to world	20.2	20.3	20.8	22.3	25.8	31.4	36.6	42.3	44.9	10.5
of which										
871 Optical instruments	1.1	1.2	1.2	1.3	1.6	1.9	2.1	2.4	2.7	12.1
872 Medical instruments	3.0	3.1	3.3	3.5	4.8	6.1	7.2	8.5	8.7	14.3
873 Meters and counters	0.5	0.5	0.4	0.4	0.5	0.6	0.6	1.2	1.2	11.6
874 Measuring, analyzing	15.5	15.4	15.6	16.8	18.6	22.3	26.2	30.2	32.3	9.6
Memorandum:										Change 1981–89
SITC 87 share of world manufactures exports (percentages)	2.0	2.1	2.1	2.1	2.3	2.3	2.2	2.1	2.1	0.1

Source: World Manufactures Trade Data Base.

Table 5.87.2 Professional, scientific, and controlling instruments: geographic distribution of world trade, 1981–89 (percentages of total)

Country	1981	1982	1983	1984	1985	1986	1987	1988	1989	Change 1981–89
Share of exports to world										
United States	29.8	29.8	28.3	28.0	28.7	24.6	22.9	23.6	24.1	−5.7
Canada	2.0	2.4	2.5	2.5	2.0	2.0	1.8	1.5	1.8	−0.2
Japan	8.9	8.8	9.9	10.9	10.6	11.1	10.6	12.0	12.5	3.6
European Community	45.1	45.2	44.8	44.4	44.7	47.3	48.8	46.9	45.3	0.2
EC to non-EC	25.7	25.1	24.9	25.7	26.3	26.2	26.2	25.2	23.8	−1.9
Germany	16.6	17.2	16.8	16.5	16.7	19.2	19.8	19.0	18.0	1.4
France	6.8	6.4	6.4	6.3	6.7	6.0	6.7	6.3	5.8	−1.0
Italy	3.0	2.9	3.0	3.0	2.9	3.3	3.5	3.1	3.2	0.2
United Kingdom	10.7	10.8	10.7	10.7	10.8	10.7	10.5	10.6	10.1	−0.6
Other Western Europe	10.3	10.0	10.1	9.4	9.5	10.5	10.8	9.7	9.3	−1.0
Asian NICs[a]	1.0	1.1	1.2	1.4	1.4	1.6	2.0	2.7	2.9	1.9
Eastern Europe[b]	0.3	0.3	0.2	0.2	0.2	0.2	0.3	0.3	0.2	−0.1
Developing countries	2.1	2.1	2.4	2.6	2.4	2.5	2.6	3.0	3.3	1.2
Latin America	0.8	0.6	0.8	1.0	1.0	0.9	1.0	1.1	1.4	0.6
Rest of world	0.1	0.1	0.2	0.2	0.2	0.2	0.2	0.5	0.4	0.3
Share of imports from world										
United States	8.7	8.8	9.8	12.6	13.3	12.8	12.6	12.3	12.4	3.6
Canada	5.5	5.3	5.6	6.0	5.7	4.6	4.2	4.3	4.8	−0.7
Japan	4.7	4.9	5.0	5.3	5.0	4.4	4.7	5.7	6.2	1.5
European Community	39.5	40.2	39.6	37.8	37.8	39.7	42.8	41.0	40.5	1.1
EC from non-EC	19.9	20.2	20.4	19.8	19.6	19.5	20.4	20.3	20.6	0.7
Germany	8.7	8.8	8.6	8.3	8.3	9.4	9.7	9.1	8.9	0.2
France	7.0	7.1	6.9	6.2	6.2	6.5	7.4	7.1	6.7	−0.3
Italy	4.9	4.9	4.8	4.7	4.8	5.2	6.2	6.0	6.0	1.2
United Kingdom	8.5	8.9	9.4	9.4	8.9	8.2	8.3	8.2	8.1	−0.4
Other Western Europe	9.2	8.6	8.2	8.1	8.6	9.5	10.0	9.0	8.6	−0.6
Asian NICs[a]	3.9	4.6	4.8	5.3	4.1	5.0	5.3	8.0	9.1	5.2
Eastern Europe[b]	2.6	2.7	2.9	2.6	2.6	2.7	2.5	2.6	2.5	−0.2
Developing countries	23.8	22.7	21.8	19.9	20.4	17.1	16.0	14.8	13.8	−10.0
Latin America	6.9	6.0	4.3	4.6	5.1	4.1	4.4	3.9	3.8	−3.1
Rest of world	0.2	0.2	0.5	0.5	0.7	0.8	0.6	1.0	0.7	0.5

table continued next page

Table 5.87.2 Professional, scientific, and controlling instruments: geographic distribution of world trade, 1981–89
(percentages of total) (continued)

Country	1981	1982	1983	1984	1985	1986	1987	1988	1989	Change 1981–89
Export share minus import share										
United States	21.1	20.9	18.5	15.4	15.4	11.8	10.3	11.3	11.8	−9.3
Canada	−3.5	−2.9	−3.1	−3.6	−3.6	−2.6	−2.4	−2.8	−3.0	0.6
Japan	4.2	3.9	4.8	5.6	5.6	6.6	5.9	6.3	6.3	2.2
European Community	5.6	5.0	5.2	6.7	7.0	7.6	6.0	5.8	4.8	−0.8
Non-EC	5.7	4.9	4.6	5.8	6.7	6.8	5.8	4.8	3.2	−2.5
Germany	7.9	8.4	8.2	8.2	8.4	9.8	10.1	10.0	9.1	1.2
France	−0.2	−0.7	−0.5	0.1	0.5	−0.5	−0.7	−0.8	−0.9	−0.7
Italy	−1.9	−2.0	−1.8	−1.7	−1.9	−2.0	−2.7	−2.9	−2.8	−1.0
United Kingdom	2.2	1.9	1.3	1.3	1.9	2.5	2.1	2.4	2.0	−0.2
Other Western Europe	1.1	1.4	1.9	1.3	0.9	0.9	0.8	0.7	0.7	−0.5
Asian NICs[a]	−2.8	−3.5	−3.6	−3.9	−2.7	−3.4	−3.3	−5.3	−6.1	−3.3
Eastern Europe[b]	−2.3	−2.4	−2.7	−2.4	−2.4	−2.4	−2.3	−2.4	−2.2	0.1
Developing countries	−21.7	−20.6	−19.4	−17.2	−18.0	−14.6	−13.4	−11.8	−10.5	11.1
Latin America	−6.2	−5.4	−3.4	−3.6	−4.1	−3.2	−3.4	−2.8	−2.5	3.7
Rest of world	−0.1	−0.1	−0.3	−0.3	−0.6	−0.6	−0.4	−0.5	−0.2	−0.1

a. Hong Kong, Korea, Singapore, and Taiwan.

b. Including Soviet Union.

Source: World Manufactures Trade Data Base.

Table 5.87.3 Professional, scientific, and controlling instruments: bilateral trade flows, 1989 (billions of dollars)

Importer	Exporter										
	World	United States	Canada	Japan	European Community	Germany	France	United Kingdom	Asian NICs	Latin America	Other
World	44.9	10.8	0.8	5.6	20.3	8.1	2.6	4.5	1.3	0.6	5.4
United States	6.8		0.5	2.0	2.4	0.9	0.3	0.8	0.5	0.6	0.8
Canada	1.7	1.2		0.1	0.2	0.1	0.0	0.1	0.0	0.0	0.1
Japan	2.6	1.6	0.0		0.6	0.3	0.1	0.2	0.1	0.0	0.2
European Community	18.1	3.9	0.1	1.2	9.6	3.7	1.2	1.8	0.3	0.0	2.8
Germany	4.4	1.0	0.0	0.5	1.8		0.5	0.5	0.1	0.0	0.9
France	3.2	0.6	0.0	0.1	1.9	1.0		0.3	0.0	0.0	0.5
United Kingdom	3.1	0.9	0.0	0.2	1.3	0.6	0.2		0.1	0.0	0.6
Asian NICs	3.1	1.0	0.0	1.2	0.6	0.2	0.1	0.2		0.0	0.6
Latin America	1.8	1.2	0.0	0.1	0.4	0.2	0.1	0.1	0.0		0.2
Other	10.9	2.0	0.1	1.0	6.4	2.7	0.8	1.4	0.2	0.0	1.3

Source: World Manufactures Trade Data Base.

Table 5.87.4 Professional, scientific, and controlling instruments: product composition of US trade, 1981–90[a]
(millions of dollars)

Category	SITC Rev. 2			SITC Rev. 3			
	1981	1987	Change 1981–87	1987	1990	Change 1981–90	Change 1981–90
Exports	6,024	7,438	1,414	8,082	12,108	6,084	4,026
Imports	1,771	4,616	2,845	4,835	6,208	4,437	1,373
Balance	4,253	2,822	−1,431	3,247	5,900	1,647	2,653
of which							
871 Optical instruments and apparatus, nes							
Exports	96	296	200	323	463	367	140
Imports	183	374	191	374	456	273	82
Balance	−87	−78	9	−51	7	94	58
872 Instruments and apparatus, n.e.s. for medical, dental, etc., purposes							
Exports	714	1,128	414	1,938	2,879	2,165	941
Imports	273	837	564	1,205	1,523	1,250	318
Balance	441	291	−150	733	1,355	914	622
873 Meters and counters, n.e.s.							
Exports	59	44	−15	127	168	109	41
Imports	127	219	92	160	205	78	45
Balance	−68	−175	−107	−33	−37	31	−4
874 Measuring, checking, analyzing, and controlling instruments, n.e.s.							
Exports	5,155	5,971	816	5,693	8,598	3,443	2,905
Imports	1,187	3,186	1,999	3,096	4,023	2,836	927
Balance	3,968	2,785	−1,183	2,597	4,575	607	1,978

a. Data are expressed on a domestic exports, imports customs basis.

Source: US Department of Commerce.

Table 5.87.5 Professional, scientific, and controlling instruments: geographic composition of US trade, 1981–90

	Millions of dollars				Percentages of total			
	1981	1987	1989	1990	1981	1987	1989	1990
Exports								
Canada	877	1,029	1,201	1,912	14.6	12.7	11.0	15.8
Japan	538	1,027	1,589	1,552	8.9	12.7	14.5	12.8
European Community	1,983	2,801	3,911	4,176	32.9	34.7	35.8	34.5
United Kingdom	531	668	890	940	8.8	8.3	8.1	7.8
Germany	477	675	962	954	7.9	8.4	8.8	7.9
France	331	447	612	663	5.5	5.5	5.6	5.5
Italy	167	288	443	465	2.8	3.6	4.1	3.8
Latin America	831	829	1,175	1,356	13.8	10.3	10.8	11.2
Asian NICs	330	635	1,010	1,109	5.5	7.9	9.2	9.2
Other	1,465	1,761	2,038	2,003	24.3	21.8	18.7	16.5
Total	6,024	8,082	10,924	12,108	100.0	100.0	100.0	100.0
Imports								
Canada	229	482	470	527	12.9	10.0	8.0	8.5
Japan	475	1,309	1,669	1,641	26.8	27.1	28.5	26.4
European Community	660	1,784	1,991	2,155	37.3	36.9	34.1	34.7
United Kingdom	197	506	605	652	11.1	10.5	10.3	10.5
Germany	291	859	859	958	16.4	17.8	14.7	15.4
France	75	160	250	241	4.2	3.3	4.3	3.9
Italy	24	68	87	86	1.4	1.4	1.5	1.4
Latin America	136	331	560	640	7.7	6.8	9.6	10.3
Asian NICs	103	419	502	453	5.8	8.7	8.6	7.3
Other	168	510	654	792	9.5	10.5	11.2	12.8
Total	1,771	4,835	5,846	6,208	100.0	100.0	100.0	100.0

a. Data are expressed on a domestic exports, imports customs basis.

Source: US Department of Commerce.

Table 5.87.6 Professional, scientific, and controlling instruments: indices of US competitiveness, 1981–89 (billions of dollars except where noted)

	1981	1982	1983	1984	1985	1986	1987	1988	1989	Annual growth 1981–89 (percentages)
World trade										
World exports to non-US destinations	18.0	18.1	18.3	19.0	22.0	26.7	31.3	36.1	38.1	9.8
World imports from non-US sources	13.9	13.9	14.2	15.5	17.6	23.5	27.9	32.1	34.3	11.9
US trade										
Exports	6.0	6.1	5.9	6.2	7.4	7.7	8.4	10.0	10.8	7.7
Imports	1.8	1.8	2.1	2.9	3.4	4.1	4.7	5.4	5.9	16.0
Balance	4.2	4.3	3.8	3.3	4.0	3.6	3.7	4.6	4.9	
										Change 1981–89
US share of exports to non-US destinations (percentages)	33.4	33.4	32.2	32.9	33.6	28.9	26.8	27.6	28.4	–5.0
US share of imports from non-US sources (percentages)	13.0	13.2	14.5	18.6	19.3	17.6	16.9	16.8	17.3	4.3
Export share minus import share (percentages)	20.4	20.2	17.7	14.3	14.3	11.3	9.9	10.9	11.1	

Source: World Manufactures Trade Data Base.

Miscellaneous Manufactures (SITC 89)

Miscellaneous manufactures includes a wide variety of products, from baskets and brooms to xylophones. Many of the products in this group are relatively low-technology items characterized by labor-intensive production techniques. During the 1980s, miscellaneous manufactures were a relatively large and growing part of world manufactures. A significant shift in production from the developed countries to East Asia occurred during the 1980s.

Description of the Product Group

Miscellaneous manufactures is divided into a number of three-digit subcategories. The list below is that of Revision 2 of the SITC code. Revision 3 added another three-digit code, arms and ammunition (SITC 891). This subcategory includes tanks, artillery, and military firearms as well as sporting firearms, which were previously classified under sporting goods (SITC 894).

SITC

892 printed matter (newspapers, books, magazines, labels, banknotes, maps, etc.)

893 plastic articles, not elsewhere specified (food containers, flooring, stoppers, lids, etc.)

894 baby carriages, toys, games, and sporting goods

895 office supplies, not elsewhere specified (filing cabinets, pens, pencils, binders, paper clips, etc.)

896 works of art, etc. (original paintings, statuary, etc.)

897 gold, silverware, and jewelry

898 musical instruments (also includes records, tapes, and compact discs)

899 other manufactured goods (includes among other items candles, umbrellas, matches, cigarette holders, smoking pipes, artificial limbs, baskets, brooms, buttons, combs, vacuum flasks, and parachutes).

Role in World Trade

Size and Composition

This catchall category is one of the larger of the two-digit manufacturing categories. World exports were $101.8 billion in 1989 and accounted for 4.8 percent of total world manufactures exports (table 5.89.1). This was the fourth-largest share of world manufactures exports; only road vehicles (SITC 78), electrical machinery (SITC 77), and office machines and computers (SITC 75) were larger. In addition, exports of miscellaneous manufactures grew faster during the 1980s than exports of manufactures in total. The 11.6 percent average annual growth rate for miscellaneous manufactures between 1981 and 1989 placed it among the five fastest growing two-digit categories, substantially ahead of the 9.6 percent growth rate for total manufactures.

With the exception of office supplies, miscellaneous manufactures exports were fairly evenly divided among the various three-digit subcategories. The two largest subcategories, miscellaneous plastic articles and baby carriages, toys, games, and sporting goods, each accounted for roughly 20 percent of trade in miscellaneous manufactures during 1989. The smallest of the three-digit subcategories, office supplies not elsewhere specified, accounted for only 3.6 percent of miscellaneous manufactures trade in 1987. Each of the remaining three-digit subcategories accounted for between 10 percent and 15 percent of total miscellaneous manufactures exports. The relative importance of the various three-digit subcategories changed little between 1981 and 1989.

Global Competition Patterns

The European Community is the leading exporter of miscellaneous manufactures. Although its export share declined slightly during the 1980s, the Community still accounted for 44.4 percent of world exports of miscellaneous manufactures in 1989 (table 5.89.2). The Asian NICs as a group are the second-largest exporter, and they increased their export share substantially during the 1980s. The United States and Japan both experienced declining export shares during the 1980s. Thus, generally, there was a shift away from production in the European Community, Japan, and the United States in favor of production in the Asian NICs and the developing countries.

The European Community was also the largest importing region for miscellaneous manufactures during the 1980s. Its import share remained roughly constant over the period (table 5.89.2). During the mid-1980s, the United States, the largest single-country importer of miscellaneous manufactures, experienced a substantial increase in its import share, which reached 29.5 percent in 1985. By 1989, however, its import share, at 22.5 percent, was only 3.4 percentage points above the 1981 level. Japan's import share was relatively stable between 1981 and 1985 but has more than doubled since 1985. The increased import shares of the European Community, the United States, and Japan reflect the shift of production from these areas to the Asian NICs and developing countries. Virtually constant imports by the developing countries in the presence of growing world trade reduced their share of world imports substantially.

The 1981–85 decline in the US share balance to 19.6 percent was brought about largely by an increase in the US import share, which accounted for 75 percent of the deterioration. The developing countries experienced the largest change in their share balances.

Trade within the European Community accounted for the largest trade flows in miscellaneous manufactures. Exports to other EC members accounted for over half of all EC exports in 1989 (table 5.89.3). The United States, the largest non-EC market for EC exports, accounted for 23.3 percent of EC exports going outside the Community. The United States was also the most important market for exports from Canada, Latin America, Japan, and the Asian NICs. The European Community was the most important US export market, receiving 28.8 percent of the total. Canada, Latin America, and Japan were the other important US export markets.

Key Determinants of World Trade Patterns

Because miscellaneous manufactures is such a diverse group of products, it is difficult to generalize about the determinants of trade patterns for the category as a whole. Two characteristics, however, are common to many of the products in the group. First, an apparent sensitivity to changes in exchange rates played an important role in at least some segments of most of the three-digit subcategories of miscellaneous manufactures. The low-technology manufactures tend to require relatively little capital for their manufacture; hence entry and exit are easy. For these types of products, price is an important competitive factor. Thus, changes in exchange rates, which affect the relative price of goods produced in different countries, can strongly affect the competitiveness of products from different countries.

A second characteristic common to many of these products is that they are relatively labor intensive. A significant portion of the production of these products appears to have shifted from Europe, Japan, and the United States to the Asian NICs and the developing countries during the 1980s.

In some of the subcategories, other, noneconomic factors such as fashions and fads play a role in determining trade flows. The increased popularity of golf in Japan and of video games in the United States are two examples.

The following sections describe factors unique to several of the more important three-digit subcategories.

Printed Matter

Only a relatively small portion of the products and output in this category is traded internationally. Markets for printing services tend to be local or regional. A large part of the printing business consists of relatively small production runs to meet the needs of local businesses: items such as business forms, advertising circulars, labels, menus, and the like. For these jobs, quality and delivery schedules are often deciding factors, and firms are relatively insensitive to small changes in unit prices. Thus, there is little international competition for these types of printing jobs.

For the relatively small part of the printing industry that consists of large jobs (newspapers, books, and magazines), price considerations can be quite important. Here changes in exchange rates can be significant because they alter the relative prices of domestic versus foreign suppliers.

Printing has traditionally required highly skilled labor. More recently, firms have been substituting capital for skilled labor in production by introducing machinery that reduces skilled labor requirements. Operating these machines, however, still requires relatively skilled technicians. The skilled labor requirements and local nature of markets have prevented the large shift in production to low-wage areas that many of the other products in this group experienced during the 1980s.

The printing industry faces increased competition from nonprint media, for example from on-line computer information systems and encyclopedias and other reference works on compact discs. Another problem is the increased use of video shopping and other media that compete for advertising revenues, traditionally one of the greatest sources of revenues (directly or indirectly) for publishers.

Baby Carriages, Toys, Games, and Sporting Goods

Production of many of the products in this subcategory is labor intensive. As a result, manufacturing operations for both toys and sporting goods have tended to shift from the developed countries to lower-wage areas, particularly the Asian NICs and other areas in Asia.

A few large multinational (mostly US) firms control most of toy production. These companies do much of the design and development of toys in their home country but often license production to foreign producers, mostly in Asia. Fads can rapidly alter the fortunes of toy companies and strongly affect trade flows. The recent resurgence in popularity of home video games is one example. Systems and cartridges for these games are produced almost exclusively in Japan. Thus, the recent growth of sales of these games in the United States has significantly contributed to the increase in the US trade deficit in toys.

The sporting goods market can be divided into a relatively small group of high-end products, for which quality and performance are the primary purchase considerations, and a larger group of low-end products, for which price considerations tend to dominate. Developed countries continue to produce a substantial portion of the high-end products. Use of advanced materials and R&D to improve product performance is critical at the high end of the market. Because price is a less important purchase consideration for these products, companies can absorb the higher costs of domestic production.

Much of the production of low-end products has shifted to low-wage areas, with a significant portion of brand-name goods now being manufactured under license outside the home country. Production of these goods is sensitive to changes in exchange rates and to other factors affecting prices.

Production of some types of sporting equipment tends to be concentrated in certain countries. Canada, for example, is the leading producer of ice skating and hockey equipment, while Finland is noted for its cross-country ski equipment; France and Austria specialize in alpine ski equipment, and the United States is known for golfing and fishing equipment.

Role in US Trade

Recent Performance

Miscellaneous manufactures is among the most important two-digit SITC categories in US trade. US exports of $18.1 billion in 1990 accounted for 6.3 percent of US manufactures exports. Imports of $25.0 billion in the same year accounted for 6.4 percent of US manufactures imports. After sluggish growth in the early to mid-1980s, exports grew dramatically in the late 1980s (table 5.89.4). Yet, particularly in the latter part of the 1980s, the US trade balance in these products deteriorated because of even more rapid import growth. The $3.4 billion improvement in the US trade balance since 1987 compensated for only one-third of the decline between 1981 and 1987.

Except for arms and ammunition (which was reclassified into SITC 89 in Revision 3 of the SITC codes), printed matter (which has achieved a growing surplus since 1987), and miscellaneous manufactured articles not elsewhere specified, the United States normally runs trade deficits in each of the three-digit subcategories of miscellaneous manufactures.

There was a significant shuffling of the importance of US export destinations during the 1980s (table 5.89.5). The share of US exports going to the United States' two largest export markets, the European Community and Canada, stayed at roughly 50 percent. The share of US exports going to Japan and to the Asian NICs increased substantially between 1981 and 1990. Japan took 7.8 percent of US exports in 1981 and 14.1 percent in 1990. The Asian NICs' share of US exports rose from 4.9 percent to 9.5 percent over the same period. The share of US exports going to Latin America declined substantially over the decade, from 17.2 percent to 10.0 percent.

There were also substantial changes in the sources of US imports over the 1980s. The two largest sources of US imports, the Asian NICs and the European Community, saw a small decline in their combined share of US imports, from 52.4 percent in 1981 to 46.2 percent in 1990 (table 5.89.5). Canada's share of US imports also declined, from 10.0 percent to 5.1 percent during the same period. The two areas that experienced significant gains in their share of US imports were Japan and the "other" countries category (primarily China and other developing countries). Japan's import share rose from 13.3 percent in 1981 to 18.5 percent in 1990, and the share of "other" countries rose from 15.4 percent to 24.8 percent.

International Competitiveness

US international competitiveness in miscellaneous manufacturers declined during the 1980s. World exports to non-US destinations increased by 10.9 percent annually on average between 1981 and 1989 (table 5.89.6). US exports grew somewhat more slowly, increasing by only 10.5 percent annually during the same period. This caused a decline in the US share of world exports to non-US destinations, from 15.5 percent in 1981 to 14.9 percent in 1989.

World imports originating outside the United States grew 11.9 percent annually on average between 1981 and 1989 (table 5.89.6). But US imports grew substantially faster (14.0 percent annually) over the same period, resulting in an increase in the US share of world imports from non-US sources from 22.4 percent in 1981 to 26.0 percent in 1989. Combined, the decline in the US export share and the increase in the US import share resulted in a 4.2-percentage-point decline in the US share balance between 1981 and 1989.

Outlook

Key Determinants of US Trade Performance

Miscellaneous manufactures includes primarily consumer items, demand for which is particularly sensitive to changes in personal disposable income and consumer confidence. Since purchases of most of these items are easily deferred, demand declines rapidly during economic downturns or periods of low consumer confidence. With imports supplying a large share of domestic consumption in some of the important subcategories, a decline in demand also results in a substantial decline in imports.

US exports go primarily to Canada, the European Community, and Japan. Hence, economic performance and consumer confidence in these countries have important consequences for US export performance.

One of the price elasticities calculated by DRI was for miscellaneous consumer goods, which in addition to the SITC classification of miscellaneous manufactures included SITC 665 (glassware), SITC 666 (pottery), SITC 696 (cutlery), SITC 697 (household equipment of base metal), SITC 699 (miscellaneous manufactures of base metals), SITC 81 (sanitary, plumbing, heating and lighting fixtures and fittings), SITC 82 (furniture), SITC 83 (luggage and handbags), and SITC 88 (photographic apparatus, watches, and clocks). The calculated elasticity of -1.1 for this group places it in the midrange of elasticities for the different industries. This indicates that US imports would change about proportionately with changes in the value of the dollar. The import price elasticity calculated for the entire group, however, is likely to mask large differences in import price elasticities for smaller subgroupings. For some three-digit subcategories, the massive appreciation of the US dollar during the early to mid-1980s appears to have been an important factor in the rapid increase in imports.

A second factor aiding import growth was the Generalized System of Preferences (GSP), which accords duty-free entry to some imports from developing countries. Until January 1989, imports of a number of goods, including toys, games, and jewelry, from the Asian NICs entered the United States duty free under the GSP. These countries were judged to be sufficiently competitive in international markets that GSP coverage was no longer needed. Since 1989, their imports have been subject to the same tariffs as countries enjoying most-favored-nation (MFN) status. The imposition of tariffs on these countries, although they are the major source of imports in many categories, does not appear to have slowed import growth. Instead, imports appear to be shifting to other developing areas, including China, Mexico, Thailand, and the Philippines.

For this product group as a whole, differences in economic growth rates and exchange rates are the most important determinants of US trade performance. Characteristics of some of the three-digit subcategories are discussed below.

Printed Matter

This is the largest three-digit US export subcategory within miscellaneous manufactures and the only one to consistently register a trade surplus during the 1980s. Several factors help account for strong US trade performance in printed matter.

US printers enjoy several advantages over their foreign competitors that enabled them to maintain exports during the 1980s. First, the United States has been a leader in introducing new printing technologies that increase labor productivity and reduce the need for highly skilled labor. Yet despite the reduction in labor requirements and the appreciation of the US dollar in the early 1980s, production has not significantly shifted to other countries, because of the continuing need for skilled labor, the increasing capital requirements for large-scale printing operations, and the local nature of markets for much of the printing industry.

US printers also enjoy several advantages due to the nature of the market. The United States is a leading academic and business research center; this fosters the publication of a high volume of scientific and technical materials, including books and journals. The location of these publishers in the United States gives US printers an important advantage over foreign competitors. In addition, the huge size and relative affluence of the US market have led to a proliferation of highly specialized nontechnical publications that other markets are not large enough to support. Filling the demand for specialized nontechnical publications overseas thus provides another boost to US printing exports.

Although neither the advent of EC 1992 nor a free trade agreement with Mexico is likely to affect the US printing industry significantly, the free trade agreement with Canada should provide a mild boost to US printing exports. A gradual elimination of Canadian tariffs of up to 28.6 percent on printed matter and the short distance between major Canadian markets and the United States should allow US printing firms to compete more effectively there.

Baby Carriages, Toys, Games, and Sporting Goods

The explosion in imports in this subcategory reflects the importance of exchange rates in determining trade performance. The appreciation of the US dollar during the early 1980s caused a rapid shift of production of these labor-intensive products to low-wage areas. The US Commerce Department reports that in 1990 imports accounted for about 89 percent of the apparent consumption of dolls and 65 percent of apparent toy consumption.

The free trade agreement with Canada will give US manufactures additional access to Canadian markets as Canadian tariffs on toys and parts are eliminated (tariffs at the time of the agreement were up to 17.6 percent on finished toys and games, 25 percent on parts, and 22.5 percent on sporting goods). A free trade agreement with Mexico is unlikely to increase US imports overall; however, it is likely that there would be continuing changes in the sources of imports, with Mexico becoming more competitive relative to other import sources.

Musical Instruments and Parts, Records, Tapes, and Compact Discs

The vast majority of US exports in this category consists of prerecorded music (records, tapes, and CDs). US exports of musical instruments are small, consisting primarily of acoustic pianos and guitars and percussion instruments.

US manufacturers of prerecorded music enjoy an advantage in world markets because of their proximity to the US music publishing and recording industries, one of the most important in the world. Increasingly, however, prerecorded music is being manufactured overseas under license rather than being exported from the United States, thus reducing US export performance.

Near-Term Outlook

The US economy's performance will greatly affect US trade performance through 1993. The recession will keep import growth moderate in 1991 and perhaps into 1992. Exports—fueled by good economic growth in Japan and the European Community, two of the most important US export markets—are likely to continue the strong growth of the last several years. The 1991 deficit is likely to narrow compared with 1990. However, with a recovery of the US economy, imports of toys, games, musical instruments, antiques, jewelry, and so forth could well resume growth. Although the wide range of items and the sensitivity of imports to US economic conditions make projections difficult, a modest expansion of the US deficits in this product group, perhaps by $1 billion or $2 billion, seems likely by 1993. Substantial changes in the value of the dollar—in either direction—could alter the outcome somewhat. Additional dollar devaluation could increase US exports in several subcategories substantially. Imports would be less strongly affected, as moderate additional dollar devaluation is unlikely to overcome US labor-cost disadvantages for many products. A rise in the dollar's value, however, could lead to another surge in imports while cutting into US export sales.

Medium-Term Outlook

Printed matter, arms and ammunition, and miscellaneous manufactures not elsewhere specified are the only subcategories in which the United States is likely to have continuing substantial trade surpluses through the mid-1990s. US trade performance in miscellaneous manufactures beyond 1993 will be driven largely by macroeconomic factors. Economic recovery in the United States is likely to result in modest continuing increases in the trade deficit beyond 1993.

Conclusions

■ Miscellaneous manufactures, a catchall category with world exports of $102 billion in 1989, is one of the larger two-digit trade categories. It was also one of the faster growing groups. Its 11.6 percent average annual growth rate between 1981 and 1989 was substantially greater than the 9.6 percent growth rate for manufactures overall.

■ Many of the products in miscellaneous manufactures are low-technology items that require relatively little capital for manufacture; hence entry and exit are easy, and price is an important competitive factor. Fluctuations in exchange rates can cause substantial changes in trade patterns.

■ Efforts to reduce labor costs—a large part of total costs for many miscellaneous manufactures—led to a substantial shift in production during the 1980s from the European Community, Japan, and particularly the United States toward East Asia.

■ The United States experienced a substantial decline in its market competitiveness in miscellaneous manufactures during the 1980s. The rapid rise in the dollar in the early to mid-1980s caused a rapid shift in production of these price-sensitive items from the United States to Asia. While US imports roughly doubled between 1981 and 1987, imports from the Asian NICs tripled.

■ The decline in the dollar after 1985 did little to curb import growth. It does appear, however, to have greatly stimulated US exports, which doubled between 1987 and 1990.

■ Economic growth in the United States relative to its major trading partners will be a primary determinant of US trade performance in this product group through 1993. The US recession in the early 1990s reduced import demand from what it would have been otherwise.

- Economic recovery in the United States, however, is likely to lead to modest continuing increases in the trade deficit in miscellaneous manufactures for the foreseeable future, perhaps $1 billion or $2 billion over 1990 levels by 1993.

Bibliography

"As Sales Slow, US Toymakers Join Game Abroad." 1990. *Journal of Commerce* (10 December): 5A.

Chipello, Christopher J. 1990. "Toys 'R' Us Inc. Plans for Japan Trigger a Tizzy." *Wall Street Journal* (10 September): A7C.

Commission of the European Communities. 1990. *Panorama of EC Industry, 1990.* Luxembourg: Commission of the European Communities.

Gladstone, Rick. 1990. "China Trade Decision Boon for Toy, Clothes Importers." *Washington Post* (25 May): F3.

Industry, Science and Technology Canada. 1988a. *Industry Profile: Jewellery.* Ottawa: Industry, Science and Technology Canada.

Industry, Science and Technology Canada. 1988b. *Industry Profile: Sporting Goods.* Ottawa: Industry, Science and Technology Canada.

Industry, Science and Technology Canada. 1988c. *Industry Profile: Toys and Games.* Ottawa: Industry, Science and Technology Canada.

US Department of Commerce. International Trade Administration. 1988a. *A Competitive Assessment of the U.S. Sports Equipment Industry.* Washington: US Department of Commerce (March).

US Department of Commerce, International Trade Administration. 1988b. *U.S. Industrial Outlook, 1988.* Washington: US Department of Commerce (January).

US Department of Commerce, International Trade Administration. 1989. *U.S. Industrial Outlook, 1989.* Washington: US Department of Commerce (January).

US Department of Commerce, International Trade Administration. 1990. *U.S. Industrial Outlook, 1990.* Washington: US Department of Commerce (January).

US International Trade Commission. 1990. *U.S. Trade Shifts in Selected Commodity Areas, January–June 1990.* Washington: US International Trade Commission (December).

Table 5.89.1 Miscellaneous manufactures: product composition of world trade, 1981–89 (billions of dollars except where noted)

SITC Product	1981	1982	1983	1984	1985	1986	1987	1988	1989	Annual growth 1981–89 (percentages)
World exports to world	42.3	43.0	43.0	46.9	49.7	63.7	79.8	92.9	101.8	11.6
of which										
892 Printed matter	7.5	7.1	7.0	7.2	7.6	9.6	11.6	13.6	14.8	8.8
893 Plastic articles, n.e.s.	7.0	7.2	7.5	8.2	9.4	12.7	16.5	17.5	18.5	12.9
894 Toys, sporting goods	8.2	7.9	7.9	8.7	9.1	11.6	15.5	17.9	19.6	11.5
895 Office supplies, n.e.s.	1.5	1.5	1.5	1.7	1.8	2.3	2.8	3.3	3.7	11.8
896 Works of art, etc.	3.2	2.4	2.6	2.9	2.9	3.8	5.3	7.0	9.6	14.7
897 Gold, silverware, jewelry	5.9	5.7	5.6	6.5	6.3	7.5	8.5	10.5	11.8	9.0
898 Musical instruments	4.8	5.0	5.1	5.6	6.2	8.4	10.3	13.7	14.9	15.2
899 Other manufactured goods	4.3	4.2	4.4	4.6	4.8	6.0	7.6	9.0	9.7	10.7
Memorandum:										1981–89
SITC 87 share of world manufactures exports (percentages)	4.2	4.4	4.4	4.4	4.4	4.7	4.8	4.7	4.8	0.6

Source: World Manufactures Trade Data Base.

Table 5.89.2 Miscellaneous manufactures: geographic distribution of world trade, 1981–89 (percentages of total)

Country	1981	1982	1983	1984	1985	1986	1987	1988	1989	Change 1981–89
Share of exports to world										
United States	12.6	11.8	11.4	10.5	9.9	8.8	8.8	10.1	11.6	−1.1
Canada	1.3	1.3	1.5	1.6	1.7	1.5	1.4	1.5	1.6	0.2
Japan	9.8	9.9	10.4	10.5	10.7	9.9	8.4	7.7	6.9	−2.9
European Community	48.4	47.4	46.6	45.0	45.9	47.5	47.7	44.7	44.4	−3.9
EC to non-EC	25.2	24.6	24.0	24.1	24.7	23.6	22.5	21.1	21.2	−4.1
Germany	12.4	12.3	12.3	11.6	12.3	13.6	13.4	13.1	12.7	0.3
France	7.1	6.5	6.1	5.8	6.0	6.2	6.3	6.0	5.9	−1.2
Italy	10.1	10.5	9.4	9.5	9.4	8.8	8.1	7.4	7.0	−3.1
United Kingdom	8.8	8.2	8.4	8.3	8.3	8.2	9.0	8.1	8.6	−0.2
Other Western Europe	8.8	8.3	8.4	8.1	8.1	8.6	7.9	7.5	8.0	−0.9
Asian NICs[a]	11.5	14.1	14.8	16.7	16.3	16.5	17.7	18.9	16.5	5.0
Eastern Europe[b]	0.9	0.7	0.7	0.6	0.6	0.6	0.6	0.6	0.5	−0.3
Developing countries	6.3	6.2	5.9	6.8	6.7	6.3	7.3	8.5	10.2	3.9
Latin America	2.1	1.9	1.3	1.5	1.7	1.4	1.4	1.4	1.6	−0.5
Rest of world	0.2	0.1	0.2	0.1	0.1	0.2	0.2	0.2	0.2	0.0
Share of imports from world										
United States	19.1	20.6	21.9	26.9	29.5	26.7	24.5	22.6	22.5	3.4
Canada	5.0	4.8	5.4	5.4	5.1	4.4	3.9	4.4	4.5	−0.5
Japan	3.4	3.3	3.4	3.3	3.4	3.9	5.2	6.3	7.3	3.9
European Community	38.8	37.1	36.8	34.5	34.1	37.6	40.0	39.1	39.4	0.6
EC from non-EC	16.8	16.1	15.8	15.0	14.2	15.3	16.7	17.3	17.8	1.0
Germany	8.5	7.6	7.8	7.2	7.0	7.8	8.3	8.0	7.8	−0.7
France	7.7	7.6	7.5	6.7	6.6	7.5	7.9	7.6	7.5	−0.1
Italy	2.6	2.7	2.5	2.5	2.6	2.8	3.1	3.0	2.9	0.3
United Kingdom	9.3	8.9	9.0	8.8	8.5	8.8	9.3	9.6	10.2	1.0
Other Western Europe	11.4	10.6	10.7	10.2	10.2	11.2	11.3	10.6	10.5	−0.9
Asian NICs[a]	2.7	4.4	4.6	3.4	2.9	3.8	3.9	5.5	4.5	1.8
Eastern Europe[b]	1.0	0.8	1.0	0.8	0.9	0.9	0.8	0.8	0.7	−0.3
Developing countries	15.8	15.4	13.7	12.8	11.3	9.5	8.5	7.9	7.8	−8.0
Latin America	5.0	4.4	3.0	2.9	3.1	2.8	2.4	2.3	2.5	−2.5
Rest of world	0.3	0.4	0.1	0.1	0.0	0.0	0.1	0.7	0.7	0.3

table continued next page

Table 5.89.2 Miscellaneous manufactures: geographic distribution of world trade, 1981–89 (percentages of total) (continued)

Country	1981	1982	1983	1984	1985	1986	1987	1988	1989	Change 1981–89
Export share minus import share										
United States	-6.4	-8.9	-10.5	-16.4	-19.6	-17.9	-15.7	-12.5	-10.9	-4.5
Canada	-3.7	-3.5	-3.9	-3.9	-3.5	-2.9	-2.6	-2.9	-3.0	0.7
Japan	6.4	6.6	6.9	7.2	7.2	6.0	3.2	1.4	-0.4	-6.8
European Community	9.6	10.3	9.8	10.4	11.8	9.9	7.7	5.6	5.0	-4.6
Non-EC	8.5	8.5	8.2	9.1	10.5	8.3	5.9	3.8	3.4	-5.0
Germany	3.9	4.6	4.5	4.4	5.3	5.9	5.1	5.1	4.9	1.0
France	-0.6	-1.2	-1.4	-0.9	-0.6	-1.3	-1.6	-1.6	-1.6	-1.0
Italy	7.5	7.8	6.9	7.0	6.9	5.9	5.0	4.4	4.1	-3.4
United Kingdom	-0.5	-0.6	-0.5	-0.5	-0.2	-0.7	-0.3	-1.5	-1.6	-1.2
Other Western Europe	-2.5	-2.2	-2.3	-2.1	-2.1	-2.5	-3.4	-3.1	-2.5	0.0
Asian NICs[a]	8.8	9.7	10.2	13.3	13.4	12.7	13.8	13.3	12.0	3.2
Eastern Europe[b]	-0.1	-0.1	-0.3	-0.2	-0.3	-0.2	-0.2	-0.3	-0.2	-0.1
Developing countries	-9.5	-9.2	-7.8	-6.0	-4.7	-3.2	-1.2	0.7	2.4	11.9
Latin America	-3.0	-2.5	-1.8	-1.4	-1.4	-1.4	-1.0	-0.8	-0.9	2.0
Rest of world	-0.1	-0.3	0.1	0.1	0.1	0.1	0.1	-0.5	-0.4	-0.3

a. Hong Kong, Korea, Singapore, and Taiwan.

b. Including Soviet Union.

Source: World Manufactures Trade Data Base.

Table 5.89.3 Miscellaneous manufactures: bilateral trade flows, 1989 (billions of dollars)

					Exporter						
Importer	World	United States	Canada	Japan	European Community	Germany	France	United Kingdom	Asian NICs	Latin America	Other
World	101.8	11.8	1.6	7.0	45.2	13.0	6.0	8.8	16.8	1.6	17.8
United States	22.6		1.3	2.5	5.0	0.9	0.6	1.5	7.0	1.3	5.4
Canada	3.6	2.0		0.2	0.5	0.1	0.1	0.1	0.6	0.0	0.3
Japan	6.8	2.0	0.0		1.6	0.3	0.4	0.6	2.2	0.0	1.0
European Community	40.8	3.4	0.1	1.9	23.7	6.9	2.9	3.4	3.9	0.2	7.8
Germany	8.2	0.7	0.0	0.6	3.8		0.7	0.7	0.8	0.0	2.3
France	8.4	0.4	0.0	0.2	5.4	1.8		0.8	0.6	0.0	1.6
United Kingdom	8.9	1.2	0.0	0.4	4.1	1.3	0.5		1.3	0.1	1.7
Asian NICs	4.4	1.0	0.0	1.3	0.7	0.2	0.1	0.2	1.1	0.0	0.3
Latin America	2.7	1.5	0.0	0.1	0.8	0.1	0.2	0.1	0.2		0.1
Other	20.9	1.9	0.1	1.1	12.9	4.5	1.7	2.9	1.9	0.1	2.9

Source: World Manufactures Trade Data Base.

Table 5.89.4 Miscellaneous manufactures: product composition of US trade, 1981–90[a] (millions of dollars)

Category	SITC Rev. 2			SITC Rev. 3			
	1981	1987	Change 1981–87	1987	1990	Change 1981–90	Change 1981–90
Exports	5,286	6,542	1,256	9,236	18,147	12,861	8,911
Imports	8,064	19,292	11,228	19,467	25,027	16,963	5,560
Balance	−2,778	−12,750	−9,972	−10,231	−6,881	−4,103	3,350
of which							
891 Arms and ammunition (Rev. 3 only)							
Exports				2,125	3,002		877
Imports				456	545		89
Balance				1,669	2,457		788
892 Printed matter							
Exports	1,297	1,562	265	1,566	3,158	1,861	1,592
Imports	616	1,513	897	1,510	1,670	1,054	160
Balance	681	49	−632	56	1,488	807	1,432
893 Articles, n.e.s., of plastics							
Exports	744	872	128	790	1,939	1,195	1,149
Imports	816	2,888	2,072	2,386	3,142	2,326	756
Balance	−72	−2,016	−1,944	−1,596	−1,203	−1,131	393
894 Baby carriages, toys, games, and sporting goods							
Exports	1,105	885	−220	858	1,820	715	962
Imports	2,137	5,855	3,718	5,990	9,087	6,950	3,097
Balance	−1,032	−4,970	−3,938	−5,132	−7,267	−6,235	−2,135
895 Office and stationery supplies, n.e.s.							
Exports	216	179	−37	322	375	159	53
Imports	130	353	223	515	787	657	272
Balance	86	−174	−260	−193	−412	−498	−219
896 Works of art, collectors' pieces, and antiques							
Exports	340	733	393	671	2,267	1,927	1,596
Imports	2,016	1,913	−103	1,836	2,341	325	505
Balance	−1,676	−1,180	496	−1,165	−74	1,602	1,091
897 Jewelry, goldsmiths' and silversmiths' wares, etc.							
Exports	285	354	69	333	620	335	287
Imports	971	2,793	1,822	2,690	3,079	2,108	389
Balance	−686	−2,439	−1,753	−2,357	−2,459	−1,773	−102
898 Musical instruments and parts, records, tapes, etc.							
Exports	952	1,487	535	1,499	3,870	2,918	2,371
Imports	624	2,527	1,903	2,540	2,538	1,914	−2
Balance	328	−1,040	−1,368	−1,041	1,332	1,004	2,373
899 Miscellaneous manufactured articles, n.e.s.							
Exports	347	469	122	1,073	1,095	748	22
Imports	753	1,448	695	1,545	1,839	1,086	294
Balance	−406	−979	−573	−472	−744	−338	−272

a. Data are expressed on a domestic exports, imports customs basis.

Source: US Department of Commerce.

Table 5.89.5 Miscellaneous manufactures: geographic composition of US trade, 1981–90

	Millions of dollars				Percentages of total			
	1981	1987	1989	1990	1981	1987	1989	1990
Exports								
Canada	1,153	1,755	2,166	3,781	21.8	19.0	13.9	20.8
Japan	412	874	2,245	2,559	7.8	9.5	14.4	14.1
European Community	1,477	2,037	4,297	5,010	27.9	22.1	27.6	27.6
United Kingdom	544	699	1,318	1,509	10.3	7.6	8.5	8.3
Germany	297	422	1,131	1,197	5.6	4.6	7.3	6.6
France	210	284	457	621	4.0	3.1	2.9	3.4
Italy	79	142	253	309	1.5	1.5	1.6	1.7
Latin America	911	994	1,532	1,813	17.2	10.8	9.8	10.0
Asian NICs	259	450	1,383	1,726	4.9	4.9	8.9	9.5
Other	1,074	3,126	3,957	3,258	20.3	33.8	25.4	18.0
Total	5,286	9,236	15,580	18,147	100.0	100.0	100.0	100.0
Imports								
Canada	805	1,276	1,386	1,279	10.0	6.6	5.8	5.1
Japan	1,071	3,001	4,110	4,627	13.3	15.4	17.2	18.5
European Community	1,955	4,473	5,228	5,536	24.2	23.0	21.9	22.1
United Kingdom	575	1,191	1,320	1,483	7.1	6.1	5.5	5.9
Germany	298	763	879	1,005	3.7	3.9	3.7	4.0
France	286	547	747	834	3.5	2.8	3.1	3.3
Italy	567	1,404	1,681	1,553	7.0	7.2	7.0	6.2
Latin America	716	937	1,313	1,330	8.9	4.8	5.5	5.3
Asian NICs	2,272	6,773	6,596	6,040	28.2	34.8	27.7	24.1
Other	1,245	3,007	5,216	6,215	15.4	15.4	21.9	24.8
Total	8,064	19,467	23,849	25,027	100.0	100.0	100.0	100.0

a. Data are expressed on a domestic exports, imports customs basis.

Source: US Department of Commerce.

Table 5.89.6 Miscellaneous manufactures: indices of US competitiveness, 1981–89 (billions of dollars except where noted)

	1981	1982	1983	1984	1985	1986	1987	1988	1989	Annual growth 1981–89 (percentages)
World trade										
World exports to non-US destinations	34.6	34.3	33.7	34.6	35.7	47.0	60.3	71.8	79.2	10.9
World imports from non-US sources	38.0	38.6	38.4	42.8	45.8	58.9	73.8	85.6	93.4	11.9
US trade										
Exports	5.3	5.1	4.9	4.9	4.9	5.6	7.0	9.4	11.8	10.5
Imports	8.5	9.3	9.8	13.2	15.3	17.8	20.3	22.1	24.2	14.0
Balance	-3.2	-4.2	-4.9	-8.3	-10.4	-12.2	-13.3	-12.8	-12.5	
										Change 1981–89
US share of exports to non-US destinations (percentages)	15.5	14.8	14.6	14.2	13.8	12.0	11.6	13.0	14.9	- 0.6
US share of imports from non-US sources (percentages)	22.4	24.2	25.6	30.9	33.5	30.2	27.6	25.9	26.0	3.6
Export share minus import share (percentages)	-6.9	-9.4	-11.0	-16.7	-19.7	-18.2	-16.0	-12.8	-11.1	-4.2

Source: World Manufactures Trade Data Base.

General Bibliography

Auerbach, Stuart. 1990. "Bureaucracy, Shortages Slow U.S. Ventures." *Washington Post* (27 May): H1.

Bank of Japan. 1989. "Balance of Payments Adjustment in Japan: Recent Developments and Prospects." *Special Paper* no. 178, Research and Statistics Department. Tokyo: Bank of Japan (May).

Cline, William R. 1989. *United States External Adjustment and the World Economy.* Washington: Institute for International Economics.

Collins, Susan M., and Dani Rodrik. 1991. *Eastern Europe and the Soviet Union in the World Economy.* POLICY ANALYSES IN INTERNATIONAL ECONOMICS 32. Washington: Institute for International Economics (February).

Dunne, Nancy. 1990. "US Industry Forecast Optimistic with Exports Predicted to Grow." *Financial Times* (31 December): 1.

Faltermayer, Edmund. 1990. "Is 'Made in the U.S.A.' Fading Away?" *Fortune* (24 September): 62.

Hiatt, Fred. 1990a. "Trade Surplus Is Not Negative Factor, Panel Suggests to Japan's Government." *Washington Post* (1 June): A32.

Hiatt, Fred. 1990b. "Japan Turns Debate on U.S. Trade Upside Down: Surplus May Be Good." *Washington Post* (3 June): A35.

"The Incredible Shrinking Deficit." 1990. *The Economist* (25 August): 57.

Japan Economic Institute. 1991. *Japan's Expanding U.S. Manufacturing Presence: 1989 Update.* Washington: Japan Economic Institute (18 January).

Kotkin, Joel. 1990. "Europe '92: It Won't Be a Threat to Our Future." *Washington Post* (20 May): B1.

MIT Commission on Industrial Productivity. 1989. *The Working Papers of the MIT Commission on Industrial Productivity.* Vol. 2. Cambridge: MA: The MIT Press.

Moreno, Ramon. 1991. "Taiwan's Trade Surpluses." 1991. *FRBSF Weekly Letter.* San Francisco: Federal Reserve Bank of San Francisco, Research Department (1 February).

Murray, Alan, and Urban C. Lehner. 1990. "What U.S. Scientists Discover, the Japanese Convert—into Profit." *Wall Street Journal* (25 June): 1.

National Association of Manufacturers, International Economic Affairs Department. 1986. *U.S. Trade Balance at a Turning Point: Can We Eliminate the Trade Deficit by 1990?* Washington: National Association of Manufacturers (June).

Office of Management and Budget. 1987. *Standard Industrial Classification Manual.* Washington: Office of Management and Budget.

Organization for Economic Cooperation and Development. 1990. *The Export Credit Financing Systems in OECD Member Countries,* 4th ed. Paris: Organization for Economic Cooperation and Development.

Peter D. Hart Research Associates. 1987. *A Survey of Attitudes Among U.S. Manufacturers.* Washington: Peter D. Hart Research Associates (August).

Porter, Michael E. 1991. "Green Competitiveness." *Scientific American* (April).

Richards, Evelyn. 1990. "Few Markets for Soviet Technology." *Washington Post* (27 May): H1.

Thurston, Charles W. 1991. "US Hopes to Double Exports' Share of GNP." *Journal of Commerce* (15 March): 3.

Truell, Peter. 1990. "Dollar Depreciation Has its Limits." *Wall Street Journal* (31 December).

US Congress, Office of Technology Assessment. 1988. *The Defense Technology Base, Introduction and Overview.* Washington: Office of Technology Assessment (March).

US Congress, Office of Technology Assessment. 1989. *Holding the Edge: Maintaining the Defense Technology Base.* Washington: Office of Technology Assessment (April).

US Congress, Office of Technology Assessment. 1990. *Making Things Better: Competing in Manufacturing.* Washington: Office of Technology Assessment.

US Department of Commerce, International Trade Administration. 1984a. *A Competitive Assessment of the U.S. Manufacturing Automation Equipment Industries.* Washington: US Department of Commerce (June).

US Department of Commerce, International Trade Administration. 1984b. *A Competitive Assessment of the U.S. International Construction Industry.* Washington: US Department of Commerce (July).

US Department of Commerce, International Trade Administration. 1985a. *A Competitive Assessment of the U.S. Automotive Parts Industry and the U.S. Aftermarket for Japanese Cars and Light Trucks.* Washington: US Department of Commerce (March).

US Department of Commerce, International Trade Administration. 1985b. *A Competitive Assessment of the U.S. Flexible Manufacturing Systems Industry.* Washington: US Department of Commerce (July).

US Department of Commerce, International Trade Administration. 1987. *A Competitive Assessment of the U.S. Robotics Industry.* Washington: US Department of Commerce (March).

US Department of Commerce, International Trade Administration. 1989a. *A Competitive Assessment of the U.S. International Construction Industry.* Washington: US Department of Commerce (February).

US Department of Commerce, International Trade Administration. 1989b. *An Examination of Potential Capacity Constraints on U.S. Manufacturing Exports.* Staff Report. Washington: US Department of Commerce (February).

US Department of Commerce, International Trade Administration. 1990. *U.S. Foreign Trade Highlights, 1989.* Washington: US Department of Commerce (September).

US International Trade Commission. 1991. *The Likely Impact on the United States of a Free Trade Agreement with Mexico.* Washington: US International Trade Commission (February).

Wyss, David A., and Roger E. Brinner. 1991. "The Economic Consequences of the Peace." *U.S. Forecast Summary.* DRI/McGraw-Hill (March).

6

Questionnaire Survey Results

6

Questionnaire Survey Results

Description and Methodology

To determine manufacturers' views on the prospects for US performance in international trade, a questionnaire survey of US manufacturing firms was conducted. Data were collected on managers' views about the outlook for capital investment, exports, and imports.

Approximately 2,400 questionnaires were distributed through 10 trade associations. A total of 687 usable returns were received, for a response rate of 28.6 percent. The participating trade associations and the number of usable responses received from each were the following:

American Iron and Steel Institute (15 responses)
Construction Industry Manufacturers Association (20)
Chemical Manufacturers Association (99)
Electronic Industries Association (64)
Manufacturers Alliance for Productivity and Innovation (138)
Motor Equipment Manufacturers Association (95)
National Association of Manufacturers (113)
National Machine Tool Builders Association (103)
National Forest Products Association (24)
Rubber Manufacturers Association (16)

With the exception of the Chemical Manufacturers Association and the Manufacturers Alliance, whose members were surveyed in the fall of 1989, the survey was conducted between May and July of 1990. Thus the results do not reflect any changes in attitudes toward the future that may have occurred since mid-1990. Specifically, the survey does not reflect any changes resulting from the

Iraqi invasion of Kuwait, the ensuing oil price increase, or the 1990–91 recession, which developed after the survey was administered.

All of the firms surveyed are manufacturing firms. To the extent that they are importers, they import mostly parts, components, and raw materials, although some may import part of their product line in finished form for sale in the United States. Nevertheless, their responses should be seen as reflecting primarily their views on foreign versus domestic inputs to their own manufacturing processes, rather than their views as importers of finished goods.

The mail survey questionnaire addressed four categories of issues:

- export expectations and constraints

- factors influencing imports

- capital investment and US-based production capacity

- exchange rate effects.

The survey results for each issue are summarized in the following sections.

Export Expectations and Constraints

Several of the questions concerned expected export performance, the importance of exports as a share of total US sales, the effects of prospective changes in market conditions in various areas of the world, and factors affecting export performance, such as exchange rate fluctuations and globalization of world markets. Below each question is presented as it was posed in the survey and is followed by a brief summary of the responses.

Question 1 *Compared with 1989 levels, what is the outlook for your company's exports from the United States (including to foreign affiliates/parents) for 1990 and for 1993?*

At the time of the survey, firms generally appeared to be only moderately optimistic about export opportunities over the next three to four years, as table 6.1 shows. The median change in exports expected by all firms between 1989 and 1993 was an increase of 20.0 percent (the mean expected increase was 37.1 percent), a modest change that translates to only a 4.7 percent mean annual growth rate. Of the 325 firms responding to this question, 259 expected an increase in exports with a median value of 20.0 percent and an average (mean) increase of 50.1 percent. Results for the 24 firms reporting that they expected a decline in exports over the period were a median decline of 12.0 percent and an average decline of 21.0 percent.

Table 6.1   Respondents' expected changes in US exports, 1993 versus 1989 (percentages)

	All firms	Firms with annual US sales of:		
		Less than $500 million	$500 million to $1 billion	More than $1 billion
Median value	20.0	20.0	15.0	0.0
Average value	37.1	44.4	21.6	10.6
No. of responses	325	251	32	42

Table 6.2   Respondents' US exports as a share of total US sales 1981, 1989, and projected 1993 (percentages)

	All firms	Firms with annual US sales of:		
		Less than $500 million	$500 million to $1 billion	More than $1 billion
Median value				
1981	5.0	5.0	5.0	10.0
1989	10.0	10.0	5.0	12.0
1993	15.0	15.0	11.0	12.0
Average value				
1981	14.2	19.7	11.9	13.5
1989	21.2	21.2	12.3	16.2
1993	23.8	26.7	15.4	15.7
No. of responses				
1981	289	227	30	32
1989	342	266	33	43
1993	322	255	30	37

By 1993, the larger firms in the sample (those with annual US sales greater than $1 billion), which supply the great bulk of US exports, expect an average increase in exports of 15.3 percent for the four-year period. The smaller firms, in contrast, expect an increase of 43.2 percent on average, for an annual increase of about 9.4 percent. Generally, the larger firms—which are already usually significantly involved in export markets—do not see opportunities for large increases in exports from the United States.

Question 2   Exports from the United States, including exports to foreign parents and affiliates, are about what portion of your company's US sales (1981, 1989, and 1993)?
Responses to this question indicate that the smaller firms are increasingly export oriented. For all respondents, the median value for exports as a percentage of total US sales increased from 5.0 percent in 1981 to 10.0 percent in 1989 (table 6.2). A further increase to 15.0 percent was anticipated by 1993. The median increases are substantially smaller than the mean increases because a small number of firms export all or nearly all of their production.

Neither the median nor the average response of the larger firms, however, indicates that they foresee their exports from the United States becoming a larger percentage of their US sales than in 1989.

Table 6.3 Portion of respondents' foreign sales met by US exports, 1981, 1989, and projected 1993 (percentages)

| | | Firms with annual US sales of: | | |
	All firms	Less than $500 million	$500 million to $1 billion	More than $1 billion
Median value				
1981	98.1	100.0	48.0	12.0
1989	82.0	100.0	74.0	15.0
1993	80.0	95.0	74.0	13.0
Average value				
1981	62.1	67.7	50.9	24.8
1989	60.7	68.2	40.0	26.4
1993	60.8	67.3	42.6	23.2
No. of responses				
1981	263	211	29	23
1989	319	251	33	35
1993	302	244	30	38

The answers appear to be consistent with those to the previous question. That is, the larger firms, which reported quite slow export growth rates, see their export sales remaining constant relative to their US sales. The smaller firms, which foresaw higher export growth rates, see exports becoming a larger portion of their US sales.

Question 3 In meeting foreign demand, what portion of your company's total foreign sales comes from US export sales (1981, 1989, and 1993)?

As a group, the respondent firms meet the majority of foreign demand by exporting from the United States. The average share of foreign demand met by exports changed little from 1981 to 1989, remaining at about 60 percent (table 6.3). Again, however, there is a substantial deviation between the mean and the median. While the mean share of foreign demand met from export sales was 62.1 percent in 1981, the median was 98.0 percent. This indicates that although most small firms supply all of their foreign demand from domestic production, a small number of large firms rely heavily on overseas production to meet that demand. Moreover, whereas the mean changed little from 1981 to 1989, the median indicates that there has been a significant decline in the share of foreign demand met by exports: from 98.1 percent in 1981 to 82.0 percent by 1989.

Results differed significantly by size of firm. Larger firms, which typically have direct investments abroad, rely much less heavily on exports from the United States to meet foreign demand than do small firms. The median for smaller firms (US sales less than $500 million) was 100 percent of foreign sales coming from exports from the United States.

However, there is a marked difference when the firm size rises above annual US sales of $1 billion. Firms in this category reported that in 1989 an average

Table 6.4   Respondents' estimation of impact of 1985–90 dollar depreciation on 1990 export performance (percentages of total responding)

		Firms with annual US sales of:		
	All firms	**Less than $500 million**	**$500 million to $1 billion**	**More than $1 billion**
Solely responsible for improved performance	1.3	1.4	0.0	0.0
Significant factor in	26.2	26.0	25.0	27.1
Somewhat important	42.8	42.8	41.7	45.8
No significant effect	29.4	30.0	33.3	27.1
Total	100.0	100.0	100.0	100.0
No. of responses	361	277	36	48

of only 15 percent of foreign sales were generated from US exports. These respondents foresee a modest decline to 13 percent by 1993. The mean values for the exporters in this group were 24.8 percent, 26.4 percent, and 23.2 percent for 1981, 1989, and 1993, respectively.

Generally, the results seem to indicate a basically stable, perhaps modestly declining portion of foreign sales satisfied by exports from the United States. This is consistent with the trend toward serving major foreign markets by locating production in those markets, usually through direct investment.

Question 4   *To what extent has the fall in the dollar since 1985 contributed to your company's current export performance?*

A. solely responsible for improved performance

B. significant factor in improved performance

C. somewhat important

D. no significant effect.

Although very few respondents reported that the dollar decline since 1985 was solely responsible for improved performance, a significant minority—over one-quarter—considered it a significant factor in the improvement (table 6.4). About 70 percent of respondents reported that the decline in the US dollar has been at least of some importance in improved export performance in recent years. The largest share of firms—almost 43 percent—reported that the decline in the dollar was somewhat important in improving export performance. Only about 30 percent of all respondents reported that the dollar decline had no significant effect. The results are surprisingly uniform across the three categories of firm size.

Table 6.5 Respondents' long-run export expectations (percentages of total responding)

| | | Firms with annual US sales of: | | |
	All firms	Less than $500 million	$500 million to $1 billion	More than $1 billion
Significantly more exports	25.3	29.6	11.1	12.5
Somewhat more exports	50.1	50.0	55.6	45.8
About the same level of exports	17.0	14.6	33.3	22.9
Decline in exports	8.1	6.2	0.0	18.8
Total	100.0	100.0	100.0	100.0
No. of responses	358	274	36	48

Question 5 *Do your long-run (mid-1990s and beyond) strategic plans for US-based production envisage:*

A. significantly more exports from US

B. somewhat more exports

C. about the same exports

D. a decline in exports.

The responses to this question, summarized in table 6.5, support the responses to question 1 (table 6.1), with a substantial majority—roughly 75 percent of the respondents—projecting either somewhat more or significantly more exports in the long run. Most of the remaining respondents—17.0 percent—anticipate exports to remain about the same. Only 8.1 percent of all respondents reported expecting a decline in exports.

There were, however, important differences in the responses depending on firm size. Almost 30 percent of the firms with US sales under $500 million see significantly more exports in their mid-1990s strategic planning; only 12.5 percent of those with sales greater than $1 billion made the same response.

It is noteworthy that among the larger firms that are the principal US exporters, the percentage expecting a mid-1990s *decline* in exports (18.0 percent) is larger than the percentage expecting significantly more exports (12.5 percent). Nevertheless, almost half of the larger companies (45.8 percent) expect exports to increase somewhat.

Question 6 *What effect do you anticipate by the mid-1990s on your company's US-based production resulting from successful completion of EC 1992, the single European market? (Please indicate all applicable answers.)*

Exports to the EC
A. it will enlarge EC markets, increasing US exports

Table 6.6 Respondents' anticipated effects of EC 1992 on US-based production (percentages of total responding)

Effect on:	All firms	Firms with annual US sales of:		
		Less than $500 million	$500 million to $1 billion	More than $1 billion
US exports to EC				
Increase exports	28.2	29.3	27.8	25.0
No change in exports	53.9	52.9	61.1	58.3
Decline in exports	18.2	18.1	11.1	16.7
Total	100.0	100.0	100.0	100.0
US exports to other markets				
More difficult	25.1	22.5	38.9	23.4
No effect	74.7	77.2	66.1	76.6
US investment in EC				
Increase	59.7	59.6	58.3	66.7
No effect	39.3	39.5	41.7	38.3
No. of responses	360	276	36	48

B. no significant effect on exports to the EC

C. exporting to the EC will be more difficult; exports will decline

Exports to Other Markets

D. increased competitiveness of EC production will make exporting to third countries more difficult

E. no significant effect on US exports to third-country markets

Investment

F. it will motivate increased direct investment in the EC to serve that market

G. no significant effect on direct investment in the EC.

Over one-fourth of the respondents believe that the advent of EC 92 will enlarge EC markets and increase US exports (table 6.6). Over half see EC 1992 having no significant effect on US exports to the European Community. Just under one-fifth of the respondents see it reducing US exports to the European Community. Although the answers varied by firm size, about one-fourth of the respondents saw successful completion of the European Community making it more difficult for them to export into third-country markets. The remaining three-fourths indicated no significant effect on exports to third countries.

A majority—59.4 percent—believe, however, that the advent of EC 1992 will spur direct investment in the European Community to serve that market. Only 39.3 percent see it as having no significant effect. The responses to this question do not vary much by company size.

Question 7a *What effects do you anticipate by the mid-1990s on your company's operations resulting from democratic reforms in* former *East Bloc nations?*

A. have recently exported to these nations and plan to increase export sales

B. have recently exported to these nations but do not expect any change in export sales

C. have recently exported to these nations and expect export sales to fall

D. have not exported to these markets, but plan to

E. have not exported to these markets, and have no current plans to.

Question 7b *What effect do you anticipate by the mid-1990s on your company's operations resulting from growth in* Pacific Rim ASEAN *nations?*

A. have recently exported to these nations and plan to increase export sales

B. have recently exported to these nations but do not expect any change in export sales

C. have recently exported to these nations and expect export sales to fall

D. have not exported to these markets, but plan to

E. have not exported to these markets, and have no current plans to.

The answers to questions 7a and 7b indicate that firms are substantially more familiar with export markets in the Pacific Rim than with those in Eastern Europe. Just over 75 percent of respondents reported they had not exported to the former Eastern bloc countries, while fewer than 30 percent reported that they had not exported to the Pacific Rim countries (table 6.7). Although respondents have less experience exporting to the former Eastern bloc countries, nearly half of those that have not exported to those countries reported that they plan to do so.

Generally, in the summer of 1990 respondent firms appeared optimistic about the prospects for greater exports to the Eastern bloc. Over 80 percent of firms that have exported to this region reported that they plan to increase export sales there.

Firms were also optimistic about increasing exports to Pacific Rim. Nearly 80 percent of firms with experience in exporting to these countries reported that they plan to increase exports to the region (table 6.7).

As might be expected, the larger firms were more likely to have exported to both the former Eastern bloc countries and the Pacific Rim countries. For ex-

Table 6.7 Respondents' anticipated change in exports to Eastern bloc and Pacific Rim ASEAN countries by mid-1990s
(percentages of total responding)

		Firms with annual US sales of:		
	All firms	Less than $500 million	$500 million to $1 billion	More than $1 billion
Eastern bloc				
Have recently exported, expect increase	19.3	13.5	47.2	27.3
Have recently exported, expect no increase	3.8	2.9	8.3	9.1
Have recently exported, expect decrease	0.4	0.0	0.0	0.0
No exports, but plan to	37.5	41.8	25.0	18.2
No exports, no plans to	39.0	41.8	19.4	45.5
Total	100.0	100.0	100.0	100.0
No. of respondents	255	208	36	11
Pacific Rim ASEAN				
Have recently exported, expect increase	57.4	53.1	72.2	90.9
Have recently exported, expect no increase	11.3	13.4	5.6	0.0
Have recently exported, expect decrease	3.8	3.3	5.6	0.0
No exports, but plan to	12.1	13.4	5.6	0.0
No exports, no plans to	15.1	16.3	11.1	9.1
Total	100.0	100.0	100.0	100.0
No. of respondents	256	209	36	11

ample, over 50 percent of firms with US sales of $500 million or more reported that they had exported to the Eastern bloc. Fewer than 20 percent of firms with sales of less than $500 million reported sales to this market. Similarly, over 80 percent of the firms with sales of over $500 million reported previous sales to the Pacific Rim region, compared with about 65 percent of the smaller firms.

Question 8 *Please indicate on a scale of 1 to 5 (with 1 the most important and 5 the least) the importance of each of the following factors in holding back growth of US exports in your product areas.*

1 2 3 4 5   a. export market not important enough to justify devoting major attention

1 2 3 4 5   b. results of earlier dollar decline not yet reflected; need more time to expand exports

1 2 3 4 5   c. the existing dollar exchange rate

1 2 3 4 5   d. uncertainty about future dollar exchange rates

1 2 3 4 5   e. lack of knowledge about foreign markets

1 2 3 4 5   f. export controls

1 2 3 4 5   g. lack of competitive export financing

1 2 3 4 5   h. capacity constraints

1 2 3 4 5   i. expected continued globalization of markets and production; need to produce in major markets

1 2 3 4 5   j. foreign quality

1 2 3 4 5   k. foreign service and flexibility in meeting needs

1 2 3 4 5   l. foreign import barriers

1 2 3 4 5   m. other (please describe).

Two factors in responses from the group as a whole stood out as limiting export growth. The item most frequently cited as important was foreign import barriers, with 44.7 percent of the respondents ranking this as 1 or 2 (table 6.8). Not far behind was the expected continued globalization of markets and the need to produce in major markets. This factor was ranked 1 or 2 by 40.2 percent of respondents. Third most important was foreign service and flexibility in meeting needs (31.4 percent ranked it 1 or 2).

The results change significantly, however, when disaggregated by annual sales levels. Whereas the smaller companies—those with annual US sales of less than $500 million—rank foreign import barriers as the most important factor inhibiting US export growth, the larger firms rank globalization first. Of firms with annual sales over $1 billion, 59.2 percent ranked globalization as extremely or very important; 42.9 percent gave import barriers equivalent rankings. Of firms in the $500 million to $1 billion sales range, 56.4 percent gave globalization

Table 6.8 Respondents' rating of factors holding back export growth (percentages of total)

	Extremely important	Very important	Important	Modestly important	Not important	No. of respondents
			Percent rating factor as:			
Export markets too small	9.5	13.3	21.3	20.3	35.6	399
Lags in adjustments to exchange rate changes	0.8	6.6	25.6	34.0	33.0	394
Current exchange rate	4.8	13.3	35.2	33.4	13.3	398
Uncertainty about future exchange rates	3.8	14.2	27.0	36.4	18.6	393
Lack of knowledge of foreign markets	9.8	19.8	22.6	22.9	24.9	398
Export controls	8.0	14.8	21.0	24.5	31.8	400
Lack of competitive export financing	5.8	11.4	19.2	28.8	34.8	396
Capacity constraints	5.3	9.5	17.3	26.0	42.0	400
Continued globalization	16.3	23.9	28.1	19.1	12.6	398
Foreign quality	6.7	18.2	26.2	26.2	22.7	401
Foreign service	8.5	22.9	31.2	20.4	17.1	398
Foreign import barriers	19.8	24.9	21.1	24.9	9.3	398
Other	50.0	20.0	3.3	1.7	25.0	60

Table 6.9   Respondents' anticipated change in imports for use as inputs to production or for direct sale, 1993 versus 1989 (percentages)

	All firms	Less than $500 million	$500 million to $1 billion	More than $1 billion
		Firms with annual US sales of:		
Median value	0.0	0.0	0.0	0.0
Average value	10.9	12.1	9.4	3.4
No. of responses	296	213	32	40

one of the top two ratings; only 25.6 percent did so for import barriers. Thus, among the major exporters that responded, the "expected continued globalization of markets and production; the need to produce in major markets" is clearly seen as the number one factor inhibiting future export growth. The least important factor listed was "results of earlier dollar decline not yet reflected; need more time to expand exports." Only 7.4 percent ranked this factor 1 or 2. Confirming the response to question 14 (see table 6.14), the next least important factor limiting the growth of exports was capacity constraints (14.8 percent ranked it as 1 or 2).

Factors Influencing Imports

The questions on this issue parallel those asked about exports. Questions were asked to determine trends in the use of imported parts and components by firms, the factors influencing their decisions to import, and the factors firms see as most important in maintaining the level of US imports.

Question 9   Compared to 1989, what is the outlook for your company's imports of parts, components, assemblies, intermediate, and completed products for inputs to US-based production or for direct sale in the United States (including from foreign affiliates/parents)?
A significant number of firms—roughly 25 percent of the total—reported that they had no imports of the type described; hence they are excluded from the results reported in table 6.9. The median firm among those remaining expects no change in imports between 1989 and 1993 (table 6.9). Among those firms anticipating an increase (136 firms, or 45.4 percent of the total), the median increase was 15.0 percent. Among those anticipating a decline (27 firms, or 9.2 percent of the total), the median drop was 30.0 percent. The remaining 136 firms (45.4 percent) expect no change between 1989 and 1993.

These mixed results, as evidenced by significant differences between the mean and the median responses, seem to indicate some modest continuing increase

Table 6.10   Respondents' estimation of share of US sales accounted for by imports, 1981, 1989, and projected 1993 (percentages of total)

		Firms with annual US sales of:		
	All firms	Less than $500 million	$500 million to $1 billion	More than $1 billion
Median value				
1981	1.0	0.0	2.0	2.0
1989	3.0	3.0	3.0	3.0
1993	4.0	5.0	5.0	2.0
Average value				
1981	7.7	8.2	3.7	9.0
1989	10.7	11.9	5.4	8.2
1993	10.8	11.7	6.2	8.7
No. of responses				
1981	327	258	29	30
1989	370	286	31	42
1993	355	277	30	37

in imports by US manufacturing firms. This conclusion stems from the fact that although just under half the respondents expected no change in imports by 1993, the same number expected increases, and only 9.2 percent expected decreases.

Question 10   What percent of your company's total recent and expected US sales (sales by the US portion of the company, including its exports) is represented by imports to the United States of parts, components, intermediate, and completed products, including imports from foreign parents and affiliates (1981, 1989, and 1993)?
Firms reported a small increase in imports as a percentage of US sales between 1981 and 1989 (table 6.10). Imports were on average 7.7 percent of US sales in 1981, and 10.7 percent by 1989. Both the median and the average responses indicate that imports by manufacturing firms represent only a relatively small percentage of their US sales, and little change is anticipated through 1993.

Question 11   What have been recent trends (since the 1985 dollar decline) in your company's foreign procurement of parts, components, assemblies, intermediate, and completed products for inputs to US-based production or for direct sale in the United States?

A. foreign procurement increasing relative to domestic production

B. foreign procurement about the same relative to domestic production

C. foreign procurement declining relative to domestic production

D. not applicable, no significant foreign procurement.

Table 6.11 Trends in foreign procurement since 1985 reported by respondents (percentages of total responding)

	All firms	Firms with annual US sales of:		
		Less than $500 million	$500 million to $1 billion	More than $1 billion
Increased procurement	18.8	17.0	32.4	16.7
No change in procurement	29.5	29.2	32.4	29.2
Decline in procurement	14.1	15.1	8.1	12.5
Not applicable	37.6	38.8	27.0	41.7
Total	100.0	100.0	100.0	100.0
No. of responses	387	312	37	48

Nearly 38 percent of the respondents reported that they had no significant foreign procurement (table 6.11). About half the other firms reported that their foreign procurement has remained about the same relative to domestic production. Combined with the results for question 10, responses to this question indicate that, on balance, the dollar decline that began in 1985 had not reduced imports by respondent firms. In fact, the data indicate further modest increases in the use of imported components. In every category of firm size, a larger portion of respondents see imports increasing relative to US sales rather than decreasing by 1993.

Question 12 *To what extent did the fall in the dollar affect your company's foreign procurement?*

A. solely responsible for changes

B. contributed significantly

C. somewhat important

D. no significant effect.

The fall in the dollar since 1985 seems to have had relatively little influence on firms' decisions about foreign versus domestic sourcing. A majority of the respondents reported that the dollar's decline had no significant effect on their foreign procurement (table 6.12). An additional 22.5 percent reported that it was somewhat important. Only a relatively small fraction of all respondents reported that the decline of the dollar contributed significantly to or was solely responsible for changes in the company's foreign procurement.

However, almost 30 percent of the respondents with sales greater than $1 billion and 45 percent of the firms with sales of $500 million to $1 billion reported that dollar decline had contributed significantly or had been somewhat important in affecting foreign procurement. At a minimum, dollar depreciation may have headed off further expansion of foreign procurement.

Table 6.12 Respondents' assessment of impact of 1985–90 dollar depreciation on foreign procurement (percentages of total)

	All firms	Firms with annual US sales of:		
		Less than $500 million	$500 million to $1 billion	More than $1 billion
Solely responsible for changes	1.0	1.0	0.0	0.0
Contributed significantly to changes	7.5	7.6	5.3	4.3
Somewhat important	22.5	19.9	39.5	25.5
No significant impact	69.0	71.5	55.3	70.2
Total	100.0	100.0	100.0	100.0
No. of responses	387	302	38	47

Question 13 *Please indicate on a scale of 1 to 5 (with 1 being the most important and 5 the least) the importance of each of the following factors in holding up the level of US imports in your product areas.*

1 2 3 4 5 a. results of earlier dollar decline not yet fully reflected; need more time to switch to US sources

1 2 3 4 5 b. current dollar rate still facilitates imports

1 2 3 4 5 c. foreign suppliers are selling below cost to retain US markets in hope of regaining competitiveness

1 2 3 4 5 d. uncertainty about future dollar exchange rates motivates staying with established foreign suppliers

1 2 3 4 5 e. no US source of supply for some product line items/components

1 2 3 4 5 f. US capacity constraints force foreign sourcing

1 2 3 4 5 g. foreign quality is very competitive

1 2 3 4 5 h. foreign service and flexibility in meeting needs is very competitive

1 2 3 4 5 i. other (please describe).

Three factors stood out as important in holding up the level of imports (table 6.13): the absence of a US source of supply for some product line items or components (34.5 percent ranked this as 1 or 2 in importance); high foreign quality (30.6 percent ranked this as 1 or 2 in importance); and foreign suppliers selling below cost to retain US markets (26.0 percent ranked this as 1 or 2 in importance). Almost 17 percent ranked "current dollar level still facilitates imports" as 1 or 2, and nearly 48 percent ranked it 1, 2, or 3.

Among the least important factors were "results of earlier dollar decline not yet fully reflected; need more time to switch to US sources" (only 6.6 percent ranked this as 1 or 2 in importance); uncertainty about future dollar exchange rates (12.5 percent ranked this as 1 or 2 in importance); and US capacity constraints (14.5 percent ranked this as 1 or 2).

Table 6.13 Respondents' rating of factors holding up level of US imports (percentages of total)

			Percent rating factor as:			
	Extremely important	Very important	Important	Modestly important	Not important	No. of respondents
Earlier dollar decline not yet reflected	1.9	4.7	23.5	33.1	36.7	362
Current exchange rate	4.1	12.8	30.9	30.1	22.1	366
Foreign suppliers selling below cost	10.5	15.5	20.2	27.7	26.0	361
Uncertainty about future exchange rates	2.5	10.0	23.8	31.0	32.7	361
No US source of supply	16.3	18.2	16.6	17.4	31.5	362
US capacity constraints	5.0	9.5	16.4	22.3	46.8	359
Foreign quality	9.2	21.4	32.9	18.9	17.5	359
Foreign service	6.1	16.4	24.4	26.7	26.4	360
Other	26.9	15.4	5.8	5.8	46.2	52

Table 6.14 Respondents' assessment of effects of lack of US production capacity on US imports (percentages of total responding)

| | All firms | Firms with annual US sales of: | | |
		Less than $500 million	$500 million to $1 billion	More than $1 billion
Significant factor	7.4	8.4	5.4	2.0
A factor, but not significant	14.9	13.8	13.5	25.2
Not a factor	77.2	77.2	81.1	72.8
Total	100.0	100.0	100.0	100.0
No. of responses	407	321	37	49

Capital Investment and US-Based Production Capacity

Questions in this section were designed to obtain information about firms' investment plans, the types of investment to be made, and factors influencing investment decisions.

Question 14 *Does a lack of US capacity inhibit your company's exports, require it to import items that you would prefer to make or buy domestically, or hold down your sales in the US market?*

A. yes, lack of US capacity is a significant factor

B. yes, but it is not a significant factor

C. lack of US capacity is not a factor.

At the time of the survey (summer 1990), lack of capacity was not a significant factor affecting exports or imports for over 90 percent of the firms. More than three-quarters of all respondents reported that a lack of capacity was not a factor at all in their trade performance (table 6.14). Another 14.9 percent reported that a lack of capacity affected them to some degree but not significantly. Only 7.4 percent of respondents rated it a significant factor, and among large firms only 2 percent so rated it.

Question 15 *What are your firm's plans for additions to US-based production capacity over the next several years?*

A. adding capacity to increase *share* of US market

B. adding capacity to handle export growth

C. adding capacity only to match trends in *overall* US market growth

Table 6.15 Respondents' reported reasons for planned additions to US-based production capacity (percentages of total responding)

| | | Firms with annual US sales of: | | |
	All firms	Less than $500 million	$500 million to $1 billion	More than $1 billion
To increase share of US market	46.6	46.9	46.2	51.0
To handle export growth	22.1	23.1	15.4	22.4
To match overall US market growth	24.7	22.8	15.4	42.9
No increase planned	20.2	21.3	28.2	2.0
Plan to decrease capacity	6.8	7.7	5.1	15.4
No. of responses	408	320	39	49

D. do not anticipate adding capacity

E. plan to decrease capacity.

Slightly fewer than half of all firms reported that they plan to increase US-based capacity to increase their share of the US market (table 6.15). An additional 24.7 percent reported that they were adding capacity to match trends in overall US market growth. Just over one-fifth of respondents reported plans to increase US capacity to handle export growth. Because firms could indicate more than one reason for adding capacity, these responses do not necessarily indicate that export growth was the primary reason for the increase. Instead, they indicate that only 24.7 percent of the respondents saw it as a factor in a decision to increase capacity. The remaining firms have no plans to increase capacity (20.2 percent) or plan to decrease capacity (6.8 percent).

Question 16   Of the total amount to be spent next year for plant and equipment, about what portion will go to each of the following? What portion of that spending will be devoted to pollution abatement?

A. investment in overseas facilities

B. modernization of US facilities

C. new construction of US facilities

Survey results indicate that plant and equipment spending is heavily biased, with two-thirds of all spending going to modernization of US facilities (table 6.16). The next-largest share was set for new construction in the United States, and the smallest to investment in overseas facilities. Of total spending on plant and equipment, firms estimate that just over 11 percent is for pollution abatement.

The answers, however, differed markedly by firm size. Generally, the larger firms plan to spend a substantially larger share of investment on overseas facilities

Table 6.16 Respondents' reported planned distribution of 1991 plant and equipment investment spending (percentages of total investment)

| | | Firms with annual US sales of: | | |
	All firms	Less than $500 million	$500 million to $1 billion	More than $1 billion
Investment in overseas facilities	9.6	6.8	19.4	19.6
Modernization of US facilities	66.6	71.0	59.9	42.9
New construction of US facilities	17.9	16.7	19.9	26.8
Total	100.0	100.0	100.0	100.0
Of total, portion for pollution abatement	11.3	11.1	9.2	12.7
No. of responses	408	320	39	49

and new construction than the smaller firms. Firms with annual US sales of over $1 billion, for example, plan to allocate an average of 19.6 percent of investment spending to overseas facilities, but firms with annual US sales of less than $500 million plan to allocate an average of only 6.8 percent. Similarly, the larger firms plan to allocate 26.8 percent of investment to new construction, compared with 16.7 percent for the smaller firms.

The responses concerning the portion of total investment devoted to pollution abatement were quite consistent across firm size.

Question 17   On a scale of 1 to 5 (with 1 being the most important and 5 the least) please indicate how important the following are in making investment decisions that would increase your US-based production capacity.

1 2 3 4 5   a. projected domestic demand
1 2 3 4 5   b. projected global demand
1 2 3 4 5   c. projections of foreign/US supplies
1 2 3 4 5   d. current level of the dollar exchange rate
1 2 3 4 5   e. uncertainty about future dollar exchange rates
1 2 3 4 5   f. cost of capital, US versus alternative foreign plant sites
1 2 3 4 5   g. uncertainty about future environmental and other regulations
1 2 3 4 5   h. uncertainty about US tax laws and regulations
1 2 3 4 5   i. "globalizing" of production favors producing in the markets to be served, rather than US exports
1 2 3 4 5   j. other important factors (please describe).

As might be expected, by far the most important factor in the investment decision was projected domestic demand, with 64.9 percent of the firms ranking it extremely important (table 6.17). An additional 23.6 percent considered it very important. The other significant factors influencing the investment decision (listed in order of importance) are projected global demand (44.3 percent of the firms

Table 6.17 Respondents' rating of factors affecting decision to increase US-based production capacity (percentages of total responding)

	Percent rating factor as:					
	Extremely important	Very important	Important	Modestly important	Not important	No. of respondents
Projected domestic demand	64.9	23.6	7.5	2.4	1.7	424
Projected global demand	18.7	25.6	26.8	22.7	6.2	422
Projections of foreign and US supplies	8.9	17.4	36.7	23.4	13.5	414
Current exchange rate	5.5	14.8	33.7	33.4	12.6	419
Uncertainty about future exchange rates	3.1	11.4	25.2	39.3	21.0	420
Relative costs of capital	6.4	15.2	21.7	32.6	24.0	420
Uncertainty about future environmental regulation	14.0	19.4	29.1	24.9	12.6	422
Uncertainty about future US tax law and regulation	8.8	15.7	31.8	32.5	11.2	421
Globalization favors foreign investment	14.6	26.9	27.3	19.4	11.8	417
Other	34.8	15.7	7.9	5.6	36.0	89

ranked it 1 or 2), globalizing of production (41.5 percent ranked it 1 or 2), and uncertainty about future environmental and other regulations (33.4 percent ranked it 1 or 2, and an additional 29.4 percent ranked it as 3).

Interesting differences emerge, however, when the responses are sorted by firm size. For example, whereas only 41.5 percent of all respondents ranked globalization of production as extremely or very important in their US investment decisions, disaggregation produces the following results: firms with sales less than $500 million, 40.8 percent; $500 million to $1 billion, 46.7 percent; sales greater than $1 billion, 52.0 percent. These results seem to support the idea that the larger firms, with broader international investment opportunities, are more inclined to see the United States as only one alternative in their investment plans.

Interesting differences are also evident in the responses on the item "uncertainty about US tax laws and regulations." Of the total respondent group, 24.5 percent ranked this factor as extremely or very important. However, 26.6 percent of firms with sales less than $500 million, 18.4 percent of those with sales $500 million to $1 billion, and only 14 percent of firms with sales greater than $1 billion ranked this factor that highly.

One obvious interpretation of these responses to the globalization and tax questions is that as firm size and foreign direct investment and participation in global markets become relatively more important, investment decisions on individual markets relate more strongly to the individual market concerned and less to international conditions. That is, a company with worldwide investments makes new investments in the United States primarily to serve the US market, and is less affected by uncertainty about US tax laws and regulations than are companies without a global presence.

Exchange rates were ranked as the least important factors listed. Only 20.3 percent of the firms gave a 1 or a 2 rating to the current level of the dollar exchange rate, and only 14.5 percent of the respondents gave a 1 or a 2 rating to uncertainty about future dollar exchange rates. It is difficult to interpret the relatively low concern of respondents about current and future dollar exchange rates. It may indicate a continued focus of US firms on US markets, supplemented by direct investment in important foreign markets to serve those markets. Among the firms with sales over $1 billion—most of which have significant direct investment abroad—only 10 percent ranked exchange rates as 1 or 2, perhaps indicating that their foreign direct investment insulates them from exchange rate effects to some extent.

Exchange Rate Effects

The questions in this area were designed to determine the potential response of companies' exports and imports to further changes in the dollar exchange rate.

Table 6.18 Respondents' estimation of effects of further significant dollar depreciation on exports (percentages of total responding)

		Firms with annual US sales of:		
	All firms	Less than $500 million	$500 million to $1 billion	More than $1 billion
Major increase in exports	26.9	28.1	20.5	20.4
Minor increases in exports	40.8	38.5	46.2	49.0
No significant effect	23.0	22.7	28.2	26.5
Not applicable, do not export	9.4	11.0	5.1	4.1
Total	100.0	100.0	100.0	100.0
No. of responses	404	317	39	49

The responses should be interpreted in the light of exchange rates prevailing in the summer of 1990. At that time, according to Federal Reserve statistics, the yen was in the range of 138 to 154 to the dollar. The German mark was at 1.57 to 1.68 to the dollar.

Question 18 A recent study by the Institute for International Economics indicates that to eliminate the current account deficit by 1992 would require the US dollar to depreciate substantially against the currencies of our major trading partners. For example, the study projects the required adjustment would be to about 100 yen and to about 1.5 deutsche marks to the dollar.
Should it occur, how would additional dollar depreciation of this magnitude affect the following:
Exports from your company's US-based production?

A. major increases

B. minor increases

C. no significant effect

D. not applicable, don't export.

At the time of the survey, respondent firms believed that additional dollar depreciation of the magnitude described would significantly help their exports. A majority of firms reported that exports would increase, with 26.9 percent expecting a major increase and an additional 40.8 percent a minor increase (table 6.18). The remainder either anticipated no significant effect (23.0 percent) or reported that they did not export (9.4 percent). It is particularly important that over 20 percent of the firms with US sales over $500 million believed that substantial dollar depreciation would lead to major export increases.

Table 6.19 Respondents' estimation of effects of further significant dollar depreciation on imports of production inputs and finished goods (percentages of total responding)

	All firms	Firms with annual US sales of:		
		Less than $500 million	$500 million to $1 billion	More than $1 billion
Major decrease in imports	9.9	11.4	2.6	4.6
Minor decrease in imports	26.0	22.7	34.2	30.6
No significant effect	33.9	31.5	55.3	36.7
Not applicable, do not import	30.8	35.0	7.9	28.6
Total	100.0	100.0	100.0	100.0
No. of responses	404	317	38	49

Question 19 *Should it occur, how would additional dollar depreciation of this magnitude affect the following:*
Imports by your company of foreign parts, components, assemblies, intermediate and finished products?

A. major decrease, return to US-based production

B. minor decrease, return to US-based production

C. no significant effect; foreign procurement as before

D. not applicable, no significant imports.

The survey responses indicate that the additional devaluation would increase exports considerably more than it would replace imports. The firms surveyed are manufacturing firms that import primarily parts and components and assemblies as inputs to their own production processes. Only 9.9 percent of respondents indicated that their imports would undergo a major decrease as a result of the additional dollar depreciation (table 6.19). A minor decrease was projected by 26.0 percent; 33.9 percent reported that there would be no significant change in foreign procurement, and 30.8 percent reported that they have no significant imports.

The larger firms—those that typically have significant foreign direct investments—were less likely to see a major change in imports as a result of additional dollar devaluation. Only 3.4 percent of firms with annual US sales of $500 million or more indicated that a dollar depreciation would result in a major decrease in their imports, as compared with 11.4 percent of firms with annual US sales of less than $500 million.

Question 20 *Should it occur, how would additional dollar depreciation of this magnitude affect the following:*
Investments by your company in US production facilities?

Table 6.20 Respondents' estimates of effect of significant further dollar depreciation on investment in US facilities (percentages of total responding)

		Firms with annual US sales of:		
	All firms	Less than $500 million	$500 million to $1 billion	More than $1 billion
Major increase in investment	22.1	25.3	12.8	8.2
No significant effect	77.9	74.7	87.2	91.8
Total	100.0	100.0	100.0	100.0
No. of responses	404	316	39	49

A. significant increase to expand US-based production

B. no significant effect on investments in US-based production.

Slightly more than three-fourths of respondents indicated that additional devaluation would have no significant effect on investments in US-based production facilities (table 6.20). The remainder, 22.1 percent, said there would be a significant increase in such investment.

Question 21   *Should it occur, how would additional dollar depreciation of this magnitude affect the following:*
Investments by your company in foreign-based production?

A. significant decrease in foreign-based production and investment

B. no significant effect on foreign investment

C. increased concern about volatility of exchange rates increases foreign investment.

As with investment in US-based production, a large majority of firms (86.3 percent) reported that additional devaluation would have no significant effect on their investments in foreign-based production (table 6.21). Another 9.2 percent said that investment would increase, and 4.7 percent said it would fall.

Conclusions

■ There is only modest optimism for increasing export sales in the near to medium term, especially among the larger companies that are the big exporters. Companies with annual US sales in the $500 million to $1 billion range foresee increases at an average annual rate of only 5 percent through 1993. Companies with annual sales of over $1 billion see even more modest

Table 6.21 **Respondents' estimates of effect of significant further dollar depreciation on investment in foreign-based production**
(percentages of total responding)

	All firms	Firms with annual US sales of:		
		Less than $500 million	$500 million to $1 billion	More than $1 billion
Major decrease in investment	4.7	4.0	5.3	4.2
No significant effect	86.3	85.8	89.5	89.6
Increase in investment	9.2	10.2	5.3	6.3
Total	100.0	100.0	100.0	100.0
No. of responses	379	303	38	48

growth of 3.0 percent per year. Looking to the mid-1990s and beyond, one-fourth of respondents anticipate significantly more exports from the United States. Among companies with annual sales over $1 billion, however, only 12.5 percent gave this response.

■ Generally, firms expect their exports to increase marginally relative to their US sales. However, they also anticipate that a modestly declining portion of their foreign sales will be met by exports from the United States; this would be consistent with the trend toward servicing major markets by production located in those markets, usually by direct investments.

■ There is also some evidence that firms anticipate a small increase in the use of imported parts and components in production in the near to medium term. This would be consistent with the continuing globalization of markets, wherein firms increasingly consider suppliers outside the United States.

■ Almost 70 percent of respondents indicated that the decline in the US dollar that began in 1985 has been of at least some importance to improved export performance. More than one-fourth (26.2 percent) indicated that it has been a significant factor.

■ The dollar decline appears to have had relatively little influence on respondents' decisions about foreign procurement. Some 70 percent indicated that it had no significant effect on their procurement. In fact, those indicating that their foreign procurement increased relative to US sales since 1985 (18.8 percent) modestly outnumber those indicating that it declined (14.1 percent).

■ It also appears that additional dollar depreciation would have a greater impact on exports than on imports. Over one-fifth of respondents that are exporters with annual US sales over $500 million foresaw major export increases from further depreciation to about 100 yen and 1.5 deutsche marks to the dollar. Fewer than 5 percent of those companies saw that depreciation as leading to major import decreases and a return to US-based production.

- Respondents indicated that added dollar depreciation would also have some effects on investment plans. One-fourth of companies with annual sales under $500 million indicated that dollar depreciation to 100 yen and 1.5 deutsche marks to the dollar would induce them to significantly increase investment to expand US production facilities; 10 percent of companies with annual sales over $500 million gave the same response.

- The two most important factors restraining export growth were foreign import barriers and expected continued globalization of markets and production. Disaggregation of the responses, however, indicates that, for the larger firms that are the major exporters, globalization is the most important factor inhibiting export growth. Of firms with annual US sales greater than $1 billion, 59.2 percent indicated globalization of production as an extremely or very important factor holding back export growth. That is, to be competitive in important foreign markets, US firms locate production in those markets rather than serve them by exports from the United States.

- On balance, respondents expect EC 1992 to enlarge the EC market and expand US exports. Over half (53.9 percent) foresee no significant effect on US exports to the European Community. But 28.4 percent see increases, and only 18.2 percent see declines.

- One-fourth of the respondents see increased competition from the European Community as making it more difficult to export to third countries, but three-fourths see no significant effects. A majority, however (59.4 percent) believe that EC 92 will motivate increased direct investment in the European Community to serve that market.

- Respondent firms reported low rates of imports of parts, components, assemblies, and finished products relative to their US sales. The 1989 median ratio of imports to sales was 3.0 percent in the respondent group as a whole, an increase from 1.0 percent in 1981. Moreover, the projected 1993 median for the group as a whole was 4.0 percent, indicating expected continuing growth of imports relative to US sales.

- Respondents ranked the lack of a US source of supply as one of the most important factors holding up the level of imports in their product areas. This indicates that substantial changes in market conditions will be required for US production to replace imports in some product lines. Competitive foreign quality ranked second.

- Responses concerning decisions about investment in US-based capacity indicate that the dominant decision factor and concern of US manufacturers is the outlook for the US market and that export markets are of only secondary importance. Globalization of production—the need to serve foreign markets by producing in those markets—was the third-ranking factor in investment decisions, but 41.7 percent of all respondents ranked it as extremely or very important in their US investment decisions. The portion assigning these descriptions increased with firm size. Among firms with sales over $1 billion, 52.0 percent considered globalization of production extremely or very important.

- At the time of the survey, only a small minority (7.4 percent) of respondents saw lack of capacity as a significant factor limiting exports. More important, only 2 percent of firms with US sales greater than $1 billion—the major exporters—labeled it significant.

- Firms with US sales of under $500 million invested 6.8 percent of their plant ₁and equipment spending in overseas facilities, but firms with annual sales of over $1 billion put an average of 19.6 percent of their investments abroad. Respondents expect to use an average of 11.3 percent of their plant and equipment spending on pollution abatement in 1991.

7

Key Findings and Policy Implications

7

Key Findings and Policy Implications

This chapter summarizes the key findings of the study. The first section presents the study's findings about the role of manufactures trade in current account performance and the outlook for US current account balances. The second section summarizes recent US trade performance and the near-term outlook on a product group-by-product group basis. The third section summarizes key findings about manufactures trade performance through 1993 and beyond. The concluding section identifies some of the implications of the study's findings for US economic policy, domestic as well as international.

Manufactures Trade and US Current Account Performance

The detailed examination of recent and projected current account performance leads to several broad conclusions.

> Manufactures trade has been and will continue to be the critical determinant of US trade and current account performance.

The huge 1981–87 deterioration in the US current account was reflected primarily in a decline in US manufactures trade performance. Similarly, the 1987–90 improvement in the US current account was primarily in manufactures trade. A detailed examination of the components of the current account shows that manufactures trade must also provide the great majority of any improvement in the current account in the foreseeable future.

> Neither expanded net exports of services or agricultural goods nor increased profits of the foreign affiliates of US firms offer a solution to US current account deficits.

The actual and potential role of services trade in the US external accounts is frequently overrated. There is little reason to believe the United States has a significant, enduring comparative advantage in services trade. Improvements in

531

services trade balances are not assured, and any feasible improvements will make only modest contributions to reducing current account deficits. Moreover, further deteriorations in the international investment income account are likely to offset most, if not all, of any prospective gains in services. Although the United States is a major agricultural exporter, there is little likelihood of major gains in its agricultural surpluses. US-owned foreign firms are doing well in foreign competition, but only their profits, which make up a very small fraction of their foreign sales, add to US current account receipts. Manufactures trade, still $73 billion in deficit in 1990, must be the primary source of future improvements in the US current account.

The dominant role of manufactures in US trade is not unique among industrialized countries. Changes in manufactures trade flows and balances are the primary counterpart to large changes in net international capital flows. Put another way, except for oil, major changes in the trade performance of industrialized countries will typically be manifested in their manufactures trade accounts.

Manufactures trade is the fastest growing, most changeable, and by far the largest component of world goods and services trade. Large oil price increases in the past have dramatically altered international trade and capital flows. Typically, however, manufactures trade is the "swing factor" in world trade flow patterns, the primary means by which net international resource transfers are accomplished. For industrialized countries, large net capital outflows—net foreign lending—typically translate into large manufactures trade surpluses, and large net capital inflows—net borrowing—into large manufactures trade deficits.

The dominant role of manufactures in trade among industrialized countries, the globalization of manufactures production, and the potential for rapid shifts in production locations among countries also make manufactures trade the primary means through which national economies compete. Policies that alter net international capital flows or a country's competitiveness in global markets (e.g., by altering the exchange rate) therefore have greater effect on the manufacturing sector than on sectors more insulated from foreign competition.

In a world where most goods are readily tradeable and most services are not, manufacturing is the sector most exposed to foreign competition. It is the primary interface of the US economy with the world economy. Manufacturing can be thought of as a relatively narrow segment of the US economy that absorbs the major portion of the trade effects of changes in net international capital flows caused by changing US and foreign economic policies and changing economic performance.

Manufacturing's contribution to US international transactions is not limited to merchandise trade. US manufacturing firms earn substantial net international income from their foreign investments and from the licensing of their technology.

The dominant role of the manufacturing sector in US international transactions is enlarged by the direct investments abroad of US multinational companies. In 1990 US manufacturing parent companies received $22.9 billion in investment income from their foreign affiliates and $1.9 billion in service charges and fees. Manufacturing also collected $8.6 billion in royalties and license fees from abroad. These receipts are a heritage from earlier periods when US manufacturing was dominant in world markets. The substantial $27.6 billion surplus produced in these categories in 1990 significantly bolstered US current account performance. These surpluses are, however, unlikely to expand much further and could gradually diminish, reflecting the waning global position of US manufacturing.

> Manufacturing's key role in US external transactions and its vulnerability to foreign competition will continue to increase as the world economy becomes more integrated and as world trade expands more rapidly than world output.

Total US goods and services trade as a share of GNP rose from 10.5 percent in 1960 to 19.8 percent in 1981 and 20.6 percent in 1990. The role of manufactures trade in total trade has also been growing. From 1981 to 1990 manufactures trade rose from 53.2 percent of goods and services trade to 62.5 percent. In 1981 manufactures trade was 64.3 percent of merchandise trade, rising to 79.2 percent by 1990. In 1981 it was 10.5 percent of GNP, rising to 12.9 percent by 1990. This growth will continue and will increase the vulnerability of the US manufacturing sector to foreign competition, the importance to the United States of manufacturing's international competitiveness, and the need for greater focus on the effects of US policies on manufacturing's competitiveness.

> Some US economic policies may have different—even contrary—effects on the manufacturing sector than on other sectors of the economy.

Policies that trigger large net capital inflows may appear in the short term to be good for the economy as a whole, lowering interest rates from what they otherwise would have been, and thus allowing more rapid growth in aggregate consumption and investment. Focusing solely on the macroeconomic effects, however, obscures the effects on those sectors that are more integrated into the international economy. For example, during most of the 1980s—a period of heavy US external borrowing—the US construction, retail and wholesale trade, and financial services industries generally did well, at least temporarily. But at the same time the large net capital inflows had their counterpart in large manufactures trade deficits, which depressed the manufacturing sector's output and employment. The overly strong dollar and the resulting strength of foreign competition held down new investment in non-defense-oriented manufacturing. Instead, the net capital inflows supported high rates of investment in sectors insulated from foreign competition: office buildings, hotels, and the retail and financial sectors.

The portion of the manufacturing sector not engaged in defense production shrank in size relative to US consumption of manufactured goods and relative to the sectors that were enjoying a boom. In addition, manufacturing's capital stock continued to age, and the competitiveness of US-based production declined. Today, however, the overbuilt sectors that boomed during the 1980s are stagnant or shrinking, and the nondefense segment of manufacturing will have to expand and be revitalized by new investments to produce the trade surpluses that will be required if the US external accounts are to be again balanced without the crutch of continuing dollar decline. Because it is the sector most exposed to foreign competition, manufacturing is also the sector most immediately affected by changes in explicit taxation, in mandated programs that constitute implicit taxes, and in other governmental laws, rules, and regulations that raise the costs of US-based production compared with foreign production. In the face of foreign competition, manufacturing is less able to pass on added costs than are those industries less exposed to foreign competition. The immediate effect may be to discourage investment in US-based manufacturing, relative to investment in other sectors more insulated from foreign competition, and relative to investment abroad.

Compared with 1990 levels (setting aside the temporary, largely recession-induced improvements in 1991), US manufactures trade performance is unlikely to improve markedly in the foreseeable future. Without significant improvement, the United States will continue to experience current account deficits of 1 percent or more of GNP through 1993.

Absent some dramatic economic event that alters normal capital and trade flow patterns, and setting aside the temporary effects of foreign contributions to offset the costs of the Gulf War, this study finds that the United States will make little progress, if any, in reducing its current account deficits during the 1990–93 period. The effects of earlier dollar depreciation have waned. Improvements in manufactures trade during 1991 were largely related to the US recession and in part will be given up when the economy recovers, with subsequent substantial gains unlikely. The modest 1989–90 dollar decline will exert some further positive effect in 1992, but absent major additional exchange rate movements, changes in US trade balances by 1993 will be modest and very much a function of relative US-foreign economic growth rates. Slow US growth relative to foreign economies would help to narrow the US trade deficits, but is in itself undesirable and is unlikely to make major reductions in the deficits from 1990 levels by 1993.

Manufactures trade performance has improved significantly since 1987. However, despite a return of the dollar exchange rate to its levels of 1979–81, when the United States enjoyed manufactures trade and current account surpluses, US-based manufacturing is not yet sufficiently competitive in international markets to avoid current account deficits. An additional manufactures trade balance improvement of about $100 billion from 1990 levels—about $75 billion from 1991 levels—would be needed to eliminate the US current account deficit by 1993.

The 1990 US manufactures trade deficit was $73.5 billion; in 1991 it was $47.7 billion. Analysis of the likely growth and composition of US external transactions indicates that a balanced US current account by 1993—a hypothetical performance target chosen to provide analytical perspective—would require an improvement in manufactures trade performance of about $100 billion over 1990 levels. This would result in a manufactures trade surplus of about $25 billion.[1]

The $100 billion improvement from 1990 performance in manufactures trade needed to eliminate the US current account deficit is equivalent to about 1.8 percent of 1990 GNP. In 1991, a recession year, performance improved by some $25 billion. Thus, despite dollar exchange rates roughly equivalent to those of 1979–81, US-based manufactures production is not yet sufficiently competitive in international markets to avoid incurring further debt to foreigners. In no small measure, lagging performance compared with 1981 can be attributed to a decline in the purchasing power of Latin America and the OPEC countries. Nevertheless, assuming a continuation of the existing economic climate, US deficits of 1 percent or more of GNP will continue, in contrast to the surplus of 1981.

US manufacturing output has grown strongly during recent years and is about the same portion of GNP as in 1981. However, this is not a relevant indicator of the international market competitiveness of US manufacturing. To eliminate or sharply reduce US borrowing from abroad and the drain on future US living standards of subsequent servicing of the foreign debt, US manufactures will have to win significantly larger shares of both US and foreign markets.

Summary of Past and Projected Manufactures Trade Performance

Analyses of aggregated trade data and the results of the individual product group analyses lead to several more specific conclusions about the outlook for US manufactures trade.

---

1. Although current account deficits at the 1990 level could probably be sustained for a long period—perhaps even indefinitely—we believe that a return to current account surpluses is desirable to enhance future living standards. (For a similar assessment, see Bergsten 1988, 125.) We also believe that accepting continuing large manufactures trade deficits is probably inconsistent with the revitalization and improved international competitiveness of US-based production that is essential if the manufacturing sector is to make its full contribution to rising US living standards.

Market Share Performance Summary

Table 7.1 summarizes US market share performance in the 21 product groups assessed in this study, which together constitute well over 90 percent of US manufactures trade. The table also includes six groups that make up the majority of the remainder of US manufactures trade. The US share of world manufactures exports to non-US destinations was 15.8 percent in 1989, down from 18.5 percent in 1981. The US share of world manufactures imports from non-US sources meanwhile rose from 18.0 percent in 1981 to 20.9 percent in 1989.

US export shares ranged widely across industries in 1989, but there were few areas of US export dominance. US shares of world exports to non-US destinations (table 7.1) ranged from 2.1 percent (travel goods, SITC 83) to 49.1 percent (aircraft, SITC 792). The United States had export market shares of over 20 percent in only four product groups. The 49.1 percent US share in aircraft (SITC 792) is high, but it is down from 1981, and the world market is relatively small. The same is true of professional and scientific equipment (SITC 87). Export market shares also topped 20 percent in power-generating machinery (SITC 71) and office machines and computers (SITC 75), both large world export items. But US import shares were also large in these two product groups, with the result that both categories showed trade deficits. From 1981 to 1989 the US export market share increased in only one category, footwear (SITC 85), from 2.0 percent to 2.4 percent.

US shares of world imports from non-US sources in 1989 ranged from 8.4 percent (textiles, SITC 65) to 36.5 percent (footwear, SITC 85) and tell a different story. The US share of world manufactures imports from non-US sources was over 20 percent in 12 of the 27 product groups. In three groups (office machines and computers, SITC 75; road vehicles, SITC 78; and footwear, SITC 85) the United States absorbed over 30 percent of total exports of the rest of the world. From 1981 to 1989 the US shares of world imports from non-US sources grew in 20 of the 27 categories, and declined in only 7.

Table 7.2 provides another means of summarizing the US competitive position. The United States has the largest individual-country share of total world imports in 23 of the 27 product groups summarized in the table. Given that it is by far the world's largest single economy, substantial US predominance in world manufactures import shares is to be expected. There is, however, no similar predominance in the US share of world manufactures exports. The United States had the largest 1989 share of exports in only three product groups: power-generating machinery (SITC 71), aircraft (SITC 792), and professional and scientific instruments (SITC 87). The table also highlights Germany's dominant role in manufactures trade, with the largest market share in 8 of the 23 product groups. Japan, in contrast, holds the largest export share in only 6 product groups, the same number as the Asian newly industrializing countries (NICs).

Table 7.1 United States: manufactures export and import shares and share balances, 1981 and 1989 (percentages)[a]

SITC Product group	1981			1989			1981 share minus 1989 share		
	Exports	Imports	Balance	Exports	Imports	Balance	Exports	Imports	Balance
All manufactures	18.5	18.0	0.5	15.8	20.9	-5.1	-2.7	2.9	-5.6
of which:									
5 Chemicals	20.0	9.5	10.5	16.1	9.9	6.2	-3.9	0.4	-4.3
61 Leather	9.1	12.5	-3.4	8.4	10.5	-2.1	-0.8	-2.0	1.3
62 Rubber manufactures	12.5	16.3	-3.8	8.6	19.5	-10.8	-3.8	3.2	-7.0
63 Cork and wood	10.2	20.4	-10.2	8.4	17.7	-9.3	-1.8	-2.7	0.9
64 Paper and paper products	13.8	17.2	-3.4	9.7	17.3	-7.6	-4.1	0.1	-4.2
65 Textiles	8.9	7.7	1.2	5.2	8.4	-3.2	-3.7	0.7	-4.4
66 Nonmetallic mineral manufactures	8.8	17.2	-8.4	6.1	17.4	-11.3	-2.7	0.2	-2.9
67 Iron and steel	5.5	19.7	-14.2	4.1	12.0	-7.9	-1.4	-7.7	6.3
68 Nonferrous metals	9.9	22.1	-12.2	8.2	16.8	-8.6	-1.7	-5.3	3.6
69 Manufactures of metal, n.e.s.	14.5	14.6	-0.1	9.4	18.2	-8.8	-5.1	3.6	-8.7
71 Power-generating machinery	31.1	18.3	12.8	27.3	28.1	-0.8	-3.8	9.8	-13.6
72 Specialized industrial machinery	29.2	12.9	16.3	16.5	15.7	0.8	-12.7	2.8	-15.5
73 Metalworking machinery	18.0	17.6	0.4	11.6	16.7	-5.1	-6.4	-0.9	-5.5
74 General industrial machinery	20.8	10.8	10.0	14.8	15.7	-0.9	-6.0	4.9	-10.9
75 Office machines and computers	39.5	20.1	19.4	28.0	30.8	-2.8	-11.5	10.7	-22.2
76 Telecommunications and sound-reproducing equipment	13.1	27.1	-14.0	12.4	29.7	-17.3	-0.7	2.6	-3.3
77 Electrical machinery	19.2	19.2	0.0	18.6	24.0	-5.4	-0.6	4.8	-5.4
78 Road vehicles	16.8	27.0	-10.2	13.5	31.6	-18.1	-3.3	4.6	-7.9
792 Aircraft	55.4	19.8	35.6	49.1	19.1	30.0	-6.3	-0.7	-5.6
81 Plumbing and heating equipment	11.5	7.5	4.0	6.7	17.3	-10.6	-4.8	9.8	-14.5
82 Furniture and parts	7.7	14.3	-6.6	5.7	22.7	-17.0	-2.0	8.4	-10.4
83 Travel goods, handbags	4.6	33.0	-28.4	2.1	31.7	-29.6	-2.5	-1.3	-1.2
84 Apparel and clothing	4.5	23.1	-18.6	2.6	29.9	-27.3	-1.9	6.8	-8.7
85 Footwear	2.0	31.6	-29.6	2.4	36.5	-34.1	0.4	4.9	-4.5
87 Professional, scientific, and controlling instruments	33.4	13.0	20.4	28.4	17.3	11.1	-5.0	4.3	-9.3
88 Photographic apparatus	16.3	20.2	-3.9	12.0	21.1	-9.1	-4.3	0.9	-5.2
89 Miscellaneous manufactures	15.5	22.4	-6.9	14.9	26.0	-11.1	-0.6	3.6	-4.2

a. Export shares are shares of world exports to all non-US destinations; import shares are shares of world imports from non-US sources.

Source: WMTDB.

Table 7.2 World market shares of the principal exporting and importing regions, 1989 (percentages of total)[a]

SITC Product group	Exports						Imports					
	United States	Japan	EC Total	EC Outside EC	Germany	Asian NICs	United States	Japan	EC Total	EC Outside EC	Germany	Asian NICs
5 Chemicals	14.7	5.9	58.4	24.5	**17.8**	2.5	8.4	5.8	46.0	12.7	**9.8**	9.0
61 Leather[b]	7.5	2.9	47.7	20.9	8.3	10.7	9.7	2.5	47.5	22.2	8.7	**18.4**
62 Rubber manufactures	7.2	**17.0**	54.8	18.9	14.7	7.4	**17.5**	3.3	43.3	10.6	11.8	3.2
63 Cork and wood	7.0	0.5	33.8	10.4	8.9	9.4	16.4	12.2	46.1	22.9	11.9	5.8
64 Paper and paper products[c]	8.1	3.1	38.3	10.6	13.9	1.9	15.8	2.3	54.4	26.1	10.7	6.8
65 Textiles	4.8	6.8	49.5	17.3	13.5	**16.0**	7.9	5.5	45.9	15.0	11.1	**11.5**
66 Nonmetallic mineral manufactures	5.1	4.6	50.9	26.5	8.7	4.7	16.2	7.1	42.7	18.6	6.6	5.2
67 Iron and steel	3.6	15.1	50.9	19.6	15.4	5.9	11.6	5.1	41.6	11.1	10.9	9.9
68 Nonferrous metals	6.9	3.1	35.1	10.9	10.7	2.1	15.5	13.7	45.7	22.3	12.9	8.8
69 Manufactures of metal, n.e.s.	7.9	8.3	52.7	21.5	18.9	11.3	16.3	2.8	42.8	13.2	9.8	4.9
71 Power-generating machinery	**21.3**	14.3	42.9	22.2	14.4	2.4	**21.3**	2.7	36.4	17.7	7.8	6.5
72 Specialized industrial machinery	14.2	14.6	52.4	28.5	23.2	2.8	13.4	2.4	34.2	11.1	5.6	10.7
73 Metalworking machinery	9.9	21.5	48.6	28.2	24.1	4.0	15.1	2.4	33.9	14.5	8.3	11.7
74 General industrial machinery	12.8	15.5	53.5	26.2	22.0	3.2	13.2	2.5	37.1	11.5	7.6	9.2
75 Office machines and computers	21.0	**21.2**	35.0	9.9	7.7	15.0	**23.0**	3.9	46.4	24.7	10.6	6.0
76 Telecommunications and sound-reproducing equipment	8.9	**31.8**	21.9	9.7	7.2	20.1	**27.1**	3.0	32.7	20.4	7.9	8.7
77 Electrical machinery	14.8	**19.5**	36.3	15.5	14.0	13.1	**19.7**	3.8	33.7	14.7	8.3	15.0
78 Road vehicles	9.7	**23.4**	47.9	15.6	21.9	2.6	**28.2**	1.9	39.2	8.4	7.4	2.4
792 Aircraft	**44.6**	0.7	43.0	23.5	13.7	0.7	11.5	3.4	38.3	19.8	**16.2**	6.9
81 Plumbing and heating equipment	6.0	2.0	67.0	22.6	20.9	3.9	16.1	2.2	50.4	11.0	13.2	3.0
82 Furniture and parts[d]	4.5	1.5	59.3	22.4	15.5	9.0	21.4	5.0	46.1	11.3	12.6	1.7
83 Travel goods, handbags	1.4	0.8	32.7	20.2	3.9	**37.8**	**31.2**	14.3	32.9	21.6	9.8	5.2
84 Apparel and clothing	2.3	0.6	32.3	11.7	6.1	**28.4**	**29.1**	10.0	42.7	22.8	16.3	1.1
85 Footwear	1.5	0.2	41.6	16.4	4.2	**32.8**	**35.8**	4.8	39.0	14.0	14.0	2.2
87 Professional, scientific, and controlling instruments	**24.1**	12.5	45.3	23.8	18.0	2.9	12.4	6.2	40.5	20.6	8.9	9.1
88 Photographic apparatus	9.7	**27.2**	34.4	15.7	11.2	10.2	17.6	5.6	39.4	22.1	9.7	14.5
89 Miscellaneous manufactures	11.6	6.9	44.4	21.2	12.7	**16.5**	**22.5**	7.3	39.4	17.8	7.8	4.5

a. Numbers in boldface indicate the largest share for each product group.

b. Italy has the largest export share at 19.3 percent.

c. Canada has largest export share at 14.9 percent.

d. Italy has the largest export share at 20.4 percent.

Source: WMTDB.

But except for photographic equipment (SITC 88), which at $33 billion was only 1.6 percent of total world manufactures exports, the product groups in which Japan leads are very large in world trade, whereas the Asian NICs excel in products with somewhat smaller shares of world trade. These data also underscore that Japan's large trade surpluses stem not only from its large manufactures exports but also from its very small manufactures imports.

Summary of Product Group Performance Projections

The matrix in table 7.3 summarizes the results of the 1993 trade balance changes projected in the individual product group analyses of chapter 5. The results are judgments based on analyses of all the empirical quantitative data and qualitative information collected, including the questionnaire survey data.

Projecting 1993 trade balances in individual product groups, some of which are quite small, is clearly an uncertain process. Some product groups, for example, are particularly sensitive to US economic growth rates or to changes in exchange rates. In others, technologies, fashions, or comparative advantages in production locations can change rapidly. There are many other variables that cannot be accurately foreseen. For example, a continued healthy recovery of Latin American markets, where the United States still retains a strong competitive position, would significantly boost exports of some US manufactures. All in all there is clearly ample opportunity for these individual projections to be wrong, and many will be wrong. Nevertheless, there is much to be learned from assessing the outlook in individual product groups and from a summation of these outlooks.

Table 7.3 projects only relatively modest improvements in some product groups and continued worsening in some others. Taken as a whole, the individual product group assessments project a net improvement from 1990 to 1993 in manufactures trade performance—and in the current account—of probably less than $10 billion but not more than $20 billion, well below the $100 billion this study projects would be needed to eliminate the US current account deficit by 1993, although perhaps adequate to restrain demands for protectionist measures if the overall performance of the economy is satisfactory. This overall assessment of the prospects for improvement in US trade and current account balances is quite similar to the projections of a number of other analysts utilizing econometric models.[2]

---

2. For example, in a revision of earlier estimates, William R. Cline (1991) of the Institute for International Economics projects an improvement of $30 billion to $40 billion in the current account by 1993 and an essentially balanced current account by 1995. The majority of the improvement foreseen by 1993 is expected to come from an improvement of $20

Nevertheless, the results in table 7.3 do not fit the image of a US manufacturing sector that is fully competitive with those of Japan and Western Europe. Indeed, some readers may be surprised at the mix of modest improvements and continuing declines among individual product groups. The continuing declines in some product groups are not in themselves surprising. In a dynamic, highly competitive world economy the competitive positions of individual industries and products will be constantly changing as comparative advantage shifts and as new products and new producers emerge. The structure of a competitive US manufacturing sector for the 1990s will be different from that of the 1980s or the 1970s. These dynamics notwithstanding, however, an important conclusion to be drawn from an overview of the individual product group analyses is that there are few, if any, products important in world trade in which a US leadership position seems likely to emerge or to be enhanced in the 1990s. Instead, without further dollar depreciation, in the face of increasing foreign competition and the continuing emergence of new producers, and without higher levels of US investment in manufacturing R&D and plant and equipment, a weakening of the overall US position seems more likely as the years unfold beyond 1993.

US Manufactures Trade Performance: Specific Findings

The most likely near-term prospect is that improvement in US manufactures trade will stagnate at about the levels of 1990–91, leaving the current account well short of the gains needed to restore it to balance.

To generate the $100 billion trade balance improvement from 1990 levels required to balance the current account by 1993 will require manufactures exports to grow about 9.5 percentage points faster than manufactures imports in each

---

billion to $30 billion in merchandise trade, notwithstanding a $9 billion increase in the oil import deficit. Cline's work does not provide separate projections for manufactures trade but implies a manufactures trade performance improvement by 1993 of about $30 billion to $40 billion. Cline's model, however, assumes continued progress in meeting the 1990 budget agreement. It also anticipates real dollar depreciation of roughly 1.0 percent to 1.5 percent annually.

In its October 1991 *Review of the US Economy*, however, DRI sees the US merchandise trade deficit for 1993 at a level $14 billion above that of 1990, including a $7 billion enlargement in oil imports and a further $21 billion increase in the merchandise trade deficit in 1994. The IMF's *World Economic Outlook* sees the US current account deficit rising to $98.5 billion in 1992, $6 billion above the 1990 level, but provides no later projections. The July 1991 *OECD Economic Outlook* more optimistically projects a 1992 US current account deficit of only $58 billion and provides no forecast for 1993. As in the Cline projections, manufactures trade is not separately identified in any of these forecasts. Oxford Economics USA, however, in its June 1991 *U.S. Economic Prospects*, projects 1993 and 1994 manufactures trade deficits of $82 billion and $81 billion, respectively, compared with an actual $73 billion deficit in 1990. Although the forecasts vary, collectively they imply no significant change in the 1993 manufactures balance compared with 1990.

Table 7.3   United States: manufactures trade balance, actual and projected changes, 1981–93 (billions of dollars)

SITC Product group	1990 Exports	1990 Imports	1990 Balance	Change in balance 1981–87	Change in balance 1987–90	Projected balance change, 1990–93 More than −5	−5 to −3	−3 to −1	−1 to +1	+1 to +3	+3 to +5	More than +5
5-9 Manufactures	297.8	388.8	−91.0	−152.5	41.7							
of which:												
5 Chemicals	39.0	22.5	16.5	−1.5	7.1		X					
61 Leather	0.9	0.9	−0.0	−0.3	0.2				X			
62 Rubber manufactures	2.1	3.5	−1.5	−1.2	0.6				X			
63 Cork and wood	1.2	2.1	−0.9	−0.8	0.5					X		
64 Paper and paper products	5.0	8.5	−3.5	−3.3	0.6					X		
65 Textiles	4.9	6.4	−1.5	−3.9	1.4							
66 Nonmetallic mineral manufactures	3.1	9.9	−6.8	−4.0	−0.0				X			
67 Iron and steel	3.4	9.9	−6.5	0.6	1.4				X			
68 Nonferrous metals	5.2	9.8	−4.6	−1.6	1.0				X			
69 Manufactures of metal, n.e.s.	5.9	8.9	−3.1	−5.1	1.4				X			
72 Specialized industrial machinery	15.3	12.9	2.3	−11.6	4.2				X			
73 Metalworking machinery	2.7	3.7	−0.9	−1.5	−0.1					X		
74 General industrial machinery	15.7	14.5	1.2	−9.2	4.3							
75 Office machines and computers	24.7	26.9	−2.2	−6.0	−2.5			X				
76 Telecommunications and sound-reproducing equipment	9.1	22.3	−13.2	−10.6	2.5					X		
77 Electrical machinery	28.2	33.6	−5.4	−10.3	3.1					X		
78 Road vehicles	29.4	72.2	−42.9	−39.7	8.8	X						
79 Other transport equipment	31.8	7.3	24.5	−0.8	12.5						X	
81 Plumbing and heating equipment	0.7	1.2	−0.6	−0.7	0.0				X			
82 Furniture and parts	1.6	5.0	−3.4	−3.5	0.6				X			
84 Apparel and clothing	2.5	25.5	−23.1	−13.1	−3.8			X				
85 Footwear	0.5	9.6	−9.1	−4.0	−1.8				X			
87 Professional, scientific, and controlling instruments	12.1	6.2	5.9	−1.4	2.7					X		
89 Miscellaneous manufactures	18.1	25.0	−6.9	−10.0	3.4					X		

Source: Historical data, US Department of Commerce.

year from 1991 through 1993. Starting from a very low base, US export growth did average 10.5 percentage points above import growth over the 1987–90 period. But despite favorable conditions in 1990—a relatively weak dollar, a slow US economy, relatively strong growth rates abroad—the margin between US export and import growth rates dropped to 7.5 percentage points in 1990, and the manufactures trade deficit narrowed in 1990 by only $19 billion, to $73.5 billion. In 1991 the deficit narrowed to $47.7 billion, a $25.8 billion improvement that reflected an increase in exports of 9.5 percent and an increase in imports of only 1.1 percent. The low import growth rate was in large measure induced by the recession of 1991. Imports are likely to grow rapidly as the US economy recovers, narrowing the gap between import and export growth rates.

Neither the product group analyses nor the questionnaire survey of manufacturing companies support expectations of export growth remaining substantially greater than import growth over the next few years. The product group analyses indicate that, without significant additional dollar decline or US economic growth rates significantly below those of major competitors, US manufactures trade performance will stagnate by 1993, after some temporary improvement, probably at a level somewhere between the 1990 deficit of $73 billion and the 1991 deficit of $48 billion. Performance thereafter could gradually deteriorate again.

In testimony before the Subcommittee on Trade of the House Committee on Ways and Means on 23 March 1992 (US Congress 1992), C. Fred Bergsten cited the results of projections by William R. Cline at the Institute for International Economics, which indicate very little change in the 1992 trade and current account deficits over 1991. Bergsten characterized the latter as "probably stuck at a plateau of $50 billion to $100 billion—only 1 percent to 2 percent of GNP but still a substantial drain on the economy and requiring steady annual increases in our net foreign debt."

> The $41.7 billion manufactures trade balance improvement that occurred between 1987 and 1990 was concentrated in a relatively few product groups that can be expected either to worsen or to realize only modest further improvements in the next few years. There are no other evident "big winners" that can be expected to provide major gains in the years just ahead.

Five product groups—aircraft, road vehicles, chemicals, general industrial machinery, and specialized industrial machinery—together contributed $36.9 billion of the $41.7 billion 1987–90 improvement in manufactures trade performance, or about 88 percent of the total. Projections indicate, however, that these same five product groups taken together are unlikely to yield further improvement by 1993.

The $12.5 billion gain in the aircraft balance from 1987 to 1990 has almost played out the potential in that product group, with perhaps a further improvement of $3 billion or $4 billion still to come by 1993. The 1987–90 improvement was not a result of improved US competitiveness from dollar depreciation or other US advances, but came from an expansion of the world market for large transport aircraft. Nor would moderate further dollar depreciation much influence US performance in the next few years: given the substantial backlogs in orders for large transport aircraft, trade balances for the next year or two are very much a function of production capacity and delivery schedules. Larger future gains will be inhibited both by the relatively small size of the world aircraft market and by the growing strength of competition from the EC Airbus consortium.

The trade performance of road vehicles, which contributed $8.8 billion to the 1987–90 gains, is likely to worsen, as discussed below. The chemical industry, which from 1987 to 1990 contributed a $7.1 billion gain, is likely to give up its record 1991 performance and fall back to balances at or below those of 1990. General and specialized industrial machinery together contributed $8.5 billion to the 1987–90 improvement, and further gains are likely but will be relatively modest. Gains in several other product groups will continue, but none are likely to be spectacular. And there are no other product groups that offer realistic prospects of stellar US performance in international markets.

> With $72.2 billion in 1990 imports and a $42.9 billion deficit, road vehicles continues to record the largest single US product group deficit. Given the size of this deficit and limited export opportunities in other product groups, a major reduction in US manufactures trade deficits will almost certainly involve significant improvement in this element of US trade. This is unlikely in the next few years, even though recent Japanese actions may signal a less aggressive targeting of US automobile markets, and despite the increasing international competitiveness of US automobile production.

There are structural US road vehicle trade deficits with Canada, Germany, Mexico, and Japan. The major portion of a significant reduction of the road vehicles deficit, however, must involve trade with Japan. The 1990 deficit with Japan was $25.9 billion, down about $4 billion from 1987 levels. Because US automobile export prospects are limited, major improvements in this product group will come about primarily by US-based production capturing a greater share of the US domestic market. This is likely to involve increased production of Japanese vehicles in the United States. However, increased US production by Japanese transplants will increase US imports of parts and components from Japan, reducing the positive effects on the US trade balance.

A reduced US automobile deficit with Japan will also require a decrease in the number of finished vehicles imported from Japan, as well as the movement of parts and components production to the United States. Japanese investment and production plans, however, seem to indicate that rising Japanese automobile production in the United States is intended mostly to supplement, not replace, exports from Japan, allowing for an increased Japanese market share. That combination could push the US vehicle and parts deficits with Japan to new highs into the mid-1990s. On balance, the deficit with Japan in vehicles, parts, and engines is likely to worsen in the next few years, by about $5 billion by 1993. Japan's recent commitment to limit its automobile exports to only 1.65 million units in Japan's fiscal year 1992 could slow this expansion, and may signal recognition of a need to accelerate the expansion both of the assembly of automobiles and of the production of parts and components by Japanese-owned plants in the United States.

Road vehicle production is highly capital and technology intensive. Over time, investment in new plant and equipment and the employment of new technologies and management techniques, much of these perhaps from Japan, can probably once again make US-based production cost competitive. Additional dollar depreciation, particularly against the Japanese yen, would probably speed the transformation.

> The United States is widely perceived as competing best in high-technology products. World markets for these goods, however, are quite limited, and competition is intensifying. Moreover, because most high-technology items can be equally or more efficiently produced abroad, US leadership in the development of technology does not ensure trade surpluses for the United States in the resulting products.

The United States excels in the production of aircraft, with a 49.1 percent share of 1989 world exports to non-US destinations. The global 1990 US surplus in aircraft trade was the largest US single product group surplus, almost as large as the US bilateral road vehicles and engines deficit with Japan.

The world aircraft market grew more slowly than world manufactures exports during the 1980s, and competition intensified with the introduction of Airbus and the entry of some developing countries into aircraft production. European governments are unlikely to give up hard-won market share achieved through their coordinated development and production of aircraft through Airbus. The already large US market share, growing competition from Airbus, and the limited world market inhibit further large US gains. At $53 billion in 1989, world aircraft exports were only 2.4 percent of world manufactures exports and one-fifth the size of world automobile exports.

Also, only 60 percent to 70 percent of the export price of large aircraft, in which US strength lies, reflects value added in the United States. This highlights the increasing globalization of production of the components—engines, airframes, electronic parts—that make up a large transport aircraft.

Professional and scientific instruments is the only manufactures product group other than aircraft in which the US share of world exports tops that of any other country. With a 1990 surplus of $5.9 billion, this product group is one of the few big US winners. But at $44.8 billion in 1989, world exports of this equipment were only 2.1 percent of world manufactures exports. With an already strong 1989 export market share (28.4 percent of world exports to non-US destinations) together with rising US imports and increasing Japanese and Asian NIC export shares, prospects for very large additional US gains are slim.

A $16.5 billion surplus in 1990 and an $18.9 billion surplus in 1991 are evidence of US strength in chemicals, in many respects a high-technology industry. But US chemicals trade performance is likely to wane as industrializing countries bring new capacity on stream. Not only will this new capacity incorporate the latest technology, but in several cases it will draw on low-cost feedstocks, diminishing the competitive position of US-based production. The new capacity is also expected to increase global supplies more rapidly than the likely growth of global demand.

Strong performance in R&D and technological leadership in developing new products are essential to strong manufactures trade performance, especially in high-technology industries. But inventing new products and manufacturing them are different undertakings. Leadership in developing new technologies does not alone ensure that the resulting products can be produced competitively in the United States. US companies have often been unable to translate new inventions or technological leads into competitive US-based manufactures production. For example, despite US technological prowess in computers, the United States runs deficits in its computer trade. Similarly, inventing or taking an early technological lead in videocassette recorders, numerically controlled machine tools, integrated circuits, and televisions has not led to trade surpluses in these items.

There are relatively few product groups with large world export values in which the United States is sufficiently competitive to benefit from gradual modest changes in the global macroeconomic climate that are likely to occur in the next few years. On the other hand, the United States now runs structural trade deficits in several product groups that loom large in world trade. Exchange rate changes sufficient to restore balance to this latter group of industries are not the answer: depreciation of the dollar of such magnitude as to bring the entire current account into substantial surplus—an unlikely prospect—would be required.

Substantial changes in trade balances might be motivated by moderate exchange rate and growth rate changes in general and special industrial machinery, iron and steel, power-generating machinery, and electrical machinery. Even in these products, however, the gains may prove quite limited.

US-based production has regained a high degree of competitiveness in general and specialized industrial machinery. US trade performance in these two product groups combined improved by $8.5 billion from 1987 to 1990. The world market in these products is large: $199.8 billion in 1989, or 9.5 percent of world manufactures exports. US import shares remain well above earlier levels, however, and despite the improvement since 1987, these two product groups in 1990 produced a combined surplus of only $3.5 billion. Both industries are price sensitive, and a significant portion of US-based production has migrated abroad, adding to rising production capabilities in other countries.

Export growth rates in these two product groups were waning in the first half of 1991. Exports were up only 6.0 percent for general industrial machinery, compared with 19.0 percent for the first half of 1990. Exports of specialized industrial machinery in the first half of 1991 grew by 5.3 percent, compared with 12.0 percent for the first half of 1990. Both of these export growth rates are probably inadequate to make much headway against the increase in US imports that will come with a return of even moderate US economic growth rates. Without further significant dollar decline against major competitor currencies, including the yen, the United States is unlikely to recoup its 1981 world export market shares or to diminish its shares of world imports in these two categories to near 1981 levels. The effects of earlier dollar declines appear to be largely spent.

Similarly, export gains in the very large and important electrical machinery category, which constituted 7.6 percent of 1989 world manufactures trade, are fading, falling to 8.2 percent in the first half of 1991, which is less than half the first-half 1990 rate and one-fourth the 1988 gain over 1987.

In several other product groups, the growth of structural deficits, manifesting a high degree of dependency on foreign suppliers, has been ongoing for many years but was accelerated by the overly strong dollar of the 1980s. There are several examples, the most important of which is road vehicles (discussed above). The integration of US and Canadian production and markets virtually guarantees an annual US bilateral deficit of at least $8 billion. This deficit will fluctuate, generally enlarging when the US automobile market is strong, but will also be affected by the product mix of sales of the Big Three US automakers, because Canadian production specializes in some types and models.

The structural automotive deficit with Japan is even larger, inasmuch as the dominant portion of demand for Japanese vehicles will not be satisfied by US-based production for at least several years but will continue to be met by imports. The $25.9 billion 1990 deficit with Japan, incurred in a poor sales year, is likely to be near its low point for the foreseeable future, although a particularly weak 1991 will probably result in a modest further temporary shrinkage.

There is also, in effect, a structural deficit in automobile trade with Germany. Although the resulting US deficit is much smaller, demand for German automobiles appears to be firmly lodged in US consumer psyches, probably ensuring an annual deficit of $5 billion or more unless the deutsche mark appreciates substantially above its level of mid-1991, or unless the new Japanese luxury models make a major encroachment on German sales in the United States (with no net gain for the US trade balance). A modest annual road vehicle and parts deficit with Mexico also seems assured.

The list does not, however, end with automobiles. There are a number of other manufacturing industries, many of them labor intensive, in which the United States clearly has lost competitive advantage. For example, large, chronic deficits can be expected in apparel, footwear, paper and paper products, electronic parts and components, furniture, and miscellaneous manufactures, including toys, games, and musical instruments. Production of these items has largely moved offshore and is unlikely to return in the foreseeable future. Dollar depreciation against the currencies of the developed countries does not significantly affect these deficits, which are incurred primarily with developing nations. Moreover, as the currencies of current suppliers like Taiwan and Korea appreciate against the dollar, other industrializing, low-wage countries such as China will take their place.

Another industry in structural deficit is consumer electronics. Because Japan now dominates consumer electronics design and marketing, US trade balances in this product group are vulnerable to a continuing series of fads in new consumer electronic products. Just as early Japanese dominance in VCRs cost the United States tens of billions of dollars in trade deficits, so it is likely that large deficits will be incurred in succeeding new products. For example, 1992's fad may be the mini-compact disc Sony Walkman. Later in this decade Japanese leadership in high-definition television could result in very large US deficits, unless recent technological advances in the United States can be successfully applied by US firms.

The surviving US production of iron and steel and manufactures of metal is more competitive than in earlier years, but the remaining competitive domestic capacity is inadequate to meet US needs, and substantial deficits will persist. Many of the imports in these product groups now come from developing countries. This lack of adequate US capacity and of any realistic prospect for rebuilding it all but guarantee structural deficits in these industries.

The 1990 US deficits in the product areas with structural deficits discussed above totaled over $115 billion. Some of these deficits can only be expected to increase given a reasonably strong US economy. In others, modest deficit reductions may be possible but will be difficult to achieve. Persistent deficits in some sectors are, of course, a normal situation. Indeed, they are the manifestation of comparative advantages among nations. In industries where the United States is in profound structural deficit, it is useless to expect exchange rate changes to restore trade balance: any depreciation of the dollar sharp enough to eliminate the deficits in these industries would also render the strongest US industries supercompetitive and produce a significant surplus in the overall current account. For political as well as economic reasons, that is not likely to happen, nor indeed would such an extreme fall in the dollar's value be desirable, given the impact it would have on US living standards.

All this is not to say, however, that depreciation of the dollar against *some* currencies is not desirable. As discussed below, there is evidence that the Japanese yen remains significantly undervalued in dollar terms when the appropriate real exchange rate measure is used.

> Growing natural resource limitations ensure continuing deficits in some US manufactures.

With US sources of several nonferrous metal ores depleting, and environmental regulations and transportation costs discouraging the importation of ores for smelting, US deficits in refined nonferrous metals will continue. These deficits will fluctuate with the unit prices of the commodities imported and with the demand for imports, which is essentially a function of US economic growth rates. The weak position of the US nonferrous metals industry also contributes to a weakened US competitive position in some basic manufactures from metals.

Diamonds offer another example of the effects of natural resource limitations. In 1990 the US deficit in precious and semiprecious stones (mostly diamonds) was $4.2 billion. As prices rise and US affluence grows, this deficit can only grow.

> Production capacity—the ability of the existing production base to meet the demands of both domestic and export markets—is not in general an important limitation on US manufactures exports. Lack of a significant production base in some types of products (for example, consumer electronics) will, however, inhibit improved trade performance by holding up the level of imports.

A small portion of the questionnaire survey respondents (chapter 6) did indicate lack of capacity to be a factor inhibiting their exports and holding up their imports, but these restraints appear to be limited to selected individual products with relatively small export markets. It is difficult to find significant examples where a reduction of US consumption would be required to make production available for export that is now preempted by the needs of domestic US markets. There are, of course, several product lines in which there is little or no US-based production because would-be investors perceive that such production would not be competitive. But, by way of contrast, the largest single US deficit category is road vehicles, an industry with substantial overcapacity in the United States. Plants of US companies are being retired while a large volume of imports continues and newer, more modern Japanese plants are being built in the United States. In essence, the US capacity problem in automobiles and several other products is not the inhibition of exports due to lack of supply; rather the problem is one of lack of capacity that is competitive in US and foreign markets.

There have been important changes since 1981 in the geographical composition of world demand for manufactured goods. Some of these changes have been unfavorable to US trade.

The decline in US trade performance that began in 1981 and the limited recovery to date reflect in part lagging purchasing power in the Latin American and OPEC countries. In 1981, 19.5 percent of US manufactures exports went to Latin America, much of it paid for by heavy Latin American borrowing. Another 9.9 percent went to OPEC countries, flush with cash from high oil prices. The United States held on to its large share of world exports of manufactures to Latin America from 1981 to 1989, but that market along with many other developing-country markets shrank during the 1980s. In 1990 Latin America took only 14.5 percent of US manufactures exports, the OPEC countries only 3.3 percent.

US manufactures exports to Latin America declined during most of the 1980s, but in 1990 they were up to $43.2 billion, compared with $32.7 billion in 1981. US exports to Latin America rose significantly in 1991, particularly to Mexico. Even with this recent increase, however, the growth of the Latin American market lags far behind that of world markets. Had Latin America's growth of manufactures imports from the world kept pace with world growth in manufactures trade, US exports to Latin America would have been about $35 billion higher in 1990 than they actually were. US exports to OPEC countries did even less well and in 1990 were only $10.2 billion, still well below the $16.3 billion level of 1981.

Even the recovery of both markets to 1981 levels would not eliminate the US current account deficit. In any case, in neither market is there any assurance of strong growth over the next several years, although increasing acceptance of economic reforms in several Latin American countries is raising optimism about the area's prospects (see Williamson 1990). To restore current account balance, the United States will have to increase its exports to other markets from 1990 levels to make up for the loss of purchasing power in these two groups of countries.

Ongoing changes in the product composition of US and world manufactures trade also appear unfavorable to the United States.

As the US and world economies mature, the composition of demand for manufactured goods is shifting away from industrial materials (chemicals, SITC 5, and basic manufactures, SITC 6) to finished goods (machinery and transportation equipment, SITC 7, and miscellaneous manufactures, SITC 8). US international market competitiveness has remained strong in chemicals and has not declined greatly in industrial materials, but has suffered major reverses in finished goods, with US finished-goods imports increasing much more dramatically than US exports.

Unless reversed, the decline in competitiveness in finished goods suggests that achieving any given US trade balance will be increasingly difficult. Continued maturation of the US and world economies and a resumption of US economic growth will lead to a resumption of growth of US imports of finished goods that will not be compensated for by US export gains in industrial materials and is unlikely to be matched by compensating US finished-goods export gains. It appears that the decline in finished-goods competitiveness is, in large measure, the result of investment in US manufacturing falling behind that of foreign competitors, a situation that will not be quickly reversed. Moreover, improved market competitiveness through price changes induced by exchange rate movements is more difficult to achieve in finished goods, with their differentiated product characteristics, than in the relatively more homogeneous industrial materials.

The extensive globalization of world markets and production in recent decades is evidence that many large firms have found production in foreign markets a more effective way to compete in those markets than by exporting from the home country. In a world of stiff competition for manufactures markets, some firms and workers will lose and some will gain from continued flows of foreign direct investment. On balance, however, these flows are likely to be in the best long-term interest of US workers, firms, and the current account.

US manufactures trade is dominated by the exports and imports of multinational corporations. About two-thirds of US manufactures exports in 1988 were shipped by US- and foreign-owned multinational firms, and almost one-fourth of US manufactures exports that same year were from US parent firms to their own affiliates abroad.

The intense international competition in many manufacturing industries and the globalization of markets and production have led many large firms to view production at sites close to their overseas markets as essential to remaining viable in those markets. Asked to indicate the importance of various factors in making investment and location decisions, 52 percent of our questionnaire survey respondents with annual sales over $1 billion cited "globalizing favors foreign investment" as extremely or very important. A somewhat larger share (59 percent) listed globalization as an extremely or very important factor in holding down the growth of US exports.

Investment in foreign-based production offers firms several advantages over exporting from the home country. Among the potential benefits are reductions in a variety of costs, including transportation and often wage costs; the ability to provide better service to customers; and insulation from unpredictable exchange rate movements and other factors (such as stricter regulation or higher taxation) that may make the home country a less desirable environment for manufacturing.

When US multinationals invest in foreign-based production capacity, obviously the resulting production will replace some US exports. But if those exports would otherwise have been replaced by foreign-owned and foreign-based production, then investment abroad by US multinationals offers a better alternative both from the perspective of the company concerned and from that of US workers and the overall US current account. At a minimum, the profits from the firm's overseas operations, when repatriated, will contribute to the US international investment account; royalties from the licensing of technology to the foreign affiliate, together with other fees and charges, provide additional earnings. But the advantages go well beyond these earnings from foreign production: foreign manufacturing affiliates of US firms also obtain many of their inputs from the parent firm. These exports from the United States would probably have been forgone, and the associated jobs would have been lost, had a wholly foreign firm captured the market. Similarly, direct investments by foreign firms in the United States may preserve US production of goods that would otherwise be imported, although in this case profits and royalties flow outward, and these and the already noted propensity of foreign affiliates to import from the home country work to the detriment of the US current account. Nonetheless, foreign direct investment, in either or both directions, offers US-based production in some manufacturing industries its best chance of remaining internationally competitive.

Extensive foreign direct investment appears to have made a palpable contribution to the competitiveness of certain US industries. For example, chemicals is perhaps the most globalized of all major manufacturing industries. US chemical companies have $38.7 billion in direct investments abroad, and foreign direct investments in the US chemical industry alone total some $41.7 billion. Chemicals is also one of the most internationally competitive of US industries, adding over $20 billion to the US current account in 1990 both through net exports ($16.5 billion) and through net investment income, royalties and license fees, and service charges ($3.6 billion). Both US direct investments in foreign chemical production and foreign investments in the US industry are widely credited with maintaining and enhancing the US industry's strength in world markets. The US chemical industry has been able, because of its large overseas investments, to amortize its enormous R&D expenses over a vastly larger sales base than the domestic market alone would provide. At the same time, foreign investment gives the US industry access to much of the latest foreign technology and stimulates competition in the US market.

In analogous fashion, Japanese direct investment in the US automobile industry has arguably reduced the deficit in that product group by many billions of dollars from what it would have been had Japanese automobile firms supplied the same number of vehicles in the form of imports. Of course, the same mitigating factors apply as for US direct investment abroad: the profits from the

Japanese transplants' sales boost the Japanese, not the US, net international investment balance, and their inputs are more likely to come from Japanese sources than if the same units were produced by US-based firms. Even so, the automobile industry is one in which US employment would be much less and the US trade balance much worse without foreign investment.

> As foreign firms continue to expand their overseas production and to assert technological leadership in domains where US firms were formerly dominant, foreign direct investment in the United States will in all likelihood play a key role in trimming and eventually eliminating the US current account deficit. This will come about largely in response to economic forces, but political factors will play a role in setting the pace of this movement.

Foreign direct investment in the United States increased dramatically during the second half of the 1980s, although its growth slowed sharply in the early 1990s. Dollar depreciation from current levels and other US macroeconomic changes that help to narrow the current account deficit would be likely to motivate the movement of much additional foreign-based production to the United States.

The book value of foreign direct investment in the US manufacturing sector already approaches that of US manufacturing direct investment abroad. However, the earning potential and hence the market value of foreign operations in the United States remain well below those of US firms' operations abroad. In addition, foreign subsidiaries in the United States, which are in general more recently established than US subsidiaries abroad, tend to import a relatively larger share of their inputs from the home country (Graham and Krugman 1991). These considerations indicate that it will be some years before the extent of US production by foreign multinationals matches the overseas production of their US counterparts. In the meantime, this greater capacity of US than of foreign multinationals to engage in production outside the home country leaves foreign firms more reliant at the moment on exports to serve the US market than are US firms in serving foreign markets.

> Even as some US firms have led the world in the direction of globalization of markets and production, many firms that are potential exporters remain preoccupied with the domestic market. Their lack of commitment to exporting represents a missed opportunity to make substantial inroads in the US current account deficit.

Many US companies have never had the export orientation common to their foreign competitors. The US market has long been so large that US firms often have tended to concentrate on domestic opportunities and to treat foreign markets as residuals. Forty-four percent of questionnaire respondents noted "export market not important enough to justify devoting major attention" as an important, very important, or extremely important factor holding back export growth. Other factors than the perception of meager opportunities abroad also make firms reluctant to commit substantial resources to exporting: for example, 45 percent of our respondents cited "uncertainty about future exchange rates" in the same three importance categories, and 44 percent cited US export controls as an extremely important, very important, or important factor inhibiting export growth. These perceptions indicate that restrictive and unpredictable government export control policies and macroeconomic policies that lead to an overly strong dollar are important inhibitors of an expansion of US exports. As the US economy recovers from the 1991 recession, the increase in domestic demand may lead some firms to abandon any export initiatives the recession pressed on them and to revert their focus to US markets.

> Many foreign firms are strongly endowed with the aggressive export orientation that their export-shy US counterparts lack. The United States, still the world's largest single-country market and the largest importer of manufactured goods, remains the number-one target of many foreign exporters, despite a gradual secular weakening of the exchange rate of the dollar and increasing US political pressures for protectionism.

The United States, which absorbed 20.9 percent of manufactures exports by the rest of the world in 1989 and led the world in imports in 23 of 27 manufactures product groups, is very often the most logical single target market for exporters in other countries, particularly the newly industrializing countries. The export-led growth strategies of these countries are usually implemented primarily through exports of manufactures. The size and affluence of the US market, its uniform standards, excellent transportation and communications systems, and unmatched wholesale and retail trade distribution systems typically offer prospective exporters unmatched sales volume opportunities and economies of scale in marketing and distribution. Once foreign companies successfully penetrate the US market, they are loath to give up their market share and will struggle hard to retain it. Indeed, for some the US market may become so important, absorbing such a large portion of their total output, that they literally cannot afford to lose it.

> A larger part of the $146.8 billion decline in US manufactures trade performance from 1981 to 1987 was accounted for by increased import penetration of the US market than by shrinking US world export shares. Limitations on the US ability to increase exports imply that a major if not the dominant portion of any large improvement in US manufactures trade performance will be accomplished by replacing foreign-based production for the US market with US-based production.

Over the 1981–87 period the US share of world manufactures exports to non-US destinations declined from 18.5 percent to 14.5 percent. The US share of world imports from non-US sources (non-US exports) rose from 18.0 percent in 1981 to 27.0 percent in 1985, before falling to 22.8 percent in 1987. In 1988 and 1989 the US export shares increased and the import shares declined. By

1989 the US export share was 15.8 percent, still 2.7 percentage points less than its 1981 share, and the 1989 US import share was 21.0 percent, 3 percentage points higher than in 1981, for a combined 5.7-percentage-point share balance decline. Over the decade of the 1980s the export shares of the major industrial countries have typically declined modestly as the Asian NICs and many developing countries enlarged their roles in world manufactures trade or entered world manufactures markets for the first time. For example, Japan's share of world manufactures exports declined from 14.6 percent in 1981 to 12.8 percent in 1989, and the EC share of exports to non-EC destinations fell from 23.6 percent to 18.8 percent. Some decline in the US export share was therefore to be expected. There has not, however, been a matching decline in the US import share from 1981 levels.

Analyses of market-share data indicate that returning to balance solely by means of export expansion would require US export shares even higher than those of 1981. But in a world of increasing competition in manufactures, with new producers continuing to come on stream, there are relatively few product groups in which further major US export-share gains can be realistically expected, let alone export shares topping those of 1981. Instead, significant improvement will require both increases in US export shares and decreases in US import shares.

In terms of benefit to the domestic economy, recapture of increasing shares of the domestic market is as beneficial as an equal amount of export expansion. There are several factors that are likely to make recapture of domestic markets a faster and surer means of improved trade performance than export expansion. One is simply that wresting US market share from foreign competitors ought to be easier than beating the same competition in their own or in third-country markets: if a company cannot win in its home market, how can it expect to win in foreign markets? Another factor is the already-noted lack of commitment of many US companies to exporting and their tendency to treat foreign markets as a residual.

The automobile industry is a prime example of a product group in which trade performance improvement is most likely to come from recapture of the US market by US-based production. The large US road vehicle and engine deficits ($44 billion in 1990) are most unlikely to be significantly reduced by an expansion of US exports. Instead, a large reduction in this deficit, which as noted above is probably essential to any major further reduction in the US manufactures trade deficit, will come about primarily by the movement of Japanese production for the US market to the United States—that is, by Japanese direct investment in the United States. Consumer electronics is another high-deficit product group in which the US market is supplied mostly by foreign-based production, and in which significant deficit reduction is likely to have to come about less from expanded US exports than from additional foreign direct investments in the United States.

Enhanced market competitiveness of US-based production in world markets—the ability to sell enough in US and foreign markets to balance the current account—depends fundamentally on improved US price competitiveness, including quality and product performance considerations. The relevant measure of this competitiveness is the relative prices of those goods that matter to US trade—not broad purchasing power parity calculations. Productivity gains are preferred over dollar depreciation as a source of competitiveness improvements, because depreciation puts downward pressure on US living standards. But US productivity gains have so far been inadequate to score advances on key foreign competitors large enough to eliminate US current account deficits.

Changes in US macroeconomic policies and US saving and consumption rates are essential to improving US trade performance. But US and foreign buyers will switch from foreign- to US-made products not because of these changes in themselves, but only if they make US products more price competitive, including considerations of quality, style, and performance. Price competitiveness is best measured, not by comparing US and foreign prices across the whole gamut of goods and services—the purchasing power parity approach—but by the relationship between prices in US and foreign markets of those goods that loom largest in US trade. Given the dominance of manufactured goods in US trade, it is these goods that figure most strongly in the calculation.

In fact, it is the relative prices of goods in a handful of manufacturing industries—for example, road vehicles and consumer electronics—that exert most of the pull on the US current account toward or away from balance. Since much of US trade in these industries is with Japan, to say that US production in these industries lacks price competitiveness is to say that changes in the yen-dollar exchange rate must be considered as at least part of the solution.

There is a case to be made that the yen remains undervalued against the dollar despite the sharp rise in its value since early 1985. In his 23 March 1992 testimony before the House Ways and Means Subcommittee on Trade, C. Fred Bergsten cited evidence that the yen still needs to appreciate by at least 25 percent against the dollar (i.e., to about 100 yen to the dollar) to restore US industry to competitiveness in world markets (US Congress 1992). The product group analyses of this study lend support to this conclusion. Bergsten also noted that the yen appeared to be similarly undervalued against the European currencies.

US productivity gains at rates faster than those of competitors are the preferred means of achieving increased price competitiveness without exerting the downward pressure on US living standards that comes from dollar depreciation. During the 1980s, although US manufacturing productivity growth appeared quite strong, so did that of several key foreign competitors. The gains in the US manufactures trade account in the 1987–90 period were largely the result of dollar decline.

If sustained US productivity gains that exceed those of competing nations cannot be achieved, further dollar depreciation is preferable to more industry- or product-specific measures to restore competitiveness, because depreciation at least allows market forces to sort out which industries will benefit from the resulting expansion of efforts and replacement of imports, thus permitting resources to be allocated among industries most efficiently.

> Continuing large US manufactures trade deficits and the prospect of little or no improvement in performance over the next several years—notwithstanding a dollar exchange rate that has returned to levels that earlier generated manufactures trade surpluses—indicate there has been a significant decline in the international competitiveness of US-based manufactures production compared with 1981, the year of the last US manufactures trade surplus.

Analyses in this study show that the competitiveness of US-based manufacturing has declined relative to that of foreign competitors, and that US manufacturing's ability to contribute to rising US living standards has slipped over the last decade. Real dollar exchange rates of the 1988–90 period were roughly comparable to those of 1978–80. During the earlier period the United States ran a cumulative manufactures trade surplus of $23.6 billion, equivalent to 3.1 percent of US manufactures exports and imports for the period. But from 1988 to 1990 the United States incurred a cumulative trade deficit of $271.3 billion, equivalent to 13.7 percent of US manufactures exports and imports during the period. In large measure, as previously noted, the decline manifested itself in worsened performance in finished goods (SITCs 7 and 8), a rapidly growing and increasingly important factor in world trade.

Moreover, export and import price data indicate that exchange rate movements and other factors have only marginally lowered the relationship of US export prices to US import prices in manufactured goods compared with the 1982–84 period, when the US dollar was overly strong. This evidences an ability of some competitors, particularly Japan, to absorb much of the effects of dollar decline, partly through higher productivity growth rates. In other cases it may reflect an ability to sacrifice fat profit margins. In still other cases it may reflect the emergence of new low-cost suppliers.[3]

> Recently reported comparisons of US and foreign manufacturing productivity gains show the United States lagging behind some key competitors, while others are excluded from the statistics. These results and recent US levels of spending for capital investment and R&D in the manufacturing sector give little reason to expect that productivity gains in the years just ahead will provide the basis for marked improvements in the market competitiveness of

---

3. For a discussion of the pass-through of exchange rate changes in more aggregated terms, see Krugman (1991, 33).

US manufactures. Any improvement is likely to have to come from further depreciation of the dollar, although slow or negative US growth rates could improve the trade balance.

Recent data comparing US and foreign manufacturing productivity gains have been widely heralded as signaling a turnaround in US competitiveness: these data show the United States besting 9 of 11 other countries of the Organization for Economic Cooperation and Development (OECD) in the 1980–89 period. Even if accepted at face value, however, the data are at best inconclusive. The data indicate that US manufacturing productivity rose faster than comparable rates in countries that provide 34.6 percent of US manufactures imports and at rates below those of competitors that provide 27.3 percent of US imports, including Japan. The OECD data, however, do not include countries that in 1990 provided 38.1 percent of US manufactures imports—a group that includes the Asian NICs and other increasingly competitive industrializing countries. On the export side, the rate of US productivity increase exceeded those of competitors representing 41.5 percent of US exports but was less than those of competitors representing 16.7 percent of US exports.

Recent patterns of US and competitor investment in R&D and manufacturing plant and equipment and the existing state of competition in major product groups indicate that future US manufacturing productivity gains are unlikely to be sufficient to restore or significantly improve US competitiveness in key product areas in the years immediately ahead. Examination of disaggregated investment spending data reveals that there was not an "investment boom" in US manufacturing during the 1980s. Moreover, much of the manufacturing investment that did occur was in defense- rather than consumer-oriented industries. Plant and equipment modernization in the manufacturing sector did not occur at a rate that is likely to provide sustained improvement in the international market competitiveness of US manufacturing. The net capital stock increased only very modestly and continued to age. The rapid technological obsolescence of computers and some other modern equipment demands higher rates of investment than were necessary in earlier years to keep pace with foreign competitors.

From 1981 to 1989 the manufacturing sector's net capital stock rose by only 0.8 percent, retail trade's by 5.2 percent, and services' by 6.2 percent. The investment boom occurred instead in sectors other than manufacturing, including some now-overbuilt services sectors: retail and financial services, shopping malls, office buildings, and the like.

The greater global competitiveness of US firms and US-designed products than of US-based production in most industries supports the conclusion that the diminished market competitiveness of US-based manufactures production is not attributable primarily to US management. Rather it is evidence that the general environment for manufacturing in the United States has declined relative to that of foreign competitors, lowering investment in manufacturing below the level needed to increase market competitiveness through new products and productivity gains.

The sales and earnings of US manufacturing's direct investments abroad exceed the sales and earnings of foreign investments in the United States. If America's trade balance were measured on the basis of ownership rather than production location, the large US manufactures trade deficits would be transformed into large trade surpluses.[4] This ability of US companies to compete better than US production implies competitive disadvantages in the latter compared with foreign alternatives, a situation that can only be resolved by improving the general environment for manufacturing in the United States.

Lagging investment in US manufacturing compared with other sectors during the 1980s suggests that investors recognize that investment in manufacturing has been less attractive (because of tax policies favoring nonmanufacturing investment, a too-strong dollar, and other reasons) than other US investment alternatives. Similarly, lagging levels of investment in US manufacturing compared with manufacturing investment in Japan and other major trading partners indicate that investment in US manufacturing is considered less attractive than manufacturing investments in key foreign competitor economies.

> Although most of the US current account deficit can be accounted for by deficits in oil trade and in a relatively few manufacturing industries, this is not to say that the United States' competitiveness problems can be resolved by initiatives, public or private, targeted toward these or other particular sectors or industries. A more comprehensive approach is called for that recognizes the dynamic interdependence of US manufacturing industries and the deterioration of the broader investment environment for manufacturing.

Our examination of individual product groups makes apparent the integrated and interdependent nature of US manufacturing—the presence of a chain of primary and intermediate products and processes and trade among industries. Although a major portion of the swings in US trade balances is concentrated in a relatively few product groups, the products included embrace essentially the whole spectrum of manufacturing's output, from many of the seemingly mundane components in automobiles and unsophisticated industrial machinery to the high technologies employed in building wide-bodied jet aircraft. Given these interdependencies, successfully manufacturing a product in the United States will typically require strong, competitive supplier industries and a high level of manufacturing know-how in a wide range of manufacturing industries. This is only likely to result from improvement in the general economic environment for manufacturing, affecting the entire spectrum of US-based manufactures pro-

---

4. Kravis and Lipsey (1989) found that, as of 1985, US-owned firms in the aggregate had not suffered any decline in global market share.

duction, compared with foreign-based production alternatives. Neither the overall manufactures trade performance problem nor the problems of any particular industry will be permanently solved by initiatives directed at particular technologies or specific industries or sectors.

Improvement instead depends largely—but by no means solely—upon steps to motivate increased US investment in R&D and plant and equipment across the range of US manufacturing industries. Of course, not every manufacturing industry will prosper or even survive in such an improved environment, but market forces should most efficiently sort out which are best able to compete and which are not.

Macroeconomic policies—fiscal and monetary—are an important determinant of the investment climate and of any comprehensive approach to improve the environment for manufacturing in the United States. However, the decline in international competitiveness that has occurred in most US manufacturing sectors is unlikely to be reversed by fiscal and monetary policies alone.

Macroeconomic policies were important factors in the growth of large US manufactures trade deficits in the 1980s. The nearly universal decline in the trade performance of individual manufacturing product groups during the 1981–87 period was the mirror image of macroeconomic policies—a lax fiscal policy and stringent monetary policy—that greatly strengthened the dollar and resulted in large net capital inflows. Similarly, the recovery since 1987 in individual product groups has been quite broad-based as the dollar has declined.

Fiscal and monetary policies aimed at further reducing and eventually eliminating the need for net capital inflows are a necessary condition, but are not likely in themselves to restore US manufacturing's ability to compete in international markets to earlier levels without continuing dollar depreciation. Macroeconomic policy tools are unlikely to arrest the secular decline in the productivity of US manufacturing relative to its competitors.[5] The return of the dollar to its levels of the early 1980s, when the United States enjoyed manufactures and current account surpluses, has not eliminated US trade deficits. The better overall US performance in industrial supplies than in finished goods is a manifestation of the poor relative performance of the more labor-intensive segments of US-based production and the need for increased productivity. The latter will require, among other things, increased investment in R&D and plant and equipment and improvements in human capital.

An improved general environment for investment in US-based production would speed investment in US manufacturing by US-owned companies as well as increased foreign

---

5. Krugman (1991, 21) cites a general agreement that there has been a secular decline in the trade value of the dollar on the order of 2 percent per year or less.

investment in US manufacturing. Both will be vital to an improved market competitiveness of US-based manufacturing achieved without continuing dollar depreciation.

For US manufacturing to prevail in an increasingly competitive global marketplace will require a new recognition of manufacturing's central role and its vulnerability to foreign competition. It will also require new, positive policies that create a more attractive US environment for R&D and investment in a wide range of US manufacturing activities. That R&D and investment can be expected to come from both foreign and domestic sources: given the increasing frequency with which foreign firms hold the technological lead in important products and processes, their participation in a reinvigorated US manufacturing sector is to be encouraged.

Policy Implications

The Critical Role of Government Policies

This study has identified a broad decline in the international competitiveness of US-based manufacturing. Because, as we have seen, a strong manufacturing sector is essential to overall US international competitiveness and to improving standards of living in the United States, the fact of such a decline is a matter of paramount concern.

The loss of US manufacturing competitiveness stems from many causes. In part it simply reflects the fact that foreign manufacturing is much better now than it was in the early postwar period. US management and labor, perhaps resting on their laurels from earlier decades of manufacturing dominance, also have no doubt contributed to lagging US performance. There are doubtless many other factors at work. But US government policies—primarily those of the federal government, but also those of state and local governments—have also had important effects on manufacturing's past performance and will certainly play a key role in its future competitiveness.

What can federal, state, and local governments do to improve the trade performance and international competitiveness of US manufacturing? Government largely decides in what kind of environment businesses must function and compete. It taxes and subsidizes. It regulates extensively. Its decisions profoundly influence what can be profitably produced and what cannot, and what can be exported or imported and what cannot. It sets health, safety, pollution control, pension benefit, and myriad other standards that in in no small measure determine the costs of doing business.

These things have always been the proper domain of government. But what is new and perhaps insufficiently appreciated by many is that the *global* environment—which no single-country government alone can determine, but in which US manufacturing must compete—has changed dramatically. On the one hand, the United States is now more dependent on international trade than ever before. It must import increasing shares of its oil and other raw materials consumption. It is also increasingly dependent on foreign technologies. These imports must eventually be paid for by exports; net capital inflows can finance net imports only temporarily.[6]

At the same time, the foreign competition that US-based producers face is tougher than ever before. When the United States held a dominant position—in many cases a monopoly—in world manufactures production, US-based production was much less sensitive to the costs imposed by taxes, environmental and other regulations, health insurance and pension costs, and other programs mandated by state and federal governments. US firms could often absorb higher costs than their foreign counterparts and still prevail. Today, however, US manufacturing is no longer so much stronger than its foreign competitors that domestic economic policies can be made independently of international considerations. Policy decisions can impose such a heavy cost on US manufacturers as to price their products out of world markets.

In addition, the costs imposed by government policy can determine investment decisions to a far greater extent than in previous decades. US-based production today has few enduring advantages over many alternative production sites in other countries. In a world where US and foreign production locations compete on a much more equal basis, the balance can tip in favor of the location that imposes the lower regulatory and other policy-related costs.

The increased foreign competition facing US manufacturers did not result solely from the spontaneous profit-maximizing efforts of foreign firms. The governments of many of the United States' competitors, recognizing the central role of manufactures trade, consciously direct their policies toward providing within their borders an economic environment that attracts high levels of investment in manufacturing. These countries actively seek a strong domestic manufacturing sector not only for the employment, value-added, and living-standard benefits of a strong international trade position, but also for its catalytic effects on other sectors of the economy. They therefore use a variety of means to encourage investment in manufacturing, sometimes including outright subsidies but typically more subtly employing fiscal, monetary, tax, regulatory, trade, and other policies toward this end. When a number of developed and developing countries

---

6. See, for example, Feldstein (1992).

adopt these practices, the result is an intense international rivalry to attract manufacturing investment and to develop national strength in manufacturing.

US economic policies, meanwhile, have tended to focus primarily on current employment and economic growth rates, rather than on the longer-term health and strength of manufacturing in international competition. Indeed, the United States has too often followed policies that actually put manufacturing at a disadvantage compared with other sectors. During the 1980s, for example, an ill-considered mix of fiscal, monetary, tax, and regulatory policies triggered an extended consumption boom and in some sectors (but not manufacturing) an investment boom as well. The result was, in aggregate terms, a rapidly growing economy with low rates of unemployment. But these high levels of consumption and investment were financed in large measure by a net inflow of foreign capital that caused the dollar to become overvalued. The overly strong dollar seriously eroded the US manufacturing sector's international competitiveness, produced huge manufactures trade deficits, shifted substantial manufacturing production to foreign countries, reduced US manufacturing employment, and discouraged investment in US based manufacturing.

Now, in the 1990s, several of the sectors that boomed during the 1980s find themselves overbuilt and shrinking (contributing among other things to the savings and loan crisis), yet investment in a diminished manufacturing sector remains inadequate to restore its competitiveness to earlier levels. To correct that inadequacy and to have a chance of restoring US manufacturing to a position of world leadership, US policymakers must recognize the increased sensitivity of US manufactures trade to policy changes. Also required, however, are new, positive policies designed to create a more attractive environment in the United States for R&D and investment in a wide range of manufacturing activities.

Policy Alternatives

Although the role of governments, as we have seen, is critical, there is no simple policy solution—no quick fix. Just as the US trade deficit and the loss of US manufacturing competitiveness in the 1980s were the result of an accumulation of neglectful policies (and some unfortunate events) over a number of years, so the elimination of the deficit and the restoration of competitiveness will require the persistent application of a combination of sound policies—macroeconomic and microeconomic—over an extended period. Merely to continue current policies would be to lock in recent adverse trends and by default to rely on a persistently declining dollar just to maintain whatever competitiveness US goods still have in US and foreign markets.

If there is no silver bullet, nonetheless one broad and perhaps obvious, but difficult-to-implement, recommendation emerges from this study:

> Successfully competing in an ever more integrated and competitive world economy— balancing the US external accounts without the prop of a continually depreciating dollar— will require that policymakers focus consistently on the effects of US policies on the international competitiveness of US business and industry, and in particular on the ability of US-based production of manufactured goods to compete in domestic and foreign markets.

A key factor in the decline of US manufacturing's competitiveness has been lagging private investment in R&D and plant and equipment: the US capital stock grew more slowly in manufacturing than in other sectors in the 1980s, and more slowly in US manufacturing than in other countries' manufacturing sectors. Restoring healthy levels of investment is by no means the whole answer, but it is a critical part of the answer and one where government can have a profound impact. Many other changes are required, such as the adoption of more effective management and motivational techniques. These, however, are not likely to be much facilitated by government actions but are instead up to management to take on its own (Porter 1992). Also, to be sure, a healthy infusion of new public investment—improvements in education, transportation, communication, and other aspects of the nation's infrastructure—would also contribute to US manufacturing's international competitiveness. But without higher levels of private investment in manufacturing industries themselves there is little hope of closing the gap with foreign competitors.

There are probably many reasons, not all of them economic, why investment in US-based manufacturing has fallen. But because government has such a large effect on the economic environment in which business functions, it is reasonable to suspect that government policies have played a very important role in restraining investment. The entire array of microeconomic policies that together determine the climate for manufacturing—tax, regulatory, export control, environmental, and others—is likely to have had the long-term effect of reducing investment in manufacturing below that required to maintain competitiveness. In addition, the macroeconomic—fiscal and monetary—policies of the 1980s clearly resulted in an overly strong dollar that reduced US competitiveness in US and foreign markets, caused large net foreign borrowing, and motivated the movement of some US production abroad—effects that persist in attenuated form today.

Even if one rejects this cause-and-effect assessment, the government policy tools identified above remain the main ways by which a more favorable environment for investment can be shaped. Looking ahead, to create an environment that will improve US trade performance and stimulate significantly higher levels of manufacturing investment, US policymakers should pursue four broad objectives:

Give the manufacturing sector due consideration in the formulation of US strategy in international negotiations and elsewhere.

US international trade negotiations should pursue the adoption of better trade practices by all countries and the reduction of barriers in all forms of trade. But in assigning priorities and in making deals, negotiators should bear in mind that manufactures trade will continue to be the largest and most variable element in US and world trade, and therefore the single most important factor in US trade performance. The focus on services and agriculture in the current Uruguay Round talks in the General Agreement on Tariffs and Trade may well produce significant liberalization in these sectors, but the greater prominence of manufactures in US trade suggests that still more critical areas for agreement lie elsewhere.

Follow macroeconomic policies that eliminate the need for large net external borrowing and the accompanying current account and manufactures trade deficits.

Investors have not forgotten the overly strong dollar of the 1980s and its effects on the competitiveness of US-based manufacturing. Sustained high levels of investment in US manufacturing will be more likely if investors feel confident that the dollar overvaluation, large net capital inflows, and manufactures trade deficits that began in the 1980s are eliminated and prevented from recurring. A return by the United States to net international lending and manufactures trade surpluses would provide an important stimulus to investment in US-based manufacturing. Avoiding wide fluctuations in the US lender-borrower status and the resulting costly disruptions to the manufacturing sector should be an important US policy goal.

Carefully examine each new legislative and regulatory proposal for its effects on the international competitiveness of US manufacturing.

The incremental effects of each new microeconomic intervention on costs and competitiveness may be small, but their cumulative effects can be great. These cost increases must be either passed on to customers in the form of price increases or borne by the affected businesses; choosing the latter course reduces profits and ultimately capital formation.

When the firms on which these costs are imposed are insulated from foreign competition, domestic resource reallocations occur, but the ill effects largely end there. But the same cost increase has different, additional effects on firms that are exposed to foreign competition: it adversely affects those firms' international competitive stance.

To take an example, new environmental regulations may require dry cleaning establishments to acquire new, nonpolluting means of disposing of their chemical wastes. Either the owners of dry cleaning businesses or the consumers of dry cleaning services, or both, will ultimately pay the attendant costs. To the extent the new regulations result in price increases, they may reduce the nation's consumption of dry cleaning services and may shift resources out of dry cleaning and into other industries. But the costs of compliance will not disadvantage domestic producers of dry cleaning services relative to foreign producers that do not face similar requirements, because it is normally impractical to import dry cleaning services.

Now consider a US industry that does compete with foreign producers, at home or abroad. If the costs of the new environmental regulations on that industry are greater than those that foreign-based producers must pay, the US industry is placed at a disadvantage, imports will increase and exports decrease, and manufacturing jobs will be lost. Investment in US-based manufacturing and R&D will become less attractive than investment in other, more insulated US industries—and less attractive than investment in foreign-based production.

Exchange rate movements and other adjustments internal to the economy can theoretically offset these added costs in the long run and restore investment in the affected industry. The effects of those adjustments may, however, be a long time in coming, and the delays may add greatly to the ultimate costs of adjustment. For example, while adjustment is occurring, foreign competitors with higher levels of R&D and investment in plant and equipment may strengthen their hold on US and foreign markets. They may even achieve technological breakthroughs and productivity gains that will be increasingly difficult and costly to match. Domestic manufacturing skills may be eroded and industries may disappear, further raising the difficulty and cost of restoring competitiveness.[7]

The Omnibus Trade and Competitiveness Act of 1988 established a mechanism—the "competitiveness impact statement"—for reviewing the impact of new government initiatives on US competitiveness. This provision of the law has seemingly been ignored, however. Consistent compliance with this provision, as recommended by the Competitiveness Policy Council in its first annual report (1992), would bring a focus to the competitiveness issue that would help prevent the inadvertent impairment of US competitive strengths by ill-considered government actions.

Reexamine the effects of existing tax, regulatory, and other policies on US-based manufacturing.

In assessing the effects of policy initiatives on international competitiveness, policymakers need to consider not just the incremental costs of each proposal

---

7. See Krugman (1991, 14–15) for a discussion of hysteresis—the tendency for lost markets to prove difficult to recapture after the exchange rate changes that caused their loss in the first place have receded.

and how they compare with those imposed on foreign competitors. They need also to consider the total environment for investment in US manufacturing that has resulted from the cumulative effects of prior legislative and regulatory actions.

The environment for investment in US-based manufacturing is, as we have seen, in no small measure the product of a vast number of government laws, rules, and regulations. Item-by-item comparisons of US laws, rules, and regulations with those of other governments for their impact on competitiveness may be useful but are likely to be inconclusive: more favorable treatment by countries abroad in one tax or regulatory domain may or may not be offset by less favorable treatment in others. Yet it would be an impossible task to analyze comprehensively the thousands of laws and regulations and their interactions that together shape the US investment environment, and compare that with the counterpart interacting laws and regulations of dozens of competitors. It is sufficient to note that when all incentives and disincentives to investment in the United States have been weighed by the capital markets, their response has been to invest less in US-based manufacturing than is desirable. The capital markets have thus provided a pragmatic, nonacademic demonstration of the need to improve the environment for investment in US-based manufacturing. Therefore, rather than embark on an unending and inconclusive series of one-by-one comparisons of US and competitor-country policies, the best approach seems to be to accept the capital markets' verdict and to reexamine those policy levers with the most potential for changing investor behavior. Analysis of tax policy—the kinds, levels, and initial incidences of taxes chosen to execute a given fiscal policy—is one particularly important means of exploring how to improve the environment for businesses. US policymakers need to recognize not only that tax policy now plays an important role in shaping the amount of investment within the United States and its allocation between manufacturing and other sectors, but also that it affects the allocation of international investments in manufacturing between the United States and other countries.

A widely held view among the general public in the United States favors heavy taxation of businesses, in the belief that much of the country's tax burden can be laid on the shoulders of large corporations with deep pockets. Yet corporations are, of course, inanimate legal constructs. Far from bearing the ultimate burden of the taxes they pay, they simply pass these costs on to the real people who interact with and within the corporation in various ways: to customers as higher prices, to employees as lower wages, or to shareholders as lower profits. Lower profits indeed affect not only shareholders but everyone in the economy by indirectly raising the cost of capital and lowering corporate R&D and capital investment spending.

Significant changes in the US tax structure will be very difficult to achieve given these widespread misperceptions. However, some changes that should be further investigated include increased R&D and investment tax credits, increased reliance on consumption taxes as an alternative to other forms of taxation, and revisions to the alternative minimum tax laws that especially adversely affect capital-intensive manufacturing industries.

The Outlook for US Manufacturing

A redirection of the focus of US policy to give greater emphasis to manufacturing, as called for in this study, will not come about easily. Indeed, it is likely to require a fundamental change in public and policymakers' perceptions and attitudes. Some continue to regard manufacturing primarily as a generator of pollution, an adversary to be regulated, and a source of tax revenues. If major changes in government policies are to occur, US-based manufacturing will have to be seen instead as a national asset to be sustained and enhanced.

Achieving such a change in attitudes will be difficult, because there is little chance of a visible crisis developing that will focus attention on US manufacturing's relative decline. Continuation of current policies and investment levels will probably *not* result in a discrete, clear-cut disaster that exposes the error of past ways for all to see. The trade and current account deficits will not necessarily expand from present levels and may even narrow in a context of slow US economic growth, further dollar decline, and gradual relative erosion of US standards of living.

In any case, manufacturing will not disappear from US shores whether or not the United States adopts policies designed to compete with other countries for investment in manufacturing. Indeed, manufacturing would survive in the United States even in a even less friendly and sympathetic political and economic environment than the present one, because there is no other way of paying for the net importation of a large portion of US consumption of manufactured goods as well as oil.

Manufactured goods production still accounts for about one-fifth of US GNP on a current-dollar, value-added basis. An accurate accounting is difficult, but if one includes the value of inputs from other sectors, manufacturing probably accounts for something like 30 percent of GNP. By this reckoning, if net imports of manufactured goods were to rise to, for example, only 10 percent of total consumption, the manufactures deficit would then be equivalent to about 3 percent of GNP. Three percent of 1991 GNP would have been $170 billion. Such a deficit, in combination with the US deficit in energy, could not be sustained indefinitely, but would generate economic and political forces that would narrow the manufactures trade deficit.

Thus, a large US manufacturing sector will survive under almost any circumstances, simply because in the United States no other sector has the potential to generate sufficient exports to pay for the net importation of a very large portion of US manufactured goods consumption. A manufacturing sector large enough to supply the great majority of US needs will somehow be kept viable, and manufactures trade deficits will be held to sustainable levels by adjustments in the US and foreign economies. The adjustments on the US side would probably include a consistently depreciating dollar to restrain imports and pump up exports, declining relative wages in manufacturing, the substitution of this cheapened labor for capital, and sufficiently slower US growth to suppress import demand.

Manufactures trade deficits therefore can, at most, provide only a relatively small portion of total US manufactured goods consumption. The postindustrial US society in which US manufacturing shrinks dramatically—seen by some as a means to rid the United States of the pollution manufacturing generates—is unattainable.[8] However, the *kind* of manufacturing sector that survives and the contribution it makes to the US economy will be importantly influenced by the investment environment as shaped in no small measure by government policies. A US manufacturing sector in which investment levels lag behind those of the United States' major trading partners is likely not to be a world-class competitor but a second- or third-rate sector, with lower productivity gains than many of its competitors and fewer new products and processes. It is likely also to be increasingly foreign owned and employ more and more foreign technology. In short, US manufacturing would survive an unfavorable environment, but it would lag behind other countries that choose to provide a more favorable investment climate, and it would not realize its full potential to contribute to the growth of US living standards.

The best prospects for a dynamic, world-class US manufacturing sector will be provided by US policies that create a more favorable environment for investment in US-based R&D and US-based production. Of course, there are no guarantees. Other factors will also be important in deciding the outcome of the competition among industrialized and industrializing nations for manufacturing leadership. But federal and state government policies will do much to shape the outcome, and the wrong policies and a shortfall in investment can ensure the continued decline of US manufacturing and the attendant costs to the US economy as a whole.

Bibliography

American Council on Capital Formation. 1991. *Economic Effects of the Corporate Alternative Minimum Tax.* Washington: American Council on Capital Formation Center for Policy Research.

---

8. See *Business Week*, 3 March 1986, 57, and Renner (1992).

American Council on Capital Formation. 1992. *U.S. Environmental Policy and Economic Growth: How Do We Fare?* Washington: American Council on Capital Formation Center for Policy Research.

Bergsten, C. Fred. 1988. *America in the World Economy: A Strategy for the 1990s.* Washington: Institute for International Economics.

Cline, William R. 1989. "The Dollar, the Budget, and US External Adjustment." Washington: Institute for International Economics (mimeographed, April).

Cohen, Stephen S., and John Zysman. 1987. *Manufacturing Matters: The Myth of the Post-Industrial Economy.* New York: Basic Books.

Competitiveness Policy Council. 1992. *First Annual Report to the President and Congress: Building a Competitive America.* Washington: Competitiveness Policy Council.

Feldstein, Martin. 1992. "The Budget and Trade Deficits Aren't Really Twins." Paper presented at the annual meeting of the American Economic Association (January).

Heim, Joseph A., and W. Dale Compton, eds. 1992. *Manufacturing Systems: Foundation of World Class Practice.* Washington: National Academy Press.

Kravis, Irving B., and Robert E. Lipsey. 1989. "Technological Characteristics of Industries and the Competitiveness of the U.S. and Its Multinational Firms." *NBER Working Papers 2933.* Cambridge, MA: National Bureau of Economic Research.

Krugman, Paul R. 1991. *Has the Adjustment Process Worked?* POLICY ANALYSES IN INTERNATIONAL ECONOMICS 34. Washington: Institute for International Economics.

Porter, Michael E. 1990. *The Competitive Advantage of Nations.* New York: The Free Press.

Porter, Michael E. 1992. "Investment Behavior and Time Horizon in American Industry," confidential draft paper. Boston: Harvard Business School (February).

Renner, Michael. 1992. "Creating Sustainable Jobs in Industrial Countries." In Lester R. Brown, ed., *State of the World 1992: A Worldwatch Institute Report on Progress Toward a Sustainable Society.* New York: W. W. Norton, 138–54.

US Congress. House of Representatives. Committee on Ways and Means. Subcommittee on Trade. 1992. *United States International Competitive Position in the Motor Vehicle and Motor Vehicle Parts Sector,* hearings, 102 Cong., 2nd sess., 23 March.

Williamson, John. 1990. *The Progress of Policy Reform in Latin America.* POLICY ANALYSES IN INTERNATIONAL ECONOMICS 28. Washington: Institute for International Economics.

Appendix

Appendix: Methodology and Statistics

Trade Data Bases

This study utilizes two forms of empirical data: world trade data and US trade data. The world trade data are drawn from a World Manufactures Trade Data Base (WMTDB) constructed for this study and described below. The US trade data are from official US Department of Commerce sources in three forms:

- US trade data from the Bureau of the Census in Standard International Trade Classification (SITC) format, Revision 2, for 1981–88

- US trade data from the Bureau of the Census in SITC format, Revision 3, for 1983–90

- US international transactions (current account) data, from the Bureau of Economic Analysis of the US Department of Commerce, in National Income and Products Account (NIPA) format.

The World Manufactures Trade Data Base

To quantify world manufactures trade by individual product group, a large electronic data base was constructed for use in this study. Detailed current data in a standardized SITC format for electronic processing are not available from all countries of the world. Not all nations report trade data to the United Nations in the prescribed SITC format (for example, Eastern Europe and the Soviet Union had, at the time the WMTDB was compiled, their own separate nomenclature). Furthermore, the reporting of many developing countries often is delayed for several years, lacks detail, and is of very poor quality. To provide the most recent information in the disaggregated form required for this study, the WMTDB was constructed using the mirror-image technique.

The WMTDB includes data obtained from the Organization for Economic Cooperation and Development (OECD) describing the world trade of 24 reporting countries for the period 1979 through 1989. These data were supplemented by data covering Taiwan for 1982–89 and Korea for 1988 and 1989. By the mirror-image method, the WMTDB was constructed by entering into it the exports to the world of the 26 reporting countries and the imports of the reporting countries from nonreporting countries (i.e., all other countries).

When this method is used, a country's exports and imports consist of those reported by that country. The trade of nonreporting countries is constructed from the data provided by the reporting countries. That is, the imports of nonreporting countries are constructed from the exports to them recorded by the reporting countries. Similarly, the exports of nonreporting countries are constructed from imports from them recorded by the reporting countries.

This method provides an admittedly imperfect picture of world trade because it does not capture trade *among* nonreporting countries, for example, among the Eastern European or the Latin American countries. Nevertheless, the WMTDB provides the best picture of trade that can be put together given the limitations imposed by current reporting practices. Moreover, comparisons with world trade data from the International Monetary Fund's *International Financial Statistics* (IFS) and data compiled by the General Agreement on Tariffs and Trade (GATT) show that the WMTDB constructed for this study consistently captures more than 90 percent of world merchandise trade and an even higher percentage of world manufactures trade.

The OECD data used in constructing the WMTDB are those in the OECD's *Foreign Trade by Commodities: Series C, SITC format, Revision 2*. Data to the three-digit level of detail for manufactures trade (SITC 5 through 9) for each of the years 1979–89 were obtained for the 24 OECD countries. The study, however, generally utilizes only 1981–89 data from the WMTDB. Similar SITC Revision 2 data were also obtained for Taiwan and Korea. The OECD countries are Belgium and Luxembourg (which are reported as one country), Denmark, France, Germany, Greece, Ireland, Italy, the Netherlands, Portugal, Spain, the United Kingdom, Austria, Finland, Iceland, Norway, Sweden, Switzerland, Turkey, Canada, the United States, Japan, Australia, and New Zealand.

OECD Series C data are available for each reporting country's domestic and foreign exports. Imports are on a c.i.f.-value basis (which includes the cost of insurance and freight as well as the cost of the good itself). This introduces a minor distortion into the data. Because of the method of construction, both the imports and the exports of nonreporting countries are valued on a c.i.f. basis. This is typically 4 percent to 4.5 percent greater than the customs valuation, which does not include insurance and freight.

The collection and processing by the United Nations of trade data from the countries used in this data base is a time-consuming process, as is the additional work on the data by the OECD. Normally, data for the entire group have been available eight or nine months after the end of the year. Reporting for 1988 and 1989, however, was further delayed by the conversion of international trade data reporting to the harmonized-code system. As a result, in April 1991, complete 1989 data for four countries in the data base (Italy, Norway, Canada, and

Turkey) were not yet available. The data for these countries were simulated by indexing—at the two-digit level of detail—the actual 1988 exports and imports of these countries by the actual 1989 percentage change over 1988 performance. This preserves the integrity of the data in quantitative terms (total exports and imports) to the two-digit level of detail, but does not perfectly reflect changes that may have occurred within two-digit categories in the country composition of the exports and imports of these four countries. Instead, the simulation assumes the same country composition of exports and imports of these four countries for 1989 as in 1988.

The WMTDB data are all expressed in US current dollars. The data thus reflect both the effects of any global inflation that may have occurred *and* the effects of exchange rate movements against the dollar, the *numeraire* currency. The exchange rate effects can be particularly significant. For example, other things being equal, dollar depreciation raises the calculated dollar value of trade transactions conducted in foreign currencies when those transactions are converted to dollar terms. Other things being equal, dollar appreciation also lowers the calculated dollar value of the trade transactions of other countries. Thus, if US exports were 15 percent of total world exports and exports by other countries were 85 percent of the total, and if there were no changes in the value of foreign transactions in the foreign currencies, a dollar decline of 10 percent against all currencies would raise the calculated dollar value of the exports of other countries by 10 percent and thus would raise the total of world exports by 8.5 percent. As a result, the calculated US share in this example would decline from 15 percent to 13.8 percent.

US Department of Commerce Data

The WMTDB is supplemented in this study by US Department of Commerce data to provide more timely and more detailed information about US trade with the world. External transactions of the United States are summarized in the US current account using NIPA data formulations prepared by the Bureau of Economic Analysis. Included in these NIPA data are statistics on merchandise trade. This formulation of merchandise trade for purposes of the NIPA accounts and the resulting valuation do not, however, agree exactly with the total valuation of merchandise trade as reported by the Bureau of the Census for purposes of detailed trade analysis.

The data utilized in this paper in disaggregated analyses of manufactures trade performance are official Bureau of the Census data in SITC format. The data series utilized are domestic exports and imports on a customs basis. Domestic exports do not include the reexport of imported items on which no significant domestic processing has been performed. Hence domestic exports from this series will differ modestly from the category domestic and foreign exports. Also, unlike the WMTDB data, imports as recorded in the Census data are on a customs basis and do not include insurance and freight costs.

These choices were made to conform with standard US Commerce Department reporting practices, but they may result in minor differences between the US exports and imports in the tables using Commerce Department data and similar statistics drawn from the WMTDB data base. In addition, the total for manufactures exports on a domestic-exports basis is somewhat smaller than the total for domestic and foreign exports typically used in aggregate presentations of merchandise trade. Manufactures trade balances calculated using domestic and foreign exports will thus result in smaller deficits and larger surpluses than balances calculated using the domestic-exports data. These differences do not impair the analysis if—as is done in this study—consistent series are utilized in making comparisons. Each table in this study indicates the data formulation it utilizes.

An important change in SITC nomenclature occurred during the 1981–90 period that is the focus of this study. Beginning in 1989, US Commerce Department data are available only in the new Revision 3 format. However, a concordance process allowed the conversion of prior (Revision 2) data to the Revision 3 format. The US Commerce Department used that concordance to provide data in Revision 3 format for the period beginning in 1983. Thus, for this study, US Department of Commerce Revision 2 trade data were available to the three-digit level of detail for 1979–88 and in Revision 3 format for 1983–90. The WMTDB data provided in this study are, however, in Revision 2 format for the entire 1981–89 period.

For practical purposes, except for chemicals, Revision 3 makes few changes at the two-digit level of detail. That is, except within the chemicals group (SITC 5), relatively few items migrate from one two-digit category to another as a result of Revision 3. In several two-digit categories, however, new three-digit subcategories are added or definitions are changed, and a number of items migrated from one three-digit subcategory to another within the same two-digit group.

The reader should be aware of these differences, which are considered in the analysis. The point is that, where significant nomenclature changes have occurred, one cannot be confident that the data for years before 1988 are consistent with the data for years after 1988. Tables providing disaggregated two-digit data typically provide the 1987 quantities in both Revision 2 and Revision 3 format. Where 1981–87 changes are presented, both the 1981 and 1987 data points use Revision 2 data. Where 1987–90 changes are presented, both data points utilize Revision 3 data.

One final statistical quirk complicates the analyses. For all years through 1989, an underreporting of exports to Canada in detailed US trade product data was compensated for by an adjustment addition to SITC 99, "undocumented exports." During the 1980s this category reflected growing omissions of US exports to Canada across all commodity groups, due to inadequate customs reporting procedures at the US-Canada border. For 1987 this omission was estimated at about $11 billion, and by 1989 it was nearly $20 billion. As a result, the trade balance with Canada in individual product groups through 1989 does not fully reflect US exports. Bilateral US balances with Canada in individual product groups are flawed in that, to the extent of the underreporting in that product group, deficits are overstated and surpluses understated.

In 1990, however, the US Department of Commerce began using Canadian import data as the basis for recording US exports to Canada (countries typically have tighter data collection procedures for imports than for exports because of tariff and other import requirements). Beginning in 1990, disaggregated data thus presumably reflect a full reporting of US exports to Canada. It should be noted, however, that one effect of these events is that calculations of 1987–90 changes in US-Canada trade reflect not just actual 1987–90 changes but also the one-time effects of eliminating the underreporting of exports to Canada in the 1990 data. That is, although the 1987 detailed data at the two-digit level understated exports by about $11 billion, the 1990 data presumably reflect US exports accurately. The effect in individual two-digit product groups may be a calculated change in US-Canada trade that is somewhat different from what actually occurred. However, when spread across some 35 manufacturing categories and a roughly equivalent number of nonmanufacturing categories, the $11 billion total estimated underreporting of exports for 1987 is likely to introduce only relatively small distortions in most individual two-digit categories.

Country Groupings

In the country groupings used in tables and text in this study, the European Community consists of the present 12 member countries, not just those that were members during the years represented in the data. The Asian NICs are the four newly industrializing countries of Taiwan, Hong Kong, Singapore, and Korea. As defined in this study, Latin America includes Mexico as well as the countries of South and Central America.

SITC 9 Product Groups

Manufactures trade is typically defined to include SITCs 5 through 9. The detailed analysis in this study does not include SITC 9, which in Revision 2 nomenclature is described as "commodities and transactions not classified according to kind" and includes the following subcategories:

91 Postal packages not classified according to kind

93 Special transactions not classified according to kind

94 Animals, not elsewhere specified

95 Firearms of war and ammunition therefor.

Except for SITC 95, military items, these categorizations are not sufficiently descriptive to allow an analysis by product. As is evident from table 3.3, the great majority of arms trade is not reported in SITC 95 but is included in other relevant product groups or submerged in SITC 93, special transactions. The SITC 9 series is also sometimes used by individual countries for reporting of non-monetary gold transactions, coins, and low-value shipments. It can also be used to record adjustments for such factors as the underreporting of US exports to Canada.

In any event, the SITC 9 group did not lend itself to detailed analysis both because of the lack of specific descriptions of the products involved and because of the changes in usage of the various subcategories. For example, in 1987 US exports in SITC 98/99, low-value shipments, were $15.1 billion and mostly consisted of underreporting of exports to Canada. When this underreporting was eliminated in 1990, SITC 98/99 exports dropped to $6.5 billion.

Market Shares

This study makes extensive use of trade share calculations as a means of gauging the relative competitiveness of a country's industries in international and domestic markets. These trade share data can provide a useful, albeit imperfect, after-the-fact measurement of the changing ability of a country's industries or products to compete in world markets—that is, the ability of a country's manufacturing industries to compete in its home market and the global market.

Export Shares

A country's world export share is calculated in this study by dividing its exports to the world by world exports to the world. Both statistics are drawn from the WMTDB. Export shares calculated in this manner can provide a crude measure of a country's exporting abilities compared with those of other countries at a given point in time. Changes in shares over time may also provide evidence of trends in a country's ability to compete in foreign markets. The measurement has two basic flaws, however.

First, exchange rate changes affect the measurements. Other things being equal, a declining dollar enlarges the calculated values of foreign transactions and lowers the calculated US share, even if no volume changes have occurred. Similarly, dollar appreciation will, other things being equal, increase the calculated US export share and decrease the share of others.

Second, because the economies and international trade of many developing countries tend to grow more rapidly than those of the United States and other developed countries, diminishing US and other developed-country shares of total world exports and imports are a natural and not-undesirable result. That is, the United States and other developed countries could end up with a smaller piece of a bigger pie. A declining export share is, therefore, not necessarily a bad omen.

Import Shares

Additional useful information can be provided and the shortcomings of export share balances can be mitigated by calculating import shares and export share minus import share balances. The import share for each country is calculated as that country's imports from the world divided by all countries' imports from the world. Like the export shares, the import shares reflect distortions introduced by exchange rate movements and the growth of trade and the world economy. But both shares should be similarly affected by these changes, and, other things being equal, a country's export and import shares should move roughly in parallel as a result. If, for example, dollar appreciation is increasing the calculated export shares, then it should have similar effects on import shares. If rapid world economic growth and trade growth are decreasing a country's export shares, then the same factors should have similar effects on its import shares and on the import and export shares of major competitor countries.

In an integrated world economy, the import share also provides a crude measure of the changing ability of a country's domestic industries to compete in their own home market, although in itself the import share does not indicate the degree of penetration of the domestic market by imports. The import share also provides a measure of the dependence of the rest of the world on the market of the country for which the import share is calculated. That is, the import share is an indicator of how important a country's imports are to world exporters.

Share Balances

Export-minus-import share balances, defined as the difference between a country's export and import shares, are a third analytical tool. They provide both a measure of whether a country is a net exporter or a net importer and a rough indicator of its changing trade competitiveness. Increasing share balances may signal improving market competitiveness; declining share balances may signal declining trade competitiveness.

The export-minus-import share balance thus provides a useful measure of changing competitiveness that mitigates the flaws of export or import shares used alone. Share balances for a given point in time provide a simple indicator of the relative market competitiveness of one country compared with another in individual product groups. Changes in share balances provide a measure of whether performance is worsening or improving. Moreover, examination of the export and import shares can show whether changes in share balances stem from changing performance in exports or imports.

It is important, however, to recognize what is being measured. Share balances are simply a crude, after-the-fact measurement of the ability of a country to compete in foreign and domestic markets in a particular product group during the indicated period. Negative balances are not necessarily bad and in any case may not be correctable. For example, declining US domestic metal resources probably dictate that the United States' negative share balances in nonferrous metals will grow. Similarly, imports of some other products may be essential not only to domestic consumption but also to exports of other, perhaps more sophisticated and higher value-added products. Finally, increasing share balances do not necessarily indicate an improvement in national welfare if, for example, they are achieved by dollar depreciation rather than by improved productivity or product quality. Nor do they indicate an improving situation if they are the result of cuts in needed imports forced by lack of purchasing power—the situation in many developing countries.

US Share Calculations

Share balances are routinely calculated and displayed in this study for the United States using the method described above. However, to assess US competitiveness in world and US markets more precisely, US export (import) shares are also calculated using world exports to non-US destinations (imports from non-US sources) as the denominator.

Because US imports in many product groups constitute a relatively large portion of total world trade, including US imports (world exports to the United States) in total world exports could unduly influence and distort the calculation of US export shares. The best measure of US ability to compete in world markets is the US share of world exports to *non-US* destinations, that is, the market actually available to US exporters. Without the deletion of US imports from the denominator, growth in US imports at a rate higher than the world export growth rate would, in itself, result in a lowered US export share.

For similar reasons, inclusion of US exports (world imports from US sources) in total world imports can distort the calculations of US import shares and should be deleted from the denominator to arrive at the best indicator of the US share of world imports. In addition to improving the accuracy of US import shares, this provides a more accurate statistical indicator of the dependency of the rest of the world on the United States as an export market.

To summarize, export shares, import shares, and share balances have several limitations but can provide useful indicators of the relative strengths of countries and regions in competing for domestic and international markets. The shares and share balances can be helpful not only in assessing relative positions at given points of time but also in assessing trends and in judging whether changes stem from export or import performance. They do not, however, provide a measure of a country's international competitiveness in any welfare sense. That is, they do not provide a measure of how or why export or import share positions are achieved, why changes are occurring, and whether those changes are in the country's best interests.

The 1993 Product Group Projections

Each of the product group analyses in this study includes a projection of the expected 1993 trade performance for that group. It should be recognized that these projections are not the result of an econometric model but are subjective judgments that draw upon the information gathered from analysis of quantitative data, survey questionnaire responses, discussions with industry experts, and various other sources.

The projections were made under the following general assumptions:

- Through 1993, the dollar exchange rate remains essentially unchanged from May 1991 levels.

- The US economy returns to positive but relatively low growth rates of about 2.5 percent by mid-1992.

- Oil prices return to pre-Gulf crisis levels, subsequently increasing at rates roughly equivalent to US inflation.

- There is no major global economic downturn; the economies of other developed countries generally perform well.

The judgments reported here could not be subjected to rigorous mathematical testing. They did, however, incorporate the information provided by a set of elasticities developed by Data Resources, Inc. (DRI). The elasticities are taken from DRI's World Trade Model, developed by David Blond. The sectoral analyses of this study did not build formal models with the DRI elasticities, but used them to aid in qualitative assessments of the responsiveness of each sector's trade to macroeconomic conditions. DRI's estimates are presented in table A.1.

The elasticities are interpreted as in the following example: for the category "other chemicals," the data indicate that if the consumption component of US GNP increases by 1 percent, then US import demand (measured in dollars) for the products in this category will increase by 1.4 percent. Growth in the investment component of US GNP has a small effect (-0.1) on the import demand for these products (because they are not investment goods). If the price paid for US imports of "other chemicals" increases by 1 percent, the US demand for these products falls by -0.8 percent. Such a change in the price that the United States pays for imports might be caused by a fall of 1 percent in the US dollar exchange rate, if foreign suppliers pass through the entire price change.

The next five columns of table A.1 show how world import demand responds to similar factors. We interpret foreign imports from the United States as an exact proxy for foreign demand, as the model was estimated based solely on trade with the United States. Growth of 1 percent in the consumption component of world income leads to a 0.5 percent increase in US exports of "other chemicals." According to the next column, growth in world investment leads to a drop in demand for US exports. The next three columns show how a change in the price of US exports in major US export markets affects demand for those exports; that is, a 1 percent rise in the price of US exports in foreign markets will cause a drop in demand for those exports of between -0.2 percent and -0.4 percent.[1] Such a price change could be caused by a 1 percent rise in the dollar exchange rate if that change is fully passed through into the prices of US exports abroad.

Note that, for most product groups, Canadian demand for US exports is more responsive to the foreign price of US exports than is demand in other countries (see the last column), indicating that the US economy is more closely integrated with the Canadian economy than with the Northern European or the Japanese economies.

These estimates have several distinct advantages over earlier ones, particularly for the purposes of this study: the DRI elasticities are estimated on 1980s data; they correspond roughly to this study's SITC categories; they cover almost all industries; they use the same data as this study; and they include elasticities for world import demand.

---

1. The Northern European aggregate consists of Germany, France, the United Kingdom, Belgium and Luxembourg, the Netherlands, Sweden, Norway, Austria, and Switzerland.

Table A.1 DRI import price and demand elasticities

WSTS (a)	Approximate SITC Rev. 2 equivalent	Short descriptor	Elasticity of US import demand			Elasticity of world import demand				
			Consumption (b)	Investment (c)	Import prices (d)	Consumption (e)	Investment (f)	Import prices Japan (g)	N. Europe (h)	Canada (i)
24	51*,52,53	Other chemicals	1.4	−0.1	−0.8	0.5	−0.4	−0.2	−0.3	−0.4
25	54,55	Pharmaceuticals	1.7	0.0	−0.6	1.3	0.1	−0.4	−0.4	−0.5
15	56	Fertilizers	0.1	0.3	0.2	−5.3	1.6	−0.6	−1.0	−1.9
26	57,58,59	Plastics, etc.	1.3	0.0	−0.4	1.1	−0.4	−0.1	−0.5	−1.9
27	61,62,65*	Textiles, leather	1.2	−0.1	−1.1	1.4	−0.1	−0.9	−0.4	−2.0
28	64	Paper	1.7	0.1	−0.9	0.1	0.3	−0.2	−0.9	−0.3
49	658,659	Furnishings	0.8	0.4	−1.5	−0.9	1.3	−1.0	−0.9	−3.9
14	661,27*	Cement, etc.	1.9	0.2	−1.6	1.0	0.0	−0.6	−0.2	−1.4
29	66*,69*	Other manufactures	0.1	0.3	−1.1	−0.2	0.3	−0.5	−0.5	0.3
56	66*,69*,81-3,88-9	Consumer goods	1.7	0.2	−1.1	1.1	0.3	−0.4	−0.7	−2.6
30	67	Iron and steel	0.3	0.3	−1.8	1.0	0.2	−0.8	−0.3	−3.2
31	68	Nonferrous metals	1.7	−0.1	−0.6	1.4	0.4	0.0	−0.2	0.8
43	713,749.3	Engines, shafts	1.2	0.0	0.2	0.0	0.2	−0.3	−0.6	−0.6
53	71*,72*,73*	Light machinery	0.9	0.7	−0.6	0.3	0.3	0.2	−0.3	−0.2
32	71*,72*,73*	Heavy machinery	1.4	0.4	−0.5	1.3	−0.1	0.3	−0.9	−1.9
34	72*,74*,78*,79*	Transport and construction	0.6	0.6	−1.5	−1.7	0.4	−1.0	−0.3	1.9
46	751	Office equipment	0.5	0.1	−1.6	1.0	−0.6	−0.3	0.6	−1.3
42	752	Computers	2.3	0.1	−1.7	2.1	0.0	−0.7	−0.3	1.8
55	75-77*	Telecommunications and electronics	2.4	0.2	−1.0	2.4	−0.3	−0.5	−0.3	−1.5
45	76*	Audio and video equipment	1.7	−0.9	−2.9	n.a.	n.a.	n.a.	n.a.	1.8
47	771-3	Electric machinery	1.6	0.7	−0.1	0.4	0.3	0.1	−0.1	1.8
48	775	Appliances	1.5	−0.1	−1.4	1.3	−0.3	0.6	−1.2	−5.9
41	776,778	Parts, semiconductors	1.0	0.2	0.0	0.9	0.1	−0.6	0.1	−0.8
35	781	Automobiles	1.5	0.0	−1.8	5.1	1.3	−1.2	−3.7	−9.0
44	784	Auto parts	1.6	−0.3	−0.1	1.1	0.2	−0.4	−0.6	1.5
54	785	Motorcycles	1.0	−0.3	−5.0	5.4	−1.5	−1.9	−2.2	−8.9
37	792,793	Aircraft and ships	−1.2	0.3	−0.3	0.6	1.0	0.9	0.0	0.6
50	84	Apparel	1.9	0.1	−1.4	n.a.	n.a.	n.a.	n.a.	n.a.
51	851	Footwear	1.3	0.3	−1.5	n.a.	n.a.	n.a.	n.a.	n.a.
52	87	Scientific equipment	0.8	−0.1	0.0	0.7	−0.1	0.0	−0.3	−1.6

n.a. = not available; a. WSTS numbers are DRI's rearrangement of SITC codes. An asterisk by an SITC code indicates that only part of that group is included in the corresponding WSTS code; b. Elasticity of US import demand with respect to the consumption component of US GNP; c. Elasticity of US import demand with respect to US investment; d. Elasticity of US import demand with respect to US import prices; e. Elasticity of world demand for imports from the United States with respect to world consumption; f. Elasticity of world demand for imports from the United States with respect to world investment; g. Elasticity of Japanese demand for imports from the United States with respect to US export prices in Japan; h. Elasticity of Northern European demand for imports from the United States with respect to US export prices in Northern Europe; i. Elasticity of Canadian demand for imports from the United States with respect to US export prices in Canada; Source: DRI.

Index

Aerospace Industries Association of
America, 404
Agricultural equipment and machinery,
trade in, 250, 252, 262, 266
Agriculture, 11, 30–33, 44, 57, 531–32
Aircraft, 394–415, 536, 542
 Asian NICs, trade in, 408–10
 Canada, trade in, 408–10
 determinants of US trade
 performance, 398–99
 determinants of world trade
 performance, 395–97
 developing countries, trade in,
 408–09
 Eastern Europe, trade in, 408–09
 European Community, trade in, 395,
 408–10
 France, trade in, 408–10
 geographic composition of US trade,
 400, 413
 geographic distribution of world
 trade, 395, 408–09
 Germany, trade in, 408–10
 global competition patterns, 395,
 408–10
 Italy, trade in, 408–09
 Japan, trade in, 408–10
 Latin America, trade in, 408–10
 product composition of US trade,
 400, 411–12
 product composition of world trade,
 395, 407
 product group description, 394
 United Kingdom, trade in, 408–10
 United States, trade in, 395–98, 400,
 410, 414–15, 544
 world manufactures export shares,
 47, 536
 world trade, 395–97, 407–10,
 414–15

Alperowicz, Natasha, 140
Aluminum, 211, 216–17, 221–22, 226,
230
American Apparel Manufacturers
Association, 438
American Paper Institute, 156
American Textile Manufacturers
Institute, 171
Animals, live, trade in, 45
Apparel, 429–46
 Asian NICs, trade in, 431, 441, 443
 bilateral trade flows, 431, 443
 Canada, trade in, 431, 441, 443
 determinants of US trade
 performance, 433–35
 developing countries, trade in, 441
 Eastern Europe, trade in, 441
 European Community, trade in, 431,
 441, 443
 France, trade in, 431, 441, 443
 geographic composition of US trade,
 432, 445
 geographic distribution of world
 trade, 431, 441–42
 Germany, trade in, 431, 441, 443
 global competition patterns, 431,
 441–43
 Italy, trade in, 441
 Japan, trade in, 431, 443
 Latin America, trade in, 431, 441
 product composition of US trade,
 431, 432, 444
 product composition of world trade,
 430, 440
 product group description, 429–30
 United Kingdom, trade in, 441, 443
 United States, trade in, 431–33, 441,
 443, 444–46
 world trade, 430–31, 440–43

Appliances, trade in, 95–96, 347–48, 351, 359
Architecture, private services transactions, 28
Armaments, trade in, 48–49, 95–96
Artificial resins, trade in, 95–96
Asian newly industrializing countries (NICs)
  aircraft, trade in, 408–09, 410, 413
  apparel, trade in, 431, 441, 443
  chemicals, trade in, 142–43, 144, 146
  computers, trade in, 318
  geographic composition of US trade, 320
  geographic composition of world trade, 316
  electrical machinery, trade in, 343–44, 356–57, 358, 360
  export share taken by US, 56
  exports, 53
  footwear, trade in, 447, 448, 457, 459, 460
  furniture, trade in, 417, 424–26
  general industrial machinery, trade in, 288, 296, 298, 300
  imports, 51, 53
  instruments, professional, trade in, 463, 464, 466, 471–72, 473, 475
  iron and steel, trade in, 193, 197, 198, 204, 205, 206, 208
  Japanese share of world exports to, 55
  metal manufactures, trade in, 234, 235, 243, 245, 247
  metalworking machinery, trade in, 270, 271, 281, 283, 284
  miscellaneous manufactures, trade in, 489–90, 491, 493
  nonferrous metals, trade in, 227, 229, 231
  nonmetallic mineral manufactures, trade in, 186, 188, 190
  office machines, trade in, 316, 318, 320
  paper, trade in, 149, 158–59, 160, 161
  road vehicles, trade in, 364, 385–86, 387
  sound-reproducing equipment, trade in, 336, 338, 340
  specialized industrial machinery, trade in, 263, 265, 267
  telecommunications equipment, trade in, 336, 338, 340
  textiles, trade in, 164, 173–74, 175
  world manufactures export market shares, 55–56, 536
  world manufactures trade shares, 50
Atwell, Wayne, 223
Auerbach, Stuart, 495
Austin, Gordon T., 184
Automobiles. See Road vehicles

Baby carriages. See Miscellaneous manufactures
Barnett, Donald, 200–01
Basic manufactures, 148–248, 549
Belgium, manufacturing productivity, 104
Bergsten, C. Fred, 38–39, 112, 542, 555
Betts, Paul, 404
Beverages, trade in, 45
Bilateral trade flows
  aircraft, 395, 410
  apparel, 431, 443
  chemicals, 124–25, 144
  computers, 303, 318
  electrical machinery, 343, 358
  footwear, 448, 459
  furniture, 417, 426
  general industrial machinery, 287, 298
  instruments, professional, 464, 473
  iron and steel, 193, 197, 198, 206
  metal manufactures, 235, 245
  metalworking machinery, 271, 283
  miscellaneous manufactures, 479, 491
  nonferrous metals, 211, 229
  nonmetallic mineral manufactures, 180, 188
  office machines, 303, 318
  paper, 150, 160
  road vehicles, 365, 387
  sound-reproducing equipment, 325, 338
  specialized industrial machinery, 251, 265

telecommunications equipment, 325, 338
textiles, 164, 175
Blustein, Paul, 383
Boeing Commercial Airplane Group, 404
Bookbinding machinery, trade in, 262, 266
Borrowing, foreign, effect on manufacturing sector, 36, 564
Bourke, William, 223
Boyle, Thomas F., 112
Brinner, Roger E., 497
Brown, Warren, 383
Building products, trade in, 181, 185, 189
Business services, trade in, 14, 28

Campbell, Gary, 223
Canada
    aircraft, trade in, 408–09, 410, 413
    apparel, trade in, 431, 441, 443, 445
    Asian NICs share of world exports to, 55–56
    chemicals, trade in, 142–43, 144, 146
    computers, trade in, 316, 318, 320
    electrical machinery, trade in, 343–44, 356–57, 358, 360
    EC share of world exports to, 54–55
    export share taken by US, 56
    exports, 53
    footwear, trade in, 457, 459, 460
    furniture, trade in, 424–25, 426, 427
    general industrial machinery, trade in, 296, 298, 300
    imports, 53
    instruments, professional, trade in, 464, 466, 471, 473, 475
    iron and steel, trade in, 193, 197, 198, 204, 205, 206, 208
    Japanese share of world exports to, 55
    manufactures trade share, 79–80, 82
    manufacturing productivity, 104, 105
    metal manufactures, trade in, 235, 243, 245, 247
    metalworking machinery, trade in, 271, 281, 283, 284
    miscellaneous manufactures, trade in, 489–90, 491, 493

nonferrous metals, trade in, 211, 227, 229, 231
nonmetallic mineral manufactures, trade in, 186, 188, 190
office machines, trade in, 316, 318, 320
paper, trade in, 149, 150, 158–59, 160, 161
road vehicles, trade in, 364, 385–86, 387, 389–90, 543
sound-reproducing equipment, trade in, 336, 338, 340
specialized industrial machinery, trade in, 251, 263, 265, 267
telecommunications equipment, trade in, 336, 338, 340
textiles, trade in, 173–74, 175, 177
US share of world exports to, 54
world manufactures trade shares, 50
Cane, Alan, 312
Cantwell, John, 112
Capital flows, and manufactures trade, 57–58, 532
Carroll, Irwin, 260
Castings, trade in, 203
Cement, trade in, 181, 185, 189
Chandler, Clay, 383
Chemical Manufacturers Association, 156
Chemicals
    Asian NICs, trade in, 124–25, 142–43, 144
    Canada, trade in, 142–43, 144
    composition of world trade, 46, 141
    determinants of US trade performance, 132–35
    determinants of world trade performance, 125–29
    developing countries, trade in, 142–43
    Eastern Europe, trade in, 142–43
    European Community, trade in, 125, 142–43, 144
    France, trade in, 124, 142–43, 144
    geographic composition of US trade, 130, 146
    geographic distribution of world trade, 124, 142–43
    Germany, trade in, 124, 125, 142–44

Chemicals *(continued)*
global competition patterns, 123–25,
142–44
globalization of industry, 551
Italy, trade in, 142–43
Japan, trade in, 124, 142–43, 144
Latin America, trade in, 124, 142–43,
144
organic, world export shares, 48–49
product composition of US trade,
129–30, 145
product composition of world trade,
123, 141
product group description, 121–22
United Kingdom, trade in, 124,
142–43, 144
United States, trade in, 129–35,
142–43, 146–47, 542, 545, 549,
551
world manufactures export shares, 49
world trade, 122–29, 141, 147
Chhabra, Jasbir, 223
China, 57, 106, 177, 448, 547
Chipello, Christopher J., 487
Civil engineering equipment, trade in,
250, 252, 262, 266
Clausing, Don P., 312
Clay and clay products, trade in, 181,
182, 185, 189
Cline, William R., 34–35, 39, 171, 438,
495, 539
Clothing. *See* Apparel
Coins, trade in, 95–96
Collins, Susan M., 495
Coloring materials, trade in, 95–96,
130, 145
Commercial services, trade in, 43–44
Commission of the European
Communities, 171, 184, 223, 240,
333, 353, 404, 421, 438, 454, 469
Commission on Industrial Productivity,
495
Communications services, trade in,
27–29
Competitiveness
international, measurements, 69–74
of US manufacturing, 63–68, 71–74,
101–03
Competitiveness Policy Council, 565
Compressors, trade in, 287

Computer Business Equipment
Manufacturers Association, 312
Computers, 303–14
Asian NICs, trade in, 316, 318
bilateral trade flows, 303, 318
Canada, trade in, 316, 318
determinants of US trade
performance, 307–09
determinants of world trade
performance, 303–05
developing countries, trade in, 316
Eastern Europe, trade in, 316
European Community, trade in, 316,
318
France, trade in, 316, 318
geographic composition of US trade,
305, 320
geographic distribution of world
trade, 303, 316–17
Germany, trade in, 316, 318
global competition patterns, 303,
316–18
Italy, trade in, 316
Japan, trade in, 316, 318
Latin America, trade in, 316, 318
product composition of US trade,
305, 307, 319
product composition of world trade,
303, 315
product group description, 303
United Kingdom, trade in, 316, 318
United States, trade in, 306, 316, 318,
321, 322, 545
world trade, 303–05, 315–18, 321
Construction materials, trade in, 189
Construction services, trade in, 11,
27–29
Consulting services, trade in, 27–29
Cooling and heating equipment, trade
in, 287, 288, 295, 299
Copper, trade in, 211, 215–16, 221,
226
Cork manufactures, trade in, 48, 95–96
Cotton fabric, trade in, 172
Council on Competitiveness, 140, 312,
332, 353, 404
Cowhey, Peter, 332
Crandall, R., 200
Crude materials, trade in, 45
Current account, 19–39, 98–101

Cutlery, trade in, 242, 246

Dammert, Alfredo, 223
Data processing machines, trade in, 48–49, 95–96
Data processing services, trade in, 28
Data Resources, Inc., 119, 540
Denmark, 104
Developed countries, manufactures trade shares, 79–80
Developing countries
    aircraft, trade in, 408–09
    apparel, trade in, 441, 445
    chemicals, trade in, 142–43, 146
    computers, trade in, 316
    electrical machinery, trade in, 343–44, 356–57
    footwear, trade in, 457
    furniture, trade in, 424–25
    general industrial machinery, trade in, 296
    import shares, 50–51
    instruments, professional, trade in, 471
    iron and steel, trade in, 193, 204, 205
    metalworking machinery, trade in, 281
    miscellaneous manufactures, trade in, 489–90
    nonferrous metals, trade in, 227
    nonmetallic mineral manufactures, trade in, 186
    office machines, trade in, 316
    paper, trade in, 149, 158–59
    road vehicles, trade in, 364, 385–86
    sound-reproducing equipment, trade in, 336
    specialized industrial machinery, trade in, 263
    telecommunications equipment, trade in, 336
    textiles, trade in, 164, 173–74
Diamonds, trade in, 185, 548
Disaggregated analysis, advantages and disadvantages, 6–9
Dornbusch, Rudiger, 112
Duncan, Ronald C., 201, 223
Dunne, Nancy, 495
Dyeing materials, trade in, 48–49, 95–96, 130, 141, 145

Eastern Europe
    aircraft, trade in, 408–09
    apparel, trade in, 441
    chemicals, trade in, 142–43
    computers, trade in, 316
    electrical machinery, trade in, 343–44, 356–57
    footwear, trade in, 457
    furniture, trade in, 424–25
    general industrial machinery, trade in, 296
    instruments, professional, trade in, 471
    iron and steel, trade in, 193, 204, 205
    merchandise trade shares, 32–33
    metal manufactures, trade in, 243
    metalworking machinery, trade in, 281
    miscellaneous manufactures, trade in, 489–90
    nonferrous metals, trade in, 227
    nonmetallic mineral manufactures, trade in, 186
    paper, trade in, 149, 158–59
    road vehicles, trade in, 364, 385–86
    sound-reproducing equipment, trade in, 336
    specialized industrial machinery, trade in, 263
    telecommunications equipment, trade in, 336
    textiles, trade in, 173–74
    world manufactures trade shares, 50
Econometric models, limitations, 7–9
Educational services, trade in, 27–29
Electrical distribution machinery, trade in, 343, 359
Electrical machinery, 342–61
    Asian NICs, trade in, 343–44, 356–57, 358
    bilateral trade flows, 343, 358
    Canada, trade in, 343–44, 356–58
    composition of US trade, 359
    determinants of US trade performance, 344, 349–54
    developing countries, trade in, 343–44, 356–57
    Eastern Europe, trade in, 343–44, 356–57

European Community, trade in, 343–44, 356–58
France, trade in, 343–44, 356–58
geographic composition of US trade, 344, 360
geographic distribution of world trade, 343–44, 356–57
Germany, trade in, 343–44, 356–58
global competition patterns, 343–44, 356–58
Italy, trade in, 343–44, 356–57
Japan, trade in, 343–44, 356–58
Latin America, trade in, 343–44, 356–58
product composition of US trade, 344, 345, 347, 348, 349, 359
product composition of world trade, 343, 355
product group description, 342–43
United Kingdom, trade in, 343–44, 356–57, 358
United States, trade in, 343–44, 356–57, 358, 359–61
world trade, 355–58, 361
Electromedical equipment, trade in, 343, 347, 351, 359
Electronic Industries Association, 333
Electronic parts, trade in, 343, 348, 351–52, 359
Electronics Industries Association, 312, 333
Employment, manufacturing, 12
Engineering services, trade in, 28
Essential oils, trade in, 48–49, 95–96, 130, 145
European Community
aircraft, trade in, 395, 408–09, 410, 413
apparel, trade in, 431, 441, 443, 445
Asian NICs share of world exports to, trade in, 55–56
chemicals, trade in, 125, 142–43, 144, 146
computers, trade in, 316, 318, 320
electrical machinery, trade in, 343–44, 356–57, 358, 360
export share taken by US, 56
exports, 53
footwear, trade in, 447, 448, 457, 459, 460

furniture, trade in, 416, 424–26, 427
general industrial machinery, trade in, 287, 288, 296, 298, 300
imports, 51, 53
instruments, professional, trade in, 463, 464, 466, 471–72, 473, 475
iron and steel, trade in, 193, 197, 198, 204, 205, 206, 208
Japanese share of world exports to, 55
manufactures trade shares, 79–80, 83
metal manufactures, trade in, 234, 235, 243, 245, 247
metalworking machinery, trade in, 270, 271, 281, 283, 284
miscellaneous manufactures, trade in, 489–90, 491, 493
nonferrous metals, trade in, 211, 227, 229, 231
nonmetallic mineral manufactures, trade in, 180, 186, 188, 190
office machines, trade in, 316, 318, 320
paper, trade in, 149, 150, 158–59, 160, 161
road vehicles, trade in, 364, 385–86, 387, 389–90
sound-reproducing equipment, trade in, 324–35, 336, 338, 340
specialized industrial machinery, trade in, 250, 263, 265, 267
telecommunications equipment, trade in, 324–36, 338, 340
textiles, trade in, 164, 173–74, 175, 177
US share of world exports to, 54
world manufactures export market shares, 54–55
world manufactures trade, 52–53
Exchange rates
disaggregated analysis and, 8
oil exports and, 57
price and volume effects on exports and imports, 88–93, 545–47
US–Japan, 555
Explosives, trade in, 48–49, 95–96, 141
Export growth rates, manufactures trade, 98–100

Export flows
  Asian NICs, 53, 55–56
  European Community, 53–55
  Japan, 53, 55–56
  United States, 52–54

Faltermayer, Edmund, 495
Fans, trade in, 287
Fee, Jonathan M., 438
Feldstein, Martin, 561
Fencing, composition of world trade, 242
Fertilizers, trade in, 48–49, 95–96, 123, 141, 145
Film rental income, 27–29
Financial services, trade in, 27–29
Finished goods, US competitiveness in, 85–86, 549–50
Fish, trade in, 11
Flamm, Kenneth, 312
Flemings, Merton, 201
Floor coverings, trade in, 172
Food. See Agriculture.
Food processing machinery, trade in, 262, 266
Footwear, 447–61
  Asian NICs, trade in, 447, 448, 457, 459
  bilateral trade flows, 448, 459
  Canada, trade in, 457, 459
  China, trade in, 448
  determinants of US trade performance, 450–52
  developing countries, trade in, 457
  Eastern Europe, trade in, 457
  European Community, trade in, 447, 448, 457, 459
  France, trade in, 457, 459
  geographic composition of US trade, 449, 450, 460
  geographic distribution of world trade, 448, 457–58
  Germany, trade in, 457, 459
  global competition patterns, 447–48, 457–59
  Indonesia, trade in, 448
  Italy, trade in, 457
  Japan, trade in, 457, 459
  Latin America, trade in, 448, 457, 459
  Malaysia, trade in, 448

  product composition of US trade, 448, 450, 460
  product composition of world trade, 447, 456
  product group description, 447
  Thailand, trade in, 448
  United Kingdom, trade in, 457, 459
  United States, trade in, 450, 457–60, 461
  world manufactures export shares, 48–49, 536
Footwear Industries of America, 455
Foreign aid, in current account, 21
Foreign direct investment, 550–52
Forestry products, trade in, 11
France
  aircraft, trade in, 408–09, 410, 413
  apparel, trade in, 441, 443
  Asian NICs share of world exports to, 55–56
  chemicals, trade in, 124, 142–43, 144, 146
  computers, trade in, 316, 318, 320
  electrical machinery, 343–44, 356–57, 358, 360
  EC share of world exports to, 54–55
  export share taken by US, 56
  exports, 53
  footwear, trade in, 457, 459, 460
  furniture, trade in, 416, 424–26, 427
  general industrial machinery, trade in, 296, 298, 300
  imports, 53
  instruments, professional, trade in, 466, 471, 473, 475
  iron and steel, trade in, 193, 197, 198, 204, 205, 206
  Japanese share of world exports to, 55
  manufacturing productivity, 104
  metal manufactures, trade in, 243, 245, 247
  metalworking machinery, trade in, 281, 283, 284
  miscellaneous manufactures, trade in, 489–90, 491, 493
  nonferrous metals, trade in, 211, 227, 229, 231
  nonmetallic mineral manufactures, trade in, 186, 188, 190

France *(continued)*
office machines, trade in, 316, 318, 320
paper, trade in, 149, 158–59, 160, 161
road vehicles, trade in, 364, 385–86, 387
sound-reproducing equipment, trade in, 336, 338
specialized industrial machinery, trade in, 263, 265, 267
telecommunications equipment, trade in, 336, 338
textiles, trade in, 173–75
US share of world exports to, 54
world manufactures trade shares, 50
Furniture, 416–28
Asian NICs, trade in, 417, 424–26
bilateral trade flows, 417, 426
Canada, trade in, 424–26
determinants of US trade performance, 419–20
determinants of world trade performance, 417–18
developing countries, trade in, 424–25
Eastern Europe, trade in, 424–25
European Community, trade in, 416, 424–26
France, trade in, 416, 424–26
geographic composition of US trade, 419, 427
geographic distribution of world trade, 416, 424–25
Germany, trade in, 416, 424–26
global competition patterns, 416–17, 424–26
Italy, trade in, 416, 424–26
Japan, trade in, 416, 417, 424–26
Latin America, trade in, 424–26
product group description, 416
United Kingdom, trade in, 417, 424–26
United States, trade in, 416, 417, 419, 424–26, 428
world manufactures export shares, 48–49
world trade, 416, 418, 423–26, 428

Games. *See* Miscellaneous manufactures
General Agreement on Tariffs and Trade, 43–44, 438, 564

General Aviation Manufactures Association, 404
General industrial machinery, 286–301, 542
Asian NICs, trade in, 288, 296, 298, 300
bilateral trade flows, 287, 298
Canada, trade in, 296, 298, 300
determinants of US trade performance, 289–90
determinants of world trade performance, 288
developing countries, trade in, 296
Eastern Europe, trade in, 296
European Community, trade in, 287, 288, 296, 298, 300
France, trade in, 296, 298, 300
geographic composition of US trade, 288–89, 300
geographic distribution of world trade, 287, 296–97
Germany, trade in, 287, 296, 298, 300
global competition patterns, 287–88, 296–98
Italy, trade in, 296, 300
Japan, trade in, 287, 288, 296, 298, 300
Latin America, trade in, 296, 298, 300
Mexico, trade in, 300
OPEC, trade in, 300
product composition of US trade, 288–89, 299
product composition of world trade, 287, 295
product group description, 286
United Kingdom, trade in, 296, 298, 300
United States, trade in, 287–89, 298, 299–301, 542, 545–46
world trade, 287–88, 289, 295–98, 301
Generators, trade in, 359
Geographic composition of US trade
aircraft, 400, 413
apparel, 432, 445
chemicals, 130, 146
computers, 305, 320
electrical machinery, 344, 360
footwear, 449, 450, 460

furniture, 419, 427
general industrial machinery, 288–89, 300
instruments, professional, 466, 475
iron and steel, 195, 197, 198, 208
metal manufactures, 237, 247
metalworking machinery, 272, 284
miscellaneous manufactures, 482, 493
nonferrous metals, 212, 231
nonmetallic mineral manufactures, 180, 190
office machines, 305, 320
paper, 151, 161
road vehicles, 366, 368, 376, 389
sound-reproducing equipment, 326, 340
specialized industrial machinery, 255, 267
telecommunications equipment, 326, 340
textiles, 166, 177
Geographic distribution of world trade
aircraft, 395, 408–09
apparel, 431, 441–42
changes in, 549
chemicals, 124, 142–43
computers, 303, 316–17
electrical machinery, 343–44, 356–57
footwear, 448, 457–58
furniture, 416, 424–25
general industrial machinery, 287, 296–97
instruments, professional, 463, 471–72
iron and steel, 193, 204, 205
metal manufactures, 234, 243–44
metalworking machinery, 270–71, 281–82
miscellaneous manufactures, 478, 489–90
nonferrous metals, 211, 227–28
nonmetallic mineral manufactures, 180, 186
office machines, 303, 316–17
paper, 149, 158–59
sound-reproducing equipment, 324, 336–37
specialized industrial machinery, 250, 263–64

telecommunications equipment, 324, 336–37
textiles, 164, 173–74
Germany
aircraft, trade in, 408–09, 410, 413
apparel, trade in, 441, 443
Asian NICs share of world export to, 55–56
chemicals, trade in, 124, 125, 142–43, 144, 146
computers, trade in, 315, 318, 320
electrical machinery, trade in, 343–44, 356–57, 358, 360
EC share of world exports to, 54–55
export share taken by US, 56
exports, 53
footwear, trade in, 457, 459, 460
furniture, trade in, 416, 424–26, 427
general industrial machinery, trade in, 287, 296, 298, 300
import-export ratio, 50–51
imports, 53
instruments, professional, trade in, 463, 466, 471–72, 473, 475
iron and steel, trade in, 193, 197, 198, 204, 205, 206, 208
Japanese share of world exports to, 55
manufacturing productivity, 104, 105
metal manufactures, trade in, 234, 243, 245, 247
metalworking machinery, trade in, 270, 271, 281, 283, 284
miscellaneous manufactures, trade in, 489–90, 491, 493
nonferrous metals, trade in, 211, 227, 229, 231
nonmetallic mineral manufactures, trade in, 186, 188, 190
office machines, trade in, 316, 318, 320
paper, trade in, 149, 150, 158–59, 160, 161
road vehicles, trade in, 364, 366, 385–86, 387, 389–90, 543
sound-reproducing equipment, trade in, 336, 338
specialized industrial machinery, trade in, 263, 265, 267

Germany *(continued)*
telecommunications equipment, trade
in, 336, 338
textiles, trade in, 173–74, 175, 177
US share of world exports to, 54
world manufactures trade, 47, 50,
50–53, 536
Gladstone, Rick, 487
Glass and glassware, trade in, 182, 185,
189
Global competition patterns
aircraft, 395, 408–10
apparel, 431, 441–43
chemicals, 123–25, 142–44
computers, 303, 316–18
electrical machinery, 343–44, 356–58
footwear, 447–48, 457–59
furniture, 416–17, 424–26
general industrial machinery, 287–88,
296–98
instruments, professional, 463–64,
471–73
iron and steel, 193–94, 204–06
metal manufactures, 234–35, 243–44
metalworking machinery, 270–71,
281–83
miscellaneous manufactures, 478–79,
489–91
nonferrous metals, 211, 227–28, 229
nonmetallic mineral manufactures,
180, 186–88
office machines, 303, 316–18
paper, 149–50, 158–59
plastics, 123–25, 142–44
road vehicles, 364–65, 385–87
sound-reproducing equipment,
324–25, 336–38
specialized industrial machinery,
250–51, 263–65
telecommunications equipment,
324–25, 336–38
textiles, 164, 173–75
Globalization of world markets, 550–52
Goldfarb, Debra, 312
Gooding, Kenneth, 223
Government, and sectoral composition
of GNP, 11
Government policy toward
manufacturing sector, 35–37, 559–68
Government services, in current
account, 23–24

Graham, Edward M., 38, 112, 333
Grain, trade in, 32–33, 57
Guenther, Gary L., 279
Gulf crisis, and merchandise trade, 32

Haggerty, Peggy, 260
Hand tools, trade in, 234
Handbags, trade in, 95–96
Handling equipment, trade in, 295
Harper, Douglas C., 156
Hayward, Keith, 404
Health Industry Manufacturers
Association, 353
Heating equipment, trade in, 287, 288,
289, 295
Heating fixtures, trade in, 48, 95–96
Heavy electrical equipment, trade in,
345–46, 350, 359
Hiatt, Fred, 495
Hickok, Susan, 112
High-technology goods, 544–45
Hochswender, Woody, 438
Hogan, William T., 201
Hong Kong, 50, 52
Hoop, trade in, 203, 207
Household electrical equipment, trade
in, 359
Howell, Thomas R., 171, 439
Hysteresis, 565

Import-export ratios, 50–51
Indonesia, 448
Industrial machinery. *See* General
industrial machinery; Specialized
industrial machinery
Industrial materials, US competitiveness
in, 85–86
Information services, trade in, 28
Ingots, trade in, 203, 207
Inorganic chemicals, trade in, 95–96,
123, 130, 141, 145
Institute for Defense Analysis, 313
Instruments, professional, 462–76
Asian NICs, trade in, 463, 464, 471,
471–72, 473
bilateral trade flows, 464, 473
Canada, trade in, 464, 471, 473
determinants of US trade
performance, 466–67
developing countries, trade in, 471

Eastern Europe, trade in, 471
European Community, trade in, 463,
    464, 471–72, 473
France, trade in, 471, 473
geographic composition of US trade,
    466, 475
geographic composition of world
    trade, 463, 471–72
Germany, trade in, 463, 471–72, 473
global competition patterns, 463–64,
    471–73
Italy, trade in, 471
Japan, trade in, 463, 464, 471–72,
    473
Latin America, trade in, 464, 471,
    473
product composition of US trade,
    465, 474
product composition of world trade,
    463, 470
product group description, 462
United Kingdom, trade in, 471, 473
United States, trade in, 463, 464,
    471–72, 473, 474–76
world trade, 463–65, 470–73, 476
Insurance, trade in, 11, 27–29
Internal combustion engines. *See* Road
    vehicles
International competitiveness, trade
    performance measurements, 69–74
International investment income
    account, 21–23
International Iron and Steel Institute, 201
International Lead and Zinc Study
    Group, 224
International Monetary Fund, 112
International transactions, US,
    summary, 19–20
Interviews, methodology, 5
Investment income, international, 20,
    23, 533
Investment trends, US, 106–08, 557, 563
Iron and steel
    Asian NICs, trade in, 193, 197, 198,
        204, 205, 206
    bilateral trade flows, 193, 197, 198,
        206
    Canada, trade in, 193, 197, 198, 204,
        205, 206

determinants of US trade
    performance, 195–200, 206, 208
determinants of world trade
    performance, 194
developing countries, trade in, 193,
    204, 205
Eastern Europe, trade in, 193, 204,
    205
European Community, trade in, 193,
    197, 198, 204, 205, 206
France, trade in, 193, 197, 198, 204,
    205, 206
geographic composition of US trade,
    195, 197, 198, 208
geographic distribution of world
    trade, 193, 204, 205
Germany, trade in, 193, 197, 198,
    204, 205, 206
global competition patterns, 193–94,
    204–06
Italy, trade in, 193, 204, 205
Japan, trade in, 193, 197, 198, 204,
    205, 206
Latin America, trade in, 193, 197,
    198, 204, 205, 206
product composition of US trade,
    194, 207
product composition of world trade,
    193, 203
product group description, 192
United Kingdom, trade in, 193, 197,
    198, 204, 205, 206
United States, trade in, 193–95, 196,
    197, 198, 204, 205, 206, 209, 547
world manufactures exports,
    percentage, 48–49
world trade, 193–94, 203, 209
Islam, Shafiqul, 39
Italy
    aircraft, trade in, 408–09
    apparel, trade in, 441
    Asian NICs share of world exports to,
        55–56
    chemicals, trade in, 142–43, 146
    computers, trade in, 316, 320
    electrical machinery, trade in,
        343–44, 356–57, 360
    EC share of world exports to, 54–55
    export share taken by US, 56
    footwear, trade in, 457, 460

Italy (continued)
furniture, trade in, 416, 424–26, 427
general industrial machinery, trade in,
296, 300
instruments, professional, trade in,
466, 471, 475
iron and steel, trade in, 193, 204,
205, 208
Japanese share of world exports to,
55
manufacturing productivity, 104
metal manufactures, trade in, 243,
247
metalworking machinery, trade in,
281, 284
miscellaneous manufactures, trade in,
489–90, 493
nonferrous metals, trade in, 227, 231
nonmetallic mineral manufactures,
trade in, 186, 190
office machines, trade in, 316, 320
paper, trade in, 149, 158–59, 161
road vehicles, trade in, 364, 385–86
sound-reproducing equipment, trade
in, 336
specialized industrial machinery, trade
in, 263, 267
telecommunications equipment, trade
in, 336
textiles, trade in, 173–74, 177
US share of world exports to, 54
world manufactures trade shares, 50

Japan
aircraft, trade in, 408–09, 410, 413
apparel, trade in, 431, 443, 445
Asian NICs share of world exports to,
55–56
chemicals, trade in, 124, 143, 144,
146
computers, trade in, 316, 318, 320
electrical machinery, trade in,
343–44, 356–57, 358, 360
EC share of world exports to, 54–55
export share taken by US, 56
exports, 53
footwear, trade in, 457, 459, 460
furniture, trade in, 416, 417, 424–26,
427
general industrial machinery, trade in,
287, 288, 296, 298, 300

import-export ratio, 50–51
imports, 51, 53
instruments, professional, trade in,
463, 464, 471–72, 473, 475
iron and steel, trade in, 193, 197,
198, 204, 205, 206, 208
manufactures trade share, 79–80, 83
manufacturing productivity, 104,
105–06
metal manufactures, trade in, 234,
235, 243, 245, 247
metalworking machinery, trade in,
270, 271, 281, 283, 284
miscellaneous manufactures, trade in,
491, 493
nonferrous metals, trade in, 211, 227,
229, 231
nonmetallic mineral manufactures,
trade in, 186, 188, 190
office machines, trade in, 316, 318,
320
paper, trade in, 149, 150, 158–59,
160, 161
road vehicles, trade in, 364, 366, 370,
385–86, 389–90, 543
sound-reproducing equipment, trade
in, 325, 326, 338, 340
specialized industrial machinery, trade
in, 263, 265, 267
telecommunications equipment, trade
in, 325, 326, 338, 340
textiles, trade in, 164, 175, 177
US share of world exports to, 54
world manufactures export shares,
55–56, 536
Japan Economic Institute, 313, 495
Japan Electronics Industry Development
Association, 313, 333
Johnson, Matthey, 224
Julius, DeAnne, 112

Kellaway, Lucy, 201
Kirsis, Karlis, 201
Knitted fabrics, trade in, 172
Kolarik, W. F., Jr., 112
Korea
EC share of world exports to, 54–55
export share taken by US, 56
iron and steel, trade in, 208

Japanese share of world exports to, 55
road vehicles, trade in, 370
US share of world exports to, 54
world manufactures trade, 50, 52, 547
Kotkin, Joel, 495
Kravis, Irving B., 558
Krugman, Paul R., 112, 333, 556, 561, 565

Lace, trade in, 172
Latin America
  aircraft, trade in, 408–09, 410, 413
  apparel, trade in, 431, 441, 443, 445
  Asian NICs share of world exports to, 55–56
  chemicals, trade in, 124, 142–43, 144, 146
  computers, trade in, 316, 318, 320
  electrical machinery, trade in, 343–44, 356–57, 358, 360
  EC share of world exports to, 54–55
  export share taken by US, 56
  exports, 53
  footwear, trade in, 448, 457, 459, 460
  furniture, trade in, 424–25, 426, 427
  general industrial machinery, trade in, 296, 298, 300
  impact of declining purchasing power, 535, 549
  imports, 53
  instruments, professional, trade in, 464, 466, 471, 473, 475
  iron and steel, trade in, 193, 197, 198, 204, 205, 206, 208
  Japanese share of world exports to, 55
  manufactures trade shares, 78–82
  manufacturing productivity, 106
  metal manufactures, trade in, 243, 245, 247
  metalworking machinery, trade in, 271, 281, 283, 284
  miscellaneous manufactures, trade in, 489–90, 491, 493
  nonferrous metals, trade in, 211, 227, 229, 231

  nonmetallic mineral manufactures, trade in, 186, 188, 190
  office machines, trade in, 316, 318, 320
  paper, trade in, 149, 150, 158–59, 160, 161
  road vehicles, trade in, 384, 385–86, 387
  sound–reproducing equipment, trade in, 336, 338
  specialized industrial machinery, trade in, 251, 265, 267
  telecommunications equipment, trade in, 336, 338
  textiles, trade in, 173–74, 175, 177
  US share of world exports to, 54
  world manufactures trade shares, 50
Lawrence, Robert Z., 112, 383
Lead, 217–18, 222, 226
Leadbeater, Charles, 201, 404
Leather, trade in, 48–49, 95–96
Leather machinery, trade in, 262, 266
Legal services, trade in, 28
Lehner, Urban C., 495
Levin, Doron P., 383
License fees, 24, 26–27
Lighting fixtures, trade in, 48–49, 95–96
Lime, trade in, 181, 189
Lipsey, Robert E., 558
Living standards, US, 14, 64, 535

Machine tools, trade in, 280, 284
Macroeconomic analysis, advantages and disadvantages, 7–9
Maeda, Shunichi, 224
Malaysia, 360, 448
Management services, trade in, 27–29
Man-made fiber, trade in, 172
Manufactures trade shares, 47–57
Manufacturing
  composition, US, 9–10
  economic role, 9–15, 531
  effect of foreign borrowing on, 36, 532
  employment, 12
  environment for, 557–60
  government policy and, 35–37, 533–34
  in gross national product, 11–12, 533

Manufacturing *(continued)*
  interface with world economy, 36,
    532
  and living standards, 14, 535
  outlook for, US, 531–35, 567–68
  productivity, in industrialized
    countries, 104–06
March, Artemis, 279, 405
Marcus, Peter, 201
Mardones, Jose Luis, 224
Market share parameters, manufactures
  trade, 100–01
Martinez, Christian, 224
Marx, William B., Jr., 333
Massachusetts Institute of Technology,
  140, 495
Mechanical handling equipment, trade
  in, 287, 288, 299
Medical services, trade in, 28
Medicinal products, trade in, 48, 95–96,
  123, 130, 141, 145
Metal manufactures, 233–48
  Asian NICs, trade in, 234, 235, 243,
    245
  bilateral trade flows, 235, 245
  Canada, trade in, 235, 243, 245
  determinants of US trade
    performance, 238
  determinants of world trade
    performance, 235–36
  Eastern Europe, trade in, 243
  European Community, trade in, 234,
    235, 243, 245
  France, trade in, 243, 245
  geographic composition of US trade,
    237, 247
  geographic distribution of world
    trade, 234, 243–44
  Germany, trade in, 234, 243, 245
  global competition patterns, 234–35,
    243–44
  Italy, trade in, 243
  Japan, trade in, 234, 235, 243, 245
  Latin America, trade in, 243, 245
  product composition of US trade,
    237, 246
  product composition of world trade,
    234, 242
  product group description, 233–34
  United Kingdom, trade in, 234, 245

  United States, trade in, 234–37, 245,
    246–47, 248
  world trade, 234–36, 242
Metal storage containers, trade in, 242,
  246
Metalworking machinery
  Asian NICs, trade in, 270, 271, 281,
    283
  bilateral trade flows, 271, 283
  Canada, trade in, 271, 281, 283
  determinants of trade performance,
    274–76
  developing countries, trade in, 281
  Eastern Europe, trade in, 281
  European Community, trade in, 270,
    271, 281, 283
  France, trade in, 281, 283
  geographic composition of US trade,
    272, 284
  geographic distribution of world
    trade, 270–71, 281–82
  Germany, trade in, 270, 271, 281,
    283
  Italy, trade in, 281
  Japan, trade in, 270, 271, 281, 283
  Latin America, trade in, 271, 281,
    283
  product composition of US trade,
    273, 284
  product composition of world trade,
    270, 280
  product group description, 269–70
  Soviet Union, trade in, 270, 271
  United Kingdom, trade in, 281, 283
  United States, trade in, 270, 271,
    272–74, 281, 283, 285
  world manufactures export shares,
    48–49
  world trade, 270–72, 280–83, 285
Methodology, 4–5
Mexico
  apparel, trade in, 445
  Asian NICs share of world exports to,
    55–56
  chemicals, trade in, 146
  electrical machinery, trade in, 360
  EC share of world exports to, 54–55
  export share taken by US, 56
  furniture, trade in, 427

general industrial machinery, trade in, 300

Japanese share of world exports to, 55

metal manufactures, trade in, 247

nonferrous metals, trade in, 231

nonmetallic mineral manufactures, trade in, 190

paper, trade in, 161

road vehicles, trade in, 370, 389–90, 543

sound-reproducing equipment, trade in, 340

telecommunications equipment, trade in, 340

US share of world exports to, 54

Microeconomic analysis, advantages and disadvantages, 6–7

Milbank, Dana, 279

Mineral fuels, composition of world trade, 45

Mineral manufactures

composition of US trade, 189

composition of world trade, 185

nonmetallic, world manufactures export shares, 48–49

Mining

manufacturing sector use of, 14

sectoral composition, 11

in world goods and services trade, 44

Miscellaneous manufactures, 477–94

Asian NICs, trade in, 489–91

baby carriages, trade in, 480–81, 484–85, 488, 492

bilateral trade flows, 479, 491

Canada, trade in, 489–90, 491

determinants of US trade performance, 483–85

determinants of world trade performance, 479–81

developing countries, trade in, 489–90

Eastern Europe, trade in, 489–90

European Community, trade in, 489–90, 491

France, trade in, 489–90, 491

games, trade in, 480–81, 484–85, 488, 492

geographic composition of US trade, 482, 493

geographic composition of world trade, 478, 489–90

Germany, trade in, 489–90, 491

global competition patterns, 478–79, 489–91

Italy, trade in, 489–90

Japan, trade in, 491

Latin America, trade in, 489–90, 491

musical instruments, trade in, 485, 488, 492

printed matter, trade in, 480, 484, 488, 492

product composition of US trade, 481, 492

product composition of world trade, 478, 488

product group description, 477

sporting goods, trade in, 480–81, 484–85, 488, 492

toys, trade in, 480–81, 484–85, 488, 492

United Kingdom, trade in, 489–90, 491

United States, trade in, 481–82, 489–90, 491, 494

world trade, 478–81, 488–91, 494

Mitchell, Jacqueline, 383

Moreno, Ramon, 495

Morita, Akio, 333

Morsch, Brian A., 260

Motor Vehicle Manufacturers Association of the United States, 383

Motorcycles, trade in, 363, 384, 388

Motors, trade in, 359

Mowery, David C., 405

Multinational corporations, 533, 550–53

Murray, Alan, 495

Musical instruments, trade in, 485, 488, 492

Nails, trade in, 242, 246

Nasar, Sylvia, 112–13

National Academy of Engineering, 201, 313, 333, 405

National Academy of Sciences, 313

National Advisory Committee on Semiconductors, 353

National Association of Manufacturers, 495

National Electrical Manufacturers
Association, 353
National Machine Tool Builders
Association, 273, 279
National Research Council, 184
Natural resources, 548
Netherlands, 104, 146
Nickel, trade in, 216, 221, 226, 230
Noellert, William A., 171, 439
Noetstaller, Richard, 184
Nonferrous metals
Asian NICs, trade in, 227, 229
bilateral trade flows, 211, 229
Canada, trade in, 211, 227, 229
determinants of US trade
performance, 214–19, 230
determinants of world trade
performance, 212
developing countries, trade in, 227
Eastern Europe, trade in, 227
European Community, trade in, 211,
227, 229
France, trade in, 211, 227, 229
geographic composition of US trade,
212, 231
geographic composition of world
trade, 211, 227–28
Germany, trade in, 211, 227, 229
global competition patterns, 211,
227–28, 229
Italy, trade in, 227
Japan, trade in, 211, 227, 229
Latin America, trade in, 211, 227, 229
product composition of US trade,
212, 216–19, 230
product composition of world trade,
211, 226
product group description, 210–11
United Kingdom, trade in, 227, 229
United States, trade in, 211, 212–14,
226, 227, 229, 230, 231, 232, 548
world manufactures export shares,
48–49
world trade, 211–12, 226, 232
Nonmetallic mineral manufactures
Asian NICs, trade in, 186, 188
bilateral trade flows, 180, 188
Canada, trade in, 186, 188
determinants of US trade
performance, 181–83

developing countries, trade in, 186
Eastern Europe, trade in, 186
European Community, trade in, 180,
186, 188
France, trade in, 186, 188
geographic composition of US trade,
180, 190
geographic distribution of world
trade, 180, 186
Germany, trade in, 186, 188
global competition patterns, 180,
186–88
Italy, trade in, 186
Japan, trade in, 186, 188
Latin America, trade in, 186, 188
product composition of US trade,
180–82, 189
product composition of world trade,
179, 185
product group description, 179
United Kingdom, trade in, 186, 188
United States, trade in, 180, 186, 188,
189, 191
world trade, 179–80, 185, 191
North American Electric Reliability
Council, 353
Norway, manufacturing productivity,
104
Nunez, Wilson Peres, 313
Nuts, trade in, 242, 246

Office machines, 303–21
Asian NICs, trade in, 316, 318
bilateral trade flows, 303, 318
Canada, trade in, 316, 318
determinants of US trade
performance, 307–09
developing countries, trade in, 316
European Community, trade in, 316,
318
France, trade in, 316, 318
geographic composition of US trade,
305, 320
geographic distribution of world
trade, 303, 316–17
Germany, trade in, 316, 318
global competition patterns, 303,
316–18
Italy, trade in, 316
Japan, trade in, 316, 318

Latin America, trade in, 316, 318
product composition of US trade,
305, 307, 319
product composition of world trade,
303, 315
product group description, 303
United Kingdom, trade in, 316, 318
United States, trade in, 305–06, 316,
318, 319–21, 322, 536
world trade, 303–05, 315–18, 321
Office of Science and Technology Policy,
405
Oil
effect on world goods and services
trade, 44
impact of exchange rate, 57
international investment income, 22
prices, 58
US import bill, 33
Omnibus Trade and Competitiveness
Act of 1988, 565
Organic chemicals, trade in, 95–96,
123, 130, 141, 145
Organization for Economic Cooperation
and Development (OECD), 5, 47,
201, 224, 313, 496, 557
Organization of Petroleum Exporting
Countries (OPEC), 79–80, 82, 300,
445, 535, 549
Orr, James, 113
Oxford Economics USA, 540

Paper
Asian NICs, trade in, 149, 158–59,
160
bilateral trade flows, 150, 160
Canada, trade in, 149, 150, 158–59,
160, 161
composition of world trade, 149, 157
determinants of US trade
performance, 151–53
developing countries, trade in, 149,
158–59
Eastern Europe, trade in, 149,
158–59
European Community, trade in, 149,
150, 158–59, 160
France, trade in, 149, 158–59, 160
geographic composition of US trade,
151, 161

geographic distribution of world
trade, 149, 158–59
Germany, trade in, 149, 150, 158–59,
160
global competition patterns, 149–50,
158–59
Italy, trade in, 149, 158–59
Japan, trade in, 149, 150, 158–59,
160
Latin America, trade in, 149, 150,
158–59, 160
product composition of US trade,
150, 161
product composition of world trade,
149, 157
product group description, 148
United Kingdom, trade in, 149,
158–59, 160
United States, trade in, 149, 150–51,
158–59, 160, 161, 162
world manufactures export shares,
48–49
world trade, 149–50, 162
Passenger fares, 24–26
Pearls, trade in, 182–83, 189
Peck, Merton, 224
Pei-Tse Wu, 438
Perfume, trade in, 48–49, 95–96, 141,
145
Peters, Anthony, 201
Peterson, Peter G., 39
Petroleum. *See* Oil
Pharmaceuticals, trade in, 48–49,
95–96, 123, 130, 141, 145
Phonographs, trade in, 335, 339
Photographic equipment, trade in,
48–49, 95–96
Pig iron, trade in, 203, 207
Pipes, trade in, 203, 207
Plastics, trade in, 48–49, 95–96,
122–35, 141, 142–44, 145–47
Platinum, trade in, 214–15, 220, 226
Plumbing fixtures, trade in, 48, 95–96
Plummer, Christopher, 201
Porter, K. E., 224
Porter, Michael E., 496
Postindustrial society, 13–15, 568
Poterba, James, 112
Pottery, trade in, 182, 185, 189

Power-generating machinery, trade in,
48–49, 95–96, 536
Precious stones, trade in, 182–83, 189
President's Commission on Industrial
Competitiveness, 113
Printed matter. *See* Miscellaneous
manufactures
Printing machinery, trade in, 262, 266
Product composition of US trade
aircraft, 400, 411–12
apparel, 431, 432, 444
chemicals, 129–30, 145
computers, 305, 307, 319
electrical machinery, 344, 345, 347,
348, 349, 359
footwear, 448, 450, 460
general industrial machinery, 288–89,
299
instruments, professional, 465, 474
iron and steel, 194, 207
metal manufactures, 237, 246
metalworking machinery, 273, 284
miscellaneous manufactures, 481, 492
nonferrous metals, 212, 216–19, 230
nonmetallic mineral manufactures,
180–82, 189
office machines, 305, 307, 319
paper, 150, 161
road vehicles, 365, 368, 388
sound-reproducing equipment, 326,
339
specialized industrial machinery, 251,
266
telecommunications equipment, 326,
339
Product composition of world trade
aircraft, 395, 407
apparel, 430, 440
changes in, 549–50
chemicals, 123, 141
computers, 303, 315
electrical machinery, 343, 355
footwear, 447, 456
general industrial machinery, 287,
295
instruments, professional, 463, 470
iron and steel, 193, 203
metal manufactures, 234, 242
metalworking machinery, 270, 280
miscellaneous manufactures, 478, 488

nonferrous metals, 211, 226
nonmetallic mineral manufactures,
179, 185
office machines, 303, 315
paper, 149, 157
road vehicles, 363, 384
sound-reproducing equipment, 324,
335
specialized industrial machinery, 250,
262
telecommunications equipment, 324,
335
textiles, 164, 172
Product group descriptions
aircraft, 394
apparel, 429–30
chemicals, 121–22
computers, 303
electrical machinery, 342–43
furniture, 416
general industrial machinery, 286
instruments, professional, 462
metalworking machinery, 269–70
miscellaneous manufactures, 477
nonferrous metals, 210–11
office machines, 303
paper, 148
sound-reproducing equipment,
323–34
telecommunications equipment,
323–34
textiles, 163
Production capacity, US, 548
Productivity, in industrialized countries,
104–06
Public relations, services transactions,
28
Public utilities, 11
Pulp mill machinery, trade in, 262, 266
Pumps, trade in, 287, 288, 289, 295
Pyrotechnic products, trade in, 48–49,
95–96, 145

Radetzki, Marian, 224
Radiological apparatus, trade in, 347,
359
Radios, trade in, 335, 339
Railway track, trade in, 203, 207
Real estate, 11

Refractory products, trade in, 181, 182, 185, 189
Reich, Robert B., 113
Resins, trade in, 48–49
Resnick, Rosalind, 438
Retail trade, 11
Ribbon, trade in, 172
Richards, Evelyn, 113, 496
Roach, Stephen S., 113
Road vehicles, 362–93
  Asian NICs, trade in, 364, 385–86, 387
  bilateral trade flows, 365, 387
  Canada, trade in, 364, 385–86, 387, 389–90
  determinants of US trade performance, 369–73
  determinants of world trade performance, 367–68
  developing countries, trade in, 364, 385–86
  Eastern Europe, trade in, 364, 385–86
  European Community, trade in, 364, 385–86, 387, 389–90
  France, trade in, 364, 385–86, 387
  geographic composition of US trade, 366, 368, 376, 389
  Germany, trade in, 364, 366, 385–86, 387, 389–90, 546
  global competition patterns, 364–65, 385–87
  globalization of production, 365–67, 388–90
  Italy, trade in, 364, 385–86
  Japan, trade in, 364, 366, 385–86, 387, 389–90, 546, 551–52
  Latin America, trade in, 364, 385–86, 387
  Mexico, trade in, 389–90
  product composition of US trade, 365, 368, 388
  product composition of world trade, 363, 384
  product group description, 362–63
  United Kingdom, trade in, 364, 385–86, 387
  United States, trade in, 364, 366, 368–69, 374–77, 379, 385–86, 387, 391, 392, 543–44, 546, 554

world manufactures export shares, 48–49, 536
world trade, 369, 391
Rodrik, Dani, 495
Roller bearings, trade in, 299
Royalties, in services account, 24, 26–27, 533
Rubber manufactures, trade in, 48–49, 95–96
Rutter, John, 113

Scientific instruments, trade in, 47, 95–96
Scott, Bruce R., 113
Screws, trade in, 242, 246
Sebenius, James K., 39
Semiconductor devices, trade in, 359
Semiprecious stones, trade in, 182–83, 189
Services, trade in, 11, 12–15, 20, 23–29, 531–32
Shapiro, Eben, 438
Silva, Enrique, 224
Silver, trade in, 211, 214–15, 220, 226, 230
Singapore, 50, 52
Skapinker, Michael, 353
Society of Japanese Aerospace Companies, 405
Sound-reproducing equipment, 323–41
  Asian NICs, trade in, 325, 336, 338
  Canada, trade in, 336, 338
  determinants of world trade performance, 325
  developing countries, trade in, 336
  Eastern Europe, trade in, 336
  European Community, trade in, 324–35, 336, 338
  France, trade in, 336, 338
  geographic composition of US trade, 326, 340
  geographic distribution of world trade, 324, 336–37
  Germany, trade in, 336, 338
  global competition patterns, 324–25, 336–38
  Italy, trade in, 336
  Japan, trade in, 325, 336, 338
  Latin America, trade in, 336, 338

Sound-reproducing equipment
(continued)
product composition of US trade,
326, 339
product composition of world trade,
324, 335
product group description, 323–34
United Kingdom, trade in, 336, 338
United States, trade in, 325, 326, 336,
338, 339–40
world trade, 324–25, 335–38, 340
Specialized industrial machinery
Asian NICs, trade in, 251, 263, 265
Canada, trade in, 251, 263, 265
determinants of US trade
performance, 253–55
determinants of world trade
performance, 251
developing countries, trade in, 263
Eastern Europe, trade in, 263
European Community, trade in, 250,
263, 265
France, trade in, 263, 265
geographic composition of US trade,
255, 267
geographic distribution of world
trade, 250, 263–64
Germany, trade in, 250–51, 263–65
Italy, trade in, 263
Japan, trade in, 263, 265
Latin America, trade in, 251, 263,
265
product composition of US trade,
251, 266
product composition of world trade,
250, 262
United Kingdom, trade in, 263, 265
United States, trade in, 250–51, 253,
263, 265, 266–68, 542, 545–46
world trade, 250–51, 262–65, 268
Sporting goods. *See* Miscellaneous
manufactures
Staelin, David H., 333
Standard Industry Classification, 10
Steel. *See* Iron and steel
Steindel, Charles, 113
Stereos, trade in, 335
Strongman, John E., 224
Summers, Lawrence, 112
Sweden, manufacturing productivity,
104
Switchgear, trade in, 343, 359

Taiwan, 5, 50, 52, 54–55, 56, 547
Takeuchi, Kenji, 224
Tan, C. Suan, 224
Tanning, 48–49, 95–96, 130, 141, 145
Taxation, 565–67
Telecommunications equipment, 323–41
Asian NICs, trade in, 336, 338
bilateral trade flows, 325, 338
Canada, trade in, 336, 338
determinants of world trade
performance, 325
developing countries, trade in, 336
Eastern Europe, trade in, 336
European Community, trade in,
324–26, 338
France, trade in, 336, 338
geographic composition of US trade,
326, 340
geographic distribution of world
trade, 324, 336–37
Germany, trade in, 336, 338
global competition patterns, 324–25,
336–38
Italy, trade in, 336
Japan, trade in, 325, 336, 338
Latin America, trade in, 336, 338
product composition of US trade,
326, 339
product composition of world trade,
324, 335
product group description, 323–34
United Kingdom, trade in, 336, 338
United States, trade in, 325, 326, 328,
336, 338, 339–40, 341
world manufactures export shares,
48–49
world trade, 324–25, 335–38, 340
Telecommunications services, trade in,
28
Televisions, trade in, 335, 339
Textile machinery, trade in, 262, 266
Textile yarn, trade in, 95–96, 172
Textiles
Asian NICs, trade in, 164, 173–74, 175
bilateral trade flows, 164, 175
Canada, trade in, 173–74, 175
composition of US trade, 166, 176
determinants of US trade
performance, 167–68

determinants of world trade
performance, 165
developing countries, trade in, 164,
173–74
Eastern Europe, trade in, 173–74
European Community, trade in, 164,
173–74, 175
France, trade in, 173–74, 175
geographic composition of US trade,
166, 177
geographic distribution of world
trade, 164, 173–74
Germany, trade in, 173–74, 175
global competition patterns, 164,
173–75
Italy, trade in, 173–74
Japan, trade in, 164, 175
Latin America, trade in, 173–74, 175
product composition of world trade,
164, 172
product group description, 163
United Kingdom, trade in, 173–74,
175
United States, trade in, 164, 165–66,
172, 173–74, 176, 178, 536
world trade, 164–65, 172, 178
Thailand, 448
Thomas, Paul R., 224
Thurston, Charles W., 496
Tilton, John E., 202, 224
Tin, trade in, 219, 226, 230
Tobacco, trade in, 45
Tools, trade in, 237, 242, 246
Toys. See Miscellaneous manufactures
Tractors, trade in, 250, 262, 266
Trade balance measurements, US,
69–74
Trade outlook
aircraft, 398–403
apparel, 433–37
chemicals, 135–38
computers, 311–12
electrical machinery, 344–52
footwear, 450–53
furniture, 419–21
general industrial machinery, 289–92
instruments, professional, 466–68
iron and steel, 195–200
metal manufactures, 238–39
metalworking machinery, 274–77

miscellaneous manufactures, 483–86
nonferrous metals, 214–22
nonmetallic mineral manufactures, 183
office machines, 306–07, 309–10
paper, 151–55
road vehicles, 369–80
US–Japan, 374–79, 389–90, 392–93
sound-reproducing equipment,
326–28, 330–31
specialized industrial machinery,
253–58
telecommunications equipment,
326–31
textiles, 167–70
Trailers, trade in, 363, 384, 388
Transformers, trade in, 343, 359
Transistors, trade in, 359
Transmission shafts, trade in, 299
Transport equipment, trade in, 45, 46,
48–49, 85–86, 95–96
Transportation services, trade in, 11, 14,
24–26, 44
Travel account, 24–26, 44
Travel goods, trade in, 48–49, 95–96
Trucks, trade in, 363, 384, 388
Truell, Peter, 171, 496
Tubes, trade in, 203, 207
Tumazos, John C., 202

Unilateral transfers account, 21
United Kingdom
aircraft, trade in, 408–09, 410, 413
apparel, trade in, 441, 443, 445
Asian NICs share of world exports to,
55–56
chemicals, trade in, 124, 142–43,
144, 146
computers, trade in, 316, 318, 320
electrical machinery, trade in,
343–44, 356–57, 358, 360
EC share of world exports to, 54–55
export share taken by US, 56
exports, 53
footwear, trade in, 457, 459, 460
furniture, trade in, 417, 424–26, 427
general industrial machinery, trade in,
296, 298, 300
imports, 53
instruments, professional, trade in,
466, 471, 473, 475

United Kingdom *(continued)*
iron and steel, trade in, 193, 197, 198, 204, 205, 206, 208
Japanese share of world exports to, 55
manufacturing productivity, 104, 105
metal manufactures, trade in, 243, 245, 247
metalworking machinery, trade in, 281, 283, 284
miscellaneous manufactures, trade in, 489–90, 491, 493
nonferrous metals, trade in, 227, 229, 231
nonmetallic mineral manufactures, trade in, 186, 188, 190
office machines, trade in, 316, 318
paper, trade in, 149, 158–59, 160, 161
road vehicles, trade in, 364, 370, 385–86, 387
sound-reproducing equipment, trade in, 336, 338, 340
specialized industrial machinery, trade in, 263, 265, 267
telecommunications equipment, trade in, 336, 338, 340
textiles, trade in, 173–74, 175, 177
US share of world exports to, 54
world manufactures trade shares, 50
United States
agricultural products, trade in, 30–33
aircraft, trade in, 395–97, 408–09, 410
apparel, trade in, 431, 441, 443
Asian NICs share of world exports to, 55–56
chemicals, trade in, 142–43, 144
competitiveness in manufactures, 71–74, 555–68
computers, trade in, 316, 318
defense sales, 23–24
deficit, manufactures trade, 13
electrical machinery, trade in, 343–44, 356–57, 358
employment, manufacturing, 12
EC share of world exports to, 54–55
footwear, trade in, 457, 459
foreign aid, 21
foreign borrowing, effect on manufacturing sector, 36
furniture, trade in, 416, 417, 424–26
general industrial machinery, trade in, 287, 288, 296, 298

government services, 23–24
instruments, professional, trade in, 463, 464, 471–72, 473
international investment income account, 21–23
investment trends, 106–08
iron and steel, trade in, 193, 197, 198, 204, 205, 206
Japanese share of world exports to, 55
lack of export orientation, 552–53, 554
license fees, 24, 26–27
living standards, 14
manufactures trade, 30–35, 70, 531–40
manufacturing productivity, 104
metal manufactures, trade in, 234, 235, 243, 245
metalworking machinery, trade in, 270, 271, 281, 283
mineral fuels, trade in, 30–33
miscellaneous manufactures, trade in, 489–90, 491
natural resources, 548
nonferrous metals, trade in, 211, 227, 229
nonmetallic mineral manufactures, trade in, 186, 188
office machines, trade in, 316, 318
oil imports, 33
paper, trade in, 149, 150, 158–59, 160
passenger fares, 24–26
"postindustrial society," 13–15
as primary export target, 553
private services, trade in, 27–29
product composition of manufactures trade, 94–98
productivity, 555–57
road vehicles, trade in, 364, 366, 385–86, 387
royalties, 24, 26–27
services account, 12–15, 23–29
sound-reproducing equipment, trade in, 336, 338
specialized industrial machinery, trade in, 250–51, 263, 265
telecommunications equipment, trade in, 325, 336, 338
textiles, trade in, 164, 173–74, 174

transportation services, trade in, 24–26
travel account, 24–26
unilateral transfers account, 21
University of Michigan Transportation Research Institute, 383
Utilities industry, 14

Video recorders, trade in, 339, 545

Wexner, Leslie H., 439
Wharton Econometric Forecasting Associates, 202
White, Joseph B., 383
Wholesale trade, 11
Wire, trade in, 203, 207, 242, 246
Wolff, Alan, 171, 439
Wood manufactures, trade in, 48–49, 95–96
Worker output in manufacturing, 12
World Bank, 439, 455
World Manufactures Trade Data Base, 43–46
World trade
  aircraft, 395–97, 407–10
  apparel, 430–31, 440–43
  chemicals, 122–29, 141
  commercial services, 43–44
  computers, 303–05, 315–18
  electrical machinery, 355–58
  footwear, 447, 456
  furniture, 416–18, 423–26
  general industrial machinery, 287–88, 295–98
  instruments, professional, 463–65, 470–73
  iron and steel, 193–94, 203
  metal manufactures, 234–36, 242
  metalworking machinery, 270–72, 280–83
  miscellaneous manufactures, 478–81, 488–91
  nonferrous metals, 211–12, 226

nonmetallic mineral manufactures, 179–80, 185
office machines, 303–05, 315–18
paper, 149–50
plastics, 122–29, 141
product composition, 45
road vehicles, 363–68, 384–90
sound-reproducing equipment, 324–25, 335–38
specialized industrial machinery, 250–51, 262–65
telecommunications equipment, 324–25, 335–38
textiles, 164–65, 172
World trade patterns, determinants
  aircraft, 395–97
  chemicals, 125–29
  computers, 303–05
  furniture, 417–18
  general industrial machinery, 288
  iron and steel, 194
  metal manufactures, 235–36
  metalworking machinery, 271–72
  miscellaneous manufactures, 479–81
  nonferrous metals, 212
  office machines, 303–05
  plastics, 125–29
  road vehicles, 367–68
  sound-reproducing equipment, 326
  specialized industrial machinery, 251
  telecommunications equipment, 326
  textiles, 165
World Trade Service model, Data Resources, Inc., 119
Wyss, David A., 497

Yano, Ichiro, 202
Yarn, trade in, 48–49
Young, Andrew, 140
Young, Ian, 140

Zinc, trade in, 218–19, 222, 226, 230

Other Publications from the
Institute for International Economics

POLICY ANALYSES IN INTERNATIONAL ECONOMICS Series

1 **The Lending Policies of the International Monetary Fund**
John Williamson/*August 1982*
$8.00   ISBN paper 0-88132-000-5   72 pp.

2 **"Reciprocity": A New Approach to World Trade Policy?**
William R. Cline/*September 1982*
$8.00   ISBN paper 0-88132-001-3   41 pp.

3 **Trade Policy in the 1980s**
C. Fred Bergsten and William R. Cline/*November 1982*
(out of print)   ISBN paper 0-88132-002-1   84 pp.
Partially reproduced in the book *Trade Policy in the 1980s.*

4 **International Debt and the Stability of the World Economy**
William R. Cline/*September 1983*
$10.00   ISBN paper 0-88132-010-2   134 pp.

5 **The Exchange Rate System**
John Williamson/*September 1983, rev. June 1985*
(out of print)   ISBN paper 0-88132-034-X   61 pp.

6 **Economic Sanctions in Support of Foreign Policy Goals**
Gary Clyde Hufbauer and Jeffrey J. Schott/*October 1983*
$10.00   ISBN paper 0-88132-014-5   109 pp.

7 **A New SDR Allocation?**
John Williamson/*March 1984*
$10.00   ISBN paper 0-88132-028-5   61 pp.

8 **An International Standard for Monetary Stabilization**
Ronald I. McKinnon/*March 1984*
$10.00   ISBN paper 0-88132-018-8   108 pp.

9 **The Yen/Dollar Agreement: Liberalizing Japanese Capital Markets**
Jeffrey A. Frankel/*December 1984*
$10.00   ISBN paper 0-88132-035-8   86 pp.

10 **Bank Lending to Developing Countries: The Policy Alternatives**
C. Fred Bergsten, William R. Cline, and John Williamson/*April 1985*
$12.00   ISBN paper 0-88132-032-3   221 pp.

11 **Trading for Growth: The Next Round of Trade Negotiations**
Gary Clyde Hufbauer and Jeffrey J. Schott/*September 1985*
$10.00   ISBN paper 0-88132-033-1   109 pp.

12 **Financial Intermediation Beyond the Debt Crisis**
Donald R. Lessard and John Williamson/*September 1985*
$12.00   ISBN paper 0-88132-021-8   130 pp.

13 **The United States–Japan Economic Problem**
C. Fred Bergsten and William R. Cline/*October 1985, rev. January 1987*
$10.00   ISBN paper 0-88132-060-9   180 pp.

14 Deficits and the Dollar: The World Economy at Risk
Stephen Marris/*December 1985, rev. November 1987*
$18.00   ISBN paper 0-88132-067-6   415 pp.

15 Trade Policy for Troubled Industries
Gary Clyde Hufbauer and Howard F. Rosen/*March 1986*
$10.00   ISBN paper 0-88132-020-X   111 pp.

16 The United States and Canada: The Quest for Free Trade
Paul Wonnacott, with an Appendix by John Williamson/*March 1987*
$10.00   ISBN paper 0-88132-056-0   188 pp.

17 Adjusting to Success: Balance of Payments Policy in the East Asian NICs
Bela Balassa and John Williamson/*June 1987, rev. April 1990*
$11.95   ISBN paper 0-88132-101-X   160 pp.

18 Mobilizing Bank Lending to Debtor Countries
William R. Cline/*June 1987*
$10.00   ISBN paper 0-88132-062-5   100 pp.

19 Auction Quotas and United States Trade Policy
C. Fred Bergsten, Kimberly Ann Elliott, Jeffrey J. Schott, and Wendy E. Takacs/*September 1987*
$10.00   ISBN paper 0-88132-050-1   254 pp.

20 Agriculture and the GATT: Rewriting the Rules
Dale E. Hathaway/*September 1987*
$10.00   ISBN paper 0-88132-052-8   169 pp.

21 Anti-Protection: Changing Forces in United States Trade Politics
I. M. Destler and John S. Odell/*September 1987*
$10.00   ISBN paper 0-88132-043-9   220 pp.

22 Targets and Indicators: A Blueprint for the International Coordination of Economic Policy
John Williamson and Marcus H. Miller/*September 1987*
$10.00   ISBN paper 0-88132-051-X   118 pp.

23 Capital Flight: The Problem and Policy Responses
Donald R. Lessard and John Williamson/*December 1987*
$10.00   ISBN paper 0-88132-059-5   80 pp.

24 United States–Canada Free Trade: An Evaluation of the Agreement
Jeffrey J. Schott/*April 1988*
$3.95   ISBN paper 0-88132-072-2   48 pp.

25 Voluntary Approaches to Debt Relief
John Williamson/*September 1988, rev. May 1989*
$10.95   ISBN paper 0-88132-075-7   80 pp.

26 American Trade Adjustment: The Global Impact
William R. Cline/*March 1989*
$12.95   ISBN paper 0-88132-095-1   98 pp.

27 More Free Trade Areas?
Jeffrey J. Schott/*May 1989*
$10.00   ISBN paper 0-88132-085-4   88 pp.

28 The Progress of Policy Reform in Latin America
John Williamson/*January 1990*
$10.95   ISBN paper 0-88132-100-1   106 pp.

29 The Global Trade Negotiations: What Can Be Achieved?
Jeffrey J. Schott/*September 1990*
$10.95   ISBN paper 0-88132-137-0   72 pp.

30 Economic Policy Coordination: Requiem or Prologue?
Wendy Dobson/*April 1991*
$11.95   ISBN paper 0-88132-102-8   162 pp.

31 The Economic Opening of Eastern Europe
John Williamson/*May 1991*
$11.95   ISBN paper 0-88132-186-9   92 pp.

32 Eastern Europe and the Soviet Union in the World Economy
Susan M. Collins and Dani Rodrik/*May 1991*
$12.95   ISBN paper 0-88132-157-5   152 pp.

33 African Economic Reform: The External Dimension
Carol Lancaster/*June 1991*
$10.00   ISBN paper 0-88132-096-X   82 pp.

34 Has the Adjustment Process Worked?
Paul R. Krugman/*October 1991*
$11.95   ISBN paper 0-88132-116-8   80 pp.

35 From Soviet disUnion to Eastern Economic Community?
Oleh Havrylyshyn and John Williamson/*October 1991*
$11.95   ISBN paper 0-88132-192-3   84 pp.

36 Global Warming: The Economic Stakes
William R. Cline/*May 1992*
$12.00   ISBN paper 0-88132-172-9   128 pp.

37 Trade and Payments After Soviet Disintegration
John Williamson/*June 1992*
$11.95   ISBN paper 0-88132-173-7   96 pp.

BOOKS

IMF Conditionality
John Williamson, editor/*1983*
$35.00   ISBN cloth 0-88132-006-4   695 pp.

Trade Policy in the 1980s
William R. Cline, editor/*1983*
$35.00   ISBN cloth 0-88132-008-1   810 pp.
$20.00   ISBN paper 0-88132-031-5   810 pp.

Subsidies in International Trade
Gary Clyde Hufbauer and Joanna Shelton Erb/*1984*
$35.00   ISBN cloth 0-88132-004-8   299 pp.

International Debt: Systemic Risk and Policy Response
William R. Cline/*1984*
$30.00   ISBN cloth 0-88132-015-3   336 pp.

Trade Protection in the United States: 31 Case Studies
Gary Clyde Hufbauer, Diane E. Berliner, and Kimberly Ann Elliott/*1986*
$25.00   ISBN paper 0-88132-040-4   371 pp.

Toward Renewed Economic Growth in Latin America
Bela Balassa, Gerardo M. Bueno, Pedro-Pablo Kuczynski, and
   Mario Henrique Simonsen/*1986*
(out of print)   ISBN paper 0-88132-045-5   205 pp.

Capital Flight and Third World Debt
Donald R. Lessard and John Williamson, editors/*1987*
(out of print)   ISBN paper 0-88132-053-6   270 pp.

The Canada–United States Free Trade Agreement: The Global Impact
Jeffrey J. Schott and Murray G. Smith, editors/*1988*
$13.95   ISBN paper 0-88132-073-0   211 pp.

World Agricultural Trade: Building a Consensus
William M. Miner and Dale E. Hathaway, editors/*1988*
$16.95   ISBN paper 0-88132-071-3   226 pp.

Japan in the World Economy
Bela Balassa and Marcus Noland/*1988*
$20.00   ISBN paper 0-88132-041-2   306 pp.

America in the World Economy: A Strategy for the 1990s
C. Fred Bergsten/*1988*
$29.95   ISBN cloth 0-88132-089-7   235 pp.
$13.95   ISBN paper 0-88132-082-X   235 pp.

Managing the Dollar: From the Plaza to the Louvre
Yoichi Funabashi/*1988, rev. 1989*
$19.95   ISBN paper 0-88132-097-8   307 pp.

United States External Adjustment and the World Economy
William R. Cline/*May 1989*
$25.00   ISBN paper 0-88132-048-X   392 pp.

Free Trade Areas and U.S. Trade Policy
Jeffrey J. Schott, editor/*May 1989*
$19.95   ISBN paper 0-88132-094-3   400 pp.

Dollar Politics: Exchange Rate Policymaking in the United States
I. M. Destler and C. Randall Henning/*September 1989*
$11.95   ISBN paper 0-88132-079-X   192 pp.

Latin American Adjustment: How Much Has Happened?
John Williamson, editor/*April 1990*
$34.95   ISBN paper 0-88132-125-7   480 pp.

The Future of World Trade in Textiles and Apparel
William R. Cline/*1987, rev. June 1990*
$20.00   ISBN paper 0-88132-110-9   344 pp.

**Completing the Uruguay Round: A Results-Oriented
   Approach to the GATT Trade Negotiations**
Jeffrey J. Schott, editor/*September 1990*
$19.95   ISBN paper 0-88132-130-3   256 pp.

Economic Sanctions Reconsidered (in two volumes)
Economic Sanctions Reconsidered: History and Current Policy
(also sold separately, see below)
Economic Sanctions Reconsidered: Supplemental Case Histories
Gary Clyde Hufbauer, Jeffrey J. Schott, and Kimberly Ann Elliott/
1985, rev. December 1990

$65.00	ISBN cloth 0-88132-115-X	928 pp.
$45.00	ISBN paper 0-88132-105-2	928 pp.

Economic Sanctions Reconsidered: History and Current Policy
Gary Clyde Hufbauer, Jeffrey J. Schott, and Kimberly Ann Elliott/
December 1990

$36.00	ISBN cloth 0-88132-136-2	288 pp.
$25.00	ISBN paper 0-88132-140-0	288 pp.

Pacific Basin Developing Countries: Prospects for the Future
Marcus Noland/*January 1991*

$29.95	ISBN cloth 0-88132-141-9	250 pp.
$19.95	ISBN paper 0-88132-081-1	250 pp.

Currency Convertibility in Eastern Europe
John Williamson, editor/*September 1991*

$39.95	ISBN cloth 0-88132-144-3	396 pp.
$28.95	ISBN paper 0-88132-128-1	396 pp.

Foreign Direct Investment in the United States
Edward M. Graham and Paul R. Krugman/*1989, rev. October 1991*

$19.00	ISBN paper 0-88132-139-7	200 pp.

International Adjustment and Financing: The Lessons of 1985–1991
C. Fred Bergsten, editor/*January 1992*

$34.95	ISBN cloth 0-88132-142-7	336 pp.
$24.95	ISBN paper 0-88132-112-5	336 pp.

North American Free Trade: Issues and Recommendations
Gary Clyde Hufbauer and Jeffrey J. Schott/*April 1992*

$42.50	ISBN cloth 0-88132-145-1	392 pp.
$25.00	ISBN paper 0-88132-120-6	392 pp.

American Trade Politics
I. M. Destler/*1986, rev. June 1992*

$35.00	ISBN cloth 0-88132-164-8	400 pp.
$20.00	ISBN paper 0-88132-188-5	400 pp.

Narrowing the U.S. Current Account Deficit: A Sectoral Assessment
Allen J. Lenz/*June 1992*

$40.00	ISBN cloth 0-88132-148-6	640 pp.
$25.00	ISBN paper 0-88132-103-6	640 pp.

The Economics of Global Warming
William R. Cline/*June 1992*

$40.00	ISBN cloth 0-88132-150-8	416 pp.
$20.00	ISBN paper 0-88132-132-X	416 pp.

SPECIAL REPORTS

1 **Promoting World Recovery: A Statement on Global Economic Strategy**
by Twenty-six Economists from Fourteen Countries/*December 1982*
(out of print)   ISBN paper 0-88132-013-7   45 pp.

2 **Prospects for Adjustment in Argentina, Brazil, and Mexico: Responding to the Debt Crisis**
John Williamson, editor/*June 1983*
(out of print)   ISBN paper 0-88132-016-1   71 pp.

3 **Inflation and Indexation: Argentina, Brazil, and Israel**
John Williamson, editor/*March 1985*
$12.00   ISBN paper 0-88132-037-4   191 pp.

4 **Global Economic Imbalances**
C. Fred Bergsten, editor/*March 1986*
$25.00   ISBN cloth 0-88132-038-2   126 pp.
$10.00   ISBN paper 0-88132-042-0   126 pp.

5 **African Debt and Financing**
Carol Lancaster and John Williamson, editors/*May 1986*
(out of print)   ISBN paper 0-88132-044-7   229 pp.

6 **Resolving the Global Economic Crisis: After Wall Street**
Thirty-three Economists from Thirteen Countries/*December 1987*
$3.00   ISBN paper 0-88132-070-6   30 pp.

7 **World Economic Problems**
Kimberly Ann Elliott and John Williamson, editors/*April 1988*
$15.95   ISBN paper 0-88132-055-2   298 pp.

Reforming World Agricultural Trade
Twenty-nine Professionals from Seventeen Countries/*1988*
$3.95   ISBN paper 0-88132-088-9   42 pp.

8 **Economic Relations Between the United States and Korea: Conflict or Cooperation?**
Thomas O. Bayard and Soo-Gil Young, editors/*January 1989*
$12.95   ISBN paper 0-88132-068-4   192 pp.

FORTHCOMING

A World Savings Shortage?
Paul R. Krugman

Who's Bashing Whom? Trade Conflict in High-Technology Industries
Laura D'Andrea Tyson

Sizing Up U.S. Export Disincentives
J. David Richardson

The Globalization of Industry and National Economic Policies
C. Fred Bergsten and Edward M. Graham

Trading for the Environment
John Whalley

U.S. Taxation of International Income: Blueprint for Reform
Gary Clyde Hufbauer

The Effects of Foreign-Exchange Intervention
Kathryn Dominguez and Jeffrey A. Frankel

The Future of the World Trading System
John Whalley

Adjusting to Volatile Energy Prices
Philip K. Verleger, Jr.

National Security and the World Economy
Ellen L. Frost

The United States as a Debtor Country
C. Fred Bergsten and Shafiqul Islam

International Monetary Policymaking in the United States, Germany, and Japan
C. Randall Henning

The Economic Consequences of Soviet Disintegration
John Williamson

Reciprocity and Retaliation: An Evaluation of Tough Trade Policies
Thomas O. Bayard and Kimberly Ann Elliott

Global Competition Policy
Edward M. Graham and J. David Richardson

The Dynamics of Korean Economic Development
Soon Cho

Equilibrium Exchange Rates: An Update
John Williamson

The United States and Japan in the 1990s
C. Fred Bergsten, I. M. Destler, and Marcus Noland

Toward Freer Trade in the Western Hemishpere
Gary Clyde Hufbauer and Jeffrey J. Schott

The New Tripolar World Economy: Toward Collective Leadership
C. Fred Bergsten and C. Randall Henning

Korea in the World Economy
Il SaKong

The Costs of U.S. Trade Barriers
Gary Clyde Hufbauer and Kimberly Ann Elliott

Comparing the Costs of Protection: Europe, Japan, and the United States
Gary Clyde Hufbauer and Kimberly Ann Elliott, editors

The Politics of Economic Reform
John Williamson

Third World Debt: A Reappraisal
William R. Cline

The New Europe in the World Economy
Gary Clyde Hufbauer